THE JUDICIOUS EYE

The Judicious Eye

Architecture Against the Other Arts

Joseph Rykwert

THE UNIVERSITY OF CHICAGO PRESS

CHICAGO AND LONDON

The University of Chicago Press, Chicago 60637
Reaktion Books, Ltd, London EC1V 0DX

© 2008 by Joseph Rykwert

All rights reserved. Published 2008

Printed in the United Kingdom

17 16 15 14 13 12 11 10 09 08   1 2 3 4 5

ISBN-13: 978-0-226-73261-9 (cloth)
ISBN-10: 0-226-73261-4 (cloth)

Library of Congress Cataloging-in-Publication Data

Rykwert, Joseph, 1926–
    The judicious eye / Joseph Rykwert.
    p. cm.
    Includes bibliographical references and index.
    ISBN-13: 978-0-226-73261-9 (cloth : alk. paper)
    ISBN-10: 0-226-73261-4 (cloth : alk. paper) 1. Architectural design.
    2. Public spaces. I. Title.
    NA2750R99 2008
    720.1—dc22

                                                            2007039957

Contents

Paul Delaroche, *L'Art Gothique*, an 1841 study for the hemicycle frieze at the Ecole des Beaux-Arts, Paris.

Preface

Painting and sculpture once counted with architecture as 'visual arts', or did so well into the nineteenth century and even the twentieth. They were usually taught in the same vocational or university schools, books about them occupied adjoining library shelves; their practitioners belonged to the same guilds, clubs or academies; and their combined skills shaped the man-made environment. Since the middle of the twentieth century, however, the impact of painting and sculpture on how the man-made environment looks and feels has been weakening.

Architecture was hobbled as the public realm shrank and receded, pressured by private interests. As soon as electricity became generally available, city centres (Piccadilly Circus in London, Times Square in New York, the Ginza in Tokyo) were swathed in coloured lights and electronic billboards which often masked buildings and obtruded private and even explicitly anti-social advocacy on the civic forum. Tobacco or alcohol advertising, for instance, urged the consumption of products which the governments of many countries now consider damaging to public health – and worse. Visual interest in the architect's work sometimes operated only above the level of the billboards and signs – above the sixth or seventh floor.

Architects often exercise design skill only on the outer surface of the buildings put up in world-city centres, since their plan and section are predetermined by the demands of developers and by building regulations. Glazed or mirrored air-conditioned rectilineal blocks are the most common shape for office buildings, since this has been accounted the most profitable; within, there is rentable accommodation from the top to the ground – which may sometimes be varied by retail space.[1] Even public entry rarely gets much of the floor area, which considerations of security shrink into insignificance. Concentration on the technical refinement of surface and on fiscal calculations has imposed such rigour on designers that variations on the basic shape can only be arbitrary. Sheer size gratified the ambitions of tower-builders for a while, but increasingly owner-developers and their designers have become concerned, like their nineteenth-century predecessors, with the 'image' of the building – with the impact its outline makes on the urban silhouette, so that even the square-plan high-rise has occasionally been crowned by some 'feature'. The sheer tedium, which this kind of building induced, pushed and pulled the profitable parallelepiped in different directions before the twenty-first century even began, and this has prompted designers to slide the containing planes apart or model them into some allusive shape (the wind-inflated sail is a common model), while at the same time the various energy crises in the latter part of the twentieth century have required the 'greening' of high-rises. This, in turn, has resulted in further variations of shape and outline.

For all that, each tall building is constrained to a form which advertises either the developer's or its designer's peculiar (and usually private) concerns. Yet the flashing, constantly changing billboards and the neon festoons still provide the charge of visual excitement which we expect in a city.[2] One of the complaints about the 'boredom' of East European centres under Communist regimes arose from the absence of just such variegated and conflicting appeals from city walls – the buildings were, of course, no more exhilarating than those of the capitalists. Dirigist authorities had learnt how to emulate advertising, but substituted politically exhortative billboards in its place. Their message was uniformly bland and conformist, even if their formal effect on the urban scene was not all that different from that in the 'free world', where the explicit intention of public advertising was the stimulation or even the arousing of conflicting expectations to be assuaged by specific consumption. Conflict and irritation, 'daring' and provocation are essential stimuli to visual excitement.

Billboards, lights, advertising perform a role contrary to old-style public art, which was either 'contained' within the architecture or elevated by it – physically – on a pedestal. It was often intended to provide a form of counterpoint to – or accord with – a building. Advertising, which violates articulated surfaces and is often vast in scale, might therefore be considered a kind of licensed and profitable ulcer or canker on the body of the city fabric. The smears and sprays of graffito-makers differ from it only in that they are individualistic and unlicensed and therefore do not produce revenue. Those who suffer public advertising gladly, and even claim to take pleasure in it, need not be censorious (as they often are) about the presence of graffiti. Oddly enough, no sober account of the visual impact of advertising in the city has yet been done.[3]

The *Défense d'afficher* notice on a French city wall.

That advertising was a disruptive, disfiguring presence was already recognized by the lawmakers of many countries during the second half of the nineteenth century. Ironically enough, the French often joke about the 'best-known law in France', the one forbidding advertising, since the slogan 'DÉFENSE D'AFFICHER. Loi du 29 Juillet 1881' is painted or stencilled in large letters on such walls as are public property and must be left unscathed. That stern and negative provision is in itself an advertisement, imposed as part of the liberal regulations which circumscribed press censorship. The same law also led to the creation of the advertising kiosk or bollard, the cylindrical hoarding which may originate in Second Empire Paris, but which became a common device in many European (and some Latin American) cities. Paradoxically, soon after that law was passed, 'serious' artists were drawn into advertising, and some painters, particularly the creative users of lithography (Toulouse-Lautrec, Steinlen, Bonnard and the Beggarstaff Brothers[4]), produced posters for singers and actors, for periodicals and humble domestic products, for soaps or patent foods, which adorned those very bollards as well as many blank (and privately owned) city walls. The Cubists notoriously absorbed advertising into their pictures; in fact, the techniques of *collage* (and later of *montage*) depended on the charm of the commonplace and the use of different-level communications:

> You read leaflets, catalogues, posters that chant aloud
> That is your poetry this morning – and for prose you have the newspaper . . .

So Guillaume Apollinaire summed it up in *Zone*.[5]

At the private level of the home, a very different but related change took place after the First World War, since industrial and graphic design had come to dominate things of everyday use: clothes, knives and forks – even food[6] which we buy packaged and wrapped. 'Artists' were often expected to provide drawings and models in the past for many such objects – at the luxury end of the market at any rate: furniture and hangings, even fireworks and time-pieces. Since the practitioners of industrial and graphic design were often (until recently) trained as architects, such endeavours may be regarded as rogue by-products of architecture.[7]

On the other hand, those people who call themselves 'artists' have, during the last decades of the twentieth century, become engaged in a host of activities whose principal characteristic is defying the commonplace, and their status as well as their 'job description' has undergone enormous (and increasingly rapid) change. 'Artists' have become a self-defined class of workers, fabricators of anything exhibited or that can be marketed as 'art'; most of those whose work is shown in the smarter galleries and museums would, if pressed, describe themselves, with more or less justice, as fighting the forces of reaction, convention, banality.

That avant-garde of the second half of the twentieth century was shown the way by Marcel Duchamp. He commented once that his most enduring legacy was the invention of the ready-made.[8] The gist of that procedure was for an artist to designate any object (usually man-made) as 'a work of art' by his mere say-so, though he sometimes 'assisted' them by combining two or more pieces. I will discuss the implications of this process when I come to it chronologically. Here I merely wish to point out that after he screwed a bicycle wheel to a wooden stool and signed his first urinal, Duchamp ironically and punningly labelled a metal dog-comb *peigne* as a token of having finally renounced painting.[9]

Several of Duchamp's other early efforts were as ironic and witty: he bottled 'Paris Air' in thin glass flacons, and labelled toilet water with photographs of himself in drag, titled – with another underhand pun – *Belle Haleine.* His successors tended to be more crass: nearly forty years after the first ready-made had been 'assisted', Piero Manzoni (to quote a famous instance) marketed a package containing an empty balloon for 'artist's breath'; the buyer could inflate it himself, or pay extra for the artist to fill it with his 'artistic' breath. Even more famously, Manzoni canned his own faeces and sold the numbered cans as *Merda d'artista/Merde d'artiste/Künstlerscheisse/Artist's Shit*, the quadrilingual label assuring the buyer that the 50 grams it contained were 'freshly preserved'.[10]

Duchamp provided the exemplar from which many were to generate their own choices – and so licensed a short cut. Producing a work of art, so the old academic teaching ran, was threefold. First came the *concetto*, the kernel idea which was the product of the artist's intellectual *habitus* or mind-set; secondly the *magistero*, the craft or mastery by which the mind-set was translated into the work; and lastly the *effetto*, the product or work proper which established the artist's relation with a spectator/consumer.[11] If the *magistero* can be reduced to the act of choosing, then the ready-made has collapsed *concetto* into *effetto*. Or, as a critic of our time has it, 'the image of the artist has changed radically. Increasingly, it is the artist's idea, not his technical prowess that is important'.[12] The technical prowess, the *magistero*, is, of course, what the spectator receives through his eyes and his fingertips, that on which his judgement operates.

Variations played on the Duchampian method have led to a heterogeneity in making 'art', so that any judgement of quality by a spectator who wishes to compare and criticize (or just appreciate) has turned into an awkward business. The ready-made has become a model for artists who emulate the master by collapsing making into choosing, and it has also obliged many of them to devise a *shtick*[13] (or more than one, since it may involve the wrapping of large buildings in plastic sheeting, the casting of full-size plaster negatives of domestic interiors, the sawing of timber houses into sections or the exhibiting of footballs in aquaria – or yet the moving of large masses of earth to create a sculpture that is virtually a landscape) that becomes their signature. Finding and naming a ready-made has become one method of working among many others. Suitably publicized, painting in oil on canvas can seem another daring innovation.

'The future avant-garde', a recent critic said, 'will not be concerned with form, in any case, but with desire',[14] and this notion certainly applies to developments of the last quarter of the twentieth century – which could for the purpose of art history begin with the Paris events of 1968 and the institutional shake-up which followed it. A class of theorists-critics has claimed to identify the fronts on which the 'avant-garde' campaigned – feminism, post-colonialism, 'gay pride' and suchlike. The hidden premise in the statement is one that has become familiar enough: that the only art which has validity must be identified as 'avant-garde', and that the business of the avant-garde is to combat the (presumably) permanently retreating *arrière garde* of some unspecified enemy forces. That quandary was already implicit in the coining of the term. Charles Baudelaire mistrusted what he called 'moustache-wearing metaphors' worthy of 'fogeys and bar layabouts'. He added to his list

> militant poets and avant-garde writers. This addiction to military metaphors does not point to valiant minds, but ones made for discipline, that is for conformity . . . belgian minds which can only think in crowds.[15]

I quote Baudelaire's misgivings because I have some sympathy with them. The history of the arts of the past two centuries cannot just be read as a teleological procession culminating in the avant-garde of desire. The succession of movements, such a reading implies, may be so presented that important figures are often discarded, and major works that cannot be conveniently fitted into the process are ignored; or alternatively, as a dialectic in which every movement is treated as a thesis to be countered by the antithesis which follows it.

Architecture will not fit neatly into either narrative (as I will try to show), since neither will sustain an account of the withdrawal of public attention from the common realm in our affluent society, or the neglect of representation or figuration in our buildings – and the gradual exclusion of works of art from them. This has generated an unease that has inspired various essays at achieving a unified sensory-mental experience throughout the nineteenth century, whether in terms of synaesthesia or simultaneity, or yet through the socially transforming *Gesamtkunstwerk*, or even the *Totaltheater* which I will have occasion to consider later.

Many of the battles avant-gardists fought were real enough: the forces at which they tilted were convention, institutional inertia, atrophied ways of working. For the many artists who accepted the avant-garde label, it inevitably acquired a political dimension: the enemy was the bourgeoisie, and their weapons were defiance and satire. Such artists were active in political and social revolutions, and some of the great achievements of the period were forged in the turmoil of political events – an example is Jacques-Louis David's *Tennis Court Oath*, which I will consider in the first chapter. At other times opposition to the bourgeoisie and its values was co-opted, even disarmed by the very opponents against whom the avant-garde had been fighting, and so became aestheticized. Art politics have sometimes tended to what used to be called 'radical chic'.

The context in which artists and their patrons operate is therefore unstable and confused. Both public and private patronage is often piloted by the counsel of 'experts' in or out of committee. Such advice may be offered by museum directors (who may have a large public subvention at their command), art critics and historians, exhibition curators – and less commonly by private collectors. Most work by successful artists continues, in any case, to be produced on a contractual basis for art dealers, who in turn depend on groups of collectors, themselves (since the late twentieth century) often speculative investors who need to value their acquisitions objectively and to whom criteria suggested by historic patination, origins and taste (even exercised at second hand – all the things Walter Benjamin summed up as *aura*) have become irrelevant as prices have risen. Indeed, whole collections may be stored in warehouses or even bank vaults – they become futures.

Artists' works are therefore 'rated' – like stocks in the market – and the rise and fall of art prices is avidly reported in the financial pages of newspapers, while art investors sometimes buy whole exhibitions of a young artist's work to control his or her value. The ratings often depend on the quantity and the stridency of the discussions the works provoke and not on the quality of the objects themselves. Which implies – or so it seems to me – that the market value of the 'art product' has to carry some disruptive charge analogous to advertising if the work is to be regarded as notable 'art' and so engage the attention of the public and even of experts. The economic machinery of the art-market is not new, and I hope to show how its development through the nineteenth century is relevant to my theme.

Some architects have assumed other artists' ways of presenting themselves, and have separated architecture from those institutional and public functions which always defined it in the past. They have done so by isolating certain obviously 'art' aspects of their concerns from the full range of their activities, which – paradoxically – gives their projects (when they are drawings) the status of (nearly extinct) easel pictures, to be framed and hung on walls.

Small-scale models turn into 'abstract' sculptures, whose reference to any future and 'full-size' construction bears no relation to their charm. On this showing the architect's activity as a builder becomes almost irrelevant to his new status.

This leads to a blurring of categories, which, you may think, is no bad thing. In my discussion of some twentieth-century artists, you will note that several of them considered their work an essential reduction, a sublimate of architecture. At the same time, the standard products of the really successful architectural offices in the latter part of the twentieth century are the inert and mute corporate buildings I mentioned at the beginning of this introduction. They have come to be regarded with distaste by the lay public (and with discomfort by many other architects and critics), provoking periodic media flurries of anti-architect aggression.

Hence recurrent calls for some redemptive sacrifice. One form it has taken is the one per cent (marginally more – or less – in different countries) of costs to be spent on 'works of art' in any public building. Even this token concession is often circumscribed. In France, where 'public' works of art have long been ordered by state-appointed commissions, the practice was abolished by well-meaning politicians early in the twentieth century because of the 'reactionary' taste of such commissions – but reinstated in 1982 when the state took it upon itself to protect avant-garde artists from the conventional attitudes of architects and local authorities. Such a 'percentage for art' concession may seem a feeble approach to what is one of the plaguing problems of the arts, but it is nevertheless a real witness to social unease, as is the protest of architects who claim exemption from it because their building is itself 'the work of art'.[16]

The relationship of the architect to painters and sculptors (and the various other artists) has, for all that, been deformed by a nostalgic conviction that whenever he does build, and whatever his 'avant-garde' credentials, an architect may need to associate his work with some paintings and sculptures if he wants his building to be 'enriched', to be considered complete according to old norms which are still respected by some institutional patrons.

Institutional patronage may even provide art for public spaces without regard to the buildings that line it. The architect may not even be consulted, as was the case with Richard Serra's huge, 18-metre-long and 3-metre-high *Tilted Arc*, first commissioned for the Federal Plaza on Foley Square in Lower Manhattan by the US Government Service Agency through the National

Endowment for the Arts, who appointed a committee of experts to identify the appropriate artist. Soon after the *Tilted Arc* had been installed, local protest became urgent and after legal proceedings it was removed from the plaza, cut into three pieces and warehoused. The architects were not consulted by the 'experts' in committee and were barely mentioned in the long and widely reported trial.[17]

Much new art cannot play such a role as the *Tilted Arc* because it requires a novel kind of space to be perceived – or at any rate consumed. The productions of some artists, as I have suggested, have so grown in size that museums have had to swell exponentially to accommodate them. Others operate on a scale which requires the appropriation of large tracts of ground; yet others demand special installations in which the full impact of their works can monopolize the sensibilities of their admirers.

Any consideration of public space in the affluent city remains fraught therefore: artists have lost interest in it; architects seem to have abdicated control over it; while sociologists keep on telling us that we must have a rich and varied street life in what remains of it.

In some cities the citizens themselves have taken an initiative. As from 1 January 2007 all electronic advertising – and even billboards – have been limited in the streets and squares of São Paulo in Brazil, the country's biggest city. This may be a straw in the wind, or it may be one of those protests that are too radical to succeed. It is, in any case, a negative move and will need sustained positive action in the public realm to register a long-term success.

I hope, in this book, to set out the reasons for the separation of the responsibilities for the public realm and its consequent loss of dignity. Of course, everyone who writes a book hopes to change something – his or her situation, that of his profession, or tribe or city – or even the way the world works. More modestly, I hope to invite my readers to consider whether the reconstitution of a usable public space, so often talked about, is possible or even desirable in a city in which so much social and political activity is, in any case, conducted over the electronic media. To that end I propose to consider the stages by which the present situation has been reached, and so have to begin my story two centuries ago, at the end of the *ancien régime*, when the conflict we now experience first declared itself.

Dominikus and Johann Baptist Zimmermann, The Pilgrimage Church, Die Wies, South Bavaria, 1744–57.

ONE

The Fall of the Old Régime

The skills of the industrial and the graphic designer grew as a by-product of architecture by way of the division of labour and of the rise of mass-production at the end of the eighteenth century. Robert Adam may well have been the first 'designer' who realized that a new mechanical casting and assembly process could be such a precision instrument as the old craft workshops could not rival: hence his long and fruitful collaboration with Matthew Boulton, 'the most enterprising man in Birmingham'.[1]

Although he is now mostly remembered for his partnership with James Watt, Boulton was honoured in his time as one of the prominent citizens of Birmingham who were intent on raising the low reputation of its manufactory. The corruption 'Brummagem' had long been a byword for counterfeit coins and cheap, tawdry goods – the town already had a virtual monopoly of metal button and screw production at the end of the seventeenth century.[2]

To raise the tone and improve the taste of the local community and of its products, the great type-designer and Birmingham printer, John Baskerville, joined Boulton and Watt and other local notables (Erasmus Darwin, Josiah Wedgwood and Joseph Priestley among them) in the Lunar Society, so called because it met at the full moon to enable members who lived far away – as Josiah Wedgwood did – to ride home by moonlight.[3] To that same end Boulton undertook to copy, emulate and recast objects, mainly antique ones – such as the Greek vases in Horace Walpole's possession – as well as many metal statues and statuettes which he borrowed from other collectors. For his part, Josiah Wedgwood, the founder of the British ceramic industry (who had both John Flaxman and George Stubbs design for him), made sure that he obtained early pulls of the colour plates from the

Josiah Wedgwood, a black basalt vase with pseudo-antique relief, *c.* 1780.

much-heralded forthcoming publication of antique vases that Sir William Hamilton had collected during his embassy in Naples. These Wedgwood emulated – even calling his newly refurbished works 'Etruria' – since he believed that the vases (which we now know to have been Campanian and Greek) were in fact Etruscan.[4]

The Adam brothers, James and Robert – who at that time were the most successful architects in Britain, and highly efficient organizers and entrepreneurs – were able to commission decorative pottery plaques from Josiah Wedgwood, painted panels from Giovanni Battista Cipriani, Antonio Zucchi and Angelica Kauffmann, as well as furniture from the Chippendales (father and son) to complete the interiors of such buildings as Kedleston and Syon House. Yet Boulton alone could give the Adams a precise control on all the metal fittings and ornament other workshops could only approximate. Fittings that came off a production line were (by implication, at any rate) interchangeable, and could therefore not carry any specific reference: their connection to antique sources had to be generic and conventional. This was important because the effect of the Adam interiors was – to some extent – dependent on snaring volumes in a network of precise and crisp lines that articulated the walls and was also picked up by the ceiling or vault: the ceiling pattern was in turn reflected in the stone or wood inlays or, failing that, in a specially woven carpet on the floor. This was already evident at Osterley Park, the Tudor mansion on the western edge of London which the Adam brothers transformed through the 1760s and the '70s; it was made quite explicit in some of the plates in the Adam brothers' own publication of their work, particularly those of the state rooms of Derby House in Grosvenor Square, in London.[5]

Carmine Pignattari (after Giuseppe Bracci), dedication page to 'the Fellows of the Royal Society of Art', from Pierre-François d'Hancarville, *Collection of Etruscan, Greek and Roman Antiquities from the Cabinet of the Hon.ble Wm. Hamilton*, vol. II (Naples, 1770).

From the 1760s onwards, the Adam brothers also practised a version of assembly-line ornamental casting in stucco and fibrous plaster – a modified form of the method they had developed in metal with Boulton – since they realized that new composite materials would allow them to apply similar ornament on exteriors, and the ever-improving stuccos were considered an acceptable substitute for stone. Moreover, the early ornamental roundels and panels were soon elaborated into complete friezes, and even allowed the reproduction of statues on a modest scale.

Curiosity about new methods of production and new technology, the insistence on a tight control of the smallest detail (door-handles, key-escutcheons), as well as their consciousness of creating a school (if not a style), distinguished the Adam brothers from contemporaries whose work some-times looked like theirs, either an enemy, Sir William Chambers, or a friend, Charles-Louis Clérisseau, or yet James 'Athenian' Stuart or (in the following generation) Thomas Wyatt or Henry Holland and George Dance. This manner

The Adam brothers'
Etruscan Room at
Osterley Park,
Middlesex, *c.* 1775.

was elaborated in France by Richard Mique (working for two successive French queens, first Maria Leszczynska and then Marie-Antoinette) at Versailles and at Saint-Cloud, and was even carried to Russia by Clérisseau (working from Paris for Catherine II) and by Charles Cameron, an Adam follower.

All this makes the Adams the true progenitors of twentieth-century industrial design. Their 'style' relied on two other factors: one is the use of large areas of varnished, shiny surfaces – wood veneers, mirror, glass panels – edged by thin, highly figured framing pieces in which the work supplied by 'decorative' (and assuredly minor) artists was valued much as polished woods (or mirrors or pottery decorations), while another factor in the formation of their style was the enthusiastic appropriation and quotation of the new antiquity of the archeologists.[6]

The Adams were both conscious and explicit about their procedure: the most obvious feature of their decorations, the grotesque, they describe as

> that beautiful light style of ornament used by the ancient Romans . . .
> by far the most perfect that has ever appeared for inside decorations

and which has stood the test of many ages . . . [which] requires not only fancy and imagination in the composition, but taste and judgement in the application; and when these are happily combined, this gay and elegant mode is capable of inimitable beauties . . . [7]

In fact, their 'grotesque' was not based directly on antique precedent, but mediated by the example of Giambattista Piranesi, their friend and mentor, who extolled it as the antique exemplar most suitable for imitation in interiors. Ornament in private houses, he argued, did not need to be symbolic or allusive, but could follow an artist's whim, unlike that of public works. He showed how Egyptian, Etruscan and Roman, as well as 'Grecian' ornaments, might be applied not only to walls and chimney-pieces, but also to clocks, sideboards and sedan chairs. Piranesi had assumed a 'freedom' in the treatment of antique and exotic detail which gave all of them equal status; whatever their origin, borrowed historical elements or motifs were reduced to the level of surface patterns. In fact, he assimilated them (by implication) to 'nature's jokes' such as shells or 'figured' stones – which were enthusiastically collected, and had already provided artists with intriguing models during the seventeenth century.

Grottesche had become an important decorative device two and a half centuries earlier, at the time of Raphael and his school, when the *grotte*, the buried rooms of Nero's Domus Aurea and the baths of Titus, were discovered and recorded – as the Adam brothers well knew.[8] What had made these patterns particularly fascinating was their status as the only authoritative antique precedent for the interior articulation of walls. They allowed artists, moreover, to play with levels of reality as well as of reference: painted vignettes could in

Door furniture design by the Adam brothers, *c.* 1775.

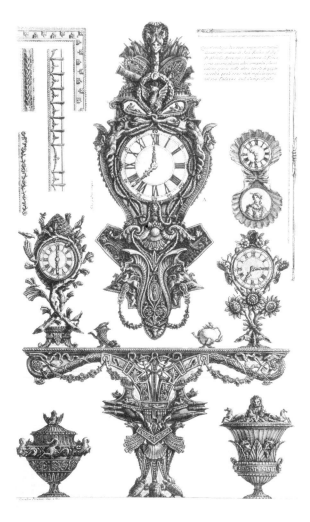

Giovanni Battista Piranesi, plate from the *Diverse maniere d'adornare i cammini* (1769).

turn be framed in stucco relief, or yet in painted imitation of cameo and embossing, and might be enclosed in an overall relief-and-fresco composition. *Grottesche* therefore became a favourite vehicle for elaborate emblem games of recondite iconographic elaboration.[9] Perugino, Mantegna and Correggio, Giulio Romano and even (on the Sistine Chapel vault) Michelangelo practised more or less complex forms of *grottesca*. Towards the end of the sixteenth century, these were developed both by the Caracci (in the Camerino and the Gallery of the Palazzo Farnese, 1595–7; 1597–1604) and by Pietro da Cortona, whose ceilings (in the great salon of the Palazzo Barberini, 1633–8; or in the

Aeneas gallery in the Palazzo Doria-Pamphilj in Rome, 1651–4; or yet the Palazzo Pitti in Florence, 1637–40) show the most exuberant flowering of *grottesche*. Some of these ceilings were engraved and were known throughout Europe. In all of them the formal elaboration is nourished by an iconographic complexity – which in the more extreme examples can be fiendishly baffling.

In England (and in the north of Europe more generally), this play with levels of reality had not been welcomed at first. Rosso and Primaticcio introduced *grottesche* in the Italianate Palace at Fontainebleau. However, the first artist outside Italy to use them on a large scale was Charles Le Brun, the prince of French decorators, in the Louvre and at Versailles. Some engravers of the next generation – notably Daniel Marot and Jean Bérain – ironed out the complex interweaving in which the Roman Baroque masters had gloried, so that all the elaboration is reduced to a pretty patterning which, with a little twisting and a little 'naturalism', turns into something rather different. 'Grotesque' became 'Arabesque' and so was denied its antique origin, as well as any complexity of internal reference.[10]

The French Academy dictionary defines 'arabesques' as 'Sortes d'ornaments qui consistent en des rinceaux & en feuillages faits de caprice'; 'grotesque' is not very different though more specific: 'figures imaginées par le caprice d'un peintre, dont une partie représente quelque chose de naturel, & l'autre quelque chose de chimérique'.[11] But then 'Arabesque', with its suggestion of abstract forms, was also associated with 'Turkey' carpets, known throughout Europe since the Middle Ages, and was given a new currency with the prodigious growth of a fashion for orientalia – Turkish, Persian, Arabic – but also Indian and Chinese, even Japanese at the end of the seventeenth century. The two notions are often confused – hence the Adam brothers' chauvinistic (but well-informed) disclaimer:

> The French, who till late have never adopted the ornaments of the ancients . . . have branded those ornaments with the vague and fantastical appellation of arabesque, a style which, though entirely distinct from the grotesque, has, notwithstanding, been most absurdly and universally confounded with it by the ignorant.[12]

What the Adams there condemned is, of course, what we now call rocaille.

Arabesque did indeed turn into rocaille, which appeared here and there as the centralizing authority of Louis XIV was declining, so that the panoply of state ritual for which Charles Le Brun had designed the overpowering interiors in the Louvre and at Versailles was also withering. The lords of the Régence during his great-grandson Louis XV's childhood and teens – first the Duc d'Orléans (1714–23) then Cardinal de Fleury (1726–43) – were to have quite a different view of what was required of the arts by way of policy and setting for state functions – as did the young king. Still, Versailles had served its purpose: it dominated not only all France, but also the rest of Europe, and many European courts had near ruined themselves emulating its grand manner.

Rococo is born of diminution; *travail de rocaille* was condensed to 'Rococo', presumably to rhyme with another 'unclassical' manner, *barocco*.[13] Rococo interiors offered a graceful, undemanding, quasi-naturalistic and explicitly unhistorical garnish and framing without all the intricate, emblematic apparatus of the *grottesche*. Its motifs were flowing water, shells, windblown leaves and branches, driftwood – earmarks of Venus or even animals – some of them fantastic.[14] It was easy to incorporate various oriental bits: Chinese *famille rose* or celadon vases, Indian rock crystal and Japanese lacquer panels were set into rocaille ormolu framing. As far as that goes, the Adams were right.[15]

Framing might be silver or gold, but the mirrors and the shiny surfaces created a new kind of light, emphasized by French windows whose reflections on the highly polished parquet floors diffused an upward glow. Dormers and lanterns – anything producing a top light – were therefore avoided. These novel effects could not have been achieved without the help of a new technique for casting plate glass perfected just before 1690 at Saint-Gobain. In combination with the colourless potash-lime glass that had been devised in the time of Rudolph II in Bohemia, it allowed enlarged window panes and vastly improved mirror surfaces. This new kind of glass became an essential element in light fittings: sparkling cut-glass candelabra and sconces were always set low, hung well clear of the ceiling to prevent soot stains or untoward shadows on faces. Special varnishes gave painted wood mouldings a glossy finish like that of porcelain.[16]

The apparatus of ceiling paintings on which the grand style relied also withered – or at least shrank – while tapestries were much favoured. Doors were high (like the windows) and emphasized by painted panels within their tall frames – *sovraporte*, overdoors. Panelling would sometimes extend up to the ceiling or vault, and include roundels or spandrels – these were the province of painters like Watteau and Boucher, and later of Chardin and Fragonard.

This manner depended on a profusion of decorative elements – furniture and showpieces. The interior volumes 'flowed' into each other. This interiority, the intimacy, is often presented as female and enticing. In a short story, 'La Petite Maison', Jean-François de Bastide gives an account of a seduction operated entirely by means of a Rococo house and its garden, detailing the working of the charm through the interior and its colours.[17] That sense of intimacy may be one reason why so few Rococo monuments have survived intact: the Petits Appartements at Versailles, the Hôtel de Soubise in Paris, and the Amalienburg palace at Nymphenburg outside Munich (by François Cuvilliés and Dominikus Zimmermann) are the most remarkable. How they looked to their inhabitants may perhaps be learnt more reliably from Boucher's or De Tory's paintings than from the monuments themselves.

At Versailles and in the Hôtel de Soubise, the architects worked within existing structures; where the exterior is also new, as at Amalienburg, it might usually be plain and monochrome and give little notice of the opulent interior spectacle. True Rococo public buildings are also very exceptional – most such projects, such as Gilles Oppenordt's and Juste-Aurèle Meissonier's competition designs for the façade for St Sulpice in Paris, remained on paper. Of those executed, almost the only one which really deserves the name is the Zwinger in Dresden, which Mattheus Pöppelmann began about 1720 for Augustus the Strong of Saxony and Poland (perhaps according to the king's sketch design). The Dresden Zwinger was an extravagance; an adjunct to the royal-electoral palace, it was primarily intended as a setting for spectacles and festivals – and Rococo was a manner much favoured by designers of great gala events. The central pavilion of the Zwinger is practically a rocaille interior turned inside out, even if it could not quite do without the apparatus of the orders, however garnished and broken.

Augustus was the prince for whom the secret of Chinese porcelain was discovered by an alchemist, and for whom a vast collection of brilliant-cut diamonds (a cutting technique as new as that of plate glass) was also formed. The Saxon monarchs then exported rocaille to their other court in Warsaw,

Balthazar Neumann and G. B. Tiepolo, the Kaisersaal ('The Emperor's Room') in the Residenz, Würzburg, c. 1750–52.

and it met a quite different ornamental vocabulary in the east of Poland. The Greek Catholic cathedral of St George in Lviv (designed as a Basilian monastery by an Austrian, Bernard Merderer, who assumed a more fashionable, Italian-sounding name, Merettini) is perhaps the least familiar meeting point of rocaille and 'Byzantium'.[18]

At about the same time, towards the end of the 1730s, the Prince-Bishop of Würzburg commissioned Balthazar Neumann to build him a magnificent palace. About a decade after it was built, Giovanni Battista Tiepolo was brought in to paint over the 'prepared' white rocaille-modelled vaults of the grand staircase, as well as the imperial reception rooms. In spite of the passage of time, that palace stands as one of the last occasions where the masterpiece of a great painter is deliberately married to the work of an outstanding architect to create an eloquent volume. Tiepolo even painted Neumann into the staircase ceiling,

26

reclining on the line of the cornice, supported by a gun barrel in a posture which is obviously an ironic token of his admiration.

Splendid though it is, the Würzburg Residenz already suggests a certain relaxation – ceremonial, if not yet financial. For all their grand manner, Neumann and his eastern contemporaries, Pöppelmann, Fischer von Erlach and the brothers Asam, adapted the elastic rocaille vocabulary to the columns and window surrounds of their grandiloquent palaces sometimes quite sparingly, and they were always articulated by the use of the orders. To the peasants of the Rhine and Danube valleys in the next generation, that same courtly style would seem to offer a dazzling vision of heaven,[19] a vision that did very well for them. However, French designers and theorists at the same time were involved in sharp and rapid changes in perception and ideas, which led to what has come to be known (in the twentieth century) as Neoclassicism.

Classic to Neoclassic

Neoclassicism: the label might be recent, but it does represent a movement which spread quickly through all of Europe. As its name suggests, the renewal of antique inspiration was prompted by several archeological portents earlier in the eighteenth century: the revisiting of long-abandoned Paestum/ Poseidonia in the south of the Campania; the sporadic recovery of material from the ruins of Herculaneum and of Pompeii just south of Naples by more or less consistent excavation from the 1760s onwards; and the publication of increasingly accurate accounts of the architecture of Greece throughout the second half of the eighteenth century. The most famous and influential prophet of the doctrine was a Prussian (who had passed through Saxony), the Abbé Johann Joachim Winckelmann.[20] He lived first in Rome as a member of Cardinal Passionei's, then of Cardinal Albani's household, and became the Papal Commissioner for Antiquities while writing his vast history of ancient art. The German text appeared in Dresden, that Rococo capital, in 1764.[21] His most famous essay, 'On the Imitation of the Ancients', had already been published there in 1755. Henry Fuseli, the Swiss pastor turned painter and publicist – by then established in London – translated that essay rather well into

English,[22] and even though it had a cold reception at first, it became one of several publications which helped to formulate the notion of a new-antique way of approaching art. Moreover, it was Winckelmann's monumental *History* which took up, universalized and transmitted to the late eighteenth and the nineteenth centuries a conception of style borrowed from Vasari. Each period passed, like a human body, through four ages: origin, growth, change, while the fourth was its fall into decrepitude and decay. An alternative reading of style a little later in the book makes the division threefold: necessity has to be satisfied first, then beauty can be sought, and finally abundance and superfluity announce decay. Winckelmann's account of Greek art was based on the second schema, and it allowed him to develop a systematic history of art which could be regarded as equal to any other historiography of his time. It made him the father of the discipline, which has, ever since, been framed in stylistic terms.[23]

Earlier (in the sixteenth and seventeenth centuries), writers on art preferred words like *maniera* rather than 'style'. And the important distinction in kinds of *maniera* was not so much between early, middle and late as between better and worse. For Vasari wrong was – in painting – the 'old', the stiff 'Greek' manner like that of the icon painters, while right was the new-ancient way which originated with Cimabue and Giotto; in architecture, wrong was the German way of building with pointed arches, while right was the antique way with semicircular ones, and with cylindrical columns. This simple usage consecrated by Raphael's and Michelangelo's circle (and only given general currency by Vasari)[24] lasted for a century and a half. It depended, of course, on a unified conception of antiquity in which the Greeks and the Romans, but also the Egyptians and Babylonians, Jews and Phoenicians, were thought to have built in the same way – the way which had been codified by Vitruvius. This belief was sustained by another, more venerable doctrine, which had been formulated in ancient Greece and had the authority of Plato: that there was a coherence between simple linear proportions and musical harmonies, and this proof of architecture out of nature had been constantly reiterated in Vitruvius' book.

A way of building that followed such precepts was therefore thought wholly consonant with reason. It could also be harmonized with Scripture, and therefore with Divine revelation. If the temple which King Solomon built in Jerusalem and the Bible described as having been designed according to direct Divine command could be shown to have been in accord with the precepts laid down by Vitruvius (several writers attempted to do this), then surely the way of building he described was not only antique and noble, but also Christian and virtuous. Vitruvius' description of ancient ways of building thus had the authority both of revealed religion and of nature. Belief about the tight triple guarantee of revelation, nature and antiquity may not always have been universally held, yet since the middle of the fifteenth century it had been powerfully argued in these terms. By the end of the seventeenth century, however, this vision of a unified antiquity had already been marred by the discovery and the detailed study of an increasing number of 'classical' monuments, some of which did not seem to follow the Vitruvian rules.

Travellers had been reporting that Greek buildings were very unlike Roman ones, and that Turks and Arabs, and (moving further afield) the Indians, Chinese – and even the Native Americans – had splendid buildings which seemed to bear little or no relation to those rules. As for the belief in

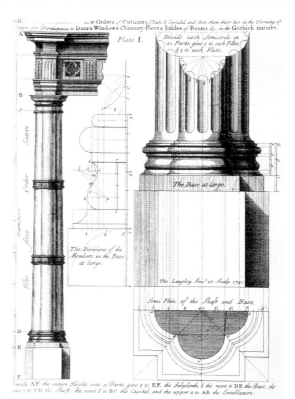

Batty Langley, a Gothic version of the Doric Order from *Gothic Architecture, Improved by Rules and Proportions* (1747).

the harmony between musical and linear proportion, that was broken in the circle of Descartes and never quite restored in spite of the heroic efforts of great men (Isaac Newton was one) who re-stated the ancient beliefs about the harmony of nature. Newton was also one of the Scriptural commentators who wanted to return the Jerusalem temple to its unquestioned pre-eminence among the buildings of the past – in opposition to the sceptics who saw it as only one of many ancient monuments of analogous authority.

Some concluded therefore that architecture had no positively binding rules drawn from divine revelation, nor from the imitation of nature, nor even from the restoration of tragically ruined ancient grandeur, but was subject to the much more fallible and arbitrary governance of human fancy, which had indeed to be bound – or at least reined in – by taste. Taste was an arbiter to which appeals had been made repeatedly throughout the seventeenth and eighteenth centuries – but whose nature was also constantly disputed;[25] and which, in any case, had to be formed in the school of the ancients – or so most of those involved agreed.

Towards the end of the eighteenth century the authority of ancient 'classical' precepts, or even of a generalized 'classical' style, had receded. A new imperative – the construction of nationhood – required a national style (such as the Gothic in England and France) which would speak not only of an un-antique barbarity, but also of the old heroism and forgotten splendour that was implicit in Winckelmann's picture of the ancient Greeks. Moreover, the increasingly attentive examination of medieval buildings showed that some of them were the result of technical and even design skills which were independent of and quite different from (some suggested that they were equal, or even superior in some ways) those of the ancient Greeks and Romans. Indeed, some eighteenth- (even seventeenth-!) century builders conceived of Gothic-type vaulted and buttressed structures masked in good-taste ornament on the antique model.[26] In England the apparent arbitrariness of Gothic ornament could be exploited both as the source of an alternative set of the 'orders' or as a 'national' alternative to the frivolities of Rococo – as it was by Horace Walpole at Strawberry Hill, and later, on a much larger scale, by William Beckford at Fonthill 'Abbey'.

Once the variation of styles had been established in historical terms, it could be refined. In the course of the eighteenth century, the manner of a time past came to be not merely judged – because different and therefore inferior

– by some absolute standard, but related to a particular historical condition: it could now also be young, mature and overgrown. In a way Winckelmann was taking up not only Vasari's rather general scheme, but a notion which – particularly in Germany – was becoming almost a war cry: it was that every nation had its own spirit, an inner coherence which translated that sense of time and place into the literature and art of a people. A nation's arts were therefore not merely a softening of the savage condition and an opening to universal beauty, but also (perhaps principally) the way in which a people became conscious of its true being through its history.

Some nations, it seemed – to Winckelmann certainly – would have a spirit, and therefore an art, superior to others. Such had been the Greeks who had taught all subsequent peoples about liberty and nationhood. Moreover, their art was produced in a tonic and hardy climate. It was therefore an art which needed to be emulated for political and ethical as well as artistic reasons. Winckelmann had used the 'noble simplicity and calm grandeur' of the Greeks to point up and castigate the faults not only of the arts, but even of the society of his own time, so that, following him, an idealized vision of the past came to be used by artists as a strong form of social criticism.

Yet the art of the Greeks was also known to have followed a historical path – from the rude archaic to the decadent and capricious Hellenistic. Its emulators should look only to the art of the best period. It is now easy to fault Winckelmann's connoisseurship, of course, and show that he took some secondary Hellenistic products – and even Roman copies – for high 'classic' works; even in his lifetime, his prescriptions for art and for society were sharply contested. Appropriately enough, it was another protégé of the Saxon court, Anton-Rafael Mengs, also resident in Rome, who would paint the manifesto of the new art, a rather stiffly neo-Raphaelesque *Parnassus* or *Apollo and the Muses* on the vaulted ceiling of the *salone* in the villa of their Roman patron, Cardinal Albani.

In Rome also, and within Winckelmann's own circle of acquaintance, the great antiquarian-engraver Giambattista Piranesi – the same who had befriended the Adam brothers – had lauded the superior art of the Etruscans as a true Italic art independent of Greece, but more ancient, being directly derived from Egyptian precedent. Moreover, Etruscan art was true to materials, while Greek architecture could never be free of the taint of imitation, since

Vitruvius' account of it spoke insistently of Greek ornament being based on the imitation of wood construction in stone.[27]

The Etruscan or Tuscan manner exalted by Piranesi seemed to him also to have been that of the ancient red and black painted vases (as he kept on pointing out). The vase images were therefore truer representations of it than could be got from texts and ruins, and therefore more ethnically authentic than any provided by the Greeks. Piranesi's views were retailed to many artists resident in Rome, and when Jacques-Louis David went there as a young painter in 1774, it was Etruscan antiquity that made the greatest impression on him.[28] When he returned to Paris, he built himself an 'Etruscan' house; and when he planned his *Oath of the Horatii* in 1782, he went back to Rome in order to have antiquity, Roman-Etruscan antiquity, about him. Roman republican virtue seemed an even more exalted civic model than that of Athens.

Of course, in the generation before David, the Parisian court and public had already been conditioned by the revival of the antique. The taste of the French court was then guided by the Marquise (later Duchesse) de Pompadour who was declared the king's 'official' mistress in 1744. She was to be a friend to Diderot and d'Alembert, Montesquieu and Buffon – with Voltaire as her court-poet and the Physiocrat Quesnay as her private physician; she was a protector of Rousseau and of the *Encyclopédie*, as well as the patron of a gamut of artists – from the frivolous Boucher to the moralizing Greuze. She would join a new antiquarian passion to the sobriety appropriate to her devotion to St Mary Magdalene – which makes the fact that she is frequently associated with Rococo very misleading.[29] Her home, the Hôtel (now Palais) de l'Elysée, was in a parish dedicated to the archetypal repentant sinner, and that church, finally rebuilt under Napoleon, would become a crucial monument in my story. At her behest, her brother, Abel Poisson, created Marquis de Marigny, was trained to be Director of Buildings (a post he retained after her death – at the king's insistence) by being sent on an Italian study journey with the engraver Charles-Nicolas Cochin and the architect Jacques-Germain Soufflot, whose masterpiece, the church of Ste Geneviève (known as the Panthéon after 1800) was built by Louis XV as a shrine to the patron saint of Paris. Its free-standing portico, large plain glass windows and sparse ornament made it the exemplary building of the new sober manner. The first stone had been laid in September

Elevation du Pavillon de Louveciennes du coté des Jardins.

Claude-Nicolas Ledoux's garden facade for the Château de Louveciennes, 1770–71.

1764, the year Madame de Pompadour died, and it was not quite finished at the time of the Revolution. Marigny's appointment made him the effective chief patron of the arts in the kingdom. The lessons that the arts were to teach at that point were to be ethical rather than mythical or cosmological, and were not proclaimed by intricate and enigmatic emblems (whether set in a framing of elaborate grotesque as Giambattista Tiepolo's or more plainly framed, as Anton-Rafael Mengs') but in the crowded, didactic and sentimental canvases of Greuze, or the heroic – and free-standing – statues of Houdon and Pigalle. These were statues and paintings done for exhibition and for display as isolated, sometimes even movable objects – they were no longer moulded into the wall-plaster or set in niches. The ornamental patterns (abstract now, and quite undidactic for their part) were stiffened and hardened on antique (preferably Greek and/or Etruscan) precedent.

The church of the Madeleine is not, as she had hoped, Madame de Pompadour's main architectural monument.[30] She is more closely associated with the pavilion of Petit-Trianon in the gardens of Versailles, which the king built for her, although it was incomplete when she died. The principal court architect, Ange-Jacques-Gabriel, managed to distil the French planning experience into a miniature palace of the strictest elegance, which – with its discreet but knowing use of rustication and giant columns – became a manifesto of Pompadour classicism. Its gardens were also in the Pompadour spirit, famous for housing an elaborate and scientifically classified botanical collection.[31]

33

Madame du Barry, who succeeded Madame de Pompadour as the king's reigning mistress five years after the latter's death, would favour another brilliant architect, Claude-Nicolas Ledoux. She may have come across him when he built the notorious 'Temple of Dance' for Mademoiselle Guimard. This was a rather luxurious house with a private theatre (its solemnity and pretence shocked Diderot – especially in view of the disreputable character of the *ballets-roses* performed there – and Fragonard was to decorate its central public top-lit, duplex vaulted dining room. Whatever the differences between them,[32] Fragonard abandoned the project, and she then commissioned the young David, then still a rising pupil of Joseph-Marie Vien, to finish the decorations.

Unfortunately nothing – except a few drawings and engravings – survives of Mademoiselle Guimard's pavilion, but about the same time, 1770, Ledoux was asked to design another one at Louveciennes, near Marly, for Madame du Barry. While Madame du Barry's pavilion does not have the fiendish ingenuity of Mademoiselle Guimard's in plan, it shares with it a very sober, a deliberately antique air. The complex play of shapes within a simple rectangle is emphatically articulated and unified by an obtrusive order, both inside and outside. The dining room is a cube opening into two lateral apses with small musicians' galleries, much-mirrored, though with an allegorical ceiling by

Claude-Nicolas Ledoux, interior of the Café Militaire, 1762.

34

Joseph-Nicolas Guichard. All sculpture and painting is contained within the thinnest rectangular frames – or sometimes in unframed wall sinkings. Three salons face the garden: one is an oval, to have been lined with tapestries; another, a cube 'king's room', is all columns and statues; while the third is an apsed room, whose main features were to be the four large compositions especially commissioned from Fragonard. For various reasons, Mme du Barry also found them unacceptable and they were returned to the artist, to be replaced by more sober, more 'antique' compositions by Vien.[33]

Grateful for the expeditious construction of her much-admired pavilion, Madame du Barry had Ledoux named to the lucrative supervision of buildings for the salt monopoly. He designed several silo-warehouses and a centre at Arc-et-Senans near Besançon, the most important of his executed buildings to survive. Perhaps the first monumental factory, it includes tied housing for the workers in a hemicycle which creates the perimeter of the complex. It is closed by the diameter made up of the salt-pans and the administration buildings, and at the centre of that diameter is a huge director's house from which the whole energy of the enterprise seems to stream. The hemicycle was to be duplicated on the other side of the diameter in an ideal future. Indeed, Ledoux' major published work is the project for a utopian city radiating over the surrounding landscape out of the oval.

It is obvious that Ledoux's whole attitude to ornament was as different from that of the Rococo decorators as it was from the Adam brothers, in spite of superficial resemblances. It is in fact the very opposite of theirs. The Adams generalized and conventionalized ornament, while Ledoux was always looking for ways to charge it with ever more specific and even with allegorical reference. His first signed work, the interiors of the Café Militaire of 1762, already shows this.[34] For all his ingenious use of corner mirrors from floor to ceiling – which multiplies the volume and turns the ornamental frames into quasi-structural elements – the gilt fasces of lances wreathed with bays and crowned by plumed helmets, the shields and the relief panels are to be 'read' as showing the military users of the café taking their victorious repose.

Ledoux had a great many more noble and public commissions – palaces in Paris for the Princes de Montmorency and the Duc d'Uzès and for the Comte d'Hallwyl, and in Normandy for the Marquis de Livry, as well as the theatre at Besançon, the law courts (or Parlement) and the prisons at Aix-en-

Provence.[35] His major executed work, however, apart from the Saline at Arc-et-Senans – were the toll-gates of Paris, built in the decade before the Revolution: they involved an elaborate sculpture programme, since all of them were to be decorated with statues and reliefs that would refer, allegorically, to the cities to which they led. The toll tax and the wall with its barrier gates (that ensured its exaction) was one of the hated impositions of the financial administration of the expiring monarchy. Several of the gates were destroyed in the days after the fall of the Bastille. The Fermiers-Généraux, who administered such taxes, including the most brilliant associate of Ledoux in this enterprise, the chemist Antoine Lavoisier – were guillotined in May 1794, some weeks before the Thermidor events. The same events presumably saved the life of Ledoux himself (who had been in prison since the end of 1793). Later, many of the surviving barriers fell victim to Baron Haussmann's plans in the 1860s, and only four have survived into the twenty-first century.

In the decade left to him after the Terror, Ledoux built nothing, though he returned to a position of honour. He went on elaborating the project for his ideal city, whose buildings were to carry a carefully articulated and highly allusive charge which was sometimes entirely moulded by his conception of it as a narrative continuity. So the conciliation court (which he called *Pacifère*) was a cube – a symbol of Justice – and its walls were to be inscribed with the fine sentiments of Socrates and other sages on panels separated by the bundled rods of lictors; they are the token of its authority – not unlike the bundled lances of

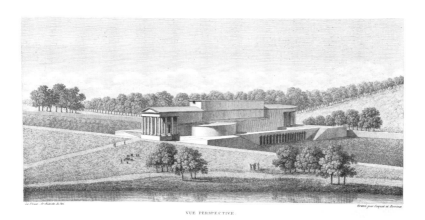

VUE PERSPECTIVE

Claude-Nicolas Ledoux, perspective view of the 'Oikéma' at the Saline de Chaux, *c.* 1774–9.

36

Claude-Nicolas Ledoux,
plan of the 'Oikéma' at the
Saline de Chaux.

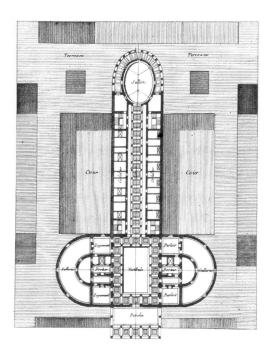

the Café Militaire. A quite different building, the *Oikéma*, was intended by
him to awake virtue in the young by displaying vice to them: brutally put, it
was a public brothel. The plan was in the shape of a phallus, a colonnaded
oval salon at its tip, while two hemicycle galleries formed its base; ranges of
cabinets particuliers line a long, clear-storied (and therefore top-lit) passage.
The walls of the building are blind, and it is entered through a portico and an
atrium. The proliferation of public buildings and monuments to commemorate and represent the institutions of a reformed society was to ensure its harmonious working – so harmonious that the city required no prisons or other
places of punishment.[36] Very few architects in the next generation followed or
developed the full implications of Ledoux's 'symbolic' method – yet he was
not alone in desiring 'signifying' buildings, an *architecture parlante* (as one of
his critics was to call it later).[37]

   While Ledoux was building his first great houses (Hallwyl, d'Uzès), another
French architect, Jean-Charles Delafosse, published his *Nouvelle Iconologie
Historique*, and he proposed a form of ornament based entirely on serial allegory;
countries, seasons, moods, the functions of the building, each had their

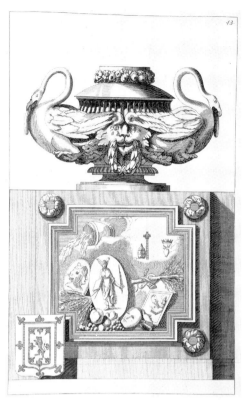

Jean-Charles Delafosse, 'A Monument Symbolizing the Origin of Paganism', from *Algemeen Kunstenaars Handboek*; engraved by Jan de Witt, 1768.

Jean-Charles Delafosse, 'An Urn Symbolizing Scotland', from *Algemeen Kunstenaars Handboek*.

appropriate set of emblems. Although Delafosse's few surviving projects (only two modest Parisian houses were built, it seems) were grand in scale, his book does not really propose whole buildings, but only allegorized features – of which some are of the new severe kind, with fluted half-columns, brutal rustication and large areas of plain wall; others are just bits of rocaille with a little narrative added. His book was published in France, reprinted in a reduced form in Holland – and had wide circulation. Allegory returns as a subject of the greatest interest to some of the artists of the last quarter of the eighteenth century.[38]

An even more popular collection of designs than Delafosse's was published by the engraver-architect Jean-François de Neufforge, beginning in 1757.[39] He provides a survey of type designs from small town houses to palaces and cathedrals, and some explicitly 'symbolic' buildings – like a triangular temple

Jean-François de Neufforge, plan and elevation of the Temple of the Arts related to Architecture, from his *Recueil*, Supplement 1772.

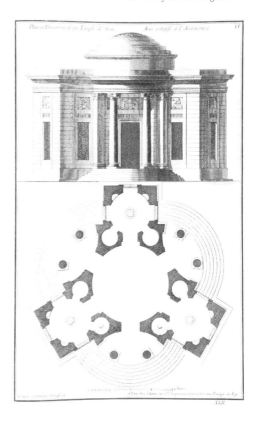

dedicated to the three arts (presumably painting, sculpture and architecture) and a square-in-circle building symbolizing the year and the four seasons. Both Delafosse and Neufforge indicate more or less elaborate sculptures on their buildings. Delafosse was explicitly concerned with detailed iconography, while Neufforge merely indicates the presence of statues and reliefs, particularly reliefs in friezes – though not on flat surfaces, but on curved niches and even wrapped around a cylinder separated from its base by a convex moulding and crowned by a spire as a 'floating' element. That, of course, is how Ledoux also uses them. In his drawings and engravings, he rarely indicates more than their outlines, perhaps because he expected to work with artists of repute.[40]

Etienne-Louis Boullée, a few years older than Ledoux, and like Ledoux and Neufforge a pupil of Jacques-François Blondel, the leading architect-teacher of his day, was consumed by a different reforming zeal; he took up Newtonian notions about light, and attempted to found his system on it. With reductive, stringent logic, he argued that regular forms (in which the play of light is more evident) are superior to irregular ones. The form in which the maximum variety of surface is paired with the greatest conceptual unity – the sphere – must therefore be supreme, his unstated postulate being the 'classic' reconciling of unity with variety, often regarded as the prime condition for beauty in a work of art. Many of his vast projects (recorded in elaborate watercolours) are based on the use of the sphere and the hemisphere, and he was almost entirely uninterested in surface embellishment. Unlike Ledoux, he paid only a token attention to the five orders; he rejected their primacy as a mainstay of design. He was not a prolific builder, but his visions were overwhelming in scale. Like Ledoux, he was a painter first and almost a reluctant architect.

In England, the 'figural' reaction to the wilful arbitrariness of both rocaille and Adamesque pseudo-antique was much more restricted. The only important public monument it produced was Newgate gaol in London, designed and built by George Dance the Younger about 1770 as a vast, heavily rusticated, blind-windowed and barely articulated block broken only in the middle of one side for a central and equally rusticated but many-windowed house for the director and the administration, and flanked by squat Piranesian, chain-wreathed pavilions – terror-inspiring entries for male and female convicts.[41] The architectural interest of Newgate lay entirely in its use of formal and iconic devices; it was built just as the design and planning of prisons were to undergo a number of important modifications.[42]

There had been a literary recoil which was much more powerful and effective. In 1757 the young Edmund Burke, before entering on his political

Contract drawing for Newgate prison, detail of west front, George Dance, London, 1769.

career, published a slim volume, *On the Sublime and the Beautiful.* The book was taken up quickly all over Europe, and Dance must have been aware of it. In England it became the manifesto of a new attitude to nature and landscape, and was coupled with another notion, that of the 'Picturesque', a kind of domesticated Sublime. It became the slogan of a whole school of garden and landscape design which was exported all over the world, perhaps most successfully to the United States.[43]

The most powerful immediate effect of this view of the Sublime, however, was on philosophers who practised the new discipline, Aesthetics. In his *Critique of Judgement* (which was not published until 1790), Immanuel Kant proposed a searching account of the beautiful and the Sublime. It derived, as he put it himself, from his transcendental exposition of aesthetic judgements, and a balanced relation between taste and feeling – in contrast to the merely psycho-physiological notion of it that he had found in Edmund Burke's little book.[44] This sharp division often made in the second half of the eighteenth century between the building and its ambient landscape may almost seem an anticipation of Kant's distinction.[45]

The Sublime before which Kant and Burke may have experienced awe and a helplessness as before the uncontrollable was very different from the pity and terror with which Greek tragedy and its neo-Greek emulations purged the spectators. There was new apprehension of the uncanny, the *Ungeheuer,* of the uncontrollable both in nature and in passion to which the ancient epics and other 'rude' arts gave access and which had been too long neglected by artists; it chimed with the new sense of storm and stress, *Sturm und Drang,* which possessed many German writers and artists.[46]

Sign and Experience

The quest for ways of transmitting inner, intense experience directly in works of art, unmuffled by precedent or convention, was also driven by a fear that the social fabric was at breaking point – and in France it would indeed crash in 1789. Yet the mechanism of allegory and the gods of antiquity had not quite been abandoned. Winckelmann himself in his last major summa, *Monumenti Antichi Inediti,* which he published himself in Rome in 1767, devoted the first of the two volumes to mythology, ritual and history proper, while the history of ancient art is relegated to the second volume, where it is packaged with the plates.[47] The fragmentation of that 'classical' past, which sharpened the historical perception of some figures of myth and allegory, also contributed to a weakening of historical continuity in the late eighteenth and early nineteenth centuries, as I shall try to show: Roman began to be distinguished from Greek, Greek from Etruscan, and all these from Egyptian – and so on, but there was also a growing sense that behind all the different facets or masks of antiquity, behind the different myths which sustained and glossed them, there was some underlying and more elemental truth.

The very notion of 'the Antique' which artists had come to Rome to study had also become unstable in any case, since the very foundation of architecture and its legitimacy (as of all human institutions) could no longer rely on the force of precedent transmitted and emulsified by tradition. Perhaps only the primitive conditions in which society (and the arts with it) had first arisen could be a guarantee of the reform which would harmonize the lessons and precepts of antiquity to the dictates of nature – and therefore of necessity. In France, leading theorist-critics realized this: Viel de Saint-Maux considered that building forms could be derived from the symbolism of number and geometry; Le Camus de Mezières translated the old doctrine of character represented in the features, even the mouldings of buildings, into a teaching which derived forms from the attempt to inspire such sentiments in the viewer.

In Germany, only a few individuals were conscious that the realm of the Sublime held social and emotional powers to which only art could give access. The young Goethe, the sharpest of these observers, was disconcerted – when visiting the tent erected on an island on the Rhine near Strasbourg for the wedding, by proxy, of Marie Antoinette and Louis XVI in 1770 – to find its throne room hung with tapestries representing the loves and misfortunes of Jason, Medea and Kreusa. Goethe feared these allegories were an appalling presage: his Strasbourg contemporaries – who saw only the rich and elaborate tapestries, not the images on them – found his unease ridiculous, though it turned out to have been fully and tragically justified.[48]

Goethe had gone to Strasbourg to take his degree, and there met a young Lutheran pastor who had studied with Kant in Königsberg, Johann Gottfried Herder. It was the beginning of a long, if troubled friendship. One of its first fruit came of their together observing the elaborate cathedral appreciatively – and it led to their re-evaluation of the Gothic architecture their neo-Greek teachers had taught them to despise. Goethe's very first and anonymous publication, *Von Deutscher Baukunst*, was a paean to the presumed – and quasi-mythical – builder of the cathedral, Erwin von Steinbach, which turned into an attack on French Neoclassical theory.[49] For his part, when still a young curate in Riga, Herder visited the Jägelsee (in what is now Latvia), where he watched girls collecting magic herbs on a St John's Eve, and heard one of them intoning an old song which the others would take up, in chorus, while they danced ritually around barrels of burning pitch. He felt then that he was witnessing 'antiquity still alive in the present', and it was this discovery that he was to call *Volksdichtung*[50] – a kind of poetry which had a direct access to the instinctive and archaic wisdom of a people, whose raw expression did not need to be constrained by taste or by any of the laws that may govern beauty. It may be a mere accident of history that Herder had his remarkable insight a few months after Gottfried Lessing published his *Laokoon* – which stated, rather elaborately, that while the Greeks may scream in poetry, they will only sigh in sculpture, since beauty in the figural, visual arts requires the containment of emotion.[51]

This experience in 1765 initiated Herder's search for a poetry which directly expressed experience, which arose almost 'spontaneously' from the people – a poetry of necessity, as it were. It allowed the language of a specific group to bridge the chasm between an individual, inevitably determined by his national-cultural context, and the infinite, universal ideal of humanity, and it suggested the possibility of some meta-symbolism from which all particular expressions were developed. It was Goethe, however, who formulated the new doctrine of the symbol for succeeding generations – in opposition to that of allegory:

> Symbol changes appearance into the Idea, the Idea into an image, so that the Idea remains ever and unceasingly effective and intelligible; and even articulated in every language it remains inarticulate.
>
> Allegory transforms appearance into a concept, the concept into a picture, yet so that the concept is limited and completed in the picture, in which it is fully contained and articulated.[52]

J. W. von Goethe,
'Monument to Good
Fortune', Weimar, 1777.

Herder had an analogous apprehension when he first visited Goethe's garden in Weimar, and saw the monument or altar the poet had erected to Good Fortune or Luck: a sphere over a cube. It seemed to Herder that Goethe had reached some elemental level of symbolism in this little garden figure that spoke directly to the spectator: the altar was a true symbol that reached some level deeper than any allegory, that it stood beyond the veil of language, incarnating, as it were, Goethe's own distinction between allegory and symbol.[53]

Beauty could be attained in allegory, but the Sublime was beyond its reach. However, the Sublime in art could be symbol. Kant's distinction between the sublime and the beautiful (which he had so carefully made in his Third *Critique*)[54] also became, in a much coarser and even violent form, the essential postulate for a new, emphatic, agonistic view of the artist's role. Striving after the Sublime seems to have eclipsed the quest for beauty which had inspired several of Kant's contemporaries – notably Goya.

In 1774 the young Francisco Goya, returned recently from Rome – where he seems to have gravitated to the Mengs–Winckelmann circle[55] – was appointed court painter and sent to Saragossa to decorate the vaults and walls of a domed shrine that Ventura Rodriguez, a Rome-trained architect, had recently completed. It had been inserted into the bleak and emphatic church of Nuestra Señora del Pilar.[56] It is not clear when he met the architect, but they seem to have been on excellent terms, and Goya painted him holding a drawing or engraving of the plan of this very project. The Saragossa paintings were greeted with great enthusiasm by contemporaries. Goya had already, in 1772–3, carried out a large fresco cycle on the *Life of the Virgin* at the Charterhouse of Aula Dei outside the town; in these very hieratic paintings, the scenes are set in a defined and screened, rather Poussinesque space unlike that of the liquid, acidly coloured and often cruelly edgy, cartoons for the royal tapestry works.[57]

Twenty years later, in 1794–8, the Italian-born Don Felipe Fontana was finishing the little church of San Antonio de la Florida, which he had conceived in a rather Roman *barocchetto* manner of almost Winckelmannian sobriety. Goya, by now quite deaf, was commissioned to decorate its domes and vaults. He does not seem to have developed as close a relationship with (the already aged) Fontana as he had with Ventura. His use of the interior space goes against the conventions of the preceding generations. Goya moved the *Adoration of the*

Francisco de Goya,
*The Miracle of St
Anthony of Padua*
(1798) in the dome of
San Antonio de la
Florida, Madrid, 1798.

Trinity (a theme which Baroque and even Rococo painters would have painted into the dome) in the apse, over the altar. The dome of the church carries the scene of a miracle of St Anthony in Lisbon, the composition crowded around the edge, the whole painted very quickly, with all the verve and the sharp colouring of the tapestry cartoons. The figures are grouped behind a thin balustrade which circles the cornice, and look either up at the saint or down at the spectators. *Putti* and angels support the drapes below the asymmetrical miracle, and the whole tonality of the frescoes brightens upwards towards the lantern. The use of light, the relaxed colloquialism of gesture, and the distribution of the figures show Goya's involvement in Enlightenment illuminism and correspond to the Erasmian piety that also informs his 'mystical' pictures.[58] For himself he painted the 'black' pictures of the *Quinta del Sordo* that display a cruel and haunted private world to which some commentators have vainly attempted to give a consistent and esoteric interpretation.[59]

From the Saragossa frescoes to the tapestry cartoons, there is a lightening of the palette and a freeing of the brushwork until it becomes more fluid than Tiepolo's – but there is always a bite to them, and it becomes evident in San Antonio de la Florida where the space is almost twisted by the images. However, in the 'black' paintings, Goya was the harbinger of a radical change in the attitude of artists towards their own art, one which would inflect the stormy developments of the next half century. Like his contemporary Beethoven, Goya carried his deafness as a stigma and a necessary mark of his isolation. His frenzied activity as an etcher and lithographer depicting the horrors of his own time and the stupid cruelty of the world were a partial response.

Johann-Heinrich Füssli (whom I mentioned earlier as Henry Fuseli, Winckelmann's translator) was a Roman visitor more or less contemporary with Goya and with David. While David, like Goya, studied the antique and the Seicento, Füssli (who, of course, had also studied it) was by then obsessed by Michelangelo. Shortly before David began his heroic *Horatii*, Füssli, on his way back from Rome in 1778, had painted (for the town hall in Zürich) a tribute to the martial virtues of his own nation according to a newly revised version of legendary Swiss history. His painting showed the representatives of the three original cantons swearing their foundation oath on the Rütlisberg. William Tell, allegedly present on that occasion (though he is not shown in Füssli's picture), was to be cast in legend as the Swiss Brutus[60] (Roman and

Greek heroes were useful prototypes for national ones), since 'classical an-tiquity', as Mona Ozouf has pointed out, 'was also the youth of history'.[61]

Like his more 'advanced' contemporaries, Füssli regarded antiquity as the only true model for representing 'primitive' conditions – which included Northern legend and literature. Painters could draw themes from Shakespeare and Milton, and the *Nibelungenlied* – but above all from Ossian.[62] Although he was amongst the more 'visionary' artists, yet Füssli cast his images in forms which sometimes owed as much to antique precedent as did David's – as may be seen in his almost literal adaptation of the figures from a Greek vase (in the Hamilton collection – which I mentioned earlier) to illustrate the passage in Hamlet about the poisoning of the King of Denmark by his brother – an antique formal model adapted to serve a 'national' narrative.[63]

The Ancient Republic

Some architects of the time – Boullée and Ledoux are obvious examples – may have seen themselves as painters (if only in metaphor). Many painters, for their part, had architecture, especially a renewed antique architecture, play an active part in their compositions. Jacques-Louis David painted the *Oath of the*

Jacques-Louis David, *The Tennis-Court Oath*, *c.* 1790, pencil, ink and sepia wash on paper.

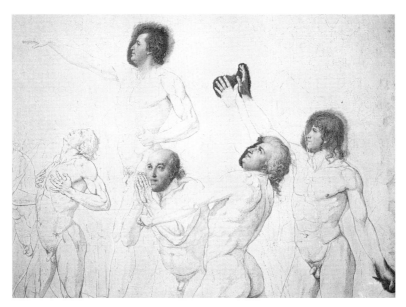

Fragment of the incomplete 1790 painted version of David's *Tennis-Court Oath*, charcoal, pencil and oil on canvas.

Horatii to a generous royal commission. As was usual with such works, it was exhibited in the Salon of 1784. Patronage notwithstanding, David's painting celebrates popular solidarity: the oath is a founding act of nationhood, emulating perhaps Füssli's heroes in his Zürich painting, who also raise their arms heavenward in an affirmation of ethnic sovereignty.[64] In the Salon of 1789, only weeks before the fall of the Bastille, David was to exhibit an even more 'revolutionary' painting. It showed one of the first consuls of the Roman Republic, Brutus, witnessing the return of the bodies of his sons who had conspired with the exiled kings and whom he had condemned to death. David set that scene again in a 'primitive-Roman' architecture, even more 'correct' than that of the house of the Horatii. And this, too, was painted to a royal commission.[65]

The inspiration of those two major Salon paintings had come from the theatre: Corneille for the *Horatii*, Voltaire and Alfieri for the *Brutus*. In Voltaire's play, David's friend, the greatest French actor of his day, François-Joseph Talma, played a minor part wearing a toga and a 'Roman' headdress that David had arranged for him.[66] Mme Vigée-Lebrun, already a very successful portrait painter at the time, though only in her twenties (she had painted the queen frequently by then), indeed thought David's passion for antique detail enhanced

48

his genius. She, too, was a great admirer of Talma (as well as a friend of David, though not a republican at all) and was equally enthusiastic about re-living, re-experiencing the antique. A homespun enactment of it was an impromptu 'antique' dinner party she arranged with her brother after reading passages from a fashionable account of ancient Greece: the Abbé Barthélémy's *Voyage du Jeune Anacharsis*.[67] They prepared some dishes described in the book, wrapped themselves in white shifts, wreathed their heads, borrowed some 'Etruscan' (i.e. Greek) vases from a friendly collector, and welcomed their guests with a chorus by Glück sung to lyre accompaniment.

It is easy to belittle antico-mania and revolutionary propensities after the event, yet David's contemporaries saw the two salon paintings as prophetic: 'Brutus et les Horaces dont le génie a dévancé la révolution', an enthusiast of David's art, Emmanuel de Pastoret, preached to the Jacobins in 1790. That speech was occasioned by his attempt to find the funds to commission a vast canvas commemorating another oath, that of the *Jeu de Paume*. It was to be a painted monument to a crucial event in the history of the Revolution: on 20 June, 1789, the deputies of the Tiers Etats and some clergy, who had declared themselves a 'National Assembly', were barred by the king from their chamber in the palace. They retired to a rickety nearby tennis court where they swore an oath that they would not depart until they had voted a constitution. That oath would come to be considered the foundation act of the new French state. The painting, which was intended as a commemorative evocation of the event (rather than an accurate depiction of it), was to be vast, 24 x 35 feet (7.32 x 10.67 m); during the various debates about the commission, a number of persons well known to have been absent therefore claimed the right to be represented as participants, and in the same discussions no one objected that the president of the Third Estate, the brilliant playwright and astronomer Sylvain Bailly, is shown facing out of the picture at the viewer rather than at the assembled deputies who are grouped behind him. Emulating Bailly, the deputies raise their arms in a gesture which recalls, inevitably, that of the Horatii in David's painting of 1785.

Certainly, David and his contemporaries made the connection forcibly. In the Salon of 1791, the *Oath of the Horatii* was re-exhibited together with his *Brutus* (now associated with the Terror, even though it was finished and shown before the fall of the Bastille) to accompany a large preparatory drawing for the

Jeu de Paume.[68] The painting which was to follow that drawing had been commissioned by the Jacobin Club as a gift to the National Assembly, to be hung 'in the place where it holds its deliberations' (as yet undefined). However, the Club was not rich, and the painting expensive – so that even the artist's costs in materials and assistants were beyond its means. It was therefore to be paid for by a subscription for an engraving of it. Although David's bid to find a new form of patronage attracted a great deal of attention and fervour, the subscription did not even raise a tenth of the estimated cost of the painting. What is more, by the time he had begun to brush in the detailed portrait faces of the nude gesturing heroes for the final version, several prominent figures of the *Oath* – notably the central figure, Sylvain Bailly, who had also been Mayor of Paris briefly, had been guillotined (Bailly on 12 November 1793). Others had badly tarnished reputations even earlier: Mirabeau was disgraced for secret collusion with the court. The painting was never finished and survives only in cut-up fragments. A large (much later) painted copy

John Singleton Copley, *Death of the Earl of Chatham*, 1779–80, oil on canvas.

after the drawing now hangs in the actual Tennis Court at Versailles, witnessing to that shabby little building's moment of glory.[69]

The episode is crucial in the economy of art, even if David was not really innovating but following the English practice of selling reproduction (engravings, of course) rights to paintings.[70] This had not always been very profitable in Britain either, and painters would also derive income from the gate money (sometimes quite a lot) by displaying a large painting publicly in a an appropriate hall or even a special marquee. Pictures exhibited in this way were not histories or allegories, but 'reportage', preferably sensational paintings which recorded recent events and relied for their effect on a combination of real portraits of the witnesses and the participants – who in many cases would also have been known to the exhibition visitors. The most successful of these was John Singleton Copley's *Death of the Earl of Chatham* of 1781, painted within a year of Chatham's death, crowded with portraits of the peers and exhibited near the Palace of Westminster where Chatham had collapsed and died. It made Copley a fortune, even if he found it impossible to sell the canvas later.[71]

The five years of turmoil which followed the Revolution (1789–94) were neither favourable to French building, nor for the public commissioning of paintings, though they were certainly busy ones for what might be termed the politics of art. David himself was elected (after several abortive candidatures for the Assembly) to the Convention in 1792. He changed his political colours gradually, moving to more radical positions, as did the Jacobin Club of which he was a member. He had voted for the death of the king and had Robespierre's confidence.[72] Having become – as far as art was concerned – the most powerful man in France, he led the attack on the Académie Royale des Beaux-Arts, which allowed him to work out his resentment at various slights; its monopoly over the Salons was quashed, its property confiscated, the teaching of the various arts interrupted. His polemic was not merely personal and political, however, since his dogmatic primitivism set him in sharp opposition to the 'academic' teaching of art schools in western Europe as it had been formulated in the seventeenth century and developed in the eighteenth, based on a universalizing of the human figure as a model – or rather a type – of perfection; but the type did not refer to a living body – it was mediated, 'seen through' the antique – which meant, in effect, Hellenistic and Roman sculpture.

The Theatre of Revolution

Festival decorations and the renewal of the theatre had favoured the assertion of a new manner, if not in painting and sculpture, then in architecture. In 1789, when the Estates met at Versailles (before they took the Tennis Court oath and turned themselves into the National Assembly), they had done so in a sober but stately and vaulted Doric hall built into the Palace by Pierre-André Pâris, architect of the Menus-Plaisirs, the royal agency which dealt with performances, stage sets and interior decoration. The governments, first royal and later republican, would finance the many revolutionary festivals that were designed and arranged by David and his associates, who purloined and 'stiffened' that Menus-Plaisirs manner. The 'primitive-Roman' architecture of the houses he had painted into the *Brutus* and the *Horatii* and the accessories and the dresses of his models anticipated the solemnity of the various feasts all over France, such as the festival of the new deity proclaimed by the Revolution, called of the 'Supreme Being', which, like those of the Federation, was held on the Champ de Mars – as well as the funerals (the reinternments of Voltaire and Rousseau notably) in the secularized church of Ste Geneviève, renamed the Panthéon.[73] The Panthéon was to play an increasingly important part in these doings.[74] In April 1791 the Constituent Assembly voted to make burial there a civic canonization.[75] The ringing slogan *Aux grands hommes la patrie reconnaissante* – which, as an acronym AGHLPR still decorates its pediment and the uniforms of the staff – was coined in the speech which proposed that change. The original sculptures and bas-reliefs of the church were destroyed in the first secularization, as was the tympanum sculpture. Meanwhile, the building had other troubles: the main piers already showed cracks when the centring of the pendentives and the crossing arches were first struck in 1776, and had to be reinforced. Quatremère de Quincy, sculptor turned art politician, in a revolutionary mood, had all the windows in the walls blocked to make them more solid and, by making the lighting indirect, the atmosphere of the building became more solemn (or so he thought). This, of course, made the walls – which Soufflot had not articulated with pilasters – into large flat surfaces like those of later academic building.

Burials and re-burials in the Panthéon were among the many and frequent shows and processions which were an essential part of the Revolution's

Rousseau'an inheritance. At the end of his long lettter to d'Alembert defending his home city, the Republic of Geneva, for its exclusion of theatre (which reinforces social inequality) and of actors (whose work inevitably condemns them to a life of duplicity and inclines them to moral turpitude), Rousseau asks rhetorically:

> Are there to be no spectacles in a Republic? On the contrary . . . there are to be many. They were born in Republics and it is only in them that they are truly festive. . . But let us not favour those exclusive shows which shut a few people up under a dark vault . . . No! O you happy people, such are not your festivals! You should gather in the open air . . . Raise a pole in a square, and garland it with flowers, gather the people and you have a festival. Go one step further, make the spectators themselves into the spectacle. Let each person see himself and love himself in others and so let them be more closely united . . .[76]

That was a lesson which Robespierre had certainly learnt: to make the spectators themselves into a spectacle. Hence the multiplication of the festivals of the revolutionary religion, solemn funerals, anniversary celebrations. David became Robespierre's hierophant, his producer and master of ceremonies, working sometimes as a 'consultant' behind the scenes. At a less exalted level, David also provided the Revolution with its accessories. The furniture that appears in David's paintings was made up by the most famous *ébéniste* of the time, Georges Jacob,[77] who also became the furniture maker of the hall of the Convention. Even the 'Phrygian' bonnet, the red cap of liberty, may go back to a pre-revolutionary painting of David's.[78]

When the Convention moved from Versailles to Paris, it reopened in a new hemicycle built into the old palace theatre, the Salle des Machines of the Tuileries, designed by the revolutionary Jacques-Pierre Gisors, even if the semicircular layout, the high colonnade and zenital lighting followed the model of the sober, neo-antique anatomy theatre in the Ecole de la Chirurgie.[79] Although the assembly hall was a bit makeshift (the statues which ornamented its walls were all painted simulations), the hemicycle found favour and was copied when the chamber was enlarged and rebuilt in the Palais-Bourbon. Two centuries later it still serves the Chamber of

Coloured woodcut of
Jean-Baptiste Guy de
Gisors' Convention Hall
in the Palais des
Tuileries, 1793 (since
destroyed).

Deputies. With its obvious division into left and right, it became the model
for many parliamentary chambers all over the world – a curious fate for an
emulation of an anatomy theatre.

Revolutionary politicians had, of course, taken the importance of the arts
for granted, but were never sure what to do about them. The Assembly, first
National and then the Convention, separated or united the arts according to personal and political considerations. Various proposals for reform were ventilated
and partially applied. A republican and patriotic institute was to group artists,
philosophers and scientists in one national body which continued in a modified
form through the Empire and the Restoration. However, once the Directory took
over, the exaltation of 'permanent' revolution had to be slaked. 'Qu'on termine la
Révolution', Madame de Staël insisted. The whole of life would not, could not,
after all, be remade as a work of art on the model of antique virtue.

Those years of Revolution and Terror notwithstanding, David's populous
studio continued as an assembly point for the more brilliant of the young:
Isabey, Gros, Gérard, Girodet, Ingres were all his students. There were also a
number of sculptors (who were soon to find employment under the Empire),
since sculpture had no alternative master at the time, even though the
Assembly and its committees were forever decreeing statues of Virtues and of
Liberty or the Nation to be erected in public places, and the various festivals
required further figures of the Supreme Being. Such statues were almost
always temporary and made of cheap materials – which may have been just as
well, since few sculptors of any real distinction worked in France. Augustin

Pajou seems to have done most of his work before the Revolution, while Jean-Baptiste Pigalle, whose nude statue of the aged Voltaire was prophetic of an unsentimental verism in portraiture, died just before it; Joseph Chinard acquired some political reputation, having been arrested by the papal police while at the Academy in Rome, but he was no master. Jean-Antoine Houdon, though saved from the guillotine by adapting his *St Scolastica* as an allegory of Philosophy,[80] never achieved the prominence he had acquired in the last decade of the monarchy during the Empire.

Napoleon's favourite sculptor – who had indeed come to dominate the European scene – was the Venetian Antonio Canova (1757–1822). His heroic nude statue of the emperor has finished ignominiously as a decorative trophy in Apsley House (the Duke of Wellington's London home). Apart from the innumerable Napoleonic busts emulating the officially sanctioned ones by Houdon and Chauvet, the only imperial sculptural monuments to survive their patron are the triumphal arch of the Place du Carrousel,[81] and the bronze victory column on the Place Vendôme that replaced an equestrian statue of Louis XIV (thrown down in 1792). The vicissitudes of that statue and the column are well known, though it is worth recalling here that its destruction in 1871 was ordered by the master of the Realist school, Gustave Courbet – of whom more later.[82] None of the sculptors in David's circle could remotely rival the reputation of Canova, or his successors, the Dane Bertil Thorvaldsen (1768/70–1844, who spent most of his career in Rome) and the German Gottfried Schadow, who had a constant flow of royal Prussian commissions. Both Canova and Thorvaldsen were called upon for monuments of the great and famous; both designed papal tombs in St Peter's (Canova of Clement XIII and XIV; Thorvaldsen of Pius VII) and both found white marble the supreme vehicle for their vision, which still owed most to that ideal of 'noble simplicity and calm greatness' formulated by Winckelmann. As against David's teaching, they believed that anatomical detail had to be subsumed to the simplicity of type and the passage of surface through movement and articulation.

When the Consulate and then the Empire replaced the Directory, David transferred his loyalty to Bonaparte. As he tried to reform everyday dress under the Terror,[83] so he designed the fancy uniforms and plumed hats of the Directory, and therefore considered that the design of the costumes for the Consulate and the Empire was also his due. He saw himself as Bonaparte's art expert, perhaps minister. But Bonaparte rejected David's costumes, and the Consular uniforms were modelled on those of the end of the monarchy. The direction of the arts went instead to Dominique Vivant-Denon, who had been a family friend of the Beauharnais (though he had also long been a friend of David), and the chronicler of Bonaparte's great Egyptian expedition. Eventually, the emperor also appointed Vivant-Denon director of all imperial museums.[84] This is one of the first cases of a museum director placed in such a 'modern' position of power.

Revolution into Empire

David had set out to celebrate the new mood of national conciliation after the end of the Terror in another huge canvas, which showed the Sabine women enforcing the peace between the Romans and their aggrieved menfolk, fathers and husbands. He is said to have conceived it in prison and to have begun working on it during a wretched period of his life after the fall of Robespierre and the fiasco – financial as well as political – of the unfinished *Tennis Court Oath*. Having lost a number of his assistants, he had to finish the painting 'in silence and solitude' to get the compensation that he had sought for the abandoned *Oath*. He therefore decided to follow the practice of British and American artists and to exhibit the picture to paying visitors himself. From the government he got a subvention of 4,000 francs for the frame, and a space in the old Academy of Architecture in the Louvre, where it was on display from 21 December 1799 until sometime in 1804. Visitors were charged 1.80 francs for entry and the ticket was an explanatory pamphlet written by the painter.[85]

Although it was the first time an exhibition of this kind had been organized in France, it went on attracting crowds (about 2,000 a week) so that David earned 650,000 francs by it. It was not only to be a new way of showing paintings and giving a painter the financial reward and a dignity he did not have before – it required the viewer to approach the picture reverentially, to examine the details of the narrative as they were set out in the explanatory text, to take in the whole vast composition (5.22 x 3.85 m), for which purpose David had a large mirror hung at the other end of the room. The mirror-image

Antoine-Jean Gros,
Self-portrait, 1795,
oil on canvas.

(so contemporary observers thought), especially when seen at some distance in the large exhibition room, mingles the figures in the painting with those of the visitors, enhancing its verisimilitude, since other members of the public could be seen in the reflection as if they had the same kind of reality as those of the painting.[86]

The Sabine theme moreover required him (or so David thought) to be even more 'primitive' than in his previous acclaimed 'antique' masterpieces; he is said to have let fall a self-critical comment to one of his assistants about his over-reliance on anatomy and on 'classical' sculpture in earlier pictures, and his desire to concentrate on the outline of limbs as well as profiles in the manner of 'Etruscan' vases and pre-Pheidian relief sculpture.

That apparently casual remark was taken up as a slogan by the small group of 'primitives' in his studio. They were led by his brilliant and charismatic pupil Maurice Quay.[87] He was to die very young, in his early twenties, but the ideas which he formulated and championed were inspired by a group who called themselves 'primitives' or 'thinkers' and were sometimes known as 'Barbus'. These 'Primitives' interpreted the master's self-critical remark as a call to purity – not only of art, but of intention. Quay himself was both very good-looking and rather pious – notable in irreligious, post-revolutionary Paris. The group adopted a particular, pseudo-antique flowing form of (Phrygian!) dress; they grew their hair and beards long (hence the soubriquet *les Barbus*), which led to awkward scenes with the police.[88] Even the emperor was drawn into the discussion: interviewing Quay who had been recommended by David as a drawing teacher for some Bonaparte children, Napoleon is reported to have asked: 'why do you dress in a way which separates you from everybody?' To which the painter answered 'To separate myself from everybody'.

The Barbus would even raise police suspicion by setting up common lodgings and studios in an abandoned convent – that of the Visitation nuns – at the foot of the hill of Chaillot, a district then frequented by some of the politically disaffected. The group clearly considered ideas of a new direction in the arts to require a different, even a communal way of life and this would suggest more general social reform, of which that of dress was a foretaste. I will have more to say about that in the next chapter.

TWO

New Empire, New Style

Louis XVI, King of France, having been re-titled King of the French in September 1791, was beheaded two years later. The Revolutionary Republic was ruled – if that is the word – by conflicting committees until the Directory was established in 1794 as a kind of premier-less cabinet. Meanwhile, the Republican armies were extending the frontiers of Liberty. In Italy they were commanded by General Bonaparte, originally Napoleone di Buonaparte, younger son of a minor Corsican noble, advanced stormily from lieutenant in 1786 to general in 1793. One of the five Directors (the *ci-devant* Comte), Paul de Barras, procured the command of the Italian army for him, and introduced him to Joséphine de Beauharnais, whom he married in 1796. Joséphine had a grander background than her new husband, but a shady past. Born in the colonies, in Martinique, she was self-consciously Creole, assertively so at times. Under the Directory she was one of the *merveilleuses*, with Mmes Récamier and Tallien, ladies of dress as extravagant as their reputation was dubious. Joséphine had been the acknowledged mistress of Barras, but had some lustre as the widow of a victim of the Terror, a Conventional – who had also been a scion of the old nobility, so that she knew how to assume the ways of the old court. All this gave her social standing, even if of an ambiguous kind. Her marriage changed all that. She was now surrounded by a court herself – from which she had to banish many of her louche old friends.[1]

In November 1799 a *coup d'état* set three consuls in the place of the Directory – with Bonaparte as one of the three; he became First Consul and Consul for Life in 1802, Emperor of the French in 1804. I have noted the dates to indicate the vertiginous speed of his rise from second lieutenant to emperor, from petty provincial notable to world ruler in less than a decade.

After another decade of absolute power, by the time he was 45, all was over and he was in exile on St Helena.

The new structure of government he established required some visible social context to mediate and represent it, and called for an assertive new style, different from that of the old monarchy. Assertion was also needed because both emperor and empress were social marginals and both of them were, moreover, notoriously short.[2] The style was in effect created for Napoleon by David – with the architects Pierre-François Fontaine and Charles Percier – almost against his will. The First Consul was an artillery officer, and at first favoured graduates of the old Ecole des Ponts et Chaussées, seeing himself as a promoter of utilitarian public works such as fountains and waterworks.[3] Even before assuming the imperial title, however, and the trappings of dynastic monarchy, Napoleon realized that something more emphatic than the undemonstrative and useful might be required.

One business of a court, after all, is to set a fashion. For that – and Joséphine seems to have realized this before Napoleon – interiors, accessories, images were needed: Percier and Fontaine were at hand, as were David and his pupils. Charles Percier and Pierre-François Fontaine had been in Rome together at the time of David's second visit there. When Percier was appointed to design sets for the Paris Opéra in 1793, he had his close companion (who had taken refuge in England – where he had seen and appreciated the work of the Adam brothers) appointed with him. They had already worked together as furniture designers and decorators, and they had been employed both by Ledoux and by Gisors.

Their ascent was as rapid as that of their employers. Mme Récamier had her rooms decorated by Louis Berthault, one of their associates (and was painted by David reclining on that famous day-bed made by Jacob to their design),[4] while they designed the rooms of the Marquis de Chauvelin (who had been ambassador to London), in which some of David's pupils executed decorative friezes.

Since she had bought the house which Claude-Nicolas Ledoux (the same who had worked for Mme du Barry) had originally designed for David's friend, the actor Talma, whom I mentioned as a guest at Mme Vigée-Lebrun's 'antique' dinner, Chauvelin turned out to be Joséphine's neighbour. The house, though stylish, had to be adapted to her needs, and fashionably so.

Charles Percier and Pierre-François-Léonard Fontaine, Library at Malmaison (*c.* 1800–02); engraving after Ch. Percier and P.-F.-L. Fontaine, 1801.

The painter Jean-Baptiste Isabey (more likeable than the rather dour David) introduced Percier and Fontaine to her. They had had a quick social success through their interior designs, but their status changed rapidly when Fontaine had the temerity to contradict Napoleon, the victor who wanted the works of art he had taken as indemnity from the pope at the treaty of Tolentino displayed as trophies under the dome of the Invalides. Fontaine told him that it was the right place for captured flags but would not do at all for works of art; they should be shown to full advantage, he thought, in the Louvre. That was in 1799.[5] Though startled by such direct contradiction, Napoleon was rather taken with the pair and from then on they were constantly in government service. Percier was to die in 1838, but Fontaine continued in various official capacities until 1849, when he was 86.

Meanwhile, the associates had become the empress's court architects. After the Paris house, they designed the interiors of her country mansion at Malmaison, and eventually became the devisers of all the settings of the new empire – more interiors at Saint-Cloud and the Tuileries, the coronation, the great military pageant afterwards (which came to be called the distribution of the Eagles) and (after the divorce from Joséphine) the organizers of the emperor's triumphal second wedding to the Austrian Emperor's sister, Marie-Louise von Habsburg. And they were adept at such work. The new imported colonial woods, particularly mahogany from the Caribbean, provided excellent backgrounds for the bright, ormolu or gilt, more or less mass-produced metal ornaments they devised. Even the humblest pupils in David's atelier were well trained in providing the appropriate painted detail.

Setting for the New Power

Percier's and Fontaine's working methods were very different from those of Ledoux (which I mentioned earlier) when he worked with Fragonard or Vien. Their decorative schemes, though conceived and presented according to linear conventions developed in the previous generation, required that undecorated walls, whether of wood or stucco, remain as blank – therefore white – areas in the presentations, while the ormolu rosettes and fronds, as well as the painted decorations, were fully detailed and made dense, dark patterns. This inverted tonal values: it dematerialized areas of dark, richly figured mahogany, which remained white in drawings and engravings, while decorated friezes and ceilings, however pale, became a complex web of lines. The Percier and Fontaine style depended also on their having passed the exalted symbols of antiquity – the sphinxes and torches, the trophies and crouching lions, palmettes and stars – through the Piranesi–Adam sieve, reducing them to mass-produced metal attachments or to patterns woven into figured silks or yet printed on wallpapers. As in the work of the Adam brothers, these motifs were not expected to carry any specific message, but to provide a background of generalized association; their overcrowding and the resulting devaluation were deliberate.[6]

The Empire style was diffused throughout Europe by Percier's and Fontaine's publications: even Napoleon's enemies, such as Emperor Alexander I of Russia, subscribed to them. The first five plates of the most popular one, their *Recueil*, show the house of the painter Isabey – and it may be assumed that he painted the decorations himself within the frames the architects had established. The same was presumably true of the decorations for the Spanish royal palace at Aranjuez painted by Girodet, Bidauld and

Ch. Percier and P.-F.-L. Fontaine,
engraving of a room in the Palace of
Aranjuez, near Madrid, from Percier
and Fontaine, 1833.

Thibault, or those at Saint-Cloud by Prud'homme. Apart from the cabinet-maker Jacob, no other collaborators are mentioned by name in their publication, so that the reader is free to assume that everything else – all the arabesques, finials, figures and so on – was executed by 'decorative' artists according to the architects' drawings. Inevitably, the *Recueil* did not claim to give a complete account of their work, but presented select examples intended to influence (as they said in the preface) the taste and the 'industrial arts' (the term is theirs) of their contemporaries with a view to creating a complete style of interior, clothes and ornament in harmony with the architecture, since these relatively trivial objects make up the clothing on the body of the building.

Nor was antiquity their only source. In fact, they regarded 'classical' antiquity critically and deplored as vulgar the fashion for the Doric orders without bases used on shopfronts and gate-lodges by their contemporaries. Precedents to which they appealed are certainly varied. The sphinxes and hieroglyphs that recur constantly in their work allude to one of Napoleon's glories: his conquest of Egypt in 1798; but when they had to decorate the cathedral of Notre-Dame for Napoleon's coronation, the outside was quickly decked out in an elaborate apparatus of Gothic flummery.[7]

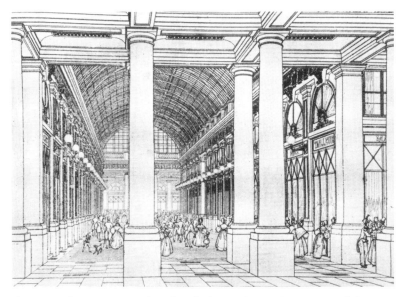

Ch. Percier and P.-F.-L. Fontaine, The Galerie d'Orléans, Palais Royal, Paris, engraved after a drawing by Fontaine, 1833.

For all his utilitarian prejudice, the first consul/emperor came to thirst for *grandeur*. Even before his assumption of the hereditary title, he was planning various public works. A group calling itself the 'Commune des Artistes' had been charged with reassessing the use of confiscated royal and religious properties: they produced a 'Plan des Artistes'. One of its main proposals was the driving through of a road connecting the Place de la Concorde with the eastern entry into Paris at the old Porte St Antoine-Bastille. The Rue de Rivoli was built by Percier and Fontaine as its first instalment, and ran as far as the Palais-Royal;[8] it was extended during the Second Empire, but there were projects connecting the eastern entry of the Louvre with the Porte St Antoine and further east – to Vincennes as well. A new church on the site of the Madeleine was begun, and the Rue Napoléon (now Rue de la Paix) laid out between it and the Place de la Concorde. Triumphal arches were planned: one at the Carrousel has already been mentioned; another and much bigger one, Chalgrin's vast and plain one at the Etoile, which was not finished until 1836 (and whose decoration will have to be considered later), was projected. Individual buildings were dwarfed by other achievements: the improvement of the water supply and new fountains, the embanking of the river and the building of four bridges – including the cast-iron Pont des Arts.[9] But the most remarkable – or perhaps bizarre – monument was the 15-metre-high elephant on the Place de la Bastille modelled by Charles-Antoine Bridan, a sculptor of some success but no great reputation, even though it was to be the largest public sculpture in the city by far; Percier and Fontaine were not involved in this – in fact, Napoleon had thought of building another triumphal arch there.[10]

Of course, Napoleon's deeds also had to be recorded and monumentalized more immediately in paintings. Though he was finicky and quite well informed about mythology, the emperor despised and distrusted allegory. David had to paint out the figure of Fame hovering over the Emperor in *The Distributions of the Eagles,* one of the two paintings he finished (of the four that were planned) to record the instauration of the empire – the other being the *Sacre,* the imperial coronation.[11] The whole of that event was enmeshed in problems and ambiguities.

Napoleon was not the Emperor of France, but of the French – of the nation, not of the land; Louis XVI had already been compelled to change his title by the National Assembly. Napoleon, for his part, would adopt the title of emperor to avoid claiming the inheritance of the various Philips, Charleses, never mind the sixteen Louis, and to appeal to the imperial authority of Charlemagne (whose alleged sword he wore at the coronation).[12] Merovingian gold cicada, found in the tomb of King Childeric (mistaken for bees), became part of the imperial insignia. This mix of the Gaulish and the Egyptian with Greek trophies and nymphs was meant to evoke a syncretic-mythological world of ideas of which many of his artists were certainly aware. Again, the Gothic coronation trappings of Notre-Dame reflected Percier's and Fontaine's involvement with the collection and recording of medieval monuments for the Musée des Monuments Français, which the antiquarian Alexandre Lenoir had put together in the deconsecrated convent of the Petits-Augustins; it was to become (and still is) the home of the Ecole des Beaux-Arts.[13]

David's *Coronation* scene was played out against a setting designed by Percier and Fontaine, and the same is true of the *Distribution of the Eagles.*[14] The *Sacre* is the most valuable commemoration of the event, since all the imperial regalia have since been destroyed and the jewellery distributed. Nor was the imperial ritual ever re-enacted. Like all David's vast canvases, the

Sacre was also painted as a Salon picture and was given the emperor's explicit approval when he visited the painter in his studio to view it: 'Vous avez deviné toute ma pensée, David, vous m'avez fait chevalier français.'[15]

Percier's and Fontaine's legacy was more complex than their part in the creation of the Empire style. Early in their career they had designed a splendid palace for the National Institute – that body which the Revolution had intended to replace the old academies. This very large, very schematic project, not unlike many that were done for academic competitions in the previous half-century, was never built. Their friend Jacques-Nicolas-Louis Durand seems to have used it in his lectures at the Ecole Polytechnique as an example of how an architect articulates a programme and marries it to a geometric analysis of the structure. He also published it as the specimen of a new and – he claimed – universal design method, which consisted of analysing any programme by means of an axial diagram. A grid is imposed on the site once the prime planning decisions have been made to establish the placing of walls and columns. His method was taken up all over the world.

Durand was professor of architecture at the Ecole Polytechnique, which had been formed in 1794 by the Convention just after the end of the Terror; he remained in that position for thirty-nine years, through all the changes of government. The curriculum required every student to give a portion of his time to architecture, which, for most of the first thirty years of the school's existence, was taught by Durand himself. His teaching, summed up in a volume extracted from his lectures, became a vade mecum not only for his students, but for all Europe. Durand's method was based on the recognition that all building design operates with three kinds of form: the highest and abstract kind are the prime geometric solids (of which the sphere, uniting as it does the maximum of unity with the maximum of variety, is the most perfect; in this, Durand adopted the 'classical' teaching of his mentor, master and kinsman – Etienne-Louis Boullée). The lowest were the contingent forms which arise from the nature of materials and the process of manufacture. Reconciling them are those third intermediate forms which are derived from historical examples, and which the architect must use to mask the mismatch between the two extremes.

Durand's method was quickly taken up by others. David Le Roy, the first to have published (in 1755) a survey of ancient Athenian architecture, opened a school in the Louvre – and soon both Percier and Fontaine joined the staff.

It then moved across the river, to the ex-Petits-Augustins convent, as did its neighbour in the Louvre, the painting school. Both schools sent their best students once more to Rome, where French authorities (after 1802) acquired much grander quarters in the Villa Médicis (which they still own), even if respective notions of the role the artist and architect pupils would play in society increasingly diverged.[16]

The belief that Durand's median 'historic forms' could provide the only legitimate ornament was accepted by virtually all the professors at the Ecole des Beaux-Arts when it was finally established. All permanently located painting and sculpture in buildings would be subordinate to this rule. Nor would there be any need to invent new ornamental forms. This did not encourage architects to seek collaboration with painters and sculptors, since 'true', 'fine' artists, even if willing to fulfil a literary or political programme (as David certainly was), looked askance at the suggestion that their work was 'ornamental'. The patronage of the Empire, on the other hand, required huge, but almost journalistic celebrations from artists – for which David's and Girodet's canvases were the model, and this created a short-lived but influential school of anecdotal chronicle painting. Following David, artists saw even their most monumental and epic productions as independent objects, to be found a dignified home in a museum or institution after it was finished. Of its nature, such painting could not ask for any permanent location, since it would always be replaced in public attention by the representation of some new 'great event'.

On the other hand, the attempt to create a universal design method out of the Empire style through the Ecole Polytechnique, which was certainly suited to the linear presentation which Percier and Fontaine had perfected, helped to break spatial continuity by rejecting painting and sculpture as irrelevant to a utilitarian one, as Hegel, a few years later, was to reject any future for architecture since it had no continuing intellectual consistency or even interest.

When the Bourbons were fully restored after the hiccup of Napoleon's return from Elba for his last 'hundred days', they still could not or would not – and perhaps did not need to – kill off the 'Empire style': but they did bloat it. A contemporary commentator noted of the decorations around Louis XVIII's bed in the Tuileries that 'the trophies and fleurons accorded with the King's obesity'.[17]

The king and his brother and successor, Charles X, retained Napoleon's architects – Percier and Fontaine – in the service of the crown; they needed that continuity in the background much as they needed Talleyrand (and even briefly Joseph Fouché – Napoleon's infamous police chief) for the stability of administration and foreign policy they could provide. Percier and Fontaine had worked for the allied invading armies even before Napoleon went into final exile after Waterloo. By then they were international celebrities, and some of the allied commanders were on good terms with them; they were the stars of a dominant Parisian elegance still associated with the Bonaparte family – with whom several of those same commanders rather ostentatiously went on associating.[18] The work of the office was hardly interrupted by political upheavals and their partnership continued unbroken. Only the shrine of expiation for the crimes of the Revolution – a domed church and a cloister Louis XVIII had built over the cemetery where the victims of the guillotine were summarily buried – was undertaken by Pierre Fontaine alone; Charles Percier, still true to his republican sentiments, would not collaborate on such an ostentatiously anti-Revolutionary project.[19]

For the most prominent cousin of the two last Bourbons, the Duc d'Orléans, who would become King Louis-Philippe (after the fall of Charles x in 1830), Percier and Fontaine had – before his accession – designed public spaces in his main Parisian house, now called the Palais-Royal, in which they also built (just before his elevation to the throne) a glazed shopping arcade. It was by far the most splendid of its kind in Europe at the time, and replaced the highly successful but ill-famed wooden market-barracks built over the foundations of a gallery that had been planned there as part of the major rebuilding of the whole complex by a much older architect, Victor Louis. It made the palace a profitable source of revenue for the Orléans princes in two generations.[20]

The Rule of the Fragments

The France of the Bourbons, however gently treated by its conquerors, was in retrenchment after the grandeur of Napoleon and his collapse. One public mark of the defeat was the return of all those works of art Napoleon had exacted as indemnity in Italy, of which the four Roman bronze horses from St Mark's in Venice were the most conspicuous. They had been harnessed to

The Aegina Pediment in the Alte Glyptothek, Munich.

the chariot which crowned the triumphal arch in the Tuileries, also
designed by Percier and Fontaine.[21] These horses turned out to be the mere
avant-garde of a great invasion of Western Europe by antique sculpture.
Lord Elgin, when ambassador to the Sublime Porte, revived a seventeenth-
century French ambition to remove what had remained of the Parthenon
cornices and pediments – and with them one of the caryatids from the
Erechtheion. He brought the sculptures to London in 1808 and sold them to
the nation in 1816. In 1812 yet another group of sculptures, the Late Archaic
pediment of the Temple of Aphaia at Aegina, was sold at auction on Malta
to the highest bidder – who happened to be the crown prince (who became
king in 1825), Ludwig I of Bavaria. After they had been rather drastically
restored in Rome by Bertil Thorvaldsen, they were provided with a dignified
setting in the new Glyptotek designed by Leo von Klenze (who had been a
pupil of Percier at the Ecole des Beaux-Arts).[22] The Glypthotek in Munich
and the new British Museum in London (where the Elgin Marbles were
housed after 1819) therefore became the pilgrimage sites of a new vision of
neo-primitive art.

The very presence of the Elgin Marbles in Britain provoked agitation, for which the curious and irritant figure of Benjamin Robert Haydon was a focus. The enthusiasm which the first glimpse of the Parthenon marbles stored in the garden shed of Elgin's house in Park Lane inspired in him resembled a lasting religious conversion. It led him to fight ferociously for a revival of British monumental fresco painting. Like David a decade earlier, he turned away from the prevalent teaching of the academic 'grand style', which – for him – was enshrined in Joshua Reynolds's *Discourses*. To Reynolds the summit of all figurative art had been the 'history picture', by which he did not mean the costume set-piece (which, as I suggested in the previous chapter, was becoming increasingly popular by the end of the eighteenth century – though it was gradually being displaced by the contemporary event), but 'history' in the old academic sense, a narrative painting whose action was made explicit through the relationships, expressions, gestures and dress of the figures. He was fighting a rearguard battle, however, much as his German contemporaries would also do, since the painting of history, with its universalist and rhetorical pretensions, would be inexorably displaced by the painting of anecdote – historical anecdote to be sure, and often moralizing – but with a concentration on details of the period and the textures of fabric for which the old history painting had no need.[23]

In the *Discourses* – which may be taken as the foundation document of the British Royal Academy's teaching – Reynolds had already said: 'no taste can ever be formed in manufacturers; but if the higher Arts of Design flourish, these inferior ends will be answered of course.'[24] The academic argument that all artists should be trained to do something approaching history painting, while the crafts should be pulled up to the level of 'high art', was maintained by Haydon against the various attempts to create a class of mechanical, 'industrial' and ornamental draughtsmen through training schools. There 'life' drawing, whether from casts of antique sculpture or from the posed model (central to all academic training), would not be taught. Like David, Haydon sought the direct inspiration of a 'primitive' antiquity (represented by the Marbles) and of anatomy (to be learnt through dissection on the cadaver) in his diatribe against the academies.[25] Haydon was not interested in the argument for a revival of medieval methods and practices then being advanced in Germany, which would only be echoed in the next English generation – that of Pugin and Ruskin. The best (if not the only possible) training for an artist was that imparted by a master to his pupils in the working atelier; all academic training, Haydon argued, was perverse.

Haydon's harping, strident polemics in favour of a national school of design were – or so he said – also the direct result of his confrontation with the Parthenon marbles. His agitation for a national design school had a ready audience, since it was felt – among some industrialists, and even in government circles – that abroad (particularly in France) these things had been better arranged. Much of that agitation was confused by a translation problem which has bedevilled the issue of design ever since: an Ecole du Dessin is a drawing school, not a school for designers as some thought in Britain. *Dessin*, *Disegno* means, primarily, drawing in artist's parlance. These terms were not synonymous with 'design' applied to industry. The profession of 'Industrial Design' has therefore grown up in Anglo-Saxon countries in a manner analogous to the German *Kunstgewerbe*, but in Latin languages the terms 'designer' and 'design' had to be taken over from English when the need for them arose in the twentieth century.[26]

Eighteenth-century academic teaching – the complaint was increasingly insistent – was producing a sub-proletariat of unemployed and unemployable 'high' artists. Diderot had already reported that complaint, as made by Chardin, and it was often quoted.[27] And yet in Paris at the time these large numbers formed the body of competent draughtsmen available to the manufacturers of decorative objects – for weaving and printing patterns, for wallpapers and tapestries. The standard of skill was of a level which could not be rivalled elsewhere. While Chardin's complaint was registered in 1765, Jean-Jacques Bachelier in 1762 had already founded a school of ornamental drawing (later it became the Ecole des Arts Décoratifs, which also taught 'academic' drawing); by 1771 it had 1,500 pupils. James Barry, an Irish painter who in fact spent his working life in London as an early protégé of Edmund Burke, reported this and other such figures in his *An Inquiry into the Real and Imaginary Obstructions to the Acquisitions of the Arts in England* of 1775. His 'inquiry' had been stimulated by his grand tour and provoked – in part – by manufacturers' complaints about the inferiority of British fancy goods, which were being displaced by French ones in the world market. Barry saw the decay of design as an aspect of the impoverishment of the arts in general, and he attributed such difficulties partly to the marginalizing of the arts at the Reformation, and

James Barry, *The Distribution of Premiums by the Society of Arts*, *c*. 1789–1801, oil on canvas, from the cycle *The Progress of Human Culture*.

partly to the excessive mechanical-commercial atmosphere of the country, but rejected the Winckelmann-derived notion that the climate of Britain was an obstruction. Like Reynolds and Haydon, he considered that the excellence of the minor arts was wholly dependent on high standards in the major ones.[28] In this, and in his attack on the Academy's apparent monopoly of training, as well as in his ambition to work on a vast and monumental scale – which he only realized partially in the decoration of the rooms Robert and James Adam designed for the (soon to be Royal) Society of Arts in the Adelphi – he foreshadowed many of Haydon's ideas and ambitions.

While Haydon, inspired by the Elgin Marbles, was agitating for the creation of a new school of monumental fresco-painting, their very presence in the country was a factor in the relation between artists and architects. Since the Marbles were seen as a nonpareil, *the* supreme works of art, they could not be equalled by any living artist. This reversal of the Renaissance argument that antiquity could be equalled, perhaps even surpassed, was made just when sculpture was becoming conspicuous by its absence from public buildings – portraits always excepted. At the same time, mechanically produced casts were becoming increasingly common and accepted by architects as a near-antique surrogate, and this inevitably changed the views of many artists about their social role and about their education.

Although this phenomenon was general, it declared itself first in Britain, where the re-planning of central London under the Prince Regent continued after his succession to the throne as George IV in 1820. It was dominated by the creation of Regent Street as a main ceremonial thoroughfare between his principal residence at Carlton House, overlooking St James's Park, and his suburban villa in Regent's Park to the north.[29] The new sites which the layout of the street created were farmed out to developers, who wanted the road finished quickly – as did the prince. Stone would, of course, have been preferred to brick for such prominent buildings, particularly for churches and other institutions, but the rapid growth of London and the new economies of construction demanded cheaper and quicker materials. Various artificial stones and forms of stucco that had been devised in the previous half-century became the staple exterior finish of brick. The near-standardized early mouldings and ornamental panels (such as those devised by the Adam brothers) proliferated into figured friezes, pinnacles and even statues. This development is associated with the work of John Nash, Decimus Burton, the Cubbitt brothers – and even John Soane.

Nash was the most successful architect of them by far. He planned Regent Street and the park to which it led; he designed, among many other things, the Regent's Park Terraces, which skirted and therefore defined the park, and many of the buildings that lined it. He also provided the original project for a palace on the site of old Buckingham House, and built a rather showy residence for himself in Lower Regent Street, whose main apartment was a long art-gallery. To fill it he commissioned copies of Raphael's pseudo-antique *grottesche* in the Vatican, as well as of 'modern' masterpieces by Titian, Caravaggio, Guido Reni and Guercino; for sculpture he had only antique examples copied – the *Apollo Belvedere* and other Hellenistic statues. There were no original

73

Interior of the Nash House gallery, 14 Regent Street, London, in an engraving by T. Kearnan after John Britton and Augustus Pugin, *Illustrations of the Public Buildings of London*, 1828.

works by contemporary artists among them. Yet Nash was on very good terms with several painters: Sir Thomas Lawrence and Benjamin West, Joseph Farrington, even Turner – which last had stayed with him in Cowes several times. As for sculptors, he was marginally involved in the commissioning of cast decorations from Flaxman and a statue of the king from Sir Francis Chantrey. In spite of all that, he seems to have bought very little of his contemporaries' work or ever – in any real sense – collaborated with any of them.[30]

As I noted earlier, in the great age of stucco a number of plaster amalgams were patented. Their main use was as wall-covering. But plaster could be moulded, cast and even carved, and became the most common ornamental vehicle. During the first half of the nineteenth century, Highgate and Bloomsbury, Belgravia, Paddington and Kensington were covered with huge estates of stuccoed or partially stuccoed buildings designed or commissioned by the Cubbitt brothers.

Of the three Cubbitt brothers who made London into a stucco city, Thomas was the shrewdest and most enterprising, while Lewis was the most architectural. Thomas's achievement as a planner of urban sanitation and of open spaces needs no celebration here, though it has to be said that – as far as the use of cast ornament was concerned – he was both more prolific and more conventional than Nash.[31]

Nash's main rival, Sir John Soane – less successful, not so seductive – was by far the most distinguished of the group. The art gallery he designed at Dulwich for Sir Francis Bourgeois, himself a painter of distinction, is one of the first purpose-built art galleries anywhere. Although he was on friendly terms with many more artists than Nash, Soane also did not collaborate with them on buildings. There is a record of his wishing to commission two large paintings (presumably on canvas – of the victories at Waterloo and Trafalgar) to be hung in the Royal Gallery of the House of Lords that he had himself designed. He had intended to give them to the crown, but although the gift seems to have been accepted, the huge pictures were painted directly on the walls of the rebuilt Gothic interior by Daniel Maclise after the destruction of all Soane's work in the Palace of Westminster during the fire of 1834.[32]

Soane was a discriminating collector of old master drawings and paintings, and the patron of painters and sculptors. Unfortunately, the one commission he gave to a great contemporary artist, his friend Turner – that in 1826 for the picture-room in his own house – ended sadly. He was to reject the canvases which, as he wrote to Turner, 'did not suit the place or the place the picture' and commissioned instead a much tamer *capriccio* by the now largely forgotten Sir Augustus Callcott.[33] Though both he and his wife had bought Turner's paintings, and Soane had even helped the painter to design Sandycombe Lodge, the small house in Twickenham in which he lived – and he continued to be on good terms with Turner and went on buying pictures from him after this incident – he had his own designs, built and unbuilt, commemorated in elaborate watercolour rendering, mostly by one watercolourist, Joseph Michael Gandy. The walls of his house, however, were crowded with the antiquities, the copies and the casts he had collected, and the most prominent sculptural ornaments he used (and that repeatedly) in two of the Bank of England domes and (for himself) both at Pitzhanger Manor and at his house in Lincoln's Inn Fields were Coade-stone copies of the caryatid that Lord Elgin had brought from Athens.[34]

James Burton, architect, developer and contractor, was the Cubbitts' one serious rival and their and Nash's occasional collaborator. His tenth son, classically christened Decimus, was born in 1800, a year after Lewis Cubbitt; he died in 1881. His most memorable works were done early in his life, in the 1820s: the stone screen and triumphal arch (both now at Hyde Park Corner) and the stucco Athenaeum Club in Pall Mall. All these, and the ornamental panoply of that arch, which had been intended to provide the main entry into Buckingham Palace, were not completed as he designed them. The screen at Hyde Park Corner was given an elaborate frieze based on that of the Parthenon one – virtually a copy – done by a Paisley/Glasgow sculptor, John Henning. Another one was carved for the Athenaeum some years later.[35]

Nash, the Cubbitts, Soane and finally Burton made much use of large exterior sculptures which could by then be produced mechanically in the form of stucco decorations. What had begun in the eighteenth century as a patrician fashion for displaying the trophies of the Grand Tour as copies – when originals could not be procured – filtered down to the middle classes and even those lower in the social scale, since the new manufacturing processes could replicate – more or less accurately – not only exemplary masterpieces like the Parthenon marbles, but also 'national', Gothic antiquities. This certainly avoided the expense and trouble involved in commissioning the work of contemporary artists.

THREE

In Many Colours

Both Britain and France – the Revolution notwithstanding – were similarly centralized imperial powers whose architecture dominated the world scene. Germany was divided, politically as well as economically: the whole country had suffered the Napoleonic buffetings. This was true of Bavaria, Saxony and the minor states, though it had perhaps been most grievous for Prussia, whose dominance of the German states, assured by Frederick II's policies, had been frittered away by a cultivated but ineffectual nephew and successor, Frederick William II and his fickle ministers. The first half of the next reign, that of Frederick William III, coincided with the Napoleonic wars. The king and his very popular wife, Queen Louise, had to spend some time in exile. Yet these years were also governed by two highly articulate, brilliant and energetic reformers: Baron Heinrich von Stein (who had the queen's ear) and General Gerhard von Scharnhorst, aided in turn by General (later Field-Marshal) August Neidhardt von Gneisenau (Blücher's chief of staff at Waterloo). They revolutionized the class system (by abolishing serfdom and reforming land tenure), education, the civil service and finally the army – so that in spite of its many early defeats the Prussian forces were stronger at the end of the Napoleonic wars than they had been at the beginning – as became obvious on the fields of Leipzig and Waterloo.

The figure of Frederick II was the great model to those reformers. In 1796 the Berlin Academy of Fine Arts declared a competition for a monument to the great Frederick – and although the king selected the cheapest of the six schemes (none was in fact executed), much the most ambitious of them, the one by the young Friedrich Gilly, provoked a great deal of comment when it was exhibited at the Academy.[1] Gilly was a brilliant and industrious youth

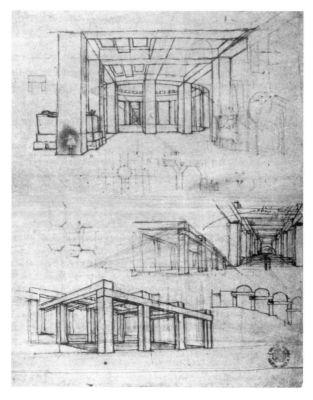

Friedrich Gilly, *Project for a Loggia*, date uncertain. Pen and ink drawing, destroyed.

Friedrich Gilly, *Project for a Monument to Frederick the Great*, 1797. Watercolour, destroyed.

whose project took the form of a pale and luminous Doric temple set on a base-ment of gloomy, almost megalithic funereal vaults. His passion for Greek antiquity alternated with – or was allied to – a passion for a national and Gothic past; his very brief life (he died at 28, in 1800) was dominated by his

Friedrich Frick, view of the ruins of Marienburg Castle, Prussia, *c.* 1803, etching with aquatint after Friedrich Gilly.

having come upon – in the course of travels with his father David, himself a distinguished architect in charge of Prussian ancient monuments – the castle of the Teutonic Knights (or Knights of the Cross) at Marienburg on the Vistula.[2] His enthusiasm for the integrity of the construction, for a wholly Germanic identity of style in architecture, was paralleled by an equally power-ful movement in the other 'fine' arts, whose gospel was a brief but eagerly read publication by a friend of Gilly's, the poet-painter Wilhelm Heinrich Wackenroder (another quickly burnt-out figure – he died in 1798, aged 25), the 'Meditations of an Art-loving Monk', which he wrote (in part) with his school friend, Ludwig Tieck. This rather nostalgic, yet novel document consisted of a rhapsodic mix – eulogies of artists, particularly of Dürer ('Master Albrecht . . . on account of whom I am glad I am a German'), Raphael, Francesco Francia, Leonardo, Piero di Cosimo – in the form of letters, essays and poems – even hymns. Wackenroder formulated a new and original vision of the artist as a somewhat isolated figure who needed to withdraw from the social melée to achieve the concentration his calling required. His was an allegedly auto-biographical picture of the total devotion of an artist to his art – a devotion which finally demanded his (fictitious) retirement to the cloister; it is sometimes considered the foundation text of the whole Romantic movement.[3]

The Artist as a Monk

Ludwig Tieck, bosom friend and close collaborator of Wackenroder, was – finally – his posthumous editor. Tieck was to die in 1853, a much-honoured but by then rather stuffy figure who is now mostly remembered as the co-translator of Shakespeare with Wilhelm von Schlegel. But he had in fact been a prolific man of (and about) letters all his life, and had performed the same posthumous editor's office for two other much greater young writers: Heinrich von Kleist and Novalis.[4] He had also spun a 'romance' from some of Wackenroder's ideas – *Sternbald's Wanderungen* – which appeared in 1798, the year Wackenroder died. Its hero, a fictional pupil of Dürer, makes a romantic pilgrimage round the ateliers of the Netherlandish painters of the time. In spite of adopting a more popular tone, Tieck's never equalled the success of Wackenroder's deliberately recondite book.

Christian-Friedrich, Ludwig Tieck's brother, had been – for three years – a pupil in David's atelier. During his time there, he modelled a head of the dying Wackenroder in relief – presumably from drawings he had done from life.[5] Although he was familiar with many of the great literary figures of his time (he had stayed with Madame de Staël and Wilhelm von Schlegel at Coppet; Goethe had engaged him to do decorations for the castle at Weimar), his rather demanding personality, his meticulous connoisseurship (he became director of sculpture of the Berlin Museums) and slow method of working prevented his succeeding to the towering position of his teacher, Gottfried Schadow. Yet he was to be a constant collaborator of Karl Friedrich Schinkel – of which more later.

That the artist should work in 'communities' or even 'communes' was a new, heady and 'romantic' idea – and it appealed to that notion of art as a religious, even a kind of monastic calling which Wackenroder had urged; it was an idea which persisted later, even when (as was often the case) medieval guild practice was invoked. Of course, such 'communities' had been anything but monastic; they were not about faith or chastity (never mind obedience), but about an exclusive devotion to art, in a hostile, bourgeois society, often accompanied with romantic entanglements.

It may well have been Christian-Friedrich Tieck who introduced David's disciples to Wackenroder's notion that the artist was a kind of monk – or they may simply have been developing such ideas in parallel. It is almost impossible to disentangle these relationships now; at any rate, the group of David's pupils whom I mentioned earlier and who retired to Chaillot in 1800 had broken up soon after the death of Quay.[6] In 1803 their friend Charles Nodier (he was twenty at the time) fictionalized the rebellious experience of the Barbus in a 'Gothic' tale, *Le Peintre de Salzbourg* (which he followed with a brief and aphoristic *Méditations du Cloître*), about a twenty-year-old artist who dies during a flood (and the reader is left to make up his mind whether it was accident or suicide), which owes much to Goethe's *Werther*. But Goethian melancholia (French interest in German ideas and German literature was then at its height) is grafted onto the quasi-monastic ideal of the Quay circle. 'I declare bitterly and with fear: Werther's pistol and the executioner's axe has already decimated us. THIS GENERATION RISES AND IT DEMANDS CLOISTERS.' *Cette génération se lève et vous demande des Cloîtres* is the strange conclusion of Nodier's *Méditations*. Like Wackenroder's, Nodier's cloister would provide the young with a refuge both from political catastrophe and oppressive government – and also from the frustration imposed by coarse and moneyed patronage.[7] Nodier turned an old institution, the Library of the Arsenal – of which he became director in 1824, and where he stayed until his death in 1844 – into his private and particular cloister. His 'at homes' became the rallying point of the young romantics, sometimes known as *Le Cénacle* about 1830 – as Gautier, Hugo and even de Musset witness.

Within a few years of Wackenroder's death, a more influential German 'sect' of artists was formed. It all began when young Johann Friedrich Overbeck (himself born in 1789) was entered (on the advice of Wilhelm Tischbein, Goethe's painter friend) in the Vienna Academy, directed at the time by Heinrich Füger, who – for his part – had been a pupil of both Anton-Rafael Mengs and of Jacques-Louis David in Rome.

Overbeck rebelled not only at the academic discipline he found in the Academy, but also at Viennese frivolity. He came of a long line of Lübeck pastors and bankers and his ideas – already exalted – had been informed by reading

Johann Friedrich Overbeck,
Self-portrait, 1809, oil on canvas.

Wackenroder and Tieck, so that they echoed some of the notions which had been formed and propagated by the Barbus. He made common cause with a brilliant but consumptive artist, Christian Philipp Pforr.[8] With four other fellow students, they founded the Sankt-Lukasbund, a 'brotherhood' or 'order' of St Luke in 1809 – about the time of Napoleon's entry into Vienna. It was dedicated to the revival of a true Christian art, modelled on the art of Raphael and his predecessors as a 'classical', Italianate precedent, as well as on a national, German art of which Dürer was the herald. Dürer's canonic status was new: writing to Lavater, the great physiognomist, in 1780, Goethe still felt that one could not express admiration for him too openly.[9] The rebellion against the academic dominance of the 'colourists', of Titian and Rubens in the teaching of art, was also rejected in Britain at the time, though Blake in his scurrilous notes on Sir Joshua Reynold's academic *Discourses* did vindicate Dürer's greatness.[10]

The admiration for 'primitive' drawing by David and his pupils prompted them to look at Greek vase-painting as a stylistic model, and re-established Raphael's role as the ideal artist. It is echoed by the rehabilitation of 'Gothic' Dürer as a model for northern European painters. The duality which an admiration for both Dürer and Raphael among artists suggests is paralleled by a somewhat different duality, even a tension, which architects never quite resolved – that of an appeal to 'primitive' Greece on the one hand, and to nationally rooted Gothic on the other. As archaeologists and philologists explored both Greek and German antiquity in ever greater detail, the nature of the appeal inevitably shifted. Yet the return to Raphael – with its clear preference for line over *sfumato,* the insistence on the primacy of local colour and the deliberate neglect of the effects of light and distance – was still considered a guarantee and source of innovation and of modernity at the beginning of the nineteenth century.

In Vienna the young artists had found a more high-minded master than Füger: Friedrich Eberhard von Wächter, who had studied both in Paris and Rome.[11] He was the link to 'Raphaelite' and even more the 'pre-Raphaelite' art of Italy; Overbeck and Pforr left the Vienna Academy for Rome in 1810 to establish an artists' commune, which soon moved into the Irish Franciscans' half-abandoned house, Sant'Isidoro, on the lower slopes of the Pincian Hill,[12] where they were joined (shortly before Pforr's early death) by Peter Cornelius, and a little later by Julius Schnorr von Karolsfeld, Friedrich Wilhelm Schadow (son of the Berlin sculptor) and Philipp Veit (stepson of Friedrich von Schlegel).[13] Their setting-up house in a monastery may have been a deliberate – or perhaps only a half-conscious replication – of the Barbus' rebellion, but their dogmatic insistence on the revival of true fresco technique was their own.[14] Overbeck became a Catholic in 1813, and stayed on in Rome until his death in 1869. The Romans quickly gave the Brotherhood the nickname 'the Nazarenes', and it referred to their long hair modelled on the self-consciously Christ-like self-portrait of the 33-year-old Dürer 'with a fur cloak'. The Nazarenes' own cloaks, which they always sported, had been 'designed' by Pforr.[15]

As a group, they were much better connected than the Barbus. Crown Prince Ludwig of Bavaria (the very same one who had bought the Aegina marbles in 1812, and would soon succeed, as King Ludwig I) saw a lot of them in Rome in 1824 while on a journey south with his favoured architect, Leo von Klenze (they visited the Greek antiquities in Sicily); he even sported their eccentric costume.[16] But the Nazarenes' first collective commission came from the Prussian consul-general, Jakob Solomon Bartholdy,[17] and it was for a series of frescoes in the Palazzo Zuccari at the top of the Spanish Steps. They chose to illustrate the biblical account of the story of Joseph.

The cycle was greeted with enthusiasm: both Antonio Canova, then the dominant figure of the Roman art world, and Bertil Thorvaldsen admired it, as did other artists – Italians and tourists. Canova's admiration was generously and instantly translated into active support: he bought a painting by Overbeck, and since the Vatican Galleries were being extended under his guidance (and he had already recommended fresco as the most suitable form of decoration), he commissioned Veit to decorate one of them. In 1817 the group was then approached by the Marchese Carlo Massimo to decorate his 'casino' in the gardens near the Lateran Palace with scenes from the epic poets: Dante, Ariosto, Tasso. While the Bartholdy frescoes only took two years, the much more ambitious ones at the Casino Massimo took ten.

Meanwhile, the Nazarenes also attracted a good deal of attention among Italian artists; in the 1830s a group centred on a prolific Roman painter, Tommaso Minardi, who called themselves 'Purists', became sufficiently articulated to be recognized as a 'movement' and late in 1849 actually produced a 'manifesto' written by a pupil of Minardi, the very learned and prolific writer Antonio Bianchini, who was also popular as a journalist. Pietro Tenerani, a sculptor, Minardi as well as Overbeck (who by then had become a figure of authority in Italy), signed a manifesto; it declared that the group looked to Orcagna and Giotto as their models, particularly to Giotto. 'Sublime conceptions', Minardi had years earlier (in 1834) told the Roman Academy of St Luke 'are found in Giotto's work rather than Raphael's', but by then there was an articulate opposition to the Nazarene and Purist archaizing.[18]

Such a renewal of medieval sources was obviously directed against the preceding generations, against the smoothness and polish of Mengs so admired by Winckelmann and emulated in sculpture by Canova and Thorvaldsen. Even if they began looking at medieval models towards the end of their careers, these two sculptors certainly considered the past as a unified, idealized country which had 'classical' antiquity at its heart.

But the generation at the turn of the century was discovering that there were very different regions within that country, that even the 'classical' past was not one country but several, each with its own art and language, its own *Kunstwollen* (as Alois Riegl was to call it later in the century). Some found this discovery disconcerting; others were excited by it: David's passion for the Etruscans was one indication of how this would affect artists. The Nazarenes'

Franz Louis Catel, *Ludwig of Bavaria Drinking with the Nazarenes*, 1824, oil on canvas.

unqualified admiration for Raphael weakened when they discovered authentic Dürerian German-ness. The further emulation of the fresh colours and the planar constructions of Italian painting before Raphael was to belong to the next generation.

Such a historicist concern with a specific episode in the past to which an appeal could be made about present problems is often treated as a facet of the general movement called 'Romanticism'. More than a hundred meanings have been given to that word, but the Nazarenes' use of it returns that over-used label to its old sense, a reference to the early medieval spoken or sung tales in the vulgar tongue, the *romance* speech of southern France, against the written text, which would almost always be in Latin. As in the French idealization of nation over country (to which I referred earlier), so – in a minor key – the Nazarene ideal of German nationhood is a symptom of that same emotional and mental cast.

Gilly had already shown the way in which it might be taken up in building. Following him in April 1828, a youngish architect, Heinrich Huebsch,

Joseph Anton Koch, a section from the *Dante* frescoes in the Casino Massimo, Rome, 1827–9.

dedicated a pamphlet, *In welchem Style sollen wir Bauen?* to a gathering of Nazarene sympathizers convened in Nuremberg to commemorate the 300th anniversary of Albrecht Dürer's death. He did it as a token of solidarity, since he could not be present himself. They were 'his friends and fellow-artists . . . who have worked together to free painting and sculpture of the bonds of antiquity', and he was, in this pamphlet, 'doing the same for architecture', which was (in his view) lagging behind the other arts. His little book instantly became a subject of discussion and polemics. Huebsch had already made his name as an architectural controversialist by attacking Alois Hirth's Vitruvian musings (Hirth was the most authoritative interpreter of antique architecture at that time) in a publication on Greek architecture.[19] He had himself been in Italy and Greece – and in Rome, where he had fallen in with the Nazarenes and was particularly close to Pforr.[20] The early Christian basilicas inspired an enthusiasm which freed him from the tutelage of his master (and predecessor as the leading architect of Karlsruhe), Friedrich Weinbrenner, who had met Hirth in Rome a generation earlier – and been

86

swayed by him and the young French architects with whom he came into contact there to turn his home city into a capital of the new 'revolutionary' and international neoclassicism.

Huebsch was looking to a rational style which could incorporate the new building techniques (which he calls, a little pompously, *technostatik*), especially cast-iron structure. He was also calling for a style suitable for the German climate and building materials – so that it would be a truly national one. Surprisingly, his model was 'Byzantine' architecture, which for his purposes includes the early basilican buildings in Italy as well as the Romanesque ones in Germany. His examples are the twelfth-century Rhineland abbey of Maria Laach and the rather obscure little basilica of Santa Balbina overlooking the Baths of Caracalla from a spur of the Aventine in Rome.[21] His argument was seen as having great force: Huebsch's contemporaries thought that it had been realized in some of Friedrich von Gaertner's Munich buildings, particularly in the Ludwigskirche – which was to be frescoed by Peter Cornelius at a later date.[22] The *Rundbogenstil* he advocated certainly made an impressive showing in its bid to be accepted as the German national style.

An Art for New Nations

Such a style was expedient for the nationalist movement which grew rapidly in Germany in the wake of Napoleon's campaigns as many smaller and feebler *ethne*s were discovering their political identity. In the course of the nineteenth century a recognition of separate ethnicity would increasingly convert into a demand for sovereignty: cultural autonomy was just not enough. Such a demand was inevitably pitted against the homologizing and aggrandizing tendency of the imperial powers. The partitions of Poland, the absorbtion of Hungary, Bohemia-Moravia and the Southern Slav 'Triune kingdom' (Bosnia, Croatia, Dalmatia) into a hereditary Habsburg Austrian (which replaced the elective Holy Roman one in 1804) empire, for their part, bred a host of 'victim' nations for which the Scots and later the Irish were in some way seen as archetypes.[23] The nobility of the victims – and their unwilling acquiescence in their subjection to the imperial conglomerates – attracted a great deal of sympathy among the liberal bourgeoisie of the great powers. Although it could not always be translated into political action, its cultural-artistic demonstration assuaged the unease this ambivalence provoked. It also deflected attention from the quick and usually brutal acquisition of overseas possessions in Africa and Southern Asia, mostly by France and Britain.

The expansionist Russian Empire, having swallowed most of Poland, made some reparation for it by fermenting disaffection among the Orthodox subjects of the Sultan; the resulting Serb insurrection of 1804, and the Greek one of 1820–21, led to the foundations of sovereign Serbia and Greece, later of Bulgaria, Romania and Albania. Meanwhile, two major fragmented nation-states, the German and the Italian, were working towards economic and political unity, which they both achieved in tandem – in 1870–71. For those two fragmented nations, the notion of a national style had a particular appeal.

The lost cause of the Stuarts and the two risings of their followers, in 1715 and 1745 (the last ruthlessly suppressed), exercised a strong attraction over the history and romance-conscious youth at the end of the century. The direct Stuart line died out in 1820 or thereabouts, while the Hanoverian Georges were firmly ensconced on the throne after 1745–6. The novels of Sir Walter Scott had fanned the smouldering – antiquarian and literary, not political – enthusiasm for the lost Stuart cause and the sturdy, remote, enthrallingly primitive Scottish past. Perhaps it was a measure of Scottish political atrophy that George IV could assume tartan dress (which had been banned in Scotland after the 1745 rising) when he visited Edinburgh in 1822.[24]

The festivities for that occasion had in fact been organized by Sir Walter Scott. He was *the* best-seller of his day: 'the King of Romance', Robert Louis Stevenson would call him. Librettos for Rossini (*Elisabetta, La Donna del Lago*), for Donizetti (*Lucia di Lammermoor*), Bellini (*I Puritani*) and even Bizet (*La Jolie Fille de Perth*) are only the best known and still performed of the operas drawn from his novels and witness to his international appeal.

Scottish particularism did not sap Britain's confidence in her empire and her rapidly growing industrial might in which the Scots played a part quite disproportionate to their numbers. Its newly rich industrial and commercial entrepreneurs, much like German nationalists (both aristocratic and bourgeois – particularly in Saxony and Prussia), were ambitious to rediscover a national manner, a native style that would be independent of direct Italian and French-filtered Italian models. Again, two possible sources offered themselves: the more obvious Gothic one – appealing to the heroic past of a nation, a past celebrated in medieval epic and legend – or the 'classic' one, invoking a more generalized and immemorial, an exemplary but equally heroic primitivism. The Scottish past of Ossian or the ancient German one of the *Nibelungenlied* could, after all, be set beside Homer's lays. In the course of the 1830s and '40s, such ideals about a heroically 'classic' past became associated with the Dorian tribes – particularly the Spartans – as models of righteousness and of discipline. Much was made of the supposed northern origin of these Dorians, and such aspirations involved both architectural styles and the themes of 'history' paint- ing. In Britain, which had bought and first exhibited the Parthenon marbles, the 'Dorians' were seen by some critics as providing a stimulus for the creation of a 'National school of history-painting' or even of 'fresco-painting'.[25]

Accident focused all these issues on a single building when the old Houses of Parliament – also known as the Palace of Westminster – were destroyed in a spectacular blaze (of which Turner left the most splendid eye- witness account; Constable drew it less dramatically). A competition was declared for a new building which, the conditions demanded, was to be 'in a Gothic or Elizabethan style'.[26] The issue had arisen a little earlier, when some parliamentarians objected to the 'style' of the new Law Courts which Sir John Soane had built in 1822–4 onto Westminster Hall, completing the façade with a neo-Palladian ordering of the 'Stone Building' which John Vardy (perhaps under William Kent's direction) had initiated in 1755. Critics called it an offence to the 'national taste'. A select committee of the Commons demanded the demolition of the facade and its replacement with a castellated one, with pointed windows emulating those of New Palace Yard. Soane hated it and offered to replace it at his own expense – but was refused.[27]

Back to the Sources

The winning project in the Palace of Westminster competition was in that very same 'National Style' the competition demanded and Soane disliked. It was a co-production by the otherwise Italianate Charles Barry, with the assis- tance (often fraught and later contested) of the very 'Gothic' (and rather 'gothic'-sounding) Augustus Welby Northmore Pugin. Pugin is a crucial

A.W.N. Pugin, *The
Nineteenth Century
Found Wanting*,
colophon of
Contrasts (1836).

figure. The son of a Huguenot immigrant at the time of the Terror, a child
prodigy, he had devoured the novels of Walter Scott in his early teens. Soon he
turned from his juvenile devotion to Scott and a 'romanced' past to more serious
political concerns as he became increasingly and painfully conscious of the
economic evils and proletarian misery that industrialization had brought.
Progress seemed to him, as it did to many of his contemporaries, illusory. For
this medievalist social reformer, Scott's nostalgia was displaced by a political
and religious conviction when he read the very anti-Protestant historian,
Father John Lingard, whose *History of England* began publication in 1819.[28]
Another, more powerful, influence was the Tory radical journalist and historian
William Cobbett; with Cobbett, Pugin saw the Reformation as the source of
much of the evil in contemporary society, particularly the demise of monastic
agriculture in the sixteenth century which had preceded the enclosure of common land and the consequent creation of the urban proletariat in the eighteenth.[29] Another source, more closely echoing his enthusiasm for medieval

architecture, were the writings of Count Montalembert, whose liberal tendency within Catholicism was very much his own – he was one of the few well-placed English Catholics who hoped for a corporate conversion of the newly formed Tractarian party in the Church of England.[30]

The evils of contemporary industrial and capitalist society were – in Pugin's view – compounded by Whig liberalism and latitudinarian religion. They were evident in the artistic indiscipline of his time, the lack of a common style that was exaggerated both by mass-production and the excessive use of ornament – stucco, of course, but iron as well. The use of cast and moulded ornament by Soane and Nash (for whom his father, Augustus Charles, had worked a good deal) came in for his particularly scathing caricature and comment. His remedy for present ills – both political and artistic – was a return to the state of affairs that existed just before the Protestant Reformation so as to start again as if the intervening period was an error which could be expunged. His revival of the architecture of the late fifteenth century was not a matter of taste, but a moral and a political crusade – his hero during that period was Savonarola. He hoped to bring about a return to the social and economic conditions which that architecture housed and represented; and that, of course, was the 'style' in which he clothed Barry's winning competition project for the Houses of Parliament. Pugin's endeavour is near-contemporary to Huebsch's attempt to jump-start a German national style by returning to 'Byzantine' architecture. Both believed that style could be updated to suit modern techniques and conditions – though Huebsch had none of Pugin's fiery reforming zeal, or his volcanic energy, which made him vastly prolific both as an architect and a propagandist.

Besides the exterior and interior fitting out of Parliament, Pugin designed and built entire cathedrals (Southwark, Birmingham, Killarney), parish churches, monasteries (in one of which, at Ramsgate, he spent his last days and was buried), palatial houses; he was a fussy and insistent controller of details, not only of masonry and woodwork, but – like Percier and Fontaine a generation earlier – of furniture, wallpapers and fabrics, as well as of very elaborate silverware, especially of the ecclesiastical kind. Unlike Ruskin and Morris in the following generations, to whom style was very much a result of craft conditions, he seems to have been unconcerned about the working methods that produced them (often using machinery), even if he was almost obsessive about historical accuracy. Somehow his collaborators and the craftsmen he employed always disappointed: 'I have spent my life thinking of fine things, studying fine things, designing fine things and realizing very poor ones', he wrote bitterly towards the end of his life. Yet his historicism was maintained on principles from which he never deviated and which he stated clearly in his *True Principles of Pointed or Christian Architecture*. The book was the text of a course of lectures he delivered to Catholic seminarians and was first published in 1841. His two primary injunctions sound surprisingly 'modern':

1st, that there should be no features about a building which are not necessary for convenience, construction and propriety;
2nd, that all ornament should consist of enrichment of the essential construction of the building.

He also took the opportunity to inveigh against 'brummagem' (he meant cheap reproductions of Gothic church objects, used inappropriately in domestic interiors),[31] against the use of landscapes and perspectives or cast

A.W.N. Pugin, *Brummagem Gothic*, from *True Principles*, 1853.

shadows instead of flat patterns on surface coverings, and against any appeal to 'classical' (which he usually called 'pagan') precedent more generally. Although he was not often quoted, these principles about the relation between structure and ornament – and his conviction that repetitive patterns of any kind must eschew any effect of relief – became the guiding principles of British (and many European) designers into the twentieth century. Nearly a hundred years after his death, W. R. Lethaby, one of the most acute critics of art and design, wrote:

> The critical work of Pugin was continued on a higher plane and univer-salized by Ruskin into a general philosophy of art. Architects now had a theory, but they repudiated it and put their faith in learning about past styles and designing for show, instead of in the practice of sound human building . . .

and this observation still seems quite true even though both Ruskin and Morris were curmudgeonly in their expressions of contempt for Pugin and his work.[32]

In his earlier book, *Contrasts*, Pugin had drawn a wretched picture of his own times – industrial blight in cities, inhuman treatment of the poor, ecclesiastical indifference and corruption as against the wonderful (and of course highly glamourized) state of affairs in 'the age of faith'. In all his elaborately illustrated publications, he relied on outline engraving as much as Percier and Fontaine had done.[33] Moreover, he had very little (good or bad) to say about contemporary painting and sculpture or about any individual artist. In his own projects, he would prepare drawings of the statues for masons to carve and painters to paint or stencil instead of appealing to 'independent' painters or sculptors – since there was none, as yet, who worked in a style he might favour. There was one exception, 'Great Overbeck, the Prince of Christian painters', the only artist to whom he defers in *Contrasts*. Pugin knew him by repute and from engravings, and was finally to meet him in person in 1842, on a visit to Rome. There he also met and brought back to England an Italian Overbeck disciple, Enrico Casolani, who worked with him during the last decade of his life – which made him, arguably, the first British Pre-Raphaelite, even if Pugin would later find him rather lazy.

The Barry and Pugin parliamentary buildings had already been partially built when Prince Albert, who became Queen Victoria's consort after their marriage in 1840, started to take British royal patronage of the arts in hand. As a pupil of Wilhelm von Schlegel and the Fichtean jurist Theodor Perthes in Bonn, the Prince Consort was also familiar with the new German art. He admired the Nazarenes. As President of the Fine Arts Commission, he worried much about how to proceed with the Houses of Parliament fresco project. Inevitably perhaps, he consulted Peter Cornelius, who modestly referred him to a young Scottish painter, William Dyce, as the person best qualified to supervise such an enterprise.[34] When a competition for the new paintings and sculptures was finally declared, Dyce was one of the artists selected. Haydon, who saw the project as the summation of his life's work (and the focus for the incipient school of native fresco painting for which he had so long agitated), was rejected – and that rebuff contributed to the decline which drove him to suicide two years later.[35] Dyce's work on the Palace of Westminster was to deteriorate physically because of his inexperience and others' neglect, but while working in the new building he did manage to achieve an easy (or as easy as possible) relation with Pugin.

Dyce had met Cornelius in Rome, where, as a brilliant teenager, he had visited the Nazarenes at Sant'Isidoro during his first, almost obligatory study-trip of 1825. The introduction had been affected by the scholar-ecclesiologist and diplomat, Baron Bunsen. As a high churchman, Dyce was passionately interested in theology and church order, as well as the externals of worship; he also happened to be an accomplished organist and a composer of talent, and one of the revivers of early polyphonic music. He was a skilled chemist. At a time when the Tractarians[36] occupied much of British intellectual life, his interest in liturgy and music (as well as in painting and sculpture) echoed those of some of the best minds of his time. The role played by Dyce in this Anglican movement was in some ways analogous to Pugin's service to the Roman Catholic community.

On that first Roman visit, Dyce had painted a *Virgin and Child* 'in the style of Perugino'. Overbeck and Cornelius both admired it – so much so that they raised a subscription to keep him there when he was recalled by his family.[37] But return to Scotland he did, and in fact seems to have neglected his proto-pre-Raphaelite past for a time and registered a quick success as a fashionable portrait artist in the manner of Raeburn.[38] He also remained deeply involved in debates about the training of artists, a matter that was to consume as much of his energy as it did Haydon's. After touring the important art schools of Europe in 1837–8, he was appointed head ('Superintendent') of the new Government School of Design at Somerset House. Impressed by what was being done in Paris and Lyons, and even more so by the German schools, he had very much approved of the reforms which Gustav Waagen had carried out in Prussia where he wanted to transform the design school into a community of craftsmen.[39] Dyce's Roman friend, Peter Cornelius, was by then also a leading academic, the director of the Kunstakademie in Düsseldorf.

The Board of Trade, as the main authority in the matter of artists' training, was not quite sure whose advice (as between Haydon, Dyce and the advocates of schools tied to industry) to heed, and the politicians who became embroiled in the matter (Haydon was very good at involving them) did not have clear views either way. At any rate, 21 'industrial' art-schools were founded between 1843 and 1852, but in the end, the whole matter of connecting art with both craft and industry went to the sidelines, even if many artists found it a burning topic and it was to provide the ground on which the Arts and Crafts movement would later flourish. Despite other vigorous moves, it never became an important factor in British industrial development.[40]

In Bavaria things were indeed very different. Ludwig I was determined both to Italianize and to medievalize his – royal since 1803 – capital on his return from his 'Grand Tour', and started a (some say disastrous) restoration of the churches in his lands, removing anything 'redolent of the wig and the pigtail' – anything we would now call Baroque or Rococo – of which there was fortunately more in Bavaria than he could wreck. He was aided in this first by the antiquarian Carl Heideloff and then by the (sometimes reluctant) Klenze and Gaertner. It was all 'applied art-history rather than art proper'.[41] The king was determined to employ and encourage local architectural talent (he ennobled both Klenze and Gaertner) and to honour the brilliant painters he had met in Rome, whose ideas about the nature of monumental art he found inspiring, even if his architects were not always entirely in sympathy. Ludwig became very active as a patron, collector, restorer. Antiquity was not neglected: the spanking new Durandian, neo-antique Glyptothek designed (1816–30) by the king's travelling companion, Leo von Klenze, was to house (in the first place) the Aegina pediments which he had

Julius Schnorr von Karolsfeld, lithograph after his composition in a mass-market edition of the *Nibelungenlied, c.* 1900.

bought at auction, then his other Greek sculptures. Klenze later (1826–36) also designed the (now Alte) Pinakothek to exhibit some of the masterpieces from the royal collection.[42] It was done in a Venetian Renaissance manner, and is sometimes quoted as the first real attempt to revive the style.

Peter Cornelius (already established in Düsseldorf) was commissioned to fresco the vaults of the Glyptothek, though in fact his cartoons were executed by assistants and his work proved unpopular;[43] another of the Roman Nazarenes, Schnorr von Karolsfeld, was already working in the Munich Residenz, which had also been designed (1825–39) by Leo von Klenze in a severe Palazzo Pitti-like Tuscan style. Like Cornelius, Schnorr had trained a team of assistants who worked with him on an even larger fresco cycle with subjects patriotically drawn from the *Nibelungenlied*, various versions of which had been published in the later eighteenth century.[44] Cornelius' most important Munich commission, however, were the frescoes in the Ludwigskirche that Friedrich Gaertner had designed in a new Romanesque-Byzantine

96

Rundbogenstil. The centrepiece was a *Last Judgement* comparable in size (in fact, it was even larger) to Michelangelo's fresco in the Sistine Chapel; projected in Rome in 1834 it was executed two years later on the wall of the church. These frescoes also had a mixed reception. Even Cornelius' friend, the king, found them 'too hieratic'. Such coolness caused a breach between artist and patron and Cornelius moved to Berlin – where, he thought, he would find a really committed protector in the person of the well-informed and talented Prussian king, Frederick William iv.

Klenze, even more than his more eclectic Munich contemporary, Gaertner, found – as King Ludwig did – the Nazarene style too stark and sober for their architecture. Karl Friedrich Schinkel, who may be considered the dominant German architect of the nineteenth century, and had already acquired a great reputation as a scenic painter during the period of the Napoleonic wars, acted as his own artist. He treated painters and sculptors as the executants – not just of his programmes but of his preparatory paintings and his outline drawings, much as Pugin did. He wanted the 'art-embellishment' of his buildings to follow precise specifications. His great contemporary, the sculptor Gottfried Schadow, records modelling figures from Schinkel's drawings for the cornice of the Neue Wache.[45] Later, Schinkel

Karl Friedrich Schinkel's outside staircase, Altes Museum, Berlin.

worked more with Friedrich Tieck, whom I have already mentioned as a pupil of David – and he came to rely on Tieck for much of the detailed ornament of his buildings.

The Altes Museum is perhaps Schinkel's most famous project. Its main facade, a great colonnade of Ionic columns, was intended by him to be seen as the Berlin equivalent (since Berlin was deliberately turning itself into 'the Athens on the Elbe') of the Athenian Painted Stoa that had flanked the Agora and been a centre of philosophical discussion as well as of commercial life. Schinkel, who considered himself as important a painter as he was an architect, knew exactly what he wanted for its decorations, and around 1830 had provided large gouache projects of the frieze-like compositions which were to be painted in fresco on either side of the main open staircase through the widely spaced colonnade. They were to represent the mythical world as it proceeded from sunrise to night, personified in a sequence from Apollo to Jupiter on one side; answering it was a frieze showing the development of humanity on earth as it passed through the cycles of the seasons.

In 1841, at the time Schinkel died, they had not even been begun. Peter Cornelius, who had been lured to Berlin to fresco a *Campo Santo*, an official cemetery of Prussian royals and notables (together with Felix Schadow, the sculptor's son and their disciples), was meanwhile directed to execute Schinkel's decorations.[46] In the event, the king would feel so humiliated and broken by the rebellion of 1848, which echoed, in Berlin, the more violent Paris events of that year, that nothing came of the *Campo Santo*.[47]

Klenze and Gaertner, Gilly and Schinkel, exact contemporaries of the Nazarenes, all had associations with the Parisian milieu, as did Christian-

Details of the proposed frescoes in the 'Vorhalle' of Karl Friedrich Schinkel's Altes Museum, Berlin, gouache on paper, 1825–8.

Friedrich Tieck. These associations were personal. Schinkel had been in Paris at the time of Napoleon's *Sacre* and admired Percier and Fontaine, who – for their part – sent him an autographed copy of their works in the Louvre in 1826 when they were published in Count de Clarac's account of the museum and its contents. Klenze and Gaertner had actually studied with Percier and Fontaine, and were therefore inevitably influenced by Durand's account of a universal design method.

In 1831 the Durand *Abrégé* was translated and published in German.[48] Although Schinkel regarded the design method of the *Abrégé* primarily as the basis for a new kind of classicism which would also absorb Gothic elements – many of his painted fantasies, after all, as well as a few of his buildings, were Gothic or even 'rustic' – to the Munich architects it provided a compositional method which allowed them to manage different stylistic exercises, and (as a by-product) gave them large, plain wall areas which, like medieval churches, could be (and in Munich were) covered with paintings. Of course, Durand – though mostly working in a shorn classicism – had no definite stylistic allegiance. He liked early Christian basilican plans, and among his many engravings there were some Italianate, Tuscan-Quattrocento-type elevations. Apart from stylistic or even compositional precepts, his 'positive' attitude to the nature of materials and forms of construction was taken up by a number of German architects, notably by Huebsch in his advocacy of the future *Rundbogenstil*.

Durand's method claimed and achieved the universality on which German architects had relied, and they applied it both at home and when working in Greece with equal enthusiasm (as did their Scandinavian and Greek colleagues, or Russian and Polish architects or those French ones who were exported to North Africa, South-East Asia or Brazil). English and American architects learnt his principles indirectly from the most popular building manual, Joseph Gwilt's *Cyclopaedia of Architecture*, first published in 1835 and frequently reprinted throughout the nineteenth century. These principles were, of course, taught quite dogmatically at the Ecole Polytechnique by Durand until his retirement in 1830, and by his pupils after him, but they were also taken over as the basis of systematic teaching at the Ecole des Beaux-Arts. Since the design method they offered rested on apodictic assumptions, it could not be questioned and required neither discussion nor yet revision. Its monopolistic pretensions had a double effect: on the one hand they dampened theoretical discussion – which could not be allowed to impugn the rationale of the method; on the other, they allowed and even stimulated an increasing elaboration of those presentation techniques which would become the touchstone of academic teaching in the nineteenth century. Richly rendered (in watercolour and gouache) presentation drawings acquired a decorative, even pictorial status quite independent of the realities of any building they might be proposing. In the plans and sections, interior volumes became negative, pale spaces against the darkening, heavily coloured, graded background and the solid, inert mass of the structure. Such projects made only token concessions to works of art – sculpture or painting – as a complement of the architect's work. And since Durand regarded ornament wholly as a matter of convention which always depended on historical precedent, the method was treated as a kind of underlay which would guarantee essential proprieties while allowing complete stylistic freedom. Yet the situation involved a paradox: since Durand's obsessional insistence on the structural and formal priority of the column over any other architectural element left large areas of wall behind the colonnades blank (as I suggested), they seemed to invite – if not paintings – at least polychromatic articulation.

The reductive banality of Durand's theory was not universally popular under the Empire and was certainly not acceptable to the historians and theorists who took power under the new monarchy – even if his method was widely practised by working architects throughout Europe and America by this time. The application of his method produced buildings with large areas of blank,

David d'Angers, projected pediment for the Palais-Bourbon, 1837.

unarticulated wall which were a challenge to French architects – and artists as well.

Yet many of those buildings with imposing colonnades and blank walls initiated under the Empire were continued under the Bourbon restoration and its successor, the July Monarchy. The stock exchange, the Bourse, had been begun under Napoleon by Alexandre Brongniart (another pupil of Boullée) as a 'temple of Money', while Pierre Vignon (a pupil of Ledoux) had been charged with transforming the Madeleine into a 'temple of the *Grande Armée*'. It is hardly surprising that Victor Hugo called the church, returned to its original dedication, 'the second volume of the Bourse'. Across the Place de la Concorde and the Seine, the *ci-devant* Palais-Bourbon, which now housed the Chamber of Deputies, had been given an even more solemn, twelve-column portico-frontispiece towards the river, designed by Bernard Poyet. It is his major surviving work. Its outsize pediment remained empty until about 1830, when a relief by David d'Angers representing the Tennis-court Oath – explicitly based on David's projected painting – was rejected for political reasons in favour of a bland allegorical group by Jean-Pierre Cortot. On the pedestal walls that frame the monumental stair stand isolated statues of *Minerva* (for wisdom) and *Themis* (for justice) originally commissioned from Philippe-Laurent Roland and Jean-Antoine Houdon respectively; they are now so weathered as to be barely recognizable and are anyway thrust into the background by the later, banal statues of statesmen and legislators at street level.[49]

At right angles to the axis of the Place de la Concorde and opposite the Tuileries the Champs-Elysées stretched up to the Etoile hill. There had, in the time of Louis XV, already been a project for a vast bronze elephant to face down the avenue – and other projects for various monuments. Napoleon, having

Henri Labrouste, reconstruction of the 'Basilica' at Paestum, pen and ink on paper, 1828–9.

overcome his early distaste for triumphal arches, had Percier and Fontaine build him one at the Carrousel as part of his whole Louvre project; a bigger one at the Etoile was to close the vista and was designed by Jean-François Chalgrin, who had also designed the nearby basilica of St Philippe-du-Roule. Its blank piers were to be decorated with trophy reliefs and it was to be crowned with a quadriga. By 1815 the piers were 20-metre-high unsightly stumps, and Louis XVIII was advised by Bernard Poyet, the designer of the Palais-Bourbon portico, to pull them down. However, the king decided to complete the arch and Napoleon's vast funereal chariot was drawn through it when his body was returned to Paris from St Helena.[50]

Blank walls also seemed a glaring reproach during the Restoration and the July Monarchy. The three dry and pompous Corinthian porticoes – of the Bourse, the Madeleine and the Palais-Bourbon – as well as the great triumphal arch seemed to cry out for dignified painted and sculptural vesture. In the past the decoration of churches had taken decades, even centuries, as a matter of course, but after the Revolution undecorated churches were considered shamefully unfinished. Napoleon's successors had strong views on such matters. Charles x and Louis-Philippe patronized the various corporations in Paris and in the provinces, and took charge of the public buildings begun under the Empire by providing them with seemly decorations. Charles x had a real concern for the matter, and after his fall the most powerful statesmen of the period,

François Guizot and Adolphe Thiers (both of whom had written art-criticism before coming to power), involved themselves in the enterprise and the resultant disputes. Even Louis-Philippe, who had been a drawing master in exile, could claim to be an informed critic and patron.

The Madeleine was one of the problem buildings: the temple exterior discordantly sheltered an interior articulated into three domed bays, and its 'pagan' face was not really considered suitable for a church. Decoration therefore became a crucial matter. Sculptures were gradually added over several decades – some by Antoine-Louis Barye and François Rude. The painter who was now emerging as the dominant French master, Ingres, was offered the decoration of the apse and high altar, but he refused[51] and the commission went to a pupil of Ingres, Jean-Claude Ziegler – apparently at Thiers' insistence. Ziegler had met Peter Cornelius and learnt the technique of fresco from him.[52] The Madeleine, elaborately decorated, never cohered, however. The business of providing public buildings – and especially churches – with

Jacques-Ignace Hittorff, lithograph reconstruction of the 'Temple of Empedocles' at Selinus, 1851.

a suitable dressing of statuary and painting would go on worrying and perplexing French artists as well as the authorities.

Several of the most influential architects of the time – Jacques-Ignace Hittorff among them – saw Byzantine mosaics as the true successors of antique polychromy. Hittorff was an Alsatian (born in Cologne), who chose to take French nationality after Napoleon's defeat. He was a pupil of Percier, and he joined (and in 1818 succeeded) Jacques Bélanger as director of the Menus-Plaisirs. A study journey to England (now obligatory for artists because of the Elgin Marbles, which Delacroix and Géricault had also visited), and later an extended tour of south Italy and Sicily, convinced him that the architecture of antiquity was polychrome.

The Colour of Regret

The word *polychrome* may have been coined by Quatremère de Quincy, whom I mentioned earlier as the 'restorer' of the Panthéon,[53] and he was particularly interested in Greek self-colouring (gold, ivory, etc) sculpture, for which there was plenty of literary but no archaeological evidence as yet. The art section of the old Imperial Institute (with whose regulations Napoleon even found time to tinker during the frantic Hundred Days) had been renamed the Royal Academy of Fine Arts in March 1816 and constituted an advisory body to the government and regulated the appointment of teachers, the giving of prizes, the setting of competitions – as well as governing the French Academy in Rome. Quatremère de Quincy, a sculptor by training and friend of David and Canova, became the first 'Perpetual Secretary' of the Paris Academy in 1816 and remained in that powerful position until 1849. During that time he published a number of papers which argued for the reconstruction of the famous polychrome sculptures of antiquity.

Since the Paris Academy governed the Roman one – which determined official commissions and distinctions – Quatremère's views had the force of rules. Against innovators he declared that all useful examples of ancient architecture could be found in the Italian peninsula, and any attempts to look for architectural precedent in Greece (or worse, Turkey) was both an extravagance and an act of wilful insubordination. Against innovators (including some of Durand's disciples) he maintained his belief in the metaphoric power of architecture, the authority of proportional rules and the example of antiquity – in which polychromy had been an important feature.

The argument about polychromy would rage for twenty years, between 1820 and 1840 and even later. It was taken up in Britain by Charles Robert Cockerell and Thomas Donaldson, and in Germany by Gottfried Semper, though it was most acrimonious in France. In the 1830s Hittorff was arguing for a much more garishly coloured architecture, both for restoring old buildings and for designing new ones, than Quatremère and his allies (convinced that colour was applied by a refined, laborious encaustic process) would allow.[54] In 1825 he had decorated Reims Cathedral for the coronation of Charles X. Elaborate, panelled canvas hangings were painted with imitation tessellated mosaic panels to make the cathedral appear similar to the elaborately decorated Norman basilica at Monreale near Palermo, which Hittorff had once surveyed and described – and which he proposed as an ideal of the polychrome church. A sharp, full-bodied polychromy was associated with renewal, even with protest at this time.

The first attempts to rebel against the universal design method initiated by Durand, but also against the Academic *diktat* more generally, came from within the institution which propagated it. In October 1826 Quatremère de Quincy, while reiterating the well-worn platitudes about beauty and proportion in a commemorative address at the Ecole des Beaux-Arts, was shouted down by students. That was the preliminary rumble of mutiny. The ferment between the Paris headquarters and the Rome Academy culminated in a full strike that hit the Ecole in 1830.[55]

Architects were also affected by this mood. In the months before the July revolution, a group of younger ones made common cause with other artists. Léon Vaudoyer, one of the rebels at the French Academy in Rome, writing to his father Laurent (who directed an atelier at the Beaux-Arts), suggested that the conflict in which he and his friends were engaged, 'was nothing other than that which rages between Victor Hugo and the classicists in literature, and which also rages in painting . . . Why should architecture not launch its own little revolution?'[56] He saw an analogous movement in painting: Ary Scheffer, Paul Delaroche (who was to specialize in scenes from French and English medieval history), as well as Delacroix, were recognized by the time of the July events as the leaders of the 'Romantic school'. Indeed, most artists and writers in France who identified themselves as 'Romantic' also took the liberal side during the last days of the legitimist monarchy, either as republicans or at least as Orléanists. In so far as Romanticism was a definable movement rather than a sentiment as I suggested earlier – a bundle of associations – it is concerned with the specificity of history as against the generality of myth, and with negative rules: defiance of the unities of place and time, breaking the hierarchy of genres, and the direct setting-out of emotion at the expense of formal rules. 'Le romantisme . . . n'est à tout prendre, si l'on ne l'envisage que sous son côté militant, que le *libéralisme* en littérature' summed up Hugo at the time in his preface to *Hernani*.[57] The first night of that play, 25 February 1830, turned into a riot, with opposing claques applauding and hissing lines and episodes. Théophile Gautier, sporting a bright red waistcoat, was the famous leader of the pro-Hugo claque. Four months later Charles x was overthrown and replaced by his cousin, the Duc d'Orléans, who reigned as Louis-Philippe – and the term avant-garde now moved from army language into the arts.[58]

Not that these labels were ever precise. Ingres considered himself 'classic', though it was the 'Romantic' critics who saved his *St Symphorien* (a painting of which more later) from opprobrium; Delacroix, for his part, may have been considered the leader of the 'Romantic' movement, yet he could say of himself that he considered himself 'truly classic', and rejected the common association with the arch-Romantic composer Hector Berlioz, whose music he cordially disliked, as he disliked Hugo's writings.[59]

The brightest *pensionnaires* at the French Academy in Rome during the 1820s, Léon Vaudoyer (just quoted, the most articulate of them), Louis Duc, Félix Duban and Henri Labrouste (a pupil of Léon's father, Laurent Vaudoyer) joined in the attack. Henri Labrouste had arrived in Rome in 1824. By 1830 he had already submitted a number of more or less conformist *envois* (the set of drawings pensioners had to submit regularly to Paris as a proof of their talent and assiduity) when some of Paestum (which were his final offering) 'hit' the Academy. There were a number of sticking points: he chose to work on a Greek (as against a Roman) site even if it was located in Italy; his use of polychromy was aggressive and – most objectionably – he had restored the so-called Basilica, now known as the Temple of Hera i, as a civil building and given it a hipped roof instead of pediments, and decorated it with military trophies and a large number of (entirely invented) graffitoed and painted inscriptions.[60] The director of the Academy, the painter Horace Vernet, thought highly of Labrouste's submission, while Quatremère did not. The correspondence which ensued when Labrouste's drawings were rejected by the Paris Academy was so acrimonious that Vernet offered his resignation twice, first under the old administration and again after the July events. Louis-Philippe had put the scholar-statesman François Guizot briefly at the interior ministry and in charge of the Academy's affairs – so it was to Guizot that Vernet submitted his resignation on 7 September 1830 – and it was, of course, rejected. In fact, Guizot made the Rome school independent of the Academy in Paris and also appointed the committee (of which Labrouste was a member) to reform teaching at the Ecole des Beaux-Arts.[61] On his return to Paris, Labrouste was not only appointed to the reform committee of the Ecole but also opened his own atelier there on 1 August 1830, where his students included many of the young rebels whom the eccentric Petrus Borel had recruited for the *Hernani* claque.[62]

Some of that original claque, in particular Théophile Gautier (still a painter) – and Borel (still an architect), started a kind of spontaneous commune, *Les Jeunes France*, devoted to the most morbid, satanic and funereal forms of Romantic behaviour (Borel would later call himself 'le Lycanthrope', the wolf-man), and they eventually and appropriately moved to the Rue d'Enfer in the Quartier Latin (there had been a slow but general movement of 'arty' Paris to the Left Bank once the Ecole des Beaux-Arts was established there), and had their rooms suitably decorated.[63]

However, the group eventually broke up, and another – rather more cheerful and sanguine – formed around Gautier. He shared a celebrated *garçonnière* in the Impasse de la Doyenné, near the Théâtre Français, with the poet Gérard de Nerval (translator of Goethe), the illustrator-engraver Camille Rogier and Arsène Houssaye (who was to become director of the same theatre after 1848). For the house-warming party in November 1835, the apartment was painted with landscapes by the (already famous) Camille Corot and Théodore Rousseau, with Druidic figures by the poet-painter Célestin Nanteuil, and bacchanal scenes by the precocious and brilliant seventeen-year-old pupil of Ingres, Théodore Chassériau. After a few years the landlord evicted the troublesome tenants and whitewashed the decorations, some of which were saved by Gérard de Nerval when the whitewash had been removed.[64]

The monochrome pomposities of post-Durandian building with their large areas of blank wall were the challenge which directed attention to a Nazarene approach to public art, to their concern with fresco. An alliance between the school of Ingres and the Nazarenes is not always acknowledged, even though French critics called Overbeck the 'German Ingres'. But the more 'advanced' of them were not all enthusiastic about the Nazarenes. Théophile Gautier – who had been so active in defence of Hugo's Cromwell, and had been at the centre of the Impasse de la Doyenné group – was distinctly cool: in a long essay on Peter Cornelius, the fruit of an extended visit to Munich, he dismisses any comparison between his Pinakothek frescoes and the wall and ceiling paintings by Ingres and Delacroix:

> An account of a painting by Cornelius will seduce you; indeed, you could hardly imagine anything finer; but look at it and you will be astonished by the feeble or savage composition; the idea has remained an idea, it has not assumed the forms. Esthetically, it's admirable; plastically it is very bad. We dare not say detestable since we respect an established reputation.[65]

Ingres would give some face value to the association. He had met Overbeck in Rome, and several of Ingres' pupils were involved with the Nazarenes – and this alliance produced some very popular essays in decorative painting. When St Germain l'Auxerrois (facing the Louvre, and therefore the king's parish church) was restored and refurnished in the most precise late medieval manner by the antiquarian-architect Jean-Baptiste Lassus in the reign of Louis-Philippe, Emmanuel Amaury-Duval (who had seen much of the Nazarenes' work and knew several of them personally, though he considered their work inferior to that of Ingres, his master) made its decoration a Nazarene-type homage to Fra Angelico. Even closer to the Nazarenes were some pupils of the Barons Guérin and Gros.

A group of them would decorate the rather Durandian parish church, Notre-Dame de Lorette, which Hippolyte Lebas built in the newly-developing district below Montmartre in fresco and encaustic.[66] Near Notre-Dame de

The interior of
J.-I. Hittorff's
church of St Vincent
de Paul, Paris,
1844, showing the
encaustic frescoes by
Hittorff and Picot.

Hittorff, St Vincent
de Paul, elevation of
the portico showing
proposed painted
panels by Pierre-Jules
Jolivet, 1844,
from *L'Architecture
Polychrome chez les
Grecs* (1851).

Lorette was the rather bigger basilican church of St Vincent de Paul that Hippolyte's son, Jean-Dominique, designed with Hittorff, by then his brother-in-law. The two neighbouring churches became the joint manifesto of the new, the renewed 'primitive' church, neither slavishly Roman like the Madeleine, nor archeologically 'early Christian', but modern-antique in the Durandian mode.[67] Its decoration was to be a model of coherence. Once again, Ingres turned the commission down, and it went to one of his most prolific students, Hippolyte Flandrin,[68] who was to become the most enthusiastic and successful decorator of Parisian buildings in the 1840s and '50s.

Linear, Nazarene-type art was much favoured by the French establishment at the time – though by no means exclusively.[69] The king and his advisers knew their obligations: Eugène Delacroix's commemoration of national unity during the July revolution of 1830, *Liberty Guiding the People*, was bought by the state; his two great Salon pictures, *Dante and Virgil* of 1822 and *The Massacre at Scio* of 1824, although not generally favoured by the press, provoked two very enthusiastic articles by the young Adolphe Thiers.[70] Thiers' enthusiasm was translated into active patronage under the July Monarchy, during which he was one of the king's confidants, and at times the effective prime minister.[71]

Delacroix was engaged to create a number of large and prominent painted cycles at public expense. The first (begun in 1833) were the ceilings of the Salon du Roi and the library for the Chamber of Deputies in the Palais-Bourbon; there followed the Library of the Luxembourg Palace for the Senate, and the chapel of the Holy Angels in the church of St Sulpice – and, most conspicuously, the Galerie d'Apollon in the Louvre. By that time he was considered by some to be the greatest painter of his generation (in France, according to Baudelaire, at any rate). In all of these public commissions he never collaborated on any building that had been begun by a contemporary architect, although he did work with several restorers.[72] Apart from a strong antipathy to Percier and Fontaine (he found their style dry and mean), as well as to Hector Lefuel and Victor Baltard,[73] and occasional objections to the post-Durandian pretence to have fixed the rules of antique architecture, there is not much notice of architecture in his journals. The 'Gothicists' – Lassus, Viollet-le-Duc he considered outright enemies. He was more at his ease with more eclectic 'Romantics', with Duban and Vaudoyer.

Ten years younger than Delacroix, Flandrin had spent his early years in Rome (having gained the Grand Prix as a student) and become a disciple of Ingres, but had also fallen in with the Nazarenes. His belief in the primacy of line, which Ingres so powerfully inculcated, would have made him very receptive to their ideas. His first commission in 1838 (at the very time when Delacroix, who really detested Flandrin's work, was painting in the Palais-Bourbon) was for a chapel in the church of St Séverin on the Left Bank that was also being restored by Lassus. For many years he worked on the much larger abbey church of St Germain-des-Prés nearby, where he is commemorated by a monument.[74]

Though less familiar than St Germain-des-Prés, Flandrin's work in the new basilica of St Vincent de Paul which Hittorff built (with Jean-Baptiste Lepère) was more innovative and truly polychrome: the church had a wide apse and an open timber roof painted in primary colours; inside, Flandrin (working with another artist, François-Edouard Picot)[75] decorated the balustrade-frieze with a procession echoing the processional mosaics of the Ravenna basilicas (Hittorff, as I said earlier, had always considered mosaic the Christian successor of ancient polychromy). Flandrin was also keen to find the modern, durable successor of mosaic, one that would demand new techniques. As luck would have it, the prefect of the Seine who promoted (and profited from) the urban developments to which the two new churches (Notre-Dame de Lorette and St Vincent de Paul) catered was one Comte Gérard Chabrol de Volvic, on whose hilly, volcanic lands (now better-known as a source of mineral water) a lava was found which provided an ideal ground for enamel. Hittorff became enthusiastic about the process, which came to be called *lave d'Auvergne* or *Volvic*. Shiny, brightly-coloured *Volvic* panels by another pupil of Baron Gros (and much Flandrin's inferior), Pierre-Jules Jolivet, were attached to the porch wall of St Vincent de Paul. Objections were immediately made to the harsh colours and to the nude figures of Adam and Eve and the whole lot was stripped off in 1860 and moved to a warehouse, where they still remain. But the removal and the controversy, as well as Hittorff's enthusiasm, left its mark on the French architecture of the succeeding decades, though paradoxically it was more influential on the use of self-colouring polychrome materials as wall-surfacing than on the employment of artists to provide ornament for new buildings.[76]

But polychromy did not seem to need great artists. The new polychrome buildings could not boast anything more glorious than Flandrin's processional friezes. Meanwhile, the same Chassériau, who as a precocious seventeen-year-old disciple of Ingres had decorated the walls of Jeune-France for Gautier and Borel, had taken his distance from his master and passed to the camp of his greatest opponent. Even before the break, Gautier was comparing him to Delacroix, and since Delacroix had no formal atelier, Chassériau, having befriended him, is sometimes considered the artist who transmitted his lessons to the next generation. He was well connected politically; and it seems that it was the decisive influence of that great social thinker (and at that time a deputy), Alexis de Tocqueville, which got him his first major mural commission, the decoration of the great stairway of the Cour des Comptes building, which was adapted about 1840 by Jacques Lacornée.[77] The Cour was largely destroyed to make way for the present Gare d'Orsay, so that only parts of the paintings have survived, though drawings for them and fragments of the three largest ones, *Peace Protecting the Arts and Agriculture*, *Order Providing for the Costs of a War* and *Commerce Reconciling the Nations* help to reconstruct the rather bland allegories; though brilliantly executed, they still seem very much enlarged easel pictures. Much of his other work was destroyed, but two younger painters, Pierre Puvis de Chavannes and Gustave Moreau, considered themselves his disciples and assured his fame throughout the nineteenth century. Moreau's mourning for his friend took the form of an early masterpiece, *The Young Man and Death*, which he showed in the Salon of 1865.[78] Moreau withdrew from public view in the following decade and re-emerged as the master of lush mythological fantasies which were closer to Rossetti and Burne-Jones than his Impressionist contemporaries. He became one of the most influential teachers of his generation (Matisse and Rouault were his pupils). Puvis de Chavannes for his part became the great maker 'of beautiful paintings in ugly buildings', which began when a now largely forgotten architect, Arthur-Stanislas Diet, asked him to paint some panels for the Museum of Picardie he was designing in Amiens; like all other Paris decorative paintings they were painted on canvas and fastened to the wall. He seems never to have worked in fresco successfully, though he developed techniques of preparation and tinting which assimilated his canvases to fresco painting.

In the following decade – and in the next administration – Chassériau had two further commissions for paintings in existing buildings: for the baptistery of the church of St Roche in the Rue Faubourg St Honoré (which Robert de Cotte had built a century earlier), where he (unfortunately) painted directly onto stone, and shortly before his early death (aged 37, he died in 1856), for the much more conspicuous but relatively small elongated conch in the apse of the church of St Philippe-du-Roule.

In all of these paintings he concentrated on grouping the figures in the manner he had learnt from Ingres. And yet in the Cour des Comptes and even at St Roche the composition is only marginally concerned with the volume around it. St Philippe was different, though: it had been conceived by Chalgrin (the designer of the triumphal arch at the Etoile) as an early Christian-type basilica. The church had been enlarged and was being finished by Victor Baltard at the time,[79] who was almost certainly involved in awarding the commission for the *Descent from the Cross* in 1852–3 to Chassériau. It turned out to be his last wall painting: the 'classic' organization of figures, which still owed something to Ingres, is now animated by Tintoretto-like energy and drama, making it one of his finest works; at St Philippe du Roule he seemed to work in complete independence of Baltard, who preferred tamer polychromy to 'high art' in his later buildings.

Two or three years older than Baltard, Henri Labrouste became the most influential of those Roman Academic rebels of 1830 who gradually moved into positions of power under the July Monarchy. With Félix Duban he was made architect of the new Ecole des Beaux-Arts buildings in 1832.[80] It was they who added the central hall for the ceremonial distribution of prizes and other solemnities in the shape of a hemicycle, which – since Gondoin's anatomy theatre in the Ecole de Médecine (about 1770) and the revolutionary and post-revolutionary Chamber of Deputies – became an increasingly popular form for assembly rooms.

Such hemicycles inevitably required a new form of decoration, and various devices were tried. Inscriptions were much favoured: one prizewinning Beaux-Arts project of 1835 has the sweeping back wall of the Chamber of Deputies inscribed with all the names of the members of the Constituent and Legislative Assemblies, as well as the Convention. The blank facade of the same project is inscribed with the text of the constitution. In the real

M. A. Marc, drawing of Paul Delaroche's hemicycle frieze of 1838–41 at the Ecole des Beaux-Arts, Paris.

Chamber of Deputies in the Palais-Bourbon, the curved back of the hemicycle is an Ionic colonnade and the columns alternate with vapid statues and reliefs. The chamber has long been dominated by a tapestry copy of Raphael's *School of Athens* over the speakers' tribune, to be 'read' as the exemplar of rational debate.

In the hemicycle of the Beaux-Arts, Paul Delaroche, newly returned from an Italian journey (and perhaps as a compensation for the loss of the Madeleine decorations), was commissioned in the same year to cover the entire curved back wall with a long frieze. Between 1838 and 1841, at the height of the fresco revival, Delaroche painted it in oil and on canvas to show a relaxed grouping of selected great painters and sculptors of past times arranged (by analogy to Raphael's *School of Athens* – though with a sideways look at Ingres' *Apotheosis of Homer*) as a dialogue between the masters of *disegno* and those of *colore*. Such groups of 'major' artists were to become an increasingly popular subject for monumental buildings: Cornelius' frescoes in

Engraving from Gourlier, Biet, Grillon and Tardieu, *Choix d'Edifices publics . . .* (Paris, 1825–50) of a section through the Bibliothèque Ste Geneviève stairwell, showing the copy of the *School of Athens*.

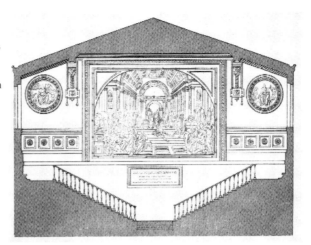

the loggia of the Alte Pinakothek in Munich and the reliefs on the Albert Memorial in London were both concerned to select and to display 'canonic artists'. Delaroche's hemicycle was regarded with particular reverence by his contemporaries, and after a fire in the Ecole at the end of 1855 (in which it was

Henri Labrouste, staircase of the Bibliothèque Ste Geneviève, showing the Balze brothers' copy of *Raphael's School of Athens*.

not damaged), Duban built a high-level viewing-box opposite the painting to allow the visitors a panoramic view.[81]

The shape and outline of Delaroche's composition were dictated by its location. Other artists were less fortunate. Labrouste was notoriously reluctant to engage with 'major' artists, even when he was given public and 'conspicuous' commissions. He had attracted much attention when, in 1840, he designed the settings for the 'Return of the Ashes', that triumphal funerary procession of Napoleon's coffin when it was reburied under the dome of St Louis des Invalides.[82] But by then he had also been asked to design his first public building, the new Bibliothèque Ste Geneviève beside the Panthéon.

The Bibliothèque Ste Geneviève project was crucial on many counts. At the time Labrouste was working on it, art was, after all, supposed to be dead (or at least dying), and among the arts, architecture was said to be the most moribund. This doctrine was preached in Berlin where Hegel had announced their demise repeatedly, definitively and magisterially in the course of his lectures on Aesthetics – to which I will return.[83]

The Point of No Return

How much was known in France about Hegel's ideas in this matter is not clear; certainly Victor Cousin, who was to teach philosophy at the Sorbonne (he was created a peer in 1832, and made a minister soon after), had met Hegel in Heidelberg and liked him best of all the German philosophers he encountered; during his visit (1824–5), he attended some of Hegel's lectures, some of which were probably the ones about Aesthetics. Whatever Victor Hugo may have learnt of Hegel's ideas about the state of the arts and of their future (from Cousin, who was a friend), he also argued the demise of architecture from rather different premises – from which he deduced the argument of the famous chapter that he added to later editions of *Notre-Dame de Paris* and which is called '*This* will kill *that*', 'Ceci tuera cela'.

Hugo's contention was that the cheap and widely distributed printed book, his *ceci*, would succeed the cathedral (even the public building in general) *cela* as the chief vehicle of social communication. He needed no overarching metaphysical Idea or Spirit to move any great dialectical process to such an end, but contended that he felt obliged to add the historical-theoretical chapter to an already very popular novel so as to make the French public sensitive to the glories of its medieval architecture; though, clearly, his argument was more complex and more ambitious.[84] *Notre-Dame* is a discursive text, whose narrative line (and even plot) depends on the way in which the cathedral is perceived by its users, as well as on the way it inflects the space of the city.

It seems clear now that a 'definitive' publication was held up until Labrouste and Hugo had worked through the text, which Labrouste had been invited to read – in proof or perhaps even in manuscript. Having worked with Hugo on the details of his forecast, Labrouste made it a starting point for the design of the Bibliothèque Ste Geneviève. An oblong two-storey stone structure, it lay east–west, parallel to the church dedicated to the same saint which had been re-named Panthéon (as I remarked earlier), and whose bare, unarticulated interior was a constant challenge to painters.

Projects for decorating the Panthéon therefore proliferated. The most famous and complete was that of the 'philosopher-painter', the Lyonnais Paul Chenavard, a close friend and frequent companion of Delacroix. In spite of their long friendship, Delacroix was open in his scepticism about the work of his 'learned but unhappily all too cold' friend.[85] After the revolution of 1848 Chenavard convinced the interior minister, Alexandre Ledru-Rollin (a fellow Freemason), that he should be allowed to turn the walls of the building into a vast, grisaille narrative showing the progress of humanity from chaos to its future destruction and its 'eternal return'; it was a scheme which depended on German philosophers of history – notably Schelling – but also chimed with the musings of the utopian writers of his time, Saint-Simon and Charles Fourier, whom he included as figures in some of the compositions. The paintings were to be largely grey, barely heightened with colour here and there, to contrast with an architecture which he wanted brightly polychromed and gilt. The intention was to make the building as little as possible like a church, so that the dun sobriety of the wall paintings would emphasize their philosophical nature. It was a missionary and extremely ambitious project. Chenavard further proposed that the metropolitan Parisian one be surrounded by twelve regional Panthéons, and that his composition be published in photographic reproductions as a kind of tract for his syncretic religion – a great novelty in

1848. Had Chenavard's work remained in place, the library and church/ex-church would have been one of the most decorated interiors of the time. And yet there was no attempt to link them by any urban 'furniture' and – apart from the names on the library elevation – the interior elaboration drawn out of the buildings failed to promote the creation of a cohesive urban ensemble.

As it happened, Louis Napoleon became prince-president in 1849, and by 1851 he was emperor and the Panthéon became a church again. What was executed of Chenavard's paintings (which were on canvas) went into storage, and he did little work after that, while the building had to wait another generation to receive more painting.[86]

Labrouste avoided similar problems in the library by conceiving the decoration of the building integrally with its structure. He had based his rather solemn exterior pilaster arcades on those of Alberti's Tempio Malatestiano at Rimini, of which he had done a careful measured drawing. The arcade rose from a heavy basement crowned with a frieze of garlands punctuated by blackened metal *paterae* that stamp the building with the joined initials 'SG', reproducing the seal that the library stamped on its books. That Italianate echo gave the building its main formal organization. Each bay was filled by a panel crowned by a thermal window within the arch. These panels were to carry 801 (when the list would be complete) names coloured in red. These names, beginning with Moses, ended, in 1848, with that of Jons Jakob Berzelius, a Swedish organic chemist who died that year. A number of places were left blank (for future heroes) and were filled gradually. The names featured on the façade were to inform the potential reader about the books he or she might expect to find in the cases on the interior of the same wall.

The arched central entry, flanked by two lamps (carved in bas-relief) which signify the light of knowledge to be found within, opens into a stone-panelled hall. Above the high stone wainscot, the walls are painted as a botanical garden by Alexandre Desgoffe – another pupil of Ingres.[87] The plants were contractually specified, and the sky above them continued into the ceiling, while the grid of iron beams that support it is painted green to stand out against that blue ceiling and make the hall into an artificial garden of Academe. Opposite the entrance, the main staircase up into the reading room was to be dominated by busts of Gutenberg and his associates. Although the original sculpture programme was modified, much of Labrouste's plan was carried out.[88] Overlooking that stairway from the top landing is – again – a full-size copy of Raphael's *School of Athens*, painted by two favourite pupils and assistants of Ingres, the brothers Paul and Raymond Balze.

Labrouste had originally intended to have that space painted with terrestrial globes. The placing of the *School of Athens* there, an appropriate enough afterthought, was almost accidental and was probably suggested by an unnamed acquaintance. The Balze canvas was one of many they painted as part of a project to copy all Raphael's fresco work in the Vatican at full size (but in oil on canvas), for display in Paris. It was a government commission (which Thiers had intended for Ingres personally) to the brothers Balze, with no thought of Labrouste's library. The finished canvases were exhibited in the Panthéon, in 1847 – just before Chenavard started working there – to much approval (including both Gautier's and Delacroix's!), and the *School of Athens* was bought for the library at Labrouste's behest.[89] Having got the big canvas, Labrouste asked the Balze brothers for some smaller Raphael copies, roundels, but he also commissioned an original cartoon for a Raphaelesque tapestry of *Learning* which now backs the issue desk in the centre of the main hall.

That hall, the main reading room, is divided into two aisles by slender cast-iron columns which carried the iron ribs of the light vault, plastered-over papier-mâché. The cast-iron columns stood on stone bases carved with herm-like figures by Louis Desprez (a sculptor whom Labrouste had met in Rome during his time at the Villa Médicis) following the drawings supplied by Labrouste (with smiling day faces to the east, and wrinkled night faces to the west). The insistently 'bookish' character of all this ornament almost suggests that Labrouste inverted Hugo's argument by turning the building into a book. In fact, Hugo himself withdrew the most pessimistic parts of his forecast, and even claimed that his hope was to stimulate a revival of architecture, of a kind that Hegel, for his part, would have found unthinkable.

Yet the use of the Raphael copies, the drawings for the sculptures and the specification of plants for the hall all suggest that Labrouste was unwilling or unable to engage with any artists who might surprise him, as was his older contemporary Schinkel, and much in the same way as Rossini rejected singers' *fioriture* and the trills which they regarded as legitimate improvised ornaments on the written score.[90] The artists' works in the library were not merely contained within tight limits, as were the friezes and interior panels that an *ancien régime* architect, say Ledoux, would offer to the sculptors and painters who collaborated with him, but Labrouste's decorators had to work within constraints almost as binding as those Schinkel gave Cornelius and Tieck in Berlin. 'Pre-planned', 'pre-existing' images, copies of recognized master-pieces, were almost comparable to John Soane's use of prefabricated Coade-stone caryatids a decade earlier.

The part Ingres (who was to do a portrait drawing of Labrouste)[91] played in all this is obscure: he did visit the Bibliothèque Ste Geneviève before it was completed to inspect his pupils' work, and there is even a rumour that he was asked to allow (and refused) a copy of his most famous monumental paintings, the *Apotheosis of Homer* to be placed where the globes (and later the *School of Athens*) were to go.[92] For all that, he preferred paintings to be 'working' parts of buildings rather than museum exhibits. As the 'natural' successor of David, he also painted the vast 'historical' canvases, called *machines*, which were expected of him – though for no specific location; but unlike David he had also painted decorations in a number of older buildings, where he was called upon to work with architects – mostly restorers – and these collaborations did not pass without conflict. His relations with architects were not always cordial.[93]

Christ Handing the Keys to Peter and *The Vow of Louis XIII* for the eight-eenth-century cathedral of Montauban, his home town, were much praised at the Salon of 1824 when they were exhibited before being hung rather than installed. In the same Salon Delacroix exhibited the *Massacre at Scio*.[94] In 1834 the *Martyrdom of St Symphorien* was commissioned for Autun Cathedral by the Minister of the Interior, who happened to be the same Adolphe Thiers who was Delacroix's patron. The programme was supplied by the bishop, but Ingres' treatment was considered by 'classical' critics excessively melodram-atic and almost 'Michelangelesque' (not a term of praise at the time!) in its articulation of the human body.[95] In any case the painting was no altar-piece, or affixed to the wall, but framed and hung in the south transept of the twelfth-century building.

Although Ingres had always insisted that his works should be incorporat-ed in buildings, his experiences were not happy. There was painted glass (which was executed at Sèvres – and wrongly called 'stained glass') for the small chapel of St Ferdinand, built in 1842–3 by Percier and Fontaine to com-memorate the Duc d'Orléans, oldest son and heir of Louis-Philippe, tragically

J.A.D. Ingres, *The Age of Gold*, 1842–7, oil on plaster, behind the 'copy' of Pheidias' Athena statue by Pierre-Charles Simart (1855), Château de Dampierre.

killed in an accident, and very similar windows for the Orléans funerary chapel in the Castle at Dreux.[96] All this was relatively small scale, but he had hoped for an opportunity to execute a large monumental painting. He therefore invested much energy in what he came to regard as one of his most important undertakings, the two very large walls in the vaulted hall now called Salon de Minerve in the castle at Dampierre which Félix Duban (the same who collaborated with Labrouste on the Ecole des Beaux-Arts) was adapting for the learned and pious Duc de Luynes. For more than a decade, beginning in 1839, Ingres worked on the paintings intensively, living in a *dependance* of the castle where Madame Hittorff used to come and embroider with Madame Ingres while the master was at work.

Ingres had forbidden anyone (including the duke) to see the paintings before they were finished. One wall of the hall was taken up by an elaborate figurative composition in a sylvan setting, the *Age of Gold*, which he managed to complete. It was to be answered from the opposite wall by an equally complex figural grouping against the background of an Ionic temple (for which only the architectural setting, very like the one at the back of the *Apotheosis of Homer* was done). The duke had taken Ingres at his word and waited to be admitted – to the painter's annoyance – but once he had examined it, he objected to the number of nudes in the *Age of Gold* and asked to be released from his contract. He had them shrouded with heavy velvet drapes, and positioned in front of them a restored version of Pheidias' gold-and-ivory Athena, about ten foot high, which Pierre-Charles Simart (who had earlier modelled some of the medallions and panels that are part of Duban's 'grotesque' framing decorations) had sent to the Exposition Universelle of 1855. Though unfinished and shrouded, the paintings were known about, of course, and attracted great curiosity.[97]

Meanwhile, Hittorff was forever failing to get Ingres involved in his most ambitious schemes – Ingres had refused commissions for decorating both Notre-Dame de Lorette and the interiors of the church of St Vincent de Paul that Hittorff had designed (as he had refused to decorate the apse of the Madeleine). The only product of their collaboration is a toy, a paper-on-copper panel of the *Birth of the Muses*, painted for the scandalously expensive model of the wholly polychrome Doric Temple of the Muses that Hittorff designed for Prince Napoleon Bonaparte (nephew of Napoleon III, and known as Plon-Plon) as a homage to his mistress, the great actress Rachel, whose statue (as Melpomene, also polychrome) by Jean-Auguste Barre was its centre. Barre was responsible for the other ornaments of this 1-metre-high miniature building, which was a finished product and not a proposal. The main structure was wooden, plastered, painted, decked in ivory and gilt bronze. The colours, if not quite as aggressive as in some of his earlier restorations of Greek temples, are nevertheless much more solid than in his executed 'modern' polychrome buildings.[98]

The polychrome arguments paradoxically coincided with a time when the leading painters (witness both Delacroix and Ingres) felt unease with architects and their works. An interesting episode is registered by Delacroix, who found himself sitting next to Isabey at the funeral of Baron de Menneval (once Napoleon's secretary) on 22 April 1850, in the church of Notre-Dame de Lorette. The polychromy round the altar of the church had been largely done by Hittorff himself. Delacroix and Isabey, whatever their differences, were so absorbed by their violent distaste for polychrome architecture that they paid little attention to the proceedings. They agreed on the way out that the shadows thrown by the mouldings were ornament enough for interiors, and that the tonalities of these paintings deformed the space. Gold ground destroyed the modelling of painted figures . . . and so on. The drenching rain that day obviously added to their ill humour.[99]

Their distaste could have been echoed by many other artists who had a high view of their calling and its public nature, and no insight into the causes which shifted their social and cultural situation. To many it seemed like a symptom of that decline of the arts to which I referred earlier, and of which Hegel was the prime interpreter. His majestic account of the development of the arts (and their inevitable decline) opens with what he terms the symbolic period, that of the 'oriental' kingdoms of Egypt and Mesopotamia. That first period was dominated by architecture. It gave way to the 'classic' one in which sculpture, particularly that of the human figure, was dominant. Since the human form was the only one in which the Idea can truly become phenomenon, the classic period is uniquely splendid. This had the inevitable effect of pushing Architecture into the background and favouring the other arts – which was crucial for Hegel's systematic account. He had made his own Kant's notion that the recognition of beauty in any one thing is that with which aesthetic discourse is primarily concerned. That recognition of beauty depends on an apprehension of finality without purpose, without any sense of instrumentality or adaptation to any use (*Zweckmässigkeit ohne Zweck*). Architecture, on this view, the earliest and therefore the heaviest and earthiest of the arts, is also the most remote and least accessible to true aesthetic apprehension, since it is inevitably mired in *Zweck*.[100]

Hegel's third, the Romantic period, which corresponds to the Christian era, being the era of Incarnation is also the most concrete, and it is dominated not by one, but by three remaining arts. The first of these is painting, which (though related) is distinct from sculpture as it has colour but no 'spatiality'. Music follows next and the Romantic era is completed by the most spiritual of all the arts, poetry – in which the sensory element is entirely subdued by inner meaning.[101] It was a belief to which some of his followers, notably Karl Marx, gave general currency.

In spite of Hegel's prophecy, the arts would not lie down – not even architecture.[102] Architects, however, saw such decline of their cultural (and in some ways also social) status as an imminent threat. Their collective answer was to bureaucratize. The organizing of the profession was an international phenomenon of the decade between 1835 and 1845. The Royal Institute of British Architects was founded in 1836, and the American Institute of Architects (abortively) about the same time;[103] in France the Société Centrale des Architectes was incorporated in 1843. It was presided over by Victor Baltard (the same who had completed Chalgrin's basilica of St Philippe-du-Roule), though its authorization and bureaucratic status were negotiated by the smooth and omnipresent Hittorff. All this coincided almost exactly with the demonstrative withdrawal of artists from the regulated exchanges of society and the constitution of a Bohemia – or, alternatively, the formation of an avant-garde – which allowed them to work in relative isolation.[104]

It coincided, too, with the tacit but general acceptance of Durand's design method (in spite of all the criticisms) and of its main assumptions: the priority of columns over walls, the prevalence of the grid as a compositional base, the absolute value of elementary geometrical solids – and its alienation of painting and sculpture. The increasing popularity of cast iron as a structural material, combined with exterior walls of brick or stone, provided almost ideal structures for such grid planning. However vocal the dissenters became (particularly the admirers of Gothic architecture), it was difficult to escape the pervasive Durandian doctrine in which ornament was both subordinate and conventional. Polychromy could substitute 'high' art, but in some rather frightening way, it seemed as if Hegel's views could be seen as true.

FOUR

Religious Attention, Aesthetic Attention

Architects were working themselves into the bourgeois social fabric as 'professional men', constructing a role that assimilated them to physicians, dentists or lawyers. This role would therefore be qualitatively different from that of sculptors, painters and other artists, who – for their part – were exploring the dangerous frontiers of experience and could be excused such social lapses as deviant behaviour.[1] Attention to works of art, 'aesthetic attention', came increasingly to be considered as quite separate from everyday experience, even though the word had lost the specificity it had in the eighteenth century.[2]

The short life of Philipp Otto Runge illustrates the problem which this development set some of the most brilliant artists of the time. Runge was a slightly older contemporary (1777–1810) of the Nazarenes. Like some of them, he had read Wackenroder and talked to Ludwig Tieck – at length. Like several of them, he died young. The similarity ends here, since he took an entirely different direction, having no patience either with their Romanist sympathies or with any hankering after a medieval past.[3]

On the contrary: Runge saw himself as the harbinger of a wholly new art, which would offer itself to the viewer in immediate apprehension, and he initiated a very different (though parallel) development in the art of the nineteenth century to the one I described in the last chapter. Were the artist (as Runge taught) to approach nature with the innocent wonder of a child, a wholly new art would become manifest, an art which would need no allegorical key, no historical or literary system of reference, but would appeal to the viewer directly, and would guide him only by a systematic use of colour. His early years were restless. From Swedish Prussia where he was born, he moved to Copenhagen, at the time one of the centres of a new, severe classicism, but soon abandoned it for Dresden.

Dresden may have been an Electoral capital, but it was a small town (it would not reach 100,000 inhabitants until about 1850) whose cultural importance in the first half of the nineteenth century was partly due to the aggressive patronage of previous Prince-Electors, who assumed the hereditary title 'King of Saxony' in 1806. In spite of their unsuccessful military ventures (mostly against Sweden and Prussia, and later in favour of Napoleon), they promoted sensible commercial and industrial policies (harnessing water-power for the textile industry, for instance) that made Dresden an important centre.[4]

One result of this aggressive royal patronage was the first systematically arranged art and antiquities collection, on which Count Francesco Algarotti (Frederick the Great's friend and an international 'art expert'), Mengs, and Winckelmann (both of them German, though living in Rome) had worked. The court also actively promoted a thriving operatic company. Ludwig Tieck (who seemed to appear anywhere there was artistic excitement) moved there about the same time as Runge, and in 1821 was to become the *dramaturg* (the artistic director) of the Court Theatres.

The young Tieck had in fact moved to Dresden in 1801, about the same time as Runge, and introduced him to the ideas of his friend Novalis, but also to the writings of the seventeenth-century mystical and theosophical writer Jakob Boehme, who had impressed many eighteenth-century thinkers, especially the Pietists.[5] The colour-system Runge then developed was grounded in Boehme's alchemical intuition. Like Boehme, he adored a God who was the ground of all being rather than the transcendent sky-father of more conventional religion – a God of the inner voice, whose presence could be experienced in the very forms of the land, in plants, in all that the senses perceive – God immanent in all nature.

Colour as Mystery

From Boehme, Runge learnt the particular apprehension of unity between the experience of colour and that of sound, which led him to build up a set of correspondences between colour and other percepta.[6] Historic polychromy had nothing to do with his ideas: they had a different ancestry, since they were a variant of a timelessly ancient trope rooted in an immemorial part of human

Philipp Otto Runge, colour circle, *c.* 1810, after his *Hinterlassenen Schriften*, 1840–41.

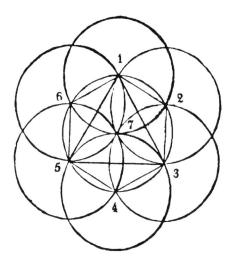

Philipp Otto Runge, colour circle, *c.* 1810, after his *Hinterlassenen Schriften*, 1840–41.

experience – witness Noah's wonder at the rainbow. It had been a challenge to thinkers, at least since Plato made it the theme of the myth of Er the Armenian at the end of the *Republic*.[7] The intuition that there was a close relationship between colour and sound had oscillated between explanations based on the refraction of light or – alternatively – ones based on the composition of pigments. During the sixteenth and seventeenth centuries, the emphasis on the pigment aspect was a little neglected, since the refraction of light was being assiduously investigated. Isaac Newton, the greatest of such investigators, appealed to a proportional account of colour in his *Optics* in order to overcome his anxiety at the way the ancient notion of an exact analogy between linear measure and sound was being set aside by recent French rationalists. Cherished ideas, ideas which claimed scriptural authority and were the traditional guarantee of a belief that the order of art could reconstruct the order of creation, were being revised. Association was being set above any other factor in the reception of sensation. Even the consciousness of beauty was reduced to pleasurable association. Paradoxically, Isaac Newton himself had been inspired by René Descartes, the most powerful advocate of association, to find a 'natural' correspondence between the proportional quantities of the seven hues he distinguished in the spectrum and the notes of the octave; Descartes' analysis of the chromatic scale in the form of a circle led Newton to revalidate the old analogy between quantity and sound through the 'secondary' phenomenon of colour.[8]

But Runge – inspired by Boehme and another seventeenth-century polygrapher and emblematist, Georg Philipp Harsdoerffer[9] – appealed to that different, though equally venerable tradition which had as its point of departure the mixing of pigments rather than the analysis of light. Runge knew about this – perhaps at second or third hand – through the eighteenth-century writings of a Parisian Jesuit, Louis-Bertrand Castel, who had provided an equally systematic account of the analogy of colour to sound – different, since it operated with five basic colours: black and white (which were not part of Newton's scheme); red, yellow and blue. These last three, with the intervening ones, produced the twelve hues which corresponded to the notes of the chromatic scale. Castel, for his part, had claimed that he was only developing the ideas of two seventeenth-century members of his Society: the German (though Rome-based) polymath Athanasius Kircher, who had in turn elaborated those of François d'Aguilon, an Antwerp mathematician and philosopher (or Aguilonius; he had been Rubens' frequent collaborator).[10] The two Jesuits had formulated colour systems, and they both presented them as a diagram of interlaced arcs, much in the way that musical theorists had presented musical scales since antiquity.

Castel had applied his theory to the construction of a colour-clavichord, described in a book which became quite celebrated. When he originally launched this *claveçin oculaire,* he had meant to operate a keyboard linked to a series of different coloured prisms with light passing through them, but this turned out to be too difficult technically, so that his instrument was reduced, in about 1730, to a keyboard that operated colour paper pop-up tapes coordinated with the 'tangents' which plucked the clavichord strings;[11] some twenty years later he devised another, refined and improved version of it, using lights and transparencies. The poet-scientist, Erasmus Darwin, may have seen a display of the more powerful of the two instruments in the Soho Concert Rooms in 1757.[12] A version of Castel's original publication had already been translated into German by the great composer Georg Philipp Telemann in 1739.

Runge, who may have known either Telemann's or some other German publication which later took up Castel's ideas, wanted to 'moralize' the Jesuit's scheme. To him white and black signified light and darkness, and their moral correlatives, good and evil; the three primary colours stood for the persons of the Trinity (blue for the Father, red for the Mediator and yellow for the

Consoler). But the same colours also corresponded to the three sentiments which the human soul experiences towards God through faith: will, love, longing. Such considerations, and his own understanding of light, led him to formulate a very different systematic presentation of colours from those of his predecessors; he showed them as a sphere with black and white at its poles, neutral grey at the centre. The three primary hues then are apices of an equilateral triangle which is inscribed into the circle of the sphere's equator. Runge's was the first convincing attempt to construct a representation of hue and of tone in three dimensions. It was to be developed much further in the twentieth century by the American painter Albert H. Munsell and the German physicist Wilhelm Ostwald.[13] Classifying colours within the three-dimensional body that Runge had proposed has now been generally accepted as the best way of ordering and sorting any range of hue and tone – it is still used by many paint manufacturers.[14]

Runge's was a pigment-based and anti-Newtonian system, yet he would not take sides in the Franco-British quarrel between colour as pigment and colour as light.[15] Although he had arranged his hues around an equilateral triangle (which suggested a sixfold organization), yet the Newtonian sevenfold was also a key notion for him as a fulfilment of his hexagonal colour scheme, developed by inserting the secondary orange, violet and green between the primary colours – and then splitting violet into purple and scarlet. That much is clear from his letters to his brother and to Ludwig Tieck,[16] as well as to Goethe, with whom he corresponded (without agreeing) about colour theory, but who also admired him and collected his paintings. Yet while Goethe's colour theory is almost entirely physio-psychological (since he considers only what happens 'in the eye' to be relevant to the perception of colour), Runge's classificatory system is deductive and tightly geometrical. The contrast between them is an aspect of that

> passage from the geometrical optics of the seventeenth and eighteenth centuries to physiological optics, which dominated both the scientific and philosophical discussion of vision in the nineteenth century.[17]

In his rather sporadic writings, Runge returns constantly to the theme of an analogy in perception through the different senses, an analogy which would be called *synaesthesia* later.[18] It is, of course, a commonplace of recent historical writing that Enlightenment thinkers were motivated by a powerful urge to classify and separate – while Romantic ones (however you circumscribe the term 'romantic') were constantly seeking the opposite, some nuclear phenomenon which would point them to a total and unifying experience. Goethe's postulation of the morphological kernel of all organic matter – his *Urpflanze* – was, in a sense, paralleled in the search by artists of the period for a synaesthetic *Urkunstwerk* – some archaic, primal work, in which all the arts would collaborate and whose unifying force would in turn act as a social cement.

In the matter of synaesthesia, Runge's approach was more ambitious and more thoroughgoing than that of many of his contemporaries; he considered the analogy between musical composition and painting much in the way in which another contemporary writer whom he came to love, Novalis, maintained that 'all senses are, in the end, one single sense'. And that 'one sense leads us, like our one world, to all (other) worlds by degrees'.[19] The works which most explicitly display and explore his ideas are a group of panels which he called the *Four Times of Day*, compositions to which he devoted most of his time in the last decade of his life. Sometimes he spoke of them as a symphony in four movements; but at other times he also suggested – more mundanely – that the four panels were to decorate a hypothetical room, where they could be 'linked by arabesques', by ornaments which he proposed to design himself. He even suggested that this room would be in a separate building of its own, which, he implied, might have a 'national' character; in any case, the room and its decorations survive only as descriptions of the interior.

Of the four paintings only one was nearly finished before Runge died; the others are known from sketches and line-drawings which have been engraved.[20] He had no doubt that there was a correspondence between musical tones and the colours or the shapes he used; not, of course, to any specific notes or to the sound of any instruments which the senses might appreciate separately – but that the composition of colours was an analogue of symphonic harmony. His aim was to incorporate this intuition in a new form of monumental art in which landscape would replace the allegories and elaborations of history painting.

English artists about this time were increasingly devoting their energies to landscape in their practice, a genre which had been considered subsidiary

Philipp Otto Runge, *The Morning*, the large version, 1809–10, oil on canvas.

by the Royal Academy and by most theorists, and a secondary element in the history painter's equipment – much like still life. More than any other artist, Constable was affected by this shift of categories. While eighteenth-century British landscape gardeners had created parks to emulate Claude's and Gaspar Dughet's views in the Roman Campagna, the English painters who first looked at the countryside *through* such parks moved beyond them.

'A gentleman's park is my aversion. It is not beauty because it is not nature', wrote John Constable in 1822.[21] His own attention to cloud-formations and other meteorological phenomena was almost anatomical.[22] Several other artists of the time turned away from the history painter's traditional obsession with human anatomy to an equal passion for other aspects of creation: George Stubbs to the anatomy of the horse and Alexander Cozens to the mechanism of pictorial imagination.[23] Landscape now also invited a new kind of literary as well as pictorial attention: not the inhabited or cultivated (even if Picturesque) landscape of the eighteenth century, a *natura naturata* (as in the *Lyrical Ballads*), but an untamed and threateningly Sublime one as in Goethe's *Harzreise im Winter*, or yet in James Ward's large canvas of *Gordale Scar*. Runge's concern to set landscape (as he defined it) at the centre of all artistic activity reflected a general development in his time.

Burke's juvenile *Enquiry into the Origin of our Ideas of the Sublime and Beautiful* of 1757 was something of a watershed, and although its influence was slow in Britain, it was translated into German and taken at face value both by Kant and by Hegel as I pointed out earlier. Germany had no recent comparable native 'landscape school' to the British one, even if near contemporaries of Constable (very unlike their British ones, however) turned up in Rome just before 1800 to work at heroic and brilliantly lit views of the Campagna, pictures which sometimes seemed like cut-out overlays, elaborated as a stage set almost as if they were viewed through a telescopic lens – or, less anachronistically – a *camera obscura*.[24] Their very sublimity chimed in with the ideas of many contemporaries: in discussing the term 'Landscape', Johann Georg Sulzer, the Zürich critic, considers terrifying and Sublime nature 'as the origin of the idea of deity'.[25]

The New Landscape

Runge's conception went well beyond the practice of such predecessors or of his contemporaries. Caspar David Friedrich, the artist to whom he felt closest, devoted himself wholly to the painting of landscape, but his art was far removed from that of the German emigrés in Rome – or of the Nazarenes. Like Runge, he cultivated the interiority of a new art based on an apprehension of God's immanent presence and His revelation of Himself in the natural world, though that approach led the much longer-lived Friedrich to paint landscapes in which very few figures were present, and most of them were seen from the back looking *at* the landscape, in the same direction as both the artist and the spectator.[26]

In Runge's exalted conception, the notion of landscape had to be redefined entirely: it was not merely a view over a stretch of more or less evocative countryside, however. Only that art which included the human figure was worthy of such designation. He went much further, and considered that only a painting in which Divine immanence could be *directly* sensed, one without any of the apparatus which history painting seemed to require, was worth doing at all. That was true landscape. In his view, Michelangelo's *Last Judgement* stood at the summit of historical composition – its grandeur due (at least in part) to the way the rocks and trees were interchangeable with human bodies. A new form of landscape began with Raphael's *Sistine Madonna*, since for all its concentration on the figure, it had loosened itself altogether from content-loaded history painting.[27] *The Sistine Madonna* was the centre of the Electoral collection in Dresden. This new form of landscape would be truly, romantically symbolic as Goethe had defined the term.

Friedrich, for his part, was commissioned by Graf von Thun-Hohenstein to provide an altarpiece for the new private chapel of his castle at Tetschen. It was his first commission as well as one of his first oils. The landscape/altarpiece made one iconic concession – there was a crucifix in it, though it was also seen from the back, looking out over the view. The chapel was finished 'in the Gothic style' and Friedrich also designed a gilt frame for his wintry painting. The predella showed the conventional 'all-seeing eye' flanked by clearly standard Eucharistic symbols: corn-sheaves and clusters of grapes. A pointed arch was made of two palm boughs, on which *putti* heads were mounted, and was to 'fit in' with the Gothic interior. Conventionally framed, the piece could not quite rise to Runge's Sublime pretensions. Nevertheless, it was much debated at the time, and was contrasted with the work of more commonplace, 'literary' religious artists. Some considered that it established Friedrich's claim (which probably did not interest Runge overmuch) that a landscape could replace a history painting as a central devotional or liturgical icon.[28]

The Tetschen altarpiece was an exceptional work for Friedrich, most of whose activity was studio painting. A loner, he looked inside himself as much as at the countryside for the landscapes he wanted to paint and had never been friendly with the Dresden critics, who, for their part, were not kind to him. Yet he was appointed to a professorship at the Dresden Academy at the height of his fame, in 1817, and continued in it until a stroke incapacitated him in 1835.

The New Total Theatre

The social-artistic life of Dresden was organized round a club, the Kunstverein, which the anti-social Friedrich himself never joined. Its president was the merchant-friend of the Nazarenes Johann Gottlob Quandt (his wife's portrait by Overbeck is one of the most celebrated paintings of the movement) and his successor was the polymath court physician Carl Gustav Carus, who was himself a talented painter, a psychological theorist of the new landscape, one of Friedrich's most committed patrons, as well as a prominent apostle of Goethe's morphological theories.[29] The musical scene was equally lively: in 1816 Carl Maria von Weber became royal *Kappelmeister*, called to Dresden specifically to organize and inspire the new German-language opera which had been founded in opposition to the old Italian one – and soon joined the Kunstverein. Weber had long been fascinated by the dramatic possibilities of composing operas to German librettos of a high literary quality, but he had also been very interested in the amalgamation of genres in the opera.[30]

Some time later, in 1834, a young, ambitious and forthright Hamburg architect, Gottfried Semper, was engaged as director of the School of Architecture in the Royal Academy, and he was to stay in Dresden until exiled for his involvement in the revolution which spread to Saxony in 1849. He had published some polemical essays on polychromy in ancient architecture, and was well aware of the Parisian battles about the colouring of ancient and medieval buildings and sculptures provoked by Quatremère de Quincy's and Hittorff's publications; he was in correspondence with Hittorff, who considered himself an ally of Semper.

His own interests never coincided with the mystical interiorities of the new landscape, and he showed little concern for the work of the older painters who were his colleagues in the Dresden Academy – either Friedrich or his friend and neighbour, the Norwegian Johan Christian Dahl, or even Carus,[31] though he was much involved in the social life of Dresden where his closest friend among Dresden artists was the sculptor (Friedrich August) Ernst Rietschel, who had been named professor at the Academy two years before him and had married Carus' famously beautiful daughter. Semper soon became a prominent figure of the clubby Kunstverein. The one artist who most engaged him during his Dresden days, however – and was to do so for the rest of his life – was neither painter nor sculptor, but a musician: Richard Wagner, who became Weber's indirect heir at the Dresden opera. Since both Wagner (and later Robert Schumann) were also members of the Verein, music – and opera especially – was much debated there.

As Weber had foreseen, opera became the genre which united poetry and music with dance, but also with the visual arts. It served as a focus for discussion about unity among all the arts from the mid-eighteenth century onwards. The analogy between architecture and music had some small part in this: that 'architecture was frozen music' was a saying attributed to Goethe, though Hegel credited it to Friedrich von Schlegel,[32] and Madame de Staël affirms it as her own in *Corinne*. For Kant, in his role as the father of aesthetics, those two arts were at the edge of his system: architecture, because it was too closely determined by utility, and music because it defied the classificatory impulse, since 'she spoke with many impressions without concepts'. Music (he said) 'proceeds from impressions to unformulated ideas'.[33] Kant's system did not have the dialectical dynamism of Hegel nor did the confining of an art to the edges imply any historic superannuation.

That Kantian sense of unease at music's lack of definition is in sharp contrast to the appeal which music had for the thinkers and artists of the following generations. It inspired Goethe's aphorism that 'the dignity of art seems to appear most explicitly in Music: since there is no material in her that has to be accounted . . . [it] is at once form and content; she heightens and ennobles everything that she expresses'.[34] One consequence of making music the paradigm of the arts was the concentration of aesthetic attention on the momentary and fleeting, on the work of art as a phenomenon in time, so that the permanent or – at any rate – immobile shaping and the stable occupation of space (the prime operation of architecture) was inevitably sidelined. Sculpture, for all its solidity, was often described as a petrifying, a concentration of dance, while painting could offer a background against which any dramatic action might be played out. Such a view makes them essential contributions to opera as the only total work of art. Architecture, on the other hand, was held only to provide a container and a shelter for such actions as demanded aesthetic attention, and therefore could not engage the art-bent spectator in an analogous way.

Gottfried Semper, Dresden opera house, lithograph, 1835–41.

Problems of staging and of opera occupied Semper a great deal – not only because of his friendship with Wagner, but because one of his most prominent buildings in Dresden was the Royal Court Theatre, which was primarily designed to present opera. Opened in 1841, the building was an instant success: the king knighted him; he was granted a personal box in perpetuity; and he also became the architect of the next big royal commission, the Gemäldegalerie, the art gallery which was to house the growing royal collection centred on Raphael's *Sistine Madonna*, which – as the most famous of its treasures – was given its own central, domed chamber.

The Court Theatre was elaborately decorated, both inside and out. Much of the exterior statuary was by Semper's friend Rietschel and other Dresden contemporaries, the figures being of the (by now) canonic literary figures from Shakespeare to Goethe. The outer walls of the building were also sgraffitoed, a form of decoration which Semper much favoured, in which a light plaster is laid over a dark one and the patterns scratched or gouged out of it, exposing the dark layer below – or vice versa. For the interior, Semper imported several French decorative painters, some of whom he had met on a theatre-study expedition financed by the Saxon court; they would remain his friends and would continue to work with him when he was exiled to London. In fact, the Dresden decorations were rather conventional; in the case of the elaborate grotesques, they were mostly done (as were the exterior sgraffiti) from his designs; being the mere vesture of the building, they did not invite special attention.

The stage arrangements, on the other hand, were quite new and startling. Semper clearly understood the new operatic requirement for a sunken and virtually invisible (though perfectly audible) orchestra which would not distract the audience from the stage action and the setting. The proscenium arch was doubled – to allow for concealed lighting between the two arches – and this helped to heighten concentration on the spectacle. Since the Dresden auditorium was one of the first to be successfully lit by gas, it could be easily dimmed during performances. Perhaps most important to Wagner, Semper had devised a way of transforming the 'orchestra' of the ancient theatre into the modern apron stage, so bringing the performance further out into the auditorium.

Richard Wagner had come to Dresden (from provincial Riga and a fiasco in Paris) with his *Rienzi* in October 1842. He presented the *Flying Dutchman* three months later with (only) modest success, but was nevertheless appointed royal *Kappelmeister* and gave brilliant performances of Glück and Mozart, first in the old German opera and later in Semper's theatre (where *Tannhäuser* would be first performed in 1845). He also threw himself into the nationalist-liberal milieu of Dresden: Semper, his friends the Devrient family (singers-actor-managers) and later Michael Bakunin (one of the fathers of philosophical anarchism) were part of the circle in which he moved. His image is now so

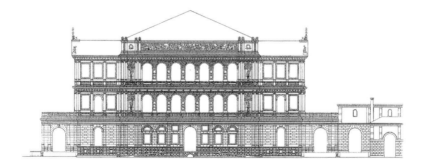

Gottfried Semper, Dresden opera house, steel engraving, 1835–41.

much that of a musician that it is easy to forget that he considered himself a man of letters whose operas were settings of his own verse libretti. He was also very much a political being, a left-winger – a view that challenges the enthusiasm of the political right (of various colourings) for his work in the last century. His ideas of what the theatre was about were formed by his reading of Greek tragedy (in translation), though by the time he reached Dresden, he was increasingly fascinated by national – that is German – and Norse myth. He was convinced, in any case, that myth alone could provide suitable subjects for music drama. Jacob Grimm's *Deutsche Mythologie*, which had appeared in 1835, invited his enthusiasm, and in Dresden he turned to the *Nibelungenlied* as a possible source of libretti. Late in 1848 the text of *Siegfrieds Tod* was ready and was read to a group of friends (Semper among them).[35]

Yet he had also taken a keen interest in philosophy. From general idealistic notions borrowed from Schelling, he moved to a reading of Hegel (particularly the *Philosophy of History*), and by the time he wrote the *Flying Dutchman*[36] he had developed his own obsessive concern with 'salvation' through love, renunciation and the negation of the will. He discovered Ludwig Feuerbach, a pupil (but no disciple) of Hegel, who had developed a sensualist, episodic naturalism in opposition to his teacher, whom he considered idealist. Feuerbach saw the *Philosophy of History* as a 'theology' by another name, and wanted to dissolve it in an anthropology, an 'anthropocentric' materialism in which the idea of God was a projection of human nature and human longing. Wagner had already entertained similar ideas before he came across Feuerbach,[37] but was loath to accept a Hegelian belief in the unconditional primacy of poetry over the arts. Later he was to write 'Art and Revolution', 'The Work of Art of the Future' (which he dedicated to Feuerbach – and which deliberately echoed the title of one of Feuerbach's books, *The Foundations of a Future Philosophy*) and 'Opera and Drama'. He owed much to Feuerbach's dialectical form of argument, and found his polemic against Christianity and against reliance on authority extremely sympathetic, but above all he appreciated his making the aesthetic experience of the sensory world the primary act of the mind.[38]

The populist and incendiary teaching of 'Art and Revolution' proposes Greek tragedy as a model of the (collective rather than synaesthetic) *Gesamtkunstwerk* in opposition to the modern, bourgeois, fragmented commodity *Handwerk* (handwork, craft – which Wagner takes to mean wage-labour).[39] The Greek stage is exalted as the place which expresses the collective consciousness of a society which is its communal spectator; it serves a 'beautiful and strong, a free people'. An echo of Winckelmann's idealization of the Greeks is clear, and this leads Wagner to an anti-Christian polemic. Yet he also found it necessary to distance himself from any unqualified admiration of the Greeks, whose economy was based on slavery, an institution that would be completely unacceptable after the great revolution, which, he thought, was inevitable after the events of 1848–9, and which would, finally, resolve the social contradictions of earlier times.[40]

The two further essays elaborate his doctrine. The work of art should confront the whole of the society for which it is made, and it should not be constrained by the divisions between categories of artistic production. It should therefore be a *Gesamtkunstwerk* in two senses: socially, since it should appeal to and connect with (and therefore also be the product of) the whole of society, but also personally, since it should speak to all the senses and thus break down the boundaries between the arts – rhetoric and ballet, poetry and theatre, the spectacle and its visual setting.[41]

Wagner was attempting to achieve that synaesthetic *Urkunstwerk* to which (as I suggested in the previous chapter) much Romantic thinking about art was already tending. By the time he wrote the *Ring*, he had freed himself of some of Feuerbach's rather imprecise and inelegant formulations. In 1855 he discovered Schopenhauer, though he did so only after his three Zürich pamphlets had already been published. Wagner read and re-read Schopenhauer constantly, even daily, and became his most enthusiastic and effective disciple and advocate. For his part, Schopenhauer never became a Wagnerite and was not even curious to hear his music. The two never met.[42]

From Schopenhauer Wagner took the bold (if ultimately neo-Platonic) hypothesis that art helps man to rise from sensation to an apprehension of type; through suffering and self-sacrifice, he can then overcome the harrowing accidents of individuality to arrive at a state of repose, a notion which Schopenhauer in fact associated with Indian (especially Buddhist) thinking, in which he had been passionately interested. Wagner also welcomed the teaching that will, that desire, is more powerful than intellect. In Schopenhauer's view music is not just the highest of the arts, but is a meta-art.

Music showed forth the world without the mediation of concept, while the other arts all showed the world as representation. Such an inversion of the Kantian scheme was surely welcome to Wagner, even if a contradiction is implied by the exaltation of music to special status, since the *Gesamtkunstwerk* supposed a fellowship among more or less equal arts. At this very time Julius Schnorr von Karolsfeld was completing his *Nibelungen* frescoes in the Munich Residenz for Ludwig I,[43] and he, too, was to be wooed to Dresden when offered the directorship of the collection, attracted by its old splendour as well as by Semper's new museum building.

Bourgeois Revolution, Crystal Palace

Both Wagner and Semper were involved in the events that followed 'the Spring of the Nations' which swept into Saxony in 1849 – a year after the rest of Europe.[44] The liberal-bourgeois revolution involved several members of the Kunstverein. Semper, long a convinced republican, was active in the rising and – on Wagner's insistence – supervised barricade building. Some have even maintained that he prolonged the revolution by a few days – since his barricades were very stable. At any rate King Friedrich August II was outraged by his defecting courtiers.[45] A warrant on a charge of high treason (which carried the death penalty) was out for Semper and for Wagner. Semper escaped, making his way to Paris where he was welcomed by a few old friends, and put up by those painters whom he had employed on the Dresden theatre. But Paris had itself been rocked by the events of 1848, and work for architects was scarce. Still, he managed to complete the monograph on his Dresden theatre in spite of strained circumstances,[46] and had occasional employment on stage-sets at the Paris opera through his painter friends. Wagner's Parisian visits were morale raisers. Yet real opportunities, he began to think, would be available to him only in the United States. A depressed Semper had already forwarded his luggage and boarded the New York steamer at Le Havre when a favourable surprise offer lured him back to Paris. The offer turned out to be vague, but it did lead to a meeting with Edwin Chadwick, a senior British civil servant, who had just become a member of the Board of Health and was proposing to reorganize the cemeteries of London

during yet another cholera epidemic. Semper came to London – but his proposal did not survive parliamentary discussion and, in any case, his Italianate
manner was rejected on grounds of style. By then Gothic was preferred for
anything smacking of religion.

He thought of starting a private architectural school. Nothing came of
that either, though Chadwick did introduce him to the hyperactive Henry
Cole, who had risen very quickly from a lowly position in the civil service.
Cole was genial, energetic and efficient. Convinced of the need to provide
superior design for the masses and concerned to improve public taste, he promoted a number of design journals. Under the pen-name Felix Summerly
(which maintained his civil service anonymity), he published a series of popular guides to monuments, and in 1845 won a competition for a plain tea set,
to be produced by Minton's, the china manufacturers. It won several prizes
and was sold in thousands. The next year – about the time of the Dresden
rebellion – he visited Paris with Minton and an architect collaborator,
Matthew Digby Wyatt, to see the great exhibition of 1849. Since 1804 Paris
had hosted such shows every five years and the 1849 one marked the recovery
from the previous year's disorders. Although there was 'a good deal of taste-
less and unprofitable ornament and its architecture [was] "mesquin"',[47] yet
the design of the exhibits (of textiles particularly) was challengingly high, a
by-product of that Parisian surfeit of drawing schools which I noted earlier.

On that visit, Cole conceived the notion of a London international exhibition and foisted it on the reluctant Prince Consort. There were several

Henry Cole, Minton
tea set, wood
engraving, 1845.

antecedents for such a show,[48] but the scale of Cole's proposal was quite unheard of – and housing it was therefore a real problem. The disappointing results of a competition (in which one project, by the French engineer Hector Horeau, was also for an iron and glass structure[49]) were set aside, and after the committee had cooked up its own ham-fisted and abortive scheme, Joseph Paxton was unexpectedly and more or less directly commissioned to build the great vaulted cruciform glasshouse in Hyde Park. Paxton was the most successful conservatory designer of the day. He had been a gardener (and had risen to be agent and advisor) to the Duke of Devonshire. By 1850 he had also become a 'railway millionaire' and a director of the Midland Railway. It was during a directors' meeting that he had done his famous blotting-pad sketch on which the whole scheme was based.

Cast iron was hardly a novelty: John Nash had used it structurally – both conventionally, as in the Doric columns of Carlton House Terrace, and innovatively, as in the very thin columns of the Brighton Pavilion. Sheet glass had at last become big enough to be used in quite substantial orangeries even in the eighteenth century. Decimus Burton, scion of the entrepreneurial family, the same who had designed the Athenaeum Club, built the iron and glass Palm House at Kew in 1845–8, and Paxton himself had, in 1850, designed the conservatory at Chatsworth for the Duke of Devonshire to house the *Victoria Regia*, the largest known plant. Paxton modelled its very light structure on the plant itself, and would now use the ridge-and-furrow system he had adapted for Kensington.

The Crystal Palace was one of the largest volumes ever enclosed to date.[50] The impact it made was more a triumph of organization than of technology. The speed of erection, of disassembly and re-erection, made almost as much impression as the effect of the diaphanous envelope of the huge building. That enclosure seemed much too insubstantial both for some of its critics and for many exhibitors. The various shows were mounted in solid pavilions and large drapes were used to mitigate the excessive transparency. Nevertheless, two or three years later, the structure could be considered as belonging to a 'type of architecture which may fairly be called "modern English"'.[51]

On his introduction to Paxton, Semper – naively perhaps – hoped for employment on the interior of the palace. By that time a polychrome scheme of reds, yellows and blues, responding to the theory that primary colours equalized each other, had already been devised, as had the 'Saracenic' details for the exterior by Owen Jones.[52] Jones had long been a fellow fighter for polychromy, and had become well-known as the result of his first publication, a chromolithographic album on the Alhambra in Granada. He had measured and drawn it together with a young French architect, Jules Goury, who died of cholera there in 1834. But Goury had earlier, in 1830–32, travelled with Semper through south Italy and Greece, and may well have told Jones about Semper's ideas.

The indefatigable Cole managed to set up the South Kensington Collections (which became the Victoria and Albert Museum) while at the same time he also reformed the design schools (of which he was made Secretary) – and he did all that while designing cheap household objects for industrial production. For Semper, he managed to secure only the design of the Canadian, Danish and Turkish sections; disappointed, Semper nevertheless visited the exhibition almost daily.

It included no memorable art-works: the fine arts were confined in the programme of the exhibits to section xxx. Augustus Pugin's last work before his death was the 'Gothic Court', but that included no important new painting or sculpture. The only 'work of art' which succeeded in achieving popular fame by being displayed in the Crystal Palace was a somewhat vapid white marble nude, the chained *Greek Slave* by Hiram Powers, a now largely forgotten American sculptor. It was conceived as a celebration of Greek independence, but by 1851 irreverent commentators suggested that an ebony Virginian slave might have been more 'relevant'.[53]

For all its shortcomings and the critical attacks, however, the Crystal Palace must be considered an unqualified success – if only measured by its spin-offs. Over the next few years, glass or 'Crystal' palaces were built in Dublin, New York, Munich; world 'expositions' would become a regular feature of later Victorian life, culminating in the Paris one of 1889 that produced both the vast Galerie des Machines (which covered a much larger area than the Crystal Palace with a single, three-hinge span) and the Eiffel Tower. Like the Crystal Palace all subsequent world expositions were dedicated to Cole's proposition that art and industry could, must and should be successfully wedded.

After the exhibition closed in Hyde Park, the palace was dismounted – its

Philip Delamotte, 'Colossi of Aboo-Simbel' at the Crystal Palace, photograph, 1854.

outline is still marked by an alley of plane trees and the Albert Memorial – to be re-erected at Sydenham, where it became an architectural museum; its permanent 'artistic' fixtures included full-size plaster casts of various great monuments (such as 21-metre-high colossi of Abu Simbel in splendid polychrome). Jones was involved in the operation, but while Semper designed several infill buildings, including a pseudo-antique theatre, no project of his was built. In spite of a certain community of ideas, Jones managed to trip Semper up, apparently motivated by a mixture of chauvinism and jealousy.[54]

At any rate, Semper had been fascinated both by the machinery and the ethnography in the Crystal Palace, and this led to considerable revisions of the great theoretical work he had begun in Dresden.[55] He had enforced leisure to elaborate the text of his academy lectures further when Cole, who continued to befriend and support him, managed – finally, in 1852 – to persuade the Board of Trade that he was not a dangerous revolutionary and had him appointed Professor of Metal Ornament at the newly re-organized design school which was by then housed in Marlborough House, a royal residence on the Mall.

In his London lectures, he first gave a systematic account of building that was based on a biological analogy; he taught that all human artefacts were constituted by four processes or functions which were synthesized in the primitive hut. Masonry, the heaping up of hard units, makes a foundation; the moulding of soft material is pottery and metalwork, which makes the hearth; the fitting together of whittled fibrous bits of carpentry makes the roof and frame – and finally, the knotting and platting of rugs and hangings make the wall. Meanwhile, Semper had come across Carl Boetticher's work first published before he left Germany in 1844. Boetticher's theory was based on a distinction between *Kernform* and *Kunstform*, between 'core' or 'seed' forms and those of 'art', dangerously near (or so Semper feared) to his own ideas about the way in which ornamental forms 'clothe' a structure.[56] It led him to refine his teaching that all ornamental forms must be seen as part of the structural business of building, since they were also the products of necessity. The notion of the wall as a curtain (which was to have such momentous consequences for the Chicago architects of the following generation) led him to consider weaving to be in some way the primal art. It must have given him some satisfaction when Paxton, describing the Crystal Palace structure, suggested that the relation between glass and iron was as between a tablecloth and the table.[57]

Jones meanwhile was also advocating the view – not unlike Pugin's or even Ruskin's – that ornament grew out of a monumental architecture; that all the visual arts were historically and logically dependent on it. This was radically opposed to Semper's growing conviction (he made it the hinge of his teaching at the School of Design) that 'practical and industrial arts' preceded architecture, that painting and colouring (body painting especially) and textile developed before building. Although we know nothing of a direct encounter, Semper's highly articulated theory must have riled Jones, while Cole found it stimulating enough.[58]

Theatre as Ornament

Owen Jones' sumptuous chromolithographic publication, *The Grammar of Ornament*, which first appeared in 1856 and was often reprinted, had a brief text (much of it is in the form of aphorisms) that propagated his own theory. The bulk of the book is made up of a hundred composite plates showing ornament from different periods and peoples: of 'Savage Tribes' (which turned out to be mostly Polynesian and New Zealand); Egyptian, Assyrian and Persian; Greek and Roman; Byzantine, Arabian, Turkish, 'Moresque' and Persian again – Islamic this time. Indian, Hindoo, Chinese; Celtic, Medieval, Renaissance, Elizabethan and 'Italian' follow. The last ten plates are devoted to 'Leaves and flowers from Nature', many of which – especially those labelled

Wall decoration from the Alhambra, Granada, from Owen Jones, *The Grammar of Ornament*, 1856.

by him as 'traced from nature' – look almost as if they were pressed botanical specimens. In introducing that closing section, Jones rather oddly insists that 'the world has become weary of the eternal repetition of the same conventional forms which have been borrowed from styles which passed away . . . There has arisen . . . a universal cry of "go back to nature as the ancients did".' Yet he also recognized that mere nature drawing will not yield ornament: 'the more closely nature is copied, the farther we are removed from producing a work of art.' Only by discovering the inner principles and the geometry of natural forms will a new ornamental art arise ('all ornament should be based on a geometrical construction' is one proposition).[59]

He supports this contention by making the eighth of the ten plant plates analytical and concerned with the geometry of plants, and acknowledges in the preface a Mr C. Dresser of Marlborough House – the Government Design School, which I mentioned earlier (William Dyce had been its director) and where Gottfried Semper was teaching about that time. That Mr (later Dr) Dresser will occupy me a great deal in the next chapter.

'Although ornament is most properly only an accessory of architecture [Jones argues] and is in all cases the very soul of an architectural monument', it does not follow that a new ornamental system will have to wait for a new architecture. Elizabethan artists, familiar with imported (mostly Italian) paintings, hanging and carvings, invented ornamental forms in emulation of them, he points out:

> We therefore think we are justified in the belief that a new style of ornament may be produced independently of a new style of architecture; and moreover, that it would be one of the readiest means of arriving at a new style: for instance, if we could only arrive at a new termination to a means of support, one of the most difficult points would be accomplished.[60]

If such a doctrine seems to contradict his earlier belief in the primacy of architecture over *all* ornament, that may be due to his not having quite integrated some of Semper's teaching.

Jones, Wyatt and other members of Cole's circle had in common an interest in popular education as well as making good design widely available, while they all accepted the inevitable growth and ultimate benefits of industry and thought that the social and psychic damage done by machine labour would be mitigated in some, not too distant future. The improvement of design and the salutary power of art would play an essential part in this redemptive social process.

The irreparably alienating and enslaving consequence of machine work was, on the other hand, the prime concern of John Ruskin and his followers. During the proceedings that brought about the exhibition of 1851, he was in Venice working on *The Stones of Venice*. The first volume was published in that same year. Ruskin was also – in his way – an advocate of a polychrome architecture but one based on the use of such coloured materials as different marbles and limestones, as well as coloured glass or majolicas. The core – or perhaps more accurately, the hinge – of his book was the chapter on the 'Nature of Gothic', since it came about the middle of the second volume of the *Stones*, published two years later. It proclaimed that true Gothic ornament required six characteristics in its makers:

> savagery or rudeness; love of change; love of nature; a disturbed imagination; obstinacy and generosity.

Savageness, the characteristic which Gothic owes to its Northern origin, is not merely a consequence of climate, but an index of its nobility, which it owes to religious principle:

> For there are three kinds of ornament: servile, which subjects the executant to the design: Greek, 'Ninevite', Egyptian. In such systems, 'the workman is a slave'. Constitutional, when ornament liberates the executant but acknowledges its dependance on higher powers – Byzantine and Romanesque; and revolutionary which requires no submission from the executant – Gothic.

And Ruskin included three items of advice to anyone who wished to promote the right kind of ornament. The first is 'never to encourage the manufacture of any object that is not absolutely necessary, to the production of which Invention has no share'. The second, 'never to demand perfect finish for its own sake, but only for some practical or noble end'. And the third, 'never to encourage copying or imitating of any kind'.[61]

Such principles were obviously at odds with what was taught in the design schools or believed by most of his optimistic contemporaries, Cole, Jones (and even Semper) included. Although Ruskin's few dealings with Cole seem to have been polite enough, the gap between them was unbridgeable, and Ruskin knew well enough that it was Cole and his like who spoke directly to the men of power. Enormously successful as a writer and as a public lecturer throughout the country, and gregarious though he was, Ruskin saw himself as a lonely prophet.

Ruskin's prophesying called for the recreation of a true Gothic architecture, but he was no antiquarian medievalist; among contemporary painters, he concentrated his attention on 'the English school of landscape, culminating in Turner' (that seemed to him) 'in reality nothing else than a healthy effort to fill the void which the destruction of Gothic architecture has left'. For self-conscious medievalists, such as Overbeck and the Nazarenes, whose religiosity seemed as pasteboard to him as their drawing looked stiff, he had only a rather chilly disapproval.[62] But later he would become the eloquent advocate of a related group of artists – the Pre-Raphaelites.

The 'Pre-Raphaelite Brotherhood' was founded in 1848, probably in the studio of John Millais, in Gower Street, London. Millais had already been regarded as a prodigy beginner in the Royal Academy Schools. He had made common cause with William Holman Hunt, also a student there, who had taken the trouble to read Ruskin – something Millais (or so he later maintained) had avoided.[63] They were joined by Dante Gabriel Rossetti and William Michael, his brother. Father Rossetti, an Abruzzan, and a political refugee from the Kingdom of Naples, was then Professor of Italian at University College. Dante Gabriel had also met Holman Hunt at the Royal Academy Schools where he was a desultory student, and had apprenticed himself first to Ford Madox Brown, a more or less established painter by then, whom he admired hugely. Brown, who had been born to English parents in France, moved to Antwerp and then to Ghent, where he was taught by two latter-day pupils of David. In 1846, on the customary Rome visit, he met Overbeck and Cornelius, and on his return was involved in the decorations of the Palace of Westminster. Rossetti, disillusioned by Brown's rather matter-of-fact teaching, later worked with Holman Hunt.[64]

When a name for the group was being considered, Rossetti at first wanted

John Everett Millais, *Christ in the House of His Parents*, 1849–50, oil on canvas.

(following, he said, Ford Madox Brown) to call the group 'Early Christian' – which Hunt 'protested, saying that the term would confuse us with the German *Quattro-Centists*'.[65] At any rate its members undertook to put the initials PRB after their names when they signed pictures and to accept a guild discipline.[66] They also produced a short-lived magazine, *The Germ*, edited by William Rossetti. There was no doubt even then that Millais, only eighteen at the time, was the most 'natural' talent of the group. His picture, *Christ in the House of His Parents*, which was shown at the Royal Academy in 1850, attracted a good deal of public attention. The young Jesus was shown having wounded his hand at his father's work-bench, and the catalogue referred the viewer to a passage in Zachariah XIII:6: 'And one shall say unto him, what are these wounds in Thine hands? Then He shall answer, those with which I was wounded in the house of My friends.' The picture was conceived as a manifesto in its insistence that the conventionalities of academic teaching should be replaced by a search for the specific and particular in nature – and the bland outlines and smooth tints were broken by the intensely coloured surfaces which the new theories suggested. All this provoked general press derision.

150

Blackwood's Magazine called it 'ugly, graceless and unpleasant', while *The Times* was at a loss for words: it was 'to speak plainly, revolting'; 'mean, odious, revolting and repulsive', Charles Dickens called it in *Household Words*.[67] Nevertheless, William Dyce, the Scottish Nazarene, 'dragged' Ruskin before it and insisted that he pay attention to John Millais' painting. This brought him in touch with the Brotherhood. Their evocation of the Nazarene ethos at first seemed disagreeably 'Romanist' to the Evangelical Ruskin, but his first action on their behalf was a letter to *The Times* in their defence.

The two Rossettis were already recognized men of letters, but other painters connected with the group (though not fully fledged 'brothers') – Ford Madox Brown and William Bell Scott – were also poets of distinction. The Pre-Raphaelites were therefore seen both as a literary and a pictorial move-ment, which also had a political or even a theological colouring. The Rossettis, of course, were a family of political refugees; Hunt had always had social and political, as well as religious interests; and even the young Millais was not immune from them. Dante Gabriel joined Ruskin as a teacher at the Working Men's College which had been founded in 1854 by one of the main proponents of Christian Socialism, Frederick Dennison Maurice.

Ornament as Work

It was Ford Madox Brown who provided a monument of this particular episode in *Work*, the painting he began in 1852 and took eleven years to finish.[68] It is crammed with figures and with detail. Set explicitly in upper Hampstead, it is dominated by three brightly lit, muscular and sun-burnt navvies in the foreground, presumably digging a sewer or water main. One of them is drinking from a tankard offered by a beer-seller – who is the fourth, ambiguous, deformed, central figure. Above and behind them the top-hatted local Member of Parliament and his daughter tower over the group on horse-back. To the left, some women of different classes avoid the excavations, while to the right and in the shadow are two much paler observers, recognizably Thomas Carlyle and Frederick Dennison Maurice; they are in the picture as theorists of the value of Manual Labour.

Work turned out to be a dress-rehearsal for Brown's masterpiece: the panels illustrating the history of Manchester which he did in 1876–88 for the hammer-beam-roofed great hall of the new Town Hall, designed by the young Alfred Waterhouse (whose most famous building was to be the Natural History Museum in London). It was a unique commission from nineteenth-century city authorities in Britain, and in their colouring and their drawing the panels still owe much to Brown's Pre-Raphaelite alliance. Although they represent the history of Manchester from its Roman foundation, the later scenes deal with the city's contribution to science and technology (Dalton collecting marsh gas, the misadventures of John Kay and his shuttle) rather than its grimy realities. Noble 'work' for the Pre-Raphaelites – and in this, as in many other things, Brown sympathized with them – remained, emphatically, that which was done by the hand.

Before Brown embarked on the Manchester cycle (and was constantly repainting *Work*), a group of young Oxford undergraduates, inspired by Carlyle, Ruskin and the Pre-Raphaelites, also aspired to form a brotherhood. The complexion of the group changed with time, but William Morris, the enormously charismatic figure who took Ruskin's teaching literally, remained the central force of the movement, and in fact dominated the whole world of design and the crafts for the following half century, until his death in 1896. He managed to work as poet, painter, designer, embroiderer, weaver, ceramicist, stained-glass maker, printer, political agitator – and businessman. His closest associate, Edward Burne-Jones, was a 'brother' undergraduate. They had both intended to go into the Church, but both opted for a life devoted to art instead. Burne-Jones apprenticed himself to Rossetti (through the Working Men's College in Red Lion Square) and through him also met Ford Madox Brown, who was to be a steady collaborator. Morris decided he would be an architect, and on coming down from Oxford, was articled in the office of George Edmund Street, a leading (and perhaps the most talented) Gothicist of his generation.[69] The brothers intended to live celibate, and Morris set up home in London with Burne-Jones, in Red Lion Square, Holborn – near the Working Men's College, where he designed his first pieces of furniture very much in the manner of Augustus Pugin, which he would later despise.

Office routine turned out to be irksome – and Rossetti urged Morris to work as a painter and a calligrapher. Partly as a result of Ruskin's influence

152

and advocacy, several members of the two groups – Rossetti, Arthur Hughes, with Morris and Burne-Jones and a few others – were commissioned to carry out a cycle of paintings in the new debating chamber of the Oxford Union in 1856–7. They chose as their theme the *Morte d'Arthur*, Thomas Malory's romance, and it would become a crucial text for them. Their enthusiasm contrasts with William Dyce's dislike of the theme when, a decade earlier, it had been allotted to him as his share of the decorations of the new Palace of Westminster. However, their enthusiasm was not matched by their skill and the paintings rapidly faded. Although they were restored several times they have never looked very good.[70]

In Street's office Morris met the young Philip Webb, with whom he would work for the rest of his life. He also married the beautiful Oxford model, Jane Burden (so much for celibacy), and set about looking for a home. He decided to get Webb to build him a house at Bexleyheath in Kent. It was Webb's first independent work and Morris occupied it in 1860.

The Red House was named after the brick of which it was built – which many Victorian architects still covered with stucco. The manner Webb adopted was an amalgam which allowed a picturesque medievalism (Morris and Webb both called it 'pure thirteenth century') to incorporate the kind of commonplace, eighteenth-century detail to which the builders of the time were accustomed – such as sash windows. Webb had learnt this accommodation from his master Street, and it was practised by another successful Gothic architect of the time, William Butterfield, the favoured church architect of the Tractarians. Through the 1850s Butterfield designed, built and had decorated their main sanctuary, All Saints' Church on Margaret Street, just off Oxford Street. Like the Red House, it was built in exposed brick, but elaborately polychrome.[71] Dyce was – inevitably – their preferred artist, and he was chosen to do the main paintings of the church; but although they were much liked at the time, they soon deteriorated, as had the Oxford Union paintings, but for different technical reasons. The reredos was redone as were the side-wall paintings, and the roof decorations had to be stripped out.

The technical problems of wall painting affected almost all the grand English projects including the vast painting that G. F. Watts, 'England's Michelangelo' (as an obituarist called him), offered in 1852 to cover the huge wall of New Hall in Lincoln's Inn. He had intended a panorama of the great law-givers, perhaps emulating Delaroche's *Great Artists* in the hemicycle of the Beaux-Arts. Within a year or two, however, and in spite of many attempted restorations, it had become barely legible. The equally vast fresco for Lord Lansdowne at Bowood was cut down for storage when the house was demolished; and a similar fate met that for Lord Somers at Carlton House Terrace (now the Royal Society).[72]

The difficulty of furnishing the Red House with what was currently available led to the founding of the enterprise Morris, Marshall, Faulkner & Co. (later William Morris & Co.),[73] to which its eponymous head would devote much of his energy and funds for the rest of his life. The idea was first formulated by Brown in response to Cole's design enterprises. Brown suggested that artists should not only design household products, but also control their manufacture and marketing as Cole had done. The 'firm' (for which Brown was to do a great deal of work in fact) produced furniture, fabrics, wallpapers, stained glass (Burne-Jones as well as Webb designed much), even whole interiors. The 'works of art' tended to be hangings or stained glass, to be assertively framed against highly patterned backgrounds of textile or wallpaper. The patterns quite often (as in the 'honeysuckle') recall the 'leaves drawn from nature' of Owen Jones' *Grammar* – though Jones is never mentioned in this connection by Morris. The self-confessed, rather theoretical medievalism of the firm was translated into practice as a rather eclectic but essentially Pre-Raphaelite historicism. Their textiles and glass were derived from oriental examples, while lettering and book production were often based on Italian Quattrocento models. In fact the Morris & Co. patterns might be considered the first answer to Jones' call for a style 'based on nature'.

Butterfield's, Street's and Webb's incorporation of 'builder's Georgian' detail in medieval-picturesque groupings was eagerly taken up by many architects over the next half century. It provided the germ of the 'Queen Anne Style' which was eagerly developed by some of the best of the next generation – William Eden Nesfield and Richard Norman Shaw – both of whom used Morris & Co. to create interiors for them in the 1870s and '80s; it became the architecture of the Garden City movement. Having crossed the Atlantic, it was then taken up in the work of H. H. Richardson and the building of the Chicago suburbs.[74]

Morris had copied out and illuminated books since his undergraduate days – his own poems or texts by Virgil and Horace. The illuminations were by him too, but sometimes also by Burne-Jones or other 'helpers'. Towards the end of his life, he decided to become a printer and publisher as well. His Kelmscott Press was the first enterprise to publish books in specially designed type and on hand-made papers, setting in motion a movement which is not yet extinct. It was to have a powerful effect on the routines of commercial publishing, particularly in the Anglo-Saxon countries. One of the first books issued by Kelmscott was that chapter 'On the Nature of Gothic' I mentioned earlier, which Morris extracted from the second volume of the vast *Stones of Venice.* In the preface he added, he called it 'one of the very few necessary and inevitable utterances of the century'. He went on:

> the lesson which Ruskin here teaches us is that art is the expression of man's pleasure in labour; that it is possible for man to rejoice in his work, for, strange as it may seem to us today, there have been times when he did rejoice in it.

That lesson – that in a just society every workman would be an artist, or at least a craftsman – was the moving force of both Ruskin's and Morris' socialism. And there was another side to it: Morris was also increasingly concerned with the relation between the work of art and its public, the notion he later formulated as a question: 'What business have we with art at all unless all can share it?'[75]

Morris' son-in-law and biographer thus sums up their common teaching:

> in this chapter [*The Stones of Venice*] and in the subsequent teaching which did little more than expand and reinforce it, Ruskin laid out, once and for all, the basis for a true Socialism. For without art Socialism would remain as sterile as other forms of social organization; it would not meet the real and perpetual wants of mankind . . .[76]

The preachy teaching of Ruskin, and that of Morris following him, was to lead to a new political and economic condition under which art was to be produced, but it could only have indirect lessons for those who would not accept their premises. Cole and Owen Jones certainly wanted a new art as well, but its outlines were not clear and explicit. However, another dogmatically rationalist attempt to formulate a universal doctrine of style, in which the understanding of Gothic architecture was a prime factor (but in a quite different manner from Ruskin's and Morris') was propagated by Emmanuel-Eugène Viollet-le-Duc when he was imposed on the Ecole des Beaux-Arts by Napoleon III in 1863 as Professor of History of Art and of Aesthetics. *Entretiens*, the book, was derived from his lectures which had been shouted down by a group of students inspired, it is said, by Ingres (whom he had befriended many years earlier in Rome),[77] had wide circulation in French (and a decade later was translated into English). For many architects who were then growing up, it would become a kind of bible and would continue to be read into the twentieth century. It suggested an architecture in which brick and stone might be united in novel ways with cast-iron, always used compressively – but set obliquely in a way that was much more daring than anything Paxton or Labrouste had ever attempted. Steel was not yet widely available and the tensile strength required depended on the available wrought iron – whose use in building he regarded as a subterfuge.[78]

Reason and Ornament

Viollet-le-Duc had been a favourite nephew of Etienne Delécluze – David's pupil and chronicler – who 'received' (that is had a *salon* – though for men only) at his home. There, Viollet had made friends with Prosper Mérimée, now remembered chiefly as the author of *Carmen*. Mérimée was already a novelist of repute, seen by some as the heir of Stendhal (he was elected to the French Academy in 1844 – at a shockingly young age), as well as an able civil servant who was appointed, early in the July Monarchy, to be the administrator of the government ancient monument agency whose authority had grown in the wake of Hugo's *Notre-Dame de Paris*. Viollet was then charged with the restoration of Vézelay in 1840 and soon after that of Notre-Dame in Paris. While working on these restorations, he developed a tightly-argued and very articulated theory of architecture: every member had to be seen as part of a systematic arrangement, and every ornamental form had to be derived from structure by necessity – for the high ages of architecture, at any rate, such as fifth-century Greece and thirteenth-century France. For nationalist reasons, Viollet saw the second as the proper source for any new development, but this also had to follow the deductive method from the premises offered by the new structural necessities: iron frame construction and plate glass.

He compiled two dictionaries – one of medieval architecture, the other of medieval furniture and fittings – and they became his most extensive publications, though he did write many popular books (some intended for adolescents) about the *House of Man* or the *History of a Castle* besides the *Entretiens*. He also provided accounts of his many restorations: the city of Carcassonne and the Château of Pierrefonds (as an out-of-town residence for Napoleon III – for whom he also designed a state railway train). He made one exotic excursus: a book on Russian architecture and its ornament, presumably the result of an involvement he also owed to Mérimée, the translator of Pushkin and Gogol; it had a strange echo in the Russian Orthodox Cathedral of the Holy Trinity in Chicago that Louis Sullivan designed in 1899–1900; he would base himself largely on Viollet's survey.

Although he was not touched by contemporary Wagnerian arguments about the *Gesamtkunstwerk*, let alone the Ruskin-Morris preaching about pleasure in labour and the menace of industrial anomie, Viollet was very exercised by one of its effects – the breach between architecture and the other arts of painting and sculpture. The eye, he maintained, had to be nourished by a harmony:

> without which art cannot exist . . . But this is not the case now: the architect erects his building, and gives it certain forms that are suitable to it; then, when the building is finished, it is given over to the painter. The chief object of the latter is to secure attention to his painting . . . The architect, the painter, and the sculptor may each have displayed remarkable talent in his own department, yet the work as a whole may produce only a mediocre effect . . . These three arts conflict with, instead of aiding each other . . .

Viollet sees the ancient and medieval 'concert' of the arts persisting into the seventeenth century only to be

> broken from the moment when architecture shut itself up in the prejudice of the schools, when the painter produced pictures and not

157

paintings and the sculptor statues and not statuary. The museums and the galleries of amateurs were filled, and the public buildings were stripped of their proper ornament ... We cannot therefore boast of being a people endowed with sensibility in matters of art, since we have ceased to be convinced of the necessity of that harmony between the arts, whose very nature requires that they advance in concert.

He sums the argument up by appealing to a familiar metaphor. Painting and sculpture are 'the decorative dress of architecture – a dress made for the body to which it is applied and which cannot be left to chance'.[79]

In his *Dictionnaires* he had explored the argument in much greater detail. The separation between the builders on the one hand and the sculptors and painters on the other had been accomplished during the Renaissance, though he suggests that even in the later middle ages the very complexity of the masons' geometry detracted from the importance of the painted wall. But liberal democrat (and crypto-republican through the Empire which he served) though he was, he did not have Ruskin's social passion, or his burning conviction that there had been a social, not merely a formal, harmony about the medieval condition of the labourer which was absent from the industrial economy of their time.

Viollet-le-Duc and Ruskin were perhaps the most prolific and most widely read architectural controversialists of the mid-nineteenth century. Another is worth mentioning here: James Fergusson. An indigo trader and grower in

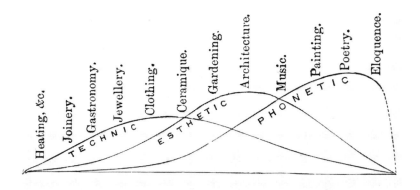

James Fergusson, 'The Three Categories of the Arts', after *A History of Architecture in All Countries* (London, 1893).

India, he retired to England when in his thirties, and involved himself in architectural controversy – though his uneasy circumstances meant that he had to accept various public and business employments. He published two books on Indian architecture before issuing his manifesto, which – echoing Pugin – he called *An Historical Enquiry into the True Principles of Beauty in Art, more especially with reference to Architecture.* About Pugin he was damning:

> Throughout his life the theatrical was the one and only branch of his art he truly understood . . . Every page of Pugin's work reiterates, 'give us the truth' . . . yet his only aim was to produce an absolute falsehood . . .[80]

The falsehood was the imitation of past style – which was abominable to him. His distaste was nourished by his conviction that truth – to material, to function, to constructional detail, to one's own age – was the architect's duty. And his view was also based on an extraordinary (for the time) knowledge of world building. Unfortunately, his manifesto was a publishing failure, while the various histories of architecture which succeeded it enjoyed great success and continued to be edited and enlarged until the twentieth century.

Unlike his great contemporaries, Fergusson was an obsessive systematizer. His *True Principles* already announced the scheme which his later books would take up again. All the arts – and crafts – are to be classed according to three quotients of beauty: technical, aesthetic, phonetic. The first two are more or less self-explanatory: adaptation to purpose, 'truth to material' and sensory gratification (due to 'artistic conception' and ornament); but the phonetic requires more comment. In the introduction to the first volume of his *History of Ancient and Medieval Architecture* there is an explicit if uninspiring account of his view:

> Carved ornament and decorative colour come within the special province of the architect . . . But one of the great merits of architecture as an art is that it affords room for the display of the works of the sculptor and painter, not only in such a manner as not to interfere with its own decorative construction, but so as to add meaning and value to the whole . . . It is still one of the special privileges of architecture that

she is able to attract to herself these phonetic arts . . . The work of the architect ought to be complete and perfect without either sculpture or painting and must be judged as if they were absent; but he will not be entirely successful unless he has provided the means by which the value of his design may be doubled by their introduction.

The formula is both chilly and ambivalent: painting and sculpture are phonetic – in that they admit of verbal explication. That, I think, is what 'meaning' is to Fergusson. But architecture does not readily translate into words: architectural forms do not speak in his conception of them. It cannot be really valued without the 'phonetic' adjuncts, but it must be judged 'as if' it were complete in itself. The great 'mistake' of the Renaissance was to confuse these categories and treat architecture itself as if it could be phonetic. These contradictions are never resolved, even though couched in Fergusson's rather flat, apparently commonsensical prose.

Yet he, like most of his contemporaries, is obsessed with another notion – the style for the age. That such a 'true' style has not yet come about he is sure. He is equally convinced that it cannot be invented. Yet progress is the law of history and he teaches that

Everything in any true art is thoroughly up to the highest standard of its period . . . As soon as the public is aware of the importance of this rule . . . a new style must be the inevitable result . . . not only perfectly suited to all our wants and desires, but also more beautiful and more perfect than any that has ever existed before.[81]

Of course, when it came to practice, the Fergusson style seems to be as pedestrian as his prose. 'Ordinary Italian' was the style he adopted for his one executed London building, the Marianne North Gallery in Kew Gardens. And 'ordinary Italian', meaning the kind of speculative builders' palazzo style which was common in the stucco building of mid-century suburbs, is his chosen manner. And yet he is damning about many of his contemporaries, those who were attempting to create a new architecture. Schinkel's *Bauakademie* in Berlin, Lewis Cubbitt's King's Cross Station are both found wanting. Semper receives the barest mention and his Dresden buildings are rejected in a paragraph, his ideas

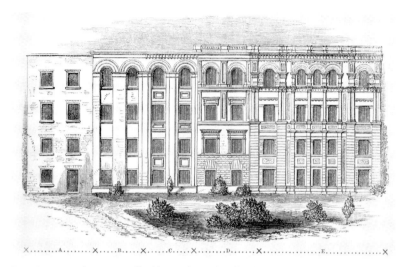

James Fergusson, 'Five stages of building with standard floor-heights' [A. Simple Warehouse; B. Civil engineering building; C. A better example of civil engineering. D. Just within Architecture. E. Architecture proper], after *An Illustrated Handbook of Architecture* (London, 1853).

never discussed. Ruskin is dismissed even more summarily than Pugin. 'His books were pretty reading, no doubt, for idle people.' The words are Fergusson's editor's, but he is surely echoing his author's conviction.[82]

During all this ferment Semper was teaching and working in London but had no part in any of it. He lived very much among German refugees – in a way rather like the post-1933 émigrés to London. However, he had his English supporters and Prince Albert had finally been persuaded to take notice of him. He was even being considered as a possible architect for a new museum to be built in Kensington (now the Victoria and Albert Museum). A model and project were presented to the prince, but got lost in budgetary and bureaucratic complexities.

Practical Aesthetics

In the meantime Richard Wagner was comfortably exiled in Zürich, where he was treated as a notable. In 1845 a new federal polytechnic school (Eidgenössische Technische Hochschule) – emulating German institutions that followed the ultimate Parisian original – had been established. Semper's

Gottfried Semper, Eidgenössische Technische Hochschule building, Zürich, lithograph.

Dresden museum, completed to his designs (in spite of the politics), was newly finished and much talked of. His name was now put forward as a possible director of architecture, and Richard Wagner, known to be his friend, was asked to make the first approach. In spite of early hesitation, Semper took to the job with great enthusiasm, and also became the designer of its very prominent building. Unfortunately, his position in Zürich turned out not to be entirely comfortable either, but he did find a society and interlocutors there, as he had in Dresden: the Dutch physiologist Jakob Moleschott and the great historian Jacob Burckhardt, then young and newly arrived in Zürich. Closest to Semper was the poet and novelist Gottfried Keller, who also happened to be the Secretary of Kanton Zürich. Princess Sayn-Wittgenstein, Liszt's companion, became a confidant during their visits. There was also the 'Young Hegelian' philosopher Theodor Friedrich Vischer, whom he had already met in Dresden and who had written a six-volume work on aesthetics whose very bulk was a deterrent even to the most committed readers. Unlike many aestheticians, he had some reputation as a poet and playwright, and was also an active, combative art (and literary) critic as well as a political figure with a chequered career, committed to party-political interests.[83] He even had a brief moment of political authority as a deputy at the ill-fated revolutionary and nationalist Frankfurt 'Professors' Parliament', the diet of 1848, after which he was put on a back burner by the university and spent some of his enforced sabbatical in writing more of his vast *Aesthetik*. It was published in instalments, between 1847 and 1855, when, like Semper, he accepted the Zürich appointment.

Vischer warned his readers against the over-smooth Winckelmann, even against the classicism of Schiller and Goethe. Shakespeare was his ideal artist. More important, he recognized the intellectual autonomy of the arts:

> There are two methods of ideation: by words and notions, and by forms. There are two ways of deciphering the universe: by letters and by images.

Political allies though they were, 'Practical Aesthetics', *Praktische Aesthetik*, Semper's pithy subtitle of his major work, *Der Stil in den Technischen und Tektonischen Künsten*, was polemically directed at Theodor.[84] Nevertheless, one thing Semper and Vischer had in common was their opposition to the formalists. Neither of them believed in any absolute and measurable guarantor of beauty. Semper's approach was, as I suggested earlier, almost positivist – as the older Vischer's would increasingly become.

Although he did successfully negotiate conditions for a more dignified return to London with Henry Cole, Zürich remained Semper's home for the rest of his life. There were important architectural commissions – including the Town Hall at Winterthur and the Zürich Railway Station. At the end of his life, he had the friendly admiration of Nietzsche and his largest commission: to design the two great Vienna museums and the extension of the Imperial Palace, the Hofburg – and the Hoftheater, which involved some compromises, but is a partial realization of his earlier projects. His London humiliations faded into the background while his ideas were absorbed into Viennese academic teaching – to have, at the end of the century, a surprising impact on those of another Wagner, the great architect Otto.[85]

The Total Work of Art

But that was later. Meanwhile, the first opportunity to apply Semper's ideas presented itself. The eighteen-year-old King Ludwig II of Bavaria succeeded to the throne in 1864 on the sudden, premature death of Maximilian II, his father. Since his early teens, the precocious and impressionable crown prince had listened to as much of Wagner's music as he could, and learnt some of his essays by heart – or so he claimed.[86] One of his first acts was to lure the composer to Munich, so as to make his capital the home of Wagner's operatic activities. Both Wagner and the king were dissatisfied with the theatres available to them and Ludwig proposed to build a new, prominent and splendid one to house 'total' performances of the (as yet unfinished) *Ring* cycle. Of course, Wagner wanted to secure this commission for Semper, to whom the most generous promises were made. Not only was there to be a stone festival theatre, but a temporary wooden one was to be built inside the Munich Glaspalast (yet another copy of the London Crystal Palace) to his design so as to allow experimental Wagnerian performances to take place in preparation for the permanent building.[87]

In the event neither the wooden theatre nor the stone one was even begun, nor was Semper ever paid for a great deal of work, so that his friendship with Wagner was in suspense for several years, particularly following the building of a rather cheap and somewhat shabby *Ring* festival theatre in Bayreuth a decade later (still with the help of Ludwig II, who presided at the opening). Wagner seemed to have no interest in the exterior or the setting, though its organization had been (and Wagner conceded as much to Semper when the frayed friendship was tentatively renewed some years later – in the salon of the fashionable Viennese painter Hans Makart) based on the Munich project.

Bayreuth did, however, finally provide Wagner with the circumstances of a near-*Gesamtkunstwerk*.[88] The operatic festivals, centring on a five-day

Gottfried Semper, design for the projected Opera for Munich (1866).

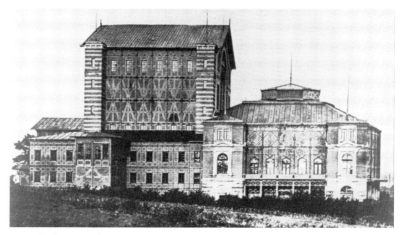

Bayreuth, the Festspielhaus, 1873–5. Otto Brueckwald (and others) on Richard Wagner's instructions.

performance of the whole *Ring*, with trumpeters summoning the audience, were projected out into the small town and involved its inhabitants as well as the crowds of 'pilgrims'. These had to be well heeled – inevitably, if they were to be able to afford the trip or pilgrimage and the hotel stay. They were therefore an elite public, quite unlike the community of Greek tragedy. The performances of the *Ring* and of the later operas were to be a social work of art involving the audience in its concentration and in its seclusion from the philistine world of the big city (Wagner, though born in Leipzig, always disliked such 'large' cities) bourgeoisie, so that it was able to provide that seamless totality of music, literary text, ballet and physical setting which the *Gesamtkunstwerk* required. The exterior of the theatre building – or its place in the urban fabric – was of no concern to Wagner; in fact, visitors arriving in Bayreuth by train could go directly to the Festspielhaus without going into the town at all. Wagner was content to accept this kind of *Kurort* placing of the theatre in a well-manicured park, though it made the therapeutic/cathartic experience closer to taking spa waters than being given a sip from the Holy Grail.

There was more than a touch of religiosity about the demands which Wagner made on his public: the unusually (for the time) dimmed theatre, the reverentially hushed audience, the cyclic, daily performances of each of the four operas that made up the *Ring* (and even more intense, the long surges of *Parsifal* from the invisible orchestra), imposed a special kind of attention. They were intended to produce an emotional involvement similar to that which liturgical prayer and pilgrimage processions had presumably aroused at an earlier time. There were further contradictions: the kind of aesthetic attention which Wagner required imposed collective participation, yet the darkened auditorium, the placing of the whole audience on a unified (if not level) *parterre*, the individual upholstered seats, all catered to the rapt *mélomane* listening with his eyes closed (to exclude, paradoxically, the distractions offered by the other senses), and that implied another problem for the composer.

The ruinous costs of the first *Ring* production were partly covered by a series of concerts at the Albert Hall in London a year later – and they provided the occasion for the only meeting between the two emulators of Norse myth, Wagner and William Morris, which latter was put next to Cosima Wagner at an official dinner.[89] Morris' interest in epic and Icelandic sagas had begun while he was working on his translation of Virgil's *Aeneid* (his plural – he would translate the *Odyssey* later). The whole subject weighed with him. When, in 1867, he was introduced to an Icelandic linguist and a writer, Erikr Magnusson, with whom he began to collaborate, he had been aware of Norse legend for some time. He made his first visit to Iceland in 1871, going round the sites of the epics by pony, and returned in 1873. Much later he would point out that the stringent conditions of the island still produced a fairer and more balanced society than capitalist distinctions of class and income allowed. The archaic direct democracy of that cold, forbidding land seemed infinitely preferable to the parliamentary government he had come to despise; he seems not to have been aware of the social problems this economic arrangement had produced. At any rate, Morris' translation of the *Great Volsung Lay* was his main literary involvement during the 1870s.[90]

Behind Morris' concern with epic was his conviction that violent social change, the revolution which Marx had foreseen (and some of his followers believed would break out in Britain first), was the prerequisite for the creation of a great art: which, like that of other epic periods, would be an art for everybody. In *News from Nowhere*, Morris provided a description of that society in a remote future – after 2003 (the date recorded in the book as that of a 'recent' building). After the coming revolution, the great – and hardly remembered – upheaval which would overturn parliamentary democracy in favour of direct government by a general strike (in which the police and the army would have sided with their own class) would also make technology subservient to social benefits, overturn the industrial division of labour and transform everyone into a craftsman-designer. His political involvement became all-consuming, so that when, in 1887, C. R. Ashbee approached him for support in his enterprise, the Guild and School of Handicraft, Morris was not interested. 'Look', Ashbee reports having said, 'I am going to forge a weapon for you.' To which Morris replied: 'The weapon is too small to be of any value.'[91]

Revolution was his way of achieving a life which would be a continuous and constant work of art, a *Gesamtkunstwerk* if you will, but it could not – unlike Wagner's equivalent – exist outside a just society. Whatever he had to say about art, Morris had no time for talk of aesthetics – nor did Ruskin before him. He was explicitly contemptuous of the term, as he was later of the 'Aesthetic movement' which sought to refine the Pre-Raphaelite ethos into an elaborate fashion which would govern furniture, fittings, clothes – and even hairdressing. As one critic maliciously remarked, his utopia looked as if everyone were dressed and had their houses furnished by Morris & Co.

For Morris, the artist-revolutionary, was also a businessman. He may have repined that the conditions of production condemned him to 'ministering to the swinish luxury of the rich', but minister he did – at his prices.[92] The revolution would change all that, but meanwhile he had to cover costs and wages, and this was all the more pressing as he came to question the rationale of his own private income – which towards the end of his life he began to consider usurious, though it dropped substantially during the 1860s in any case.

There was a bluff disregard of the spectator's attention about Morris. The objects he made, the poems and tapestries, were to be treated as tables and chairs were treated. They were to be used. In the context of the post-revolutionary society, everyone would be a craftsman and would be making them and therefore have equal access to them. Society itself would be the *Gesamtkunstwerk*. This may be why, after such events as the Oxford Union fiasco, major wall painting does not appear in his interiors, not even in the churches.

Wagner and the Wagnerians on the other hand had regarded the experience they offered as being outside the social framework, a kind of seed or kernel which, by demanding total attention, would inevitably achieve the transformation of society. Structurally, of course, Wagnerian music-drama did provide a different kind of experience from the conventional operas of the time, even the later Verdi ones in which scenes could still be divided into recitatives-arias-ballet (though *Falstaff* does offer an almost Wagnerian continuity).

But even the Wagnerian fusion was not enough for many of his contemporaries. The immanent experience which Philipp Otto Runge had wished his *Seasons* to inspire was, later in the century, to be sought through new instruments and through new forms of composition that involved unprecedented claims on experience and relied more directly on the unifying potentialities of synaesthesia. As had been the case with earlier synaesthetic efforts (with Castel's *claveçin oculaire* for instance), such developments would inevitably challenge existing technical resources. By Wagner's time such resources had become available. An avid specialist public as well as artists were creating a demand for synaesthetic performance and making high claims for the grandeur, even the mystical heights which the fusing of the senses in such an experience might offer.

FIVE

A New Century, a New Art

Wagner's achievement at Bayreuth inspired many of his contemporaries and juniors to look for a more complicit association of the arts. Techniques were devised which could act on several senses at the same time, and stimulate an experience – to be newly named *synaesthesis*,[1] which would signify 'the generality of neural psychoses in an irrational being' (in parallel to *noesis*, 'the sum of mental actions in a rational one'). The primal, even regressive nature of the phenomenon is implicit in that earliest definition.[2]

Two years later, and without using the term, Francis Galton (later Sir Francis, and now remembered chiefly as the father of that unsavoury science, eugenics) wrote extensively about what he called Mental Imagery, which included the association of numbers with shapes, numbers with colour – but also colour with sound. He found that there was little agreement about such associations among people who experienced them; in particular, he noted that people might associate quite different (though precisely described) colours with the same vowels, while no consonant prompted such visualization. Disagreements between those who had such experiences were often sharp, even acrimonious.[3] A number of other scientists considered the problem during the next two decades, but as behaviourists took over the discipline of experimental psychology (and marginalised interest in mental activities), so interest in the matter declined, to be revived about 1980.[4]

The Unifying Sensation

Some time before the term was even coined, a literal, almost a mechanical application of the *Gesamtkunstwerk* principle was devised by a younger Alsatian contemporary of Richard Wagner, Georg Friedrich Kastner. He had become very interested in recent experiments by British scientists involving sound emitted by burning gas,[5] and managed to harness it in a novel musical instrument. In 1875 he actually patented his Pyrophone, an organ of coloured glass tubes within which gas jets (whose tone was correlated to the colour of the glass) were controlled from a keyboard. Henry Dunant (to whom we also owe both the Red Cross and the YMCA) became its most vociferous advocate and demonstrated it in Paris – where it aroused a good deal of interest. But although César Franck did play on it and Charles Gounod used it in his ballet *Joan of Arc*, it was never accepted for general performance.[6] As the nineteenth century drew on, however, more or less successful (at any rate, technically) colour organs were constructed and were translated into forms of movement and of dance. The British mathematician Charles Babbage, better-known for his life-long involvement with calculating and analytical machines, would conceive an even more 'total' form of art: a ballet in which dancers and musicians in white costumes would be illuminated by coloured gas lights synchronized with the music. The risk of fire defeated the project, nor was he (or Kastner) able to resolve the problem of the yellow tinge produced by gaslight.

In linking tone directly to colour, pyrophone music certainly catered to a growing demand for an art that could stimulate a gamut of experience, an art that would not merely represent but in some way directly induce a *participation mystique* – I use that anachronistic term advisedly – in the work of art. The idea excited a great many people about that time. Madame H. P. Blavatsky, for instance, the founding genius of Theosophy, considered synaesthesia a part of the *Secret Doctrine*.[7] Two of her more adventurous followers, Annie Besant and 'Bishop' Charles Leadbeater, developed the idea in some small but highly-influential publications, in which, among other 'thought forms', they showed coloured clairvoyant 'visualizations' of the music of Mendelssohn, Gounod – and, of course, Wagner.[8]

Many of the earlier synaesthesists were obsessed by the notion implied by Schopenhauer but first articulated about 1870 by Walter Pater, at the time

Wendelin Weissheimer
playing the pyrophone,
c. 1880.

a young Oxford don and a pupil (though no disciple) of John Ruskin, that all
art constantly 'aspires towards the condition of music'.

> In [music's] consummate moments [he wrote], the end is not distinct
> from the means, the form from the matter, the subject from the expres-
> sion; they inhere in and completely saturate each other. In music, then,
> rather than in poetry, is to be found the true type or measure of perfect-
> ed art . . . which could also be an end unto itself – it requires no context
> nor any reference outside that experience.[9]

Music was therefore the 'highest' art for the followers of the art for art's
sake doctrine. *L'Art pour l'art* is often considered primarily a French product,
since the Parnassian poets of the 1860s read it back to some remarks of Victor
Hugo,[10] though Hugo himself had long abjured such views. It could also be

traced here and there in Baudelaire's writings, although he had taken a rather dogmatic and harsh stand against it:

> . . . intemperate partiality to form leads to monstrous and unforeseen disorders. When absorbed by a violent passion for the beautiful, the amusing, the pretty, the picturesque (for there are graduations of it) the notion of the just and the true vanish. The frenetic passion for art is a cancer which devours all others; and since the complete absence of the just and the true from art amounts to an absence of art, all of man vanishes: the over-development of a single faculty opens on the void. I understand the fury of the iconoclasts and of Moslems against images. I concede St Augustine his remorse at the excessive indulgence in the pleasures of sight . . . The time cannot be far when we will come to understand that any literature which does not walk fraternally between science and philosophy is a literature of homicide and of suicide.[11]

Baudelaire's attack distanced him from certain associates: Théodore de Banville, Charles Leconte de Lisle – but above all his friend Théophile Gautier, whose anti-utilitarian, anti-moralising preface to his novel *Mademoiselle de Maupin* was sometimes regarded as the 'classic' text of 'art for art's sake'. A sentence from it was even taken for its motto: 'Il n'y a de vraiment beau que ce qui ne peut servir à rien; tout ce qui est utile est laid.'[12] Some form of this belief was certainly held by Wagner and Schopenhauer, but in Britain was promoted and even dogmatized by Algernon Charles Swinburne (who had once been the intimate of Burne-Jones and Morris) as well as by Walter Pater. Of course it did not command general assent and indeed provoked some artists to fury more violent than Baudelaire's:

> Art for Art's sake! Hail, truest Lord of Hell!
>   Hail Genius, Master of the Moral Will!
> 'The filthiest of all paintings painted well
>   Is mightier than the purest painted ill!'
> Yes, mightier than the purest painted well,
>   So prone are we toward the broad way to Hell.

Tennyson thundered in answer to critics who found an excess of moral zeal in his *Idylls to the King*.[13]

'Art for art's sake' shaded off into the 'Religion of Art'. Walter Pater even applied for ordination to the Bishop of London who rejected him as a candidate on the grounds that his fancy for High Church ceremony did not offset the disadvantage of his not being a believing Christian. That 'Religion of Art', which he failed to slip into the Established Church, Pater would instil in the chosen young at Oxford;[14] Oscar Wilde, his pupil and his disciple, would preach it to the world at large. Like any effective *maitre-à-penser*, Pater provided the cult with its golden rule: 'How shall we pass most swiftly from point to point, and be present always at the focus where the greatest number of vital forces unite in their purest Energy? *To burn always with this hard, gemlike flame* [my emphasis], to maintain this ecstasy, is success in life.'[15] It was a 'religion' that also fostered the notion that the experience of works of art – whether total or not – should occur in an atmosphere of such piety as the term implied, and that the aesthetic attention which art demanded should be closely related to the sort of attention that religious observance had required in earlier times – as had already been suggested by Hegel.

By the middle of the nineteenth century theatre audiences were turning into the nearest thing to a church congregation outside established religion. This new religion of art also rapidly acquired its accompanying religiosity, of which the growing solemnity of the concert hall and the opera house was only an aspect. The capital of this religiosity was Bayreuth, but the atmosphere affected a wide variety of music lovers. Baudelaire, who admired Wagner intensely, would listen to his music with closed eyes – and be rewarded with a synaesthetic experience. Parisians could hear Wagner often at the Concerts Lamoureux (so-called after the conductor-impresario who was Wagner's most persuasive Parisian advocate) where in the 1880s, according to a brilliant if bigoted memorialist, a group of dandyish young medics occupying the cheap seats made a point of keeping their eyes shut during performances, not only for self-absorbed synaesthesia, but also for protection against the view of the philistines in the more expensive ones.[16]

Before it was even named or labelled, synaesthesia had become an aspect of the *Gesamtkunstwerk* for French Wagnerites. The most famous and most commented statement on it is Baudelaire's sonnet 'Correspondances', in which nature is conceived as a forest of symbols, a forest in which scents, colours and sounds mingle and echo each other: 'Les parfums, les couleurs et les sons se répondent.'

> There are scents there, fresh as that of a child's body,
> Sweet as the sound of oboes and green like meadows –
> And others corrupt, rich and triumphant
>
> Expansive like boundless things [*ayant l'expansion des choses infinies*]:
> As ambergris, musk, balm and frankincense –
> They sing the transport of the spirit and of the senses.[17]

That sonnet was probably written in the mid-1840s, and rewritten some ten years later. Baudelaire himself quotes the two quatrains in his essay on Wagner and *Tannhäuser*.[18] In his notes on the Salon of 1846, he provides a key to his inspiration,[19] quoting a passage from *Kreisleriana*, the satirical autobiography of the painter, caricaturist, musician and man of letters E.T.A. Hoffmann – yet another friend and correspondent of Tieck. One of his 'very scattered thoughts' ran:

> not only in a dream or in the state of distraction which precedes sleep – but especially when I have listened to much music . . . I find agreement [Baudelaire emphasizes in translating: 'une analogie et une réunion intime'] between colours, sounds and scents. It seems to me as if all of them were mysteriously engendered by the same ray of light and must unite in a marvellous concert. The scent of the dark-red carnations works its magic power on me; defenceless. I enter into a dream-like state and I hear, as from a far distance, the deep tones of the clarinet swelling and receding.[20]

The synaesthesia theme runs through nineteenth-century German and French literature. Modern readers find its mystical implications rather disconcerting, which goes not only for Baudelaire's 'Correspondances' but also for Arthur Rimbaud's equally famous and equally enigmatic 'Voyelles', which begins

> *A noir, E blanc, I rouge, U vert, O bleu: voyelles*
> *Je dirai quelque jour vos naissances latentes . . .*[21]

echoing Baudelaire's sonnet (with a touch of mockery), Rimbaud goes on to detail the pairing of each colour with a vowel.[22]

Since it concerned only two of the five senses, equivalence between sound and colour was only one (among several) forms of sensory harmony. Smell and taste, even touch would be required to make their contributions so as to turn a work of art into a total experience. In one extreme form, Joris-Karl Huysmans, in his most famous novel *A Rebours* (translated as *Against Nature*), has its hero, Jean Floressas, Duc des Esseintes, build himself a 'mouth-organ'[23] – not in the modern sense, of course, but one made up of a series of miniature liqueur-barrels for which he had a sandalwood casing made. These liqueurs are arranged according to a tonality: dry Curaçao corresponds to the clarinet, Kummel to the oboe, Kirsch to the trumpet and so on. There were even liqueurs to summon the keys – Benedictine for the minor, Green Chartreuse for the major.

Des Esseintes could use the organ to experience 'whole symphonic scores in his gullet'. Later in the novel, when the hero is afflicted by hallucinatory odours, he combats them by composing complex counter-scents which might reproduce 'a melody of Beethoven or of Clapisson',[24] or construct effects similar to some poems by Baudelaire. His experiments end in a kind of enervation, a debility for which the label 'neurasthenia' had recently been devised.[25] The country doctor who treated the duke was not aware of such a disease, however. He advised a tonic change of scene – so des Esseintes decided to visit London. As it happened, he managed to fabricate (or at least simulate) all the sensations such a journey would have procured him without actually leaving Paris. For des Esseintes and for his like, place exists only as a cluster of sensations.[26] Huysmans seemed to follow 'naturalist' precepts, so that place and person were built up through a summation of detailed observations and the superimposed clusters of sensations, much as Claude Monet translated changing, varying sensation into thick, liquid brushstrokes on such series as his 'Rouen Cathedral'. Such was the concordance between the literary and the pictorial method.

Yet *A Rebours* was anything but realist in atmosphere and construction. It was 'vaguely clerical, slightly pederast – a novel with a single personage!' and 'fell like a meteor on the literary fairground; all was fever and rage'.[27]

175

Des Esseintes was the neurotic personnage par excellence and neuroses were very much what the younger doctors of the 1870s and '80s wanted to study. They flocked from all over France (and from abroad as well) to the lectures of Jean-Martin Charcot, the *Napoleon of Neuroses* and originator of therapies by suggestion and hypnosis at the Salpétrière Hospital. These students would include the Moravian Sigmund Freud and the Hungarian Max Nordau,[28] who cordially disliked each other. Max Nordau was already well established in Paris, and had become so distressed by developments in the art world that he would write a book against recent Parisian tendencies. *Entartung* pretended to a scientific objectivity in its judgements, but was really a digest of such anecdotal evidence as he had collected in the Paris cafés, theatres and art galleries during the time he worked with Charcot. Called *Degeneration* in English, the book first appeared in German in 1889, and became a runaway bestseller in several languages.[29]

Among the things Nordau condemned out of hand was the growing interest in synaesthesia, which he (like Galton) considered regressive – and therefore inevitably degenerate. Man in general, but modern man especially, must learn to distinguish between his sensations, to classify and to discriminate among them. On this showing synaesthesia can only be considered sub-human, a recession to the unified perception of such beings as molluscs. Huysmans' des Esseintes was, of course, one of Nordau's prize exhibits,[30] but he would have no truck with the whole business of Wagnerian *Gesamtkunstwerk* either, since he regarded it as yet another symptom of regression, degenerate almost by definition.

A very striking change follows from the concept of social regression. In the late eighteenth century a return to the social 'primitive' had been proposed in the wake of Rousseau's anthropology to guarantee authenticity of thought and feeling, since it was believed that first humanity had to be concerned directly with needs and so was untainted by any dependence on repressive or deforming culture. Necessity forced a direct contact with nature herself. An adherence to 'primitive' example would inevitably help the recovery of those essential principles which would guide the renewal of art and of society. As the nineteenth century drew on, and long before Nordau's attack, a return to 'the primitive' came increasingly to be treated with distaste as a denial of progress, as a descent into degeneracy. Darwin had concluded *The*

Origin of Species with a ringing profession of faith in evolution as a beneficent force:

> . . . we may look with some confidence to a secure future of some length. And as natural selection works solely by and for the good of each being, all corporeal and mental endowments will tend to progress towards perfection.[31]

A new art, many felt, could therefore be inspired by the rapid and brilliant achievements of new sciences, particularly of biology.

The Curves of Life

When he read *The Origin of Species* a year or two after its publication, Ernst Haeckel was a young physician. It was now his gospel and he became the chief apostle of Darwinian Evolution in Germany. His many publications were to make him one of the best-known scientists in the second half of the nineteenth century. Having taken a relatively modest appointment at the University of Jena, he upgraded his institute into a centre of morphological research. His own take on evolution drew on his conviction that ontogeny recapitulates phylogeny – that the growth of the individual is the epitome of the evolution of the species to which it belongs. It so happened that a morphological study of evolution lent itself to lithographic illustration, and his monograph on *Radiolaria*, which appeared in 1862, was taken up as a textbook about these invertebrate sea-creatures, and in its second, illustrated version become a source for many artists.[32]

The sinuous forms of these protozoa had an immediate appeal to the artists of the time, as did many of his obviously tentacular figures, yet in spite of the appeal of his plates – and his ideas – to artists, Haeckel's direct entry into the literature of art was late. His *Kunstformen der Natur* did not appear until 1904 and by then the direct exploitation of natural forms for ornament was really a thing of the past.[33] In the meantime, the new century, the twentieth, which already appeared to mark the millennium as its round number seemed to promise, would see the rise of a fresh, new, healthy art which would be qualitatively different. Many hidden occult things would now be revealed. For those who were so convinced (as Nordau was) *fin de siècle* meant the bright dawning of a new age which deserved its own forward-looking art – not the dusk and murk of twilight.

Those optimists concerned primarily with the visual arts, with design in the widest sense, had long argued that any truly harmonious visual experience could be achieved only through a new style. Some believed such a style would conjure away the perils of mass-production.[34] A new style might allow artists to control the entire environment and all its different components – furniture, hangings, floor, ceiling and wall coverings, even picture-frames as well as the pictures inside them – and so make it into a continuous and harmonious artifact. The idea increased in appeal as the impact of the Industrial Revolution on everyday things led to their jostling and jarring fragmentation. Since the 1850s and '60s those who were arguing for a new style came to insist that it could not be based on any historical precedent – except by analogy: a new style had to be based on nature alone. Those discordant contemporaries – William Morris

Lithographic plate from Ernst Haeckel's *Kunstformen der Natur* showing *Discomedusae* jellyfish, 1902.

and Owen Jones – had given this notion their own, parallel reformulation in the 1860s and '70s.[35] But Morris worked in Ruskinian terms, seeking a fidelity to nature through medievalizing crafts to make that the guiding principle of his vast output, while all Owen Jones' work relates to new forms of machine production. So, his quasi-botanical plates in the *Grammar of Ornament*, which I mentioned in the previous chapter, relied on the new popularity of chromolithography for fancy book-illumination as well as for scientific illustration. The *Grammar* had provided a survey of patterns from all civilizations, and then – almost devaluing all that it had surveyed – offered a series of botanical drawings as models for future ornament, though Jones was careful to warn his readers against an excessively naturalistic, unstructured approach, which, as he pointed out, is already that of many 'decorative' designers of the time whose work he deplored. 'The more closely nature is copied the farther we are removed from a work of art.'[36] Art would inevitably have to come into it: nature cannot reveal herself directly, immediately to the artist.

Honeysuckle, from Owen Jones, *Grammar of Ornament*, 1856.

Plate showing
'1. Rosa Englenteria;
2. Rosa Muscata Alba;
3. Libanotis; 4. Cistus
Ledon Myrtifolium;
5. Herba Benedicta';
from A.W.N. Pugin,
Floreated Ornament
(1849).

One plate in the *Grammar* which attracted much attention was therefore the 'morphological' analysis of plant forms provided by Jones' young assistant Christopher Dresser, and it gave him far more fame than its modest place in the book (it was one of 112) warranted. As a lad, Dresser had entered the (then rather decrepit) Government Design School, and been promoted to teach plant drawing there in 1854.[37] When Gottfried Semper left the school for Zürich in 1855, Dresser was one of the triumvirate appointed to take over his teaching, and he gave twelve illustrated talks 'on the best mode of investigating the form and structure of biological/botanical specimens with a view to their treatment as "ornament"'.

But his aims were more radically scientific, and theoretically more ambitious; he had come under the influence of John Lindlay, Professor of Botany at University College, London, who published what was to be his best-known book, *The Vegetable Kingdom*, to much acclaim in 1846. Lindlay was the main British exponent of the morphological study of plants, which has its origin in Goethe's biological thinking. The *morphé* which gives the science its name, the Greek word for 'form', pointed to its concern with structure rather than outward appearance. Dresser had become so proficient at the morphological study of plants[38] that Jena University, specifically Haeckel's institute, awarded him a doctorate for his work on the subject in 1859, the very year Darwin published *The Origin of Species*. When Lindlay retired the following year, Dresser applied for his vacant chair, but seems not even to have been short-listed; his intense preoccupation with biology as a science and as a career would make for a brief hiatus, but he soon re-established himself, with the publication of his *Art of Decorative Design* in 1862.

Dresser was clearly of the Pugin–Cole tendency and in spite of some similarities, he had played little or no part in the Arts and Crafts movement, which was to have its efflorescence in Art Nouveau. Between that school and what I might call (with apologies to Ruskin), the Pugin–Ruskin one, there was an unbridgeable, if almost symmetrical difference. Ruskin and his disciples wanted artists involved in decoration; even 'fine' artists were to glory in their

William Morris, design for 'Honeysuckle' chintz, 1876.

status as workmen. The Cole circle – Jones, the Redgraves and most explicitly and emphatically Dresser – wanted to raise the status of the decorative, 'mechanical' designer to that of an artist, explicitly a 'fine' artist.

Dresser makes a very assertive statement about his own doctrine in the book which is the most useful introduction to it: *Principles of Decorative Design*, which he published in 1873:

> Ornamentation is in the highest sense of the word, a Fine Art; there is no art more noble, none more exalted. It can cheer the sorrowing; it can soothe the troubled, it can enhance the joys of those who make merry, it can inculcate the doctrine of truth; it can refine, elevate, purify and point onward and upward to heaven and to God.[39]

A high claim. Dresser backs it with a refusal to allow that 'taste' might be a criterion for judging ornament. Acquiring knowledge, by which he means the knowledge of the art of the past, is the only guide to judging the art of the present. And there are three principles to guide his readers to a true understanding of what is to be done: truth, beauty and *power*. The combination was so important to Dresser that he has to add:

> Long since I was so convinced that I embodied them in an ornamental device which I painted on my study door . . .

For which device, Dresser made several variant studies.

Of the three principles, truth is fairly straightforward – nothing that Ruskin would have disapproved of (no imitation, for instance, fake graining and so on), though he does not press his demands too far. Beauty is briefly outlined and it is summed up in a sentence which Dresser derived from Leon Battista Alberti, however indirectly: 'The perfectly beautiful is that which admits of no improvement', and he leaves the reader to pick up its traces throughout the rest of the book.

As for power, this is a new word in such a context, but Dresser's use of it does not seem to relate to the sense it had assumed in German philosophy during his time. Early on in his *Principles*, he hints at his own view of it by presenting two contrasting patterns: one of sinuous curves in an oval surround,

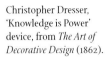

Christopher Dresser,
'Knowledge is Power'
device, from *The Art of
Decorative Design* (1862).

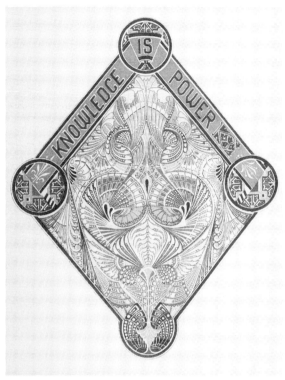

whose tendril ends are intended to be 'more or less exciting' and which displays harmonious, flowing movement; then, a few pages later, another, of which he says (in a footnote) that in it:

> I have sought to embody chiefly the one idea of power, energy, force or vigour; and in order to do this, I have employed such lines as we see in the bursting buds of spring . . . I have also availed myself of those forms to be seen in certain bones of birds . . . which give us an impression of great strength . . .

Evidently, this is the result of 'scientific' study – which, to Dresser, means primarily the application of morphological concepts from biology to design.

Though he was to publish several more books – *Studies in Design* in 1874–6, *Principles of Art* in 1881, and an invaluable book on Japan (which became one of the sources of Japonism, of which more later) in 1882 – Dresser never went back on the doctrine he proclaimed in his first book. His approach to ornament inevitably went against the two principles which John Ruskin had formulated in the *Seven Lamps of Architecture*, even if he modified them later (because they were too commonsensical – or so he said); and his first rule ran:

> not to decorate things belonging to purposes of active and occupied life. Wherever you can rest, there decorate. Wherever rest is forbidden, so is beauty.

Another principle dictates the hierarchy of nobility:

> Imitated flowers are nobler than imitated stones; imitated animals than flowers; imitated human form, of all the animal forms the noblest . . .[40]

Against Ruskin (but implicitly), Dresser presents himself as a practical man, insisting in his writings that good design will, for instance, increase the gross national income. He would therefore have no truck with German psychological and philosophical musings either. Yet he was one of the very few artists and designers in Britain to have some knowledge of German Formalist ideas, and seems, in his later writings, to have been aware of their teaching that perception – and aesthetic appreciation most particularly – responded to inherent characteristics (both primary, like harmonious measurements, and secondary, such as texture and colour) which were physically taken in by the eye.

In asides, he lets the reader see the underlying themes in his work and his thinking. His teaching is specific: the decoration of a dining room, he directs, should give the impression of richness, that of a drawing-room, cheerfulness, of a library, worth, of a bedroom (not surprisingly), repose. Yet Dresser was not explicit about how emotions were to be stimulated, nor did he offer any explanation for any direct relation between shapes and colours, which he assumes in a double-take, since the assumption that the forms recommended have permanent validity across all periods and culture is not reasoned. His first contact with Japanese art therefore – at the World Exposition of 1862 – involved no challenge to his underlying views.

Dresser was an implicit formalist, one of the many artists and scientists who believed that direct appreciation transcended any bounds set by history or culture. Abstracted from context or content, forms had universal validity; context (or content) was therefore irrelevant to the way in which forms were 'received' by the viewer; it followed that any historical interpretation of art was irrelevant to aesthetic appreciation. This approach has, as its ancestor, Johann Friedrich Herbart,[41] a pupil of Fichte, who rejected the primary Kantian postulate, the *a priori*, since he believed that notions of time and space were not innate, but arose from experience. Like all our notions, they were formed by association in a kind of chain reaction. Any idea can be received into consciousness if it tallies with previous experience, the sum of which he called 'apperceptive mass'. If a newly-met idea does not so tally, it is elided and stored in another faculty, the unconscious. But the elided idea can be retrieved by new apperceptive occurrences. Herbart's widely influential educational ideas derived from the notion of extending the apperceptive mass.

Herbart also taught – among other things – that perception depended on contrast both in time (succession) and in space (simultaneity), and he set musical harmony up as the benchmark to which all 'aesthetic' perception should refer. This idea became the foundation of later 'experimental aesthetics', which would investigate and statistically establish those preferences for abstract shapes and colours and other 'inexpressive' elements on the assumption that the way they were valued – either in art or nature – had no cultural or historical dimension. They were to be evaluated statistically in terms of the degree of pleasure the viewer received from them.[42]

Scientific assurance was much sought after by artists who were becoming increasingly aware of the irrelevance of routine academic teaching to their activities and were looking for certainty in the judgement – and even in the making – of works of art. Colour was one issue on which much research would focus, and the most important experiments were carried out by a chemist, Michel Chevreul, during the 1830s and '40s.[43] Yet Chevreul was not at all interested in its psychological effects, but rather in its complex, but calculable perceptual interrelation. He was primarily a chemist – like George Field – but working with dyes at the Gobelins works, and he became convinced that lack of contrast produced those dull colour effects in the tapestries he had been engaged to correct rather than any defects in the dyes themselves.[44]

Dresser was writing and working a generation after Chevreul, but he already used a virtually divisionist/pointillist technique to achieve his brilliant, contrasty colouring – which as he himself owned, he took from Chevreul. And the knowledge required in the matter of colour was not to be got up by studying history, but by considering the theories of colour contrast most particularly. That is why he insisted that considerations of colour could never be limited to a single room. Its scientific study fascinated any number of artists; but like Chevreul they took little interest in its psychological effects.

Colour was only one aspect of visual experience which required scientifically guaranteed procedures. Biology, particularly the measurement and morphology of growth, seemed to offer the assurance that there was a natural, even a scientific guarantee to such matters – as did the venerable enquiry into the measurements of the human body.

Leonardo da Vinci's now over-familiar drawing of a man in the square and the circle (which comments on the almost equally familiar text on human proportion in Vitruvius' treatise on architecture)[45] was engraved by the Milanese painter Giuseppe Bossi in his essay on the *Last Supper* fresco (which he reprinted separately a year later), and widely circulated. During the 1820s Gottfried Schadow spent some time taking measurements of differing human bodies – both living ones and statues by old masters – to establish a corpus of human measurements which he considered an extension of Dürer's teaching about body proportions; he published it in 1834. His portfolio was called *Polyklet* after the Greek sculptor whose statue of a young man carrying a spear had been considered the perfect incarnation of human proportion in antiquity, and who was also supposed to have written a commentary on that statue. Schadow's book proved an immensely popular handbook for artists, and was translated and published in English in 1864.[46] Meanwhile in Edinburgh, David Hay, a formalist colour theorist (whom Dresser would condemn for his 'rigid formalism' and his utopianism), became the great Scots expert on colour; having redecorated Abbotsford for Sir Walter Scott,[47] he organized the colour scheme for the National Gallery of Scotland. A 'decorative' painter by profession (in the old sense – he was known as the 'first intellectual house-painter'), he set out a system adopting the insights of George Field,[48] but also took up the ideas of a recusant history painter, Giles Hussey.[49] This allowed

David Hay, male and
female body, after *The
Geometric Beauty of the
Human Figure Defined*,
1851.

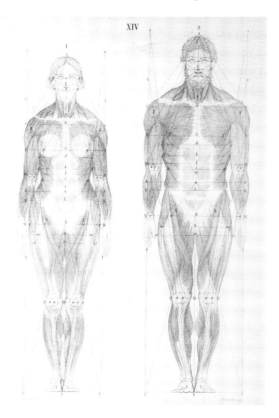

him to wed 'scientific' theories about colour with an apparently equal 'scientific' interest in proportion, particularly human proportion.

Hay was one of several variously distinguished writer-artists who worked on the subject. A sculptor and Egyptologist who had worked with Owen Jones on the Egyptian Court in the Sydenham Crystal Palace, Joseph Bonomi the younger,[50] now produced another handbook on the proportions of the body based on the measurement of antique sculptures made by John Gibson, an artist who also bid to revive polychromatic sculpture and whose 'tinted Venus' (begun in 1851) was exhibited, inside a polychrome temple designed for her by Owen Jones, at the 1862 World Exposition.[51] The shaggy, distracted Gibson cut a very different figure from the rich and sociable ('He liked the "world", and the world also thoroughly liked him'[52]) American writer, lawyer and sculptor William Wetmore Story (now remembered mostly as a chronicler of mid-nineteenth century Rome and a friend of the Brownings), who in a 'mystical', cabalistic and almost missionary book criticized all those who used a modular system based on Vitruvius – as had Bonomi – and turned to a geometrical system reminiscent of David Hay's, though much simpler, in which the differentials of triangle and square inscribed in a circle are used to dimension the body.[53]

The physician Carl Gustav Carus (whom I had occasion to mention as chairing the Dresden Kunstverein[54]) approached it from his knowledge of comparative anatomy and of morphology. Having surveyed the work of his many predecessors, Carus condemned all previous modular systems based on irrational numbers (such as Hay's because geometrically calculated) in favour of one based on whole numbers. He proposed a standard, invariant morphological module: since bodily proportions changed with growth, he took one third of the spinal column (of 24 vertebrae) as an unchanging body-module which would work for all age groups since it remained proportionally constant as the body grew, and it worked for all human types.[55]

However, perhaps the most influential of all these, because most scientific-seeming, were the arguments proposed by the poet and philosopher Alfred Zeising, who considered himself a follower of Herbart. He had accepted as a key to all aesthetic and mensural problems the speculations about a geometrical device well known since antiquity (it had been explored by Euclid),[56] and much discussed in the fifteenth and sixteenth centuries, namely the division of a line in extreme and mean measure which resulted in a ratio by which the smaller part to the bigger equalled that of the bigger to the whole. It had been dignified with the name 'Golden Section' by a German mathematician, Martin Ohm, in 1835.[57] Zeising's plea for the 'Golden Section' to be a privileged formal relationship influenced several generations of artists, historians, botanists into the twenty-first century, and was more subtly advocated by Gustav Theodor Fechner,[58] who used statistical enquiries to establish a 'natural' preference for it in what he called 'direct' (which he distinguished from the culturally dependent 'associative') experience. These enquiries were carried out without reference, it would seem, to the more stringent ones of Hermann von Helmholtz, whose *Physiologische Optik* of 1856 established the physiological basis of vision – though his work on the sensations of tone is now better known and has long been a standard work of reference.[59]

Fechner believed that the data derived from sensory experience and those held consciously could not be reduced to one another – even if they had to be considered different aspects of one reality. The relation between them, he thought, might nevertheless be given some numerical value. From such a postulate he refined the law with which his name is now associated and asserted that the *arithmetical* increase of a sensation requires a *geometrical* increase in stimulus, for which he even devised the formula s (sensation) = c log R (the 'c' constant to be determined for each sense while 'R' is the numerical value of the stimulus for it). It was his conviction, therefore, that there was a calculable relation between the stimulus offered in observation and its effect on the observer.[60] We now tend to find it difficult to believe that so many psychological 'laboratories' devoted such important research resources to this curious enterprise.

Fechner, who was radically anti-materialist (he also drew inspiration from Jakob Boehme's writings, which had been so important to Runge), was also interested in the relation between colour and sound. This he shared with many of the writers I have mentioned: Hussey and Webb, Field, Bonomi, Hay and Story. The tendency to articulate such invariant formal values was given a very important 'humanist' reading or twist when the notion of empathy was formulated. The German word for empathy, *Einfühlung*, was re-coined by the philosopher Robert Vischer in his doctoral thesis, 'On the Optical Sense of Form', which he defended in 1872.[61] The concept had been implicit in the voluminous writings of his philosopher father, Theodor Friedrich, but it was Robert who coined and launched the term.[62]

When the younger Vischer, Robert, was writing, Herbartian formalism had split into scientific, positive Fechnerian experimental psychology, while certain neo-Kantians had transformed the master's teaching into a doctrine in which experience could either be organized linguistically or sensorially – especially visually. That made the two kinds of organizing experience independent of each other, privileging the sensory kind as far as representation was concerned. The main proponent of this view, Konrad Fiedler,[63] was a man of independent means who travelled much, mostly in Italy, where he fell in with the painter Hans von Marées. Marées had left Germany for Rome and worked in a monumental, classicizing, dry manner which had closer affinity with older French painters like Pierre Puvis de Chavannes than with anyone in Germany. His masterpiece was a series of decorative panels which he painted in the new zoological station and aquarium built in Naples in 1872.

The south wall of the
Naples Aquarium
Library, decorated
by Hans von Marées,
1873.

The young sculptor Adolf von Hildebrand met Fiedler and Marées in Rome
and collaborated with Marées on the Naples project – after which they all
moved to Florence. Marées died young (in 1888), but Hildebrand settled to a
life between Florence and Munich; the Wittelsbach Fountain (1889–95) was
his masterpiece in that city.[64] Hildebrand's playful but idealizing statues
incarnated the ethos of pure visibility before the public.

While Fiedler was working out his views on pure visibility, Robert
Vischer elaborated the concept *Einfühlung*[65] to denote the way in which any
object observed is interpreted and appropriated by projecting quasi-human
intentions and even quasi-human movement onto it. It is in stark contrast to
any formalist ideas of perception (particularly of aesthetic appreciation),
which declared that inherent characteristics were directly, almost physically
taken up in perception. Empathy was appropriated by a number of designers
– Dresser, for instance – as well as writers on philosophy and psychology,

most energetically by another Leipzig teacher, Theodor Lipps, who made it one of the three fundamental forms of cognition:

> I know about myself, I know about things and I know about other egos
> . . . the first knowledge has its origin in sensory experience. The second
> is inner experience, that is the direct or the recollected backward-look-
> ing experience of grasping the ego with its certainties, demands, activ-
> ities, deeds and feelings – and with them its relationship to objects.
> The source of the third cognition finally is empathy. That has implica-
> tions well beyond cognition. I take 'empathy' in a wider sense than the
> word allows . . . [66]

Lipps goes on to detail two primary ways in which empathy grants me a relationship with objects: either to be 'against' them as it were, or yet 'enter' into them figuratively and experience my own consciousness as that of the object of my perception.

Lipps' account of empathy has inevitably become part of any aesthetic discussion. In Britain it was mediated by his disciple, Vernon Lee, and would affect Roger Fry's and Clive Bell's versions of formalist theory.[67] It was diluted and popularized for the Anglo-Saxon world (as 'tactile values') by Bernard Berenson, and following him introduced into architectural ter-minology by a member of his entourage, Geoffrey Scott – who rather sur-prisingly presented empathy as a revolutionary notion in the 1920s.[68] The empathetic doctrine was brilliantly restated and extended in psychoana-lytical terms by Adrian Stokes in the 1930s and '40s. Much more importantly, empathy has entered general philosophical discussion. It has been taken up by some of the early phenomenologists: by Moritz Geiger, Max Scheler and Eugène Minkowski – though it was perhaps more important to Edmund Husserl, who appealed to it in his account of the transcendental constitution of the object.[69]

I will have more to say about the present impact of such ideas, but however powerful, they developed in an intellectual climate in which rapid scientific advance seemed unstoppable. Darwin's profession of faith in progress which I quoted earlier,[70] was echoed by many thinkers of the succeeding decades, when biology – a relatively new science – absorbed much of the intellectual energy, and its industrial application provoked the greatest excitement. Through the late 1860s and '70s the discoveries of Louis Pasteur and Joseph Lister were transforming medical practice as well as agriculture and food production all over Europe. Biology and chemistry – biochemistry specifically – were the most engrossing (and the most popular) fields of applied science until the end of the nineteenth century.

Many of these enquiries, though exciting popular interest, did not seem to have immediate commercial or industrial relevance. It took nearly a decade for industry to see the application of a most remarkable and well-publicized discovery – the structure of carbon compounds. August Kekulé,[71] while studying architecture at Giessen, became a disciple of the great biochemist Justus von Liebig and was responsible for some of the most important contemporary discoveries transforming organic chemistry. Nasty, black and brute material – coal-tar – could be elevated almost alchemically into aromatic compounds and many-coloured dyes, so establishing a new branch of the subject.[72]

The first 30 years of imperial Germany were of quickly growing prosperity. Many industrialists (and some scientists) conscious of their contribution to this transformation considered it in an almost religious, if not an occult manner. The whole of Germany would, they thought, be turned into a laboratory and factory. It was to be the herald of a different kind of Industrial Revolution. The whole population of the new empire could be sublimated into a nation-wide community – a *Gemeinschaft* – as coal-tar was transformed into the brilliant colours of aniline dyes.[73]

Industry rather than science established the progressive mood. Intellectual tendencies were more hesitant. The search for origins, for biological genealogies, remained a powerful urge. Yet no return to a primitive condition – historical or even biological – could at this point be seen as at all 'progressive' in spite of the morphological interest in *Urformen*. There was no question of *reculer pour mieux sauter*. The dependance on the past which had moved and inspired Pugin, Ruskin, Morris and Viollet-le-Duc – or for that matter the Prussians who wanted to see themselves as the Greek 'Dorians' come-again – lost all currency in the 1870s and '80s, so that any advocacy of a return to such origins, however that could be understood, was inevitably construed as an infantilism of some kind – or worse. That is why Max Nordau could damn Haeckel with other 'degenerates' as a pedlar of 'protozoic soup' to artists, respected scientist though he was.

Nature in the Orient

The often sinuous character of botanical and zoological drawings was being echoed among the very artists Nordau so disliked by an increasing tendency towards linearity. Such patterns appear increasingly in 'art'-book illustrations, in textiles and wallpapers, even in some furniture designs between 1875 and 1890. There was even nostalgia for the uniconic, quasi-naturalistic and quite unhistorical rocaille ornaments of Louis xv's time when Watteau, Boucher and Tiepolo were painting Chinese subjects and European manufacturers had finally discovered the secrets of Chinese porcelain. Arab, Turkish, Indian and Chinese arts were becoming increasingly familiar and fashionable in the West. Contact with India and China had been intermittent since antiquity in any case, but Japan had been unilaterally cut off by the Tokugawa shoguns at the end of the sixteenth century when the Japanese were even forbidden to build ocean-going ships. By the eighteenth century Japanese products had become hard to find and the place seemed impossibly remote.[74]

The famous – or infamous – invasion of Uraga Bay by Commodore Perry and his four 'black ships' in 1854 has been interpreted as an early exercise in the imposition of a free market economy on unwilling exotics. Yet it also marks the time when Japanese art was 'discovered' and started to infiltrate the west. During the later 1850s and '60s trade increased. The Japanese art that inspired enthusiasm in the West at the time – particularly the *ukiyo-e* woodcuts – was quite unlike older 'oriental' imports. Their abbreviated, flat, stagey volumes, the powerful and taut linearity and flat areas of unbroken colour, the raw juxtapositions of powerful patterns soon had emulators in Europe and in America.

Woodcuts of the greatest *ukiyo-e* master, Hokusai, had been discovered – reputedly as discarded wrapping paper – by the engraver and decorator Félix Bracquemond in 1856 in the shop of Auguste Delâtre, a respected printer and print dealer in Paris. The following year he had put together a complete copy of one of Hokusai's drawing-books, *Mangwa*;[75] he did not know at the time that there were fifteen of these books, some of which had not yet been published even in Japan. Bracquemond was enthusiastic – and the woodcuts were much talked of in the Café Guerbois, where, following Manet, most of the lively painters of the time were *habitués*. Almost overnight they became a sensation among French artists. Hokusai had died aged 90 in 1849 and many of his pupils were still living and working. He was therefore a contemporary of Ingres, a 'modern' artist – however exotic. Soon Japanese woodcuts would become completely familiar to Western artists. The flattened space, deliberately composed in layers parallel to the picture-plane, is evident in Edouard Manet's portrait of the young Emile Zola which was shown in the Salon of 1868.[76] In one corner, on a wallboard, a photograph of his own *Olympia* is pinned next to an engraving of Velázquez's *Feast of Bacchus* and a print of Toshusai Sharaku, tokens of Manet's two favourite exemplars. The Japanese print with its light background not only provided a formal and compositional precedent, but it also hinted at the way Manet's palette would develop.

Zola was not yet the leading 'naturalist' novelist he would soon become, but very active as an art critic; he had written a passionate vindication of Manet in his account of the Salon of 1866 as part of a very contested contribution to a periodical called *L'Evénement*.[77] If Manet was obviously excited and enthralled by the compositional methods offered by the prints, so was Degas – even more explicitly; the outline drawing of silhouettes as if they were layers of stage-settings, the use of bold, abrupt diagonal movements, the almost photographic depiction of an arrested gesture, the deliberate clash of patterns, all this can be seen in Degas' work of that period. Others followed: Claude Monet, notoriously, showed his wife in an elaborately embroidered No-play kimono, coquettishly fanning herself with a Japanese fan – in a most un-Japanese pose. Other artists assumed kimonos for some occasions; Van Gogh, who traded in Japanese prints, also copied them in oil paint and used motifs from them – the flowering cherry most conspicuously; Toulouse-Lautrec had himself photographed wearing a kimono.[78]

Many painters of the next generation learned these skills; they also appreciated that the woodcuts and the paintings (which were their more refined companions) showed a world in which there seemed to be an unfamiliar harmony between the great art of painter and printmaker on the one hand, and the crafts of the potter, embroiderer, fabric-designer, lacquer-maker and metal-smith on the other, all of whom incorporated elements of the man-made environment in which the refinement of gesture was an extension. It presupposed an equally brilliant and exquisite architecture, and provided a reproach and a model to which the stuffy, crowded and ungainly Western dwellings should aspire.

Japanese minor arts had appealed to a cultivated British public before the prints had been appreciated by artists, and the Japanese government exploited this in the 1862 London World Exposition. London's prime 'oriental' shop was the *Great Shawl and Cloak Emporium* which became increasingly successful as ladies' crinolined skirts grew in volume, so that by the 1850s shawls were an indispensable item of clothing.[79] The Emporium, which had always traded in Indian and Chinese fabrics and catered to the constant curiosity about the arts of the Far East, brought many of the exhibits from the Japanese section when the 1862 World Exposition ended, and used them to open an arts-and-crafts branch. An enterprising junior employee of the firm, Arthur Liberty, who had been excited by the Japanese show, soon became the manager of the shop. When in 1875 he was refused a partnership in the wildly successful enterprise, he started on his own, having been promised the custom of many artists and architects he had met through his – and their – oriental enthusiasm.[80] All this happened just before Japan had suffered its own revolution. In 1866–8 the Tokugawa Shogunate was abolished, the Mikado resumed supreme power ('The Meiji restoration') and the prohibition on foreign trade was relaxed. European art dealers travelled out and connoisseurs soon began to complain at the debasement of Japanese wares due to overproduction.[81]

In Paris a market for Japanese (and other oriental) crafts had begun quite sporadically. By 1853 a tea-and-curiosity shop, *La Porte Chinoise*, had been established; in 1862 a Madame Desoye (or de Soye, or even just Mme Soye) established an 'Oriental' craft shop, *Curiosité*, in the Rue de Rivoli, encouraged by a Hamburg dealer, Siegfried (or Samuel) Bing, who had moved to Paris in the 1860s and whose shop was frequented by the artists I mentioned, as well as the de Goncourt and the Van Gogh brothers. All bought, but also traded in porcelain and prints. In 1888 Bing began to publish a polyglot periodical, *Le Japon artistique*, specifically devoted to Japanese crafts.

A young West Point graduate, James McNeill Whistler, had come to Paris in 1856. He resolved to become a painter, and after some preliminaries entered the atelier of Charles Gleyre (a Swiss follower of Ingres – though the studio had been that of Paul Delaroche). He was one of the first to whom

Bracquemond showed his Hokusai discovery. Whistler was one of Madame Desoye's early customers, collecting not only prints but also Japanese and Chinese blue-and-white porcelain. In Gleyre's studio he fell in with two fellow students, Edward Poynter (later President of the Royal Academy) and George Du Maurier – as well as the group which called itself *les copains* – Renoir, Bazille, Sisley; Fantin-Latour was a special friend. Without quite abandoning Paris, Whistler then moved to England in 1859[82] and, perhaps through Algernon Swinburne, struck up a friendship with Michael and Dante Gabriel Rossetti, whom he infected with his Japanese enthusiasm. It was Dante Gabriel who first drew Whistler's Japanese-looking emblem, the butterfly which became his trademark and signature. The Rossettis in turn became advocates of things Japanese and passed their enthusiasm to William Morris – and through him to the whole Arts and Crafts movement.

Whistler's first major English picture, *The Balcony*, is clearly, deliberately, enthusiastically evocative of Japanese composition with a number of female figures in flowing oriental dresses silhouetted against a light sky. He made his preparatory sketches for it look even more like Japanese woodcuts. In 1864 he painted *La Princesse du Pays de la Porcelaine*, very much a European girl, dressed in a kimono, and standing against a Japanese screen holding a Japanese fan. Although soon considered one of his finest, the picture did not find a ready owner (the girl's family did not like it) and it was bought by a dealer.[83]

One of his most munificent patrons and friend, a shipowner called Frederick Leyland (who had also been a generous patron of the Pre-Raphaelites), bought the *Princesse du Pays de la Porcelaine*, and some years later, decided to hang it in his new dining room – he had bought a vast house at 49 Princes Gate, and had had the exterior 'adjusted' by Norman Shaw. A stone-and-iron staircase by the Adam brothers was installed[84] and the house filled with other magnificent art-clutter. The dining room, which had been given rather obtrusive pendant gasoliers, was to be decorated with old Spanish embossed leather and was also to house a collection of blue-and-white porcelain. The clash between the highly figured leather and the porcelain looked painful and Whistler was asked to advise. In the absence of the owners he painted over the embossed leather, the ceiling and the gasoliers in blue and gold. It now became 'his' Peacock Room:

A pattern invented from the Eye of the Peacock, is seen in the ceiling spreading from the lamps. Between them is a pattern devised from the breast feathers.

The two patterns are repeated throughout the room . . . Beginning again from the blue floor, on the dado is the breastwork blue on gold while above, on the Blue wall, the pattern is reversed, gold on blue . . .

The arrangement is completed by the Blue Peacocks [Whistler capitalizes], on the Gold shutters, and finally the Gold Peacocks on the Blue wall.[85]

Though the *Princesse* picture was an important starting-point, it became a mere incident among all the peacockry. The Leylands were startled and furious. There was a quarrel about money. Whistler was banned from the house but the precious room remained intact.

Meanwhile, Whistler took some part in the design of his own ('The White') house in Chelsea by William Godwin.[86] Whistler and Godwin had already worked together on a 'decorative' stand at the Paris World's Fair of 1887. They popularized the use of yellow backgrounds for the blue-and-white china which, with white wainscots, became such a trademark of the 'aesthetic' style. White and pale gold frames were now a feature of art exhibitions in Britain. Nowhere else had such a close control of the domestic environment as theirs ever been achieved – it was more intrusive than that of the French masters of rocaille. Passionate attention to the details of the environment almost inevitably 'toned' paintings and sculpture into the general effect any room exercised on a visitor. Being so integrated, they seemed not to invite special attention.

The generalized fashion for everything Japanese and the enthusiasm felt for their exquisite interiors fed into the design and the decoration of the 1870s and '80s. There was a rage for reshaping even the staidest middle-class homes to accord with such trends, and many authors therefore offered advice on domestic interiors, sometimes in association with manufacturers. Christopher Dresser was one of them, even if his was the most consistent and reasoned (as well as the most profitable) approach given that his 'office' was turning out large quantities of wallpapers, fabrics, silverware, glassware and china which he could use as examples.

Much that was being produced for the fashionable interior was directly modelled on Japanese patterns, but there were many other influences. The rather undefined and eclectic Arts and Crafts movement was first given institutional prestige by an exhibition at the Grosvenor Gallery in 1881. Its main mover, Walter Crane, became a public figure.[87] Crane may have made his fame as a book designer and illustrator, but he soon received commissions for wall-papers, textiles and silverware. Through his publications, he became one of the best-known British artists in Europe and the United States. He was typical of the Arts and Crafts movement in admiring Morris (who exhibited with them) and Ruskin (though ignoring their condemnation of machine production), and became involved in left-wing politics as well as fringe activities: the reform of women's clothing, vegetarianism and community living.

An aim of the movement was to turn every room, the whole house even – which included the sculptures and the pictures, as well as every object of daily use – into an 'aesthetic' unity. Crane certainly understood that all this concentration on the continuity of the aestheticized environment inevitably weakened any attention to the individual work of art:

> Some facetious friends of William Morris once proposed to send him a circular asking subscriptions to an association for the protection of the poor easel-picture painter, since he was being frozen out by designers of wall-papers and hangings of such mere ornamental interest that people did not want anything else on their walls.
> It was a joke, but there was meaning in it . . .[88]

Pervasive though it was, the Arts and Crafts movement had no institutional centre, or even any specific programme. In any case, the severity and the dogmatism of French artists were not for them. Their ideology owed much to the 'aesthetic' religiosity that had been taught by Walter Pater, even if he was out of sympathy with Ruskin's and Morris' very demanding socio-political aims. Yet he had a wide following among the laxer Arts and Crafts rank-and-file.

I noted earlier that both Ruskin and Morris expressed their contempt for applying the word 'aesthetic' to the making of art or craft objects. Yet many of the advocates of the Arts and Crafts movement – journalists, art dealers, even manufacturers – held that their products could turn the whole life of the com-

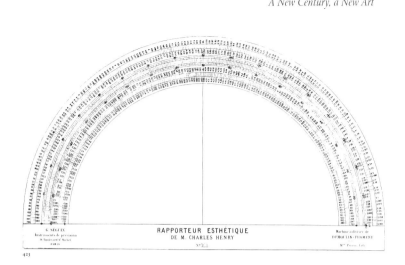

Charles Henry's 'Aesthetic Protractor', 1888–9.

mon man into an aesthetic unity. This view was ridiculed frequently in *Punch*. Dependant though it was on both Dresser and Morris for its patterns and its accessories, its ideology was unsympathetic to both of them – as it certainly was to Ruskin, who repeatedly damned the term as applied to the home or the place of work.

The Japanese infatuation endured in Paris, too. A clamorous Japanese quotation, more abrupt and striking than any by Manet or Whistler, was the 'cameo-portrait' of the anarchist critic and philosopher Félix Fenéon which the 'post-Impressionist' Paul Signac painted in 1890. Although Signac called the harshly-patterned background of the figure 'Rhythmical Angles', the spiralling forms are in fact a direct copy of a design in a Japanese woodcut kimono pattern-book which Signac owned – if reversed in direction. His hero advances, top-hat and cane in one hand, a cyclamen in the other – almost as if he were going to be whirled into the spiral. A number of critics have pointed out that the reversal of the Japanese pattern obeys a theoretical code recently formulated by his friend, the young philosopher-critic Charles Henry (or Henri Hirsch), whose 'Esthétique scientifique' was first published as a paper in a small periodical, *La Vogue*.[89] The underlying notions of Henry's theory go back to Humbert de Superville's account of invariant signs, but are now reinforced by Fechner's speculative psychophysiology as well as Helmholtz's more sober experimental findings.[90] Henry's formalism was inevitably nourished by the general nineteenth-century conviction that mental phenomena must be studied as reactions to stimuli – and that both linear forms and colours produce them.[91] Since they could be studied experimentally they could also be worked into the pattern of a picture and so ensure the appropriate response by the spectator. Henry was so convinced of this that he even had an instrument-maker in the Boulevard St Michel make (and put on sale) an 'aesthetic protractor' in which the degrees of inclination from the vertical were calibrated according to the appropriate response.

The Objective Sensation

Henry had come to Paris from Alsace in 1875 (aged 26); he was sharply and inquisitively aware of developments in German psychology and philosophy – as was his friend Jules Laforgue, a great and still underestimated poet and thinker who had been eking out a living in Berlin as French lector to the Empress Augusta. The two were close, but Henry was the ideologue. A *scientific* aesthetic approach to guide the artists of the future was his aim. His teaching was concerned with the dialectic between the two psycho-optical powers – the dynamogenous and the inhibitory ones – which govern the polarity between joy, pleasure and release for the first, pain, discomfort and withdrawal for the second. Colour, sound and even shape and rhythm could all be studied in terms of this dialectic. A passionate advocate and publicist of his own ideas, he saw himself as the methodical successor (even heir) of two earlier theorists, Charles Blanc and Humbert de Superville.

The 1880s were a propitious time for Henry's enterprise. Younger painters could no longer feel any enthusiasm for the *plein-air* approach which had led to that accumulation of sensations the Impressionists had perfected, their every paint-charged brushstroke shaped like a dash or comma, an addition to the sum of recorded effects.

Impressionism may well be the most written-about movement in painting and I cannot add to that literature usefully here. It had little or no impact on architecture and confined itself within the picture frame, and even those frames were often deliberately old-fashioned, curved, swept and gilt. Outside the frame the environment – whether natural or man-made – was the datum which the painter observed and which provided him with sensations and impressions. The paradox of this situation was that several of them, painters, particularly Pisarro and Caillebotte (but also Monet), were passionately interested and involved in recording the new urban scene, the teeming urban traffic, the arrival of steam in the city. But they were never analytic; they always recorded sensation.

The younger members of the group were now looking for a positive and scientific (preferably a mathematical) method of achieving beauty, and for some of them, even that was not enough. They demanded higher intellectual guarantees such as Henri claimed to provide. Georges Seurat was – arguably – the greatest of them. In his first mature canvas, *Baignade à Asnières*, which was shown in 1883 (and coolly received at the time – the monumental composition was seen by some critics as a mere emulation of Puvis de Chavannes), he used colour contrasts to create a new tonality. Each tone was broken into its chromatic components using both Chevreul's and Rood's systems, while the brushstrokes charged with complementary hues gave each area of colour a novel vibrancy. Seurat had first become dissatisfied with Impressionist 'comma' strokes, and he devised a technique involving the application of colour by a thin brush held at right-angles to the canvas – hence the term 'pointillism' – thereby eliminating any virtuosity of brushwork to concentrate on a scientific rendering of the effects of light through an analysis of colour-stimuli. Seurat even experimented with a white gesso ground to give each colour its true value. In order to compel a proper aesthetic concentration on the picture itself, moreover, he was the first to eschew the golden frames which the Impressionists had favoured (he found that they picked up the tonalities of yellow and orange), and having tried and rejected white frames, he extended his compositions over the mouldings, continuing the lines and colours of the picture. But a scientific approach to colour was still not enough for him. Seurat wanted to discipline his way of working further by a rigorous use of geometrical proportion, guided particularly (in his later paintings) by the Golden Section. Fechner's immediate relevance to the post-Impressionist project would therefore derive from his experimental-statistical attempt to establish a scientific justification for it as the ultimate proportion. He was convinced that the aesthetic laws he was discovering applied to visible forms, but could also work on colour and on music.

Paul Signac, *Felix Fenéon*, 1890, oil on canvas.

The effects achieved by the pointillist method are so striking that it is easy
to think of Seurat exclusively as a colourist. Yet the linearity of his composition was equally important to him. He applied a simple geometry to regulate
the picture-plane. Within the composition he dogmatically applied the teaching about psychodynamic directions as interpreted by Charles-Henri out of
Humbert de Superville. In case there was any doubt about this, he made a
brief statement about these principles in letters to Fenéon and his biographer
Jules-Cristophe, as well as his friend Maurice Beaubourg.[92] To Fenéon, who
had written a text on Signac in which Seurat was not mentioned, he protested his claim to the primacy of his 'divisionism' – and this before Henri had
arrived on the scene. In all his writings, he sets his first debt to Delacroix as
the great colourist.[93]

In fact, another quite different tendency was developing, mostly around
Paul Gauguin in the late 1880s, before his departure for Tahiti in 1891. Seurat,
in spite of occasional irritation, was an admirer. Gauguin, for his part, did
not trust the 'scientific' pretension of Seurat's method.[94] With the assistance
of a much younger painter, Emile Bernard, he developed a rather different

202

technique labelled *cloisonisme*,[95] isolating and circumscribing colour areas in a composition much as Japanese wood-engravers and medieval enamel-lists (or stained-glass artists) had done (the term is derived from *cloison*, a screen, a ridge). That radical simplification of representative, almost heraldic – as against imitative – colour was Gauguin's first and most radical lesson to his followers.

These followers also turned their attention to Chassériau's two great pupils, Gustave Moreau and Puvis de Chavannes, who seemed to hold the secret of avoiding allegory and achieving innate symbolism. Indeed, the very word 'symbol' became a slogan again; to achieve its power, the artist had to concentrate on heraldic, on 'local' colour, and this went hand-in-hand with an interest in the systematic use of geometric proportion. Most painters and sculptors who accepted the label 'Symbolist' set themselves against Impressionism and its correlative, the literary 'naturalism' of Zola. Baudelaire's 'Correspondances' was again central to their concerns, Huysmans and Mallarmé to their literary references. Gauguin taught them how to look, how to understand what they were about. He had learnt much from Cézanne,[96] and would transmit his ideas to them before he made his break with France. Emile Bernard, Paul Sérusier and Maurice Denis and later, Edouard Vuillard and Pierre Bonnard, were the most celebrated beneficiaries of his teaching.

An important group of Symbolists called themselves the Nabis. Founded in 1888, they took the Hebrew name (*Nabi, Navih*, a prophet; they even used the Hebrew plural, *Nebiim*) at the behest of Sérusier who knew some Hebrew and Arabic and was fascinated by the occult, by theosophy and by the murkier reaches of neo-Platonism. He was an enthusiastic reader of Edouard Schuré (the most verbose of the French Wagnerians and a noted occultist).[97] The Nabis took up some of the monkish externals of their predecessors (Nazarenes, Pre-Raphaelites, etc.), devised a curious mystifying jargon and had regular meetings from which women were excluded. Their nucleus was the group of Gauguin's followers, and they insisted that Symbolism would propel painting from Impressionism to a new classicism.

Their demand on a new art was best stated (as often happens) by their friend, the poet and critic G. Albert Aurier.[98] It was to be (1) *ideist* (he apolo-gized for the 'barbarous neologism'), since the expression of Ideas was to be its aim; (2) *symbolist*, since the Idea was to be communicated by forms; (3) *synthetist*, since the forms, which are signs, are so set out as to be generally understood;[99] (4) *subjective*, since the forms are not to be perceived as objects but as the sign of the Idea which the subject perceives; and (5) therefore – Aurier concludes rather surprisingly – *decorative*, since, as the ancients understood, a painting that fulfils these conditions will decorate the banal (Aurier's word) walls of man-made buildings with thoughts, dreams and ideas. Easel painting, Aurier concluded, is merely a decadent refinement. For all his insistence on the decorative nature of painting, no architects appear in this part of the story, confirming the Nabis' implied distaste for what was being built at that time. And yet, beginning with Gauguin, who was a passionate ceramist and also designed furniture, some of the group designed tapestries and embroideries; Morris' ideas were being applied at second-hand and would have some curious side-effects.

One of their associates, the Flemish painter, Jan Verkade, took the religiosity so seriously that he entered the monastery at Beuron in 1895 to become Dom Willibord.[100] Several other monks at Beuron were active artists, of whom the most influential seems to have been Dom Desiderius Lenz, an architect who built a new church in the monastery.[101] Together with some of his companions, he also executed some ambitious mosaics in the mother house of the Benedictines, Monte Cassino.

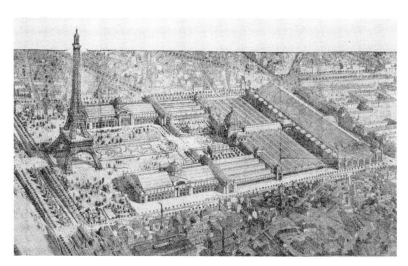

Paris, the Salle des Machines and the Eiffel Tower, lithograph, 1889.

The Eiffel Tower, Paris, photograph taken during construction, 1888.

Lenz was a dogmatic advocate of the Golden Section. Though he recognized that they would not guarantee quality, Zeising's speculations (reinforced by Fechner's experiments) had made a great impression on him. He tried to establish a 'canon' of Egyptian proportion (a perennial justification of a sacred geometry), and his approach was taken up beyond the confessional circle of his followers. In Munich, August Thiersch would make proportion the basis of his teaching of composition and would stress the use of geometrical 'regulating' lines as part of architectural speculation.[102]

During the 1880s the apprehension that a new century would overturn many old certainties provoked the sense of unease which has been identified as *fin de siècle*. The eighteenth century had finished with a bang – on the Revolution. The nineteenth century would celebrate that centenary 'positively' with the 1889 Exposition Universelle in Paris. The demand for a new style, even a wholly new art, which had been a recurrent theme throughout the nineteenth century, was becoming pressing as the end of it approached.

A world exposition was an excellent place to try it out. The centenary of the French Revolution would also assert the new-found stability and expansiveness of the Third Republic, its recovery from the disaster of 1870–71, and the growth of its heavy industry. This was explicitly demanded by the prime minister, Jules Ferry. World expositions in the past had offered theatres for structural innovation – but 1889 was to prove the most adventurous. The largest single-span structure ever was erected to house the engineering achievements of the world – the Salle des Machines on the Champs de Mars. Its daring three-hinge trusses eliminated any distinction between column and beam. Criticized – even by other engineers – for their apparent defiance of statics, the building was designed by Victor Contamin (assisted by an 'official' architect, Charles-Louis-Ferdinand Dutert). It proved enormously impressive and popular – and was known at the time as the Palais des Machines.[103]

By far the most prominent, the most debated and abused part of the complex was the main entrance to the exhibition, a giant 300-metre (1,000 feet!) tall tower. It soon became the trademark of Paris for travelogues and advertising, while the name of its designer, Gustave Eiffel, has become attached to it. At the time of the exhibition the vertical tower and the horizontal 'palace' were coupled in the popular imagination as if they were its male and female aspects. This may not have been explicit at the time, though they were jointly described as the steeple and the nave of the cathedral of the new age.[104] The label 'Art Nouveau' seems to have first been coined for them.[105]

The prefabrication involved in organizing the building, the rapidity of erection, the precise engineering – all this was debated by contemporary critics or detractors (and I will quote some), as well as by admirers. The buildings were seen as 'bare', even though they were, by our standards, quite elaborately 'decorated'. So the exterior of the Palais des Machines and its ornamental details were designed by Dutert. The glass walls of the palace were virtually unscreened, but some of the interior ceramic panelling was floreated and the structural members filigreed.

The tower, so often described as unadorned, was dominated by the four huge arches – one to each side. Eiffel himself considered them jointly as the 'triumphal arch to science and industry'.[106] It was fretted with patterns of oversize, repeated palmettes which never had any part at all in its working structure, which was made up of four pylons leaning against each other, stabilized by being tied together by the horizontal plates of intermediate floors.

The arches are therefore exclusively ornamental – in the modern sense of the word. Contamin and Dutert played with decorated infill arches and floreated ceramic panels on the interior of the 'palace', but these were much more modest than Eiffel's gigantic obtrusive 'ornamental' invention.

Of course, Eiffel had designed and built many daring structures before the tower – such as the viaducts at Garabit and Oporto – but they did not carry comparable ornamental embellishment. His tower became instantly both famous and infamous. Protests against its vast size and the dwarfing of its environment were as vociferous and strident as was the praise for the achievement. Its detail may have been mannered and striking, yet it had no immediate effect on the move for a new architecture (and a new art) for the coming century. Many agreed when a glib and prolific *boulevardier* poet described it as: 'L'idole de métal/Symbole de force inutile/Et triomphe du fait brutal.'[107] Nevertheless, in the course of the three or four years that followed, a new style involving idiosyncratic metal and glass structures decorated by a full complement of original and easily recognizable ornament appeared all over Europe.

Disparate elements (many of which I have enumerated) made up the ingredients of that new style: excitement about the new biology; curiosity about abstract, linear, sinuous eighteenth-century rocaille; an enthusiasm for things Japanese. Some elements were positive-scientific, others echoes of Arts and Crafts and of the 'aesthetic' movement – and they all came together so confusedly that it is almost impossible to disentangle the strands. Being so disparate, they needed an external powerful stimulus or catalyst to twist this amalgam into the unified biology-based style which goes by the name of Art Nouveau in Anglo-Saxon countries (after Bing's Paris shop – rather than the Eiffel Tower). In other languages the label varied: *Style moderne* (sometimes Yachting style – a term apparently invented by the brothers Goncourt) in French, *Stile Liberty* in Italian (after the Regent Street shop, though with a nudge about freedom), *Schnorkenstil* (the term had been coined for rocaille originally) or *Jugendstil* in German (after the satirical magazine *Jugend*, which was its main proponent). The mixture of liberation, commerce, novelty and journalism is of course highly appropriate to the time; the manner on the other hand, with its seductive lines, might be considered the decorative elaboration of empathy – which, as I suggested earlier, was then occupying many philosophers and psychologists.

Victor Horta, Hôtel Solvay, interior of the salon, Brussels, 1894.

The patrons of the new style were largely urban and middle-class. The cities where it flourished were newly prosperous, industrial. They needed to establish their independence of some metropolitan centre – even if Paris remained the world focus of artists' attention. Brussels was just such a rich city: gorged on the vilely bloodstained money from the Congo (the whole colony remained the personal property of King Leopold II almost until his death in 1909), it was also sustained by 'cleaner' industrial money (mining and manufacture). The full infamy of that colonial adventure would show up later, but meanwhile Belgian internal politics had led to advanced social legislation. The Brussels working population was lively, the bourgeoisie literate and curious. Seurat and Signac, Gauguin and Denis, exhibiting with a new artists' association there, Les XX, had a readier audience than they did in Paris.

The house which a young architect, Victor Horta, designed and built in 1893 for an engineer, Emile Tassel in Brussels, is heralded as an instance of Art Nouveau's instant maturity and is regarded, almost canonically, as its first full stylistic achievement. A relatively sober, symmetrical and gently undulating stone exterior is entered through a tall, glazed bay. It encloses an interior articulated by an exposed cast-iron structure. Bolts and filigreed beams are integral to the ornament, while the polychromy of walls and ceiling, a swirl of quasi-vegetative patterns of mosaic, shows Horta to have been a true, but also inventive follower of Viollet-le-Duc.

His domestic masterpiece was a slightly later and much bigger house for the textile magnate Ernst Solvay, in which every detail was made to Horta's design – even if Liberty fabrics were acceptable parts of the scheme. As a reminder of stylistic shifts and alliances, the main entrance hall is dominated by a division-ist, even pointillist painting by Théo van Rysselberghe, a disciple of Seurat (if a critical one), rather than by one of the more obvious 'Art Nouveau' heralds.[108]

King Leopold II and the court favoured a blowsy version of the Parisian Beaux-Arts manner, of which the elephantine Palais de Justice in Brussels by Joseph Poelaert (of 1866–83) is the most prominent, while Horta's clients were fellow Freemasons and members of the Belgian Workers' Party – 'we were all "reds"', he said later of himself and his clients. His most important public build-ing of that early period, the Maison du Peuple, which he designed for the Trade Union organization of Belgium,[109] was a built manifesto, with its ingeniously intricate plan, its insistent use of an exposed iron structure framing large plate-glass areas and artificial lighting by electroliers with naked light-bulbs.

Victor Horta, Maison du Peuple, Brussels, interior of assembly hall, 1895–9 (since destroyed).

A contemporary of Horta's, the young Antwerp painter Henry Van de Velde, a friend of Mallarmé and a disciple of Signac, had also been feted as a divisionist when in Paris, but found, as he matured, that he favoured increasing linearity. By the time he met another painter, Marie Sethe (who became his wife), his paintings and designs for embroidery had taken on all the sinuosity we now associate with Art Nouveau. For his new *ménage* he built himself a home (which he called Bloemenwerf) at Uccle outside Brussels in emulation of William Morris' Red House. By 1894 industry was much more receptive to decorative novelties than it had been in Morris' time. Van de Velde sympathized with Morris' politics, though not with his radical rejection of the machine. He was able to design wallpapers, curtains and door-handles for the house, as well as furniture which was instantly put into industrial production. And he went much further than Morris, designing tableware and china (and even his wife's clothes and jewellery), so that the house became a total work of art, even if not at all in the sense which Wagner had in mind when he coined the term. Linear design controlled every item of the man-made space, so that room, house, garden, and the residents themselves became the integrated 'work of art' which was to act as a social and artistic leaven, much more intensely than had been the case in Horta's buildings.

Art Nouveau proper remained of marginal influence in England, but Scotland was different. Glasgow, like Brussels, was industrially rich, self-consciously provincial, ambitious. A small group of artists around the Art School, one of whom was its architect, Charles Rennie Mackintosh, took up the challenge of the new style. Mackintosh had won the competition for the new Art School in 1894 with a project which can be read as a Nipponified version of a Scottish baronial castle. It was to be his most important building. His other works were two secondary schools and two more conventional though highly refined Gothic churches, as well as some private houses, all of them in and around Glasgow – and the series of very elegant tea-rooms for a Miss Cranston.[110] His work was received with enormous enthusiasm by European students and critics, yet he remained little known south of the border. European (particularly German) patrons may have preferred the work of other Arts and Crafts designers, particularly that of M. H. Baillie Scott – who won a much publicized international competition for 'the House of an Art-lover', which a German publisher-architect, Albert Koch, launched in 1901 –

yet Mackintosh (who was placed second) received much more publicity than the winner.[111] A cultivated Viennese businessman, Fritz Wärndorfer, who had gone to Glasgow to meet him and see his work, had him design a music room in his house. It was Wärndorfer, too, who sponsored with Josef Hoffmann and Koloman Moser an Arts and Crafts type enterprise, the Wiener Werkstätte, for which he got Mackintosh to design both trademark and stationery.

In Barcelona Antoní Gaudí had begun to develop a very personal biological manner even earlier. He was keen, too, to forge a Catalan style which would draw not only on Gothic (as it had been digested by Viollet-le-Duc), but also on Mozarabic and even Moorish elements. Working at first mainly for the industrialist Eusebio Güell, he relied on Viollet-le-Duc's positive understanding of how metal and stone could work in a structure – but he gave it a mystical interpretation. For Güell, too, Gaudí designed an estate with a private chapel, a town 'palace' and planned a 'garden-city' – which, though not an economic success, gave Barcelona an ambitious colonnaded market built into the slope of the hill-site and an incipient 'Greek Theatre' over it. The culmination of his work is the unfinished, vast church of the Sagrada Familia, begun in 1883, of which only a fragment – a transept façade and some perimeter walls – had been built when he was killed by a tramcar in 1926. The very adventurous and inventive metal and concrete structure, based on his intuitive understanding of the catenary curve,[112] was illuminated and embellished by an elaborate iconographic programme he devised for the building. It was to be carried out by himself assisted by a group of craftsmen. Gaudí taught that all ornament must be accurately figurative. He therefore incorporated hugely enlarged casts of shells and reptiles into his decorative reliefs. For the sculptures involving the human figure, he also demanded 'accuracy', a 'truth to nature', which he tried to achieve by basing his figures on photographs of live models taken from various angles.[113] His figure groups now seem strikingly conventional when compared to the welter of watery-swirly ornament in which they are set.[114] Gaudí was a fervent polychromist, of course, though he did not care for flat areas of colour or painted stucco (which required constant attention), but relied instead on glazed earthenware. Josep Maria Jujol, his most brilliant architect-disciple, looked after the polychromy, particularly the elaborate mosaics. He used bright complete tiles laid in contrasting patterns; on parts of the Sagrada Familia, in the Casa Battlló, the Güell chapel and in

William Morris and Edward Burne-Jones, *The Kelmscott Chaucer*, opening page (1896).

the famous undulating bench in the Parc Güell, the polychrome surfaces are made up of broken ceramics, glass, even bottle-tops, the whole set into concrete. It has even been suggested that Cubist collage owes something to Picasso's childhood rambles in that park.

Meanwhile, a number of other Catalan architects – notably Josep Puig i Catafalch, Lluis Domènech i Montaner (and later also Gaudí's polychromist, Jujol) – joined him in a movement which was first known as *Modernisme*.[115] Barcelona, prosperous, ambitious to be independent (and a smarter rival) of Madrid and self-conscious about its linguistic separateness, was in a sense an ideal ground for the new style to take root. Even there Richard Wagner provided a focus for its mythology. The Wagnerian Society of Barcelona was founded in 1901 to supervise the production of all Wagner's operas and the publication of Catalan versions of the librettos. Domenech i Montaner designed the Palau de Musica (1905–8) as a late flowering of Art Nouveau (it also became a home for the Wagnerians). Its parure of sculpture may have a somewhat old-fashioned and flaccid look; it is not as floral and sinuous as that of Horta or even Gaudí, yet it remains a marvellously crepuscular witness to the novelty of the New Art.

As in Glasgow and Brussels, so in Budapest and Prague the new style was enthusiastically accepted. The Obecní Dum 'Communal House' in Prague, begun by Osvald Polívka and Antonin Balšanék in 1903, was not finished until 1911. The cafés and meeting rooms at street level are elaborately carved, mosaicked and gilt in proper Jugendstil manner, though the central space of the building, a vaulted concert hall dedicated to Bedřich Smetana (which soon became the city's main assembly hall), was given a somewhat shorn and flaccid neo-baroque ornamental dress. The Obecní Dum in Prague, the Maison du Peuple in Brussels, the Palau de Musica in Barcelona, as well as Ödön Lechner's Natural History Museum and Post Office Savings Bank in Budapest and the 'Old' Theatre in Kraków by Mączyński and Stryjeński, show Art Nouveau as the face of an 'advanced' or 'progressive' and therefore politically nationalist (but culturally internationalist) liberal-bourgeois public life. Berlin, Madrid, Rome, New York, even Vienna – never mind London – had nothing comparable.

In spite of the noted British resistance to any cosmopolitan (never mind nationalist) New Art, the still teenage Aubrey Beardsley produced his own

Aubrey Beardsley,
decorated border
design for Malory's
Le Morte d'Arthur,
c. 1893–4.

manifesto in the new manner, an illustrated edition of Oscar Wilde's *Salome*. The play had been written (in French) in 1892 and was being rehearsed by the greatest actress-diva of the time, Sarah Bernhardt. Refused a licence in London, it was not performed by her until 1894 in Paris. Beardsley illustrated the published version, and also designed a specially woven cloth binding for it based on a peacock pattern.[116] He had recently visited Whistler's Peacock Room and been quite overwhelmed by its beauty. His admiration for Whistler at this point knew no bounds. Also an avid collector of Japanese prints, he seems to have limited himself to erotic ones.[117]

Beardsley, like Whistler (or even the much more politically conscious Wilde), were concerned with matters visual at the intimate scale: the houses which Godwin built for them seemed manageable. They (and even their most ambitious and successful architectural contemporary, Richard Norman Shaw) were not prepared for the energy and urban explosion which had already begun and which would transform all man-made space.

214

Its vortex was Chicago, which grew at a catastrophic rate after its great fire of 1871. The first skyscrapers rose on the edge of that windswept lake on unsuitable, unstable ground. They required great structural ingenuity, therefore – much more than the more conventional high-rise buildings which were going up at the same time on Manhattan. Most of them were decked out in a more or less eclectic, conventional and unspecifically historical dress, even if some architects were also considering the question of style actively. Their patrons were also beginning to show some interest in such matters. Although it was the capital of the meat-packing industry, Chicago was a great communication and financial interchange and the epicentre of an incipient labour movement. Much of its upper- and middle-level classes were of German origin, and the first New World performances of several Wagner operas therefore took place there. Among the architects who flocked to the city, the most searching was Louis Sullivan, who (with his partner Dankmar Adler) designed the Auditorium Building in 1886–9. The hall, which gives the building its name, was the nearest Chicago had to a great public assembly space.[118] A tower was part of the building and Adler and Sullivan established their office on its top two floors.

Though he had studied in Paris like his most prominent contemporaries, Sullivan rejected historical trappings as unworthy of the age and the unprecedented situation of the New World. Yet he was committed to the importance of ornament, and therefore independently developed a theory of quasi-natural patterns and reliefs to be carried out in terracotta and metal which owes much to Owen Jones and (as time went on) ever more to Christopher Dresser both in its morphology and in the communicative power of its ornamental detail. His rapid and floridly inventive drawings show this ebullient ornament allied to a structural bravura which none of his European contemporaries could rival.

For such ornament he did not need help from other artists, nor does he seem to have had much truck with any of them. The sculptor Augustus Saint-Gaudens, his most celebrated contemporary, worked on a number of projects by architects diametrically opposed to him, McKim, Mead and White, who were the prime American masters of the French academic manner. For Stanford White (whose scandalous career and death have often been told), Saint-Gaudens made the 18-foot-high statue of *Diana* which was the weathercock of Madison Square Garden in New York, an extravagant (but short-lived) Spanish Renaissance fun palace.[119] Ironically enough, it was for Boston Public

Library in Copley Square, a building whose organization is based on Labrouste's Bibliothèque Ste Geneviève, that a number of artists were recruited: Saint-Gaudens himself did not deliver, though commissioned, nor did Whistler (too expensive), but Stanford White, on a European visit in 1895, did suggest that his Peacock Room might be stripped out of Princes Gate and moved to Boston.[120] Charles McKim had visited Puvis de Chavannes in 1891, and convinced him to provide a series of panels for the hall of the library, which were installed among its array of marbles and quartzes, dampening their effect somewhat. John Singer Sargent and the English-settled American painter-illustrator Edwin Abbey both worked on their contributions in Abbey's Gloucestershire studios. It made for one of the few buildings in the second half of the nineteenth century where notable sculptors managed to work together with architects of note.

For McKim, Saint-Gaudens also acted as the sculpture chief of the Chicago Columbian Exposition of 1893, a huge display of temporary white marble-like buildings which his pupils peopled with fountains and statues of all shapes and sizes, most of them soon wrecked and none memorable.[121] Sullivan, who had himself contributed a long and low Transport Building to the show, thought that this mixture of pasteboard classicism and fruity statuary would put American architecture back half a century – and he was not far wrong. No other major American artist ever had occasion to work with Sullivan. Nor was this a worry to him, since the catastrophic innovation he had theorized was not morphological and ornamental but concerned the building type we now call the skyscraper. Sullivan thought that he could harness and discipline it through what he called 'artistic consideration'. 'The Tall Building Artistically Considered' was the title of an article which he published in a Philadelphia periodical in 1896. It has been so often reprinted that it has become identified with him. Sullivan was himself responsible for a number of steel-framed, elevator-serviced, tall office buildings, and his rule required that each building should be an articulated unity: it should have a base, a trunk and a crowning element. Otherwise, a beginning, a middle and an end:

> It is a prevailing law of all things organic and inorganic, of all things physical and metaphysical, of all things human and all things superhuman, of all true manifestations of the head, of the heart, of the soul,

that the life is recognizable in its expression, that form ever follows function. That is the law . . .

For all that, he demanded that it should be lofty, since

This loftiness is to the artist-nature its thrilling aspect . . . The force and power of altitude must be in it, the glory and the pride of exaltation must be in it. It must be every inch a proud and soaring thing, rising in sheer exultation that from bottom to top it is a unit without a single dissenting line . . .[122]

The tall building seen in such terms is its own monument and its own master-piece. It needed no 'accessories' since its ornament was an efflorescence of its articulation and structure. Sullivan's place in my story must therefore be – necessarily – a modest and negative one. At this point, even the most opulent and ambitious skyscrapers relied on subservient 'decorators', dispensing with the 'integral' work of artists.

New Light, New Power

A New York contemporary of Sullivan's (and of Whistler's), Louis Comfort Tiffany, the heir to a jewellery fortune, also went to Paris to become an artist, but, like Van de Velde, was sidetracked by the example of Morris and returned to the United States a skilled decorator. Following Morris, he turned his skill to making household objects – of metal and terracotta – though he worked mostly in glass, evolving various metal-alloyed pastes of quite astonishing iridescence, many of them (like Dresser's) owing something to Moorish and Persian, even Japanese precedent. The interior of the Lyceum Theater in New York, which opened in 1884, was probably his most successful public commission. Tiffany would be one of the very first designers anywhere to create special fittings to accommodate electric light during the 1880s. It is hardly surprising therefore that Dresser would make contact with him while travelling through the United States in 1876 on his way to Japan – to become, in effect, Tiffany's agent during his Japanese visit.[123]

217

While Tiffany may have been the first to realize that electric light could stimulate new forms, it was adapted quickly for the theatre, being safer and much more manageable than gaslight, and it finally did away with the existing yellow tinge. The new possibilities of synaesthesia that had been extended by the invention of gaslight (witness the pyrophone) were now expanded exciting-ly. Yet Tiffany's endeavour was a straw in a hurricane. By the turn of the century various inventors and enthusiasts had made the commercial use of electricity possible (the skyscraper, of course, would have been unthinkable without the electric elevator), so that the World Exposition of 1889 already had a number of electric installations, including the Eiffel Tower elevators and its lighting.

Elaboration of coloured, directed light related to both tone and movement was also the subject of many experiments. Electricity seemed to represent the female energy of the new age, an almost uncontrollable psychic energy. A

Chicago girl, Loïe Fuller, was the first to make electric light the prime factor in her performance, and it became the incarnation of the 'fairy electricity'. After modest, though growing success in the United States, Germany and England, first as a soubrette then as a 'novelty' dancer (all without any dance training), Loïe Fuller was a sensation from her first Paris appearance at the Folies Bergère in October 1892, when she was engaged to replace an inferior imitator. Her serpent-, butterfly-, lily-, fire- and other dances depended on movement directly related both to music and coloured, changing directed lights in which her flowing skirts and veils swirled elaborately into curved patterns so as to make them many-media performances, though still not the true *Gesamtkunstwerk*.

She could not have known the term then. The singular beauty of her act was all in the lights and the swirls, which were controlled by a mechanism of rings and batons, varieties of which she patented both in Europe and in the United States, to which music was subservient. Shorn of them, she appeared as a slightly butch, coarse-featured girl. For all that, her popularity is witnessed by some 50 films of her dances between 1893 and her death (in 1928). She herself appears in practically none of them – they were mostly made by imitators, parodists and pupils.[124] Yet writers and artists flocked to the Folies Bergère; Stéphane Mallarmé, at his most cryptic, wrote that the transition from tonalities to woven stuff was the unique enchantment which Loïe Fuller operated (and, he asks parenthetically, whether there was not anything more gauze-like than music?); but he was also conscious of another, more sinister aspect of her art: exertion, as an invention without application, implicates a rapture of art and, at the same time, an industrial achievement; it is a rapture therefore which owes nothing to nature since all is artifice.[125]

Loïe soon had powerful friends. The astronomer-occultist, Camille Flammarion, became her Parisian guide; as her interest in the technical side of her performance increased, she applied for more stage machinery patents – including one she had tried out herself in which she danced on a frosted glass plane illuminated from below. She also explored the use of ultra-violet light and phosphorescent salts on her costumes, introduced to its effects by Pierre and Marie Curie,[126] though they discouraged any thought of a 'radium' dance. She – in turn – introduced them to her other new friend, Auguste Rodin, who, in spite of their long friendship, never either modelled or drew her.

But many other artists did. Sculptures of her proliferated in plaster, ceramics and bronze. There were many imitators, even parodists undeterred by patents.[127] The artist who first served her fame, however, was Jules Chéret, called 'the Tiepolo of the billboard', who became the dominant master of the advertising poster; his chromolithograph of 1893 is one of his first characteristic products, even if the most powerful lithographed image of Fuller was perhaps Toulouse-Lautrec's print. This went through several states, printed not only with different colours, but also (appropriately) with the addition of metal and phosphorescent powders.[128]

Loïe Fuller managed to harness a formal drive of which she herself was only half aware but which seized Europe in the last decade of the nineteenth century. It is worth insisting that when she arrived at the Folies Bergère, Victor Horta had not yet built the Tassel House in Brussels, nor had Oscar Wilde written his *Salome*. The first decade of her success coincides exactly with the span of Art Nouveau. By 1900 Loïe Fuller's fame was so great that if her statue did not crown the World Fair entrance, one pavilion, the 'Palace of Dance', had a statue of her doing the Serpentine dance as its main feature. She refused to perform there herself (and had to be replaced by an imitator) since she had a special theatre built for her. The commonplace building designed by Henri Sauvage (whose later career as a leading designer of low-cost housing does not concern me here) was transformed into the image of a breaking wave by reliefs of billowing drapery by Pierre Roche, a sculptor whose statue of Loïe dancing was mounted over the entrance.

As she matured and her body stiffened, Loïe turned to choreography and teaching and to production, which began when she presented the Japanese troupe of Sada Yakko (who performed in her theatre at the 1900 exhibition and often toured with her), the first Japanese theatre company to enjoy a European success.[129] Their dances derived from the popular Kabuki tradition, but she belonged to Art Nouveau – she almost incarnated it. Later she would flirt with the avant-garde, Futurism especially.

The visitor to the 1889 exhibition had entered under the stark metal arches of the square Eiffel Tower which was spot-lit electrically. The next Parisian one, of 1900 (which celebrated the new century), was the first to be entirely lit electrically – so that Paris truly became 'the city of light'.[130] The entry had none of the thrusting energy of the Eiffel Tower: its visitors were welcomed through a

Hector Guimard, Paris
Métro station
entrance, 1899.

polychrome, curvaceous dome on a three-pronged base, crowned by the statue of a diademed lady known as *La Parisienne*. She was elegantly dressed in clothes designed specially for her by Paquin, one of the leading couturiers of the day, and had been drawn rather than carved or modelled by Jules Chéret. As for the arch itself, it was designed by a young architect, (Joseph) René Binet, who having distinguished himself as a student, chose to travel in the Orient and in North Africa rather than Rome or even Greece. This huge orientalizing confection was to be the high point of his career.[131] The Binet-Chéret-Paquin *Parisienne* is one of many giant figures which appear in more or less ornamental guise during that *fin-de-siècle* decade. They are often nude and playful, but sometimes the figure actually becomes the building.[132]

For the 1900 exhibition, Paris also reformed its public transport system. The underground railway, the trains of the Métropolitaine (known as Métro) were moved and the stations lit electrically. The network was extended and provided with metal entrances as well as pavilions at some important stations, all designed by Hector Guimard, then still a relatively young (born 1867) disciple of Viollet-le-Duc, who described himself proudly as *architecte-artiste*, though he had already been commissioned to design the housing estate still known as Castel Béranger. Guimard chose not to make the conventional journey to Italy and Greece but went instead to England, and later to Belgium; he returned with sketches of Arts and Crafts houses, as well as some of works by Victor Horta (whom he met).[133]

One of his first public commissions, quickly built in 1895, was the Ecole du Sacré-Coeur in Paris. It is a miniature realization of a project for an open market drawn by Viollet-le-Duc in his *Entretiens*. Its oblique cast-iron struts set in a stone hinge make startling v-shaped supports for the bare iron beam on which the shallow-vaulted main floors are carried. Although the space between these columns has recently been filled in, the surprising character of the struts is obvious. He owed to Viollet that almost dogmatic separation of straightforward stone walling with metal structure and garnish, though the spiky metal floreations are of his own time. He was a prolific furniture and fabric designer as well as an architect, and through that decade his forms become wilful and tense. His one really important building is a metal-structured concert hall, the Salle Humbert de Romans, which he was asked to design in 1898.[134] An octagonal steel structure was clothed in mahogany and inserted into an irregular but rectangular plan. It was demolished quickly, but during its short life was the second concert hall in Paris.

Guimard's most famous and enduring works (begun in 1899) were, however, those Métro stations designed in preparation for the exhibition year. A competition had been held and the winning one had Garnier's Opéra as a stylistic example (Charles Garnier – who died in 1898 – had appealed to the authorities to make the designs artistic, not industrial). The winning and other competition designs were, however, set aside, and Guimard was commissioned. His Métro entries were in cast metal: the gates were two stalk-like uprights that almost seemed to sway, and that curved up into buds from which flower-like glazed electric lamps protruded. Other 'branches' made the transverse, holding a panel inscribed *Métropolitain* in specially scrolled and floreated letters, all set in ornately panelled balustrades. In several stations (at the Place des Abbesses, for instance), the stalks 'grew' more robust to support a thinly mullioned glass roof. In spite of an aggressively damning press campaign, several of them – notably the one at Palais-Royal – have survived.[135]

As the Métro was further extended, new entries were needed; but in 1904 the station in front of Garnier's Opéra caused even more controversy than the earlier ones. Charles Garnier's style was back in opulent fashion, and Art Nouveau was out. A much more conventional and rigid surround to the underground entrances was now demanded. The architect of the blowsy, opulent and entirely 'academic' Pont Alexandre III (another World Exhibition project) designed the stone balustrades and cast-iron lamp standard which were adopted for later entries. Guimard's career went into reverse. His Métro designs were discontinued, and he did not receive other official commissions; his later career, when he retreated from his floreated extravagance to a sober Art Déco manner and made his way to New York, is not part of my story.

Meanwhile, new lithographic printing techniques produced vast areas of brightly coloured posters which were plastered on the advertising bollards and billboards, but also on the blank walls of the city – sometimes as multiple copies next to each other, repeated over and over so that they became the wallpaper of the 'public rooms' of the squares and boulevards, outdoor wallpapers with a difference. They provided a visual cacophony of bright colours, each one vying for the passer-by's attention. Many of them were the work of leading artists – I quoted Chéret and Toulouse-Lautrec, but they were joined by Théophile Steinlen and Alphonse Mucha (a Czech working in Paris). Their slogans and jingles entered daily speech and their bright colours were a vibrant part of the visual environment.

Mucha had arrived in Paris as a poor art student in 1887; employed by a commercial lithographic studio, he began, almost fortuitously, to work for Sarah Bernhardt at the end of 1894. For her he designed not only posters, but also jewellery, including the famous snake bracelet which curled up her arm but whose opal head with ruby eyes held a number of thin chains in its mouth, one of which was attached to an opal-and-gold finger-ring. Mucha was immediately seen by some as Chéret's heir and worked for many other smart patrons: Nestlé babyfood, Moët & Chandon champagne, exhibitions, and for other actresses. A friend of Gauguin, he held classes with Whistler and collaborated with Rodin. In fact, he became so notable that the *style Mucha* became almost synonymous with Yachting style, and the demand for his work was such that he was compelled to produce various series of lithographic decorative panels (about half the size of his posters – mostly two metres high) which were bought as frameable and multiple pictures. Like almost everything else he did at that time, his posters showed female figures scantily clothed. The style was opulent, but the imagery conventional: four seasons, four times of day, four flowers, four jewels – and Mucha's son insisted that his father always disciplined his florid designs by submitting them to the hypnotic charm of the Golden Mean.[136]

Both generous and improvident, Mucha remained insolvent in spite of all his success. In 1895 he moved to the United States, hoping to become a fashionable portrait-painter but did not make his fortune at this either. His Parisian fame was obscured by the quick exhaustion of Art Nouveau (of which more later) with which he was identified. Since he retained a strong attachment to his people and to the Slav cause, he returned to Prague in 1910 where his first major commission was for some stained-glass windows for St Vitus Cathedral. At the end of the war, Thomas Masaryk, who admired him, asked him to 'design' the visuals of the new republic: he 'styled' Czechoslovakia in a residual Art Nouveau manner.[137] The last twenty years of his life were devoted to a series of large panels illustrating the history of the Slav (particularly the Bohemian and Moravian) peoples in the inaccessible castle of Moravske Krumlovy as an example of his patriotic devotion. It may have seemed to him the only way to create a notable twentieth-century monument.

Indeed, it became increasingly difficult to make monuments as the nineteenth century advanced, since vast, unprecedented numbers of busts and statues were inserted in almost every city – not just of kings and emperors, dictators and generals but even of poets and painters. Their very numbers made them negligible. An acute observer even remarked: 'there is nothing in the world less visible than a monument'.[138] Their declamatory tone was, in any case, no longer audible in a city dominated by the advertising poster.

The New Monuments

Most public monuments of the time – the Victory Column in Berlin, the statues of the Strausses, Schubert, the Empress Elisabeth (Sissi) in Vienna, Chopin in Warsaw, *Peter Pan* and Prince Albert's vast one in London – were set in parks, away from traffic and the street hurly-burly. None of them has had any significance in the history of sculpture – or of architecture. Exceptionally, Victor Emmanuel II of Italy was given a vast pile (now colloquially known as the Pannetone – officially as Altare della Patria) on the edge of the Capitol Hill in Rome, which has completely re-structured the traffic patterns of the city, the only royal monument to rival the Roman ones in size. Queen Victoria's own display (2,300 tons of white marble, beside the bronze and gold leaf) in London by the now forgotten, unloved duo, Sir Thomas Brock (sculptor) and Sir Aston Webb (architect), was made into a traffic island – a *rond-point* – an early importation of the French traffic-control innovation. In New York, Augustus Saint-Gaudens' equestrian statue of General William Sherman on the edge of Central Park, which stands on a base designed by Charles McKim, was considered the equal of the great

Auguste Rodin, *The Gates of Hell*, 1880–*c.* 1900, bronze.

Renaissance horsemen, *Gattamelata* and *Colleoni*, at the time; now, like Queen Victoria, it occupies a traffic circle rather than a public space and is barely noticed.[139] Many critics felt that there was a glut of monuments. Both Henry James and Oscar Wilde before him remarked that Washington 'had too many bronze generals'.[140] The notable exceptions to this rather dismal summary are the ill-fated statues by Auguste Rodin, particularly the figure of Honoré de Balzac and the collective monument to the Burghers of Calais. They cannot be discussed here without reference to another unfortunate work of Rodin's, the *Gates of Hell*. Though it commemorates no ruler or hero, it does illustrate the problems artists experienced with the genre. Rodin would produce a number of other less important monuments as well.[141] Like many working sculptors of the time, he also had some experience of 'decorative' work. During his Brussels 'exile' (1871–6), he had earned a living doing caryatids, atlantes, allegories, jewellery, furniture – jobbing stuff, much of it unsigned. On his return to Paris, when a statue known as *The Age of Bronze* was exhibited, he was accused – wrongly – of making the figure up from casts taken from a living model.[142]

To console him for those accusations, his first official commission was for a huge composite bronze gate which was to illustrate themes from Dante's *Divine Comedy* (Rodin had chosen the subject himself) and to serve as entry to a new (but not yet identified) Museum of Decorative Arts.[143] He worked on it intermittently until his death in 1918 and left it unfinished,[144] but various separate figures which were part of the assemblage – the *Thinker*, the *Three Shades* – are among his best-known works.

The first drawn and clay sketches were for a more conventional gate, with a heavily framed two-leaf door, each leaf with four separate sculptured panels. But there is no indication as to how it was to relate to a building, since there was no project for a museum, nor is any architect mentioned in connection with the commission. Hector Lefuel, who had designed the part of the Louvre extension known as Pavillon de Marsan (which now houses the museum), had died in 1880, and its formation was a long drawn-out affair. Meanwhile Rodin was receiving substantial sums for the commission and 35,000 francs had even been set aside for the bronze cast in 1885 (only to be withdrawn in 1904 since it was not yet ready).

The nature of the door and its figuration was changing meanwhile. Rodin's disciple and friend Antoine Bourdelle was uncomfortable with the high relief of an early version; if the door were to be opened, he thought, it could pick out an eye – and Rodin himself observed that it 'had too many holes'. Bourdelle's main objection, however, was that he was not sure whether the thing was a wall or a door. When a new Museum of Contemporary Art was proposed in the state-requisitioned Seminary of St Sulpice, there was a suggestion that it should be set up there like an iconostasis, framed in and supported by a white marble surround.[145]

Such a surround was a matter of concern to Rodin, who gave a great deal of attention to mouldings. The nature of the profile and modenature is very striking in his study of French cathedrals, which was published towards the end of his life and whose last 23 plates (of 100) are all of profiles and mouldings – since 'The life of modenature is that of the whole building. It carries all the power of the architect, it expresses the whole of his thinking.' It was also the female element of the building: 'mouldings are soft symphonies'.[146] Rodin never resolved the surround to his own satisfaction and the *Gate* has remained a singular and unabsorbable object.

In 1891 the Société des Gens de Lettres (at Emile Zola's insistence) commissioned a monument to Balzac, which became yet another troubled episode in Rodin's career. At least 50 studies of various sizes were made before he decided on the definitive robed figure for which a new friend of his, the Belgian architect Frantz Jourdain,[147] was to design a moulded base. Rodin took a long time to arrive at that 'definitive' form, and meanwhile a series of rows – about money and politics as well as the statue – followed. In 1898, when it was finally exhibited, the Société rejected it.

The year 1894 brought another semi-official government commission, to design a monument to the nobility of labour, virtually a building of its own. To Rodin labour was opposed to mechanical production as typified by the Eiffel Tower, and his view may owe something – however indirectly – to Ruskin. The monument was to be a white marble tower within which a vaulted spiral stairway (in emulation of the famous one at Blois) rose about a central column. It was to be lined with a series of reliefs representing all human work in microcosm; starting underground with miners and divers, it would rise to poets, artists and philosophers, so that it became effectively an inside-out version of a Roman imperial column. It was to be crowned by two winged figures known as *The Benediction*. Rodin wanted to be buried in the crypt. The monument remained at model stage, however, as exhibited at the 1900 exposition, and later attempts to fund its realization were desultory.[148]

In 1884 national subscriptions raised enough money for another work and Rodin was again approached, this time by the city of Calais, for a monument to the six leading burghers who in 1347, dressed only in a shirt and with a halter round their necks, brought King Edward III the keys of their city and implored him to break his eleven-month-old siege.[149] For a century or more the city had intended to set up a monument to these citizens. Rodin first proposed to place the group on a plinth slightly higher than the figures (which were life-size, with bases of 1.90 metres), but by about 1890 had decided that he wanted them to stand directly on the pavement before the Hôtel de Ville so that they would become part of pedestrian movement within the square.[150] Inevitably, the commissioning committee would not hear of it, and he was compelled to design a 1.5-metre socle which was later surrounded with metal railings. Although this group suffered the usual troubles and indignities, it was completed in his lifetime. Damaged during the First World War, it was restored – and in 1923–4 – re-sited directly on the paving in front of the old town hall as Rodin had intended.[151]

As he 'designed' it, the *Burghers of Calais* was an anti-monument: those commemorated were not famous and recently dead, but quasi-mythical

Auguste Rodin, *The Burghers of Calais*, 1894–5, bronze.

heroes 'caught' at a crucial moment of their story. Their living fellow-citizens were invited to mix with them and so be raised to their epic level. The *Gates*, the tower and the Balzac statue have been interpreted as showing the failure of any monumental rationale.[152] They certainly demonstrate the disassociation between artist and builder, though the matter does not seem to have concerned any later commentators. More importantly, perhaps, they show the inability of the urban environment to absorb such refractory, indigestible features – and that is what Rodin had attempted to remedy in the Calais figures.[153]

Secession

In Vienna, in 1902 a polychrome statue – an Olympian, idealized *Beethoven* in marble, ivory, bronze, mother-of-pearl and semi-precious stone (seated on an ornate throne), by Max Klinger, the Leipzig painter-poet,[154] dominated the fourteenth exhibition (in April–June 1902) of the Secession, to become the centre of yet another art scandal such as were more usual there than in London, Paris or Berlin. Klinger had begun to work on it in the late 1880s, though it took him a decade to complete.

Max Klinger, *Beethoven in the Vienna Secession* setting, 1902, mixed media.

The Secession dominated art in the city after its foundation in 1896–7; a Salon des Refusés it had – as the name suggests – withdrawn from the official monopoly body, the Künstlergenossenschaft, which was the exhibiting branch of the Imperial Academy. Its exit was led by the most renowned painter of the time, Gustav Klimt, and it adopted the label of a Munich group which had been similarly founded in 1892. But the Vienna group was well connected: the emperor paid an official visit to the first show, and within a year it had acquired a site adjoining the Academy for its own exhibition hall. From the outset the work of some of the leading artists admired in Vienna was shown: Rodin, of course, Puvis de Chavannes, Mucha, Whistler, Crane and the leading Belgian symbolist, Ferdinand Khnopff.

One of its first members was the architect Otto Wagner, who – in 1893 – had won the competition for the development of Vienna. It involved regulating drainage and canals as well as a new electric urban railway network. The dams and sluices, bridges and stations were all designed by him; one of the first, elaborately and florally decorated, was for the use of the emperor and his suite near Schönbrunn palace. The new consciousness of the wall as a plane, the insubstantial nature of surface ornament the use of iron-and-steel structural members as self-sufficient decorative elements were all rapidly developed by Wagner in the last decade of the century. He was very much part of the Viennese art world, and held the exalted view that Klimt was 'the greatest artist who ever walked the earth'.[155] Yet though he owned several of his paintings, Wagner never commissioned Klimt to paint in, or to decorate, any of his buildings.

Younger Secession artists included Josef Maria Olbrich and Josef Hoffman (architects and Wagner's most brilliant pupils), Koloman Moser, a painter and decorator, other painters, Alfred Roller and Adolf Böhm, their advocates, the journalists and critics Hermann Bahr, Ludwig (sometimes Lajos) Hevesi, as well as Max Burkhard, a philosopher and civil servant who had become director of the Hof- (later Burg-) theatre and who also edited their journal, *Ver Sacrum*.

The primitive-sounding name *Ver Sacrum*,[156] and the sober rooms which Josef Hoffman contributed to the first Secession show, signalled that Art Nouveau linearity was on the wane. Wagner bid farewell to it with his most extreme exercise in the genre, an apartment block (40 Linke Wienzeile – also known as the Majolikahaus) with a five-storey street elevation wreathed in

J. M. Olbrich, the Vienna Secession building, 1897–8.

glazed terracotta coils of wild rose which terminated in monumental garlands under the roof. By 1899 next door (38, Linke Wienzeile), the floral ornament is tightly restricted to leafy rectangles over the edging pilasters. Olbrich's Secession building goes a step further: plant forms, natural growth, now no longer provide direct inspiration. Olbrich wanted to invoke the stunning impression made on him by the unfinished Doric temple at Segesta in Sicily. His vegetable ornament is therefore disciplined, even constricted within the simplest geometry. Most conspicuously, the primly-spherical main dome is made of gilt bronze bay leaves (which the Viennese nicknamed 'the Golden Cabbage') hemmed in by four squarish pylons, each one decorated by the new favourite motif, the chequerboard.

Viennese society may have been repressed and conventional, and the emperor's 'Apostolic Majesty' omnipresent with his army, clergy and his civil servants, but the city had a lively and entrepreneurial bourgeoisie determined on technical progress. As capital of the multi-language empire it was also cosmopolitan. Its intellectual elite was keenly aware of developments in Europe – and in America – but, of course, most acutely of what was happening in Germany. They read Schopenhauer and listened to (Richard) Wagner, so Klimt did not lack commissions: he had (with another painter) decorated the recently completed buildings of the Kunsthistorisches Museum and the Hoftheater to much acclaim, so that when the Ministry of Education commissioned ceiling paintings for the Great Hall of the new university, Klimt was given part of the work. Like his other mural decorations, these were done on canvas and suffer some of the limitations imposed by an easel format. When they were raised in position a storm of protest against their obscurity and irrationality forced the Ministry to remove them. Klimt returned his fee; the paintings went to private collectors – and with much of Klimt's other work were destroyed in a wartime fire.

The Secession met twice yearly. In 1900, for their sixth show, they invited Mackintosh as well as Ashbee's Guild of Handicraft to present their work in Vienna.[157] The climax of their activities was the transformation of the building for the 1902 showing of Klinger's *Beethoven* statue. Josef Hoffman was charged with transforming Olbrich's interior into a 'sanctuary . . . which the visitor may not enter unprepared'. Pale and creamy rough-cast walls were punctuated with inset abstract reliefs; Klimt's pictorial frieze, set as it was

Josef Hoffman and Gustav Klimt, 1902 Secession exhibition entrance.

with stones and mother-of pearl and gold leaf, was a first essay in what his apologists were to call his *Malmosaik*.[158] It guided the visitor through side-chambers into the main hall to face Klinger's brooding *Beethoven* set against a starry background painted by Alfred Roller. At the opening, Gustav Mahler was to conduct his orchestration of the last movement of Beethoven's Ninth symphony. If only temporarily, a *Gesamtkunstwerk* had been achieved – visible music.[159]

When the exhibition and all its contents (not the statue, of course), were destroyed (as was usual with such installations), agitation (and another scandal) saved Klimt's frieze. However, the Secession now only had two more shows of importance before it went into decline.[160] An epoch had come to a close, but most of the relevant players were hardly aware of the change.

Yet violent and rapid change in the public perception of science at this very time coincided with an unexpected development. The newsworthiness of biochemistry declined and the new phase was marked by Wilhelm Konrad Röntgen's discovery of the effect of x-rays in 1895.[161] Three years later Pierre and Marie Curie announced their discovery of two new and radioactive elements, polonium and radium. These two discoveries led to what might almost be called a chain reaction, so that biology – and even chemistry – were displaced from public attention. The great decade of the new physics culminated in the first publication of the General Theory of Relativity in 1905.

When Mahler conducted Beethoven at the opening of the Secession show, he had already (1893–6) composed his third symphony, originally sub-titled, after Friedrich Nietzsche, 'Joyful Knowledge'. Its climax, the vocal part, was the setting of a 'hymn' from the closing pages of Nietzsche's *Thus Spake Zarathustra* (*Oh Mensch! Gib Acht!*).[162] Nietzsche, the most powerful witness to a more insidious and perhaps more critical change which would shake Western philosophy, had died on 25 August 1900, even if he had been interned since the beginning of 1889, following a breakdown while on a visit to Turin. His fame was just beginning to spread as dementia struck, but his brooding absence (cherished first by his mother and then by his sister) would from then on dominate the German literary and artistic scene. 'Where don't they talk about Nietzsche!' a leading German poet, Otto Erich Hartleben, complained in his diary in 1890.[163]

Zarathustra Architect

Klimt's Greek gods and heroes owe much to Nietzsche who had been a pre-cocious student of Greek literature, particularly philosophy and tragedy; the dialectic he would now read into Greek tragedy – that between Apollo, the triumphant law-giving sun-god, and Dionysus, the dark god of rapture and unreason – had originally led him to Richard Wagner, whom he adu-lated for having revived it in the total work of art, the *Gesamtkunstwerk*, which would energize and revive a bourgeois society he saw as moribund.[164] Disappointment with Wagner would eventually turn the adulation into execration, however. Through the 1880s Wagner was blamed for having debased music to the level of entertainment, and for having, unjustifiedly, taken on the manner of a genius.

Allegedly, Nietzsche's last work, *Will to Power*, was in fact concocted by his sister, Elisabeth Förster-Nietzsche, with some help from others;[165] and although it traduced his thought in many ways, it was avidly read as his last, his definitive statement. By then his work and ideas were widely discussed (the first monograph on him appeared before his breakdown).[166] What so attracted many artists (even if they had only an approximate idea of his contradictory notions) was his wit and lyrical vehemence, his damning of the commercial vulgarities of his own time, his excoriating the epistemic arrogance of scientists – but also his rejection of Kantian aesthetics. Already in the *Genealogy of Morals* he had damned Kant's ultimate aesthetic criterion, 'purposeless purpose' (*Zweckmässigkeit ohne Zweck*) by contrasting it with Stendahl's 'beauty as the promise of happiness' (which he considered more apposite and revealing).[167] In his writings he fought many battles about art – against the extremes of formalism, against 'l'art pour l'art', which he condemns repeatedly as decadent, against art as imitation and art as an imitation of life. It is about this last idea that he is as vehement as he ever gets: having yet again invited his readers to 'respect the consistency of Christianity in conceiving the good man as ugly', he adds: 'For a philosopher to say "the good and the beautiful are one", is infamy; if he goes on to add "also the true", he should be thrashed. Truth is ugly. We possess art lest we perish of the truth.'[168]

Kantian aesthetics was, he considered, concerned with art as a spectator activity – receptive only and therefore exclusively feminine. What he called for was a masculine 'grand style'. This grand style, Nietzsche taught insistently, had to be 'classical', though not, of course, like the Neoclassical Herder or Goethe had imagined,

> who claimed to have rediscovered the classical ideal – and at the same time Shakespeare! . . . [they] desired 'nature', 'naturalness'; the stupidity! To believe that classicism was a kind of naturalness!

No,

To be classical, one must possess all the strong, seemingly contradictory gifts and desires – but in such a way that they go together beneath one yoke . . . reflect a total state (of a people or culture)

and again:

[The grand style] has this in common with great passion, that it disdains to please; that it forgets to persuade; that it commands; that it wills . . . No musician has yet built as that architect who created the Palazzo Pitti . . .

Architecture, in particular, at its best reconciles dark Dionysian power with Apollinian clarity:

it is the great act of will, the will that moves mountains . . . The most powerful men have always inspired architects . . . Architecture is a kind of eloquence of power in forms . . . The highest feeling of power and sureness finds expression in a grand style. The power which no longer needs any proof, which spurns pleasing, which does not answer lightly, which feels no witness near, which is oblivious to all opposition, which reposes within itself – fatalistically – as a law among laws – that bespeaks the grand style.[169]

SIX

The Geometry of Disenchantment

Enchantment, Disenchantment

In June 1902 the vast International Exhibition of Decorative Art opened in Turin and asserted the triumph of the new style. The organizers did not realize which way the wind was blowing. But Turin, as the most energetically industrialized city in Italy, had much in common with Barcelona and Nancy, and with Brussels or Glasgow where the style had flourished, so it was an obvious setting for such an event. The poster which announced it displayed four white-robed ladies who swirled white scarves, Loïe Fuller-wise, as they pranced over a flower-strewn lawn.[1]

Many of the designers and artists I mentioned in the last chapter were invited to contribute. Walter Crane chaired the exhibition jury; Scotland had a separate section from the rest of Britain to mark the importance of the Glasgow group.[2] The pavilions were opulent, the tone of their apologists celebratory, yet the eclipse of Art Nouveau – and of the whole notion of a 'decorative art' with it – was already evident in the details. The design of the main pavilion and of the public section went out to competition, and was won by a Venetian architect, Raimondo d'Aronco, the court-architect to the Ottoman sultan in Istanbul at the time. The dome of the central hall, shored by flying buttresses, was crowned by bigger-than-life plaster ladies who acted as their pinnacles – all of it was more figurative and *mouvementé* than Josef-Maria Olbrich (d'Aronco's acknowledged master) would have endorsed. In his own work of the time, as in d'Aronco's floral ornament, a stiffening was evident, however, and panels of chessboard black-and-white pattern (also borrowed from Olbrich's Secession building) obtrude harshly into the ornamental flow that had been the blazon of the new style.[3]

In the months following the show, some of its most prominent exhibitors, without explicitly abjuring their past work or offering any account of the change, would move into a quite different mode. Peter Behrens (just over 30 at the time) was perhaps the most radical of such turncoats (and – later – the most successful of them). His contribution to the German section in Turin, the 'Hamburg Hall', was brooding, stiff and stilted – as if all the whip and tension had already drained out of his whirling lines. Melodramatically lit, it was later nicknamed 'the tomb of Superman'.[4]

Nietzsche's Geometry

Like most of his contemporaries, Peter Behrens had fallen under the Nietzsche spell, and written fulsome letters to Elisabeth Förster-Nietzsche.[5] By 1901 his unsmiling version of *Jugendstil* was hardening; its ironic-satirical aspect (the style was named from the magazine *Jugend*, which was, after all, a 'humorous' monthly) seems to have eluded him and was quite lost in the earnestness with which a new, 'national' (theatrical but sombre) style was to invigorate Germany. There was little of the laughing Nietzschean dance about it.

J. M. Olbrich,
Mathildenhöhe
exhibition
entrance,
Darmstadt,
1901.

Behrens' House, Mathildenhöhe, Darmstadt, 1901–2.

A year before the Turin exhibition Behrens had been one of the organiz-ers of an equally ambitious show, which opened in Darmstadt on 15 May 1901. The occasion was the ceremonial handing-over of a new studio building for the artists' settlement on the Mathildenhöhe (a hill overlooking the town) to its patron, Ernst Ludwig, Grand Duke of Hesse-Darmstadt. It celebrated the completion of the artists' colony and the redemption of a promise the duke had made when he inveigled them to build themselves homes on that hill. Designed by Olbrich, as was most of the settlement, its tall north-light win-dows were echoed by blank walls on the main, south-facing facade. The cen-tral, mosaicked portal in it was flanked by two giant semi-nude tufa figures (one male, one female), carved by a very successful local sculptor, Ludwig Habich.[6] On the stairway leading up to it, the ceremony – almost a ritual – was acted out. It had been staged, choreographed, designed in every detail by Peter Behrens to a vapid script by his old friend, the playwright-poetaster Georg Fuchs, and was chanted to music provided by the court conductor, Willem de Haan. *Das Zeichen*, 'The Sign', its title, was taken from the last chapter of Nietzsche's *Zarathustra*. Backed by a choir, two actors, 'man' and 'woman' (who echoed Habich's giant figures), hymned the entry of the hero,

Organizer Georg Fuchs'
performance of *Das
Zeichen*, Darmstadt,
1901.

a scarlet-robed actor who played a herald or prophet, the Verkünder – 'glowing and strong, as the morning sun' – just like Zarathustra. To the sound of trumpets he unveiled a casket containing a crystal which he then 'elevated' before the grand duke (who played himself – in gala uniform), and carried it back into the new building.

'Libretto' and music were published as part of *Ein Dokument deutscher Kunst*. The book also had an insert on hand-made paper to display Behrens's project for his Darmstadt house. Under the same title appeared a Nietzscheanly phrased (but un-Nietzscheanly servile) address to the grand duke:

> Thanks are due to him who has the great Will – and the Power – to exalt it into Action and to a beautiful grandeur . . . [and continues] We want to live laughing in our luminous times, we have forgotten our dreams, we have been awoken, we are awake. Hail, our awaker, in the sun's glow![7]

240

The address was elaborately ornamented in residually Art Nouveau (but stiffened) arabesques designed by Behrens: it had the image of a radiating crystal as a frontispiece, a crystal shaped like a diamond. 'Carbon', Fuchs proclaimed, 'though it is merely compressed dust, can be compacted tightly into crystalline diamond' – much as the gritty modern mob could be fused into a hard, unified community when transformed by art.

In the last years of the nineteenth century, or so I suggested in the previous chapter, there had been a shift in the popular perception of science: in the first two or three years of the twentieth century dry, sparkling, multi-faceted crystals would replace the dank and convoluted vitality to which *fin-de-siècle* artists looked for model and inspiration. This marked a rapid change in the fashion or, at any rate, in the mood of the time.[8] Even if Behrens made that angular crystal or diamond look like a jeweller's advertisement, it was meant to suggest radiance – the diamond was to be the beacon of a new society.

The Darmstadt festival 'scene' had been coloured by a Wagnerian vision of performance as a social generator. Georg Fuchs, Behrens' collaborator on *Das Zeichen*, was a committed 'modernist', a strong advocate of *Jugendstil* and of the Munich Sezession, as well as an enemy of the conventional stage – the peep-show box or *Gukkasten*, as he called it. Since he had addressed a pamphlet to the newly installed Grand duke urging him to patronize such an enterprise some years earlier,[9] he was called to Darmstadt when Ernst Ludwig needed a spokesman for his *Künstlerkolonie*. With his friend (and much better poet), Richard Dehmel, Fuchs had a more ambitious project which also involved Peter Behrens. Dehmel's *Mass of Life* – oratorio rather than opera – was to be staged in a hemispherical (or at any rate circular) theatre designed for it at Darmstadt. Dehmel never quite completed the *Mass*, nor was Behrens' theatre – a radical development of the Bayreuth one – ever built.[10]

Behrens, the painter and graphic designer, turned himself into a designer-architect as quickly as Van de Velde had already done – though without even a nod to the Ruskin–Morris joy-through-handwork ethos. His Darmstadt house with its relative sobriety and shapely verticality, its linear composition (all praised by several critics of the time), was favourably compared with the insistent horizontality and more exuberant forms of Olbrich's neighbouring one, and provided a better indication of his future direction than the showier Turin hall.[11] Yet Behrens' rather sinuous furniture still looked very much like that which Van de Velde had designed for himself at Uccle ten years earlier.

Olbrich, being a trained and already accomplished architect, had priority in Darmstadt by ducal favour. Feeling constrained, Behrens moved to Düsseldorf to become head of the art and design school there, taking with him the sculptor Rudolph Bosselt, one of the original Darmstadt artists. He also invited another old Munich friend, the Russian painter Wassily Kandinsky, as well as Josef Hoffman, Otto Wagner's other brilliant pupil from Vienna – though neither would come. Nor would the great Dutch architect, Hendrik Petrus Berlage, whose most famous building, the Amsterdam Beurs, the Stock Exchange, had just been finished to great acclaim. Berlage was an insistent, dogmatic explorer of geometric proportion, and the Stock Exchange was controlled by the 'Egyptian' ratio, which has three units of height to five of base (which approximates to the Golden Section), though he also advocated the 'Pythagorean' triangle, 3:4:5, in his lectures, as well as proportions derived from the square inscribed in and circumscribed by the circle.[12] To Behrens he recommended a disciple, J.L.M. Lauweriks (a committed and proselytizing theosophist). In a lecture he gave at the Zürich Polytechnic (of which he was a graduate), Berlage even illustrated the work of two of Lauweriks' Düsseldorf pupils who used geometry dogmatically; one of them, Adolf Meyer, would become Walter Gropius' partner when they left Behrens' office in 1912.[13]

Research into the validity and appeal of geometrical proportion favoured by formalist thinkers as well as the psychologists of the Fechner school had been explored by a number of German architects and teachers, and this led to its application by many architects and artists.[14] Behrens' interest in these researches helped him to move from a flowing Art Nouveau linearity (after 1901), through stern blockiness (1902–3), to a chastened (but still linear) manner, straightened by a new proportional rigorism and a dogmatic exploration of elementary geometry (after 1904), much as a century and a half earlier the Adam brothers had turned vegetative rocaille sinuosities into the geometries of a neo-antique style.

An early essay in this new manner brought Behrens up against Van de Velde. The fabulously wealthy (and then very young) patron-collector Karl-Ernst Osthaus had commissioned Van de Velde to design a sequence of interiors for his private Folkwang Museum[15] in the small Westphalian town, Hagen, but he had failed to provide a satisfactory scheme for a lecture hall. For Behrens it became an exercise in the style which he had begun to develop. In this case a square-in-circle motif and the application of an isosceles triangle of 40 degrees at the base resulted in a 2:3 relation.[16] Behrens also became the planner for part of Hagen and was commissioned to design a large Protestant church for the town (it was not built). He did complete three rather large private houses, though there were problems both of design and execution. Osthaus then had Van de Velde build him a huge villa called Hohe Warte within the Behrens plan to house his private collection – Cézanne, Vuillard, Gauguin, Maillol, as well as the German Expressionist[17] works he had bought earlier; Van de Velde also devised all the furnishing and the decoration.

Behrens went on to design and build a number of houses and some very monumental exhibition pavilions over the next few years, temporary buildings given hieratic solemnity by his assertive use of geometry as a determinant of the general shape and scribed on the exterior as ornamental traces.[18] The climax of this period is the crematorium he designed at Delsten (near Hagen) in Westphalia, a commission which also came to him through Osthaus. As the first crematorium in Prussian lands, it was to establish the 'type' – and Behrens based it (somewhat sentimentally) on the small Romanesque (or perhaps more accurately, proto-Renaissance) black and white marble church of San Miniato al Monte, on a hillside overlooking Florence, where it is surrounded by a churchyard. The hill at Delsten allowed

Peter Behrens, Delsten Crematorium, 1905–7.

for the layout of an analogous columbarium round the chapel (which was never completed), while the *campanile* of the church was transformed into the furnace chimney.[19]

As in all Behrens' buildings of the time, the crematorium walls were ornamented with (or, at any rate, articulated by) geometrical tracings – black and white marble inlays. In the interior, the apse over the tabernacular catafalque carried an (allegedly Ravenna-style) gold-ground mosaic by another friend of Behrens', the rather bookish painter Emil Weiss.[20] He also used work by Rudolf Bosselt, his Darmstadt and Düsseldorf colleague, elsewhere but always as a garnish, not integrally. He once confessed that the artist he really admired was Aristide Maillol, the most prominent French sculptor of the generation after Rodin.[21]

The Mathildenhöhe inauguration ceremonies I described earlier were Ernst Ludwig's wager in the culture stakes which mattered to some German princes as the twentieth century opened. Although Ernst-Ludwig was highly connected (his sister Alexandra was married to Tsar Nicholas II,[22] and Queen Victoria was his maternal grandmother), the ethos of his court was nourished by Nietzsche's preaching about the primacy of a coming aristocracy – not the hereditary one of blood, but a higher one of daring and power. In a prosperous pre-war period, dominated by the famously philistine emperor, Wilhelm II, cultural daring showed a certain independence and staked the claim to more exalted nobility.[23]

Darmstadt's only venerable cultural showpiece was a fine library. The town could not rival some other small capitals – notably Weimar – where Martin Luther had preached and the Cranachs (father and son) had worked; Herder had been the pastor of its main church and Goethe prime-minister; Wieland, Jean-Paul, Schiller and von Humboldt had made their home there, as Liszt would later; Wagner's *Lohengrin* was first performed in its theatre. Moreover, Nietzsche's widowed sister, Elizabeth Förster-Nietzsche,[24] had brought the demented, barely conscious philosopher to Weimar in 1897, to the Villa Silberblick, where she showed him off – 'Europe's grandest putrescence' – to assorted visitors, and where he died towards the end of August 1900.[25] The house was to be maintained as an archive and study centre as well as a monument, a pilgrimage goal. The help of his polyglot, cosmopolitan disciple Count Harry Kessler (who had assisted in casting his death-mask and closed the philosopher's eyes in his coffin) was enlisted.[26] Henry Van de Velde, whom Kessler had brought to Berlin to design his palatial apartment (which was dominated by Seurat's *Poseuses*),[27] arranged the library and public rooms. Later Max Klinger provided the marble herm crowned by a heroic portrait (based on the Kessler death-mask) to serve as its focus. Van de Velde also designed the layouts and bindings for the first luxury edition of *Zarathustra*, which Kessler was to have printed.[28]

Mrs Förster-Nietzsche also wanted to act as the hostess of a *salon*, so that the archive could be to Weimar what the Villa Wahnfried was to Bayreuth.[29] But she had problems organizing the archive, and consulted the well-estab-lished Goethe-Schiller one,[30] where she met the brilliant and charismatic Rudolf Steiner, a promising young philosopher and one of the leading experts on Goethe's scientific teachings. She invited him to catalogue her brother's (much annotated) library with a view to further collaboration and even had Steiner give her private lessons about her brother's philosophy. She also intro-duced him into the presence. He was profoundly moved – and wrote a book on Nietzsche as a critic of his times.[31]

Meanwhile, the young and vacillating Grand-Duke Ernst Wilhelm of Saxe-Weimar, who succeeded his grandfather in 1901, also saw himself in a Nietzschean role. There was talk of a 'third' Weimar (the first being Goethe's, the second Liszt's) and Elisabeth Förster-Nietzsche urged him to call on Kessler, whose critical acumen, contacts and great energy could be harnessed; he was appointed director of the Ducal Museum of Arts and Crafts (which had ample room for exhibitions), as well as ducal adviser on matters of design. At the Museum he arranged a succession of exhilarating shows: Courbet, Klinger, Lieberman, Monet, the Post-Impressionists,[32] Munch, Gauguin, Kandinsky – and Rodin – which last caused his fall: a splendid watercolour nude inscribed by Rodin to the Duke was judged obscene, and the dedication therefore an act of *lèse-majesté*. Kessler was accused of favour-ing pornography and was publicly snubbed by the duke, and so lost his court position. For all that, he continued to live in the house Van de Velde had made over for him, with its high wainscots and the decorative panels by Maurice Denis. And he remained an active, important figure in Weimar until 1933.[33]

Kessler saw his and Van de Velde's endeavours as rivalling the Darmstadt colony. He, too, attempted to entice various artists to Weimar. Dehmel (and his wife) toyed with the idea of living there – but demurred. Eduard Munch did spend time there, and painted some splendid portraits of Kessler. Hugo von Hofmannsthal (who was collaborating with him on the libretto for Richard Strauss' *Rosenkavalier*) was offered the direction of the theatre but did not stay. Van de Velde was also appointed adviser on art to the court *(Hofrat)* and survived Kessler's disgrace: he reformed the local art school and organized an Arts and Crafts one.[34] Another potential resident was the (by then famous) actress Louise Dumont and her producer husband, Gustav Lindemann, who had commissioned a new theatre from Van de Velde in Berlin. When its building was blocked by the authorities, they decided to start a festival – a prose Bayreuth – in Weimar. Local rivalries (and more ducal shilly-shallying) stymied that project as well.[35] Like Behrens' theatre for the Dehmel *Mass of Life*, Van de Velde's was an early attempt to consolidate the Wagnerian stage: the apron was suppressed, the auditorium raked, and a few boxes were set half-way up the slope.[36] His drawings and models were known to the rising producer, Max Reinhardt (who was being urged to have Van de Velde also design a theatre for him), and to Edward Gordon Craig, the son of the great actress Ellen Terry by William Godwin (I mentioned him earlier as Oscar Wilde's and James Whistler's architect), who was to become one of the most important reformers of the theatre after 1900 and whose visit to Weimar involved him in Van de Velde's projects.[37]

To focus all these disparate endeavours, Kessler wanted to create a stately, spacious Nietzsche monument in Weimar – much grander than the archive – and make it the setting for quasi-ritual gymnastic-balletic festivities. Van de Velde worked through several projects for a temple-tomb and a stadium-theatre. In front of the temple there was to be a giant statue of *Superman Apollo* by Aristide Maillol. Vaslav Nijinski, first dancer of the *Ballets Russes*, was to model for *Apollo*, while the interior was to be carved (or modelled?) into 'Dionysan' reliefs by Max Klinger.[38] Starting as a Greek-type temple, the proposal passed through several increasingly unsatisfactory stages. Van de Velde's projected temple, with its choir-gallery and organ, was thought too lumpy to prove acceptable (even to his faithful friend and admirer Kessler). In any case, Elisabeth Förster-Nietzsche vetoed it, and the duke at first opposed it, then saw it briefly as a source of profit. Even if the idea had many powerful supporters – Prince Bülow, the German Chancellor, for one, but also assorted literary notables such as André Gide, Anatole France, Gabriele d'Annunzio, Gilbert Murray, Bernard Shaw and H. G. Wells – the war intervened and nothing ever came of sculptures, temple or stadium.[39]

The programme for the monument, and its failure, must be seen in relation to the almost obsessional interest of many artists (and their audiences!) in the devising of quasi-religious, proto-religious – even anti-religious – rituals such as I described at Darmstadt after Nietzsche had announced the death of God:

> How but in custom and in ceremony
> are innocence and beauty born?

asked Yeats, echoing Nietzsche, consciously or unconsciously.[40]

Such public 'happenings' – conspicuously, the Darmstadt *Zeichen* – might, some thought, 'realize' a public and a monumental time and turn into a *Gesamtkunstwerk*. Public space was increasingly difficult to constitute and no longer offered a credible site or shelter for common experience. Some of the best minds and talents of the time became involved in developing new forms of dramatic, even balletic performance, in the hope of galvanizing a place by 'filling' it with occasions. The ritualizing of the theatre and its offshoots seemed to offer the middle and upper classes a setting for social integration and transformation. Yeats' aphorism, when he spoke of his plays as 'not drama, but the ritual of a lost faith', summed up the almost obsessive interest in the social benefits of participatory ritual as part of a religiosity without a deity;[41] it had already been implied in Wagner's demand for a building which, if not the vital public space of past centuries, would at least offer a surrogate for the common experience of public time by imposing solemn and fervent attention on the audience. Not only the familiar horseshoe plan and even the tiered, pseudo-antique semicircular auditorium (favoured by earlier nineteenth-century reformers) were suitable for Wagnerian purposes: his audience had to be unified, *gleichgeschaltet* – no barriers of class or ticketing between gallery, boxes and stalls; all, as one body, were to concentrate on the spectacle-ritual on the stage. The orchestra, too, had to be concealed under the stage-apron so as not to obstruct the view or distract from the spectacle.

Housing the *Gesamtkunstwerk*

Theatre architects or managers may not have satisfied Wagner's exacting demands, yet in the spate of late nineteenth- and early twentieth-century German theatre building, boxes were increasingly eliminated, stalls extended (following Bayreuth), while the exteriors were becoming more monumental as befitted the temples of the age.[42] The Schiller Theatre in Charlottenburg (1906) and the Munich Künstlertheater a year or two later, both designed by Max Littman, were conspicuous examples of the tendency;[43] stages, too, were being extended and mechanically equipped so that *almost* any illusion could be achieved on them; Littman – not Van de Velde – also designed the new Weimar one in an updated 'Empire' style on the grand duke's recommendation. The Weimar Republic would be inaugurated there in 1918.[44]

Looking back over this period, the great sociologist Max Weber was to state their problem clearly, warning that:

> It is the fate of our time, with all its intellectualizing and rationalizing – above all, with its disenchantment of the world – that the ultimate, most sublime values have withdrawn from the public sphere either into the other-worldly realm of the mystical life or into the fraternity of direct personal contact. It is no accident that our greatest art is intimate rather than monumental . . . When we try to force or 'invent' a sense of the monumental we get wretched monstrosities such as many of the monuments built in the last twenty years. When we try to advance new religions without a new and true prophecy, we have something profoundly similar, which will produce even worse results . . . [45]

Ritual without Dogma

In spite of such misgivings, both left- and right-wing movements had held devotional meetings with sermons and hymns and pious readings emulating the Positivist 'church' founded by Auguste Comte.[46] Mallarmé's 'hidden project', to institute a quasi-religious ceremony (quite different from Wagner's, of course, but equally solemn – if more intimate), might be considered one early extreme 'aesthetic' instance of this tendency. He had never made a secret of his belief that 'the world existed only to give birth to the Beautiful Book' (I capital-ize – as he sometimes did) and he even maintained (as he did to his young friend, Paul Valéry) that this book already existed, that it was the 'Orphic' explanation of the world'.[47] Mallarmé never succeeded in giving the Book final form, but it has been inferred from his papers. He seems to have conceived it as a loose-leaf album (of some 960 pages), sections of which would be recited or performed at regular intervals. The rustle of turning pages was to be part of the ritual, whose nature is not otherwise explained. He may have thought of it as a cosy, a domestic occasion (like a civil wedding perhaps), though he was known to admire the Oxbridge academic ceremonies he had witnessed during his English visit in March 1894. In some way his rite was analogous to the Mass, even if it needed no other music than the sound of the words – perhaps because Mallarmé himself was an enchanting, mellifluous speaker.[48] His own attitude to music had – anyway – been ambivalent, intensely conscious as he was of the sound-value of his poems.[49]

Le Livre celebrated God as a psychological, not a theological truth,[50] the intimate God 'within' – not at all the 'social' deity Comte had proclaimed or Feuerbach theorized. Mallarmé almost certainly intended the ritual reading of the *Livre* to have the transforming effect of a *Gesamtkunstwerk* on the partic-ipants, though his ritual seems too bland and withdrawn, too demure to make any impact even on an 'aesthetic' elite in the Dionysan atmosphere of the 1890s and the early twentieth century.[51]

At the other extreme, the Bolshevik party was also not immune from rit-ualist ambitions. Anatoly Lunacharsky, one of Lenin's faithful, infuriated his chief in the early days of their collaboration (1905 and after) by setting up (with the help of Maxim Gorky) a plan for 'God-building', *Bogostroitelstvo*, a religiosity for socialism.[52] In so far as a deity – even one that was a social con-struct – was involved in this 'building', Lenin found Gorky's and Lunacharsky's activities highly objectionable at the time,[53] and his successors soon ensured that any such celebrations would be dragooned into military-style parades for which there was much precedent in the gymnastic displays which were becoming increasingly popular at the turn of the century.[54]

There were many for whom such celebrations were not enough. Those whose 'disenchantment with the world' (in Weber's phrase) prompted them to seek 'the other-worldly realm of the mystical' sought a 'fraternity of personal contact'. Some of the occult movements that proliferated at the time offered just that. The most widespread of these groups, the Theosophical Society, acknowledged the Russian mystagogue Helena Petrovna Blavatsky as its founder.[55] The Society had many followers in Germany and in 1902 a branch was founded in Munich. Rudolf Steiner, Elisabeth Förster-Nietzsche's friend, had early been in contact with the group and became its secretary. Being a much more rigorous thinker than any of the Theosophist propagandists, he never quite accepted the Blavatskian revelation. Even when he was working with them, he was already promoting a rather different revelation of his own which he called anthroposophy. It continues to have a wide following, especially in Germany.[56] Since Steiner's teaching had been formulated as the result of a private revelation, it could also be divulged as he and his associates chose. Steiner was very interested in contemporary science and his teaching was dogmatically evolutionary (the biologist Ernst Haeckel was a friend, even an occasional collaborator) and he always insisted on its importance.[57] He was, moreover, very involved in contemporary art, particularly literature: Otto Erich Hartleben had been a friend and collaborator in Weimar, and as the editor of a literary magazine, Steiner befriended some Expressionist writers: Frank Wedekind and Paul Scheerbart, as well as Adolf Loos' poet friend, Peter Altenberg. Later, Christian Morgenstern became a faithful devotee.

Goethe's biology and his colour theory remained crucial to him, and he developed a psycho-occult version of synaesthesia from it. As his teaching evolved and his following grew, Steiner incorporated his message in a way of life in which a 'dynamic-biologic' agriculture combined organic methods with astrological observations. He also developed various therapeutic techniques.[58] With his wife he devised an art of performance which they called 'eurhythmy'. Eurhythmic rituals became an essential part of his cult and the Goetheanum at Dornach near Berne the central shrine for their performance. He designed it himself as two interlocking cylinders, like a giant nut, since a nut is both fruit and seed. In the interior seven columns support the stage-dome and twelve the auditorium, twelve and seven being sympathetic to each other as the sum and the product of three and four. All the columns were heavily carved to illustrate – esoterically – Goethe's poem, *Die Metamorphose der Pflanzen*, and the dome was painted by Steiner himself with heavy, symbolic, Expressionist images. Since the plays performed in the building were also written by him and eurhythmically performed, the whole of anthroposophy could be interpreted as a total work of art – and it certainly was meant to transform its audience.[59]

At the beginning of the century Munich had not yet been overtaken by Berlin as an artistic centre. It had long attracted Russian refugees of all professions and political colours. Wassily Kandinsky, the scion of a family which had opposed the oppressive tsarist regime for generations, had thought that art was a luxury which Russia could ill afford. He therefore first decided to be an economist and lawyer rather than an artist. Soon peasant customary law, which seemed more humane than the official code (derived, as it was, from Roman precedent), became a passionate interest. By analogy he came to appreciate peasant art, devotional woodcuts (*luboki* – which he collected) and the painted carvings of peasant houses. A proficient ethnographer, in the course of his studies he acquired an extensive knowledge of the art of Western Siberia and of Eskimo Shamanism. The brightly painted, icon-and-embroidery-filled peasant houses seemed the promise of a realized *Gesamtkunstwerk* to him.[60]

Having learnt from the work of Richard Wagner and Claude Monet that art could indeed transform society, he decided to become a painter when he moved to Munich in 1896, attracted by all the *Jugendstil* activities as well as its colony of Russian exiles. A prolific engraver, he was also constantly involved in 'applied art', designing metal, leather, beadwork, embroidery, even women's dresses – all implicitly part of some new and yet generalized and total work of art. He was also in contact with a number of esoteric figures: Steiner's explicit appeal to Christian mystics, particularly Jakob Boehme, he found sympathetic, as he did Steiner's interest in colour symbolism and in synaesthesia; above all it was his teaching that echoed Kandinsky's own beliefs. In a much quoted aphorism, he defined the inner content of art as a 'speaking of the invisible by means of the visible'.[61]

Kandinsky had become the animator of a dissident artists' group in Munich, a further secession from the original Munich Secession around the turn of the century. Called 'Phalanx', it organized exhibitions; the second had a large section devoted to the Darmstadt artists, while the fourth was entirely devoted to Monet. 'Phalanx' was wound up in 1904 when Kandinsky (whom Behrens had not succeeded in recruiting for his Düsseldorf school) moved to Paris. While he was impressed by Symbolist art, as well as by the paintings of the *Fauve* group, particularly Matisse, and his own work had something in common with Vuillard's and Bonnard's, he was already moving from his folkloric-*Jugendstil* manner to an increasingly abstract approach. Art-politics would absorb much of his energy. A new group now formed around Franz Marc, Paul Klee, August Macke, Alfred Kubin and Alexei von Jawlensky. There was to be a yearly publication – an almanac, *Der Blaue Reiter* – which Kandinsky edited with Marc. They gave space to the work of a musician whom they did not yet know personally (but whose music had much impressed Kandinsky), Arnold Schoenberg; one of his earliest (and most successful) compositions, *Verklärte Nacht* (published as his Opus 4), was based on a sequence of poems by Peter Behrens' friend, Richard Dehmel.[62] Schoenberg was close to the Weimar–Darmstadt Wagnerian transcription of word and mood into tonal colour, but he was also becoming well-known as a painter and exhibited with the Blaue Reiter group; Kandinsky wrote an extended essay on Schoenberg's pictures.[63]

The group, perhaps Franz Marc was the first, was also impressed by a young art historian Wilhelm Worringer; he had heard Lipps lecture in Munich, and became convinced that though the concept of empathy which Lipps and many critics and historians believed to have universal validity might describe the smooth experience of Italian (particularly Renaissance) painting and sculpture adequately, it could not account for the experience of spiky, harsh, yes, crystalline Northern or Islamic or primitive art. It thus led to wholly different formal conceptions, and Worringer sets out the conditions of abstraction which this realization requires: 'A return to the plane surface, a suppression of the organic, crystalline-geometric composition.'[64] By moving away from direct representation and making any reference to the appearance of the outside world increasingly tenuous, Kandinsky had taken a decisive step towards a form of abstraction, towards a painting which aspired to the condition of music. There was, to his mind, a constant dialogue between music and painting, since painting can allow the spectator a complete view of the work in one instant, while music is bound to the passing of time. It was a dichotomy which could be resolved only in the synthesis of dance.[65]

'Pure', 'abstract' painting (reduced to the condition of music, therefore) interested an increasing number of artists around 1910. Kandinsky even thought that such a change was implied in some of Claude Monet's later paintings. Independently it had been tried a few years earlier by Nicolas Čiurlionis, a young Lithuanian settled in St Petersburg – and a friend of Gorky.[66] It became, too, the slogan of Rayonism, the movement made up of Natalia Goncharova and Mikhail Larionov (and some later interlopers) who, like Kandinsky and other Russian artists, rediscovered folk art (popular woodcuts especially) and had the same passionate interest in theatre and dance.

Modest Moussorgsky had 'translated' the posthumous exhibition of watercolours by his friend Viktor Gartman – an architect – into a piano suite, *Pictures at an Exhibition*; some 40 years later Kandinsky 're-translated' Moussorgsky's music back into completely abstract colours and shapes.[67] He took this synaesthetic approach further, and composed whole 'operas' (or at any rate, fragmentary librettos, stage directions for scenes or 'pictures'). The texts were sometimes made up of nonsense words, while the stage instructions seem improbable. The titles insisted on their synaesthetic character: *The Yellow Sound, The Green Sound, Black and White, Violet*.[68] Performances were to be true *Gesamtkunstwerke*, and were planned as a dialogue between 'pure' visual elements – colour, sound, motion – and a puppet-like vocabulary of gesture; they were to have a liberating effect on the audience, but never in fact took place.

Musicians and synaesthetic artists had some impatience with the conventions of current building; the unity of sound, light and colour seemed to require, or perhaps even create, its own space, independent of any existing structure.

The *Blaue Reiter Almanack*[69] also published an analytical article on Alexander Scriabin's *Prometheus*,[70] the first musical composition to have a 'projected' colour part explicitly notated for a light-clavier (which was treated as if it were one of the instruments of the orchestra), perhaps the most famous single synaesthetic work. Scriabin's whole creative process seemed centred in fact on synaesthesia.

The score of *Prometheus* had been published in Moscow in 1913 bound in a flamboyant cover designed by the Belgian theosophist-painter, Jean Delville, a latter-day Art Nouveau figure. Delville's dreamy, Symbolist imagining was too smooth and old-fashioned to appeal to the Blaue Reiter group, however. Scriabin's work, on the other hand, seemed to transcend mere matters of style and taste. The *Almanack* article had been written by Leonid Sabaneyev (a pupil of Moussorgsky), who saw *Prometheus* as the logical outcome of Scriabin's development which begins with his first symphony[71] (a 'Hymn of Art as Religion'), while the third, the *Poème de l'extase*, celebrates the rapture of creation. The ecstasy of the Third Symphony title was to be induced by the music, by lights and by a concert of aromas, and Sabaneyev compares the combined effect of the different 'willed' and dominating procedures (music, the word, gesture) and the non-willed ones (light, aroma) to a solemn celebration of an Orthodox liturgy.[72]

Although it has entered several conductors' repertoires, *Prometheus* is hardly ever performed with the colour 'score'; it had been a flop at the 1911 première in Moscow since the colour-keyboard broke down.[73] Despite such technical difficulties, even *Prometheus* was not ambitious enough for Scriabin, who spent his last years planning a cosmic 'liturgy' which was to be celebrated in a hemispherical temple on a lake island so that its reflection might 'complete' the sphere. He called it *Mystère*. The temple was to be built in India with the help of British theosophists, and the 2,000 spectators it would accommodate were to be grouped hieratically round the poet-seer who would be its 'celebrant'. Nor could the building be used for any other purpose. He did not complete the score (never mind perform it), nor was there ever a hemispherical temple – which may be just as well since Scriabin believed that a performance would render the whole phenomenal world redundant.[74]

Like Kandinsky's 'operas', so Scriabin's last works went well beyond the technical possibilities of contemporary stagecraft – and indeed if these Russo-Bavarian synaesthetic experiments now seem exotic, even more extreme developments of such machinery were taking place in Britain and the United States. Two more or less elaborate electronic colour-organs were built and patented, one by a British painter, Wallace Rimington, in 1895, and another by an American pianist, Mrs Mary Hallock Greenewalt, between 1906 and 1910.[75] The most ambitious was the *Clavilux* devised by a Danish (naturalized American) folk-singer, Thomas Wilfred. He performed on it at various locations in London and Paris as well as in his own church-like 'Art-Institute of Light'. He had an enthusiastic associate in the architect who designed a studio for him on Long Island, Claude Bragdon, a friend of Louis Sullivan and a committed follower of Madame Blavatsky. In his introductory theoretic work,

Bragdon, restated – in terms parallel to Kandinsky's – the music/visual art analogy, but in relation to architecture, not dance:

> Music being purely in time, and architecture being purely in space, each is, in a manner and to a degree not possible with any of the other arts, convertible into the other . . . A perception of this may have inspired the famous saying that architecture is frozen music . . .[76]

Bragdon, writing in an overheated post-Wagnerian time, was invoking a musical experience as well as an architecture which would have been quite alien to his illustrious exemplars, Goethe and Mme de Staël. While they spoke of a fugue-like construction mirrored in the rationalities of building, Bragdon invokes a flow of sound that could be, as it were, instantly frozen into a pliable, supple, coruscating surface.

Synaesthesia became ancillary to Scriabin's explicitly, almost aggressively ritual approach. The new, electrically lit theatre could never live up to his high ambition, but it inspired radical changes and proved an instant boon to innovative producers. In Munich a Swiss theatre reformer (and enthusiastic Wagnerian), Adolphe Appia, published his call to make electric light the dominant element in stage design,[77] though the Catalan-Italian painter/designer Mariano Fortuny de Madrazo was the first to exploit it fully. He had visited Loïe Fuller's World Exposition theatre and was very taken with her use of coloured light; that same year he designed the sets and the lighting for a production of Wagner's *Tristan* at La Scala in Milan which was enormously successful and much publicized;[78] Fortuny's Wagnerian excursions made him well known to theatre people all over Europe. In 1903 he met up with Appia, who had by then devised something he called *Worttundrama* (word-and-drama – though he also meant it to include music, echoing the *Gesamtkunstwerk*), in which lighting effects 'stood in for' stage setting. The Bayreuth authorities (Wagner's heirs) were advised to consult Appia – but beyond introducing electric lighting, they (and especially the widow Cosima) found his innovations unacceptable since he believed that Wagner's stage directions could be ignored and performances managed synaesthetically. The score itself dictated the physical form of the setting, Appia thought. It led him to propose a production of Wagner's *Parsifal* – what else? – against a colourless setting which was to be lit by a synchronized colour-organ.[79] Gabriele d'Annunzio and Eleonora Duse involved him in their ambitious project to create an Italian National Theatre on the shores of Alban Lake, south of Rome, in which they proposed to return the performance of tragedy to its Dionysac power. That project also never came to anything.[80] But lighting spectacle electronically was only a primitive beginning; the new technology would, within a year or two, revolutionize the expectation of the audience.

The Cinematograph

A very different electrically powered innovation threatened, marginally at first, the very nature of spectacle – the cinematograph. It started very tentatively in the United States with Eadweard Muybridge's experiments in photographing movement (he began by recording photo-finishes at horse races). About the same time, Etienne-Jules Marey in France developed a more subtle and ingenious mechanism, the chronophotograph.[81] The well-named brothers Lumière, Auguste and Louis (already well-established manufacturers of photographic material), then found a way of recording motion on moving film using some of Thomas Edison's chemical innovations: at the first private showing in 1894–5, they merely projected some takes of workers leaving their factory in Lyons, but soon became more ambitious, and by the end of 1895 had held demonstrations of short films in Chicago and Boston, New York and Atlanta, as well as Berlin. Edison returned to the fray with his Vitascope, and for a while patents and

Jules Marey's Chronophotograph, *c.* 1885.

machinery competed. The first films were side-shows and curiosities. They showed public ceremonies – Queen Victoria's Diamond Jubilee, the arrival (1896) of the Russian imperial family in Paris and so on – or brief farces, and there was even a little very soft 'porno'. Early development of cinema-spectacle was stymied, however, by the catastrophic fire started by an early ether-vapour lamp at a great 'society' affair (an annual charity fair in 1897), in which a great many high-born and very monied figures were burnt to ashes. That event seemed to condemn the cinema, in Europe at any rate, to the lower orders.[82]

At least one philosopher saw the cinema as a metaphor of cognition operating through duration. In his first Collège de France lectures just after 1900, Henri Bergson suggested that cinematic recording was a very helpful metaphor for the cognitive process:

> Instead of concentrating on the inner development of things, we set our-selves outside them to recompose their development artificially. We take almost instant views of reality as it passes, and as they typify that reality, it is enough for us to align them on an abstract, uniform, invisible devel-opment situated in the inner mechanism of knowledge . . . Whether we are concerned with thinking the development or even of perceiving it, we do little but activate this kind of interior cine-camera.[83]

The limitations of recorded sound diminished the surrogate experience, however. Audiences were chatty and even talked back at the screen the way they might in a music hall (but not in the theatre), while projectors whirred very loudly, and sitting in the crackly dark while watching a silent screen made spectators restive. Sound was therefore required for distraction to mask the machine rumble. Meanwhile, the recording and transmission of sound also progressed: the phonoautograph became the phonograph, which in turn became the gramophone. Edison was also instrumental in this development, though the machine was clumsy and recordings too brief to cooordinate with moving images. Live music for the first films was provided at first by a piano or a small band (and even the occasional orchestra). Some actors developed ways of speaking synchronized lines from behind the screen.[84] Cue-sheets for musicians were supplied by several film-makers and even before 1914 a few movie-houses installed electric organs. The first director to attempt large-scale cinematic presentations, the vastly prolific D. W. Griffith, actually had a live orchestra touring with major films, playing a pre-arranged score (mostly quotes with link passages where required).

Although many artists were fascinated by the early film-makers such as Georges Méliès and his burlesque-trick pantomime shorts, the first great 'stars' the cinema produced were silent comedians (Charlie Chaplin remains the most famous), though there were also attempts to create 'respectable high art', soundless spectacle: Sarah Bernhardt in Sardou's *Tosca*, Réjane and Mounet-Sully in Racine's *Britannicus*. In Germany, too, Max Reinhardt was engaged in some (rather unsuccessful) silent film-making. The ambitions of cineasts became more pronounced in due course, even if the major composers or writers did not seem very interested at first. Camille Saint-Saëns composed a score for Henri Lavedan's *Murder of the Duc de Guise*, while the ambitious Italian producer Giovanni Pastrone made one of the first really dramatic films, *Cabiria*, with a script by D'Annunzio – who managed to sell a number of his plays to film producers but was only marginally interested in the process. The absence of sound also meant, of course, that synaesthetic experiments such as Kandinsky's could not be translated into film.

Cinema spectators, however chatty, were still passive assistants at the spectacle, if marginally less so than those in the theatre. The theatre (and dance even more so) had been, in Europe at any rate, a participatory and not a spectator sport. In the mid-eighteenth century the abstract *divertissement* was separated from the narrative *ballet-d'action* (itself derived from older mimes), while through the nineteenth century it developed as ancillary to opera. Certain houses demanded the insertion of ballets into existing scores even from the most illustrious composers – Wagner and Verdi.

Ballet is not all of dance in any case: Loïe Fuller, 'constantly sniffing out new ideas', had realized that new forms of movement offered her the possibility of renewal. In 1902 she sponsored Sado Yakko,[85] and that same year was joined by another American dancer, the ambitious and independent Isadora Duncan, who broke away after a few months. Like Fuller, Duncan claimed to be more or less self-taught, but unlike Fuller, it was not voluminous skirts and veils which provided her effects: she danced in sandals or barefoot in light 'classical' tunics, causing a good deal of brow-raising, particularly among balletomanes. She claimed to have recovered the secrets of

Isadora Duncan dancing,
photograph, *c.* 1910.

Greek dance as it was represented on the vases and reliefs she had examined in the Louvre,[86] and became a star in a matter of weeks after her tour with Loïe Fuller.[87]

Early in her European career she also went to Bayreuth – her inspiration, she claimed, was the trinity of Beethoven, Wagner and Nietzsche, the 'dancing philosopher'. Having been made welcome by Cosima Wagner, she startled her hostess (and the assembled company) by announcing over lunch at Villa Wahnfried that

> The Master had made a mistake, a mistake as great as his genius . . . Music-drama is nonsense . . . the speaking is the brain, the thinking man. The singing is the emotion. The dancing is the Dionysan ecstasy which carries away all . . . *Musik drama kann nie sein.*[88]

She was not shown the door, though there were troubles in Bayreuth when she appeared – she was already a great international star and remained one for twenty years.

In 1905 she danced in St Petersburg to great acclaim, returned there almost every year after that, and – intermittently – ran a dance academy in Russia. Her first visit coincided with the 'little' revolution when the Imperial ballet also had its mini-troubles. The dissident dancers (they included the choreographer Michel Fokine, and the first *ballerini,* Anna Pavlova, Vaslav Nijinski and Tamara Karsavina) admired Duncan, while her influence on the younger members of the famous Imperial company was instant and transforming.

The man who understood and exploited the new enthusiasm for exoticism and ritual was the Russian impresario Serge Diaghilev. His productions had all the barbaric splendour of an orient which may have looked alien and exotic,[89] but was more easily 'digestible' than the Far East or even Levantine Islam. Russia was unfamiliar, after all, even if several impressive Russian writers and thinkers had come west in the nineteenth century: Gogol to Rome, Turgenev to Paris, Herzen to London, Bakunin to Germany and Switzerland; yet in spite of many translations and Prosper Mérimée's eloquent advocacy, Russian art and thought were little known abroad.

In Russia itself, the art, and more particularly the architecture of the past, were not altogether familiar to artists. Icons had been covered with jewelled metal protective shields, and although their faces and hands were left bare, they were often blackened by many years' candle- smoke. Publications on the history of Russian architecture were inaccurate and scarce, and revivals had therefore to be approximative. True, one of the most prominent churches built in Moscow during the nineteenth century, the Cathedral of the Redeemer (1839–83), which commemorated the defeat of Napoleon,[90] was in an archaic Novgorod style, though much bigger than any of its models (and with added onion domes), and the city, though not the capital at that time, was at the centre of a 'national' art, but changes in official taste were displayed only in the 'Imperial' churches of St Petersburg. To design the most prominent official building in St Petersburg, the Hermitage – which doubled the area of the Winter Palace – the most famous of Bavarian Neoclassical architects, Leo von Klenze, would be summoned from Munich in 1839–40.[91]

A rich and enlightened Russian upper middle class emerged in the second half of the nineteenth century, many from thrifty and puritanic Old-Believer families who saw it as their duty as well as their social privilege to patronize native 'advanced' artists. Among them was the textile millionaire Pavel Sergeievitch Tretiakov (and his brother Mikhail), who began to collect Russian art during the 1860s and '70s. It was the time of the first 'secession' from officially acceptable academic sterility in Russia, and an important group, who called themselves 'The Wanderers',[92] took on the Tolstoyan burden of social comment, urged partly by the critic Vladimir Stasov, who invested much energy in promoting his *troika*: Ilya Repin (the son of a poor family who had trained as an icon-painter before moving to the academy – and to Paris), the sculptor Mark Antokolsky – a Jew from Wilno – and the composer Modest Moussorgsky. The harrowing historical realism of Wassily Surikov provides perhaps the best evidence of this development. Another fellow traveller, an independent spirit, the Symbolist Mikhail Vrubel, was to be a great inspiration to the artists of the next generation.

Another patron was a young Moscow iron and railway contractor, Savva Ivanovich Mamontov and his wife Elizaveta, who in 1870 bought a *dacha*-estate, Abramtsevo, some 60 kilometres from Moscow. They had often spent the winters in Rome, where they had visited monuments and expatriate Russian artists' studios such as those of Antokolsky and Vassily Polenov; they also met Franz Overbeck. The aged Nazarene inspired them with his account of an artists' community reviving medieval ideals and techniques.[93] They returned to gather a colony of composers, writers and artists as well as craftsmen at Abramtsevo, and Vassily Polenov (a painter who had ethnographic and archeological interests) became the moving spirit of the enterprise.[94] The ideals were those of Slavophile Russian populism: 'We owe a debt to the people', Savva Mamontov used to say. The couple built a hospital and a school on the estate, and later added woodworking and ceramic workshops as well as a small church which they made a centre of liturgical renewal.[95] Its interior was painted by several artists, including Repin, who made his first essay in revived 'modern' icon painting there, attempting a fusion of academic sophistication and his own early training. Vrubel became the main designer for the ceramic workshops, producing figures and pots not unlike Gauguin's. The Mamontov programme promoted a collaboration between artists and craftsmen so as to increase their familiarity with technique and so revitalize craft production (some 50 years before such an approach became part of the Bauhaus enterprise), as is evident in the outfitting and exterior facing in majolica of the church.[96]

Mamontov was himself a talented singer (as well as a sculptor) and the private readings and performances in his Moscow home soon led to the founding of a semi-professional opera. Moussorgsky, Glinka and Dargomyshsky were performed as well as Mozart. Rimsky-Korsakov was involved, as was Konstantin Stanislavsky (who was a relation), and – a little later – the very ambitious Serge Diaghilev. Much attention was given to sets and costumes, which had to be the work of painters, not professional theatre-decorators. The artist-ethnographer Nicolas Roerich (who would later mastermind *The Rite of Spring*) was part of the group. Rilke visited the estate in 1899 and sang its praises to his German correspondents.

By this time a number of collectors were putting together public and semi-public collections. The Tretiakovs presented their collection to the city of Moscow, and it became the main museum of Russian art (it still bears their name), together with a 'national style' building which Viktor Vasnetsov, one of Mamontov's principal supporters, designed in 1900. More adventurous were Ivan Abramovich Morosov and Sergei Ivanovich Shchukin – which latter invited Matisse to Moscow in 1911 and opened his gallery weekly to visitors. Their collections now form the basis of the Hermitage's holding of twentieth-century Western art. A new publication documenting this artistic ferment was launched that same year, *Mir Iskustva* (the World of Art). Its first editor was Serge Diaghilev, though its moving spirit was Alexander Benois, still primarily known as a painter. Of course, Mamontov subsidized it.[97]

Not that the court and the upper nobility took the Abramtsevo example seriously: official portraits and commemorative pictures and sculptures remained flaccid. Still, by the end of the century, officialdom began to take note. Alexander III visited the Tretiakov collection before he died and decided to have a rival show in St Petersburg (the Russian Museum), even if imperial patronage went to rather perverse arts-and-crafts enterprises, notably the Fabergé workshops, which continued to turn out the elaborate high-kitsch gewgaws (some of them mechanically ingenious) in gold, semi-precious and precious stones for the court and the higher reaches of the bourgeoisie until

1916. The Easter eggs might be considered the most vacuous example of conspicuous consumption ever conceived.[98]

For all that, radical changes were registered in Russian architecture – and
they spanned the world of Abramtsevo and the new industry. For the Russian
section of the 1900 International Exposition in Paris, the Abramtsevo workshops furnished a wooden pavilion designed by another painter-designer,
Konstantin Korovin.[99] About the same time there was also a competition for a
new luxury hotel, the Metropol in Moscow. A young English (but Russian-born)
architect who was associated with the Abramtsevo group, William Walcot, was
placed fourth, but – after some pressure from Mamontov – was awarded the
commission.[100] His residually Art Nouveau manner came to be called neo-
Russian by then: the facade is crowned by a large curved pediment which is
filled by a fairy ceramic composition by Vrubel, *The Princess of Rêverie*, while
below the attic the whole building is also girt by a tall frieze of interacting
figures, which surround the windows, and is itself edged by a deep ceramic

Lev Kekushev,
Vladimir
Shukhov and
William Walcot,
Hotel Metropol,
Moscow,
1898–1907.

band. The Metropol hotel, still operating today, was the Moscow showfront of Abramtsevo. What is rarely mentioned is that the public rooms had a prismatic-light ceiling sustained by a structure designed by Vladimir Shukhov, one of the most original and enterprising structural engineers of the time.[101]

A few months after Walcot won the Metropol hotel commission, another architect connected to the circle, Fedor Shekhtel (1859–1926), was asked to restructure the Yaroslav railway station; his version of the neo-Russian style came that much closer to Art Nouveau. He invited Korovin, Roerich and Valentin Serov to do some 'heroic' paintings in his building. Shekhtel moved even closer to a full-blooded Art Nouveau when he designed a mansion for another art-loving family, the Riabushinsky in Moscow.[102]

Aleksei Shchusev won the competition for Kazan station in 1911. He was a more explicitly nationalist designer, then best known for his historical restorations and the Martha-and-Mary Mission in Moscow, a foundation commemorating Archduke Sergei who had been assassinated in 1905. It had much in common with the Abramtsevo church and was decorated by Roerich and Mikhail Nesterov, who also designed the nuns' habits. Shchusev was to become the Vicar of Bray to Russian architecture.

When Diaghilev moved to conquer Paris, therefore, the team he would take with him was Mamontov's. Its 'pictorial' leaders were Alexander Benois, his fellow student and friend Leon Bakst, as well as Nicolas Roerich. Paris, Diaghilev knew well, was where he had to make his mark if he was to work internationally. A Russian exhibition at the Salon d'Automne in 1906 was followed the next year by a Russian historical concert at which the great bass Feodor Chaliapin (who had also been involved in the Mamontov performances) sang passages from his most famous role, Modest Mussorgsky's *Boris Goudunov*. Rimsky-Korsakov (who had reorchestrated *Boris*) was encouraged to amplify the coronation scene so as to emphasize its ritual character. It became Diaghilev's first great Western success, after which he brought over his ballet company (to which he had recruited those dissident dancers from the Imperial ballet).

Diaghilev's personal enthusiasm had moved from music to the visual arts, and he made sure his opera and ballet productions could be appreciated as unified works of art; the care taken over sets and costumes equalled that over music and choreography. Borodin's 'Polovtsian Dances' (from his opera

Prince Igor), which were performed separately as a ballet, and Rimsky's *Shéchérezade* provided the heavy orientalist atmosphere which became such a great success first in Paris and then in London. The Debussy-Nijinski *L'Après midi d'un faune*[103] was a foretaste of the revolution which the violence of Igor Stravinsky's primitive and explicitly liturgical *Sacre du printemps* carried out. That was not until 1913, and I will need to consider it in relation to the theatre in which it was performed.

Before *L'Après-midi* was choreographed, Diaghilev took Nijinski to Dresden, where in the suburb of Hellerau a most thoroughgoing and methodical dance experiment was being taught by Emile Jaques-Dalcroze who created a dance-and-music discipline he called 'Eurythmics' or 'rhythmic gymnastics', making his pupils aware of melody and rhythm by translating them, note by note, into bodily movement. He also claimed to revive the antique (more specifically Greek) dance that Isadora Duncan also claimed to teach, though Dalcroze found her method unsystematic and unhelpful.[104]

The 'institute' had been opened for Jaques-Dalcroze at Hellerau in 1910. He was joined there by Adolphe Appia. His institute was to be the central element in a garden city organized according to the ideas preached by the English founder of the Garden City movement, Ebenezer Howard, around a furniture workshop which had been started in 1899 but soon developed into a successful semi-industrial undertaking. By 1906 the factory in that German branch of the Garden City movement founded in 1902 was prosperous enough to become its economic seed, and its chief designer, the architect Richard Riemerschmid, whose very soberly modified Art Nouveau manner lent itself to industrial production, did the layout. But it needed a soul – and that soul was to be Dalcroze's eurythmic reform of education,[105] which would effectively make the whole settlement into a social transformer, a *Gesamtkunstwerk* in perpetual action involving all the inhabitants as well as the performers in the theatre.

After Peter Behrens refused the commission to design the Festspielhaus, it was handed to the young Heinrich Tessenow, who had developed a radically no-nonsense approach to building. He refined conventional elements – doors, windows, etc. – to recombine them into stark, economic yet very symmetrical and monumental compositions, a kind of sober 'classicism' which was in tune with Dalcroze's ideas.[106] The solemn portico of the school was appropriately temple-like, and its rather steeped pediment carried a relief of the yin-yang emblem. Formalized movement, whether dance or dance-like, seemed to many about this time to offer a quasi-religious but also primordial (and paradoxically also liberating, with its emphasis on the unfettered body) discipline which would offer the starting-point for a new education. A photograph of smiling children prancing on sunlit lawns was a stand-by of 'advanced' school brochures throughout the Western world from about 1910 until the Second World War. Dalcrozeian eurythmics would become the standard teaching method of many schools, though it was superseded in the second half of the twentieth century.[107]

The opening 1912 *Fest* at the Hellerau Hall centred on Adolphe Appia's 'realization' of the second act of Gluck's *Orfeus and Eurydice*. Many of the great artists and critics I mentioned earlier – Richard Dehmel and Hugo von Hofmannsthal, Karl-Ernst Osthaus, Peter Behrens and Henry Van de Velde, Wilhelm Worringer and Heinrich Wöllflin – but also Sergei Rachmaninoff and Paul Claudel, were in the audience, and Franz Kafka, Christian Morgenstern, Frank Wedekind and Igor Stravinsky were also drawn to it. Other less spectacular *Festspiele* followed in 1913, but by then the school – in spite of its success – was in financial difficulties.[108] The war put a stop to its activities and in 1915 Dalcroze returned to Geneva. The Dalcroze productions organized with Adolphe Appia as his stage-crafter achieved a monumentality which depended on the use of light and simple volume. Diaghilev, brilliant though he was, would never reduce his effects to the simplicities that Appia and Gordon Craig demanded.

Dance, any formalized movement, had come to dominate the theatre. Converted by Nietzsche, later neo-Wagnerians required something the illusionistic stage could not offer. Behrens had produced Otto Hartleben's play *Diogen* in Hagen (sponsored by Osthaus) with a stage so shallow that actors' movements took on the character of figures in a frieze and they were required to move in a stiffly stylized manner.[109] The body language of actors had to be circumscribed and was now made deliberately inexpressive. There was an enthusiastic revival of interest in the mask as well. Kessler's and Van de Velde's friend, Edward Gordon Craig, proposed the *übermarionette*, the super-puppet, as an ideal – and he publicized his ideas in a periodical, calling it 'The

Mask'.[110] In the first policy statement, the anonymous writer – presumably Craig himself:

> . . . prayed for a religion that did not rest upon knowledge or rely upon the Word . . . but brought together Music, Architecture and Movement to heal the Evil that has separated these arts and which leaves the world without a belief . . . [111]

Peter Behrens, who had established himself as a *Jugendstil* decorator and pageant-master, turned himself, as I said before, into an architect in the first decade of the twentieth century and gradually emerged as the most powerful designer in Germany (perhaps in the world!), overtaking Van de Velde and Olbrich for all their grand-ducal patronage. Ambitious and organized, he was a persuasive speaker. His rise was meteoric; by 1903 he had already met another devoted Nietzschean, a powerful industrialist and a close friend of Harry Kessler, who became one of the most influential German political thinkers of the time, Walter Rathenau.[112] Rathenau, Kessler and Behrens all saw themselves as variously embodying the characteristics of Nietzsche's 'good Europeans' as well as 'radical aristocrats'.

Peter Behrens: Turbine Hall of the AEG factory, Berlin 1909.

Lucius Bernhard (?),
publicity for the
'Flamenco' arc-lamp,
using the typeface Peter
Behrens designed for
AEG. The background is
the Turbine factory, lit
from within.

Nietzschean Production

When Behrens entered into contact with the Rathenau family enterprise, the
Allgemeine Elektrizität Gesellschaft (AEG for short) was already one of the
world's largest industrial operations.[113] How Behrens was appointed its design-
controller in 1907 is not certain.[114] At any rate, he gave up his Düsseldorf job
and moved his office to Berlin. From then on, he controlled all AEG products:
from the filaments inside the electric light-bulbs, the fans, kettles and other
electro-domestics through to doormen's uniforms and publicity (printed in a
Behrens typeface), as well as, more impressively, showrooms, factory buildings
and worker housing. His first major building for AEG was an octagonal and
church-like pavilion in the Berlin shipping exhibition of 1908, a simplified
version of the unbuilt church he had designed for Hagen. The best-known
(though certainly not the largest) of his AEG buildings is the Turbine factory, a
reduced and refined version of the Parisian Palais des Machines. Steel-framed

268

and amply glazed, it is a vaulted hall, the first steel-framed building in Germany. Le Corbusier called it 'the Cathedral of Labour'.[115]

Behrens' earlier enthusiasm for Maillol, his collaboration with Weiss and Bosselt, were also set aside in the operative investment of the AEG commission – but other architectural work came his way about that time. The most important were the (offensively ungainly) Mannesmann offices in Düsseldorf, and the much more impressive, dourly Doric-Prussian German embassy in St Isaac's Square in St Petersburg of 1910–11. This red granite 'palace' was dominated by a double statue: the *Dioscuri*, two young men, each leading a horse, by Erdmann Encke. Though he did not work with Encke again,[116] he liked the *Dioscuri* well enough to use another cast of them on the Festhalle, the central pavilion which he would design for the Cologne *Deutsche Werkbund* exhibition in 1914.

The German Werkbund, based on the English Design and Industries Association, had been founded in Munich in 1907. Behrens (with Henry Van de Velde, Theodor Fischer, Karl-Ernst Osthaus, Hermann Muthesius) was one of its founders. It set itself the task of reforming German industrial production and making it a rival to that of any other nation – and succeeded. The young Charles-Edouard Jeanneret, whom I quoted a little earlier on Behrens' Turbine factory, put it succinctly in 1912: 'Paris may be the home of art, but Germany is a huge workshop of production.'[117]

Emphasis on production from such a Ruskin-formed thinker as Jeanneret reflects a rising scepticism about the role of the Arts and Crafts movement in industrial design. The close connection between empathy, the *Gesamtkunstwerk* and Art Nouveau was deconstructed by the social thinker (and part-time art historian) Georg Simmel, another associate of Count Kessler. Simmel was only incidentally concerned with the content of the work of art or its facture, but very much with its social function – and this led him to enquire into the nature of a new *Gesamtkunstwerk*. It seemed to him that the distinction between art and craft (as he saw it) was being obliterated to the detriment of each. To his ample *Soziologie*, which was in fact a collection of essays written over the previous few years, he added an appendix on art and craft to his chapter on secret societies and associations.[118] The distinction between works of art and craft objects seemed to him existential:

Direct ornament is typical of 'primitive' people: tattooing. Its very opposite is metal and stone adornment, wholly unindividual, which anyone might wear . . . between the two lie different forms of dress.

And he goes on to explain:

> True elegance . . . draws a sphere of the general, the stylized about a person . . . If adornment is to extend the individual into the trans-individual . . . then it must, over and above its materiality, have Style. Style is ever a common property, which moulds the contents of personal life and production into such a form that it can be shared with – and is accessible to – many . . . [while] in the work of art, the more intense the personal involvement and the subjective life expressed in it, the less we care about its styles; because that is what engages the personal attitude of the spectator, so that he [or she] is, as it were, alone with it in the whole world.
>
> But, for everything which we call craft (*Kunstgewerbe*) and which is intended for many people because of its usefulness, we demand a more generalized and typical form . . . It is the greatest error possible to consider a piece of personal adornment . . . as an individual work of art because it adorns an individual.

Style, Ornament, Crime

Other writers were voicing similar scepticism. Hermann Muthesius, who had first imported the ideal of the Arts and Crafts movement to Germany and had been involved in the Darmstadt festivities, became increasingly sceptical about any craft tendency which rejected the machine: design had to contribute to changing national taste and improving production. In a series of essays, he suggested that industrial design, which he called *Sachkunst*, 'thing-art', was quite different from *Empfindungskunst*, 'feel-art' – but that fine and applied art had to interact to their mutual benefit.[119] A more subtle yet more aggressive Viennese statement of the theme took a different tone. The young (Moravian) architect Adolf Loos, who had spent some years in the United States, had returned to Vienna in 1896 and set up his own office. About the earliest project of his to survive is for a Behrens-type theatre: an oval, unified auditorium centred on a circular stage-orchestra half-in, half-out of the stage tower, the roof of the auditorium 'growing' into an ovoid, shell-like envelope.[120] Most of his early designs are for shops and private houses, though he became instantly famous for his sharp and polemical writings as a critic of art and of architecture and as a harsh enemy of Viennese custom and culture. He admired Otto Wagner's thoroughgoing rationalism, but assertively despised his two prominent pupils, Josef Olbrich and Josef Hoffman – and all the Secession (and later its offshoot, the Wiener Werkstätte) with them.

'The poor-rich man' was an early target for his scorn. In Loos' fable he had everything – but art was lacking in his life. He therefore summons a fashionable architect to make sure that everything about him can be art: he treads on art, when he is tired he sinks his head in art, his *boeuf à l'oignon* is brought to him on art, he cuts it with art and even uses art to put it in his mouth. Carpet and cushion, plate, knife and fork, all are to be art. On his birthday, his affectionate family offers him some presents – which have to be artfully accommodated, of course – and only his architect can do this; summoned, he is horrified to see the rich man wearing the slippers designed for his bedroom in his living room! As for the presents, there is just no room for them. The rich man's home is complete.

The welter of creepers which constituted 'modern' ornament is a cage for the wretched – if rich – client. It is not only constricting, Loos insists, it is also decadent.[121] In his much more famous essay, 'On Ornament and Crime', which was published in 1908, the same year as Simmel's analogous piece I have just quoted, he declared himself an enemy of all 'invented' ornament:

> The Papuan tattoos his skin, his boat, his oar – in short, anything in his
> reach. He is no criminal. A modern man who tattoos himself is either
> a degenerate or a criminal . . . Anyone tattooed who is not imprisoned
> is either a potential criminal or a degenerate aristocrat . . . [122]

To use ornament was not in itself criminal, he allowed. The most 'advanced' among us may enjoy (as he certainly did) Persian carpets or carved wood furniture of the past (Loos was particularly fond of Chippendale-style chairs),[123] but embroidering clothes or – perish the thought – designing

Adolf Loos, *Chicago Tribune competition entry*, 1922.

patterned wallpapers he compared to the efforts of the 'primitive' who scrawls a cross on the wall: the horizontal to mean female, the penetrating vertical the male. The primitive man who first traced it on the rockface may have been a genius, says Loos, but the makers of modern ornament he labels 'primitive', therefore 'degenerate' and (by association) 'criminal' (echoing Nordau and Lombroso).[124] He formulates a principle: 'the evolution of a culture is equivalent to the removal of ornament from objects of everyday use'. Van de Velde therefore becomes his archetype of the guilty designer. In a postscript addressed 'to the clown [*Ulk*] who mocked my essay "On Ornament and Crime": 'I say to you, you clown, that the day will come when to have your cell decorated by *Hofrath* Van de Velde will be considered an increase of the punishment!'

Loos not only installed much highly figured marble, patterned textiles, Persian and Turkish rugs and Chippendale-type chairs in his buildings, but like the architects of earlier centuries he was also an enthusiastic handler of 'classical' ornament. In 1910 the elegant men's haberdashery Goldman & Salacz (now known as the *Looshaus*) was designed as a plain stuccoed four-storey 'cage' or frame of rentable space. Since it faced the entrance of the Hofburg, the emperor's residence, the nudity of the stucco 'skeleton' was regarded as an affront to civic propriety by many Viennese and was the subject of voluminous, acrimonious polemics even though the 'cage' was set over a two-storey, marble- and bronze-fronted base articulated by Tuscan columns rising its full height. Later, in 1921, in his entry for the competition launched by the *Chicago Tribune*, which declared it wanted the 'most beautiful office-building in the world', Loos submitted a project in the form of a twenty-storey Doric column: he extolled it as a building 'whose beauty would be a beacon for the architecture of the future'.[125] There was no contradiction in Loos' mind between damning newly invented ornament and his using ornamental forms from the past.

Loos' modernism – like that of his friend the satirist Karl Kraus, 'the white high priest of the truth'[126] – had little room or time for the occult theatricalities of their German contemporaries. Both Loos and Kraus were clear and uncompromising about this. In a famous quasi-aphorism, Karl Kraus wrote:

> Adolf Loos and I – he literally, and I through the word – did no more than show the difference between the urn and the chamber-pot – and how culture is asserted in that distinction. Other, practical people may be divided into those who use an urn as a chamber pot and those who mistake the chamber pot for an urn.[127]

Both of them taught insistently that art needed to be free, to obey only the artist's genius, while dwellings, like clothes, had to follow the patron's needs, suit his way of life.

Loos insisted on such discontinuity: in 'Architecture', an essay of 1909, he states it in almost the same terms as Simmel:

> A house fulfills a need. A work of art has no responsibility to anybody, the house is responsible to everybody. The work of art wants to tear men out of their comfortable complacency. A house must serve comfort. The work of art is revolutionary, a house conservative . . . Man loves all that serves his comfort and hates everything that wants to bother him and tear him from the position he has achieved and assured. He therefore loves his house and hates art.
>
> *The house therefore has nothing to do with art and architecture is not to be counted among the arts? That is how it is. Only a very small part of architecture belongs to art: the tomb and the monument . . .* [128]

Discontinuity between old artefacts (carpets, furniture) and the wall surface, as well as between the wall and any work of art attached to it, was therefore a rule which all of Loos' projects had to obey. Loos' modernity thrived on that discontinuity. Painting or sculpture, the piece of music or the play – all of them *Kunst* – were not subject to necessity. He favoured artists who are now labelled Expressionist,[129] and gave unstinting loyalty to the young Oskar Kokoschka, a brilliant draughtsman and a highly literate painter who drew, painted and engraved several portraits of both Kraus and Loos. Yet that did not lead to collaboration, except in a mausoleum projected for the art-historian Max Dvořak (who died in 1921), which was not built.[130]

Oskar Kokoschka, for his part, became involved in another architectural project bigger than anything that Loos designed. This came about when a vast exhibition was planned in Breslau to celebrate the centenary of the defeat of Napoleon. Hans Poelzig, a contemporary of Behrens (and by then the most successful architect in eastern Germany, as well as the very influential director of the local Academy of Fine Arts),[131] designed a domed pavilion with long colonnades and pergolas enclosing a formal garden which now seems rather etiolated and 'classical', and therefore surprising coming from the masterful designer of so many robust industrial buildings. The main feature of the exhibition, however, was a concrete 'Centenary' hall (*Jahrhunderthalle*), conceived by the other 'major' Breslau architect, Max Berg, and it was the largest concrete construction in the world.[132] It was planned as a quadrafoil, some 95 metres across, with a central dome 67 metres in diameter over powerful sustaining arches. The stepped roofs (which give the building zenital light) were screened with very thin marble plates instead of glass. The hall was entered through a curved hexastyle portico, the thin columns carrying a flat cornice.

The Breslau authorities were determined that it should be 'culturally significant', not a mere engineering achievement. The solemn opening ceremony (not like several already mentioned) was scripted by the Expressionist playwright Gerhard Hauptman and produced by Max Reinhardt, while the area of the pendentives between the sustaining arches was to be frescoed (or at any rate painted) by Kokoschka; but negotiations ended in failure. It was to have been the most ambitious of all the artist-architect collaborations of the time.

Berg tried again to involve Kokoschka when he built a crematorium in Breslau in 1912. Kokoschka's paintings for Max Berg did not break Loos' *ukaze* – the Jahrhunderthalle was a monument, after all, but Loos, Kraus and

Simmel had all, in their different ways, challenged the attitudes of Art Nouveau designers – the Mackintoshes, Ashbees, Guimards, Tiffanies and Van de Veldes, as well as those of the Wiener Werkstätte, of Olbrich, Hoffman and their collaborators in the Secession, Gustav Klimt, Koloman Moser and Alfred Roller (who became Gustav Mahler's brilliant set-designer at the Vienna Opera). Their criticism undercut the very basis of the Arts and Crafts movement which treated paintings and sculptures as uninflected parts of the environment. Yet the assertion of discontinuity was primarily a work of cleansing, and could not lead to a grander theoretical formulation. What Elias Canetti said about Karl Kraus might apply equally to Loos:

> He was anxious . . . to be unassailable: no gap, no crack, no mis-placed comma – sentence on sentence, block on block, rise into a Chinese Wall. It is laid equally well everywhere, and cannot be faulted anywhere. But what it encloses no one really knows . . . There is no realm behind the wall, it itself is the realm . . . The blocks from which [Kraus] built it were judgements . . . which condemned all that lived in the country around . . . [133]

A stringent, controlled sobriety in clothing, design and building allowed, even invited a great freedom, an exuberance in the arts; the most famous of the group's associates, the composer Arnold Schoenberg, touched on a rather different, formally more adventurous aspect of modernism. Enlightened Viennese rationalism shied away from too much dealing with *Märchen und Mythen* – since the primitive, like the criminal, was too close to the decadent to be handled. Kraus' and Loos' distrust of psychoanalysis, 'the disease for which it claims to be the cure', is well known.[134] Yet Loos was reputed to know the giant fairy-tale cantata, Schoenberg's *Gurrelieder*, by heart, and Schoenberg, for his part, admired Loos both as an architect and as a person. Many things linked them: there was the solidarity between 'advanced' artists whose work the public rejected, and at another level, the craftsmanly ethos. Schoenberg insisted that he replaced musicians' bad aesthetics by a crafts procedure – the twelve-tone method. However, he was also a close friend and collaborator of Kandinsky over many years, and so linked his exuberant and mystical modernity to the sober, hygienic Viennese elegance of Loos.[135]

From Vienna to Paris

Loos enjoyed visiting Paris. His friends there were musicians and writers rather than architects and painters, and usually foreigners like himself rather than Frenchmen – he was not at ease in French. Kessler, too, and Van de Velde (or, for that matter, Behrens) were very much aware of and involved in the 'staid' part of the Parisian art world, with artists like Maillol and Bourdelle, Monet, Signac, Vuillard – even Matisse. An invisible barrier of rationalism, or at any rate of a certain sobriety, separated them from the two most vital and influential (and therefore most Dionysian) Parisian developments in the decade before the war: Cubism and Futurism, perhaps the most discussed episode in the whole history of art. Without adding to the mass of literature, I need to give a skeleton outline of the episode for the continuity of my argument.

Cubism is usually said to have opened with Picasso's large canvas, *Les Demoiselles d'Avignon*, which was painted in 1907,[136] while Futurism begins with a manifesto (the first of many) which Filippo Tommaso Marinetti published on the front page of *Le Figaro* on 20 February 1909 – like an advertisement. The two movements or 'isms' (as they were later called) had little in common at first. Cubism evolved quickly, during 1907–9, as a way of observing and recording phenomena. Picasso and his (then) close friend Georges Braque, working in each other's studios and looking at the same landscapes and objects, started it. The *Demoiselles*, a large canvas (whose 'motive' seems to have been Picasso's obsession with outsiders, marginal figures), may not be counted as a true Cubist painting by some critics, yet it already shows features which will distinguish all the work of the movement: defiance of linear perspective, expressive manipulation of the human body. The origins of the *Demoiselles* – and of Cubism generally – remain puzzling, although the picture has been studied and commented on learnedly and extensively, perhaps even more than those of Impressionism. Certainly within a few months of the *Demoiselles*, both Braque and Picasso had found ways of formalizing their vision as landscape, and a few months later they extended the method back to the figure – even to portraits. By 1909 Picasso had also done his first Cubist sculpture of a head.[137]

Their work became known quickly through exhibitions and the private galleries owned by Paris-based German dealer-critics, Daniel-Henry Kahnweiler and Wilhelm Uhde, as well as by the advocacy of one of the greatest of all French poets, Guillaume Apollinaire. Their method or approach obviously offered a way of accounting for perception which other artists found fascinating, so that by 1911 major painters like Fernand Léger and Juan Gris and Robert Delaunay, as well as less glorious figures such as Jean Metzinger and Albert Gleizes (who produced the manifesto of the movement, *Du Cubisme* in 1912 – after the event), Louis Marcoussis, Henri Le Fauconnier (who was also involved in the Munich Blaue Reiter group), Roger de la Fresnaye, Francis Picabia and the sculptor Jacques Lipschitz, were refracting the world through Cubist lenses; even André Derain and Henri Matisse were affected, as were the brothers Duchamp/Villon – of whom more later.

The late work of Cézanne, particularly his *Bathers*, is constantly quoted as the immediate precedent for the Cubist mutation. 'Anyone who understands Cézanne has an apprehension of Cubism', asserted that first manifesto.[138] Whatever is true about how these and other – African, Iberian – influences were absorbed, there is no doubt that by 1909–10 both founders had worked out a way of so shaping pictorial space that the picture-plane is not (as it had been since Alberti taught painters two-point perspective) a window into another world, but a material ground on (and from) which a new image of reality is built up or projected.[139] Braque (being the son of a house-decorator)[140] was more proficient than Picasso at constructing such a plane by imitating wood and marble on the canvas, though within a few months (even weeks) they both came to substitute ready-made materials for the painted ground: wallpapers, newsprint, then real pieces of wood or textile, even cane chair-seats. The technique of *collage* which they both elaborated was quickly absorbed into the Cubist approach.

Cubist painters were excited by the possibility of presenting objects and figures from more than one point, turning them, as it were, on a hypothetical axis 'in front' of a solid ground so that they could be shown from several angles at the same time:

> An object did not have one absolute form, but several – as many as
> there are planes within the limits of signification . . . if a geometry is
> to be related to the space of painters, it would have to be referred
> to non-Euclidean mathematicians, and meditate long on certain theories
> of Rieman . . .

Not that either Picasso or Braque had the leisure (or the specialist insight) to have read treatises on multi-dimensional geometry, not even the most popular ones: 'Geometry (after all) is a science, painting is an art: the geometer measures, the painter relishes.'[141]

Dimension and *Durée*

Yet almost all commentators have considered exploring the fourth dimension as part of the Cubist method. Perspective construction was based on solid Euclidian foundations resting on Aristotle's teaching that space only has three dimensions.[142] Kant had made space one *a priori* postulate of experience, and time another. Even before him, since time could be plotted as a coordinate on the Cartesian grid, it was geometrically measurable and therefore a *potential* dimension.[143] Henri Bergson, who, almost single-handedly, challenged the primacy of positivism that had dominated French thinking since Comte, opposed lived experienced time – *durée*[144] – to 'homogeneous', dimensioned and measured time. Analogously, he saw movement as the condition of all things in nature, which is in constant evolution. Stasis was therefore neither logically nor even temporarily prior to movement. Nothing can be seized, understood without a prior acknowledgement that a static image is movement arrested, which could be read (as he most emphatically did not) as a justification of the Cubist approach.[145]

Bergson was the most widely discussed philosopher in the France of the time. Picasso would have learnt of his ideas at second hand from his friend and mentor the poet Max Jacob, who was certainly familiar with them; other artists of the time absorbed them in an 'unstructured way . . . from what [they] heard and saw in the avant-garde about [them], the result being, in philosophical terms, far from consistent'.[146] The notion of time as a fourth dimension is easier to appreciate, of course, than that of a space measured in four – or more dimensions – which is what interested geometers and was the subject of much speculation. For almost a century before the Cubists there had been a spate of publications about many-dimensional space by a scattered group of brilliant mathematicians: Karl Friedrich Gauss (and his pupil Bernhard Riemann), who first considered the possibility of one-dimensional

278

and many-dimensional manifolds) in Göttingen, János Bolyai in Budapest, Nikolai Ivanovich Lobachevski in Kazan.[147] Some imaginative writers became fascinated by multi-dimensional space. Perhaps the first to work a story out of its implications was Edwin Abbott Abbott, whose *Flatlandia* managed a satire on contemporary England by recounting the adventures of a three-dimensional 'hero' in two-dimensional space.[148]

One of the greatest of French mathematicians (who happened to write elegant prose and be a brilliant popularizer), Henri Poincaré, made the distinction between *geometrical*, three-dimensional space, whose characteristics were not absolute or apodictic (as Euclid and Descartes had both supposed in their different ways) but conventional. It was therefore quite different, he maintained, from *perceptual* space, since perception allows sight, movement and touch as part of the experience. Poincaré also considered the hypothesis of a non-perceptible space beyond it.[149] This distinction may well have been known to early Cubists.[150]

Two manuals on four-dimensional geometry by a mathematician, Pascal Jouffret (which extended and 'visualized' some of Poincaré's intuitions, and also discussed Abbot's book), were certainly known to some painters. They provided fascinating diagrammatic aids for understanding the possible construction of 'super-bodies'. Copies were almost certainly 'about' in the Bâteau-Lavoir, a disused piano factory on the slopes of Montmartre where several Cubist painters worked.[151] Yet the Cubist painters' and sculptors' exploration of space represented did not stimulate any of them to attempt any novel articulation of tangible volume.

The Cubists never constituted themselves into a formal group, though there were plenty of groupuscules and collective exhibitions. Some painters were kept out of one or other; some chose to stay out (as Picasso and Braque did occasionally). Moreover, the movement was quickly 'periodized' into 'styles' as it was happening;[152] labels for various groups and manifestos proliferated, evidence of the lively and conflictual atmosphere of pre-1914 Paris. One of the original sub-groups, that around Jacques Villon[153] and his brother Raymond, moved from Montmartre to Puteaux, a suburb beyond Neuilly which gave its name (the Groupe de Puteaux) to a Cubist 'salon' where La Section d'Or was formed as an exhibition club, and a single issue of a proposed periodical was published. 'Golden Section' – also known as Φ – sounded scientific, suggesting a rigorous application of this proportion. A number of Post-Impressionists (encouraged by Charles Henri) had used it – Seurat, Signac – and, more dogmatically, Sérusier, who had also absorbed the teaching of the Beuron monks.[154] Among the 'orthodox' Cubist artists, only Juan Gris adopted it consistently at first. As the title of a group show, the name was a slogan and a theme for discussion rather than a declaration of principle.

The youngest of the three Duchamp brothers, Marcel, joined them in 1908. Like Gaston and Jacques he earned small sums by doing double-entendre cartoons for comic papers while painting solidly Fauve portraits and symbolic compositions at that time. He also began to investigate chess as a source of images (he was to become a respected tournament player during the 1920s and '30s) in a series of canvases in which he used a Cubist palette, but also appealed to some Futurist-seeming ideas about movement, though he linked them to movements of the pieces across the chessboard.[155]

At the end of 1911 he concentrated on studies of two upright figures in movement which, again, look Futurist, though he always maintained that the paintings owed everything to the Cubists and the photography of moving figures by Etienne-Jules Marey.[156] The most famous of his paintings from this time, the *Nude Descending a Staircase*, exists in a number of versions. It was offered to the Section d'Or in 1913, but accepted only after the title was changed. Two years later it was sent to the Armory Show in New York, which introduced Duchamp to his future American patrons. In spite of his obvious accomplishments, he was by then disillusioned with the imprecision of painting and with both Cubist and Futurist transformations of perceptual space. He professed to despise them and representational (which he called interchangeably 'realist' or 'retinal') painting. He wanted to reintroduce 'grey matter' into art, so that his interest now shifted to various forms of projection and quasi-engineering drawings.[157]

The Cubist revolution, though frenetic and intense, had fermented in the privacy of studios and art galleries. Futurism, on the other hand, had been launched with a fanfare before there was anything to see. Their self-appointed (and unchallenged) leader, Marinetti, could (rather like André Breton with the Surrealists later) expel artists and writers from the movement for personal as well ideological errors. He urged and bullied them to develop new techniques, new formulations. His manifesto called for a new art to exalt the automobile driver at his steering wheel, to show that 'a roaring motor-car running into machine-gun fire is more beautiful than the Victory of Samothrace'. All old art, museums, monuments were to be destroyed. He would rejoice at the 'sight of the burning bookshelves of libraries, the ragged remains of glorious canvases floating discoloured in the flood-water of the canals, re-routed to drown all museums'. Art, he said, must exalt violence, cruelty, injustice![158]

Because of their constant insistence on speed and obliquity, the Futurists were more interested in time as a fourth dimension, in exploring the movement within the object or its changing configuration to the observer walking around it. The Cubist artists for their part tended to move round their subject to consider the refraction of the surface. The artists who would make Futurism matter – Balla, Boccioni, Carrà, Severini (the last was the only one of them in Paris at the time) – had been only half-aware of Marinetti's original trumpet-blast. They were working in the wake of Italian Post-Impressionism and Divisionism. Already friends, they were taken to meet him a year later in his 'orientalist' apartment in Milan. Marinetti was constantly on the attack – against aesthetics, history, decadence – and the pervasive influence of Vienna. He claimed to have cultivated the theatrical art of being booed and whistled off the stage. By 1910 he had devised an *übermensch*-alter ego, Mafarka the Futurist. Some considered Mafarka an updated Zarathustra, but Marinetti rejected Nietzsche's 'ideal and teaching', violently, of course, for 'being rooted in the past, in Greek myth and art'.[159]

Subsequent manifestos now became more specific and contained some very sagacious criticism. In all of them dynamism, speed, the importance of the oblique and of fluidity are reasserted. The Futurists went in for all kinds of self-promotion and performances, which were often led by Marinetti in person – recitations, readings of manifestos through megaphones, 'rumorist' music, etc., intended (usually successfully) to provoke noisy responses from the public or fisticuffs with their critics. A true 'Battle of Hernani' Marinetti called one of them.[160] Manifestos followed each other – of painting, sculpture, music, literature, lust, women. A special manifesto-pamphlet addressed to the Venetians (damning love, moonlight and old Venice) was thrown from the Campanile of St Mark's at the Sunday morning crowd.[161]

The flock of artists Marinetti had shepherded turned into a cohesive group, and exhibitions followed – even in Paris, where reception was mixed.

Anonymous designer and André Mare, with ornament by Raymond Duchamp-Villon, *Maison Cubiste*, 1912.

There was a hiatus in activity when Marinetti volunteered for service (if only as a war correspondent) in the discreditable 1911 Italian colonial adventure in Tripolitania/Libya. He was an indefatigable propagandist, lecturing and performing in Germany, Britain and Russia, which had its own, flourishing and very nuanced Cubo-Futurist movement. Yet in spite of all that internationalism and modernity, the core Futurists were aggressively nationalist. 'The young call for war, the only hygiene of the world.'[162] Having agitated for Italy to enter the war (against Austria), most of the Futurists joined the army in 1915. Boccioni was soon killed in a riding accident, the architect Antonio Sant'Elia shot in battle in 1916. The movement had now lost two of its most brilliant members, though by then their allegiance to it seems to have been shaken anyway. Boccioni's last (and unfinished) major painting was an explicitly Cézannesque portrait of the great Italo-German composer Ferruccio Busoni.

As for architecture, if the Cubists did not have any, neither did the Futurists, and their perpetual turmoil seemed inimical to the stability which building demands. The Cubists made a first, tentative move when the German *Werkbund* sent some impressive material to the Salon d'Automne of 1912. Frantz Jourdain, Rodin's friend,[163] who had founded the Salon in 1902, had been very distressed that France had nothing comparable to display. He therefore persuaded a young and otherwise unknown architect-decorator, André Mare, to organize a Cubist house at the Salon.[164] Looking at it now, it seems very strange that the wonderful plethora of more or less Cubist artists working in Paris at the time should produce such a sorry result. To judge by surviving photographs, the rooms were a tame version of an Art Nouveau exhibition house, the furniture sub-Van de Velde, the walls decorated with floral papers and hung, rather disjointedly, with pictures by Marie Laurencin, Fernand Léger and Marcel Duchamp. The outside was that of a conventional *pavillon*, a mansarded suburban villa. What was to take it out of the common-place, however, were the Cubist sculptural 'hoods' over the windows and over the main door. These and all the mouldings were the work of the same Raymond Duchamp-Villon. Presenting the house in *La Peinture Cubiste,* Apollinaire pitches his tone improbably high:

> As soon as sculpture takes its leave of nature it becomes architecture
> . . . Architects and engineers should build with sublime intentions: to
> build the highest tower, to prepare a more beautiful ruin than any
> other for ivy and for time . . . Duchamp-Villon has this titanic concep-
> tion of architecture . . . Sculptor and architect, for him it is only light
> which matters . . . incorruptible light.[165]

Apollinaire's rhapsody accords ill with the suburban villa and its timidly jazzy reliefs; and coming from Apollinaire (who had been shrewdly sceptical about the Futurists, and seemed aware of what Adolf Loos was doing in Vienna – he even wanted to see an exhibition of the work of Gaudí in Paris), it reads like a piece of special pleading, particularly as he seems to take no interest in the Parisian architectural scene: Henri Sauvage, Auguste Perret, Tony Garnier simply do not impinge on his attention.[166]

Called up in 1914, Duchamp-Villon[167] made one large sculpture before he went into the army, and it remains one of the most important Cubist essays into the third dimension. *Le Cheval*, a furiously dynamic head of a horse, was done in 1913–14. The horse is really more Futurist than Cubist, and Duchamp-Villon and his brothers, with many other artists, veered between the ideas which the two (in fact, complementary) movements had invoked. Overlaps and consequent recriminations, excommunications, accusations were not unusual among both Cubists and Futurists.

Non-pictorial devices had inevitably excited Futurists. Movement had been examined intensively during the last quarter of the nineteenth century by Muybridge and Marey especially.[168] While some Futurist inventions were derived from photographic practice,[169] the new moving pictures fascinated them even more. Marinetti – with the Corradini brothers[170] and the journalist Emilio Settimelli – even made an episodic short, *Vita Futurista* in 1916, of which only some stills survive, and at the same time produced the *Manifesto of the Futurist Cinema*. 'Coloured' film was already in its first experimental stage and seemed to offer even more exciting possibilities. The Corradinis were familiar with the ideas of both Steiner and Blavastky, to which they introduced several Futurists – including Marinetti. They had also come across the Leadbeater-Besant colour-music ideas and translated them into experimental hand-coloured film set to the music of Chopin and Mendelssohn.[171]

Futurist architecture had a rather different beginning. Antonio Sant'Elia, a prolific draughtsman who built comparatively little, joined the movement in 1914. A manifesto of Futurist architecture seems to have been in preparation before that, though the circumstances of its writing and its authorship are confused; Antonio Sant'Elia certainly signed it.[172] Brilliant, visionary draughtsman though he was, excited about the use of glass and metal, about oblique lines and multi-level roads, there was a rather Viennese atmosphere about his projects for soaring and mechanical hypothetical buildings, an atmosphere quite incongruent with the Futurists' aggressively anti-Austrian stance. Many of his drawings look like the exercises of some of Otto Wagner's best pupils, while his executed work was in some ways more like that of Olbrich than of Wagner himself. Ironically enough, it was an Austrian bullet that killed Sant'Elia in 1916.

So there never was any true Futurist building in the end. Architects who had followed Sant'Elia into Futurism, the Swiss Mario Chiattone and Alberto Sartoris, did not remain faithful to its principles; only the precocious teenager Enrico Prampolini, having produced his own architectural mini-manifesto in 1913, developed a Futurist decor for the theatre and for exhibitions. Italian architecture did not 'realize' the Futurist impulse, and even painters did not remain faithful to it. After the war Balla moved into abstraction, Carrà and Severini (as well as the late joiners, Ottone Rosai and Mario Sironi) to a 'metaphysical' classicism.[173] When some young architects formed the influential 'rationalist' Gruppo 7 in 1926, they were careful to dissociate themselves from Futurist violence and unreason. In all that Cubist and Futurist excitement, which produced brilliant and enduring painting, sculpture and literature, film and music (of a kind), building seemed an oblique afterthought. The great energy which both Cubists and Futurists had invested in making a breach into the everyday was frustrated – there seemed to be no way to shift from the brilliant explosion of mimetic invention to the shaping of objects, a move which at this time was complicated by the fairly quick take-over of production by the machine. The attempt to transform industrial production by art had been made in England and in Scotland in the nineteenth century, but that movement seemed to have exhausted itself by the twentieth, even if Loos, in Vienna, could still talk of craft production, and the Secession artists, principally through the Wiener Werkstätte, were producing everyday design objects by craft methods. Only in Germany, in those last years before the outbreak of the war, did artists, designers and architects put their energy into machine-produced everyday objects – of which Behrens' AEG enterprise was by far the most important. The energy which did not go towards making a bridge from representation to the shaping of everyday things was channelled into the theatre in Paris.

In the Theatre

Much creative energy in Paris on the eve of the First World War became focused on one particular theatre building. It had no obvious stylistic connection with Futurism or with Cubism. The brainchild of Gabriel Thomas (chairman of the Eiffel Tower holding board) and a very enterprising impresario, Gabriel Astruc (Diaghilev's main Parisian backer), who knew well enough that an alternative was needed to the old and somewhat rickety Châtelet (in which Diaghilev had had his first ballet season), it had to be both more modest and more modern than the Opéra. They found a site on the Avenue Montaigne, near the Pont de l'Alma, though the theatre was in fact called, for many reasons, the Théâtre des Champs-Elysées. A distinguished patronage committee was formed with the Symbolist painter Maurice Denis as the artistic adviser. Denis suggested Van de Velde as the best architect possible: his involvement with theatre design was well-known by then, and, of course, Denis had been a friend of Van de Velde since his Divisionist days and they had worked together intermittently (for Kessler, for instance).

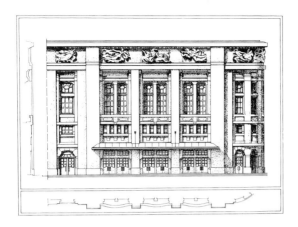

Henry Van de Velde,
elevation of the facade
of the Théâtre des
Champs-Elysées,
1911–13.

Van de Velde's original project was traditionally tripartite: a stately glazed foyer opened on the Avenue, with a smaller theatre over it, while the main auditorium was a modified cylinder articulated by three superimposed balconies (there was not room enough for the full Wagnerian *Gleichschaltung* so that the stage proper was relatively shallow). Van de Velde proposed a steel, stone-clad structure in his up-dated sober, rather blockish (but still ornamentally fluid) style; on his elevations and sections, Maurice Denis sketched the outline of his interior paintings, while Rodin's other major disciple, Antoine Bourdelle (who had been brought in by Thomas), started by drawing outlines of reliefs on the proposed facade, though in the end he re-did the drawings altogether. The Bourdelle-Van de Velde project was not greeted with enthusiasm by the committee, if Van de Velde is to be believed.

The estimates for the steel-and-stone project did turn out rather high, and Van de Velde suggested to the committee that a reinforced concrete structure be considered instead. The Brothers Perret, the most experienced and innovative concrete builders in Paris at the time, were consulted at the suggestion of another of Van de Velde's old painter friends, Théo van Rysselberge, whose Divisionist panel had made such a contrast among Horta's Art Nouveau swirls in the Hôtel Solvay in Brussels.[174] The concrete structure did turn out to be cheaper and was adopted.

The Perret brothers were not just contractors. Auguste, the architect brother of the firm, had built one of the earliest reinforced concrete frame structures in Paris in 1903: an apartment block, its exposed frame infilled with elaborately

286

floral ceramic panels, stylized and crowded, recalled some of Gaudí's harsh decorations. The formal relation of infill to frame was an expressive device, more like Olbrich's geometrized plants on his Vienna Secession building than the sinuous ornament of Perret's Parisian contemporaries. Two years later, in the Garage Ponthieu, just off the Champs-Elysées (one of the very earliest car-parking buildings), Perret abandoned floral ornament altogether: the infill elements are of plain sheet glass, while the frame is carefully attenuated by a play of mouldings and recessions, so that the historical, 'classical' references become ordering devices of (though not ornamental additions to) the facade, even if the square centre panel is a spider's web pattern of thin metal glazing.[175] It was about this time that he also began to frequent the Puteaux artists.

The way Auguste Perret filched the commission and any credit away from Van de Velde does not make for a glorious episode.[176] Van de Velde should, in

Auguste Perret, Théâtre des Champs-Elysées, 1911–13. Reliefs by Antoine Bourdelle.

any case, have realized that such an ambitious and subtle architect would not act as a mere amanuensis. Strangely enough, he seems to have accepted without demur first Bourdelle's and then Perret's radical changes to the 'decorative' character of the building, allegedly to make the project conform to the tastes of the committee, who – as Van de Velde himself put it – 'did want to do something "new" but were not free of the tradition of the "French Styles"'.[177]

If Perret did change the structure in adapting it to concrete, he did not alter the plan substantially; yet there is very little about the look of the executed building to recall Van de Velde's early drawings in which the metal frame was a structural expedient unrelated to the apparent stone facing or the elaboration of the sculptured ornament, which in a sense rivalled, even if it was subordinate to, the reliefs which were also to 'decorate' it. In Perret's building, the concrete skeleton is clearly translated into a post-and-beam figuration which organizes both exterior and interior, so that vertical elements of the frame read as columns or pilasters, the horizontals, as beams. As in the Garage Ponthieu, the implicitly 'classicizing' effect depends on the modulation of the frame and the relief of the plane surfaces. Such historical reference seems a great deal more 'digested' than Behrens' explicitly Prussian classicism of the same year.

The sculptured reliefs were part of the project from the start; they were drawn in by Bourdelle and he certainly influenced the designs. Perret's deep cornice, for instance, was intended to emphasize but never overshadow the reliefs. About their relation and some of the other figures Bourdelle was enthusiastic: 'All the sculptures have to relate to the proportions of the architecture, depend on it. . . it should seem as if the wall itself erupted into human figures', he told his students; and later, writing of the facade relief: 'In the great high-relief frieze there remains among you a young dancer born close to the great Terpsichore herself, Isadora Duncan . . . Something of the evanescently human was affixed in the laws of marble.'

Duncan and Nijinski provided the main inspiration for many of the figures in the reliefs and for the frescoes which Bourdelle executed in the theatre. Of one, 'The Dance', he wrote:

Isadora, inclining and throwing her fine head, shuts her eyes to dance from within – pure emotion . . . He, the dancer, a Nijinski, tears himself out of the marble which still imprisons him . . .

The main auditorium dome and proscenium arch were painted by Maurice Denis, while other painters (Edouard Vuillard was one) executed some subsidiary frescoes. The role and the importance of the building were clear to all of them. Bourdelle certainly knew what he was at: 'The new Cathedral, the new temple to which the crowds will flock shall be the theatre, which will unite all the arts', and so claimed the status of a true total work of art for the Théâtre des Champs-Elysées itself, with the help of the two dancers who became emblematic of the period and its ambitions.[178] Denis and Bourdelle were certainly not the most 'advanced' artists of the day, but they were respected by critics and colleagues alike,[179] while Perret was recognized as one of the fathers of modern architecture. It was certainly his most ambitious collaboration with artists of a stature analogous to his.[180]

The Théâtre des Champs-Elysées turned out to be one of the last Parisian buildings whose exterior space and interior volume were ruled by that very sense of continuity which Simmel and Loos had in their different ways theorized away. Its importance was emphasized when its 1913 opening season (which included the revival of the Debussy-Nijinski *L'Apres-midi d'un faune*) centred on one of the most famous of all theatrical scandals, the first night of the Stravinsky–Nijinsky *Sacre du printemps*. The 'book' of the ballet, as well as the sets and costumes, were all by Nicolas Roerich, an artist who may have belonged to the older world of theatre decorators, but was as passionately interested in esoteric ideas and in ritual as Kandinsky. It was Roerich who had insisted on rhythmic intensity and the ritual atmosphere which seemed to suit the 'classical' but, in a sense, also archaic interior.

That first season ruined Astruc. Scandal and ruin apart, some spectators at that first *Sacre* saw its importance clearly: Count Kessler wrote to von Hofmannsthal that Nijinski's choreography was shattering: '[it] sticks out from the choreography of Fokine like a Gauguin in a Bouguereau exhibition'.[181]

A reverse image of the relation between artist and architect was provided by a building at the other end of the world. In Chicago Frank Lloyd Wright was commissioned by a family friend to design a novel building – restaurant, open-air music-theatre, dance hall, culture centre all in one. Called Midway Gardens,[182] it had a sharp, early success, but the time was not propitious: it opened two months before the First World War broke out in Europe and was dogged by financial problems from the beginning;

bought by a brewery, it was then ruined by the prohibition of 1920–21. Midway Gardens was torn down in 1929.

Wright saw Midway as one of his masterworks, a 'synthesis of the arts'; 'painting and sculpture were to be bidden back again to their original places and to their original offices . . . The architect, himself, was here again master of them all together.' Wright speaks of the artists who worked for him generously, but usually to emphasize their devotion to him, their fidelity. There was no question, as at the Théâtre des Champs-Elysées, of independent artists expressing criticisms of the designs; the architect was the absolute master of the scene. He provided them with detailed drawings for the sculptures and the wall paintings in the idiosyncratic manner into which he had absorbed a number of influences. He was very taken with what he had seen earlier in Vienna, and the sculptures he drew owe something to the Viennese Josef Hoffman and his sculptor, Emilie Simandl,[183] and indeed referred to himself (only briefly and very occasionally) as the 'Chicago Secessionist'. This was unusual in someone who took any suggestion of influence by anyone living or recently dead very ill. There is virtually no mention of any living sculptor or painter in his autobiography.

The buildings were tough: steel-framed and brick-clad, the main restaurant hall carried a large, 20-foot-high painted panel. This was – like the sculpture – executed faithfully from Wright's designs and suggests the contemporary work of both Kupka and Kandinsky. The sculptors who were employed to carve the statues, like the fresco painters who carried out the painting, were menials; to be sure, he valued their collaboration, but the architect directed the artist's hand. One or two paintings in the side pavilions were carried out by independent Chicago artists, but their names are hardly ever mentioned in the prolific literature about Midway. Nor did they infringe on the brilliantly unified formal unity of Wright's most accomplished public building before the war.

But Chicago was not an artistic stomping-ground for European visitors – or even for East Coasters. Paris remained the capital of the art world, for all its follies and frivolities and in spite of the depradations of the war.

Van de Velde's Champs-Elysées fiasco was a real blow to his reputation. He never did any further work of importance there. Until his forced departure as an enemy alien in 1917, Weimar remained his base. Yet Van de Velde did get to build his theatre, which had a great, though brief success at the Werkbund exhibition of 1914 in Cologne. That exhibition, in a sense, is the closing episode of the period which began with the Darmstadt Fest and the Turin show. Van de Velde was not commissioned generously: a nationalist wing of the Werkbund did not want a Belgian to design this important building, but the Mayor of Cologne, Konrad Adenauer, intervened in his favour decisively.[184]

The Cologne theatre is not as ambitious as the Champs-Elysées project, but it did provide a gently raked, unified auditorium of the kind Wagner had demanded; the effect, Van de Velde says, was that of a temple. The stage was circular, and had a fixed semicircular cyclorama based on the Appia-Fortuny scheme. It was wider than the auditorium, and articulated by two columns into three openings, an arrangement which avoided the usual deep proscenium and wings as well as the proscenium arch, while the structure was concrete and subtly moulded. Ironically enough, Perret would virtually imitate it in the wooden festival theatre he designed for the Exposition des Arts Décoratifs in Paris in 1925. As for the unity of the arts, it could not show anything to equal Denis' paintings, or Bourdelle's carvings: some rather modest low reliefs were done by a young sculptor, Molly Steger, though the foyer had a striking frieze of Dionysiac figures painted by Ludwig von Hoffmann, a trusted Weimar collaborator of Van de Velde and a fine colourist.

Nor did the theatre play any important part in literary history: Goethe's *Faust* was an obvious opener; a fine production of Mozart's *Seraglio* conducted by Bruno Walter was imported from Munich. Two months after it opened, war broke out and the theatre was never used again. But it had admirers: the aspiring architect Erich Mendelsohn visited the exhibition soon after it opened. Van de Velde's theatre, he thought, was powerful in concept and expression.[185] He confessed himself its disciple while he was disappointed with both Peter Behrens' and Josef Hoffman's buildings.

Behrens' Festival Hall (*Festhalle*) was rather flaccid, vaguely 'classical'; it was entered under a replica cast of those Petersburg *Dioscuri* by Erdmann Encke and faced the solemn, u-shaped colonnade of Josef Hoffman's Austrian pavilion, its grey, fluted square pillars carrying a thin cornice, the two end pediments decorated with 'architectural' wreaths. The most momentous and striking buildings of the exhibition, however, were the virtually undecorated model

Bruno Taut, Cologne: Werkbund Exhibition (1914): Glass Pavilion, exterior view.

factory by Walter Gropius and Adolf Meyer, and Bruno Taut's pavilion of the glass industry, which turned out to be the most extraordinary (certainly the most notorious) of all the exhibits. It was a low, near-circular, faceted building. Its light steel structure was crowned by a latticed beehive dome. Walls, floors, ceilings were all of different types of glass. A cascade ran through the middle of the building illuminated at night to turn into the shining crystal of Behrens' rhapsody fifteen years earlier. Taut had worked closely with the witty and brilliant science-fiction writer, Paul Scheerbart (whom I mentioned earlier as Rudolf Steiner's friend), who was enthusiastically involved in its conception and provided the joky couplets with which the exterior was inscribed.[186]

A quite different event marked Van de Velde's presence in Cologne. A founder-director of the Werkbund, Hermann Muthesius, demanded in a public address in Cologne that the Association should henceforth impose standardization – *Typiesierung* – on all designers. German design and architecture were tending that way in any case, he said, and standardizing all products associated with the Werkbund would ensure a minimum level of taste to

292

Glass Pavilion, interior view with cascade.

make German industry world-competitive. Only industrial prototypes should be displayed or commissioned, since the individually made object was economically as well as industrially irrelevant. Shocked by the *diktat*, Van de Velde gathered a group of designers – August Endell, Hermann Obrist and the young Bruno Taut, who were joined by Walter Gropius and Richard Riemerschmid – to produce a manifesto in defence of the craft object and of a free, experimental creativity; Peter Behrens as chairman of the Werkbund and the most successful industrial designer in Germany took their side.[187]

But in August 1914 the Austrian Crown Prince Franz-Ferdinand was assassinated in Sarajevo, and all these developments were broken by the horror and turmoil of World War slaughter. 'Lamps were going out all over Europe.' When peace returned in 1918, Vienna and Berlin were no longer imperial capitals, a generation of artists and patrons had been decimated, and German artists lived the defeat bitterly. It also put an end to the dominance of dance and the hope that it begot – that dance would become the socially transforming total work of art.

Yet the demise of dance was gradual. Loïe Fuller had attempted Futurist performances just before the war. In the early summer of 1914, she presented a Cubist/Futurist *Synaesthetic Symphony* at the Châtelet using (unidentified) music by Scriabin, as well as Stravinsky's *Feux d'artifice*; the dance was part-organic, part-geometric shadow-movement against paper screens. Wartime also caused Diaghilev to move his workshops and rehearsals to Rome, where Marinetti was quick to make an alliance with him. Giacomo Balla took up Loïe Fuller's projection technique in a 1917 Futurist production of *Feux d'artifice* for Diaghilev, though like Scriabin's experiments it was dogged by technical hitches.[188] Diaghilev was still thinking in terms of ritual performances, but as the visual element became increasingly important, he (and Massine) contemplated a highly stylized, almost icon-style performance which would give the audience the experience of the Mass or of the Orthodox liturgy; he wanted to call it simply *Liturgie*. Larionov and Natalia Goncharova were enthusiastic about the sets and costumes, but Stravinsky, approached for the music, sensing blasphemy, demurred and the enterprise floundered.[189]

The final Cubist *festin* was yet another ballet mounted by Diaghilev in 1917 and shown in wartime Paris: *Parade*, choreographed by Léonide Massine on a 'book' by Jean Cocteau, to music by Erik Satie. Costumes and sets were by Picasso – and hardly Cubist, except for the 10-foot-high Cubist 'sheath-masks' for two characters called 'managers'.[190] The brilliance of the spectacle was due partly to the evident tension between the new 'classical' Picasso and his Cubist past, but also to Cocteau's passion for Futurist effects and his determination to draw themes from the circus as well as the new silent cinema into his ballet. This amalgam worked well enough between Picasso and Satie on one side, Cocteau on the other – who turned Satie's score into a quasi-Futurist musical collage with propeller and typewriter effects. At the first night there were scenes of protest at the Opéra, though now some of the protesters were Cubists.[191]

The Eclipse of Reason

Surrealism was a word born about this time. After the only performance of his play *Les Mamelles de Térésias* in 1918, at which some of the Cubists also remonstrated, Apollinaire wrote to Juan Gris to break off their friendship, and decreed: 'don't forget that the play is Surrealist and that the word Cubist has been banished altogether'. He claimed, in his preface to the *Mamelles,* to have coined the word (which he first used in his programme notes for *Parade*), to counter Cocteau's own description of it as *ballet réaliste.* By 1924 it was taken up as the label of a movement and of a periodical: *La Révolution Surréaliste.*

In so far as it was a coherent movement, it had evolved out of a group of near-neutral refugees in Zürich: Romanians (Tristan Tzara, Marcel Janco), Germans (Hugo Ball, Richard Hülsenbeck), Alsatians (Hans/Jean Arp), who first started a literary cabaret, the Cabaret Voltaire, and then a periodical, *Dada.* The periodical became the label of the group, which soon found sympathizers in Berlin and Paris. Eclectic, anti-war, internationalist, anarchist, it was radically opposed to Futurist warmongering. A Dada demonstration broke up Russolo's Rumorist concert at the Champs-Elysées in 1922. Dada was very much a literary-political rather than a visual movement, though the cabaret performed (among many other things) a play by Kokoschka as well as dances by Rudolf von Laban, who was to become the dominant theorist of dance in the twentieth century. Dada ended dramatically in July 1923 at an anthological evening which culminated in a riot during a performance of Tzara's 'play' *Coeur à Barbe*, at which André Breton (who was to dominate the inter-war Parisian art scene as the pope or *duce* of Surrealism) broke one of the participants' arms.[192]

The Dada atmosphere held for six years, while Cubism had lasted for a little more than a decade, though both formed or modified many an artist's vision. In spite of Apollinaire's *ukaze,* many painters continued to work through their Cubist inheritance: Picasso and Braque – and intermittently Léger, Gris, as well as the sculptors Henri Laurens and Jacques Lipschitz. Cubism as a 'movement' broke up at the end of the war in a series of banquet brawls (for Apollinaire, for Braque, both wounded and decorated). From then on movements and manifestos succeed each other with increasing speed and pugnacity.

The school of Paris was never cohesive, of course, and some 'Parisians' were determined to work out methods which would take them beyond any aesthetic. Marcel Duchamp had exhibited his *Nude Descending a Staircase* at the Armory Show of 1913, and he soon became a committee member of the Society of Independent Artists in New York, which, for its 1917 show, received as a submission *Fountain*, a urinal lying on its back, roughly signed on the side

'R. Mutt 1917'. The embarrassed hanging jury 'lost' it in a dark corner. As is known all too well, it was recovered when Duchamp's principal patron of the time, Walter Arensberg, asserted that he wanted to buy it – whereupon both he and Duchamp (who at first disclaimed authorship) resigned from the committee.[193] It was Duchamp's first public attempt to claim that he himself should decide what was or was not a work of art – indeed that the decision itself was the 'work'. He had begun doing so in Paris in 1913 when he first mounted a bicycle-wheel in its fork on a bar-stool: he found playing with it soothing, he said. There were some other 'assisted' inventions, but in the winter of 1914 he bought a bottle-drying rack in a street market, a common household object at the time, and turned it into the first un-manipulated ready-made,[194] making further replicas when he got to New York. More 'ready-mades' followed between 1913 and 1918: a snow shovel and a typewriter cover – as well as a metal dog-comb, the kind used to dress poodles. Their titles became part of a game, and the constant punning became one way of performing, one of the prime operations of modernity – the freeing of the concept from the phenomenon.

Everyday objects were fetishized by turning them into art-works. By inversion, Duchamp also suggested that one could use a Rembrandt portrait as an ironing-board.[195] His cool irony is far removed from the bombastic militancy of the Futurists. Ready-mades were deliberately, provocatively anti-aesthetic, or as he would say, 'anaesthetic'. What he called 'retinal' art was a swipe at everything from Impressionism to Cubism. This did not stop him offering admiring and helpful criticism to his brothers and sister Suzanne who persisted in their practice.[196] Another departure led to his last and best-known work, the *Large Glass*, which he never finished. Its kernel was a 'Cubist' dissection of a coffee-grinder which he painted for his brother Raymond, who had called on several friends to decorate his new kitchen in 1911. It was drawn as an engineering proposition, the movement of the handle shown by a series of arrows. He then showed some other objects (observed, analysed and projected), such as the three-drum chocolate grinder he had seen in a confectioner's window. He made several analytic drawings and finally a number of painted projections of it. Then there were the 'nine malic moulds' (another pun), representations of coffin-like, stiff, hollow uniforms. Painted in oil, silver foil and lead wire, these were sandwiched between two glass sheets and became one of several trial runs to the cool, elegant 'composition', the *Large Glass*, which he had already planned in 1913. In 1924, when he abandoned it, it was unfinished, and in 1926 it broke in transport, though Duchamp considered the cracks part of its facture, contributed by hazard.[197]

The complex and obscure imagery of the *Large Glass* has provoked a number of interpretations: Alchemical and Rosicrucian, Masonic and – inevitably – psychoanalytical.[198] The title Duchamp himself gave it, *The Bride Stripped Bare by her Bachelors, Even*, suggests an obsessive concern with non-consummation and makes it a paean to voyeurism and masturbation. Yet Duchamp remained the gamesman-chess player and *farceur*, as well as the shrewd ironist who always parried any univocal interpretation of his anti-aesthetic masterpiece.

The Impressionist Cathedral

Meanwhile, total aesthetic attention did, eventually and 'out of step with its time', acquire its own temple which owed nothing to Cubism or Futurism or to any of the other twentieth-century innovations, but was the work of the archetypal Impressionist, Claude Monet, who devoted much of his energies to it during the last three decades of his life. He began his water-lily paintings, the *Nymphéas* (sometimes also called *Nénuphars*) in his garden at Giverny outside Paris late in the 1890s, and worked on them until his death in 1926, altering his garden to fit the pictures. The largest, painted on canvases as long (if not as high) as David had used for his monumental compositions, were created to be given to 'the Nation', though it was not clear at first by what mechanism the gift was to be proffered or where 'the Nation' would keep them. He received much encouragement in this enterprise from Georges Clémenceau, a neighbour and a very close friend as well as a powerful patron of the arts. Clémenceau was a great national figure: prime minister in 1907–9, and much more crucially in 1917–20, chairman of the Versailles treaty negotiations. In 1920 he had been the unsuccessful Presidential candidate – after which he withdrew from politics.

Monet, whose method of recording fleeting observations invited Cézanne's envious and snide comments about his being 'only an eye – but what an eye!', had spent his maturity as an artist painting the same subjects over and over again to capture the variations of light on them and their constant colour changes in the course of a day. These formed series: 'The Haystack', 'Rouen Cathedral', 'London, the Houses of Parliament', 'Venice, the Doge's Palace from the Water'. Groups of these canvases were often exhibited together, though Monet was not committed to any one of them having a permanent home. In this the 'Water-Lilies' were different,[199] since they were planned as an outsize and semi-public ensemble from the outset: indeed a special 'church-like' (and rather unsightly) studio[200] had to be built in Monet's garden to accommodate the large canvases, which he would prop round him in a circle as he wanted them displayed.

Clémenceau used his status as the personification of French victory in the World War to have the French state buy the much debated and criticised Rouen Cathedral series – unsuccessfully.[201] Not only the fate but also the method of painting the water-lilies was different. While truth to the subject had always been an inviolate principle for Monet, the lily-pond in his garden was always carefully prepared for his painting sessions in advance: dead leaves were picked off, the plants dusted and moistened.

Their first major exhibition at Durand-Ruel in 1909 was welcomed with almost universal critical enthusiasm. Changeable and constantly shimmering images of rushes and floating lilies were shown reflected in the water: 'now the crepuscular bronze of a cloud served as a theme, now the calm of unclouded azure.'[202] In spite of Monet's reluctance, two of the canvases were woven as tapestries by the Gobelins factory. Sacha Guitry, still a very young man, made a film of Monet working in his studio, but Monet was constantly worried and he agonized over the project. Many of those large – 2 x 4-metre – canvases were furiously slashed by him and most were repainted many times.[203] He worked on them through the war, through his troubles with eyesight (cataract, tunnel vision) and family problems.

Although from 1916 onwards dealers and collectors tried to buy the 'final' pictures, Monet was not willing to sell, both because he was constantly working on them and because he hoped that they would find a permanent home in a national institution. In a way they were his meditative, near-abstract and personal war-monument. Nor were they comparable to the equally large but highly figured 'sideshow' canvases of the 'exhibition artists' whom I considered earlier: Copley, West, David, Constable, Géricault and Courbet.

These were pictures which could not be offered as a spectacle, and indeed Monet kept on referring to them as his 'decorative' panels. Yet he pursued a rather different aim consciously: he spoke of applying his paint as medieval monks illuminated books of hours. He evoked Japanese prints and eighteenth-century French painters, yet he always knew that he wanted the paintings shown in a circle of shimmering colour, as a dimensionally ambiguous surface, defying gravity.

After much negotiation and the badgering of influential critics (as well as Clémenceau's manoeuvring – to him they represented the triumph of French civility and therefore a most glorious trophy of the 1918 victory), a project to set up a special building was handed to his contemporary, the very official and respectable Louis-Bernard Bonnier. It was to be in the garden of the Hôtel Biron (now the Rodin Museum). However, the definitive installation – of 22 canvases – was made in the Tuileries Orangery by another architect, Camille Lefèvre. Neither of these were architects of great distinction, yet the installation became 'the first in the history of Western art designed exclusively for non-utilitarian, non-ceremonial visual meditation'. The Surrealist painter André Masson called them 'the Sistine Chapel of Impressionism'.[204] Monet himself had conceived them as a kind of secular temple, an enclosure whose exterior was immaterial to him, and on entering which the spectator would be taken into a flux of impressions – he would experience the volume as a sensorial, video-tactile totality in much the same way as the auditors of Scriabin's ritual were to experience his music and colour projections, or for that matter, as the listeners to the reading of Stéphane Mallarmé's *Livre* were invited to experience his endless and seamless text, his scripture, as a quasi-religious but auditory, detachedly aesthetic experience.

Scriabin, Monet and Mallarmé stand at the end of the development which Philipp Otto Runge had begun a century earlier. Each one of the three demanded that their work provide the totality of a sensory experience through which every member of the audience would be able to overcome his individuality and have access to another, an ambiguously transcendent reality. They offered a secularized version of Runge's hope that visitors to his room 'decorated' with *The Seasons* would (through their harmony) achieve that experience of the Deity who is immanent in all of nature, the Divine *Abgrund* about which Boehme had taught.

299

Both Monet's and Runge's paintings, and many between them, demanded responses which, according to Georg Simmel, proper works of art should solicit: a devoutly aesthetic attention. Even when they were monumental by intention, as Monet's *Nénuphars* certainly were, their appeal to the viewer remains intimate. André Masson's comparison to the Sistine Chapel is telling: Michelangelo's two fresco-cycles – one horizontal (and overhead), the other vertical – were the ceiling and the end wall of a room which was half-public, the pope's chapel. However, the aesthetic response that Simmel demanded was only possible when Michelangelo's frescoes were viewed on the page, as it were, either as engravings or as reproductions (unless you have the privilege of seeing them from the restorer's scaffold). The structure of the interior in the Sistine Chapel, a vault spanning a triple cube, is essential to any integral experience of the frescoes. On the other hand, Monet provided only the most generic directions for the volume which was to display his paintings, since aesthetic attention considered architecture as making only a marginal contribution. But then it was hard to imagine anyone burning with a hard, gem-like flame at the sight of a building.

Conclusion: After the Wars

The 'ten' October 'days that shook the world' in 1917 convulsed art as well as everything else: the time of revelation and redemption that many artists (and most mystagogues) had awaited had come and the 'war to end all wars' was drawing to its catastrophic close. The 'cosmic spring' when art would finally fuse with life had sprung at last. Even clear-headed modernists were ecstatic: 'a new cosmic creation has become a reality in the world'.[1]

Most actors in the October events may have taken a cooler view of the cataclysm, even if many of them claimed that they had seen it coming – some prosily, in the officially materialist tone of the day:

> what happened to society in 1917 had been realized in our work as pictorial artists by 1914 when we accepted 'materials, volume and construction' as the basis of our work.

Others put it more sonorously:

> Art, don't you see, means prophecy. Works of art are the embodiments of presentiments; therefore pre-revolutionary art is the art of the Revolution.

Vladimir Tatlin made the first remarks in an official publication, understating the nature of the change, if anything; while in the second Leon Trotsky was ironically qualifying his perceptive (if strident) criticism of the avant-garde.[2] He had, it is worth remembering, some claim to be taken seriously as a literary figure as well, though by the time his *Literature and Revolution* appeared, Lenin was dead and Stalin was edging him out.

Both had been right: Russian painters and sculptors, even theatre decorators, registered the pandemic ferment in their pre-Revolutionary work with increasing confidence. They may not have been in advance of Western Europe technically, but were aware of Diaghilev's Parisian successes and of the part Russian artists had played in German and French developments – and they were eager to participate. Marinetti's *Figaro* manifesto was printed in a Moscow evening paper within a month of its Parisian publication, and he is reputed to have visited Moscow and St Petersburg about that time.[3] But by 1914, when he did make a famous Russian lecture tour, the Cubo-Futurists (the binomial was coined there) were disillusioned with him and even devised a new *echt*-Russian label for themselves, *budetliani* (those-of-shall-it-be?) – which did not stick.

Architects, on the other hand, remained staid, conventional. The neo-Russian style had not seemed a harbinger of catastrophe to its patrons or practitioners. Academic teaching of architecture continued in Moscow and St Petersburg, where it was dominated by Alexander Benois' brother Leontii Nikolaievich. Among Benois' pupils were two architects, both about 50 in 1918, who were to influence the following generations while making few concessions to nationalism or to any kind of modernism: Ivan Fomin,[4] whose best-known pre-Revolutionary building was a Frenchified, palatial and much-colonnaded Polovtsev *dacha* of 1911–16, and Ivan Zholtovski, who was much more dogmatic; his most famous building was a gracelessly re-proportioned copy of Palladio's Palazzo Thiene of 1541 as the Tarasov Mansion in Moscow in 1905. Paradoxically, he was also the teacher of many 'advanced' young (and 'avant-garde') architects.[5]

In the decade before the war some younger architects moderated a refined classicism into post-1900 modernity – not unlike that of Peter Behrens and Bruno Paul – notably Fyodor Lidval, whose discreet Astoria Hotel on St Isaac's Square was (and still is) the most fashionable in the city, while his Don-Azov Bank built over the next two or three years in St Petersburg had the kind of sober steel construction which a group of local architects were developing before the Revolution.[6] Opposite the Astoria, also on St Isaac's Square, Peter Behrens' dourly palatial German Embassy was sacked by a crowd on the declaration of war, but seems to have made little impact on the history of Russian architecture in any case.[7]

There were austerely 'advanced' industrial and commercial buildings in Moscow and in St Petersburg, and one or two graceful houses as well. Ilya Golosov in Moscow and the three brothers Vesnin in St Petersburg had come to public notice before the Revolution with a series of conventional but elegant town and country houses. The oldest of the Vesnins, Leonid, had been a student of Benois, while Victor and Aleksander were trained as civil engineers. It was Aleksander who turned to painting before the Revolution, fraternized with the future Constructivists and became one of the first masters of avant-garde stage design. The Vesnins are also often named as leading civil engineers, while the most inventive structural designer in Russia, Vladimir Grigorevich Shukhov (who had been consulted on the building of the pre-Revolutionary Moscow stations I mentioned in the previous chapter), gets few mentions in histories of Russian architecture, even if – paradoxically – his openwork wireless transmission tower appears in the background of many photographs of new Moscow buildings.

The outbreak of the war had already changed the context in which Russian artists were working. Half the Blaue Reiter group (Kandinsky being the most prominent) had to leave Germany as enemy aliens. A number of others who were studying or working abroad – Natan Altman, Marc Chagall, Aleksandra Exter, El Lissitzky, Lyubov Popova, Ivan Puni (later known as Jean Pougny) – returned to Russia. Most of them were already known at home and had exhibited with the various groups which were all in a permanent frenzy of contention.[8]

Exhibitions, and squabbles, went on through the war period: early in 1915 a collective show called *Tramway v – The First Futurist Exhibition* was followed a few months later by *0.10* (zero-ten) which was in turn advertised as the 'last Futurist Exhibition'. That joke apart, there was a finality about *0.10*, since Tatlin, who had exhibited in *Tramway* with Kasimir Malevich, objected to showing together with him again and accused him of bungling. They even came to fisticuffs.[9] Tatlin and his allies then provocatively labelled their room: 'Show of Professional Artists', and it marked their separation as Constructivists (though they did not assume the label until 1922) from the more idealizing Suprematists. Both sides in the quarrel were affected by the notion of *zaum* – ultra sense, super reason – associated with their collaborators and fellow travellers, the Cubo-Futurist poets Velemir Khlebnikov and

Alexei Kruchenykh, both of whom taught that words have a sense beyond common understanding, that their shape on the page, their sound and materiality signify more than the meaning assigned to them in dictionaries: words are autonomous agents – much like the shapes and materials that are fused into a Constructivist assembly.[10]

Malevich himself had moved from a heavy, peasanty primitivism to radical abstraction, to what he termed non-objective art. He reduced the elements of his figuration to a square, and in 1913 arrived at what seemed like the ultimate goal – a black square on a white ground. It was to have the power of a sacred icon, and when he first showed it, he had it hung in a corner at 45 degrees to the walls like a holy picture in a peasant home. He designed sets and costumes for his friend Kruchenykh's play *Victory over the Sun*, and by the following year he was labelling his work with variants on the term 'supremus'. About the time of the October events, he went one further, painting in white on a white ground to reach the zero point of art – the extinction of painting.[11]

Malevich was one of several artists between the First World War and the end of the century who saw the end of painting as inevitable for different reasons. For much of the next decade, he was working first on drawings, then on wood and plaster models of buildings with no function, no plan and no location which he called 'architektons' and which he wanted to compose into a Suprematist city, though he left neither drawings nor instructions of how it was to be done. Their separation from use or situation asserted the autonomy of aesthetic experience and the power it would have to mould not just art, but all visual perception in some future time. Lissitzky's rather utilitarian view of building led to a break between them, even if Malevich was also designing fabric and wallpaper patterns, applying ornament to household china objects, and even producing a famous 'analysed' china teapot, which, in spite of its angular mutation, was intended for daily use.

His opponent, Vladimir Tatlin, had already met Aleksander Vesnin at art school and they started collaborating in 1910. They, too, were fascinated by the possibilities which the theatre offered. Tatlin designed sets and costumes for a Moscow production of an eighteenth-century farce, but also sets and costumes for Glinka's opera *Ivan Susanin*[12] and for Wagner's *Flying Dutchman* – 'on spec'. They were never used. Just before the Revolution, Boris Jakovlev (a Georgian painter, recently returned from Paris where he had worked with the

Aleksander
Rodchenko, Vladimir
Tatlin and Gregori
Yakulov et al., Café
Pittoresque,
Moscow, 1917.

Simultaneist group of Robert and Sonia Delaunay) involved Tatlin in the decorations and furnishing, in and out, of a locale in the basement of a Moscow theatre called Café Pittoresque. Another young artist involved in that enterprise, Aleksander Rodchenko, would often work with Tatlin in the future. For the brief period that it existed, the café became a resort of avant-garde artists and *littérateurs*.

There was involvement in these developments at the highest levels of Soviet government. In spite of all the reservations I mentioned earlier, Lenin made Anatoly Lunacharsky (who had been a Bolshevik intermittently since 1905) Commissar for Education in the first Soviet cabinet.[13] Lunacharsky, a familiar of many of the avant-garde artists, returned to Petersburg in 1917. He was, by then, well known as a dramatist and poet as well as a fluent and rousing speaker. The October Revolution he saw as having accomplished 'the greatest, the most definitive act of "god-building"'.[14] Lunacharsky's department – NARKOMPROS – was not only responsible for educational policy (as its title suggested), but was also the channel of all state patronage of the arts.[15] The primal and instant change that the events of October worked on the arts propelled the avant-garde from the margins – bohemia, café interiors or scandal-generating exhibitions – to the centres of state activity. Farcically labelled factions were replaced by official institutes and syndicates (identified by even more confusing successions of contractions and acronyms), which dispensed patronage and wielded power, so that squabbles turned into official and semi-official denunciations.

Lunacharsky moved quickly, establishing IZO, the Institute of Fine Arts[16] as part of NARKOMPROS under his friend, the artist David Shterenberg (also returned from Paris, where he had studied at the Ecole des Beaux-Arts). Patronage and monument-conservation committees (which Lunacharsky called *Collegia*) were set up in the main cities, to which he appointed the artists he favoured: so Tatlin directed the Moscow one, and was also the main mover in setting up the Museum of Artistic Culture (that is, a Museum of Modern Art), as well as the agency for the protection of ancient monuments. Cultural policy may have been centralized, but it was not co-ordinated. On Lenin's personal initiative Lunacharsky charged Tatlin (before 1918 was out) to organize 50 permanent monuments around Moscow to historic literary and political figures admired by the Revolution.[17] Within weeks of the Revolution the Free Studios, SVOMAS, were established first in Petersburg, where Tatlin reigned, and then in Moscow, but there were also a number of semi-official bodies, dedicated, in spite of Lunacharsky's explicit directive, to the unity of the 'major arts'.[18] They were transformed into the more famous VKHUTEMAS in 1920, which became VKHUTEIN in 1926.[19]

All these art and cultural activities reformed existing attitudes and practices, but film had no established precedent. Lenin and Trotsky both insisted on its importance. It appealed to a young audience, and could be treated as a kind of undogmatic party teaching. The photographic image seemed to speak to the eye directly. Projectors were installed on agitation trains which were sent into the country and in workers' clubs so that new films had to be constantly made for home consumption. Inevitably, film stock and cameras were in short supply. Almost as an expedient, ways were devised of reusing news-film so that old shots could be mounted into continuous narrative reels. It was a technique which some Futurists saw as analogous to forms of collage and which came to be known as montage. A disciple of Vladimir Mayakovsky, Dziga Vertov,[20] with Vsevolod Pudovkin (the technical master of Soviet cinema) and Lev Kuleshov (the first to practise montage) were its leading figures.

Anonymous Construction advertising Sergei Eisenstein's 1929 film *The Battleship Potemkin*, at the Metropol Cinema, Moscow.

Sergei Eisenstein studied with Kuleshov, and he was to dominate Soviet cinema during the 1920s and '30s. Trained as an engineer, he joined the Red Army as a technician in 1918 but was moved to army theatre. He was an excellent and inventive draughtsman, produced a great many stage sets and worked with Meyerhold in 1920–22, when he moved to film. The most intensely visual and cultivated (and the most ambitious) of the Russian film producers, he saw the cinema rising to the status of great art from its beginnings as entertainment as it finally offered the possibility of total synaesthesia, but also that of being an agent of social transformation – so a true realization of the Wagnerian *Gesamtkunstwerk*.[21]

To commemorate the twentieth anniversary of the 1905 navy rebellion, Eisenstein made one of the masterpieces of silent cinema, *Battleship Potemkin*. Two unlikely admirers, Douglas Fairbanks and Mary Pickford, saw it on their visit to Moscow in 1925 and immediately offered Eisenstein work in Hollywood. When German distributors took the film over a few months later, they invited the Viennese film-music specialist Edmund Meisel to compose a score. The collaboration was lively and they 'broke away' in Eisenstein's words

> from the limits of the 'silent film with musical illustrations' into a new sphere – into sound-film, where true models of this art live in a unity of fused musical and visual images.[22]

Eisenstein's next major film, still silent, celebrated the tenth anniversary of the Revolution. *October* was not a documentary but professionally acted – though takes from it are still mistaken for documentary shots and often appear in library images of the Revolution.[23]

Meanwhile, all kinds of artists were being husbanded: Chagall was sent to organize an art school in his native Vitebsk, to which he apprenticed the local house-painters who decorated the blank walls of buildings with much enlarged versions of his pictures; his colleagues there were Ivan Puni (already a follower of Malevich) and the young El Lissitzky,[24] who in turn invited Malevich.[25] Chagall's folksy Cubism got no sympathy from Malevich (an extraordinarily charismatic personality – who had meanwhile converted Lissitzky to his doctrines) and they got rid of Chagall before 1920 was out;

Natan Altman, Setting for the *Pageant of the Storming of the Winter Palace*, 1918, gouache.

Reconstruction of the Storming of the Winter Palace for the anniversary pageant of 1921.

they also had their compositions painted over Chagall's and extended over street pavings. On a visit to Vitebsk, Sergei Eisenstein remarked that they looked like 'Suprematist confetti'. Chagall returned to Moscow, where he painted a group of his best works – the frescoes in the foyer of the Jewish Theatre – but he emigrated to Germany in 1922 before settling in Paris.[26]

It is virtually impossible to convey the sense of feverish activity, the conflicts, the making, unmaking and overlapping of various bodies after the Revolution. Lunacharsky's ministry channelled all that ferment into the theatre as well as into exhibitions and demonstrations. Even if he made little reference to 'God-building' during his ministerial career, he promoted mass-crowd events, often involving avant-garde artists, investing heavily in parades and in display and he even personally assisted in their arrangement, maintaining that 'the masses are only conscious of themselves when, as Robespierre asserted, they become a spectacle for themselves'.[27]

For the first anniversary of the Revolution, the buildings and the monuments of Palace Square (*Dvortsova Ploshad*) in St Petersburg were decorated with a Constructivist composition by Natan Altman. The celebrations were to be a yearly event, though the next, even more ambitious demonstration was in fact on the third anniversary. It was organized by the producer Nicolai Evrenov with Altman, involved an orchestra of 500 players and 8,000 active participants and while the spectators were estimated at 100,000. Its culmination was a re-enactment of the October Revolution in and around the Winter Palace. Mayakovsky's revolutionary farce, the *Mystère-Bouffe*, in which the

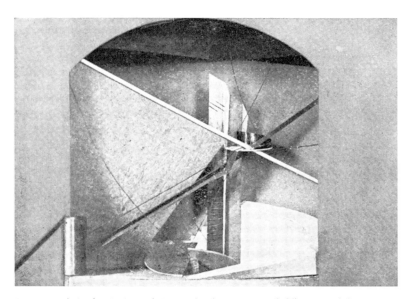

Anonymous design for a Soviet revolutionary play, done in V. Meyerhold's stage-workshop, *c.* 1920.

'unclean' revolutionaries defeat the 'clear bourgeois', and in which the athletic poet himself appeared on a trampoline suspended from the ceiling of Natan Altman's set, was also produced by Vsevolod Meyerhold on that occasion. Revived in 1921, the play failed both times.[28]

For the congress of the Third International in 1921, Aleksander Vesnin and the painter-decorator Lyubov Popova worked with Meyerhold on a vast spectacle to be held on Khodynka Field in Moscow. It was to be a mock battle between two 'cities': one a 'Capitalist Fortress' of smooth geometrical blocks, the other a very industrial-looking (lots of revolving toothed wheels) 'City of the Future'. It was to involve some 3,000 troops, tanks and armoured trains with an inevitable triumph, massed bands, a fly-over, fireworks and so on. All was to happen under tethered dirigibles carrying huge streamer-posters stretched between their mooring cables.[29]

The Congress display never happened. Yet Lunacharsky was also prepared to back and finance, for a time at least, the Proletkult movement whose theorist was his brother-in-law Aleksander Bogdanov (long associated with him and Gorky, but also with 'leftist' opponents of Lenin). Bogdanov took an extreme position, demanding the rapid development of a specifically proletarian art which would take a freely critical attitude to the art of the past, since

> Art is the most powerful weapon for organizing collective forces in a class
> society . . . the proletarian needs a new class art. The spirit of this art is the
> collectivism of labour . . . The treasures of old art should not be accepted
> passively . . . The transference of this artistic legacy must be carried out by
> proletarian critics.

And in a later essay:

> The old world . . . dressed creation up in mystical fetishism . . . The
> methods of proletarian creation are founded on proletarian labour,
> i.e., the type of work characteristic for the workers in modern heavy
> industry . . . (1) the unification of elements in 'physical' and 'spiritual'
> labour; (2) the transparent, unconcealed and unmasked collectivism
> of its actual form.[30]

There could be a cultural way to socialism, independent of either the economic or the political one, and Proletkult could act separately from the Party
and its directives. Workshops were organized to paint propaganda trains and
boats for the Agit-prop agency of Lunacharsky's ministry and carried the message of the new state to outlying districts. Painted trains or barges with
libraries and agitators, festival decorations and such like might, in the early
1920s, be organized by avant-garde artists. Even the 'biomechanical'[31] performances of classics in Meyerhold's highly ritualized versions could be
weapons of mass-propaganda. Lenin had made his distaste for Proletkult
demonstrations explicit – his taste in art was notoriously conservative. He
would have none of it; nor indeed would the more sympathetic Trotsky, who
regarded it as 'proletarian patronizing'. Bogdanov returned to medicine and
was put in charge of a haematological laboratory.[32]

But Lunacharsky, Bogdanov and Trotsky did have an agreed tactic – the
Revolution had to create a new Soviet man. Trotsky was, of course, much
higher in Lenin's counsel than Lunacharsky. He had first been put in charge
of the Foreign Ministry, and then of the Armed Forces, and was also made
Commander-in-Chief of an army whose discipline he wanted to extend to all
workers in a kind of general mobilization. For that matter, Lenin was equally
convinced that the Revolution had to be involved in the creation of a new

man. It is worth remembering that he considered Ivan Petrovich Pavlov's researches on the conditioned reflex as supporting the mechanistic psychology to which he held. Pavlov (the son of a priest and an Orthodox believer) was therefore protected until his death in 1936 and funds for his research guaranteed.[33]

The sort of conditioning provided by the avant-garde environment, Meyerhold argued, would contribute to the creation of this new 'Soviet Man'.[34] His new theatre depended – in opposition to the inward, psychological 'method' acting of Stanislavsky's Arts Theatre (in which he had been trained himself) – on precision and near-mechanical dance-like action. Actors were trained in the communicative use of body movement and gesture and were therefore also much in demand for the silent cinema.[35]

Lunacharsky had to mediate in another conflict which developed soon after the Bolshevik takeover: that between the 'left' artists and 'right' architects. He 'resolved' it by separating the artists' administration (left) from that of the architects (right), and he counterbalanced the Futurist and Constructivist control of the 'commissions' for art and festivals by entrusting the architecture sections of IZO to Zholtovski and Shchusev in Moscow. In Petersburg, Andrei Belogrud (almost as dogmatic a 'Palladian' as Zholtovski) became director of the building office, though Fomin was the most powerful figure there. Trotsky seemed to find this 'natural':

> Futurism . . . tried to express itself in the chaotic dynamic of words, then neo-Classicism expressed the need for peace, for stable forms . . .[36]

Lunacharsky echoed Trotsky's literary judgement in organizing the visual arts. Building was to be dominated by Lenin's taste, not his own. Lunacharsky theorized the duality this implied explicitly:

> Architecture does not tolerate . . . bold ventures. It is our priority, as far as architecture is concerned, to find a firm base in Classical traditions correctly understood . . . The People's Commissariat should have its architectural-art staff capable of laying the foundations of a great Communist construction drive . . .[37]

312

Vladimir Tatlin,
*Monument to
the Third International,*
c. 1919–20.

His decision institutionalized the breach between architecture and the other arts. The state and the Party wanted architecture directed to develop separately from painting or sculpture – or even spectacle, echoing the views advanced a decade earlier by Adolf Loos in Vienna.

Soviet avant-garde environment-making was therefore confined to the theatre and to spectacle for the construction of public space in the years immediately after the Revolution. Tatlin set the posthumous performances of Khlebnikov's vatic play *Zambesi*; Aleksander Vesnin, Paul Claudel's quasi-ritual *L'Annonce faite à Marie*[38] – and rather surprisingly (and splendidly!), a dramatized version of G. K. Chesterton's *The Man who was Thursday*. Lyubov Popova designed sets for Meyerhold's production of the Walloon proto-Surrealist Ferdinand Crommelynck's *The Magnificent Cuckold* and for a Russian re-working of another

French play, *The World Upside-Down*, while a lesser-known Suprematist, Vladimir Dimitriev, set *Dawn* by another Belgian writer, Emile Verhaeren.[39]

Tatlin was able to take a number of 'unsponsored' initiatives: he conceived a huge scale project in 1919 – a Monument to the Third International – which was worked out in a wood model some three metres high built in 1919–20 with some SVOMAS pupils in the old mosaic workshops of the Petersburg Academy. Its external shape was determined by twinned spirals, narrowing as they rose and supported by a lattice of struts which may well have echoed Shukhov's constructions quite deliberately. A rectilineal buttress rises through the spirals and its upper part holds a tubular element – like a vast telescope – which gives the whole monument its thrust; it was pointed to the pole star.[40] The tube rises above a cylindrical chamber, while on the stage below there is a larger tetrahedron, and below that again, at the lowest level, a yet larger cube. Three transparent solids, each housing an assembly chamber, were to turn at different speeds: the top cylinder during one day, the second, a tetrahedron, during one month, the third (and largest) during a whole year. At 500 metres, the project was to dwarf the Eiffel Tower and be painted red. Tatlin called for the exclusion of architects from its construction, which should employ only 'Constructivist engineers and artists'. The model was widely regarded as one of the trophies of Soviet art: 'It is the first time that Iron has reared like a horse and is now searching for its creative formula', wrote Victor Shklovski, one of the founders of the Formalist movement.[41] It was paraded – paradoxically – on a horse-drawn cart in Petersburg in 1920 and then moved to Moscow'[42] where it was shown in 1927 and paraded again, while in 1925 a replica was at the centre of the Grand

Vladimir Tatlin, maquette for the *Monument to the Third International* drawn on a horse-cart, Moscow, 1925.

Palais Soviet section of the Exposition des Arts Décoratifs in Paris. Tatlin himself saw it as a symbol of the age.

More privately, Lissitzky made an allegorical collage-portrait of Tatlin working on the Monument of the Third International: starting with a photograph of Tatlin at work, he projected the artist's eye as a pair of open compasses, implying a precision of hand and eye. It was a device he favoured (and used for a photo-montage in a self-portrait), but in the Tatlin composition Lissitzky imposed it on a geometrized space and inscribed it with a calculus formula; it became an icon of the period and was published in Berlin as part of a portfolio Lissitzky did with the Communist (but non-Bolshevik) writer, Ilya Ehrenburg.[43]

However, at the Tenth Party Congress of 1921, Lenin introduced the New Economic Policy (NEP for short). The early aggressive collectivization of 'War-communism' had been an economic failure, the cities were starving, the Navy was in rebellion and Lenin was determined (in the face of much 'leftist' opposition) to liberalize the lower reaches of industry and agriculture while tightening party discipline.[44] One of the immediate 'artistic' by-products of NEP was the proliferation of lively state-sponsored posters and publicity. Mayakovsky collaborated with Rodchenko on a number of slogans for the montage posters which were plastered on Moscow buildings.

The whole drive of such avant-garde endeavour had gone against the sense of Lunacharsky's *ukaze.* The boundaries between art and life (by implication therefore also between architecture, sculpture and painting) were being effaced. Graphics allowed the earliest of such essays. Lissitzky's memorable and completely abstract poster, 'Hit the whites with the red wedge' done in Vitebsk, was used as propaganda during the campaign against the 'White' armies in 1919–20. The Vitebsk school was also employed to provide propaganda for the campaign against unemployment – even Malevich did some of the (abstract) posters.[45]

The first 'visible' product of NEP was the Pan-Soviet agricultural and village industry exhibition of 1923 in Moscow, which was addressed (in part at least) to foreign investors and was the first great Soviet show of that kind. The layout and representative sections, as well as the main exhibition sheds, were designed by the 'old guard': Zholtovski, with Shchukov and Fomin. But 'leftist' artists were allowed to provide the decorative touches: there were graphics by Rodchenko, Popova, Lissitzky. Aleksandra Exter added more or less

'Constructivist' ornamental reliefs to Zholtovski's main exhibition sheds –
just before she emigrated. This display of Lunacharsky's policy of separating
art and architecture almost diagrammatically also illustrated the division of
labour between structure and ornament. Exter also collaborated on a stand
for the daily *Izvestia*, while an untried architect – and a favourite pupil of
Zholtovski's, Konstantin Melnikov – designed a more or less Constructivist
stand for *Machorka*, the common (state monopoly) shag tobacco.[46]

Meanwhile, the plans for the expansion of Moscow drawn up by MOSSO-
VIET, a local government agency, were prepared under the supervision of
Zholtovski and Shchusev. Like the Greater London plan of 1944, it borrowed
many ideas from Ebenezer Howard's *Garden Cities of Tomorrow* (which had
been translated into Russian in 1911). Lenin took a personal interest in
Zholtovski's and Shchusev's plan, but by 1922–3 he was already ailing and he
died on 21 January 1924.

Within hours of his death, the decision to embalm the body had been
taken, and within a few days the first mausoleum was ready: a wooden cube
between two spires on Red Square. Alexei Shchusev charged the same
Konstantin Melnikov to design a more or less Constructivist crystal sarcophagus to display the Lenin mummy.[47] The transformations of Shchusev's

316

project then provided a focus for Soviet monumental building. The mausoleum grew into a wooden kourgan-temple in 1926 and finally, in 1929–30, became the simplified two-tone – red (for communism) and black (for mourning) – granite ziggurat, and the ceremonial centre of the Soviet Union.[48]

The Lenin sarcophagus showed Zholtovski and Shchusev that Melnikov could work quickly; his next important commission for wooden (dismountable) stalls for the Sukharevsky (farmers') Market in Moscow showed he could also build cheaply. The stalls were arranged in radiating rows, the oblique planes of their walls stiffening the fragile structure. Melnikov went on to win another prestigious commission against eleven other competitors as a result, including that for the Soviet pavilion at the Paris exhibition of 1925. This Paris pavilion was a wooden frame-building on a rectangular plan, diagonally crossed by a stairway that rose up to and descended from a central platform. The stairway was roofed by wooden planes which crossed scissor-wise – and it became the first sample of the new Soviet architecture in the West.[49] Soviet authorities were prepared to support its export to decadent capitalist Western Europe, however much they disapproved of Proletkult and avant-garde art generally for home consumption. Soviet

Alexei Shchusev's first design for Lenin's tomb, 1924.

artists in Berlin and in Paris therefore received some official support. Of the exhibits, the most notable was the furniture for a workers' club by Rodchenko, the first show of that kind of 'utility' furniture in Paris, paradoxically for the exhibition which identified with and gave its name to the rather opulent Art Deco style.[50]

While in Paris (he seems to have enjoyed his visit, unlike other Soviet artists), Melnikov met the leading Russian émigrés and was invited by the city authorities to design a parking garage for 1,000 cars as a bridge spanning the Seine. The sloping and counter-sloping ramps of the garage cloverleafs crossed scissor-fashion like the roofs of the Soviet pavilion. In response to criticism (it is said), he supported the ramps on straining, inward-sloping statues about 15 metres high. These colossi became part of his repertory: even bigger statues appear in his competition projects for the Palace of the Soviets and the Ministry for Heavy Industry (1934) in a curious return to the use of giant human statues at the close of Art Nouveau. Melnikov's are definitely part of the architecture, however, and have no aspiration to any independent status as works of art – and he combined them with shapes based on letter-forms in his attempt to create a new symbolic art.[51]

Little industrial building or housing was done directly after the Revolution. Much was produced by offices like the 'Workshop for Proletarian Classicism' and they continued to build even after Lenin's imposition of NEP.[52] Meanwhile, a number of ambitious competition projects (which were not realized) absorbed the energy of many architects. Of those produced in 1923, the two best known are those for the Palace of Labour in Moscow and for the Pravda offices in Leningrad. Avant-garde entries by the Vesnins, Melnikov and Aleksander Golovin were widely publicized outside Russia and regarded as prestige exports. For *Pravda*

Aleksander Vesnin, competition design for the Leningrad *Pravda* offices, 1924.

Aleksander Vesnin – with his two brothers – offered a simple, rectilineal skeletal building, with a large, three-storey-high panel inclined to the spectator on which the two leading pages of the newspaper could be back-projected. Melnikov, for his part, turned in a project in which a central services column is the axis of the building from which every storey is cantilevered separately; they rotate round it in an obvious reference to Tatlin's monument. For the Palace of Labour the Vesnins suggested a sober, oval assembly building and a rectilineal office tower linked by a panoply of radio antennae, while Melnikov's project took off into a swirly Expressionist phantasy which owed something to Hans Poelzig. There was also a competition that year for the ARCOS building – a NEP-inspired, private-public finance corporation for which Golosov produced the most innovative project: a rectilineal building into which a glass cylinder was inserted to cut into the corner of the block; he returned repeatedly to this motif himself and it became an iconic element of Soviet modernity. The dynamic element of the staircase cut, dialectically, into the static structure of orthogonality.[53]

The application of avant-garde research to the everyday, to furniture, book and textile design, was allowed to proceed: Lyubov Popova and Barbara Stepanova designed wallpapers, textiles and sensible (or at any rate 'rational') clothes. So, rather surprisingly, did Tatlin – who wore them himself – and who was, in any case, passionate about transforming the everyday. Bent wood, which the Viennese manufacturer Thonet had been exploiting since the 1840s, seemed to offer unexplored possibilities which Tatlin attempted to develop using steam-bent willow rods instead of the beech used in Vienna; a springy willow chair has survived only in photographs. In the late 1920s he invested much energy in a fascinating, emblematic (if doomed) project, *Letatlin*. Invoking Icarus and Leonardo, as well as the beauty and airworthiness of the seagull and the young heron, he created a light-willow pedal-powered gliding-plane, a hauntingly beautiful object, its wings of parachute silk stretched on thin, moulded rib-fingers. The pilot was to lie prone in the wickerwork body fuselage and power it by pedalling with his feet, while he used his hands to control direction and height. It was to be the sort of object that would evoke a new Soviet society – low-energy, easy to use, cheap. Any child could have one to take him or her to school, Tatlin suggested. Several versions were made in his workshops at the Novodevitschy monastery and shown at glider meetings and air shows. A few test pilots expressed their enthusiasm for it, but the only one who actually tried to get it airborne tangled with the fuselage, as with an outsize kite, and had to be rescued.[54] When its failure became evident, Tatlin retired into book-illustration, photography, theatre sets – even painting – and neglect.[55]

Letatlin was a revolutionary dream – just the kind Lenin had no time for. Many other artists also believed that the condition of life would be altered, that gravity could be modified and even psychic adjustment could result from the new techniques. 'Dynamic' cities, cities on Mars, now became part of architectural programming. In VKHUTEIN design studio, projects were done for housing estates which would orbit the earth, on the analogy of Saturn's rings. The ideal of the *Gesamtkunstwerk* could be forgotten; works of art would no longer be needed to promote social transformation since art and life would be continuous. The convulsive changes did not shake the human condition as the utopians and the artists prophesied.

320

Historical realities decreed, moreover, that the Revolution would not sweep the world rapidly as Trotsky had taught. It had seemed at first that Eastern Europe would fall quickly with the help of the Red Army, but in the event, only Hungary achieved a European communist government and it lasted all of five months. Stalin's policy of 'Socialism in one country' was to emerge victorious.

Germany: After Versailles

In Western Europe the negotiations to settle the world after the 'war to end all wars' went on at Versailles, while the whole social framework seemed to crack and split. Before those negotiations could even begin, Wilhelm II had to abdicate all his titles the day before the Armistice.[56] Defeat provoked a great wave of revulsion in Germany: workers' and soldiers' communes took power inspired by the Soviet example, while parts of the defeated, demoralized German army opposed them violently. Since there was no sure chain of command for four or five months, detachments roamed in immediate post-war Berlin in conflict with the workers' organizations, fighting 'reds' (and Poles in Silesia). The mixture of old soldiers and volunteers was called the Freikorps. Russian help was blocked by Polish intransigence, and the 1920 defeat of the Red Army outside Warsaw checked the westward dynamic of the Revolution.

The new German Republic was instituted in February 1919, not in Berlin, shaken by aggressive army detachments and repeated Spartacist insurrections, but in the relative safety of the Weimar theatre.[57] In Berlin most artists sympathized with the workers: the Arbeitsrat für Kunst, an artists' Soviet, was founded by Bruno Taut (whose glass pavilion in Cologne I described in the previous chapter), together with some other architects, Walter Gropius and Erich Mendelsohn among them, as well as a number of (mostly Expressionist) painters and sculptors: Ernst Barlach, Erich Heckel, Karl Schmidt-Rottluf, Max Pechstein, and the German-American Lyonel Feininger. It was to advise the new Republic on artistic policy; at the same time an avant-garde artists' group, the Novembergruppe, was founded in Berlin (by Max Pechstein and César Klein to unite all 'Expressionists, Cubists, Futurists'). Mighty Behrens himself was affected by the movement. In 1919 he was one of the notables consulted on the framing of the republican constitution. His work during the war was concerned with low-cost housing – he became a recognized expert on the subject – and he was moreover insistent on popular consultation during the planning of any housing estate and on the inclusion of communal facilities in any such enterprise, while at the same time being one of the promoters of the standardization programme suggested by Hermann Muthesius.[58] His major works in the immediate post-war period depart sharply from his earlier, geometrical neo-Classicism. At the Craft Fair (*Gewerbeschau*) of 1922, the *Dombauhütte* pavilion showing church furniture (and rather 'advanced' church art) was a rectangle over which a grid of butting squares was laid at 45 degrees, breaking the walls with a jagged chevron polychrome brick inlay. Dombauhütte invokes the masons' lodge on the site of a cathedral, and the great crucifix by Ludwig Gies which dominated it recalls the great past of German art.[59]

Even before the war ended, Behrens' old assistant and protegé, Walter Gropius, now a decorated war veteran, had been recommended by Henry Van de Velde (induced to retire from the directorship of the Weimar Kunstgewerbeschule in 1917 as an enemy alien) to succeed him. He was not eager to accept, but the new (left-wing) Thuringian government seemed enthusiastic about his proposal to add an experimental section to the school, which he called Bauhaus, alluding (again) to a *Bauhütte*, a masons' lodge – which also gave the enterprise a deliberately medievalizing whiff,[60] as did the splintry woodcut 'The Cathedral of the Future' by Lyonel Feininger, which, in 1919, decorated its first manifesto-proclamation. New York-born, but settled in Weimar since 1906, Feininger was one of Gropius' earliest recruits on the staff. The manifesto called for a unity of the arts under the aegis of building, a unity which would create the 'Cathedral of the Future'. The programme pointed in a direction diametrically opposite to Lunacharsky's aims, and it was translated into practical policies by making the individual workshops – woodworking, stone carving, metal-construction, ceramics, glass, weaving, printing, the stage – into cooperative enterprises which accepted individual 'craft' commissions as well as industrial design ones. In recognition of the decline of the craft ideal however, the workshops were to be run by two masters in tandem: a craft master and a form master (the latter being a 'fine' artist) and this was to foster a smooth passage from craft-based production to an industrially based one in which form and skill would be reunited.

322

Walter Gropius, Joost Schmidt and Josef Albers, The Sommerfeld 'Blockhouse', Berlin, 1920–21.

The first collective Bauhaus product was a house in Berlin-Dahlem designed for a timber-merchant, Adolf Sommerfeld, using teak from ships' timbers (building material was still scarce) and put up by the same contractors who had worked on Behrens' Dombauhütte. The elaborate carvings were carried out in the Weimar woodworking shops. A large stained-glass window was the earliest published work of Josef Albers, while the doors and balustrades were carved by Joost Schmidt – both of them student-apprentices who were to become masters.[61]

Teaching at the Bauhaus in the early years was dominated by a Swiss painter, Johannes Itten, who instituted the idea of a 'foundation' course through which all students had to pass. He imposed methods of bodily, almost gymnastic, yoga-like exercises before any drawing or painting could be done, as well as the doctrines of a strange sect, Mazdaznan.[62] Itten's brilliant teaching methods and charismatic personality soon came into conflict with Gropius himself, as well as other colleagues. A year later an old friend of Itten, the painter Oskar Schlemmer, also joined the Bauhaus – and though he had little interest in Mazdaznan, he was fascinated by body movement and performance and was already working on the *Triadic Ballet*, a synaesthetic dance for which the young Paul Hindemith wrote the music, later to become one of the Bauhaus' most impressive though least-acknowledged achievements. Kandinsky, who could not endure life in the Soviet Union (not even under

Lunacharsky's relatively benevolent regime), moved to Germany and was recruited by Gropius, as was Paul Klee.

Meanwhile, Dada infected several German cities. The infection was carried by an original Zürich Dadaist, Richard Huelsenbeck, who moved to Berlin even before the Armistice. Max Ernst in Cologne, Kurt Schwitters in Hannover and Georg Grosz and Helmut Herzfeld (who changed his name to John Heartfield) in Berlin called themselves Dadaists, and they were joined by others, determined to undermine the 'bourgeois' Expressionists.[63] In 1920 the first Dada fair was held there and there were Dada missionary tours to other German cities: Dresden, Leipzig and so on. When Kurt Schwitters moved to Berlin (however briefly), and El Lissitzky joined them in 1922, as did Tristan Tzara, Berlin, freed of the oppressive Hohenzollern presence, really seemed the capital of the avant-garde.

In spite of all the Dada agitation, though, Expressionism still dominated the German scene. The *Novembergruppe* architects were led by Bruno Taut (the same who designed the Glass Pavilion in Cologne in 1914) and his brother Max, with another sibling partnership, the brothers Wassily and Hans Luckhardt, as well as the most visionary of them, the theosophical biologist Hermann Finsterlin; they formed a kind of sodality. Their periodical, *Frühlicht*, which also published the inner correspondence of the group, became its organ.[64]

Not all Expressionist architecture had a medievalizing flavour: at Potsdam, just outside Berlin, a newcomer from East Prussia, Erich Mendelsohn (who considered himself an heir to the Art Nouveau designers; I mentioned his admiration of Van de Velde's 1914 Cologne exhibition theatre in the previous chapter), designed an observatory, the Einstein Tower in 1918. It looks as if it had been poured in concrete, but since both cement and steel reinforcements rods were hard to come by, it had a brick core and the flowing outline was sprayed in stucco to a wood-framed wire mesh – for which 'dishonesty' Mendelsohn was (rather unfairly) criticized. The strange shape – a dome set on a several-storey tower extending into a long basement – was dictated by its programme: to provide spectroscopic data-testing of Einstein's General Relativity theory.[65]

Mendelsohn became enormously prolific in the following decades, with domestic, commercial and industrial buildings in Germany, Israel and the Soviet Union. However brilliant his drawings (and they were exhibited in art galleries to be sold as self-sufficient 'pictures') and although he was also very

Hans Poelzig, Grosses Schauspielhaus, Berlin, 1919.

involved in art-politics (he negotiated the agreement between the Arbeitsrat
für Kunst and the Novembergruppe in 1918–19), there is no sign in his buildings of any collaboration with artists, or even of giving a conspicuous place to
painting and sculpture in and around them.[66]

The most notable building in Berlin in those early days was the Grosses
Schauspielhaus designed by Hans Poelzig, its plain exterior concealing a sta-
lactite cave. Poelzig's early buildings in Breslau were later called proto-
Expressionist, though he would surely have rejected that label himself. The
Grosses Schauspielhaus was regarded by many Expressionist writers in the
first years of its existence as a perfect setting for their plays. Poelzig had no
direct links with the *Frühlicht* group, though Mendelsohn, as well as Tatlin
and Mies van der Rohe, had drawings and writings published in it.

Some Expressionist buildings, like the Einstein Tower, were not generally accessible and did not intrude on attention, though they were widely published. The most popular and public face of German Expressionism was the
cinema. German films had taken off about 1910; although Max Reinhardt had
not found film-making rewarding, one of his actors, Paul Wegener, had a
great success just before the war with *The Student of Prague*, an uncanny story

Fantastic architecture in
Robert Wiene's 1921 film,
The Cabinet of Dr Caligari.

about a Faustian pact. The 'student' of the title sells his mirror-image to a
magician for love and wealth, but with fatal consequences. This mix of E.T.A.
Hoffmann's and Adelbart von Chamisso's *Shlemiel* was followed by *The Golem*,
inspired perhaps by the best-selling thriller of the same title by Gustav
Meyrink which appeared just before the war. The first version in 1915 was
remade some years later, with sets and costumes by Poelzig.

Such uncanny ghost-thrillers became a German speciality. Just after the
war ended, a commercial film-maker was given the script of a fantastic and
subversive tale, the *Cabinet of Dr Caligari*, by two young writers, Erich May
and Karl Janowitz, who wanted the Austrian painter-novelist Alfred Kubin to
set and dress it; when he declined, it was handed to three minor artists who
produced a brilliant pastiche of an Expressionist world. Although they were
all members of the Novembergruppe, the producer bowdlerized the original
subversive concept of the film, which nevertheless may well be the best-
known Expressionist 'product': it conjured up a three-dimensional reality
which other designers and artists never quite achieved.

The business of *Klangfarbe* and *Farbmusik* which had occupied
Schoenberg and Kandinsky was now adopted by a young Expressionist archi-
tect-photographer, Walter Ruttman. He used a quartet by a young and prolific
composer, Max Butting, to construct a colour-film show (he went on to
become a master of documentary montage).[67] The dynamism implicit in
abstract forms was also fascinating to some early film-makers such as the
Swedish painter Viking Eggeling, who developed some of Kandinsky's ideas
on colour and befriended the Zürich Dadaists (he operated with light on film

326

in abstract compositions which demanded musical accompaniment), but he died very young in 1925 before he could develop this approach.

The end of the war also invoked the problem of memorials both for the winners and losers. I have had occasion to mention Monet's *Nénuphars*. In Germany individual artists were occasionally involved in such things, but architects seem to have made little contribution. A notable exception was Gropius' monument to the dead of the March rising in the Weimar cemetery. Cast in concrete, it seems built up of splintered planes.[68] Whatever it was said to evoke – flame or lightning – it certainly seems to be in the same spirit as Feininger's woodcut on the Bauhaus manifesto. Four years later, in 1925–6, Mies van der Rohe was commissioned to provide a monument for Karl Liebknecht and Rosa Luxemburg who had been murdered by members of the Freikorps in January 1919. Surrounded by the graves of other murdered revolutionaries, it was a wall in a Berlin cemetery, an oblong slab articulated into an abstract composition of asymmetrical planes, built of very corporeal, rough-surfaced (because salvaged) bricks, laid in bond, the lower edge of each plane outlined in headers so that its effect depended entirely on the articulation of the material, even though it was certainly meant to be inscribed. Affixed asymmetrically to it is a five-pointed star with a hammer and sickle and a flagpole which concede something to figuration. Some have maintained that it intended to evoke a wall against which some revolutionaries were shot.[69]

Neither monument required the contribution of a painter or sculptor.[70] The development should hardly surprise. In Russia, Malevich was working on his *architectonics*, which offered a universal 'absolute and classical, freed from any trammels of utility' model for the treatment of built solids and their artic-

L. Mies van der Rohe, Luxemburg–Liebknecht memorial, Berlin, 1926 (since destroyed).

ulation into planes by an artist, while Tatlin wanted to exclude architects in favour of artists and engineers from the construction of the Monument to the Third International. For their part, architects were building monuments which were autonomous works of art.

The change in atmosphere and styles of visualizing around 1925 paralleled that which ended the exuberance of Art Nouveau around 1902, even if the promoters and sufferers of the change were somewhat more explicit than their predecessors a generation earlier. Bruno Taut, who had been appointed city architect of Magdeburg in 1923, was already working towards a new sobriety. He abandoned his Expressionist fervours and became the great designer of *Siedlungen,* semi-enclosed housing estates which were not quite garden cities in the sense of Ebenezer Howard, whose prophetic books, published around the turn of the century, were read avidly all over Europe. Yet Howard's vision had no obvious architectural consequences. Barry Parker and Raymond Unwin, the architects preferred by the Garden City Association (a co-operative devoted to realizing his project), were the last faithful *epigoni* of the Arts and Crafts movement and worked in a modified Queen Anne manner. British art and design, which had been so exciting throughout the nineteenth century, seems to have entered the doldrums at the beginning of the twentieth. When Marinetti visited London (three times before 1914!) in his motor-car with Boccioni, he thought London thrilling but the English stuffy – and they repaid in kind. The critic and painter Roger Fry was prepared to battle for the recognition of French modern painting against an indifferent public, but would not take such trouble for the Futurists. Percy Wyndham Lewis, who had, about 1912–13, produced his first abstract canvases, launched his self-conscious emulation of Futurism, Vorticism (its review, *BLAST!* had the usual two issues, 1914 and 1915), but set himself against Marinetti and organized a barracking team of hefty young artists at one of his London lectures.

If English art was not thrilling, architecture was moribund. The last major Arts and Crafts architect, R. Norman Shaw, the master of Parker and Unwin, died in 1912 and the generation that succeeded him was dominated by a lady-like neo-Baroque which had no contact with what was happening in the visual arts elsewhere. The most successful practitioner of the manner, Sir Edwin Lutyens, became president of the then lifeless Royal Academy. One institution stands out against all this: London Transport was led by a visionary manager–engineer Frank Pick, who inspired his otherwise indifferent architects (Adams, Holden and Pearson) to adopt a sober version of the latest Dutch manner for the new Underground stations. The very ungainly building of his headquarters nevertheless sported statues by Jacob Epstein and Eric Gill as well as the young Henry Moore.

In Holland

But that was just before 1930. English sobriety and the cool which overcame the German visionaries had indeed been anticipated in the Netherlands – the country which demonstrates that social upheaval is no prerequisite of avant-garde action. The Netherlands remained neutral in 1914–18; it may have been impoverished by the sea-war, but it suffered no violent social or political cataclysm either during or after it. Building practice was lively, much of it dominated by some eclectic disciples of Viollet-le-Duc who called themselves the 'Amsterdam School', reacting to the domination of Berlage. Younger architects were developing an Expressionist manner from Berlage's principles however, while his articles and lectures, as well as his own buildings, were becoming well known abroad. Berlage was also one of the first European architects to make a study visit to the United States and he spread the gospel of Frank Lloyd Wright,[71] noting his emphatic analysis of solids into planar elements while he balanced them in plan and in volume. Berlage was also impressed by Wright's use of horizontal windows to separate a wide-eaved roof from the wall and so shape his built forms analytically. This depended, of course, on his respect for the integrity of the wall surface, and also became a basic principle of Berlage's practice. Any ornament that was carved into the wall did not project beyond the planar surface. Berlage had always had an interest in painting, and at one point or another commissioned several Symbolist artists to work in his buildings, though there was no such ferment in painting or sculpture as there was in architecture. The Maris brothers or Thorn-Prikker, even Jan Toorop and Ronald Holst (both had worked with Berlage – and he designed houses for them), may have been big in the Netherlands but they did not make much impact on world painting. There was only modest Dutch Art Nouveau excitement to equal the Belgian: Van de Velde, van Rysselberge – even Toorop – belong to Brussels, not Amsterdam.

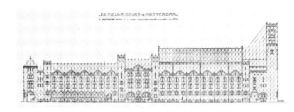

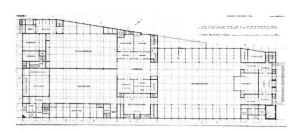

H. P. Berlage,
The Koopmansbeurs
(the Stock Exchange),
Amsterdam,
1898–1903.

Berlage also attached great importance to the use of geometrical proportion. In the previous chapter I mentioned Peter Behrens' invitation to join him in Düsseldorf and his recommendation of J.L.M. Lauwerijcks. He was an active missionary theosophist, as was Berlage, who also declared himself a socialist (a combination of occultism and left-wing politics marked most Dutch architects of the post-war generation, many of whom belonged to the club Architectura et Amicitia, which had published a sumptuous portfolio of Frank Lloyd Wright's work).[72]

Without any powerful precedent, therefore, and without any institutional stimulus, a radical understanding of the relation between architecture and the other visual arts was formulated in an irregularly published periodical review which gave its name to a movement – *De Stijl*. The initiator of the periodical and 'the mover' of the movement was Theo van Doesburg, then a relatively young man (he had been born in 1883), but its mentor and guide was Piet Mondriaan who was ten years older. Mondrian (as he – and I will follow him – would later style himself) was the son of a piously Calvinist schoolteacher and had thought of entering the ministry, but joined the Theosophical Society in 1909 instead. Though discreet about his beliefs, he remained faithful to his own version of it for the rest of his life. In 1911 he moved to Paris for the Cubist experience, although his own pictorial world only had an edge contact with Cubism, which he would later reject as 'incomplete'. For family reasons he returned to the

Netherlands in 1914, but the war kept him at home and brought him into contact with M.H.J. Schoenmaekers, a neighbour and fellow theosophist who attempted a synthesis of Hegel and Mme Blavatsky which he called New Catholicism, and whose impact on Mondrian's as well as van Doesburg's pictorial language was decisive. They broke with him later, objecting to his belief in the irrationality of the artistic act. It was Schoenmaekers who coined the term that described the new forms of creation they practised – *Nieuwe Beelding*, which has been translated as Neo-Plasticism. But another thinker, who was regarded as one of the great Hegelians of his time, and who was also a theosophist, G.J.P.J. Bolland, would instil in them the notion (which he owed to Hegel, but also to Hegel's critic Schopenhauer) that art could not rise above, could not surpass various forms of more or less imitative representation to achieve a conscious appreciation of concepts. A contemplative subject could only approach the Idea through art if and when form was entirely divorced from 'matter' in such a way that a rule or principle could be descried behind phenomenal accidents.

This became Mondrian's core belief. The subject as individual is always tragic:

> The combination of the universal (in so far as it is developed in man) with individuality (in so far as it has matured in a man) creates tragedy: the battle between them is the tragedy of life.

The tendency of modern life, de Stijl artists maintained, tends to abstraction,

> which allows humanity to overcome tragedy . . . the elimination of tragedy is the purpose of living, it is illogical therefore to protest against the New Representation,

since human intervention spiritualizes and elevates matter. The standard and the machine-made are best, Mondrian maintained – wrought iron is more spiritual than iron ore, and rolled steel more spiritual than wrought iron.

When Mondrian met van Doesburg (who had written a flattering review of his exhibition in 1915), he was already interested in publishing a periodical which would bring together the various tendencies of the time. Dogmatic and combative, he was an enthusiastic founder of groups and a joiner of movements, like André Breton (the 'founder' of Surrealism, of whom more later – but with whom he had no contact), and like Breton, an excommunicator.[73]

What the de Stijl artists all owed to Schoenmaekers was the doctrine that only the three primary colours, yellow, red, blue, in a painting or sculpture were 'objective', and that only two directions perpendicular to each other, up–down, right–left, had any legitimacy in the Neo-Plasticism they championed, to which all construction needed to be reduced. They considered their principles to be a logical deduction from recent developments in the arts (especially Cubism and Kandinsky's abstraction), and therefore universally applicable, however rooted they themselves may have been in the Dutch experience. But the movement was fissured by defections and excommunications, while some, such as the American composer Georges Antheil and Constantin Brancusi, were arbitrarily given more or less honorary membership.

In the year before de Stijl appeared, van Doesburg founded two other groups: De Anderen, with both writers and artists, and De Sphinx, a kind of artists' collaborative which was started with the architect Jacobus Johannes Pieter (always known as J.J.P.) Oud to work on a number of interiors for Oud's buildings. Oud had worked for Theodor Fischer in Munich, but like most of his Dutch contemporaries was under Berlage's authority. Doesburg began by designing tile and linoleum floor-patterns, stained-glass windows and ceramic inlays (which look rather dingy now, in spite of their primary colours) and also worked out a rather complex scheme for distributing colour according to the Golden Section for Oud's early Berlage-like houses, but soon moved beyond that early manner.

Within months of their first collaboration, Doesburg and Oud were joined by the painters Bert van der Leck and George Vantongerloo, as well as the Hungarian-born interior designer and stained-glass maker, Vilmos Huszár. Hans Arp, one of the original Dadaists, by then living in Strasbourg (where he was working with the young Max Ernst), was an active sympathizer. Architects such as Robert van t'Hoff were also part of the group, as was (briefly) Jan Wils, another admirer of Wright who had worked for Berlage. The most faithful was the young Gerrit Rietveld, trained as a cabinet-maker (by his father), who had moved to architecture. The first issue of the periodical appeared in October 1917 with a cover by Vilmos Huszár; it carried a project for terrace-houses and for a factory by Oud, which latter became 'the' iconic de Stijl project. In the same year, Rietveld produced his first chairs: each was a geometrical analysis of the chair form in thin, inclined planes, stained red and blue, which were held by an orthogonal structure stained yellow and black. The use of standard-section wood battens allowed Rietveld to develop his production method, and in 1920 to design a full de Stijl interior which included a light fitting of long tubular bulbs fitted into standard section wooden sockets so that they, too, 'became' sticks.[74]

Van Doesburg was inevitably drawn to Berlin. The Russians, particularly Lissitzky, aroused his enthusiasm: he also met Mies. The association of some de Stijl forms (particularly van Doesburg's paintings with Mies' plans) began then.[75] They were both involved in yet another magazine, '*G*', which was initiated by the Dadaist film-maker (and collaborator of Viking Eggeling) Hans Richter.[76]

Weimar

In 1921 van Doesburg went to Weimar to spread the de Stijl gospel, claiming that he had been invited by Gropius (who denied it) to teach at the two-year-old Bauhaus. He objected to its dominant Expressionism, and advertised an independent course on de Stijl-Constructivist principles, which inevitably attracted dissident students. He also organized a Constructivist-Dadaist conference with Lissitzky (by then in Berlin), Tristan Tzara, Hans Richter, Sophie and Hans Arp and the Hungarian László Moholy-Nagy (who would stay on in Weimar and become one of the pillars of the Bauhaus). In spite of their impact on the school, these events remained extra-curricular. Van Doesburg's teaching precipitated the opposition to Itten.

Gropius may have forbidden Bauhaus students to attend van Doesburg's 'free' classes, yet he still used the occasion to slip Itten and his minions out of Weimar, and his competition scheme for the Chicago Tribune Building was heavily influenced by de Stijl.[77] Van Doesburg met a Dutch Prix de Rome student, Cornelis van Eesteren, in Weimar, recruited him at once for de Stijl and began 'helping' with his final diploma work, a hall for Amsterdam University, a project which was to be rejected by his examiners. But his publicity had

worked – and in 1923, the most 'advanced' Paris dealer of the post-war period, Léonce Rosenberg, gave the group a show in his gallery, L'Effort Moderne, which centred on models and drawings of a house 'for an art-lover' by van Doesburg and van Eesteren.[78]

The two went on to do a number of projects for various buildings in which the planar analysis in colour terms dominated. By 1924 van Eesteren had been independently commissioned to design a shopping arcade with a cinema in The Hague which he developed together with van Doesburg (after which they also fell out). From 1927 van Eesteren taught at the Bauhaus and in 1929 became the city architect of Amsterdam.[79] The fullest working-out of what de Stijl meant in architecture was the house for Mrs Schroeder in Utrecht realized by Gerrit Rietveld in 1923–5, however. It was a tour de force, in which every working detail (the cat-door, the hatch for milk bottles and so on) was given the analytic de Stijl treatment; moreover, the original client lived there until her death in 1980.[80]

In that same year, 1923, the Bauhaus, constantly challenged in Weimar by citizen vigilantes as well as local government, had its first public exposure: a show of student and masters' work centred on a 'model' house designed by a young painter-teacher, Georg Muche. The living room was a double-height cube set in a single-storey square containing the rest of the accommodation; all the fittings were designed in the workshops.[81] Weimar had by then become a magnet for the avant-garde so that the exhibition was accompanied by some glittering events: performances in the city itself and in nearby Jena, where Gropius – with one of his outstanding pupils, Marcel Breuer – had rebuilt the local theatre. These events included a performance of Stravinsky's *Soldier's Tale,* as well as Paul Hindemith's setting of Rilke's *Marienlieder;* Ferruccio Busoni played his *Fantasia Contrapuntistica* and Oskar Schlemmer's *Triadic Ballet* was danced, also to music by Hindemith. The wall-painting workshops executed ambitious decorations in the public spaces of the Bauhaus, still in the original building designed by Henry Van de Velde.[82] There was an international architectural exhibition which featured the work of de Stijl masters as well as Le Corbusier.

That festival was very much part of Gropius' and his colleagues' intention to show the unity of the arts as a theme of the Bauhaus. It ran through much of the student work as well as that of the teachers. Perhaps the most famous witness to it is the 'scientifically exact' visualization of the E-Minor Fugue from Bach's *Well-Tempered Klavier* – later conceived as a proposed monument to Bach by a student, Heinrich Neugeboren, which I mentioned earlier.[83] Translating the notation into a diagram, he devised a method of modelling it in three dimensions, and although it never achieved the dignity of a public monument, it was often published. A very different but even more famous product was the 'light-space modulator' on which László Moholy-Nagy worked from 1922 (when he came to Weimar), until it achieved a kind of finality in Darmstadt in 1929. It was made of pierced metal sheet, metal screw elements, wire net, glass, all mounted on a turntable with a number of pieces revolving differentially.[84] While it neither calls on music nor uses applied colour, its movement involves time in a way which is much more compulsive and rigorous than most mobiles, and it is also concerned (as

Georg Muche, Haus am Horn, Weimar, 1923.

László Moholy-Nagy, set for a production of Offenbach's *Tales of Hoffmann*, 1929.

most mobiles are not) to relate the material object to the working of light. Moholy regarded it as his *chef-d'oeuvre* and it became the prototype for the way he used light as a stage designer – notably for Offenbach's *Tales of Hoffmann* at the Deutsche Oper.[85]

Yet Gropius never quite succeeded in establishing his 'building research workshop', even if the whole Bauhaus contributed to the new building when they were forced to move from Weimar to Dessau in 1925. A provisional building course had been started by the Swiss architect Hannes Meyer in 1927, but there was no architectural school until Meyer replaced Gropius as director in 1929. By then it was too late for it to develop fully and, in any case, Meyer, a communist, left for the Soviet Union after a year. Schlemmer and Klee both left at the same time. For very different reasons, Mies van der Rohe moved the school to Berlin shortly after becoming its last director in 1930, though Kandinsky remained its focal presence until the Nazis forced the closure in April 1934.[86] The Bauhaus had only existed for fifteen very troubled years, during which about 600 students passed through it, first in Weimar, then Dessau and finally in Berlin, yet it became the most influential and imitated art institution of the inter-war years.

Dessau, like Weimar, were both small towns in the Berlin orbit. Kandinsky was one of the many Russian intellectuals who (in various circumstances) had come to Berlin at the time, and they included Viktor Shklovsky, Marc Chagall and El Lissitzky, as well as a number of other writers. The most notable perhaps was Ilya Ehrenburg; but there were also one or two youngsters such as Vladimir Nabokov and the philosopher Alexandre Koujevnikov.[87] Ehrenburg, with Lissitzky's 'visual' help, produced the very short-lived (two issues, March–May 1922) periodical *Veshch/Gegenstand/Objet*, which proclaimed the end of Soviet isolation and carried Ivan Puni's article about Tatlin's tower.[88]

Translations of Russian and American plays filled Berlin theatres, and foreign artists settled there for the atmosphere and for cheap living since none of their currencies declined as catastrophically as the German mark, hit by war reparations and social instability. But in the immediate post-war period there was also a Soviet-German anti-Versailles understanding, confirmed by the Treaty of Rapallo in April 1922,[89] negotiated by Walter Rathenau, by then the Weimar Republic's Foreign Minister. As the heir of its founder, Rathenau was master of the AEG and had been Behrens' chief patron. He had managed to control German government finances during and just after the war, but was assassinated by a nationalist in June 1922. The mark then went into a spin which was not arrested until 1925, when some German financiers and international banks intervened to give Germany a breathing space – though only until the catastrophic international crash of 1929.[90]

The New Sobriety

The end of inflation in 1925 brought stability, and the situation of German architects changed dramatically when new credits for investment in public works and 'social' housing became available. A general shift of atmosphere in the arts was marked by the *Neue Sachlichkeit* exhibition in the Mannheim Kunsthalle. Its sub-title, 'After Expressionism', is explained in the catalogue preface: the movement was not to be seen as a statement of reaction, but of generational differences. The new artists would favour a cool, dispassionate – if observant – approach to the phenomenal world. Not for them the intense religiosity and the distortions for the sake of emotional impact of the Expressionists. They divided into a 'left' tendency which projects current experience in its tempo and fevered temperature [and a 'right'] . . . that searches for the object of timeless validity to embody timeless laws of existence; the former have been called 'verists', in the artistic sphere, one could almost call the latter 'classicists' . . . [91]

A few of the Sachlich artists had made their name as Expressionists. In the case of architecture, the change of heart was, however, much more sweeping. Some of the 'visionary' designers, who had drawn vast crystal halls for undefined ceremonies, were now using their presentation techniques of dramatized outlines and oblique light rays to display large commercial high-rises. Others, notably Hermann Finsterlin, who detested all 'boxy buildings', withdrew from architecture altogether, signing off in *Frühlicht* 3 with a proposal for a game of architectural styles (which evolve – unhistorically – from orthogonality to the trigonometric-mineral, to organic) for which he even took out a patent![92]

Bruno Taut moved to a Sachlich position steadily through 1924, and then took the initiative to create another, more open pressure group, the Zehnerring, 'The Ring of Ten' (though they were hardly ever ten). It exercised pressure on local government, but was also the theatre of a constant sparring match between the organic-functionalist Hugo Häring and the 'rationalist-structuralist' Mies van der Rohe. The Zehnerring would become the obvious German section of CIAM – of which more later.

Taut became the most prolific designer of *Siedlungen*, as I noted earlier, and with his brother Max, planned the (archly named) 'Onkel Tom's Hütte' to the south-west of Berlin, between Zehlendorf and Dahlem. It was the largest *Siedlung* to date. The thirty or so architects employed there included Hugo Häring, Heinrich Tessenow and Hans Poelzig, as well as the Taut brothers. Poelzig's notable building of the time, the Cinema Capitol, has none of the earlier stalactite-cavernous look of the Grosses Schauspielhaus, but is a soberly expressed frame structure on the outside, while the interior is rectilinearly ribbed, both walls and the coved ceiling. The cinema introduced the newly sober manner which would govern his work of the next five years: the monumental IG Farben headquarters and the equally substantial German Radio building in Berlin. Mendelsohn's work, on the other hand, maintained a stylistic continuity. At the same time as Poelzig and in the same neighbourhood, he also designed a cinema, the Universum, whose sweeping lines were not only carried by inert building materials, but also by tubular light which sustained the spatial and malleable quality of his earlier work. In 1930 he built himself a large house in which he intended to shelter musical and even theatrical performances. He had invited the French painter Amédée Ozenfant to decorate its main duplex hall with a fresco symbolic of all the arts, but was persuaded by the nervous (and more far-sighted) painter to make it a rollable-up and removable canvas.[93]

Concurrently, a younger architect, Ernst May, a disciple of Ebenezer Howard (who had worked in Britain with Raymond Unwin and after the war became responsible for much housing in Breslau), was appointed city architect of Frankfurt. He set out on a policy of rapidly building semi-prefabricated housing estates inspired by Howard's ideas. Prefabrication also meant the standardizing of some plan-forms so that the Frankfurt 'ergonomic' kitchen became world-famous. Yet in all this rapid and efficient programming, there was no time for the intervention of artists.

French artists showed more enthusiasm for the new German architecture than for the home product: on Aristide Maillol's visit to Germany in 1931, Count Kessler, whose Weimar activities I described in the previous chapter, shepherded him round the new Frankfurt. They go to the Stadion after lunch. Maillol admires the nudity. Kessler tells him it is all part of the new *Lebensgefühl* after the war: light, sun, happiness in body experience – and it is a mass-movement. The same is true of the new architecture, the new *Wohnkultur*. Later, Kessler takes Maillol to the Römerstadt Siedlung (part of May's development) and reports his comment:

> I have never seen anything like it. It's the first time I see modern architecture that is perfect . . . If I knew how to write, I would write an article about it . . .[94]

The next year, Kessler took André Gide to visit Erich Mendelsohn's house in Berlin (which they both admired). They also visited another *Siedlung* on the Argentiner Strasse designed by some of the Novembergruppe architects (Taut, Häring, Gropius – but also Tessenow). Gide, full of admiration, called it *La Cité Magique*. 'Why have the French quite lost any sense of architecture?'

he asks – and Kessler explains that this kind of architecture is not *art pour l'art* but is part of a new lifestyle.[95]

It is easy to dismiss such trust in the new lifestyle in hindsight, even if any idea of 'a new dawn' had already come to such a murky end in the Soviet Union. A year after Gide's Berlin visit, Kessler, who had lost much of his fortune in the 1929–30 crash and was in France when Hitler took power, was advised by the German Embassy in Paris not to return home. An emblematic figure of the time, he died, lonely and bitterly disappointed, in a village near Maillol's home in Provence in 1937.[96] 'New architecture, a change of heart' (to quote Auden's memorable line) would remain an aspiration for the next decade.

Until Hitler's rise German architecture would, however, be dominated by Sachlich architects. Mendelsohn was not altogether Sachlich, not quite of the Mies–Gropius–Taut team – there was something too plastic, too sweeping about his designs. In 1926–7 the Werkbund entrusted Mies with the planning of a *Siedlung* at Weissenhof, a hill on the outskirts of Stuttgart. It was not only to represent the advanced tendencies in Germany, but also to include some Werkbund oldies: Peter Behrens (who, like Mies designed an apartment block), Poelzig (a middle-class villa). The Taut brothers did a villa each, Gropius two houses (one in half-dry assembly, the other wholly prefabricated). The Weissenhof Siedlung was to be international, and included designs

Erich Mendelsohn, the Universum/Luxor-Palast cinema, Berlin, 1926–9 (interior since destroyed).

by some foreign architects: the Dutch J.J.P. Oud and Mart Stam, both of whom did terrace houses, while the Belgian Victor Bourgeois did a villa. The two most memorable contributions were a house and a terrace by Le Corbusier and Pierre Jeanneret.[97] Mendelsohn is the obvious absence from the roster.

Sculptures or paintings were not part of the programme, and a cursory look at the documentation will show that even framed easel-pictures were rare, with the exception of those in the Le Corbusier houses by the abstract painter Willi Baumeister. By 1926 Le Corbusier was recognized as one of the leaders of the new architecture, so the invitation to work on the Stuttgart exhibition is hardly surprising; he was by then identified with Paris, and Paris continued to dominate the art world, even while Berlin acted as a magnet for avant-garde figures. The developments in the two cities (though the leading figures in each were aware of what was happening in the other) therefore proceeded independently.[98] The Swiss Charles-Edouard Jeanneret flourished in the Parisian context. He had already spent some time there before the war when he had worked for the Perret brothers (before his visit to Germany) and he had moved for good to 'the capital of art' in 1916,[99] hoping for engineering and defence contracts using concrete – in which he was a bit disappointed. Just before leaving his native Chaux-de-Fonds, Le Corbusier had designed a villa for a prosperous client (the only one of his early buildings he allowed into the six volumes of his *Oeuvres Complètes*) in a spare, disciplined and classicizing manner which owed much to the Perrets and perhaps a little to Wright. Like everything he designed after 1910, that of the villa was controlled by Golden Section regulating lines.[100] Jeanneret may have first learnt the procedure from Theodor Fischer's writings, but he certainly became familiar with it in Behrens' atelier. The use of that particular geometry had been taken up by a number of Parisian artists, especially the second-generation 'Synthetic Cubists' – Juan Gris most insistently, most of whom belonged to (and exhibited with) the group Section d'Or, which I mentioned in the previous chapter.

The situation changed in yet another way during the early 1920s. Some of the artists I mentioned (of all nationalities) had been killed or died of wounds. Franz Marc, Kandinsky's closest Blaue Reiter collaborator, was shot at Verdun in 1916; Apollinaire, trepanned after a head-wound, was killed by the Spanish 'flu on Armistice day; Raymond Duchamp-Villon died from the effects of gassing the same year; Blaise Cendrars, the poet (though Swiss), had joined the Foreign Legion and lost an arm. Fernand Léger (who survived his gassing) and Georges Braque had both been wounded, as had Walter Gropius. Schlemmer and Grosz both had long gruesome war service. Most artists – on both sides of the conflict – therefore turned to forms of pacifism, which in some cases (Max Ernst and Paul Eluard for instance) became errant fraternizing. Though the Futurists also lost the architect Sant'Elia and the painter-sculptor Umberto Boccioni, Marinetti persisted in war-mongering. He joined the Fascists in 1920 (a few months after Mussolini first formed the *Fasci del Combattimento*), left them briefly, but rejoined in 1923. Meanwhile, he enlisted in the forces of the farouche decadent Symbolist poet Gabriele D'Annunzio (whose secretary he had been twenty years earlier), which occupied Fiume/Rijeka, a city the Versailles peacemakers had given to Yugoslavia. D'Annunzio's maladministration presided over a weird, two-year-long carnival in opposition to the Italian government, which, weakened by this and other factional struggles, fell to the Fascists in 1924. In spite of his nationalist posturing Marinetti retained his commitment to the 'international' avant-garde, and in 1920 organized a Rome show of the Novembergruppe.

The great excitement of the Cubist adventure had subsided during that second phase. Picasso,[101] for one, even before the end of the war, had announced his forthcoming change of mood (and his ambivalence about his own Cubist achievement) with his baroquely figured backdrop for *Parade,* which I mentioned earlier. One of Diaghilev's last collective efforts, the ballet had a 'book' by the young and very vain Jean Cocteau. The score was by that great musical eccentric Erik Satie, reviver of church modes and composer of hymnodies for imaginary occult ceremonies. Always up-to-date, Cocteau persuaded him to include Futuro-Rumorist effects: pistol-shots, a typewriter, a propeller, a siren. Picasso also designed the costumes: ironically Cubist ones for some of the stiffer characters (the 10-foot-high 'managers'), as well as some enchantingly simple ones for the others.

That backdrop showed a group of dancers – harlequins, magicians and guitarists – looking at a ballerina dancing on the back of a she-Pegasus which suckles her young. Picasso painted it in Rome in 1917, where he had gone with Diaghilev and Nijinski and where war seemed remote, even if Italy was a combatant. They visited Pompeii and met some 'friendly' Futurists.[102] At that time

Picasso also embarked on a series of meticulous, Ingres-like pencil portraits (the poets Cocteau, Apollinaire, Max Jacob; Ambroise Vollard and Daniel-Henry Kahnweiler, the art dealers). The end of the war would usher in the period of large canvases showing monumental women and groups. They were later regarded as emblematic of an insistent quest for stability and are often labelled (justifiably) neo-Classical.

Picasso's mood, as well as his lasting obsession with clowns, also made him the obvious choice to design the sets and costumes of *Pulcinella*, with which Stravinsky turned from the primal folksiness of the *Rite of Spring* and *Petroushka* to a tightly organized emulation of eighteenth-century models; it initiated his neo-Classical period.[103] Many artists needed to feel the earth solid beneath their feet, and their world at rest, so Cubism seemed superannuated.[104] Jean Cocteau, ever sensitive to the mood of his time, wrote a number of brilliant and witty essays published under the slogan-title *Rappel à l'ordre*.

To return to Jeanneret, however: soon after he moved to Paris, Auguste Perret introduced him to Amédée Ozenfant, the same who was to paint the hall of Mendelsohn's house later. Ozenfant was well established, had launched a literary-artistic review, *L'Elan* (which he turned into a broadsheet in 1916), and had an interest in the emerging motor-car industry as well as a couture house.[105] A few months after his meeting with Jeanneret, Ozenfant also met the poet Paul Dermée, a disciple and friend of Apollinaire,[106] who was already involved with the Zürich Dada group. He already ran a small publishing house with the Apollinaireian label, *L'Esprit Nouveau*. There were, of course, plenty of art-culture periodicals in Paris, several of them old-established, yet within a few weeks of their meeting, the three decided to run a review together from Dermée's premises. A series of articles setting out the principles of architecture appeared in the early issues signed 'Le Corbusier-Saugnier', using Jeanneret's new pseudonym and Ozenfant's mother's maiden name.[107] The essays were collected into a book in 1923, and quickly went through several printings. *Vers une architecture* has remained one of the foundation texts of architecture. At the same time Jeanneret also designed a concrete house-atelier for Ozenfant, his first building in central Paris and one of his first essays in a new, 'white' manner.

A month before the Armistice they had also issued a manifesto which they called *Après le Cubisme*. The occasion was a joint exhibition of paintings that launched their movement, Purism. Against the Cubists the Purists championed the integrity of every individual object. Their most accomplished paintings are still lifes (of the kind familiar from Cubist canvases): bottles, carafes and glasses, mandolins, tables and chairs – always presented frontally and superimposed. Interpenetrating was not allowed, nor was the integrity of the object 'compromised'. The outlines were controlled by the Golden Section, and this respect for the geometry of every form also led them to reject any 'expressive' deformation influenced by African and other 'primitive' arts.

Dermée was soon marginalized by his two powerful partners (they thought he was sailing too close to Dada), yet he maintained an editorial place and *L'Esprit Nouveau* became his flagship in the battle about another Apollinaireian term, 'Surrealism'. He was determined to break Breton's virtual copyright on the word.[108] Against Breton's insistence that every artistic activity must surrender totally to the dictates of the unconscious, he maintained the super-rationality of the poetic method; the team he set up against Breton's party (Eluard, Aragon, Georges Ribemont-Dessaignes, Soupault – and the shifting crowd of his followers) was a strong one: Max Jacob, Pierre Reverdy, Ivan Goll – and himself. Attitudes to design and to man-made modernity was divided as follows: the Surrealists regarded the physical environment as a theatre of dreams whose features were only as interesting as their power of suggestion, while writers whom they rejected – Jacob, Reverdy and Goll, of course, as well as Blaise Cendrars, Jean Cocteau and the painters Fernand Léger and Robert Delaunay – were fascinated by the tangibles of modernity: aeroplanes, great ocean liners, smart cars, the radio and the telephone – and therefore the new ways of building. The Surrealists also declared themselves dialectical materialists, and until many of them allied themselves with Trotsky, joined the Communist Party more or less collectively.[109]

For all *L'Esprit Nouveau*'s commitment to the avant-garde and to rationality, Purism could be read as a kind of classicism. Corbusier's early theoretical writings certainly gave this association a face value, confirmed by his dogmatic insistence on the use of the Golden Section. However, he was not the artists' architect of choice – many wanted Auguste Perret. The graphic designer Cassandre (1924), Georges Braque (1927) and Marc Chagall (1927 – not built) were the best-known artists for whom Perret designed houses; lesser known were the Russian sculptor Chana Orloff (1926) and the Polish painter Mela Muter (1928).[110]

Auguste Perret, Maison Braque, Paris (1927).

As Diaghilev's fortunes declined in the theatre, Rolf de Maré's Ballets Suédois took over the role of the Ballets Russes. Erik Satie wrote the score for the paradoxical *Relâche* (usually translated as 'no performance' – which is what the audience found plastered over the theatre on arrival, producing a double-take), with Francis Picabia doing the sets. René Clair (with Picabia and the American Surrealist painter-photographer Man Ray) devised *Entr'acte* (Interval), a film to be shown in the interval of the ballet, in which several avant-garde figures (including Marcel Duchamp playing a rooftop chess-game with Man Ray) appeared.[111] There were other memorable avant-garde silent films: Luis Buñuel and Salvador Dalí created the over-furnished sado-oneiric *L'Age d'or*, and followed it with the gentler but more perverse *Chien Andalou*, woven out of a number of dreams organized about (and shown to the sound of) a recording of Wagner's *Liebestod* – so Buñuel. The musical ambitions of cineasts then became more refined in the late 1920s.[112] René Clair commissioned a score from the neo-Ravelian Jacques Ibert for his last silent film, a hilarious version of Georges Feydeau's *boulevard* farce, *Le Chapeau de paille d'Italie*, while Léger's *Ballet Mécanique* and his *Creation du Monde* had a score by Francis Poulenc and a text by Blaise Cendrars. One of the first films on which several artists collaborated to create a visual unity was (the unfortunately feebly scripted) *L'Inhumaine* of 1924, for which Fernand Léger created the interiors, while the rather 'advanced' sets were the work of the young architect Robert Mallet-Stevens, who was already booked for the Exposition des Arts Décoratifs a year later.[113]

The Twilight of 'Isms'

That vast art and decoration show occupied both sides of the river between the Eiffel Tower and the Grand Palais during the summer of 1925. The architects who planned it and who designed many of the pavilions are now mostly forgotten, though its opulence and scale gave the name Art Deco to the high-bourgeois manner of the time. Interiors were filled with furniture and objects discreetly but richly decorated using semi-precious materials (bronze – often gilt – highly figured woods and marbles, stamped and tooled leather). The style had a short but intense life into the 1930s. Much of the 'art' which accompanied it was coy, soft-porno statuary, some of it mechanically produced, while the best-known artists of that vogue were the rubbery Tamara Lempicka and the fey Erté.[114]

The 'advanced' episodes of the 1925 Exposition are remembered out of context. I have already mentioned Konstantin Melnikov's pavilion and the Soviet section of the collective show in the Grand Palais, which had the model of Tatlin's tower as its prize exhibit. The Austrian section had an almost de Stijl construction of battens and panels called *City in Space* by a young architect-theatre decorator Friedrich (later Frederick) Kiesler; some barges moored on the river were equipped by the fashion king Paul Poiret, and decorated with specially woven tapestries designed by the painter (who doubled at the time as a textile designer), Raoul Dufy.[115] Auguste Perret built

Le Corbusier, interior of the Pavillon de l'Esprit Nouveau, Exposition des Arts Décoratifs, Paris, 1925.

a wood-frame and concrete theatre with an auditorium which was an octagon inscribed in a rectangular exterior, giving the stage a Van de Velde-like threefold configuration,[116] while Robert Mallet-Stevens did several pavilions and showed himself aware (at least formally) of what the de Stijl architects had achieved.

By then *L'Esprit Nouveau* was established enough to be given a pavilion. Though ascribed to a collective, it was largely the work of Le Corbusier. Of the two adjoining parts, one was a curved diorama showing his *Plan Voisin* for Paris and his 'vision' of a city for three million inhabitants, while the other was a duplex apartment, a 'show flat' from a project which Corbusier never developed called *immeuble-villas*. It opened on to a double-height terrace garden which incorporated an existing tree which was allowed to grow through it. A large statue by Lipschitz was part of the exhibit,[117] while a number of paintings by Léger (who also contributed to one of Mallet-Stevens' pavilions) decorated its polychrome walls, whose colours seem also to have been worked out with him.[118] Close by there was another deliberately 'modern' formal garden planned by Gabriel Gouverekian, the first of its kind, though within a year or two the informal 'English' garden became the standard 'modern' landscape type. In spite of many protests, the de Stijl artists were not offered a collective show in the Dutch pavilion, which was designed by one of the Frank Lloyd Wright's apostles, Hendrik Wijdeveld.[119]

Like the 1902 Turin show, the Paris exhibition both absorbed some of the avant-garde artists and – in a sense – undermined them. Both set out to be celebrations but acted as closures. The year 1925 marked the wane of those 'isms' of all kinds which had flourished in Paris during and after the war as they had in Germany and in Eastern Europe. That same year Lissitzky and Arp[120] produced a guidebook to them which turned out to be something of an obituary, perhaps because they had not taken account of the young Surrealists whose continuous eruptions throughout the 1930s (there were even some splutters in the 1940s and '50s) were the most public assertions of avant-garde continuity.

In the aftermath of Art Deco, van Doesburg, who had moved to Paris, was commissioned through Hans and Sophie Arp to decorate and to transform a brasserie and café concert in Strasbourg, L'Aubette, a locale that occupied two lower floors and the basement of an eighteenth-century building. The Arps and van Doesburg could not touch the exterior of the monument,[121] but the interior became a triumph of Doesburg's personal version of Neo-

Theo van Doesburg, Hans Arp and Sophie Tauber-Arp, cinema/dance-hall, Café de l'Aubette, Strasbourg, *c.* 1928; screen wall shortly after completion.

Theo van Doesburg, drawing for the screen wall of the cinema-dance hall of the Café de l'Aubette, Strasbourg, 1927.

Plasticism, for which he developed a programme he called Elementarism.[122] He was responsible for the main café at ground level and the two banqueting rooms on the floor above, while Hans Arp painted the passages and billiard-room as well as the basement with dancing 'organic' forms; his wife Sophie did the two bars and a tea-room. Though the three worked independently, van Doesburg had the overall command. Their materials were poor: linoleum floors, relief plaster coloured with house-painters' enamel (which quickly looked shabby), aluminium and chrome, some stained glass. The walls and ceilings of the main dance-hall/cinema, with its range of windows, were left orthogonal and this was stressed by the metal fixtures, the linear structure of the rods on which the lights were set, and a gallery. This orthogonality was further underlined by the layout of the booths which articulate the room and (most insistently) by the cinema screen. Van Doesburg's composition of coloured rectangles was pitched diagonally against all that orthogonality and set up a sharp and bracing rhythm against the structure. The effect of L'Aubette is therefore almost the opposite of that resolution which Mondrian considered an essential attribute of de Stijl.[123] Although it had a considerable *succès d'estime*, it led to no further commissions and in the last few years of his life van Doesburg (he died, depressed and impoverished in 1931) gave up painting for architecture and produced a number of 'ideal', almost 'Futurist' projects in the studio he designed for himself near Paris.

Inflexible Mondrian, who also designed (or rather 'arranged') studios for himself in Paris and then in New York using minimal resources (coloured papers, his own easel, the odd canvas and Spartan furniture), lived to regenerate de Stijl principles without ever abandoning essential orthogonality, and so created a new pictorial world to exalt the urban environment that he found in New York. In spite of their divergence and their conflict, Mondrian and van Doesburg had in common the search for a visual demonstration that affirmed the unity of the plastic experience.

Starting from quite different premises, Walter Gropius had become involved in an equally 'totalizing' project: the Total Theatre. *Totaltheater* was the brainchild of Erwin Piscator, by then one of the best-known German avant-garde producers, who had already worked with a number of Bauhaus figures (Moholy-Nagy had done sets for him) and become the proponent of politico-theatrical spectacle.[124] The building which he and Gropius imagined had an auditorium arena of three circles of different size, the two smaller ones swivelling eccentrically inside the larger, so that the smallest circle could become a central stage (this could even be done during a performance). The walls were screens on which images could be back-projected so that the spectator could be entirely enveloped by the setting. The stage could be full apron, a three-space proscenium as imagined by Van de Velde and Perret, or completely open. Although the building was aborted by the 1929 crash it received international publicity when Gropius was invited to present it at a theatre conference held in Rome in 1934.[125]

Gropius' trip to Rome was a prelude to his withdrawal from Germany – even though, like Mies van der Rohe, he had tried accommodation with the new powers.[126] Several other German avant-garde architects (notably Hannes Meyer with some Bauhaus pupils, and Ernst May with Frankfurt collaborators such as Martin Wagner and the Dutchman Mart Stam) worried about their political future, were seduced by plans for Soviet expansion, notably by the promise of the competition for a new manufacturing city in the Urals, Magnitogorsk, decreed as part of the (largely eastward) industrial development called for by the fifteenth Party Congress of 1927. Various schemes were advanced by Soviet architects, but their disputes led the authorities in 1931 to commission May's team as being the most pragmatic and economically sound. However, material shortages as well as the rapid changes in party policy meant that none of the 'advanced' projects was ever built.[127]

Le Corbusier, for his part, had won a competition for the Central Cooperative (Centrosoyus) Moscow building in 1929. It was under construction as the party line was changing. There had, since 1922, been an association to promote what later became 'Social-Realist' art, AKhR,[128] in opposition to the various avant-garde tendencies, and by 1928 it had the ear of authority. Many of the artists I mentioned earlier – Rodchenko and Stepanova, El Lissitzky, the Mexican Diego Rivera (in Moscow at the time), the Vesnin brothers, Sergei Eisenstein – had founded a new association, 'October', in 1928, with an exhibition in 1930 as a show of resistance. However, its catalogue, issued a year later, carried the publisher's 'apology' for 'vulgar, materialistic mistakes', and when the Central Committee of the Communist Party declared the amalgamation of all literary and artistic organizations in April 1932, the Social Realists were in power. For his part, Lunacharsky in a series of articles in 1931–2 claimed that 'classical' forms were as rational and timeless as those of geometry, and that the proletariat, now being free and organized, needed palaces which would proclaim its greatness.[129]

A number of other Soviet competitions invited international participation, of which the most important by far, historically as well as architecturally, was that for the Palace of the Soviets in Moscow (1929–31), to be built at the foot of the Kremlin, on the site of the Cathedral of the Redeemer, which had been pulled down in 1925 (only to be rebuilt as-was in 1998–9). Poelzig and Perret, Le Corbusier, Gropius, Hannes Meyer, Erich Mendelsohn were invited to compete.[130] The first prize was divided between the aged academician Ivan Zholtovski, Hector O. Hamilton (an Englishman working out of New Jersey in a commercially smoothed version of American Beaux-Arts design – it was his one moment of glory) and the young, rising Boris Iofan, working with a group of collaborators, who after four further stages was awarded the commission for an Art Deco tower with Expressionist touches, to be crowned by a 70-metre statue of the exhorting Lenin. Such competition results affirmed the end of official Soviet accommodation with its avant-garde. Meyer made his way through Siberia to Mexico and back to Switzerland, May to East Africa, Stam back to the Netherlands.

A Change of Heart

The scale and nature of the changes were not glaring at first. When CIAM summoned its 1933 conference to Moscow, unanswered protests (including one to Stalin) about the Palace of the Soviets competition project brought home to the organizers that their choice of venue may have been impolitic.[131] A ship was chartered instead to take participants from Marseilles to Athens and back. For the first time the congress included painter-sculptors – Fernand Léger and László Moholy-Nagy – who filmed a record of the occasion. On this trip, van Doesburg's old associate, Cornelis van Eesteren became the president and CIAM formulated a programme still known as the 'Athens Charter' which set out the basis of all building under four headings: dwelling, work, recreation, traffic, and this became the uniform method for analysing all projects to be presented at its sessions.

In spite of all these conflicts and obstacles, it still seemed in the second half of the 1920s and in the early 1930s that a real achievement had been made, and that the promises of the immediate post-war were being fulfilled. There would indeed be 'a new architecture, a change of heart'. That sense of it – which Count Kessler had celebrated – was obscured by the events of the 1930s and in many publications, notably in the very influential (and now notorious) exhibition organized by Philip Johnson and Henry-Russell Hitchcock at the Museum of Modern Art in New York in 1931–2 to celebrate the arrival of a new international style of architecture as a historical phenomenon free of any social or even economic implications.[132]

The twenty years (colloquially the *ventennio*) of Italy under Fascist rule provided a quirky parenthesis. At the end of the First World War the Italian avantgarde (identified with the Futurists) had lost Sant'Elia and Boccioni while another painter, Gino Severini, turned away to Parisian classicism, but perhaps the most important defection was that of Carlo Carrà, who encountered Giorgio de Chirico in 1917. Among the greatest painters of his time, Chirico (born in Greece of Italian parents) had trained as an engineer before turning to art. On moving to Munich (where he went to study painting), he also discovered Nietzsche as well as the art of the Secession; going on to Paris, he gravitated to Apollinaire's circle, returning to Italy for his military service. He met Carrà as a fellow inmate of a military hospital in Ferrara, that 'most metaphysical of cities'.

That was where a 'Metaphysical' art was born – an art whose impact depended on the alienation of everyday objects and interiors. Metaphysical disquiet in turn gave way to a more assertive Novecento 'classicism' and a quite un-Futurist (if patriotic) admiration for the monumental Italian art of the past: Giotto, Paolo Uccello, Piero della Francesca. Carrà had been an enthusiastic Futurist, like a younger ex-Futurist, Mario Sironi, an early member of the

Fascist Party. They made common cause with Giovanni Muzio, an architect whose early buildings were scholarly if ironic versions of classicism. The Novecento group had official support – their most powerful advocate was Margherita Sarfatti, a combative art-critic who was Mussolini's Egeira, so that the Novecento painters received commissions to cover areas of official walls and vaults; they also had the sympathy of the 'classical' side of German Neue Sachlichkeit.

In 1926–7 seven young north Italian architects issued a 'Rationalist' manifesto[133] in discreet opposition to the academy and to the Futurists; they claimed affinity with the Novecento artists as well as international movements – particularly *L'Esprit Nouveau* in Paris, and the Dutch and German ones. Calling for a rational analysis of programme which gave priority to structure and the evolution of new buildings types, they constituted themselves as 'the new primitives' with no pretension to 'create a style'; instead, they hoped that a style might appear through their work of analysis. Mies van der Rohe chose the project for a hotel by two of the seven, Larco and Rava, for the Werkbund exhibition at the Weissenhof Siedlung in 1927 and the group became the Italian branch of CIAM.

Although 'totalitarian' was a slogan adopted by the Fascists, it did not seem to affect the patronage of the arts. Inside the Fascist directorate, the Novecento and the 'Rationalists' had (until he was dismissed in 1933) the backing (against most of his colleagues) of a minister, Enrico Bottai, and they soon found other powerful advocates: Giuseppe Pagano, an active Fascist, and Edoardo Persico, who steered clear of power. The most brilliant of the group, Giuseppe Terragni, also an early Fascist, was commissioned in 1932[134] to design the headquarters of the party in his native Como, and the Casa del Fascio was to become one of the best-known twentieth-century buildings. It has none of the trappings otherwise associated with Fascist architecture – no 'classical' details, no speaker's tribune or tower, no propagandist sculptures, few inscriptions. Like many buildings of Gruppo 7, it was a simple geometrical body: the plan was a square, the elevation a double square made up of seven frame units horizontally, four vertically; the concrete structure was pink and marble-sheathed, as were the walls. The front was asymmetrical, two of the seven horizontal bays making a blank wall. In some of the early versions, the building does have a *campanile*, and the blank wall carries an elegantly contained inscription. In later schemes, however, this wall is covered with photo-montages of which several versions have survived, though none has been executed. An abstract composition by Terragni's painter friend Mario Radice (with whom he collaborated on some other occasions) centred on a large photograph of Mussolini, which took up one wall of the main council room.

The opening of the Casa del Fascio coincided with the tenth anniversary exhibition of the Fascist March on Rome; the large old exhibition hall of the Palazzo dell'Esposizione in the centre of the city was transformed by Adalberto Libera. Terragni and others of the '7' were responsible for the interior, which used photomontage generously and often looked very like slightly earlier ones devised in the Soviet Union. Montage was developed brilliantly in other exhibi-tions of the time, though the permanent buildings of the regime were increas-ingly in the hands of 'academic' architects. In 1933–4 the campus of Rome University by Marcello Piacentini was one of the most important regime com-missions, yet even there two of the buildings (one by Giuseppe Pagano) were distinctly 'rationalist'. The campus was centred on a large bronze *Athena* by the sculptor Arturo Martini, whose naively archaic manner was appreciated by the more perceptive academic architects, as was Sironi's and Carrà's new monu-mental style. Martini and Sironi both collaborated with Piacentini on the build-ing of the Law Courts in Milan. In Milan, too, Sironi's old associate Muzio involved him in the design of the Fascist newspaper offices.

The confused patronage of the Fascists became evident in the competi-tion for the headquarters of the party on the new Via dell'Impero in Rome, opposite the late antique ruins of the Basilica of Maxentius. A number of 'rationalist' projects were submitted, as well as a number of academic ones. Among the winners was one by a team which included both Terragni and Sironi. In 1938, just before the war, on a site adjoining the proposed head-quarters, Terragni and his colleagues, with Mario Sironi as the figurative artist, planned the Danteum, a monument which would 'realize' the *Divine Comedy* as a kind of passage rite through the building. It would have no other function. The project was promoted by a small group of literary enthusiasts who were also convinced Fascists, and was, arguably, the closest architecture got to a true Wagnerian *Gesamtkunstwerk*: the *promenade architecturale* was intended to offer an experience analogous to a transformative reading of Dante's poem. Inspired though it was by a Fascist caricature of the Ghibelline

354

Mario Sironi,
*Synthesis of Urban
Landcape*, 1919,
oil on canvas.

ideal of the just empire, Terragni's project could have been his master-piece.[135] The war intervened, however; Terragni was sent to Russia, suffered a drastic change of political heart and died suddenly in 1944. Although Mussolini had personally approved it, the Danteum was crazily eccentric to the Fascist enterprise.

Prompted by trade deficits and shortages which the League of Nations sanctions produced during the Abyssinian war, the Fascist government now promoted Mediterranean self-sufficiency, 'autarchy' – vernacular building and poor materials. Mediterranean 'rootedness' was also promoted officially in France for a short time, and a plan for a 'Mediterranean University' centred on Nice was floated in 1933.[136] A different but also 'Mediterranean' 'Guild-academy' for all the arts was promoted by the Dutch architect Hendrik Wijdeveld, the same who had designed the Dutch pavilion in the 1925 Paris exhibition. Amédée Ozenfant and Erich Mendelsohn (by then working mostly in Palestine) were involved, and they were joined by the Russian-born architect Serge Chermayeff, the Spanish sculptor Pablo Gargallo, Paul Hindemith and the British sculptor-letterer Eric Gill. Land had been bought near Saint-Tropez in 1933, but the site and the first buildings were destroyed in a forest fire in 1934, and when Pablo Gargallo died suddenly in Spain, the whole project was gradually abandoned.[137]

The 1937 CIAM conference was called in Paris. It was to consider agricultural planning as well as the integration of leisure and educational buildings into housing projects. It attracted little notice in the frantic excitement of the Paris International World Fair of that year, however, which was visited by 34 million tourists and took up the Champs de Mars as well as the Invalides esplanade, dominating the whole city. On the Chaillot hill, the old spiky and polychrome building put up for the World Exhibition of 1878 was modified:[138] the central auditorium was pulled down to open a long vista from the Longchamps roundabout through the Eiffel Tower inserted between it and the Ecole Militaire in 1889. Encased in a pale and gleaming limestone, it was renamed the Palais de Chaillot.[139] Almost parallel to it, another double 'palace' called the Palais de Tokyo (after the boulevard at the bottom of the hill) housed two new museums (the City of Paris and the Modern Art), separated by a plain but emphatic limestone colonnaded Art Deco confection, underlined for emphasis by many bland bas-reliefs and fountains descending to river level. Mellifluously oracular inscriptions specially composed by Paul Valéry and incised in its wall reiterated the 'classicism' of the complex,[140] whose orderly smoothness camouflaged the turbulence of government crises at the approach of war. Even Albert Speer, Hitler's minister and favourite architect, in Paris briefly to oversee the construction of the German pavilion he had designed, was taken aback by the 'classicism' of the official French buildings.[141]

Boris Iofan, model for the Moscow Palace of the Soviets, 1933–8 (unexecuted).

Flanking the axial view of the Eiffel Tower from Chaillot, the

German pavilion stood on one side, its inert set of tall pilasters carrying a cornice surmounted by a gilt eagle-and-swastika relief, while on the other side of the avenue, the Soviet one, designed by the same Boris Iofan who had won the Palace of the Soviets competition, was pleated like a Wurlitzer organ and crowned by a twin statue of a factory worker and a collective farm-girl thrusting their Social Realist hammer and sickle aggressively at the German eagle.[142] With the Palais de Chaillot, the two pavilions were a triple triumph of state-sponsored kitsch. Yet all was not quite so dismal. Michel Roux-Spitz designed one of the big technological exhibits, that of electricity; its hall was internally painted by the rather undervalued Raoul Dufy, while Robert Delaunay provided large external panels for the railway pavilion designed by a group of otherwise undistinguished architects.[143]

Guernica

Le Corbusier overcame the objections of the show's organizers, and was to be given space for a pavilion dedicated to the new *Temps* rather than a new *Esprit*. A square tented structure, it had 'walls' and a flat 'roof' suspended from cables passed over steel struts. Within, a thin steel grid carried a narrative collage which exhorted those in power to provide housing for the people so as to forestall a revolution.[144] Other national pavilions were memorable: the Belgian one was designed by the aged Henri Van de Velde; Sweden had an elegant metal-framed one, and Hungary a metal-sheathed one. The Finnish pavilion was done by the rising master Alvar Aalto, and was all wood and photographs. Splendid though all these were, they are not part of this story.

The national pavilion which is crucial is the Spanish one. The Civil War was then a year old. The building was a metal-framed two-storey structure designed by the young Catalan Josep Lluis Sert,[145] its outer panels covered by photomontages evoking the horrors of the war. It was 'announced' at its ramped entrance by a kind of column-totem created by the sculptor Alberto Sanchez-Perez,[146] while in the main entry hall a mobile mercury fountain devised by Sandy (Alexander III) Calder advertised one of Spain's principal mineral products. One whole wall of the hall was covered by Picasso's grisaille canvas – one of the largest he painted. A protest against the conflict, *Guernica* commemorated the first aerial bombing, that of a Basque town, by the German airforce. There were other more or less interesting works of art in that relatively small building, but what seems powerful now, 70 years after the event, is that a political conjunction prompted the unique incandescent fusion of building, painting and sculpture.[147] It was perhaps the last time that the avant-garde – architecture, painting, sculpture, graphics – came together to touch public life unforgettably.

Support for the Republic was a popular movement which mobilized most European artists, even if the misdeeds of the Spanish left now make it look a bit naive, and there was no opportunity for building or any other artistic patronage of the avant-garde beyond the propaganda posters by the Republican government in Spain. When the exhibition closed, Munich and the invasion of Czechoslovakia in September 1938 were only a year away – to be followed by the outbreak of the Second World War.

The New World

Meanwhile, a team of young Brazilians, including Alfonso Reidy, Lucio Costa and Oskar Niemeyer, architects, Candido Portinari, painter and ceramic designer, and the landscapist Roberto Burle Marx, called Le Corbusier to act as consultant on the design of the new Ministry of Education in Rio de Janeiro in 1936–7. Their creation of the ministry in the form of a glass-faced but louvre-shielded block raised on high columns, with walls decorated by brilliantly blue-tinted tiles, remains a triumph marred only by the fact that the dwarf bronze of *Perseus* by the Parisian Jacques Lipschitz attached to the prominent curved wall of the auditorium was cast one third of the intended size.[148] The same group produced an ensemble of semi-public buildings on the lake-reservoir, Pampulha near Belo Horizonte. Oskar Niemeyer designed the Casino and a parabolic-vaulted church of St Francis, whose painted reredos wall is one of Portinari's most impressive works, while the parks and gardens were laid out by Roberto Burle Marx. The same group would become the main creators of a new, inland capital for the country during the immediate post-war period, Brasilia. The inability of the more thoughtful architects of the time to provide a formal vesture for institutions – or the proper context for a vital urban development – turned this brilliant project into a bitter fiasco.

Two very different instances of state patronage between the wars concerned painters and sculptors working on buildings without involving any architects; in both cases the policy was limited to the 'beautifying' of existing structures. In 1920 a reforming statesman, Jose Vasconcelos, was appointed minister of education by the left-wing President Obregon of Mexico; he immediately promoted the state patronage of a group of 'advanced' artists. He encouraged the return of the Cubist-Surrealist-Social Realist Diego Rivera from Paris, and secured him commissions for wall paintings, including a huge one in the Palacio Nacional, the parliament building. Most famous among other painters who received prominent commissions were José Clemente Orozco and the younger David Alfaro Siqueiros, now remembered chiefly for his part in the murder of Trotsky. They all covered vast areas of wall and vault, yet none of the three worked with any innovative architects – of whom there were not many in Mexico at the time in any case since Art Deco remained the official style. The first Mexican 'modern' architects, José Villagrán Garcia and Luis Barragan, did not really establish their independent way of working until the late 1930s. Indeed, the most prominent building of Mexico City, the theatre-opera house, Palacio de Bellas Artes, had been begun by an Italian architect in 1900, during the dictatorship of Porfirio Diaz, though it was not finished until 1930; its Art Nouveau character was not modified and its most famous 'figurative' feature is a glass curtain made by the workshops of Louis Comfort Tiffany.

The 'Muralist' movement flourished until the right-wing take-over in 1925 and returned to walls and vaults when the left was voted back under Lázaro Cárdenas in 1933.[149] Orozco had gone into exile in 1925, while Siqueiros, the only true Stalinist among them, allied himself with the Trade Union movement. All travelled – and taught. Siqueiros had a studio in New York where Jackson Pollock enrolled at one point.

Diego Rivera was the most famous native New World avant-gardist, and among other commissions was asked to paint the entrance hall of the new RCA Center, the main building of Rockefeller Plaza recently finished to designs by a group guided by Raymond Hood. Rivera's explicit political imagery caused much scandal and he was asked to modify it; when he refused, he was dismissed and some months later the paintings were destroyed, though Rivera was encouraged to paint a replica of them in the Palacio de Bellas Artes and continued to work on large mural decorations (including a half-submerged painting and mosaics in the Lerma River waterworks of Mexico City). He had, in the meanwhile, met a young architect, Juan O'Gorman. Their first collaboration, in 1929–31, was the design of two interconnected concrete Corbusieran houses for Rivera himself and for his new wife, Frida Kahlo.[150] While working on another house at Anahuacali,[151] the painter suggested lining the inside of the shuttering with a pattern in coloured stones to create a mosaic which would become the facing surface of the house. O'Gorman repeated the treatment on a very fanciful house for himself and one for the American composer Conlan Nancarrow in 1947.[152]

While O'Gorman continued to work occasionally with Rivera, he was called on to design (with two associates) a new Library for the National University. The blank walls of its storage tower offered a surface of 4,000 square metres on which O'Gorman 'tattooed' (with the master's active approval) an exuberant Rivera-style, Aztec-looking, narrative-heraldic mosaic which some consider the terminal firework of Mexican Muralism.

The Mexican Muralists may only have been involved with architecture intermittently, but they were always politically 'engaged', as Diego Rivera's defiance of his New York patrons shows. And their adventure became a model for another episode of state patronage, the Federal Arts Project (FDA), under the New Deal. The post-1929 financial disasters had brought misery to much of the population of the United States, and Franklin Delano Roosevelt had been elected President in 1933 on a promise of rapid change – which he achieved. Public works sponsored by the Works Progress Administration (established in 1935) were one of the minor products of this achievement. Although the WPA had no explicit architectural policy, the New Deal did promote vast planning-building schemes, notably those of the Tennessee Valley Authority. Its 40 or more dams and the hydro-electric works connected with them were largely done by one Hungarian-trained architect, Roland Wank, who was also responsible for their remarkably handsome surfacing. His gigantic structures (unfortunately not equalled, either for quantity or quality in his later work) are forgotten by most historians of modern architecture.[153] Nor were they parallelled by any painterly or sculptural involvement.

The Works Art (later Federal Arts) Project was initiated as an attempt to find employment for indigent artists in various regional centres: symphony orchestras and jazz bands were promoted; theatre companies, music-copying schemes, commissions for writers and for painters were funded, as well as a prints workshop.[154] Murals were also commissioned for public libraries, hospitals, prisons, post offices – nearly 1,400 by the time the programme was wound down in 1943. Much of the work was cheerful and combative, and emulated Mexican models. Some of the artists involved achieved a great reputation: Arshile Gorky, for one, while Mark Rothko, Clifford Still and Philip Guston went on to become masters of post-war American Abstract Expressionism.[155] The most quintessentially American 'post-Cubist' painter, Stuart Davis, already had one or two wall paintings to his credit. Deeply committed to left-wing politics, he never joined the Communist Party and had a strong distaste for Mexican Muralist 'social realism'. He did some panels for the WPA which were not installed (and survive in museums) or have been destroyed.[156] Other painters who took part in the Project – Ben Shahn, Norman Rockwell – never slid back on the social engagement of their work. If startlingly different from each other, neither ever collaborated in a building.

Such developments hardly touched the European avant-garde in the late 1930s. André Breton, on a shabbily 'official' visit to Mexico in 1938, was put up by Diego Rivera in the house that O'Gorman had designed for him and Frida Kahlo (who hated 'the old cockroach' and rejected the 'Surrealist' label Breton offered her). Rivera and Breton formed a trio with Trotsky and went on many excursions together; Breton and Rivera combed markets for pre-Columbian figurines, to Trotsky's perplexity at their interest in such clumsy, primitive stuff. Nor is there any record of their visiting the Muralists' work – not even Rivera's own. But then Breton was not a 'visual' person (even if part of his income came from art-dealing) and he was also insensitive to music. It may have been the most obvious effect of his genius that he managed to convince the press (and the public with it) that the flame of the avant-garde only burnt pure in the Surrealist movement, and that only Surrealists could guarantee French artistic vitality – or anyone else's for that matter. They invested much energy in 'happenings', which ever fascinated the media, though it meant that 'abstract' artists (I use the term generically to include those who also called themselves 'concrete' and 'non-objective' – Delaunay and Kupka as well as Mondrian) received little publicity in comparison.

Even before the outset of the Second World War many of the European artists I have mentioned, fascinated by the New World, had moved across the Atlantic. Colonies of them settled mostly in New York (painters, some architects) and Los Angeles (musicians and writers). Some, of course – like Marcel Duchamp – already lived in New York, while two young Austrian architects (disciples of Adolf Loos), Richard Neutra and Rudolf Schindler, had gravitated to California before 1930; another Austrian, Friedrich Kiesler, who had made that brilliant 'Neo-Plastic' contribution to the Austrian pavilion at the 1925 Paris Exposition des Arts Décoratifs, was enthusiastically taken up by van Doesburg. His show was moved to New York; he settled there to become a key figure of the transatlantic avant-garde. As the staff designer of the Julliard School, he set a number of 'advanced' operas and plays while he continued to work on his project for a 'universal' theatre (rather less developed than Gropius'), as well as an 'endless' house whose interiors would be a seamless surface with no articulation into walls, floors, ceilings. His friendship with Duchamp[157] led to his designing the *Art of this Century* exhibition for the gallerist and collector Peggy Guggenheim, in which many of the New York exiles, particularly the Surrealists, took part. That exhibition made him their favourite 'decorator', and Breton involved him in their first 'return' Parisian exhibition in 1947; the Kiesler connection was Duchamp's only involvement with contemporary architecture.

Against Architecture

Duchampian indifference turned to contempt in the writings of the ethnosadist and proto-Surrealist Georges Bataille. His essay 'On Architecture', first published in the early 1930s and much quoted thereafter, was misnamed – it was not 'on' but 'against' it. Architecture was the tangible demonstration of power and social authority, the incarnation of the super-ego, says Bataille. He claimed to follow Hegel's historical dialectic to argue that art had been left behind in the development of thinking; and since architecture had been the earliest of the arts, it would also be the first discarded as it had become the art most remote from any true human need or desire. The city, Bataille conceded, will nevertheless go on requiring two (but only two) kinds of public building, the slaughterhouse and the museum, since they shelter the essential aspects of *dépense*, of expenditure – even waste. That uniquely vital social function has two faces: one sacred, awful; the other secular and restorative. As Bataille saw it, the two roles of the ancient temple – a place of slaughter and a place of prayer – have been separated in the modern world.[158]

The Surrealists may have found Bataille's obsession with fluid expenditure – with blood, mucus, excrement – repugnant, though their project needed architecture even less.[159] Of course, they called on features of the environment as essential stimuli to dreams and visionary experiences, as their writings show (say Louis Aragon's *Paysans de Paris* or even more explicitly Breton's own *Nadja* or *Les Vases communicants*), but the architectural quality of buildings was irrelevant: only their oneiric potentialities enthralled them.[160] That is why they would go on pilgrimage to visit the works of Facteur Cheval (1836–1924), the village postman of Hauterives in the Isère who devoted decades of his life to building a fantastically collaged (of shells, pebbles, other fragments) monument he called the *Palais Idéal* (as well as a tomb of the same style).[161] Maurice Nadeau's *Histoire du Surréalisme*, which includes long extracts from documents and manifestos, has not a word about any building, alive or dead, though, of course, exhibitions allowed the Surrealists the sort of environmental extravagance which commonplace, everyday existence inevitably precluded.[162] Such effects were then quickly taken up by fashion and display designers as well as by the more lively advertising agencies, sometimes to the Surrealists' indignation, much as New York art critics were scandalized by the quick absorption of Abstract Expressionist canvases into fashion photographs.

Architecture cannot be the product of rampant unconscious forces, however. Contacts between the French Surrealists and contemporary architects therefore remained minimal.[163] On their side, at any rate. Le Corbusier, for one, was familiar with the movement from its beginnings; he had been party to the 1925–6 Dermée-Breton controversy in *l'Esprit nouveau*, and even contributed to their 'house' journal, *Minotaure*; and he was well aware, too, that some of the forms he had devised might sustain an oneiric 'reading', and willing, on occasion, to 'fabricate' effects which emulated dreams, most notably in the apartment for Charles de Beistegui,[164] in which a spiral staircase descends among rocaille furniture; yew and box hedges are planted in electrically movable troughs; the lawn-paved roof-terrace has a fireplace with an oval empty picture-frame over it (through half of which you can see the Arc de Triomphe); while a periscope projects images of the Paris skyline into a *camera lucida*.[165] The extravagant playfulness of the Beistegui apartment may be something of an exception among Corbusier's works (though he was more inclined to play on ambiguities and metaphors than has generally been recognized, especially in his later work).

Before the war there had been much conflict and little avant-garde solidarity among the various artists working in Paris. But in the American exile it was different – and the various currents of émigré avant-garde artists did fraternize. Mondrian, so Roberto Matta reported, found the conversation of Surrealists more entertaining than that of Abstract painters in New York.[166] But with the end of the war, many exiles returned to Europe, and those who were seduced by America coalesced with the rising native school to create the New York art world which was to dominate the second half of the twentieth century.

The outbreak of the war found several of the 'refugee' architects taking up powerful positions in the United States. Gropius ruled from Harvard, Mies from the Illinois Institute of Technology in Chicago (where he gave a rather patronising blessing to László Moholy-Nagy's short-lived 'New Bauhaus').[167] Josef Albers, his wife Annie and some other *Bauhäusler* were involved in the founding of an avant-garde outpost in the Alleghenies, Black Mountain College, which attempted its own 'synthesis of the arts'.[168] When that failed (financially), Albers, with his disciple Gyorgy Kepes, moved to Yale in 1950 to make its art department another Bauhaus outpost; their impact on the formation of younger American artists was capital, even if their intrusion into the American scene was not always viewed benevolently by the natives. All of which was of little interest to Breton and his minions.

Many of the CIAM architects found themselves in control of reconstruction at the end of the war. More than half of the habitat in Europe, and much in Asia, had been destroyed, while housing and attendant social buildings (schools, hospitals, etc.) made a demand on architects and planners that far exceeded the supply of talent. Their matter-of-fact approach was now adopted in the reconstruction, even by stylistically historicist 'social realist' builders. Only in the United States was the bulk of the 'homes for heroes' left to private enterprise, working (usually) without the benefit of an architect – of which

Levittown became one of the prototypes.[169] As for the CIAM architects, most were self-confident, assured in their social role and position, and with little need for either counsel or formal intervention from artists.

Building the Liberal Ideal

In all this frenzy of building, commemorative monuments were not initially in demand – even if some First World War ones were updated. Yet the 'Synthesis of the Major Arts', which could be considered a quintessentially monumental proposition, became a surprisingly lively issue, and the terms 'monument', 'monumental' were given a new face value. At the eighth CIAM (1949) meeting in Bergamo, the notion that every town required a more or less monumental 'core' was introduced by the British members, conscious of their Garden City heritage which had guided the post-war planning of the New Towns around London. They (as well as their European colleagues) were also eager to relate the concept of city core to the charms of the Mediterranean town. There was therefore much talk at the time about a 'new monumentality' which would require the presence of notable works of art in public spaces.[170] That same year, 1949, Gropius (now working with a group of his students – the Architects' Collaborative) finished the Harkness Commons building for the Harvard Graduate Center, and invited the collaboration of Josef Albers, Gyorgy Kepes and Herbert Bayer (another Bauhaus pupil), Hans Arp and Joan Miró – as well as the American sculptor Richard Lippold (although he did complain that he could not find American artists equal to the task). Harkness Commons still figures in tourist guides, but is rarely mentioned in the literature of twentieth-century art, and it did not have any notable influence in the following decades – not even on Gropius' own work.

Yet Gropius had presented Harkness Commons at the Bergamo CIAM conference as the model of what a 'core' should be: a relaxed group of buildings round a courtyard, featuring (however modestly) the work of 'major' artists. It was to be a signpost to future development, and he insisted that painters and sculptors had to be part of the building team with architects from the beginning of a project, 'each influencing the other' and concluded, regretfully:

I have not seen any building yet in our period where that kind of deep integration has brought about a solution which we could consider completely satisfactory.[171]

Few other experiments in giving works of art a prominent place in a prominent public location were equally successful. For the new UNESCO headquarters in Paris, which the *Bauhäusler* Marcel Breuer designed with the Italian engineer Pier-Luigi Nervi and two French architects, Picasso painted one of his feeblest works – *The Fall of Icarus*.[172] Léger's two panels, which flank the presidency tribune in the anodyne assembly chamber of the United Nations Building in New York, are among his least impressive achievements. Often photographed and shown on television as a background to some political event, they are so bland that they are barely noticed by the room's occupants, let alone the general public.[173] Léger was much happier in his contribution to the campus of the University of Caracas in Venezuela designed by Raul Villanueva, who commissioned him to do exterior relief murals and a large stained-glass window for the library. Victor Vasarély, Antoine Pevsner, Henri Laurens, Hans Arp and Alexander Calder (who designed huge hanging planes he called 'clouds' to modify the acoustics of the Aula Magna), as well as several Venezuelan artists, all contributed to the project. That campus provided a more scattered and sparse environment than that of the Harkness Center, but the University of Caracas remains another isolated instance of an architect inviting the active collaboration of artists.[174]

Outside of the university context avant-garde artists would rarely operate in any institutional commission. Their suspicion, even scorn, had culminated in the Dada loathing of the social framework within which the carnage of the First World War had been accepted as necessary or inevitable. Since Courbet at least, the avant-garde of art militated against social hierarchy. The number of occasions on which leading artists were involved in institutional collaboration were so few, therefore, that they stand out in the history of the twentieth-century visual arts. *Pace* Bataille, the slaughterhouse has attracted little attention from either architects or artists. Late capitalism, with its focus on accumulation, would not, could not, institutionalize death and waste.

Museums, on the other hand, where expenditure is intercepted and harvested, have proliferated and expanded, adapting to the growing pressure of visitors and their expectations, as well as to the increasing bulk and variety of what artists may be producing. They have shown themselves eager to accommodate artists' demands, and will take charge of installations that cannot be contained within their walls. The museum has become that institutional establishment in which artists and their public can both feel at home. Marcel Duchamp, to return to my anti-hero, had a relationship to museums which might almost be called cosy. Even in the most refractory cases, room would be found for his products. In 1921, for instance, he had been commissioned to make an 'assisted' ready-made: a bird-cage which he filled with marble cubes that look like sugar-lumps. A cuttlefish bone is stuck between the bars (as it might be in a bird-cage) and – less congruently – a thermometer. The whole stands on a mirror; when it is lifted, its weight offers a sensory shock, since the marble cubes are very much heavier than any supposed sugar-lumps would have been, while the absurd slogan on the underside of the cage ('why not sneeze Rose Sélavy') may be read in the mirror.[175] Unloved by its patron, the object stayed with Duchamp's dealer (though photographs of it appeared in various publications) until 1935, when it was moved to the United States and exhibited with other Duchampiana – the broken *Big Glass* is the most notable of them – in the Philadelphia Museum of Fine Arts, where it has been shut away in a glass case, the inept relic of a sly jest.

It could still provoke, though. Jean-Paul Sartre damned it as typifying the *misère* of the Surrealists, who attempted to abolish any distinction between conscious and unconscious life, waking and dreaming, in objects whose very objecthood is auto-destructive.[176] Sartre's antipathy to Surrealism was well known, and he focused it on that small object, neutralized by its museum status, to show the futility of the attempt to make unconscious life the true reality.

Undeterred by this or any other criticism, in the last decades of his life Marcel Duchamp laboured at a complex construction, *Etant donné*, the final and most elaborately 'assisted' of all his ready-mades.[177] It was moved from his studio in New York after his death (in 1968) to join the bulk of his other work in the Philadelphia Museum, and housed in a bare, anonymous room which seems to offer nothing of interest to the innocent visitor.[178] A hefty, well-seasoned (and therefore shabby – from his seaside home in Catalunya) barn door in a brick surround is its only visible furnishing. The knowing will peep through two holes drilled through the door at eye-level, to be rewarded with a view (past a ruined brick wall) of a bent-back female figure proffering her pudenda. Her left arm raises a gas lamp whose light (the manual Duchamp composed for its assembly instructs)[179] is to fall directly on her sex, while her face and hair are barely visible. The background is a Swiss landscape of postcard banality which incorporates a 'novelty' waterfall. It is the great magus's last comment on the nullity of the world. As in all his nihilist exercises, its enigmatic hilarity may seem very seductive, its inner banality glossed by his showmanship and mystification.

Duchamp's work has invited more literary comment than that of any artist of the century, excepting perhaps Picasso's. In spite of Sartre's thundering, most of the artists who worked in the second half of the twentieth century have had to come to terms with him. Some have resisted or ignored him, as Sartre had urged them to do. Others have 'commented' on his work by trying to reduce the objects to their pre-*trouvé* everyday status.[180] But most have found that the *objet trouvé* has offered the exemplar from which to generate their own choices and so enlarge the scope of their activities – as I suggested in the Preface. With its punning title and its *faux-naïf* allure, the ready-made has been the archetype of the anti-institutional product, and many artists – even those who repudiate Duchamp's influence – still consider the anti-institutional stance integral to their avant-garde credentials.

All this forms part of the context in which the conflict between artists and architects has been fought. Architecture is of its nature, as Lunacharsky had insisted, intimately engaged with institutions. Without institutions and their funds, the architect's project can have no substance. The twentieth-century

Giuseppe Terragni, final design for the Casa del Fascio, Como (1932–6).

architecture of the 'isms' avoided metaphor and concerned itself primarily with the practicalities of housing – both of dwellings and of administration. Issues of social representation were tackled only on the rare occasions I mentioned earlier: the Melnikov and Golosov workers' clubs, Terragni's Casa del Fascio, or the great competitions around 1930 for the League of Nations and for the Palace of the Soviets. Recent exceptions to this commonplace, such as the casino and church at Pampulha, depend on closed, individual initiatives and are therefore very few. Post-war world-government (UN, UNESCO) or civic institutions that have built on a large scale, whether in Chicago or Tokyo, have all emulated office buildings.

Since organized religion had been the most conspicuous butt of avant-garde contempt, it is ironic that after 1945 a small group of French clergy took it upon themselves to recreate the synthesis of great art in a church context, and their inability to achieve such a synthesis redoubles the irony. In part at least, it may be due to their having started with painters, however wonderful: Braque, Bonnard, Léger, Rouault (of course). Their patronage did produce a number of outstanding works, notably Léger's cycle of stained-glass windows for the church at Audincourt (in the Doubs, on the Swiss border), for which he used rough blocks of coloured glass set in concrete. The most heralded masterpieces are the pilgrimage chapel at Ronchamp and the Dominican house of studies at La Tourette near Lyon, both designed by Le Corbusier. No independent painter or sculptor was involved in their conception or execution, however.[181] Between 1948 and 1951 the aged Matisse, hungry for any monumental commission, decorated a monochrome chapel for the white-robed Dominican nuns in Grasse, near Nice. An experienced ceramist, he drew black line images on its white-tiled walls, the only colour provided by brilliant stained glass and the almost gaudy vestments he designed for the celebrant.[182] In designing the little building, Matisse had been offered the collaboration, first of Le Corbusier, then of his more docile old friend Auguste Perret – though he chose to be the dominant artist of the project. The building and its approach are therefore architecturally insignificant.[183]

Yet the movement offered a challenge. Resentfully familiar with Matisse's chapel in nearby Vence ('why not a brothel?' he is said to have demanded – 'because nobody asked me', answered Matisse) and his old friend Braque's work in the coastal church at Varengeville-sur-Mer (near Dieppe) in

Normandy, the peppery anti-clerical Picasso decided to give several months over to providing the deconsecrated Castle Chapel on the main square of Vallauris (the Communist municipality where he had made his home) with a secular cycle about war and peace (it was at the height of the Party-promoted peace campaign), which he painted in a specially furbished studio on pliable panels to be fixed to the curves of the chapel vault, though even that never became the kind of exhilarating volume which Picasso's intense involvement with the work should have guaranteed.[184]

Picasso and Matisse were both frustrated by their exclusion from working with buildings (existing or projected) in a way which would give a proper place and value to their contribution. The times did not seem propitious for the kind of public works that might have given them a worthy place: one can only dream of a UN building realized by Le Corbusier in which Matisse stained-glass windows, like those of his coloured paper cut-outs, might have transformed and enhanced the volumes.

Though the massing of the United Nations building was approximately that devised by Corbusier, the project was neutralized as built, even the seat of world government was made to resemble a commercial office building. In fact, such institutions as have grown to a size and eminence that demanded representation as the twentieth century has moved into the twenty-first have all been private. Neither civic halls nor churches nor yet museums, they have been finance corporations, banks and hotels. New imaging techniques made possible by information technology have allowed architects to shape their buildings without reference to the unavoidable orthogonalities of building or the routine repetition of windows, columns, beams and suchlike. Developers and financial institutions increasingly require, moreover, that their major achievements become distinctive, easily identifiable elements in the urban landscape. The epicentres of such building in the early twenty-first century have been Abu Dhabi and Dubai – so the manner might be called the Emirate style. In it, buildings assume an ambivalent relation to advertising since their entire bulk is in fact a trademark. Peremptory and over-emphatic variations of plan and outline may well produce an assuefaction similar to the tedium caused by the repetitive over-refinement of high-tech, the style which dominated commercial building in the later twentieth century and to which the Emirate style is the inevitable reaction. The difference between them, however, is only skin-deep, since both styles, in so far as they signify the private appropriation of space for commerce, speak of the dominance of money. It is now more than a century since a German sociologist, Georg Simmel, whom I quoted earlier about other matters, identified one effect of a completely internalized money economy such as ours:

> by being the equivalent to all the manifold things in one and the same way, money becomes the most frightful leveller. For money expresses all qualitative differences of things in terms of 'how much?' Money, with all its colourlessness and indifference, becomes the common denominator of all values, it hollows out the core of things irreparably – their individuality, their specific value and their incomparability.[185]

The Judicious Eye

Object-buildings, whether high-tech or Emirate style, occupy the soil in the same way and make the same demands on their users. They are similarly separated by atrophied and wind-swept semi-public spaces that seem to cry out for some garnish, some tonic to articulate the ground level. That is usually provided by an out-of-scale and arbitrarily-shaped sculptural object. Some of these may even be works of quality, but in any case demand for these objects has been so insistent that a few have even been produced as multiples, and the term 'the turd in the piazza' was coined to describe them.[186] This, too, can be read as a confirmation of Lunacharsky's *ukaze* that separated the artist's way of operating from that of the architect.

Which makes for an architecture of economic and political conformity, whatever its technical virtuosity. But does not the architect have to be conformist to have his projects put up at all, I hear the reader object. The objection has some force, but the present is different in that we produce an architecture which has no reference outside itself. Even the most time-serving of buildings (the Château of Versailles is about the most obvious), is articulated by an ornamental-structural system which looks back to a venerated antiquity and suggests a promise (however empty) of social benefit. Whatever Versailles may not have been, it certainly was a public building, a stage set for the sovereign to play the spectacle of power. The history of building over the past half century, on the other hand, can be written as an account of the increasing privatization of the public realm. Perhaps this hardly matters if the politics of advanced countries are inevitably to be played out on a television screen. Versailles-type spectacle has long been superannuated by the electronic media.

Now the radical impact of electronic media on human behaviour hardly needs another rehearsal here, but I do think it might be worth noting how it has been modulated. During the 1960s and '70s the idea that the workplace would move from the urban office to a cottage in the promised global village turned out to be a mirage. In the following decades, virtual reality offered yet another intoxicating and even more exalted vision of a world in which uninterrupted electronic communication would atrophy the place of work and so make any interpersonal contacts redundant. Yet this did not quite happen either; such encounters have remained a compelling condition of all human affairs, and this is not only true of private but also of business contacts. Even in the political sphere, the ceremonial handshake photo-opportunity has become the one universal gesture of political negotiation.

The most sophisticated and influential users of electronic media have continued to demand and pursue face-to-face meetings. Our celebrity culture thrives on elaborate and glittery rituals of such higher togetherness – sports matches, pop concerts, prize awards, charity dinners – for which showy but ephemeral ad-hoc environments are often created, while the workings of real economic and political power are played out in closed committee rooms and offices in old-style, often quasi-anonymous institutional buildings. Exercise of real power seems to shun exposure. Mao, Stalin and Hitler, the three wielders of power in the last century, famously fetishized their 'ordinary' clothing. The men of true power never display its tokens: no top hats, no feathers, stars and sashes, no medals. Except for their power they look 'just like you and me'.

Against that privacy of power, popular pressure occasionally breaks out in spontaneous, or semi-spontaneous mass-marches, demonstrations which always tend to invade 'historic' urban centres: Trafalgar Square in London, the Champs-Elysées in Paris, the Lateran in Rome, Tiananmen Square in Beijing, the Washington Mall. The intention of such disruptions is to push secretive decision-making onto the open stage. The electronic media are quick to follow the human presence in such events, and so reassert, however briefly, the primacy of the public space in our affairs.

Yet these demonstrative occupations are transient, mutinous and primarily negative, even if impressive (though not always effective) in emergencies. Meanwhile, the public spaces of daily civility and governance in our constantly growing cities are neglected, atrophied, as many of us lament. Cities have always been unsatisfactory, of course, ever since their first beginnings in the Fertile Crescent five or six thousand years ago, and criticism of them has been so sustained that it can be considered a literary genre, though the complaint specific to the later twentieth century focused insistently on that atrophy of institutions in the urban fabric. From the point of view of the governed, government at any level does not so much need the transparency which twenty-first century politicians are constantly promising (without ever delivering) but visible and emphatic disclosure. At the risk of sounding nostalgic, I venture to say that this will only happen if a way can be found to show our need for and respect of public space. I think, further, that this cannot be achieved without inviting, demanding the collaboration of the arts. Whether such a development will (or even can) take place depends on political and social factors whose outlines are, as yet, barely visible.

Whatever public buildings are being built throughout the world nowadays are not about power or authority or governance – but about culture: museums, concert halls, 'art-centres'. The culture they are about is one of consumption: these are studios, halls, workshops, in which art can be isolated from the everyday in a move contrary to the aims and wishes of many of the old-style avant-garde.

Architecture can only go about providing a neutral – a more or less convenient, more or less showy container or shell for the passive business of such a culture. The word used to suggest 'the acquainting ourselves with the best that has been said and known in the world, and thus with the history of the human spirit'.[187] The classic definition sounds very quaint when most of us visit culture-houses to see what is oldest (dinosaurs, mummies) or what is most expensive (Picasso, Andy Warhol). Whether in terms of the quaint definition therefore, or of common experience, the cultural condition is of its nature receptive and uncritical. Even when such consumption and reception is merely motivated by curiosity, it automatically turns the exhibits we look at, mummies and all, into 'works of art' requiring an 'aesthetic' which has come to mean more or less conceptual attention. We have not had much of a culture of sensing or making for a century or more.

As I have suggested throughout this book, architecture has therefore been gradually separated from such activities as we consider more or less 'cultural', particularly from those other arts once classified as visual and which have had to rely increasingly on a conceptual rather than a perceptual experience. Yet, for better or worse, architecture must always rely on some form of sensory response – both tactile and visual – to be acknowledged at all. 'Architecture is judged by eyes that see, by the head that turns, by the legs that walk.'[188]

I have chronicled the gradual separation between the arts throughout this book, and I have also tried to take account of artists' awareness of the broken sensibility they have suffered and attempted to remedy. Now I note, not altogether comfortably, that the divorce has been celebrated. In a recent, thousand-page history of cultural life over the past two centuries, the whole of the man-made environment (with the exception of advertising) has been excluded from cultural attention and architecture gets barely a mention. The world of the 'fine arts' does not figure either, because of its dominance by an elitist speculative market; and although some reference to posters and book-illustration is made, the whole of industrial design, so much part of the everyday world, is excluded from culture – with architecture.[189] Perhaps more spectacularly, an insistently avant-garde history of twentieth-century art ends on a night-photograph of the Hong Kong and Shanghai Bank offices in Hong Kong. The avant-garde aspect of that photograph is its 'objectivity' – yet strangely, the name of the bank's (rather famous) architect is not mentioned at all in the book.[190] The photograph of the building may be a work of art, but the building itself does not rate as one.

And yet, and yet . . . buildings are insistent, overpowering representations of society; they tower over all of us in a metaphoric image of the dominant powers, of all that society holds valuable and holds dear. To set architecture at the margin of culture seems to me therefore to demean it and consequently corrode the other arts. That is why I have tried to investigate the way in which the situation has arisen. If, in conclusion, I return to the concerns which prompted me to embark on this book, it is because I know that my story ends at an arbitrary place in time and can have no definite ending, happy or otherwise. The strands which I have followed over the past two centuries have to be cut as we move into the present. In the future they will, of course, continue to weave into other, unpredictable patterns which will be conditioned by pressures at which, like my reader, I can only guess.

References

Preface

1 On the formula for maximum profit from building (the 'Pedersen' formula), which gave us the World Trade Center as well as thousands of other such buildings, see Carol Willis, *Form Follows Finance* (New York, 1995), pp. 142f.

2 Architects were of course aware of the problem. Lecturing at the Los Angeles University (presumably UCLA) in March 1948, Erich Mendelsohn remembers designing one of his largest buildings, the Columbus House in Berlin in 1931:

> My last actual building in Germany (1931), though my first with vertical emphasis. All window mullions are . . . structural . . . to permit maximum flexibility . . . In the course of the erection, my client demanded the introduction of *horizontal stone bands* [his emphasis] for neon advertisements. He practically makes a fortune, I lose one – architecturally!

Erich Mendelsohn, *Letters of an Architect*, ed. Oskar Beyer (London and New York, 1967), p. 169.

3 Pierre Bourdieu in *La Distinction* (Paris, 1979), pp. 370ff. touches on it, though he seems uninterested in the spatial role of advertising. The most extensive French – semiological – approach to the language of advertising, Marcel Galliot's *Essai sur la langue de la réclame contemporaine* (Toulouse, 1955), mentions no work in English or German in the bibliography. Virtually the first student of the matter, Leonard W. Doob (*Propaganda: Its Psychology and Technique*, New York, 1943, p. 158), touches on it very marginally. Vance Packard's still relevant study of the use of 'motivation psychology' in advertising, *The Hidden Persuaders* (New York, 1957), is often – unjustly – dismissed as 'popular sociology'; see also his *The Status Seekers* (London, 1959), p. 307, on the effect of advertising men on social space. A more 'respectable' treatment in John Kenneth Galbraith's *The Affluent Society* (London, 1958, reprinted 1962), pp. 128ff., and his *The New Industrial State* (London, 1967), pp. 203ff., 327f.; also in *The Astonished Muse* by Reuel Denney (Chicago, 1957, reprinted New Brunswick, 1989), pp. 204ff. The question of the advertisement in the city is virtually untouched in Jacques Ellul's otherwise very searching *Propaganda* (New York, 1971); but see pp 68f., 290f. The implications of directing advertising at children were suggested by David Riesman, *The Lonely Crowd*, with Nathan Glazer and Reuel Denney (New Haven, CT, 1967), pp. 78ff., 97f., 223ff., 301f. Scepticism of advertising copy was methodically taught in England by F. R. Leavis and his followers: see, for instance, Richard Hoggart, *Speaking to Each Other* (London, 1970), vol. I, pp. 209ff; though they have little interest in its environmental effects. Richard Ohmann's *Selling Culture* (London and New York, 1996) is much concerned with the way the environment (pp. 119ff.) is represented in advertising, but not with advertising as a force in it. E. S. Turner treats what he calls 'Open-air advertising' negatively and bluntly in *The*

Shocking History of Advertising (New York, 1953), pp.150ff., 294ff. See also Arturo Lancellotti, *Storia anedottica della réclame* (Milan, 1912). By far the most useful so far is Adam Gopnik's section 'Advertising', in Kirk Varnedoe and Adam Gopnik, eds, *High and Low* (New York, 1991), pp. 232ff.

4 The pseudonym of (later Sir) William Nicholson and his brother-in-law, James Pryde; they operated as very popular graphic and poster designers during the 1890s.

5 Guillaume Apollinaire, *Oeuvres poétiques,* ed. Marcel Adéma and Michel Décaudin (Paris, 1965), p. 39:

> Tu lis les prospectus les catalogues les affiches qui chantent tout haut
> Voilà la poésie ce matin et pour la prose il y a les journaux . . .

Zône was written in the summer or autumn of 1912.

6 A useful compendium on 'designer food' is *Album: annuario di progetto e cultura materiale,* ed. Mario Bellini, of which only one issue, 'Progetto Mangiare', was issued in 1981. Towards the end of the twentieth century the soubriquet 'designer' got attached to many unlikely products: scents, games, television programmes and so on.

7 While it can hardly be considered a statistical sample, it is indicative that among the 400 objects selected by Kathryn B. Hiesinger and George H. Markus as *Landmarks of Twentieth-Century Design* (New York, 1993) were textiles and graphics, and many objects produced anonymously by institutions – 182 were produced by architects.

8 'Ready-made' is his own translation of the French *objet trouvé.*

9 I write 'first' advisedly – after he signed and showed that first urinal in 1914, the original being lost, several replicas were procured. See Arturo Schwarz, *Tutta l'opera di M. D.* and below, chapter Seven. The irony is in the label: *peigne,* 'a comb' is a homonym of *peins,* the imperative of *peindre,* to paint, so that the title of the ready-made almost seems a command to take up the abandoned brushes again – and the irony seems almost petulant.

10 They were dated 'May 1961'. Twenty-eight of them, all signed by the artist on the label and lent by various galleries and collectors, were shown at the Guggenheim Museum in the exhibition *Italian Metamorphosis, 1943–1968,* organized by Germano Celant; exh. cat. (New York, 1994), nos 133–60. They were to be sold for their weight in gold at its current market price. I take the oxymoron 'freshly preserved' to be unintentional.

11 Cesare Ripa, *Iconologia,* ed. G. Zaratino-Castelli (Rome, 1604), p. 44. On the background of this division, see David Summers, *The Judgement of Sense* (Cambridge, 1987), pp. 120, 300ff. While Ripa's is a conveniently pithy statement of this notion, it has inspired much grander and subtler witness, as in Michelangelo's sonnet

> Non ha l'ottimo artista alcun concetto
> Ch'un marmo solo in sé non circoscriva
> Col suo soverchio, e solo a quello arriva
> La man che ubbedisce all'intelletto

in which the artist's *magistero* is the freeing of the *concetto* inherent in the stone from the superfluous brute matter. Much sixteenth-century art theory took this sonnet as a starting point.

12 Gene Younghusband, quoted by Harold Rosenberg, in *The Re-definition of Art* (New York, 1972), p. 244.

13 I use this New York Yiddishism (not in the OED but allowed by Webster) with some hesitation: but nothing else quite seems to fit the case of the artist finding the 'thing' ('routine, act, gig' – Webster) which allows him to exercise his trade.

376

14 Since this was said in a private conversation, the critic had better remain anonymous. Anyway, his forecast has already been fulfilled, and its first consequences were spelled out by Anthony Julius (2002).

15 Charles Baudelaire 'Mon coeur mis à nu', paragraph XXXIX, p. 654. I have translated 'cuistres et fainéants d'estaminet' a bit freely. The second passage (from XLI) runs: 'Les poètes de combat, les littérateurs d'avant-garde. Ces habitudes de métaphores militaires dénotent des esprits, non pas militants, mais faits pour la discipline, c'est-à-dire pour la conformité . . . des esprits belges, qui ne peuvent penser qu'en société.' Baudelaire used 'belgian' as a general term of abuse and often spelt it with a lower-case 'b'.

16 This is not an altogether new situation. When the sculptor Jacques Lipschitz suggested to Le Corbusier that he might do a relief on the curved wall of the La Roche house in the Square du Dr Blanche in Paris (now part of the Fondation Le Corbusier), the architect chided him: 'Mais vous n'avez rien compris! C'est le mur lui-même qui est l'oeuvre d'art!' (verbal communication). 'Percentage for art' was turned into a legal problem in 1993, when the California architect Eric Owen Moss claimed – through the developers who were his main patrons – that the 1 per cent for art did not apply to their rather pretentious buildings, because the buildings were indeed 'works of art' in their own right.

17 The building and plaza were the work of a successful New York office, Alfred Easton Poor, Kahn and Jacobs, and though they are not mentioned in the account of the legal proceedings, several of the witnesses made disparaging remarks about it; Clara Weyergraf-Serra and Martha Buskirk in *The Destruction of Tilted Arc: Documents* (Cambridge, MA, 1991), pp. 73, 80, 83, 97; the wife of one of the partners, Margo Jacobs, was also called as a witness and was the only one to have anything good to say about it. It seems strange that the line of defence of the *Arc* concentrated on issues of breach of contract and freedom of speech; though the celebrity of the artist is also occasionally mentioned.

One: The Fall of the Old Régime

1 That was the view of Lord Shelburne (Marquess of Lansdown after 1784, for whom they had designed Shelburne House), in a letter to the Adam brothers offering an introduction; he had convinced Boulton, who had set up his Soho works in Birmingham in 1762–3 (with a partner, John Fothergill), to buy a copy of their *Palace of Diocletian*. Boulton had entered into another partnership with James Watt in 1773–4; their first engines were produced by craftsmen, even if these were organized on a primitive kind of assembly system. See Samuel Smiles, *Lives of the Engineers* (London, 1905), vol. IV, 'The Steam Engine', 'Boulton and Watt', pp. 120ff., 146ff., 170ff, and Nicholas Goodison, *Matthew Boulton: Ormolu* (London, 2002), pp. 14ff., 42ff., 70f. The social consequence of such 'mechanical' division and the financing it involved were described by Emile Durkheim, *De la Division du travail social* (Paris, 1932), pp. 344ff. But see also Paul Mantoux, *The Industrial Revolution in the Eighteenth Century* (New York, 1961), pp. 322ff., 372ff., and Phyllis Deane, *The First Industrial Revolution* (Cambridge, 1965), pp. 87, 130. Jenny Uglow, *The Lunar Men: Five Friends Whose Curiosity Changed the World* (New York, 2002), pp. 21ff. Chambers, as might have been expected, did not exploit his early collaboration with Boulton; John Harris, *Sir William Chambers* (London, 1970), pp. 204, 253.

2 Eric Hopkins, *The Rise of the Manufacturing Town: Birmingham and the Industrial Revolution* (Sutton, 1998), pp. 84ff., and Vivian Bird, *Portrait of Birmingham* (London, 1970), pp. 56ff.

3 Uglow, *The Lunar Men*, *passim* but especially pp. 146ff., 210ff.

4 On Wedgwood and the Hamilton collection, see Brian Fothergill, *Sir William Hamilton* (London, 1969), pp. 68ff., 195ff. The early plates came from Hamilton's brother-in-law, Lord Cathcart. Uglow, *The Lunar Men*, p. 147.

5 On the decoration of Osterley Park, see J. Rykwert and A. Rykwert, *The Brothers Adam* (London, 1985), pp. 122ff. The Adam brothers passed their designs to other manufacturers, but it also seems as if Boulton, having cast a good design, traded it to other architects and builders. Goodison, *Matthew Boulton*, pp. 97ff, 240ff.

6 Indeed, their career, like that of some of their contemporaries, opened with a scholarly archeological publication: measured drawings and views of the Palace of Diocletian at Spalato/Split: Robert Adam, FRS, FSA (Architect to the King and Queen), *Ruins of the Palace of the Emperor Diocletian at Spalato in Dalmatia, for the Author* (Venice, 1764). On the publication and its history, see Rykwert and Rykwert, *The Brothers Adam*, pp. 48, 98. For their use of motifs, see pp. 68, 122, 144, 172. Diocletian's palace was chosen because it had not been fully surveyed before, and because it was relatively easy of access. Although little decorative detail had survived in the palace, there was enough to provide unusual source material and the book served as a demonstration of learning.

7 Robert Adam and James Adam, *The Works in Architecture* (reprinted London, 1931), vol. I: *1778, 1779, 1802*, p. vii.

8 Raphael's pupil and assistant, Giovanni da Udine, was reputedly the first artist to visit them, and he introduced Raphael. The earliest graffito there is dated 1493, *Roma nell'Anno MDCC-CVXXXVIII*, Antonio Nibby, *Antica*, parte II (Rome, 1838), p. 811; R. Lanciani, *The Ruins and Excavations of Ancient Rome* (London, 1897), pp. 363ff. They seem to have been neglected during the intervening period, but were excavated and recorded in the eighteenth century; see Charles Cameron, *The Baths of the Romans* (London, 1772), and Nicolas Ponce, *Description des Bains de Titus; ou, Collection des Peintures trouvées dans les Bains de cet Empereur* (Paris, 1786). However, some years before Raphael's visit (1496–1507), they were already being emulated brilliantly by Pinturicchio in the Sala dell'Udienze of the Cambio in Perugia and about the same time in the Borgia apartments in the Vatican and by Luca Signorelli in the panels of Dante and Virgil in the chapel of San Brizio in Orvieto Cathedral. Vasari describes the visit of Giovanni da Udine and Raphael and the origin of the word *grottesche* in his life of Giovanni (ed. G. Milanesi, Florence, 1906, vol. VI, p. 550). It must have occurred in the late 1490s. On the problem in general, see Friedrich Piel, *Die Ornament-Grotteske in der Italienischen Renaissance* (Berlin, 1962).

9 Vitruvius (VII, 5) seems to describe painting rather like that – though he is insistent that the painted constructions should represent buildable structures.

10 S. Fiske Kimball, *The Creation of the Rococo* (New York, 1964), pp. 28ff., so that when Corneille instructs his stage painter (in *La Toison d'Or*, V.vi) that the palace of the sun is to be decorated with *divers grands feuillages à l'Arabesque*, there is no indication that this might be the antique grotesque; and there is little in John Florio's rendering of the word in his Italian–English dictionary of 1598: 'a kind of rugged unpolished painter's worke', even if he does gloss it 'anticke worke'; Dr Johnson has no entry for 'arabesque' in his *dictionary*, and only gives the metaphoric meaning for 'grotesque', quoting Milton, Dryden and Pope. The first true grotesque decorations in Britain to have survived are William Kent's at Houghton Hall, when rocaille was already practised routinely by London furniture-makers. But see for this and what follows, Joseph Rykwert, *The First Moderns* (Cambridge, MA, 1980), pp. 60ff., 96ff., 173ff.

11 The word took on its figurative sense – meaning something deformed and ridiculous – about 1650, about a century after its descriptive introduction in France: as, for instance, in Pascal's *Lettres provinciales*, ed. H. F. Stewart (Manchester, 1920), p. 124. Much the same changes may be observed in English.

12 Adam and Adam, *The Works in Architecture*, vol. I, p. vii.

13 I have discussed this matter elsewhere: Rykwert, *The First Moderns*, pp. 120ff. Cavaliere Giambattista Piranesi, *Diverse Maniere d'Adornare i Cammini ed ogni altra parte degli Edifizi . . .* (Rome, 1769) [in Italian, English and French; the English title runs: *Divers Manners of orna-*

menting Chimneys and all other parts of houses taken from the Egyptian, Tuscan, and Grecian Architecture with an Apologetical Essay in Defence of the Egyptian and Tuscan Architecture by John Baptist Piranesi, Knight and Architect], pp. 18ff.

14 Bats' wings are a favoured motif. See Hermann Bauer, *Rocaille: Zur Herkunft und zum Wesen eines Ornament-Motivs* (Berlin, 1962), *passim*. The whole movement has strong roots in a late-medieval fascination with 'growing' architecture: on which see J. Rykwert, *On Adam's House in Paradise* (Cambridge, MA, 1981), pp. 211ff., and J. Baltrusaitis, *Aberrations* (Cambridge, MA, 1989), pp. 108ff. The use of casts of leaves and even animals in ornamental compositions in the sixteenth century needs more discussion, but what is still worth consulting (though apparently unknown to Bauer) is E. Kris, 'Der Stil Rustique: Die Verwendung des Naturabgusses bei Wenzel Jamnitzer und Bernard Palissy' *Jahrbuch der Kunsthistorischen Sammlungen in Wien* (1926), pp. 137–208. Early rocaille monsters had been developed by Stefano della Bella as cartouche inventions in the 1640s. A kind of rather fancy shell-decoration known as *travail de coquille* was considered analogous to a pebble and driftwood manner, *travail de rocaille.*

15 A useful though very brief introduction to this is Peter Hughes, *Eighteenth-century France and the East* (London, 1981); on the Chinese connection particularly, Hugh Honour, *Chinoiserie: The Vision of Cathay* (London, 1961).

16 On Etienne Martin and his *vernis*, see R. Cazes, *Le Château de Versailles et ses dépendances* (Versailles, 1910), pp. 109, 123, and I. Dunlop, *Versailles* (London, 1956), pp. 109, 125, 147, 207. On the invention of plate glass, see Ada Polak, *Glass: Its Tradition and its Makers* (New York, 1975), pp. 127ff. It was first described by a Venetian émigré, Bernardo Perrotto or Perrot, but also claimed by Louis Lucas de Nohan and André Thévert.

17 Bastide was an *homme de lettres*, who collaborated on a number of occasions with Jacques-François Blondel; the story was published in two different collections: in the first (of 1758) the heroine resists advances; in the second (of 1763), she succumbs. See Jean François de Bastide, *La Petite Maison*, trans. and ed. Barbara Briganti (Palermo, 1989), pp. 23ff.

18 It is much more sophisticated than Rastrelli's huge (and better-known) Smolny Monastery in St Petersburg or the church of St Andrew in Kiev. There are other examples in eastern Poland and the Ukraine, however – as in the cathedral of Sandomierz, where the brooding Byzantine fresco cycle of the long chancel is prefaced by a riot of rocaille side altars and organ cases in the nave.

19 See Karsten Harries, *The Bavarian Rococo Church* (New Haven, CT, 1983).

20 He was born in Prussia, though his career was prompted by Saxon patronage.

21 Translations into French, Spanish and Italian soon followed.

22 London, 1765; Fuseli was ordained to the Zwinglian ministry together with his friend, Caspar Lavater (whose *Aphorisms* he also translated into English, and whose great work on physiognomy he helped to illustrate). He was brought to Britain by Andrew Mitchell, then the British Chargé d'Affaires in Prussia. After studying painting in Italy, he settled in London after suffering a broken heart in Switzerland. He was appointed Professor of Painting at the Royal Academy in 1799 and became Keeper of the Schools there in 1804, both of which posts he held until his death in 1825, when he was buried in St Paul's. He anglicized his name in Italy, wanting to make it sound more Italian. Blake's memorable testimonial was:

> The only Man that e'er I knew
> Who did not make me almost spew
> Was Fuselli: he was both Turk and Jew –
> And so my Christian Friends, how do you do?

in *The Complete Writings of W.B.*, ed. Geoffrey Keynes (London, 1957), p. 551. The description as 'both Turk and Jew' must refer either to Fuseli's theology or his manner rather than his ethnic origins. A partial French translation of this book (by the Abbé Arnaud) had already appeared in French, in the *Journal etranger* in 1755; it was published in full in 1786.

23 Johann Joachim Winckelmann, *Geschichte der Kunst des Altertums* (Vienna, 1934), pp. 9, 25. Alex Potts, *Flesh and the Ideal: Winckelmann and the Origins of Art History* (New Haven, CT, and London, 1996), pp. 36ff. The word 'style' is familiar enough. It comes from the Greek *stylos*: a prop, a pillar or a mast; also a stick, including the kind of sharply pointed stick or metal prod for writing on wax tablets, and hence a way of writing and speaking. 'Style' therefore merged with dialect. However, the old significance of prop or column was not forgotten. 'Style' could therefore also stand for a kind of column – hence a Doric or Ionic style could refer to the dialect but also to the column type and the general repertory of mouldings and proportions associated with it.

By the time of Cicero, the word had come to mean in Latin the way in which one wrote using a stylus, one's prose style. In Greek the sense of 'stile' was never transferred to writing or 'style' in the modern sense. The root **sty* or **sta* (from which, of course, the modern 'stand') is evident in the Sanskrit *sthuma*, Persian *stuma*, a pillar. Since the Latin word is written *stilus* (short 'i') rather than *stylus*, some lexicographers derive it from *stelechos*, 'the crown of the root', 'trunk', 'stem' – from the related root **stel*, **stal*, to do with place, placing – as in the German *stelle*. In fact, the word *style* appears commonly only in relation to architecture (and the visual arts generally) in the eighteenth century.

24 An early survey of Vasari's 590 uses of the words *maniera* was made by John Grace Freeman in *The Maniera of Vasari* (London, 1867). Vasari makes a clear distinction between what is *antico* – the works of the Greeks and Romans – and what is old, *vecchio*, or everything after the reign of Pope St Sylvester (314–37 – a contemporary of Constantine) in his *Proemio* to *The Lives of the Artists*, ed. Milizia (reprinted 1973), vol. I, p. 242.

25 I have discussed this matter elsewhere: Rykwert, *The First Moderns*, pp. 36ff., 52 n.63, 92.

26 The largest and most impressive are the cathedral of Arras and the chapel of the Château at Versailles.

27 For this dispute and its ramifications, see Rykwert, *The First Moderns*, pp. 378ff.

28 It is not clear whether the young David met the aged Piranesi, who was to die in 1776. But see Georges Brunel, ed., *Piranèse et les Français* (Rome, 1978), pp. 316ff.; Paolo Marconi, *Giuseppe Valadier* (Rome, 1964), pp. 84ff. At any rate, his was one of the names Piranesi's sons cited as being supporters of the project to reprint all Piranesi's plates in Paris. Brunel, *Piranèse et les Français*, p. 416.

The Etruscan fashion was so prevalent in the years immediately before the Revolution that even the furniture that Georges Jacob made to designs by Hubert Robert for the queen's *hameau* at Rambouillet was said to be in the 'Etruscan' style: F.J.B. Watson, *Louis XVI Furniture* (London, 1960), p. 145 (no. 192).

29 It makes the curious association of Pompadour with Rococo unfair: 'Pompadour, rococo, à peu près admises aujourd'hui dans la conversation, pour désigner le goût à la mode pendant le règne de Louis XV, ont été employées pour la première fois par Maurice Quaï', in E. J. Delécluze, *Louis David: son ecole et son temps* (Paris, 1855; reprinted 1983), p. 82.

30 The project, on the site of an older church, was made after 1757 by Pierre Contant d'Ivry and was published by Pierre Patte in 1768. The foundation stone was laid in 1764, a few months after that of Ste Geneviève. A model of the portico is in the Musée Carnavalet in Paris.

31 In the next reign, Queen Marie-Antoinette had the rational garden uprooted to make way for her 'sentimental' English one; and her toy farm designed for her by Robert Mique, working with the painter Hubert Robert, one of the few real collaborations between painter and architect in that reign, was quoted as an instance of the queen's frivolity at her trial. Mique indeed was one of the few architects and artists to be guillotined, while Robert's neck was only just

saved by the end of the Terror. Cazes, *Le Château de Versailles*, p. 632. E. Goncourt and J. Goncourt, *Histoire de Marie-Antoinette* (Paris, 1859), pp. 438f.

32 The dispute may well have been about the price. But there are different versions of the story: on which see Jean-Pierre Cuzin, *Jean-Honoré Fragonard: Life and Work* (New York, 1988), pp. 152ff. However, the portrait he painted of her in 1771 (one of a series of portraits in seventeenth-century dress, now in the Louvre (cat. no. 171), ibid., is her most enduring memorial – it does not glamorize the subject, but gives her a shiny nose (Fragonard's malicious afterthought?).

A rather racier but perhaps more speculative account of the two pavilions and their decoration is given by Pierre de Nolhac, *Fragonard* (Paris, 1901), pp. 112ff., and also by Henri d'Alméras and Paul d'Estrée, *Les Théâtres libertins au xviiie siècle* (Paris, 1905), pp. 284ff. Vien was, at the time, the Director of the French Academy in Rome.

33 The theme was 'The Pursuit of Love', though they are also known as 'The Loves of the Shepherds'. Fragonard was indemnified and hung them in the house of a relative in his home town, Grasse. They are now in the Frick Collection in New York and two preliminary versions are privately owned. See Cuzin, *Jean-Honoré Fragonard*, pp. 142ff.; nos 239–44. But there were also some overdoors by Fragonard there (pp. 135ff., nos 148–51), ibid., which have been dispersed in various collections, though in the salon *en-cul de four* the overdoors were by François-Hubert Drouais, and the ceiling painted as a lightly-clouded sky by Jean-Bernard Restout. There is reason to think that two of Fragonard's compositions were to be on the curved walls of the apse, and that the whole scheme was 'integrated'; see, however, Marianne Roland-Michel, ed., *Aspects de Fragonard: peintures-dessins-estampes*, exh. cat., Gallerie Cailleux (Paris, 1987).

It is not clear what part the king, Madame du Barry herself (who in spite of her flighty reputation was passionately interested in the visual arts) or even Ledoux had in this rejection.

34 The panelling, as well as that of the salon of the Hôtel d'Uzès, is in the Musée Carnavalet in Paris. The café was called Café Godeau (after its owner) and was at the Palais-Royal end of the Rue St Honoré, but is better known as the Café Militaire. See Anthony Vidler, *Claude-Nicolas Ledoux* (Cambridge, MA, 1990), pp. 20f. A better image is in Marcel Raval, *Claude-Nicolas Ledoux* (Paris, 1946), plate 1.

35 While the builder of the prisons more or less respected Ledoux's project, the Palais de Justice as built is a cruel parody of the scheme, for which a complete set of rendered drawings – including a survey of the medieval buildings on the site destroyed before it was begun – is in the Municipal Library at Aix-en-Provence.

36 The idea of such a park was already current. Horace Walpole reports – rather patronizingly – that a visiting French nobleman (whom he does not name) criticized Strawberry Hill for its lack of socially useful as well as of edifying buildings (*Anecdotes of Painting in England, with some Account of the Principal Artists; collected by George Vertue, and now digested and published from his original manuscripts by Horace Walpole*, 4 vols, ed. J. Dallaway, London, 1828, vol. iv, p. 260). He equally patronizingly dismisses a treatise which he sees as the source of such ideas. The reference is probably to *De la Composition des Paysages . . . en joignant l'agréable à l'utile* which the Marquis René de Girardin published in Geneva in 1777; it was translated into English by David Malthus and issued in 1783.

Girardin was a friend of Rousseau and invited him to live at Ermenonville where the philosopher spent the last months of his life and where he died and was buried – on the 'Island of Poplars'; his body was disinterred and transferred to the Panthéon in 1791. Girardin was, of course, known to Ledoux: see Vidler, *Claude-Nicolas Ledoux*, pp. 322f.

37 Léon Vaudoyer, writing about Ledoux as being 'partisan de ce que on a appelé depuis l'architecture parlante' in *Le Magasin Pittoresque* in December 1852, quoted by Neil Levine, *Architectural Reasoning in the Age of Positivism* (Ann Arbor, MI, 1977), vol. I, pp. 685f. Vaudoyer

contrasted Ledoux's hectoring *parlante* architecture with a more reasonable *lisible* one, which is explicit about its arrangement and structure.

38 Jean-Charles Delafosse, *Nouvelle Iconologie Historique ou Attributs Hiérogliphyques* (Paris, 1768); *Algemeen Kunstenaars Handboek . . . en in't koper gegraveerd door Jan de Witt Jansz* (Amsterdam, n.d.). On him, see Michel Gallet, 'Jean-Charles Delafosse, Architecte' in *Gazette des Beaux-Arts* (March 1963), pp. 150ff. Emil Kaufmann, *L'architettura dell'Illuminismo* (Turin, 1966), pp. 188ff., and Sven Eriksen, *Early Neo-Classicism in France* (London, 1974), p. 170. However, the large collections of his drawings in the Musée des Arts Décoratifs in Paris and in the Cooper-Hewitt Museum in New York have not yet been studied.

39 Jean-François de Neufforge, *Recueil elémentaire de l'architecture* (Paris, 1757–62) [supplement 1780]; there are 906 plates altogether. He had been a pupil of Jacques-François Blondel, the last major theorist of the *Ancien Régime*.

40 Such as Félix Lecomte, in particular on the pavilions of Mademoiselle Guimard and of Madame du Barry. The painters, too, worked (sometimes, as in the case of Fragonard, which I mentioned earlier, unsuccessfully) without constraints by the architect. It would seem, however, that there was general agreement about treatment and subject matter between the client, the architect and the artist – who would certainly have made known his views about the way his or her work was to be 'placed', as the sequence Fragonard–David, Fragonard–Vien, first for Mademoiselle Guimard, then at Louveciennes, showed. Félix Lecomte, who had had the Rome prize (in 1761), was a senior academician who became Marie-Antoinette's favourite portrait sculptor – hardly an artist to follow the outlines provided by an architect. He was better known for two of the six statues – the others were by Pigalle and Mouchy – on the Hôtel de la Monnaie.

41 Begun in 1768, it was damaged in the Gordon Riots of 1780 when it was modified and rebuilt. Debtors, who had their own courtyard windows opened onto them, did not rate a terror-inspiring entry.

42 Apart, perhaps, from the provision of open courtyards: see Robin Evans, *The Fabrication of Virtue* (Cambridge, 1982), pp. 103ff., which also gives an account of the preliminary schemes prepared for the competition held for the building. It was won by George Dance the Elder, the actual architect's father. A somewhat similar, but even more emphatic project for a temple of justice by Delafosse – unfortunately, only a small drawing of the facade remains – is in the Cooper-Hewitt Museum in New York; on which see Emil Kaufmann, *Architecture in the Age of Reason* (Cambridge, MA, 1955), cat. no. 32.

43 As neo-antique sobriety took hold of architects' – and their patrons' – imaginations, so the sharply outlined and clearly articulated building came increasingly to act as a clearing screen between a capricious interior and a sinuously retreating or Picturesque landscape, the kind which in Continental Europe often goes by the name Anglo-Chinese; it dominated French and German – later also Italian and Spanish – ideas about gardening in the latter part of the century. An ingratiating and undemanding manner, it was quickly taken up by the rich bourgeois as well as the *embourgeoisied* gentry in Britain (it had invited the Adam brothers' condemnation). The gradually sobering increasingly classicizing eighteenth-century palaces and monasteries looked out on a nature which was sometimes quite untamed, or yet on gardens which were increasingly loosening their bounds, dissolving into more liquid forms.

44 Edmund Burke, *A Philosophical Enquiry into the Origins of our Ideas of the Sublime and the Beautiful* (London, 1757). Lessing had intended to translate it into German (letter to Moses Mendelssohn – to whom he was recommending the book – from Leipzig, 21 January 1758), though only because he was bored in Leipzig. Mendelssohn reviewed the book very favourably in *Bibliothek der Schönen Wissenschaften und der Freyen Künste*, ed. Christophf. Nicolai, Moses Mendelssohn and Christianf. Weisse (Leipzig, 1757–65), vol. III, part 2, and a German translation, *Vom Schönen und Erhebenen* was in fact published in Riga in 1773 – and

that is the version Kant used.

Kant makes the distinction towards the end of §29 of the *Kritik der Urteilskraft (Critique of the Power of Judgement),* trans. Paul Guyer and Eric Matthews (Cambridge, 2000), p. 158.

45 See Adrian von Buttlar, *Der Englische Landsitz* (Mittenwald, 1982), pp. 87f., 174ff. Rosario Assunto, *Stagioni e ragioni* (Milan, 1967), pp. 6off. Christopher Hussey, *The Picturesque* (London, 1967), pp. 55ff., 80f., 170ff. Ernst Cassirer, *The Philosophy of the Enlightenment* (Princeton, NJ, 1951), pp. 328ff.

46 But Kant, who never left Königsberg, was not acquainted with the works of contemporary artists and knew little of a new 'romantic' art.

47 Supplements were published by a Jesuit antiquarian, Simone Raffei, and in 1772, 1773 and 1778. Strangely enough, those ancient gods would regain some of their power, even if in a much diminished and modified form, in the twentieth century. The substance of that essay, written in Rome in 1764, had been published separately by Winckelmann in German: *Versuch einer Allegorie, besonders für die Kunst* (Dresden, 1766).

48 J. W. von Goethe, *Werke* (Zürich, 1962), vol. X, 'Dichtung und Wahrheit', pp. 399ff. See also Goncourt and Goncourt, *Histoire de Marie Antoinette* (Paris, 1859), pp. 15ff. The horrible stampede at the fireworks after the wedding, in which 132 persons were allegedly killed and which the authorities tried to hush up, seemed equally ominous to Goethe. It is interesting that he was scandalized by the fact that tapestries woven from the Raphael cartoons and representing the *Acts of the Apostles* were relegated to a subsidiary chamber, while the main room was given over to antique heroes of dubious propriety. The *Jason* and *Medea* tapestries were presumably those the Gobelins factory commissioned from de Tory in 1738.

Curiously enough, in that same year, 1770, Jean-Raymond de Petity published his *Manuel des Artistes et des Amateurs ou Dictionnaire Historique et Mythologique des Emblèmes, Allégories, Enigmes, Devises, Attributs et Symboles . . .* the very long title ending *Composé en faveur des Nouvelles Ecoles Gratuites de Dessein* – of which more in the next chapter. It is symptomatic of the new interest in allegory and mythology (which had been neglected in the first half of the eighteenth century).

49 *Von Deutscher Baukunst* (Strasbourg, 1770). The main target of his attack, the Abbé Laugier, was in fact one of the first theorists to appreciate Gothic architecture – though acknowledging that would have made him less useful as a butt of Goethe's attack.

50 J. G. Herder, 'Auszug aus einem Briefwechsel über Ossian und die Lieder alter Völker' of 1772, published as an appendix to the *Abhandlung über de Ursprung der Sprache* [1789] in *Herders Sämtliche Werke,* ed. Bernhard Suphan (Berlin, 1877–99), vol. V, pp. 168ff; on that visit to the Jägelsee, see Johann Gottfried Herder, *Briefe* (Weimar, 1977), vol. I, pp. 48f. Also quoted by Giuliano Briganti, *I pittori dell'immaginario* (Milan, 1989), pp. 43, 274, n. 31.

51 Lessing was in fact appealing to Longinus, *peri ypsos* (usually translated as 'On the Sublime'), XXXVI, 3

for those who prefer a gigantic statue . . . to Polykleitos' *Doryphoros,* the answer is that in a work of art we admire the skill, in a work of nature the effect of vastness. Because speech is natural to man; I may look for resemblance in a statue but in speech I demand something that rises above the human condition . . .

against Winckelmann's 'Considerations about the Imitation of the Greeks', though he does not quote Longinus till much later in this text. The whole matter of the Sublime in German thinking at this time has been studied by Karl Vietor, *Geist und Form* (Berne, 1952), pp. 239ff.

52 J. W. von Goethe, *Maximen und Reflexionen,* §749:

Die Symbolik verwandelt die Erscheinung in Idee, die Idee in ein Bild, und so, dass die

Idee im Bild immer unendlich wirksam und erreichbar bleibt und selbst in allen
Sprachen aussgeschprochen doch unaussprechlich bleibe.
Die Allegorie verwandelt die Erscheinung in einem Begriff, den Begriff in ein Bild doch
so, dass der Begriff im Bilde immer noch begrenzt und vollständig zu halten und zu
haben und an demselben auszusprechen sei.

Goethe developed this notion in discussion with Schiller and takes up certain themes from Diderot (article *Hiéroglyphe* in the *Encyclopédie*) but sets itself in a way against Kant's definition, *Kritik der Urteilskraft*, §59; ed. Hermann Kohn *et al.* (Berlin, 1922), vol. v, pp. 428ff. 'Nun sage ich: das Schöne ist das Symbol des Sittlichguten': 'Beauty is the symbol of the morally good.' But see Maurice Marache, *Le Symbole dans la pensée et l'oeuvre de Goethe* (Paris, 1960), especially pp. 104ff.

53 *Agathy Tuchy*. The form was discussed with Winckelmann's great friend, the painter Adam Oeser, at Christmas 1776, when Oeser visited Weimar. It was 'consecrated' ('geweit dem Guten Glück') on 5 April 1777. Goethe reflects in his diary: 'Da Muthos erfunden wird, werden die Bilder durch die Sachen gross; wenns Mythologie wird, werden die Sachen durch die Bilder Gross' (J. W. von Goethe, *Tagebücher*, Zürich, vol. xii, 1964, p. 38).

Oeser seemed to have something rather different in mind, and suggested that the altar would just look like one of those cannonballs abandoned at many city gates.

54 It is well known that Herder criticized Kant, sometimes harshly in his later writings, and that Kant had written a somewhat dismissive review of Herder's *Uber der Ursprung der Sprache* in 1785. Whatever his debt to Kant, Herder was too much the inductive socio-anthropologist to evoke any sympathy or even interest in Kant.

55 If only because his brother-in-law Francisco Bayeu had worked with Mengs in Madrid, and the Spanish Ambassador, D. Nicola de Azara, was one of their protectors and collaborators.

56 *El arquitecto D. Ventura Rodriguez*, exh. cat., Museo Municipal (Madrid, 1983). The drawings are nos 15 to 18. The original church was designed by Francisco Herrera *El Mozo* at the end of the seventeenth century. According to legend, the church was founded in AD 40 by the Apostle James.

57 Pierre Gassier and Juliet Wilson, *The Life and Work of Francisco Goya* (London, 1971), pp. 51ff., nos 30–33, 42–8. Ventura Rodriguez is shown once in a double portrait with the Infante Don Luis de Borbon (no. 213) and again holding the drawing (Stockholm, Nationalmuseet). There is a copy in the Academy of San Fernando in Madrid, and it was engraved several times. The cartoons are in the Prado.

58 There were, anyway, administrative reasons why Goya was freer in San Antonio than in any other of his commissions, his own house apart.

59 Gassier and Wilson, *Life and Work*, on San Antonio, pp. 139ff., nos 717–35; on the *Quinta del Sordo*, pp. 313ff., nos 115–1628. Enrique Lafuente Ferrari, *Goya: The Frescoes in San Antonio de la Florida in Madrid* (Geneva, 1955). On Francisco Bayeu's disapproval of Goya's quick working method, ibid., p. 123, and Priscilla E. Muller, *Goya's 'Black' Paintings* (New York, 1984).

60 Füssli may already have known Johannes von Müller's *Geschichte der Schweizer Konfederation* (Zürich, 1780), though the story had earlier been told in a 'final' revision of Aegidius Tschudi's sixteenth-century *Prisca Rhaetia* (1734–6). Tell, the sharpshooter, was not one of the representatives of the three original cantons and was probably a legendary figure, though he became a nationalist hero through Schiller's tragedy and Rossini's operatic version of it.

61 Mona Ozouf, *Festivals and the French Revolution* (Cambridge, MA, 1988), pp. 273.

62 Napoleon, typically, was to venerate and carry about with him (emulating Alexander the Great's use of Homer's *Iliad*) Ossian's poems in his saddle-bag, presumably in the Italian translation by Melchiore Cesarotti – whose rather easy-going hendecasyllable verses influenced Alfieri and Foscolo. Although Dr Johnson denounced Ossian's poems as an imposture,

little credence was given him – or other sceptics. The general public wanted to accept the Ossianic poems as genuine ancient documents. MacPherson entered Parliament in 1780 and made a fortune as a government spokesman for Lord North and the London agent for the Nabob of Arcot. Ossian was familiar to and popular with the *Sturm und Drang* poets.

63 In the collection of the ETH in Zurich. The homoerotic vase-drawing (now attributed to the Dinos painter; in London; BM, f.65) was reproduced by D'Hancarville in the Hamilton collection (Naples, 1766), vol. II, plate 32.

64 See Peter Tomory, *The Life and Art of Henry Fuseli* (New York, 1972), pp. 90f., no. 57, on the use of *dexterum iunctio* and the leaden, relief-like colour. Although the picture – an oil paint-ing on canvas – has remained in Zürich Town Hall, engravings of it were certainly known in Paris.

On the images of swearing an oath, see Jean Starobinski, *1789: Les Emblèmes de la raison* (Paris, 1979), pp. 66ff. The particular image of Brutus and his associates swearing vengeance by the corpse of Lucretia had already been shown several times before David painted his oath: by Gavin Hamilton – the engraving of 1768 was very popular – and by Jules-André Beaufort in 1771 (Nevers, Musée des Beaux-Arts). Albert Boime ('Le Thème du Serment: David et la Franc-maçonnerie', in *David contre David*, ed. Régis Michel, Paris, 1993; *Actes du Colloque organisé au Louvre le 6–10 Décembre 1989*, pp. 259ff., adds another set of implications to those gestures.

65 It was Jean-Chrysostome Quatremère de Quincy who criticized the building in the *Horatii* because it had arches supported directly on cylindrical columns (the house of Brutus has columns carrying a cornice). As for the columns, they have no bases, as well as 'primitive Doric' capitals. However, the cornice in the *Brutus* is definitely Tuscan, although in one early drawing for it (Musée Toulouse-Lautrec, Albi) David suggests a proper Doric cornice, with metopes and triglyphs.

66 Delécluze, *Louis David*, pp. 22f. At least a part of the audience in the theatre found his get-up comical. On the theatrical (and otherwise) sources of the two paintings, see Edgar Wind, *Hume and the Heroic Portrait* (Oxford, 1986), pp. 105ff.

67 Since *Anacharsis* was published in 1787, that was presumably the date of the party. But see *Memoirs of Mme Vigée Lebrun*, trans. Lionel Strachey (London, 1903; reprinted New York, 1989), pp. 40ff.

68 Much of this depends on Philippe Bordes, *Le Serment du Jeu de Paume de Jacques-Louis David* (Paris, 1983). David almost certainly did not witness the event, which had been recorded by many other artists: Monnet, Prieur, Janinet, Duplessis-Bertaux; many later artists (notably Ary Scheffer) attempted a non-Davidian reconstruction of the event.

The sum estimated was 72,000 livres; the subscription among the Jacobins (in the first place) brought in 5,631 livres; the last tally, which included several friends and family members (but also some strange fellows, like the Scots banker Coutts), produced another 993. David set up the vast canvas which had (of course) to be sewn from several sheets in the church of the *Feuillants*. The rent for the space was paid by public authority.

The unfinished canvas was bought by the French government for the equivalent of £100 at the *Vente David* in 1835, while Napoleon had paid the equivalent of £4,000 for the *Sacre* and £2,080 for the larger *Distribution of the Eagles*. See Gerald Reitlinger, *The Economics of Taste* (London, 1961), vol. I, pp. 294f. David collaborated with Vivant Denon (later Baron Denon) on the engraving.

69 By Luc-Olivier Merson; nearly the size of David's planned picture, it was painted for exhibi-tion in the Jeu de Paume, transformed in 1883 into the Museum of the Revolution.

70 Hogarth was the most famous English precedent: he virtually devised this form of subscrip-tion financing with the 'Harlot's Progress' about 1740. On which see Ronald Paulson, *Hogarth* (London, 1975), vol. I, pp. 301ff.

71 Of those present and invited to sit, only Chatham's enemy Lord Mansfield refused.

Copley was said to have earned £5,000 in gate money. His *Floating Batteries at Gibraltar*, exhibited in a tent at St James, made £3,000; the 'American Raffaele', Benjamin West, an immigrant from the American Colonies, like Copley, was effectively paid a retainer by George III for his history pictures, but his most famous painting remains his first major work, the *Death of General Wolfe* (of 1771 – of which he painted several versions). That canvas was also successfully exhibited. Described somewhat bombastically at the time as 'the first battle scene in modern dress', it was certainly innovative in eighteenth-century Britain and broke the heroic pseudo-antique precepts that Joshua Reynolds had recommended to the Royal Academy – and was therefore also something of a *succès de scandale*. West's pupil, John Trumbull, was urged in the same direction by Thomas Jefferson, and painted a *Surrender of Lord Cornwallis* and later the *Signing of the Declaration of Independence*, which had wide circulation in an engraved version; Trumbull was to go on to become hugely successful by depicting 'historical' scenes in modern dress. See Reitlinger, *The Economics of Taste*, I, pp. 66ff.; Wind, *Hume and the Heroic Portrait*, pp. 88ff.

72 Though his political position was more dubious than earlier writers have suggested. In 1792 he was engaged to paint a portrait of the king 'showing the constitution to his heir', even if in 1789 he had expressed his detestation of the queen. It is remarkable that his wife, who had been active in the early days of the Assembly, left him to retire to a convent, though they were reconciled after Thermidor.

André Chénier had written an Ode on the Jeu de Paume in 1791 (*Oeuvres*, ed. Gérard Walter, Paris, 1958, pp. 167ff; he also wrote an article in the *Journal de Paris* for 20 March 1792; ibid., pp. 284ff.), but withdrew his friendship from the painter in the next year: in a fragment written shortly before his death he execrates the art of the Terror:

> *Digne de l'atroce démence*
> *Du stupide David qu'autrefois j'ai chanté . . .*

When the Directory took over, David wrote a report on the financial problems, and reckoned the government – which took over responsibility for the omission – should indemnify him to the tune of 150,000 francs – which was not done: L. J. David, *Le Peintre Louis David* (Paris, 1880), pp. 344ff.

On David's rather complicated political position at the end of the Terror, see Philippe Bordes, 'Brissotin enragé, Ennemi de Robespierre: David, Conventionel et Terroriste', in Michel, *David contre David*, vol. I, pp. 319ff. Still, his dramatic exclamation when Robespierre threatened to drink hemlock, 'Si tu bois la cigue je la boirai avec toi', was widely reported, though he managed to evade the Thermidor events.

73 A corpus of illustrations in B. de Andia *et al.*, *Fêtes et Révolution* (Paris and Dijon, 1989), and Mona Ozouf, *Festivals and the French Revolution* (Cambridge, MA, 1988), especially pp. 76ff., 123, 154ff. Also see J.-C. Bonnet, ed., *La Carmagnole des Muses* (Paris, 1988).

74 The death of Mirabeau was the immediate cause – though when he was disgraced, his was also the first body that had to be removed from the Panthéon.

75 In 1806 Napoleon returned the building to the Church (in part) and in 1821 it was solemnly consecrated – it had not been consecrated before the Revolution – only to be secularized again in 1831. Reconsecrated in 1851, it was definitively secularized in 1871. Each one of the changes involved the removal of corpses as well as of decorations.

76 J[ean-]J[acques] Rousseau (*Mélanges*, III) *Citoyen de Genève à D'Alembert . . . sur son Article Genève Dans le Septième Volume de l'Encyclopédie . . .* (London, 1782), pp. 246f. Jean Starobinski, *J.-J. Rousseau: la transparence et l'obstacle. . .* (Paris, 1971), pp. 116ff.

77 In one of the most famous and intriguing examples, the portrait of Madame Récamier, which

David did not finish and kept in his studio, she is shown reclining on a couch by Jacob which was in fact a studio prop, though she did own one just like it herself. See André Schnapper, *David: témoin de son temps* (New York, 1980), pp. 174ff.

78 *Helen and Paris*, painted, paradoxically enough, for the debauched, extravagant and reactionary Comte d'Artois, later Charles x; it was exhibited in the Salon of 1787. The Trojan prince, Paris, is wearing a red bonnet (and little else). To the Salon of 1791 Mme de Genlis wore such a bonnet (presumably – it is called *bonnet de la Liberté*) conspicuously; her otherwise decorous costume is reported in the *Journal de Paris* of 29 September 1791. The sansculottes adopted a red bonnet, apparently as convict dress, in 1789, but it was not called *bonnet Phrygien* until 1792 – though the equation Trojan : Phrygian : Roman may have seemed more obvious at the time than it is now. The late antique statue in the Louvre, known then as 'Paris', was coiffed with just such a bonnet, though it showed him fully dressed. Ironically, this inverts the original implication of the picture, which meant to show the upright Spartan maiden (Helen) seduced by the effeminate Phrygian prince, echoing Gluck's opera on the subject, *Paride ed Elena*: see Wind, *Hume and the Heroic Portrait*, pp. 116ff.

For all this – and the furniture involved, see Michel Thévoz, *Le Théâtre du crime* (Paris, 1989), pp. 8ff., 29.

79 Which had been designed and built in the years 1769–74, ironically enough, by an arch-royalist, Jacques Gondoin.

80 On Chinard's sculptures and his arrest, see Thomas Crowe, *Emulation: Making Artists for Revolutionary France* (New Haven and London, 1995), pp. 145ff. Various versions of the anecdote were told: see H. H. Arnason, *The Sculptures of Houdon* (London, 1975), p. 95. The sculpture found its way to the Convention hall but unaccountably disappeared during the nineteenth century.

81 It was crowned by a quadriga to which the four antique bronze horses the Venetians had stolen from Constantinople in the Fourth Crusade (and Napoleon claimed as war reparations) were attached. After 1814 they were returned to St Mark's church.

82 Its reliefs were designed by David's pupil (and Ingres' friend and associate), Pierre Bergeret, with an Italian, Giuseppe Bosio (also known as François-Joseph), while the statue that crowned it was cast by Antoine Chaudet – a disciple (and friend) rather than a pupil of David.

83 David had his designs engraved by Dominique Vivant-Denon, which justified his presence in Paris, though as a diplomat and courtier of long standing he had been proscribed as an émigré. David had pleaded for his reinstatement, citing their collaboration. Vivant-Denon also made a large engraving of David's *Serment du Jeu de Paume*, which was not finished. See P. Bordes, *Autour de David* (Paris, 1983), p. 85.

84 Bonaparte's refusal of David's designs for 'antique' costumes was the first of his many independent 'artistic' moves; so that although David did become *premier peintre de l'Empereur*, he never assumed the role of minister of the arts such as Le Brun had under Louis xiv, and which David certainly thought his due. Delécluze, *Louis David*, pp. 237ff.

85 L. J. David, *Le Tableau des Sabines Exposé Publiquement* (Paris, 1799), pp. 356ff. The first part justifies the idea of the exhibition and accounts for its English origin, the second provides an account of the episode out of Plutarch's Life of Romulus. See Schnapper, *David*, pp. 182ff.

86 David found this device so rewarding that he used it on several other occasions; in one case he had the exhibition room hung with green velvet, so that the mirror in which the painting was reflected could be seen as floating free of the wall. Louis xviii eventually bought the Sabine picture from an agent (David having gone into his Belgian exile) for the Luxembourg in 1819. It was moved to the Louvre in 1826.

87 Schnapper, *David*, mentions Quay, pp. 189; Delécluze had spelt him Quaï but it now seems that the spelling with 'y' is preferable. See Georges Levitine, *The Dawn of Bohemianism: The Barbu Rebellion and Primitivism in Neoclassical France* (University Park, PA, 1978), pp. 46ff.

88　L. J. David, *Le Paintre Louis David*, pp. 356ff. Robert Rosenblum, 'Essai de Synthèse: *Les Sabines*', in Michel, *David contre David*, vol. I, pp. 459ff., and Thomas Crow, *Emulation: Making Artists for Revolutionary France* (New Haven, CT and London, 1995), pp. 185ff. A large painting on the same subject by François-André Vincent (now in the Musée des Beaux-Arts, Angers) was exhibited in the Salon of 1781 where David would certainly have seen it. At any rate, his income from exhibiting the *Sabines* was five times the compensation he claimed for the *Jeu de Paume*.

Two: New Empire, New Style

1　Her maiden name was Tascher de la Pagerie. She had been christened Marie-Josèphe-Rose (but known as Marie-Rose) and was the widow of General the Viscount Alexandre de Beauharnais, also born on Martinique, who had served in the American War of Independence, had been a deputy and a Jacobin but was nevertheless guillotined in 1794, three days before Robespierre fell. Marie-Rose/Joséphine had herself been imprisoned for over a hundred days. Joséphine was Bonaparte's name for her, adapting her middle name. Joseph Turquan, *The Wife of General Bonaparte* (London, 1912).

2　Mme Vigée-Lebrun on meeting the First Consul could not believe he was so small! (New York, 1989), p. 172. Both Napoleon and Joséphine were 5 feet 2 inches tall.

3　See Georges Poisson, 'Les Fontaines de Paris sous le Premier Empire', in *Urbanisme et architecture*: *Festschrift for Paul Lavedan* (Paris, 1954), pp. 295ff.

4　Her rooms at 7 Rue du Mont Blanc are described in some detail by Edmond and Jules de Goncourt, *Histoire de la société française sous le Directoire* (Paris, 1880), pp. 49ff.

5　Marie-Louise Biver, *Pierre Fontaine* (Paris, 1964), p. 21. Mme Biver's book is based on Fontaine's diary, from which his account of the episode is taken.

6　On the devaluation of specific reference in the Empire style, see Siegfried Giedion, *Mechanization Takes Command* (New York, 1955), pp. 329ff. On the importance of outline engraving about this period, see Joseph Rykwert, *The First Moderns* (Cambridge, MA, 1980), pp. 366ff. The Percier and Fontaine *Recueil* is entirely engraved in outline – as are all the albums illustrating their works.

7　For a brief account of the proceedings, the decision (against Napoleon's wishes) to have the *Sacre* at Notre-Dame, not the Invalides, the destruction of the original tent-like vestibule four days before the ceremony (and so on), see Pierre-François-Léonard Fontaine, *Journal, 1779–1853* (Paris, 1987), vol. I, pp. 84ff. On the sources of the 'national' iconography, see Jurgis Baltrusaitis, *La Quête d'Isis* (Paris, 1967), pp. 51ff.

8　Fontaine, *Journal*, vol. I, pp. 42ff. for the early projects. An early plan by Percier and Fontaine dated *l'an II* was published by Bruno Fortier in *Le Métropole imaginaire* (Brussels, 1989), p. 71.

9　Angelo Villa, 'Parigi', in Carlo Aymonino *et al.*, *Le città capitali del XIX secolo* (Rome, 1975), pp. 86ff.; Siegfried Giedion, *Space, Time and Architecture* (Cambridge, MA, 1954), pp. 613ff.; Henry Bidou, *Paris* (London, 1939), pp. 306ff.

10　The elephant, which harboured a vast number of rats, was removed to the Barrière du Trône and finally destroyed in 1846. On the elephant at the Etoile, see Pierre Lavedan, *Histoire d'urbanisme* (Paris, 1959), vol. III, pp. 354ff. On the Bastille one, Poisson, 'Les Fontaines de Paris sous le Premier Empire', pp. 301ff., Louis Hautecoeur, *Histoire de l'architecture classique en France* (Paris, 1943–57), vol. VI, pp. 51ff.; it 'realized' an older and larger bronze elephant projected for the Etoile in 1758. As happened occasionally to such large public projects, a full-size mock-up was built in canvas and plaster over a wooden frame, which by 1830 was ruined and dangerous; it is often attributed wrongly to Jean-Antoine Alavoine, who had designed the base of the elephant fountain. It was removed in favour of the bronze column designed by

Louis-Joseph Duc commemorating the July revolution and was solemnly inaugurated there – to the sound of Berlioz's *Symphonie Funèbre et Triomphale* in 1840. Edward Planta in *A New Picture of Paris* (London, 1818), p. 235, speaks of it being planned 'to be 72 foot high . . .The model is complete and is exhibited near the spot under an immense shed'. It was the subject of several imperial decrees and was to carry a pavilion, which was to be accessible and serve as a belvedere. The scale is not specified. A drawing of the elephant by Alavoine, to be cast in bronze from guns captured in Spain by an 'animalier', Antoine Mouton (known as Moutoni), was recently bought by the Louvre.

11 David kept the drawing, with the figure of Victory hovering over the Eagles (and Joséphine seated beside Napoleon – she also had to be painted out after the divorce – until his death). It is now in the Louvre.

12 The drawings of all the costumes by Isabey, framed in ornaments devised by Percier, were published by Frederic Masson in *Livre du Sacre de l'Empereur Napoléon* (Paris, 1908).

    The emperor would so far forget himself – he was, after all, to marry *en deuxièmes noces*, a niece of Marie Antoinette – that he would refer to Louis xvi as *mon pauvre oncle*.

13 This was done to rescue them from revolutionary 'vandalism', a term new-minted at the time by the antiquarian and Conventional bishop, the Abbé Henri Grégoire, for such destructive activity – or so he claimed. But in fact the term had been in use in a similar way two centuries earlier in English. See Dario Gamboni, *The Destruction of Art* (London, 1997), pp. 16ff., 35f.

14 It seems that Napoleon had no clear idea where these vast canvases were to be hung. But he did urge David to eschew themes from antiquity, and celebrate modern – by which he meant Napoleonic – events.

15 E. J. Delécluze, *Louis David: son ecole et son temps* (Paris, 1855; reprinted 1983), pp. 242, 295, 312f. In the Salon of 1810, David's *Coronation* was hung opposite Gros' livid and funereal *Battle of Eyleau*, at the first sight of which (at an earlier Salon) the emperor had pinned his own Legion of Honour on Gros' chest. Gros became the head of the atelier when his regicide master was exiled to Brussels at the Restoration and always reproached himself for not being true enough to David's precepts. Although he was created baron by Charles x much later, he is usually referred to as Baron Gros.

    David's fee for the *Sacre*, 100,000 francs, was something of a record: no British painter had received that much for a canvas about that time. The nearest was Benjamin West's *Christ Healing the Sick*, which the British Institutions bought for £3,150; they recouped all of it from the sale of the engravings. See George Reitlinger, *The Economics of Taste* (London, 1961), vol. i, p. 70.

16 During David's rule over the arts, the old Royal Academy had been destituted of its authority over art and architecture teaching. Its role was taken over by the new institute. The name and function of the Academy was restored after the return of the monarchy.

17 On Louis xviii's bed, quotation in Hautecoeur, *Histoire de l'architecture classique en France* (1955 edition), vol. vi, p. 352. For his ministry after the 'hundred days', see André Maurois, *Chateaubriand* (Paris, 1938), pp. 277ff.

18 It was well known in Paris that Tsar Alexander i much preferred the company of the ex-Empress Joséphine and her children to that of the melancholy and protocol-obsessed family of Louis xviii.

19 Marie-Louise Biver, *Pierre Fontaine* (Paris, 1964), pp.190f.

20 Ibid., pp. 192ff. The old construction, called 'Galerie de Bois', also known as the 'Tartar Camp', was built in the 1760s. It was graphically (and nostalgically) described by Balzac in *Un Grand Homme de Province à Paris*. On both constructions, see Johann Friedrich Geist, *Arcades* (Cambridge, ma, 1983), pp. 452ff.

21 They were eventually replaced by a much more 'static' quadriga by Giuseppe Bosio, which was set up during the Second Empire. But see Charles Saunier, *Les Conquêtes Artistiques de la*

Révolution et de l'Empire (Paris, 1902), pp. 140ff. The horses were, in any case, Venetian booty exacted from Byzantium during the Fourth Crusade; they may have been brought there from Rome itself and originally drawn a chariot on some Imperial triumphal arch.

Vivant-Denon had suggested that the driver of the quadriga should be a likeness of the emperor – it was commissioned from François Lemot – but Napoleon objected, and the statue was removed into storage. It is now in the gardens of Fontainebleau.

22 Klenze won the competition, but even he did three schemes: one Doric, one Ionic and one 'Renaissance'. Haller von Hallerstein also did a Doric one. In the end Klenze argued strongly for the 'middling' Ionic one, and that is the one that was built.

23 Haydon himself tells of his reception by James Northcote, then already an aged RA, whom he told he wished to be a history painter, and reproduces the older artist's answer in Devon dialect: 'Heestoricaul peinter! why yee'll starve with a bundle of straw under yeer head!', in *The Autobiography and Memoirs of Benjamin Robert Haydon*, ed. Tom Taylor (London, 1926), vol. I, p. 19.

24 Sir Joshua Reynolds, *Discourses on Art*, ed. Robert R. Wark (New Haven and London, 1975), p. 13. It is in fact the second paragraph of his first discourse, which was delivered in January 1769. But see Quentin Bell, *The Schools of Design* (London, 1963), pp. 24ff.

25 Like David, Benjamin Robert Haydon had his personal quarrel with the Academy; see Bell, *The Schools of Design*, pp. 37ff. Unfortunately, he was not gifted with a genius to equal David's. Haydon tells of his encounter with the marbles in his *Autobiography and Memoirs* (London, 1926), vol. I, pp. 66ff. He was, of course, not alone. He went with David Wilkie and then with Füssli: that was in 1808. The marbles had various other notable visitors: Mrs Siddons, John Flaxman (who, like his master, Canova, refused to have anything to do with 'restoring' them; see William St Clair, *Lord Elgin and the Marbles*, London, 1967, pp. 152, 166f.). Benjamin West also got admission; the last wrote two letters about them to Lord Elgin which were published in *Memorandum on the Subject of the Earl of Elgin's Pursuits in Greece* (Edinburgh, 1811), pp. 47ff. In 1815 Haydon was allowed to make casts, and accompanied Canova to see them; (*Autobiography and Memoirs*, vol. I, pp. 223ff.). He gave a much more racy and indiscreet account of his encounter with the marbles in a lecture which he reprinted in his *Lectures on Painting and Design* (London, 1846), pp. 203ff.

26 In Germany – particularly in Prussia and Bavaria – *Gewerbeinstitute* were being patronised by government agencies as the German states belatedly industrialized in the second half of the nineteenth century.

27 Diderot refers to Chardin's opinion in the Salon of 1765; see Denis Diderot, *Oeuvres complètes* (Paris, 1970), vol. IV, pp. 16f.

28 Burke's relation to Barry was long but not easy. They had quarrelled badly in 1774 about a portrait of Burke (as Ulysses) and Barry himself (as one of his companions) escaping from the cave of Polyphemus – which must have signified some real or imaginary danger. It was shown at the Royal Academy in 1776 – presumably after their big quarrel; and is now in the Crawford Municipal Gallery, Cork.

Barry's later publication, *A Letter to the Dilettanti Society* (London, 1797), which anticipated some of Haydon's ideas about history painting, also made some insulting accusations against the Royal Academy and several of its members, which led to his expulsion from it in 1799.

29 See John Summerson, *Georgian London* (London, 1980), pp. 177ff. Hermione Hobhouse, *A History of Regent Street* (London, 1975), pp. 28ff.

30 Summerson, *Georgian London*, pp. 132ff., 172f., 232f.; though at Cowes on the Isle of Wight, to which he moved the whole of his Regent Street gallery, he also had three landscapes by Turner, painted locally, and two pictures by West – as well as the usual copies of old masters – all of which were sold at auction after his death.

31 Hermione Hobhouse, *Thomas Cubbitt* (London, 1971).

32 Arthur T. Bolton, *The Portrait of Sir John Soane* (London, 1927), pp. 471f., for the offer. Daniel Maclise RA was commissioned to do two panels of such subjects (the *Meeting of Blücher and Wellington*, the *Death of Nelson*, both 12 foot by 45 foot in 1845 for the Royal Gallery. Soane knew and disliked Maclise who painted his portrait for the Literary Fund, which Soane hated and had destroyed (see Nancy Weston, *Daniel Maclise: Irish Artist in Victorian London*, London, 2001, pp. 99f.). They were done by a novel process, waterglass steteochromy, much advocated by the Prince Consort, which involved covering watercolour painting on plaster with a hard, artificial varnish.

    The first was greeted with enormous enthusiasm, the second (the waterglass did not last well in any case) with increasing hostility, though influential critics – such as the Rossetti brothers – were lavish in their praise. Maclise went on protesting about the damaging effects of the stained glass and the arbitrary deformations of colour and shape produced by mouldings, chandeliers and so on. Maclise's champions, the Prince Consort (at whose behest he went to Germany to learn the waterglass process in 1859) and Sir Charles Eastlake, died before the second picture was finished, and the technical defects as well as the increasing hostility are thought responsible for the artist's early death in 1870. See R.J.B. Walker, *A Catalogue of Paintings, Drawings, Engravings and Sculpture in the Palace of Westminster* (Croydon, 1988), vol. III, pp. 109ff. See also Robert Redgrave and Samuel Redgrave, *A Century of Painters* (London, 1890), pp. 430ff. (or 1947, pp. 466f.), and Weston, *Daniel Maclise*, pp. 237ff.

33 The story of his rejection of the Turner canvas does not show Soane at his best – but is an interesting comment on the 'decorative' status of the work of even the most illustrious artists of the time. Turner's picture is now in Tate Britain, and Callcott's *Passage Point* is in the north recess of the Picture Room of Sir John Soane's Museum (which was in fact finished in 1889 – though replicating the original arrangement); it was shown in the Soane Exhibition at the Royal Academy in 2000, no. 37. See Gillian Darley, *John Soane, An Accidental Romantic* (New Haven, CT, 1999), pp. 279f. On Callcott, see Redgrave and Redgrave, *A Century of British Painters* (London, 1947), pp. 373ff.

34 Though in the third of his lectures at the Royal Academy, he was rather sniffy about using caryatids in 'modern work', specifically condemning Jean Goujon's ones in the Louvre (David Watkin, *Sir John Soane: Enlightenment Thought and the Royal Academy Lectures*, Cambridge, 1996, pp. 517ff.) and Inigo Jones' projected ones for Whitehall Palace – 'nothing can be more noble or magnificent and at the same time more absurd' – which he even illustrated (fig. 79); though he excerpts from his censures the portals of the Museo Pio-Clementino and a fountain supported by male figures in the Villa Albani, without motivating his preference. One caryatid (of the original eight – the others were left in place) was brought by Lord Elgin as part of his booty.

35 John Henning (1771–1851) worked with his two sons (John and Samuel) to produce a restoration of the Parthenon frieze at Lord Elgin's – but also took some casts. Both father and son emulated it several times. St Clair, *Lord Elgin and the Marbles*, pp. 218f.

Three: In Many Colours

1 See Friedrich Gilly, *Essays on Architecture*, ed. and trans. Fritz Neumeyer and David Britt (Santa Monica, CA, 1994), pp. 6f, 129ff.

2 Ibid., pp. 25ff., 105ff.

3 It appeared anonymously in 1796 and was at once attributed to Goethe; after Wackenroder's death, his collected papers were published by Ludwig Tieck. But see Ladislao Mittner, *Storia*

della letteratura tedesca, 1700–1820 (Turin, 1964), §353ff.; also Joseph Rykwert, 'The Constitution of Bohemia', in *RES* 31 (New York, 1997), p. 122, nn. 59f.

Any definition of the 'Romantic movement' is notoriously difficult: the Schlegels already found it so. It is often read as the succession and the development of a *Sturm und Drang* tendency, a label which takes its name from Goethe's *Wanderer im Sturm* (*Werke*, ed. Ernst Beutler, Zürich, 1960, vol. I, pp. 331ff.) though it is often seen as originating in the anti-Enlightenment stance of Johann Georg Hamman; Hegel indicates this – and Benedetto Croce wanted to see the eighteenth-century philosopher (and critic of Cartesian rationalism) Giambattista Vico as a proto-Romantic figure. *Sturm und Drang* is also associated with certain proto-Romantic music: that of Wilhelm Friedemann Bach and the late work of Haydn. A bibliography of the question in Austin Warren and René Wellek, *Theory of Literature* (London, 1954), pp. 381ff. Hegel was to give the term new coinage, of which more later. In any case, it did not move from literature into the visual arts until Hegel's generation. In a way the most powerful statement of what Romanticism meant about the time of *Hernani* is set out by Hugo in the preface of a slightly earlier play, *Cromwell*. Victor Hugo, *Théâtre* (Paris, 1858), vol. III, pp. 14ff.

4 In fact he edited Novalis and Kleist with Friedrich Schlegel, Wilhelm's brother.

5 The suggestion that the head was modelled in Paris in 1798 was made by Wolfgang Becker in his *Paris und die deutsche Malerei, 1750–1840* (Munich, 1971), p. 68.

6 Although several of them – notably the Brothers Francque as painters and Charles Nodier as a writer and polemicist – had a great influence on later French intellectual life.

7 Charles Nodier, *Les Romans* (Paris, 1840), p. 238. In fact, 'Les Méditations du Cloitre' is added to 'Le Peintre de Salzbourg' by the editor or publisher (perhaps by Nodier himself) as an appendix, 'as being similar in subject and written at the same time'. It was specifically the Goethian suicide and the executioner's axe which unpeopled Nodier's world. See the discussion in Malcolm Easton's *Artists and Writers in Paris* (London, 1964), pp. 12ff. I have translated 'se lève' as 'rises', which unfortunately does not convey the rebellious implication of the French word, but it is the closest translation.

8 Though he did not die of tuberculosis, but was drowned when swimming in the Tiber.

9 'Denn ich verehre täglich mehr die . . . Arbeit des Menschen [i.e. Dürer's] der, wenn man ihn recht im Innersten erkennen lernt, an Wahrheit Erhabenheit und selbst Grazie nur die ersten Italiener zu seines Gleichen hat. Dieses wollen wir nicht laut sagen.' *Werke*, vol. XVIII, p. 487.

10 William Blake, *Complete Writings*, ed. Geoffrey Keynes (London, 1957), pp. 460f.

These notes were probably written in 1808. Reynolds had been a bit off-hand about Dürer in his third discourse.

On the coupling of Raphael and Dürer by the early Romantic artist, see Jan Biasłostocki, 'Rafael i Dürer jako Symbole dwóch Artystycznych Idea ów w Dobie Romantyzmu', in *Reflexsje i Syntezy ze swiata sztuki, Cykl Drugi* (Warsaw, 1987), pp. 168ff.

11 Where he had seen and admired the brooding work of a strange, Michelangelesque Dane, Asmus Jakob Carstens.

12 Aedan Daly, *Sant'Isidoro* (Rome, 1971), pp. 27ff. The Vienna Academy had in any case ceased functioning for a while when Napoleon's troops occupied the city in 1809.

13 He and his older brother (Jonas) Johannes were the sons of the Jewish banker Simon Veit and Brendel (later Dorothea), the daughter of the philosopher Moses Mendelssohn. They divorced and sometime later Dorothea, who had custody of her sons, married (the not yet ennobled) Friedrich Schlegel; the couple moved to Vienna, where the brothers joined them. They both converted to Catholicism about this time and went to Rome, where Johannes settled (he died there in 1854), while Philipp returned to Germany before 1840, was an influential teacher in Frankfurt, and moved to Mainz to fresco the cathedral; he directed the Städel Museum, which was also the main art academy of the town.

14 They had relied in Palazzo Zuccari on the technical help of an aged Roman plasterer who had

worked for Anton-Rafael Mengs.

15 Dated 1500, the picture is in the Pinakothek in Munich.

16 The painting of the prince and his entourage drinking in the Spanish-Portuguese inn in Rome with Thorvaldsen and some of the Nazarenes by Franz Louis Catel is in the Bayerische Staatsgalerie in Munich. The prince had made his first 'Grand Tour' in 1804–6.

17 Jakob Levi Solomon Bartholdy (the family name came from a property they had outside Berlin) was a kinsman of Felix Mendelssohn-Bartholdy's mother. He became a Protestant in 1805, served as a junior officer in the Wiener Landwehr and was appointed consul in Rome in 1815. Pensioned in 1825, he died in Rome soon after. He had been friendly with the Veit family, which made the connection; but he sympathized with the Nazarenes anyway. The frescoes have been detached and are now in Berlin.

18 Lionello Venturi, *Il gusto dei primitivi* (Turin, 1972), pp. 125ff., Corrado Maltese, *Storia dell'arte in Italia, 1785–1943* (Turin, 1960), pp. 115ff. Tommaso Minardi, on Canova's recommendation, was made director of the Perugia Academy, but also taught in Rome in the Academy of St Luke. Antonio Bianchini (1803–84): his six-volume translation of the homilies of the Greek Church fathers was his most substantial achievement, but his publishing house failed and his anthology of medieval Italian literature was not published. He was a member of Rome city council and a successful painter; his best-known work is the altarpiece showing St Giovanni de Rossi in the Trinità dei Pellegrini. Pietro Tenerani (1798–1869) was a pupil of Luigi Bartolini, then of Canova and finally Thorvaldsen's assistant; he had worked in Paris briefly during the Empire, but returned to Italy after the fall of Napoleon. The tomb of Pius VIII in St Peter's (1853), his monument to Simon Bolivar in Bogotá and the Bolivar tomb in Caracas witness to his reputation.

The Accademia di San Luca is the one still housed in the Palazzo Carpegna in Rome and had no real connection with the Lukasbund. Their common dedication is to the Evangelist St Luke, who is the patron saint of artists.

19 *In welchem Style sollen wir Bauen? beantwortet von H. Hübsch* . . . [Karlsruhe 1828], ed. Wolf Schirmer (Karslruhe, 1984). But see also his *Ueber Griechische Architektur* (Heidelberg, 1822; reprinted, with a counter-attack on Hirth, 1824). With another architect, Franz Heger, he also published in 1823 the *Malerische Ansichten von Athen*. However, he was no antiquarian, but passionately interested in iron construction and perhaps the first to try the method, associated with Antoni Gaudì, of using suspended elastic models to work out the tensile forces in a vault.

In 1847 he wrote another brief book on the relation of architecture to contemporary painting and sculpture. His designs were published in three volumes (1838, 1852, 1859) as well as a folio about the early Christian churches and their influence on contemporary church building (Karlsruhe, 1862–3; in French: Paris, 1866). A summary of the discussion in English is provided by *In What Style Should We Build?* ed. Wolfgang Herrmann (Los Angeles, CA, 1992).

20 *Heinrich Huebsch*, exh. cat. (Karlsruhe, 1983), pp. 28f.

21 Although it was reputedly consecrated by Gregory the Great in the sixth century, it had been radically restored in 1486 and again in 1600, as well as in 1813 and 1825. Huebsch must have been aware of the last restoration, at any rate. The present appearance of the church is due to yet another radical restoration – or even remodelling – by Antonio Muñoz in 1929.

22 Friedrich von Gaertner was another Munich practitioner in several styles favoured and ennobled by King Maximilian II.

23 The 'Book of the Polish Nation' and the 'Book of Polish Pilgrimage' (*Ksiega Narodu Polskiego* and *Ksiega Pielgrzymstwa Polskiego*) by Adam Mickiewicz (Paris, 1832) summarizes the argument that the victim-people – in his case the Poles – was a persecuted Messiah of all the nations who will rise again.

24 On the banning of the kilt, see H. Trevor-Roper, 'The Highland Tradition in Scotland', in *The*

Invention of Tradition, ed. Eric Hobsbawm and Terence Ranger (Cambridge, 1983), pp. 25ff. The ban on kilts and tartans was repealed in 1782. The idea of distinctive clan tartans was not launched until 1822.

The visit was recorded by J.M.W. Turner in a number of paintings and George IV was painted in full highland costume by Sir David Wilkie. See Gerald Finley, *Turner and George IV in Edinburgh* (London, 1981). His niece, Queen Victoria, could even consider herself a Stuart and (at times) a Jacobite, and often sported tartan dress, as did her consort, Prince Albert.

25 This involved some double-take: since Athens was, of course, an Ionian, not a Dorian city; but since the Parthenon was a Doric temple the style could stand for the *ethne*.

26 Soane, who had built the Royal Staircase, complained of the 'mischief' James Wyatt had done talking of a 'national style' – by which he meant a rather generalized (tending to Perpendicular) Gothic – in which style he reconstructed Palace Yard and the Speaker's House. See Arthur T. Bolton, ed., *The Portrait of Sir John Soane* (London, 1927), pp. 445ff.

27 Ibid. Howard M. Colvin, *The History of the King's Works*, vol. VI: *1782–1851*, ed. J. Mordaunt Crook and M. H. Port (London, 1975), pp. 506ff.

28 Although they were to have their ecclesiological differences later: see Michael Trappes-Lomax, *Pugin* (London, 1932), pp. 241ff.

29 See Phoebe Stanton, 'The Sources of Pugin's Contrasts', in *Concerning Architecture: Essays on Architectural Writers and Writing Presented to Nikolaus Pevsner*, ed. John Summerson (Harmondsworth, 1964), pp. 134ff. Stanton points to another, very prolific writer, Kenelm Digby, as an influence; Pugin had actually met Digby – though he does not quote him explicitly. Through Digby he may have learnt of the Schlegels' ideas.

30 The 'Tractarians' were a group of clergy and laymen who revived the rather moribund High Church tradition in the Church of England, concentrating ecclesiology, sacramental theology and liturgical 'primitivism' against the pervasive latitudinarian attitude of much of the higher clergy and the puritan individualism of the Low Church. Their main weapons were a series of publications issued in Oxford, called *Tracts for the Times* – hence the sobriquet. But see Geoffrey Faber, *Oxford Apostles: A Character Study of the Oxford Movement* (London, 1933), pp. 42f., 72f., 340ff.

Pugin – and others – were hoping for the establishment of a 'uniate' Anglican communion; this was frustrated and the Anglo-Catholic party in the Church of England came into being.

31 The principles are stated right at the beginning, on p. 1; on 'Brummagem', see chapter One, n. 2; but see A.W.N. Pugin, *The True Principles of Pointed or Christian Architecture* (London, 1853), pp. 20ff., 32f.

32 W. R. Lethaby, *Philip Webb and his Work* (Oxford, 1935), p. 66.

33 On the origins and implications of the all-pervasive linearity of presentation, see R. Rosenblum, 'The International Style of 1800', unpublished doctoral thesis, New York University (New York, 1956), and Joseph Rykwert, *The First Moderns* (Cambridge, MA, 1980), pp. 368ff.

34 This is reported by Ford Madox Hueffer in *Ford Madox Brown* (London, 1896), vol. I, p. 36. But see also Marcia Pointon, *William Dyce* (Oxford, 1979), pp. 84ff.

35 His despair at his exclusion was noted by many contemporaries: see Eric George, *The Life and Death of Benjamin Robert Haydon* (Oxford, 1948), pp. 264ff. But see above, chapter Two, pp. 14ff. Nevertheless, he was very generous in his comments on the winning cartoons – especially Dyce's.

36 The editor of the Tracts was John Henry Newman, who had been ordained in the Church of England in 1824, and edited the *Tracts for the Times, 1833–1841*. He became a Catholic in 1845, was ordained a priest in 1847 and created cardinal in 1879.

37 And perhaps even bought it. See Pointon, *William Dyce*, pp. 7ff. Curiously enough, the Redgraves, who must have known about Dyce's Italian journeys, have nothing to say about any contact he may have had with contemporary artists. But see S. Redgrave and R. Redgrave, *A Century of British Painters* (London, 1890; reprinted 1947), pp. 480ff. The Roman *Virgin and*

Child is lost, but he later painted some which seem emulations of that early success. The Prince Consort bought one dated 1845, now in the collection of HM the Queen.

38 Another Roman friend was Nicholas Wiseman – then professor of Syro-Chaldaic and Hebrew at the Sapienza, then Rector of the English College and later Cardinal-Archbishop of Westminster. It was to Wiseman at the English College that Dyce wrote about the possibility of doing large-scale devotional painting if a cathedral were to be built in England. Wiseman promised to refer this matter to 'Mr Pugin . . . and I shall say all in my power to induce him to take you into his councils, should he have any such great work in hand' (29 June 1838), quoted by Pointon, *William Dyce*, pp. 129f.

39 Quentin Bell, *The Schools of Design* (London, 1963), pp. 53, 80.

40 Ibid.; but see Haydon's expostulation in Appendix I, pp. 264ff.

41 So Cornelius Gurlitt, *Die Deutsche Kunst Seit 1800* (Berlin, 1924), p. 188.

42 He also 'designed' the fresco cycle about the history of medieval art in the southern loggias of the Alte Pinakothek. They, too, were not altogether popular: Baedeker's 'South Germany' of 1929 (p. 439) informs the visitor that they are locked up but 'may be shown on application to the custodian'.

43 In fact, Cornelius had earlier done a series of outline drawings of the *Nibelungenlied* which were engraved and first published in 1822.

44 Cornelius' major achievement was to be a great fresco cycle of 'the Christian Epic'; its non-execution led to the breach with King Ludwig in 1840; in 1863, when it was clear that his cartoons would never be executed, he told the lexicographer Hermann Grimm that it allowed him to develop his great strength as a draughtsman and the cartoons would last 'for a thousand years'. Quoted by Herbert von Einem in *Deutsche Malerei des Klassizismus und der Romantik* (Munich, 1978), p. 156.

45 Johann Gottfried Schadow, *Kunstwerke und Kunstansichten*, ed. Götz Eckhardt (Berlin, 1987), pp. 121, 586ff. The plaster figures were cast in zinc. Schadow was unenthusiastic about Schinkel's figures – although he 'quite liked them' ('die Entwürfe hätten ihn gar wohl gefallen'); elsewhere he notes that he told *Geh.Rath* Schinkel 'that in the dimensions he had indicated the figures would not have much effect. He was too much in love with his drawing to reflect on this'. And indeed the relief of the pediment, which Schadow was also meant to execute, was given to another sculptor.

46 By 1897 the paintings had been restored out of recognition; or so Hermann Ziller, *Schinkel* (Bielefeld and Leipzig, 1897), pp. 74f.

47 Schinkel's own favourite building, the Bauakademie, where he had taught and where he also lived and died (it looked across the Spree to the Museum), had sculptured decorations on the theme of architecture and its power which followed an exacting programme not only worked out but also 'designed' by him, to be executed by Tieck and his assistants. Cornelius, Tieck and Schadow were prepared to follow Schinkel's drawings and were on good terms with him. Whatever their reservations about Schinkel, neither Peter Cornelius nor Julius Schnorr von Karolsfeld ever achieved an analogous working partnership with Gaertner and Klenze, though the Munich architects never reduced painters and sculptors to mere executants. So Paul Ortwin Rave, *Genius der Baukunst* (Berlin, nd [1940?]). The building was destroyed during the war. Schinkel was familiar with the work of the Nazarenes, and on 6 September 1824 wrote to his friend Rauch from Naples about the great lessons he had learnt in Italy about sculpture and painting in buildings; he had also examined the Casino Massimo frescoes and considered that Schnorr (and presumably Cornelius with whom he had spent a great deal of time earlier that year), the 'Protestants', were much more original and fiery than the 'Catholic' Veit and Overbeck, whose work he finds anxious and constrained.

48 As *Abriss der Vorlesungen über Baukunst, gehalten in der K. Polytechnischen Schule zu Paris*. In fact, Durand was the second teacher of architecture at the Ecole Polytechnique; the course

had originally (and briefly) been given to Louis-Pierre Baltard – who later taught at the Ecole des Beaux-Arts. But the method set out in the *Précis* in its different versions is Durand's.

49   They have since been restored, though they remain outbid by the seated legislators.

50   E. M. Laumann, *Le Retour des cendres* (Paris, 1904), p. 96. A quadriga symbolizing the Revolution was added by Alexandre Falguière in 1881; of the four groups which were placed against the bare piers during the July Monarchy, one, by François Rud, is distinguished – the *Appeal to the volunteers of 1792*, popularly known as *La Marseillaise*; the others, two by Antoine Etex and one by Jean-Pierre Corot, have been neglected by criticism as well as public opinion.

51   Paul Delaroche was also considered for the commission.

52   Cornelius had also instructed a German pupil of Ingres, Henri Lehmann, and the Swiss Adolf von Stürler. Stürler went on to run an art school in Florence with one of the original neo-Nazarene 'purists', Luigi Mussini.

53   The French Academy did not admit it into the language until 1878.

54   The best discussion is by R. D. Middleton, 'Hittorff's Polychrome Campaign', in R. D. Middleton, ed., *The Beaux-Arts and Nineteenth Century French Architecture* (London, 1982), pp. 175ff. But see Quatremère de Quincy's *Dictionnaire historique de l'architecture* (Paris, 1832), s.v. *Couleur*, where he admits the possibility that the ancients used both local colour (in marbles, gilding etc.) and coloured stucco finishes, but recapitulates that true architecture needs neither of these and they can be employed only if they are not just a motley (*bigarrure*).

    On the popularity of polychrome sculpture in the nineteenth century, see Andreas Blühm *et al.*, *The Colour of Sculpture, 1840–1900* (Amsterdam, 1996), *passim*.

55   David van Zanten, 'Architectural Polychromy', in *The Beaux-Arts*, ed. Robin Middleton (London, 1982), pp. 197f. The occasion was the commemoration of Joseph-Max Hurtault, who had obtained a *premier grand prix* in 1797.

56   Léon Vaudoyer to Antoine-Thomas-Laurent Vaudoyer on 21 February 1830; quoted by Barry Bergdoll, *Léon Vaudoyer* (Cambridge, MA, 1994), p. 2. Translation modified.

57   Victor Hugo, *Théâtre* (Paris, 1856), vol. I, p. 4; on the battle, P. Brookes in D. Hollier, *Against Architecture* (Cambridge, MA, 1989), pp. 650ff.

58   See note 3, this chapter.

59   'Cet homme, me dit-il, ne sait pas se renfermer dans son cadre. Voyez Beethoven s'il en sort jamais . . . O! je sais, on me compare souvent à lui; mais . . . Je n'ai mérité ni cet excès d'honneur, ni cet indignité.' Conversation with Amaury-Duval and quoted by him, Eugène-Emmanuel Amaury-Duval, *L'Atelier d'Ingres*, ed. D. Ternois (Paris, 1996), pp. 232f.

    The remark about frames is ironic, given Delacroix's almost obsessive interest in the framing elements of his wall-paintings (even existing seventeenth-century ones) and his always remaining within them.

    As for Hugo, Delacroix's summary dismissal which he records is in one of his 'lost' notebooks, probably about 1845 (*Delacroix*, ed. H. Damisch, Paris, 1981), p. 871.): 'Les ouvrages d'Hugo ressemblent à un brouillon d'un homme qui a du talent: il dit tout ce qui lui vient', was often quoted.

60   Neil Levine in Arthur Drexler, ed., *The Architecture of the Ecole des Beaux-Arts* (New York, 1977), pp. 357ff.

61   The documents of the quarrel are set out by Henri Lapauze, *Histoire de l'Académie de France à Rome* (Paris, 1924), vol. II, pp. 189ff. It all happened just before Hector Berlioz arrived (in January 1831) as a *pensionnaire*: though, as is well known, his career there did not run smoothly, even if he got on well enough with Vernet.

    Vernet consistently protected delinquent but brilliant students, as he did Hector Berlioz – who got up to all sorts of scrapes: Guy de Pourtalès, *Berlioz et l'Europe romantique* (Paris, 1939), pp. 102ff.

62   Although Eugène Delacroix seems to have written articles for 'Romantic' student magazines,

the *Barbus* architects seem to have kept themselves to themselves. On Petrus Borel as an architectural critic, see David van Zanten, *Designing Paris* (Cambridge, MA, 1987), p. 62.

63 By the Brother Davéria and the poet-painter Louis Boulanger.

64 Enid Starkie, *Petrus Borel, the Lycanthrope* (London, 1954), pp. 122ff. Léonce Bénédite, *Théodore Chassériau* (Paris, 1931), pp. 55ff. Gautier remembered there also being a *Diana and Actaon*: *Portraits Contemporains* . . .

   Gérard de Nerval had described the *garçonnière* in the first of his *Châteaux de Bohème* in *Oeuvres* (Paris, 1960), vol. I, pp. 65ff. He is the indefatigable translator, the poet and eccentric – also famous for having a pet lobster which he took for a walk in the Luxembourg Gardens on a ribbon.

65 Théophile Gautier, 'Pierre de Cornélius', in *L'Art moderne* (Paris, 1856), p. 249: 'Une peinture de Cornélius racontée vous séduit, et, en effet, il n'est guère possible de rien imaginer de mieux; voyez la, vous serez étonné de la faiblesse ou de la sauvagerie de l'exécution: l'idée est restée une idée, et n'a pas revêtu de formes. Esthétiquement, c'est admirable; plastiquement, c'est très mauvais, nous n'osons dire détestable par respect pour une réputation consacrée.'

   The contrast of 'esthétique' and 'plastique' – the literary against the visual – is worth noting. Later German generations found him equally objectionable. Anselm Feuerbach, one of the leading painters of the next generation, writes in bitter disappointment to his father on his visit to Munich (*Ein Vermächtnis*, ed. Henriette Feuerbach, Berlin, 1911, pp. 45f.; letter undated, but 1848) not only about the sloppy drawing but also the colouring; 'von Kolorit keine Spur'. Still, he remained on good terms with Cornelius and there was talk of his painting a portrait of the older man which would be engraved and sold in Germany (*Briefe an seine Mutter*, Berlin, 1911, vol. II, pp. 477f, 481f.)

66 Lebas, a pupil of Percier, won the competition in 1823. The painters were Adolphe Roger, Victor Orsel and Alphonse Périn, who had met both Overbeck and Cornelius.

   The district became well-known for its light-hearted inhabitants – hence the word *lorette* has come to mean 'a woman of loose habits', as a dictionary puts it. As for the encaustic (hot-wax) technique, it had been re-discovered in the eighteenth century and was widely practised in the nineteenth, as were various techniques of cold-wax and emulsified wax painting.

67 This was appreciated at the time as well as much later. See, for instance, E. E. Viollet-le-Duc, *Les Eglises de Paris* (with E. Quinet, *Le Panthéon*) (Paris, 1883), pp. 95ff.

68 See Louis Flandrin, *Hippolyte Flandrin: sa vie et son oeuvre* (Paris, 1902), pp. 77ff., 127ff., 205ff. The commission was also refused by Paul Delaroche. Flandrin was, incidentally, a close friend of the Balze brothers. Ingres considered being asked to submit preliminary sketches for discussion a bit of an insult.

69 King Louis-Philippe's favourite artist was that other quasi-Nazarene proto-Pre-Raphaelite, Ary Scheffer (a Dutch pupil of Guérin).

70 That this ambitious young lawyer, who did not have any specialist knowledge of painting but was a rising political force, exposed himself in their praise fermented the cynical rumour that Talleyrand was Delacroix's natural father. This was untrue – even if his mother's familiarity with the old fox did give the gossip some credibility.

71 Raymond Escholier, *Eugène Delacroix* (Paris, 1926), vol. I, pp. 9ff., 62ff. One of Thiers' articles is quoted with approval by Baudelaire in his Salon article of 1846.

72 As Félix Duban (later one of the architects of the Ecole des Beaux-Arts) did, in the restoration of the Galerie d'Apollon, to be painted within Le Brun's decorative surrounds. Duban and (the younger) Vaudoyer were – inevitably – more sympathetic to Delacroix than their elders.

73 Eugène Delacroix, *Journal*, ed. Hubert Damisch (Paris, 1981), pp. 228: 11 March 1850. The only personal friend among architects was Alphonse de Gisors, designer of the Cour de Cassation (whose father had designed the old Chamber of Deputies) – though he did also have kind words for Duban and Vaudoyer.

74 It was being restored by Louis-François Baltard (now remembered mostly as the father of the iron innovator, Victor) who had been his contemporary in the Rome academy.

75 On the awkward relation between Flandrin and Picot at St Vincent, see Sylvain Bellenger, 'Hittorff et les peintres à l'église Saint-Vincent-de-Paul', in *Hittorff*, exh. cat., Musée Carnavalet (Paris, 1986), pp. 309ff. Hittorff gave a copy of his study of Sicilian mosaics to Picot in 1835.

76 See Claudine de Vaulchier, 'Saint-Vincent-de-Paul entre les réminiscences et l'invention 1824–44', in ibid, pp. 111, and 'Hittorff et les Laves émaillés, 1832–38', ibid., pp. 297ff. Chabrol re-activated the quarries on his estate after 1815 (he had been confirmed as Prefect of the Seine Department, to which he had been appointed by Napoleon) and used the stone for paving in Paris. The enamelling process had been devised by a porcelain painter in 1827. Chabrol himself, Hittorff and the inventor's son-in-law (curiously called Hachette) made various attempts to exploit the invention commercially, though Hittorff withdrew from the firm in 1838, as the professionalizing of architecture made his commercial involvement unacceptable. In 1833 he had sent specimens to Schinkel and King Frederic William IV (still crown prince at the time) thought of using them to face the church of St Nicolas in Potsdam that Schinkel, had begun in 1832, but nothing came of it. Charles Garnier tried one Volvic medallion in the stairway of the Opéra, but though he found its colours too hard against the white marble, he did place four such medallions among the mosaics under the dome of the *avant-foyer*: see Charles Garnier, *Le Nouvel Opéra de Paris* (Paris, 1878), vol. I, pp. 278ff. These panels, representing the music of ancient peoples, were painted by Emile Solier.

   Jules Jollivet seems to have been interested in the enamel business technically. Hittorff produced a scheme for the decoration and the first panel was put in place in 1840. Although Hachette was urged to buy larger ovens for the enamel baking, there was much delay and he became bankrupt and died in 1848, while the project was finally carried out in 1860–61. The protests began immediately and the panels were removed in a matter of months.

77 Lacornée also designed the neo-Gabriel building for the Foreign Ministry on the Quai d'Orsay, on which Chassériau's architect-brother Frédéric worked for him as an assistant.

78 It was not favourably received: a hostile critic, M. J. Claretie, noting that Moreau had been called a painter-philosopher, wrote that the painting: 'ressemble à un pastiche de Mantegna fait per un étudiant allemand qui se reposerait de la peinture en lisant Schopenhauer'; quoted by Léon Deshairs and Jean Laran, *Gustave Moreau* (Paris, 1916), p. 31.

79 Who had worked in Italy for the Duc de Luynes and organized the architectural background of Ingres' *Stratonice*. The first alterations were by Etienne-Hippolyte Godde.

80 Delacroix, *Journal, 1822–1863*, found himself at one with Jacques Duban who was to become the architect to the Louvre and with whom he worked on the Galerie d'Apollon.

81 On the painting and the disputes round the choice of the figures, see Stephen Bann, *Paul Delaroche: History Painted* (London, 1997), pp. 202f.; on Duban's platform, p. 208. The popularity of the reliefs or paintings of the great – the canonic – artists in conversational compositions is a subject which still needs investigation: but see Francis Haskell, 'The Old Masters in Nineteenth-Century French Painting', in his *Past and Present in Art and Taste* (New Haven, CT and London, 1987), pp. 90ff.

82 This event, patronized by the July monarch, Louis-Philippe, engaged the whole of France for several months. Napoleon's body was exhumed on St Helena in October 1840, taken by a French frigate to Cherbourg, and there embarked on a steam-boat, the *Normandie*; it arrived at the Pont de Neuilly at Courbevoie, was transferred to a vast mobile catafalque and processed down the Avenue de Neuilly, through the great Triumphal Arch, over the Pont de la Concorde to the Invalides. The tripod flares along the route and the fire-breathing columns, including two vast ones which held up the vast canopy at the entrance of the *cour d'honneur*, were most conspicuous. See E.-M. Laumann, *Le Retour des cendres* (Paris, 1904), pp. 119ff.

A rather irreverent (and not wholly creditable to its author) account of the event by W. M. Thackeray (under the pen-name Michael Angelo Titmarsh) in *Roundabout Papers* (London, 1873), pp. 591ff.

83 He delivered them in 1823–5, but had in fact sketched them some years earlier in Heidelberg, but the text was not published until 1835, posthumously.

84 See N. Levine in Robin Middleton, ed., *The Beaux-Arts and Nineteenth-Century French Architecture* (London, 1982), pp. 138ff. Another architect who was a lifelong friend of Hugo's was Charles Robelin who was well off – a *rentier*; and also a friend of Gustave Doré: see Jean Tild, *Théophile Gautier et ses amis* (Paris, 1951): also Maurice Dreyfous, *Ce que je tiens a dire*. Levine has even suggested that Robelin – whose main achievement was the restoration of Besançon Cathedral – introduced Labrouste to Hugo.

85 Delacroix, *Journal, 1822–63*, p. 349: 'le docte et malheureusement trop froid Chenavard' On their friendship, the sharp comment of Baudelaire in his essay on Delacroix in *Oeuvres* (1976), vol. II, p. 218.

86 Marie-Antoinette Grunewald, *Paul Chenavard et la décoration du Panthéon de Paris* (Lyon, 1977). Thirty-six small preparatory drawings, seventeen grisaille paintings (4.60 by 3.49m); the (presumably) complete cycle of forty-two panels is discussed in the article on Chenavard in Théophile Silvestre, *Les Artistes français* (Paris, 1926), vol. II, pp 107ff. The climactic one of *Palingenesis* has been cut. It was to have been a 'mosaic' 12 metres (36 feet) high in the apse, to be painted on 'volcanic' stone, presumably the same *pierre de Volvic*. The surviving drawings and painting are in the Musée de l'Art, Lyon. Of the 130 photographs, six negatives only have survived in the Musée de l'Impression sur Etoffes, Lyon.

87 (Or Degoffe), best known as a landscape painter; Paul Flandrin married his daughter Aline, who was the darling of Ingres' circle in Rome.

The space of the lower storey is largely devoted to office accommodation, two closed chambers separated by the entry hall.

88 The bust of of Ulrich Gehring (or Gering – by Louis Daumas), the first Parisian printer, was placed there after 1870 and was removed recently to allow passage into a public lavatory.

89 Fifty-two such paintings were commissioned, of which forty-four had been done by the Brothers Balze, and it had taken them some twenty years. Both brothers were decorated and given studios in the Institut. The copies of the *Logge* were placed in the Ecole des Beaux-Arts, where they still remain and where they were joined recently by those of the *Stanze* (except, of course, the *School of Athens*) and four roundels which are in the Bibliothèque Ste Geneviève. See Amaury-Duval, *L'Atelier d'Ingres*, pp. 154ff.

90 Stendhal, *Oeuvres complètes* (Paris, 1922), *Vie de Rossini*, vol. II, pp. 95ff. The singer to whose *fioriture* he objected was one of Rossini's favourites, the *castrato* Giambattista Velluti. The opera was *Aureliano in Palmyra* and the episode occurred in La Scala, Milan, in 1813. Though it is only fair to add that a century earlier François Couperin (Couperin-le-Grand) warned keyboard players in his *L'Art de toucher le clavecin* (Paris, 1716) against the bad taste displayed by those who venture to ornament the written notes.

91 This drawing was paid for by Labrouste's pupils when his atelier was closed: they were rewarded with an engraving of it, of which Labrouste's heirs still seem to hold one or two copies. I would like to thank Neil Levine for this information.

92 C. de Clarac, *Description historique et graphique du Louvre et des Tuileries* (Paris, 1853), pp. 567ff. In 1865 *Apotheosis* had been painted in 1827 as a ceiling for a room in the newly arranged (by Percier and Fontaine) museum of Charles X in the Louvre, and as part of a larger decorative scheme.

When Ingres prepared a drawing of it for the engraver, he excluded certain figures – Shakespeare and Tasso, for instance – as being too 'romantic'. He was very upset when, at the opening, the king never looked up at his painting.

Since the painting was on stucco it had to be canvas-backed when it was removed to be shown at the Exposition Universelle of 1855; it has now been returned to the Louvre, where its place on the ceiling has been taken by a copy painted by the Brothers Balze. There is a story that Delacroix inspected it carefully before it was put in place at the exhibition, and expressed his admiration of it to Ingres. When he left, Ingres ordered one of the ushers to open the windows as 'the room stinks of sulphur'. Amaury-Duval, *L'Atelier d'Ingres*, pp. 230f.

93 Ingres had strong views on the details of ornament: when his friends Hittorff (with his associate in the *Menus-plaisirs*, Jacques-François Lecointe) decorated Reims Cathedral for the coronation of Charles x in 1825 (as architects of the *Menus-plaisirs*), Percier designed a commemorative album modelled on the one that had been issued for Napoleon's *Sacre*. Ingres was commissioned to do the frontispiece (*Alliance of Religion and Monarchy*) and the portraits of the king and the archbishop in their very graceless and fulsome regalia: but he also chose to alter the surrounds very considerably – which was not popular either with Percier or the court. Henri Lapauze, *Ingres* (Paris, 1911), pp. 281ff.

94 Herbert von Einem, *Deutsche Malerei des Klassizismus und der Romantik, 1760 bis 1840* (Munich, 1978), p. 109, on the influence of Overbeck on Ingres, particularly in these paintings. *The Vow of Louis XIII*, exhibited in the Salon, marked Ingres' 'official' acceptance.

95 Charles Blanc, *Ingres: sa vie et ses ouvrages* (Paris, 1870), pp. 100ff.; Lapauze, *Ingres*, pp.143ff. Ingres was so embittered by the negative criticism (and the huge popular success of Paul Delaroche's *Execution of Lady Jane Grey*) that he vowed never again to exhibit in the Salon.

96 Victor Brongniart started these 'painted glass' workshops at Sèvres, which Louis Philippe protected; the architectural borders were supplied by the young Eugène Viollet-le-Duc. The other artists at Dreux included Delacroix (the *Pont de Taillebourg* in his *Journal*, p. 834). But medieval-type leaded stained glass, which was being revived in Britain, was introduced in France soon after. Louis Hautecoeur, *Histoire de l'architecture classique en France*, vol. V, pp. 330f.

97 According to the critic Théophile Silvestre (*Les Artistes Français*, vol. II, p. 33), Ingres said of these paintings:

> I set down the composition of the *Apotheosis of Homer* in one day; I prepared for three and a half years and painted in nine months *The Vow of Louis XIII* . . . *The Martyrdom of St Symphorien* is the picture on which I have worked more than on any other and on which I reckon most for my reputation with posterity . . . the *Age of Gold* and the *Age of Iron* will never be finished . . .

The whole sad story of the master's intermittent six years' work (1843–9 – giving the text of the different agreements between Ingres and the duke) is told by Blanc, *Ingres*, pp. 121ff., 135ff.

While Delacroix did not have such conflict with architects – perhaps because he managed to keep his distance – Ingres was familiar with a number of them: he befriended and drew the young Charles Robert Cockerell in Rome and beside Labrouste had made drawings of Couderc-Gentillon, Provost, Baltard, Destouches and inevitably Hittorff whose familiars served as models for some decorations which Ingres painted in the Hittorff house.

98 Prince Napoléon-Charles-Joseph-Paul Bonaparte, son of King Jerome, styled himself (it caused problems, of course) Napoleon Bonaparte; he was nicknamed Plon-plon in Paris. His liaison with Rachel (Elisa Rachel Felix), the greatest French actress of her day, was public; they had two illegitimate (but acknowledged) sons. The model, which is now lost, was exhibited in the Salon of 1859; see *Hittorff*, exh. cat., pp. 259ff. Contemporary photographs of it are in the Cabinet des Estampes of the Bibliothèque Nationale in Paris, and a set of coloured renderings in the university library in Cologne. It was an expensive present: 800,000 francs. Ingres' panel, a gouache

on paper, deposited on copper without its frame and setting, is now in the Louvre: it is some-time called *The Birth of Erato*.

99 Delacroix, *Journal*, p. 232.

100 On the implications of this notion for Hegel's ontology, see Charles Taylor's comments in *Hegel* (Cambridge, 1975), pp. 468ff.

101 A recent commentary on Hegel's lecture and the artists of his time is Beat Wyss' *Die Trauer der Vollendung* [1985] (hideously rendered in English as *Hegel's Art History and the Critique of Modernity*, Cambridge, 1999), especially pp. 106ff.

102 Beat Wyss, *Trauer der Vollendung* (Munich, 1989), pp. 140ff.

103 Though the final incorporation was in 1857: 'climaxed nearly thirty years of ineffective efforts at being recognized as professionals'. John Burchard and Albert Bush-Brown, *The Architecture of America* (Boston, MA, 1961), p. 111.

104 On the 'Constitution of Bohemia', see J. Rykwert, 'The Constitution of Bohemia', *RES*, 31 (Spring 1997), and Jerrold Seigel, *Bohemian Paris* (New York, 1986), pp. 3ff.

Four: Religious Attention, Aesthetic Attention

1 See J. Rykwert, 'The Constitution of Bohemia', *RES*, 31 (Spring 1997).

2 A useful index of the change is the articles 'Aesthetik' and 'Aesthetisch' in Johann Georg Sulzer's dictionary, *Allgemeine Theorie der Schönen Künste . . .* (Leipzig, 1792; pp. 47ff.) he makes the distinction that *eigentlich*, it means *die Wissenschaft der Empfindungen, welche in der griechischen Sprache Αισθησες gennant werden*. But he considers that at the time he wrote, it had come to signify *die Wissenschaft, welche sowohl die allgemeine Theorie, als die Regeln der schönen Künste aus der Natur des Geschmacks herleitet*.

3 He met the young Overbeck (who was on his way to study in Vienna) in Hamburg in 1806: Philipp Otto Runge, *Hinterlassene Schriften*, ed. 'by his older brother' (Hamburg, 1840–41; reprinted Göttingen, 1965), vol. II, pp. 500f. It is, however, also true that Wackenroder during the trip to Bamberg in 1793 (which he meant to make with Tieck – who couldn't go in the end) was impressed with the majesty of Catholic church services (W. H. Wackenroder and Ludwig Tieck, *Outpourings of an Art-Loving Friar*, trans. Edward Mornin, New York, 1975, p. 521) which he describes in extensive and puzzled detail to his parents. But see also Alfred Robert Neumann, *The Evolution of the Concept* Gesamtkunstwerk *in German Romanticism* (PhD thesis, 1951; Ann Arbor, MI, 1996), p. 120. Schelling was also to see the liturgy as the ideal, synaesthetic drama which acted as a social cement, however diminished it was in his own time: *der Gottesdienst, die einzige Art wahrhaft öffentlicher Handlung, die der neueren Zeit und auch dieser späthin nur sehr Geschmälert und beengt geblieben ist. Werke* (Stuttgart, 1859), vol. V, p. 736.

4 The patronage of the two Augustuses, father and son, was very different. Augustus II loved jewels and was a sucker for antiquities, not all of them genuine. He also promoted the discovery of porcelain and established the first European porcelain works at Meissen and then at Dresden. Augustus III and his (rather eccentric) minister, Count Brühl, fanatically 'acquired' many of the Este pictures from Modena, the *Sistine Madonna* from Piacenza, etc. 'It soon came to be regarded not only as the most magnificent in Germany, but – with the exception of the Louvre – as the richest in the world'. So (Ivan Lermolieff) Giovanni Morelli, *Italian Painters* (London, 1893), vol. II, p. 121.

5 The Pietist movement, a renewal of Lutheran religious practice aiming at a greater intensity of inner life and charitable practice against the doctrinal schematism of the Church establishment, grew during the second half of the seventeenth century mostly in Saxony and Hesse. Bochme was one of its first promoters, but it owes its 'label' to Philip Jacob Spener, an Alsatian pastor whose *Pia Desideria* of 1675 demanded (among other things) the formation of

the movement as a 'church within the church'.

6   Tieck had, in one of his early 'dramas' (*Leben und Tod der heiligen Genoveva*) of 1799, attempted to overlay Boehme's colour symbolism on a curiously stilted, quasi-liturgical narrative.

7   *Republic* X; 614 bff. It has been the subject of interminable speculation. This Er, son of Armenius, was already identified with Zoroaster by Clemens Alexandrinus (*Strom*, V, 14). The issue of synaesthesia became very important in the second half of the nineteenth century and will be considered in detail in the next chapter.

8   See John Gage, *Colour and Culture: Practice and Meaning from Antiquity to Abstraction* (London, 1993), Nuremberg, *passim*, but especially pp. 227ff.

9   Whose *Geschichtspiegel* (1654), he found very inspiring: Runge, *Hinterlassenen Schriften*, vol. I, pp. 183f. But see Irmgard Boetther in *Deutsche Dichter des 17. Jahrhunderts* by Harald Steinhagen and Benno von Wiese (Berlin, 1984), p. 304. Harsdoerffer had certainly read Athanasius Kircher, as is clear from his *Deliciae Mathematicae et Physicae . . . der Mathematischen und Philosophischen Erquickstunden*, 3 vols (Frankfurt, 1636–51). Boehme is very emphatic about black, white and the three primary colours: most explicitly in his *Mysterium Pansophicum oder Gruendlicher Bericht von dem Irdischen und Himmlischen Mysterio*; first published in 1620; seventh text, *3ff. (See *Alle Göttliche Schriften*, Stuttgart, 1730; reprinted 1957), vol. IV, 8, pp. 105f. In fact, Boehme's five colours are blue, red, green and yellow, with white as the fifth colour and quintessence. Black does not belong to this *mysterium* – it is a mystery of its own, available only to those who 'have the speech of nature' which is opened to them by the Holy Spirit.

10 On François d'Aguilon as an illustrator and interlocutor of Rubens, see Christopher White, *Peter Paul Rubens* (New Haven, CT and London, 1987), pp. 146ff., 150f. Goethe was well informed about them, though he used their work a little tendentiously in the historical introduction to his *Farbenlehre*. See his *Werke*, ed. Ernst Beutler (Zürich, 1964), vol. XVI, pp. 431ff., 441ff.

11 It was a great curiosity. The polymathic Count Algarotti suggested that soon ladies would be able to wear ribbons 'composed by Paisiello', while more seriously, Denis Diderot returned to it many times. In the *Encyclopédie*, he had himself written an extended article on the *Claveçin oculaire*, and although he is clear about its technical difficulties, defends it: 'cette machine ingénieuse que peu de gens ont vue, dont plusieurs ont parlé et dont l'invention ferait bien l'honneur à la plupart de ceux qui en ont parlé avec dédain'. More seriously, elsewhere he considers it as a device to teach the deaf about music, and even sound in general. 'Lettre sur les Sourds et Muets', in *Oeuvres complètes*, ed. Chronologique, introduction by Roger Lewinter (Paris, 1969–73), vol. II, pp. 531ff. He returns to it in the 'Rêve d'Alembert' (vol. VIII, p. 97) and even in the slightly salacious 'Les Bijoux Indiscrets' (vol. I, p. 765).

12 It is not certain that the London version was actually operated; one Georges Guyot (presumably the inventor and physicist, whose four-volume *Nouvelles Récréations physiques et mathématiques* (Besançon, 1769–70) was known to Goethe (vol. XVI, pp. 654ff.), suggested a further refinement, adapting the recently invented Argand lamps which much impressed Darwin. The best account of Castel's instruments and their technical problems is in Gage, *Colour and Culture*; and again in Martin Kemp's *The Science of Art* (New Haven, CT and London, 1990), pp. 287ff. See also Erasmus Darwin, *The Botanic Garden*, part II (London, 1789 [part I, which was illustrated by Henry Fuseli, is dated 1791]), pp. 127ff.

13 Ostwald discusses his meeting with Munsell, and the importance of Runge's model in his autobiography, *Lebenslinien* (Berlin, 1926–7), vol. III, pp. 60ff., 360ff., though Ostwald criticized Munsell for his excessive reliance on Helmholtz as well as for his placing the primaries on the ecliptic, not on the equator of his colour-sphere.

   An earlier attempt to find a three-dimensional 'colour-body' (in his case, a pyramid) by the Berlin mathematician Johann Heinrich Lambert is compared unfavourably to Runge's sphere by Goethe (*Werke*, vol. xvi, pp. 640f.). But see Gage, *Colour and Culture*, pp. 108ff.

14 Runge's announcement of his formulation was a book with a long title, which begins: *Farben-Kugel oder Construction der Verhältnisse aller Mischungen der Farben zu einander . . .* and ends: *nebst einer Abhandlung über die Bedeutung der Farben in der Natur von Hm. Prof. Henrik Steffens von Halle* (Hamburg, 1810). Steffens was a Danish biologist. The division into three colours had already been considered by Robert Waller in an early edition of the Royal Society's *Philosophical Transactions*, according to Hermann Helmholtz, *On the Sensations of Tone* (London, 1885), p. 64.

15 Although Castel is not mentioned, Newton's colour ideas are discussed sympathetically in Runge, *Farben-Kugel*, pp. 102ff.

16 Writing to Tieck (in April 1803) he shows a regular hexagon generated by six circles and adds: 'Das ist die erste Figur der Schöpfung. Die 6 ist nach dem Sündenfall nicht verstanden, und wird nicht verstanden bis der kommt wo alles zum Licht zurücklehrt, das ist, der siebente Tag . . . '. Runge, *Hinterlassenen Schriften*, vol. i, pp. 40f. The sevenfold colours are discussed in vol. i, pp. 105ff.

17 Jonathan Crary, *Techniques of the Observer* (Cambridge, MA, 1990), p. 16.

18 So, for instance, he relates different material qualities to each art: relation or figuration correspond to architecture; so does beat or rhythm; movement or form to sculpture and to melody; physical materiality to painting and to tone. Runge, *Hinterlassenen Schriften*, vol. i, pp. 189ff. The word appears in the nineteenth century to signify both the occurrence of a common feeling in several individuals or, alternatively, a sensation experienced in one part of the body when the stimulus is applied to another. But see chapter Five, note 1.

19 Novalis (Friedrich von Hardenberg), *Schriften*, ed. J. Minor (Jena, 1907), vol. ii, pp. 114; cf. p. 192.

20 What remains of them is housed in the Kunsthalle in Hamburg: *Morning* exists in a smaller preliminary version (1808; Inv. no. 1016) and a rather different final full-size but unfinished one (1809–10; Inv. no. 1022). There are also highly finished ink drawings for all four times (Inv. nos 34177 *Morning*; 34177 *Noon*; 34170 *Evening*; 34181 *Night*) done in 1803, which show the project in its primitive version.

21 John Constable, *Correspondence*, ed. R. B. Beckett (Ipswich, 1962–8), vol. vi, p. 98., cf. Keith Thomas, *Man in the Natural World* (London, 1983).

22 Kurt Badt, *Constable's Clouds* (London, 1950).

23 George Stubbs' work on the anatomy of the horse is well known; Alexander Cozens' very brief *A New Method of Assisting the Invention in Drawing Original Compositions of Landscape* (London, 1786; reprinted 1977) is much less familiar.

24 The best known were Joseph Anton Koch (who later worked with the Nazarenes and influenced their ideas on the subject) and Johann Christian Reinhart. On Koch and Reinhart, see Cornelius Gurlitt, *Deutsche Kunst seit 1800* (Berlin, 1824), pp. 113ff., and Rudolf Zeitler, *Klassizismus und Utopia* (Stockholm, 1954), pp. 165ff.

25 Johann Georg Sulzer, *Allgemeine Theorie der Schönen Künste* (Leipzig, 1792–3), *s.v.* 'Landschaft'; vol. iii, p. 146. But Burke's ideals had long been current: *di mezzo alla tema esce il diletto* – 'out of fear springs pleasure' italicizes Piranesi, *Diverse Maniere d'Adornare i Cammini ed Ogni Altra Parte degli Edifizi Desunte dall'Architettura Egizia, Etrusca e Greca* (Rome, 1769), p. 10.

26 See Gustav Pauli, *Die Kunst des Klassizismus un der Romantik* (Berlin, 1925), pp. 99f. These have come to be known as *Rückenfiguren*; on which, in the painting of Friedrich and his contemporaries, see Joseph Leo Koerner, *Caspar David Friedrich* (London, 1990), pp. 240ff.

27 See Wolfgang Roch, *Philipp Otto Runges Kunstanschauung* (Strasbourg, 1909), pp. 66ff.

28 The painting for the chapel of Schloss Tetschen (and therefore known as the Tetschener Altar, though Tetschen is now called Děčin, in the Czech Republic) was begun for King Gustav iv of Sweden (whose troubles led to his deposition in 1809); the unfinished picture, which was Friedrich's first important oil painting, was commissioned explicitly as an altarpiece by the

owner of the castle, Graf Franz-Anthon von Thun-Hohenstein, in 1808. The elaborately carved frame was designed by Friedrich himself and carved by a local sculptor, Karl Gottlob Kühn. A preliminary drawing for the picture in its setting is shown and discussed by Koerner, *Caspar David Friedrich*, pp. 47ff. It is now in the Kupferstichkabinett in Dresden, while the picture is in the Gemäldegalerie. The controversy is summarized by Timothy Frank Mitchell, 'Philipp Otto Runge and Caspar David Friedrich', Indiana University, PhD thesis (Indianapolis, IN, 1977), pp. 222ff. (digest in *Art History*, X/3 (1987), pp. 315ff.).

On the place of the painting in the development of the 'uniconic' religious landscape painting, see Charles Rosen and Henri Zerner, *Romanticism and Realism: The Mythology of Nineteenth-Century Art* (New York, 1984), pp. 51ff.

29 C. Gustav Carus, *Neun Briefe über die Landschaftsmalerei geschrieben in den Jahren, 1815–1824 zuvor ein Brief von Goethe als Einleitung* (Dresden, 1831; reprinted 1923), *passim*, but especially pp.61ff. On his morphological explorations and proportional theories, see chapter Five.

30 Tieck therefore overlapped with Weber who was its *Kappelmeister* until 1821 – he died on tour in London, in 1826.

31 On Carus (as painter) and Dahl, see Cornelius Gurlitt, *Die Deutsche Kunst seit 1800* (Berlin, 1924), pp. 100ff.

32 Though Hegel thinks of it in relation to 'classical' architecture, which is considered dependent on a priori deduction, and not on imitation: *Ästhetik* (Berlin, 1965), vol. II, pp. 52f.

33 Immanuel Kant, *Kritik der Urteilskraft*, §53.

34 Goethe, *Werke*, VIII, p. 314; in 'Wilhelm Meisters Wanderjahre'.

35 At this very time, Julius Schnorr von Karolsfeld was completing his *Nibelungen* frescoes in the Munich Residenz for Ludwig I.

36 In fact, the *Flying Dutchman* was drawn from a text of Heinrich Heine which may have recalled a play he saw in London in 1826 (*The Flying Dutchman or the Phantom Ship* by Edward Fitzball). Heine's account of the legend (in the sixth chapter of his *Memorien des Herrn Schnabelewopsky*) may, in Wagner's mind, have overlaid the impression of the near-shipwreck of the boat which carried him from Riga to London in 1839. Wagner probably also owes his account of the Tannhäuser legend to Heine (as well as Tieck and E.T.A. Hoffmann). The libretto of *Flying Dutchman* was bought by the Paris Opéra, and to Wagner's chagrin passed to a now-forgotten composer, Pierre-Louis Dietsch – who would later conduct the first performance of the revised *Tannhäuser* in 1861.

Wagner sent the manuscript of the *Ring* to Schopenhauer (who did not care for the *Dutchman* and *Lohengrin*, both of which he had seen), who suggested that Wagner should abandon music and devote himself to literature, for which he was obviously more gifted.

37 Unlike his contemporary, the positivist, Auguste Comte, who developed a church with a clerisy and a liturgy to perpetuate his social doctrine. See Frank E. Manuel and Fritzie Manuel, *Utopian Thought in the Western World* (Cambridge, MA, 1979).

38 Richard Wagner, 'Das Kunstwerk der Zukunft' in 'Die Groszten Reformatischen Schriften der Züricher Epoche' (bibliographical data, pp. 106ff.) in *Die Hauptschriften*, ed. Ernst Bücken (Stuttgart, 1956), pp. 108ff.

39 The term *Handwerk* had quite a different sense for Goethe: see Karl Muthesius, *Goethe und das Handwerk* (Leipzig, 1927); esp. pp. 29ff. on his pleasure in the practical details of building.

40 Richard Wagner, *Gesammelte Schriften und Dichtungen*, 3rd edn (Leipzig, n.d.), vol. III; 'Die Kunst und die Revolution', pp. 8ff.; 'Das Kunstwerk der Zukunft', pp. 42ff.; 'Opern und Drama', pp. 222ff. On *Handwerk*, see pp. 24ff.

Curiously enough, both Marx and Engels disapproved of Wagner's view of prehistoric mores in the *Nibelungenlied*: see Karl Marx and Friedrich Engels, *Selected Works*, vol. II, p. 199. Marx was shocked (if Engels is to be believed) by Wagner's view of the old gods as guilty of lewd behaviour, 'promiscuity spiced with incest' as Marx put it in a letter to Engels of 1882.

'In primaeval times', he adds, 'the sister was the bride and that was moral'. The issue is given a long note by Engels in the fourth edition of 'The Origin of the Family'.

41 Harald Szeeman, ed., *Der Hang zum Gesamtkunstwerk* (Arrau, 1983), pp. 197ff.

42 Ernest Newman, *The Life of Richard Wagner* (New York, 1937), vol. II, pp. 430ff.

43 The painter's son Ludwig was to become Wagner's favourite *Heldentenor* and was the first *Tristan* in 1855; but see also note 35.

44 A Viennese wit of the time observed that were he to be told that the end of the world was coming to Vienna, he would move to Dresden, where it was sure to come ten years later.

45 Henry Cole, visiting Dresden in 1851, reports that the king, interpellated on Semper's behalf, replied that if he ever got hold of his architect, he would 'hang him in his own theatre' . MS notes quoted by Harry Francis Mallgrave, *Gottfried Semper: Architect of the Nineteenth Century* (New Haven, CT and London, 1996) p. 173. I have relied on Mallgrave's book for much that follows.

46 Published by the prestigious house Vieweg in Brunswick in 1849.

47 Matthew Digby Wyatt's report on the exhibition quoted by Peter Berlyn and Charles Fowler in their *The Crystal Palace: Its Architectural History and Constructive Marvels* (London, 1851), pp. 18f.

48 A good account of antecedents was already given by Berlyn and Fowler, *The Crystal Palace*, pp. 15ff.

49 On which see *Hector Horeau, 1801–1872*, exh. cat., Musée des Arts Décoratifs (Paris, 1977), cat. no. 22.

50 The name was devised by the journalist Douglas Jerrold, a friend of Paxton who was the editor of *Punch*.

51 Offered by analogy to Early English by Samuel Phillips in *Guide to the Crystal Palace and Park* (London, 1854), p. 24.

52 'The primaries of equal intensities will harmonize or neutralize each other in the proportions of 3 yellow, 5 red, 8 blue – integrally 16': Proposition V in 'An Attempt to Define the Principles which should regulate the employment of colour in the Decorative Arts' of 1852, in his *Lectures on Architecture and the Decorative Arts* (London, 1863), pp. 12ff., 20. These principles Jones ascribes to the trinitarian paint-manufacturer and theorist – John Constable's friend, George Field – whose work closely parallels that of his better-known French contemporary, Michel Chevreuil. The parallel to Runge's colour theory was pointed out by Gage, *Colour and Culture*, pp. 221ff.

The story of the Paxton introduction and the disappointment is told by Wolfgang Herrmann, *Gottfried Semper: In Search of Architecture* (Cambridge, MA, 1984), pp. xi, 36ff.

53 Jeffrey A. Auerbach, *The Great Exhibition of 1851: A Nation on Display* (New Haven, CT and London, 1999), pp. 114ff. On the sculpture and its many copies, see Vivien M. Green, 'Hiram Power's Greek Slave: Emblem of Freedom', *American Art Journal* (Autumn 1982), pp. 31ff.

54 Mallgrave, *Gottfried Semper*, p. 208.

55 The substance of the lectures Semper was giving at the Academy seemed to him to provide the material for an innovative treatise on all the arts.

56 Herrmann, *Gottfried Semper*, pp. 139ff. Carl (Gottlieb Wilhelm) Boetticher published *Die tektonik der Hellenen* in Berlin, 1844–52. But see also Wolfgang Herrmann, *Der Theoretische Nachlass in der ETH Zürich* (Zürich, 1981), pp. 26ff., 113f.; for direct quotations, pp. 119f., 167f.

57 Adolf Max Vogt, 'Gottfried Semper und Joseph Paxton', in ETH Zürich, *Gottfried Semper und die Mitte des Neunzehnten Jarhunderts* (Zürich, 1976), pp. 175ff. Wolfgang Herrmann, *Gottfried Semper: In Search of Architecture* (Cambridge, MA, 1984), pp. xiff.

58 Herrmann, *Gottfried Semper*, pp. 72ff.

59 Owen Jones, *The Grammar of Ornament* [1956] (London, 1867), pp. 154ff. The 'Aphorisms', which were published separately several times, are on pp. 5ff.

60 Ibid., p. 154.

61 John Ruskin, *The Works of John Ruskin*, ed. E. T. Cook and A. Wedderburn (London, 1903–12), vol. x, pp. 180ff.; *The Stones of Venice* (London, 1851–3), vol. II, pp. 151ff.

62 John Ruskin, *Modern Painters* (London, 1860–69), vol. IV, 3, §7.

63 John Guille Millais, *The Life and Letters of Sir John Everett Millais* (New York, 1899), vol. I, p. 61.

64 William Sharp, *Dante Gabriel Rossetti: A Record and a Study* (London, 1882), pp. 11ff. Brown's Belgian masters were Jakob Franz Gregorius and Peter van Hanselaere.

65 Millais, *The Life and Letters of Sir John Everett Millais*, vol. I, p. 49. Presumably these 'Quattro-Centists' were the Nazarenes.

66 The original Brothers beside Millais and Hunt were Dante Gabriel and Michael Rossetti, Thomas Woolner (a sculptor best known for the bust of Tennyson) and James Collinson. Arthur Hughes, Frederic Sandys and the poet Coventry Patmore were among the 'sympathiz-ers' and Ford Madox Brown was a sceptical but benevolent observer. Holman Hunt, Rossetti and Millais all tell of the foundation differently; whether the foundation meeting in Millais' studio ever happened is not now clear. Elizabeth Prettejohn, *The Art of the Pre-Raphaelites* (London, 2000), pp. 23ff.

67 All (and more) quoted by Millais, *The Life and Letters of Sir John Everett Millais*, vol. I, pp. 74ff.

68 On this 'secular altarpiece': see Tim Barringer, *Men at Work, Art and Labour in Victorian England* (New Haven, CT, 2005), pp. 21ff.

69 George Edmund Street (1824–81) was also an architect favoured by the Tractarians; a pupil of Giles Gilbert Scott, a learned Gothicist, his most important building was not a church, but the new Law Courts in London.

70 Unlike the decorations of the roof which William Morris restored himself in 1875. But see Prettejohn, *The Art of the Pre-Raphaelites*, pp. 100ff.

71 C. L. Eastlake, *A History of the Gothic Revival in England* (London, 1872), pp. 252f., 384. Dyce's wall paintings had deteriorated so much that they had to be restored in 1864; in spite of that, by 1909 they were covered over by somewhat etiolated panel-painted copies by Ninian Comper.

72 Wilfrid Blunt, *'England's Michelangelo': A Biography of George Frederic Watts* (London, 1975), pp. 96ff. Though it is only fair to add that the house had been internally rebuilt by Albert Speer's office when it was being used as the German Embassy in the 1930s.

73 P. P. Marshall was a surveyor friend of Madox Brown; Charles Faulkner a mathematics don at Oxford who doubled as a decorative painter.

74 See Mark Girouard, *The Queen-Anne Style* (London and New Haven, CT, 1977), passim.

75 First formulated in a letter to the *Manchester Examiner* in the *Manchester Guardian* (*Examiner*), 14 March 1883. Quoted by Fiona McCarthy, *William Morris: A Life for Our Time* (New York, 1995), p. 467. Morris liked the sentence and repeated it often.

76 J. W. Mackail, *The Life of William Morris*, new ed. (London, 1901), vol. II, p. 135.

77 Unlike the fiery Romantics who shouted down Quatremère de Quincy some thirty years earlier, these were young fogeys defending the academic orthodoxy of their teachers.

78 But this had to follow the deductive method from premises provided by new structural necessities.

79 (*Entretiens*), *Discourses on Architecture*, vol. I, pp. 250ff. The following quotation is from the article 'Peinture' in the *Dictionnaire raisonné de l'architecture* (Paris, 1854–68), vol. VII, pp. 56ff.

80 James Fergusson, *History of the Modern Styles of Architecture*, 3rd edn, by Robert Kerr (London, 1891), vol. II, p. 100 and note.

81 James Fergusson, *A History of Architecture in All Countries*, 3rd edn, by R. Phené Spiers (London, 1893), vol. I, pp. 37ff., 46.

82 Fergusson, *A History of Architecture*, vol. I, p. 123. On the *Bauakademie*, ibid., vol. II, pp. 202f.; on Semper in Dresden, pp. 211f. On Fergusson's projects, see J. Mordaunt Crook, *The Dilemma of Style* (London, 1987), pp.128ff.

83 In 1844 he had been suspended from the chair at Tübingen (to which he had just been appointed) after his inaugural lecture on the place of Aesthetics in university teaching. This would hardly seem to invite revolutionary incitement, though it was considered an intellectual threat by the Würtemberg establishment who treated any remark on the master as suspect – those were the days of the young Hegelians.

84 Theodor Vischer had suggested, when in Dresden, and in a collection of essays that he published in 1844, that the *Nibelungenlied* could be the perfect subject for the truly German opera – Wagner may have picked that suggestion up from Vischer.

85 See Otto Antonia Graf, *Otto Wagner* (Vienna, 1985), vol. I, pp. 275f., II, pp. 606, 705f. He returned to Semper both for ideas and for themes; Otto Wagner, *Modern Architecture* (Los Angeles, CA, 1988), pp. 13f., Longer discussion by Mallgrave, *Gottfried Semper*, pp. 368ff. His self-proclaimed motto *sola domina artis necessitas* is an extrapolation from Semper's essential teaching.

86 Newman, *The Life of Richard Wagner*, vol. III, pp. 212, for an extended account of their doomed relationship.

87 Mallgrave, *Gottfried Semper*, pp. 252ff.; Newman, *The Life of Richard Wagner*, vol. III, pp. 386ff., 409ff. The Glaspalast had been built in 1853–4.

88 See Edouard Schuré, *Le Drame musical: Richard Wagner et son oeuvre*, 3rd edn (Paris, 1894), pp. 294ff. It provides a piously Wagnerite account of the theatre, and Semper is not even mentioned. But see Mallgrave, *Gottfried Semper*, pp. 262ff., for a salutary corrective to Wagnerolatry on this subject. The Ring cycle has been repeated yearly.

    The town already had an opera house from the time when it was the capital of the Margraves of Brandenburg-Kulmbach. It was built in the 1740s by the court-architect, Joseph St-Pierre, with interiors by the Bibbienas. It was, of course, too small (and quite inappropriate) for Wagner's purposes.

89 See McCarthy, *William Morris*, pp. 353, 372f. Morris also attended a rehearsal with the Burne-Joneses, sitting in the box beside Wagner's, who was there with the doyen Germanophiles of the day, George Eliot and G. H. Lewes.

    It is worth noting (in parenthesis), that George Eliot had been Feuerbach's English translator. The Burne-Joneses were committed Wagnerians. They attended several concerts and befriended Cosima, who called on them and was drawn by E. B.-J.; she made them a present of a cast of Beethoven's death-mask. G[eorgina] B[urne]-J[ones], *Memorial of Edward Burne-Jones* (London, 1907), vol. II, pp. 79f. In fact, Morris had not initiated the revival – Rossetti had attempted a version of the *Nibelungenlied* before 1850. But Morris, like Ruskin before him, hated Wagner's music.

90 He even proposed to translate the Persian epic, the *Shahnama* of Firdausi, though he abandoned the project.

91 C. R. Ashbee, *Journal*. Quoted by Alan Crawford, *C. R. Ashbee* (New Haven, CT and London, 1985), p. 26.

92 Norman Shaw, though he disliked him personally and thought he overcharged, nevertheless used Morris furnishings in many of his interiors, as did his disciples. McCarthy, *William Morris*, pp. 412ff.

Five: A New Century, a New Art

 1 Later (and more commonly) known as synaesthesia (p. 386 n.). It was probably coined by St George Jackson Mivart, a distinguished, if perverse 'evolutionary biologist' in his book *The Cat*, which first appeared in London in 1881. The *American Journal of Psychology* (VII, 90) ascribed the word to the French psychic investigator Théodore Flournoy – whose paper was

called 'Enquête sur l'audition colorée'; on which, in relation to Galton's investigations, see Frederic W. H. Myers, *Human Personality and its Survival of Bodily Death* (London, 1903), vol. I, pp. 222f, 565ff.; vol. II, pp. 270f. The *Trésor de la langue française* dates the first French use of *synesthésie* to 1888, without quoting a source. In fact, the French term seems to have been coined by a physician, Jules Millet, in *L'Audition colorée* (thesis presented to the Faculty of Medicine at Montpellier in 1892, or so Victor Ségalen in his *Synesthésies et l'école symboliste* (Paris, 1981) (though written about 1900 – by 1913 he called it his *péché de jeunesse*), p. 55, n. 1. A number of other words had been used for the phenomenon. Yet another oculist, F. Suarez de Mendoza (*L'Audition colorée: étude sur les fausses sensations secondaires physiologiques*, Paris 1892, suggested the term *pseudo-photesthésie*; another one, Chaballier, suggested *pseudo-chromesthésie*.

As a footnote on a footnote, it might be worth noting that half a century later Charles Ogden (I. A. Richards and James Wood in *The Foundations of Aesthetics*, 2nd edn, New York, 1925, pp. 7, 72ff.) suggested that the word implying, as it does, the satisfaction of all senses, might be used to signify beauty in general. German writers did not appeal to Greek and called it *Farbenhören*, which is not in Grimm but appears in recent dictionaries (such as the *Duden*). The French called it *audition colorée* – which, as far as the *Trésor* is concerned – has to be considered a 'morbid phenomenon' – as has the parallel *audition gustative*.

The empirical investigation of the phenomenon begins in a sense with John Locke's account of the man blinded in childhood (in fact, the mathematician Nicholas Saunderson, though Locke does not name him), saying that the sound of trumpets corresponds to the colour scarlet. The idea was developed by a scholar-journalist of Leipzig, Johann Leonhard Hoffmann (*Versuch einer Geschichte der malerischen Harmonie überhaupt und der Farbenharmonie insbesondere...* Halle, 1786), who built up an elaborate scale of correspondences between colour and sound and compared the painter's setting of the colours on his palette to the orchestra tuning. Goethe appreciated his scepticism about Castel's *clavichord* (*Werke*, ed. Ernst Beutler, Zürich, 1948–64, vol. XVI, pp. 682ff.). It has been recently suggested that synaesthetic perception may be sufficiently unusual to be considered a neurological disorder. The case examined was of a subject who saw taste in terms of touch. See Richard E. Cytowic, *The Man Who Tasted Shapes: A Bizarre Medical Mystery Offers Revolutionary Insights into Emotion, Reasoning and Consciousness* (New York, 1993). Cytowic has also contributed to *Synaesthesia: Classic and Contemporary Readings*, ed. Simon Baron-Cohen and John E. Harrison (Oxford, 1997). The matter was the subject of intense scientific curiosity between 1870 and 1910, and although interest declined for the next seventy years, it has again become very interesting to neurologists and psychologists. Synaesthesia has two aspects: 'constructed' by artists in the way I have been describing, and an involuntarily experience by select individuals (currently calculated at about 1 in 25,000, though there may be more). It sometimes occurs in families and may therefore be genetically determined. It does not seem to have a direct relation either to intelligence or to artistic ability, and although variants of tone-colour vision may be the most common, connection of hearing with taste, taste with touch and so on are also known. Curiously enough, Nordau's commination is not mentioned in the recent publications.

2 Mivart, *The Cat*, idem.

3 Francis Galton FRS, *Inquiries into Human Faculty and its Development* (London, 1883, 2nd edn, 1911; I quote from the reprint of 1928), pp. 57ff. for mental imagery generally, pp. 105ff. for colour association.

4 See a brief summary of recent discussion in *Synesthesia: The Strangest Thing* by John Harrison (Oxford, 2001), pp. 25ff.

5 The three scientists, Michael Faraday and John Tyndall as well as Sir Charles Wheatstone; although they are mostly remembered for their electrical discoveries, they were all interested more generally in the phenomena of sound. Wheatstone's acoucryphone, which he invented

in the 1820s, took up seventeenth-century ideas of resonance and worked by transmitting sound vibrations over distance; though, in fact, his main contribution to music was the invention of the concertina in 1829, the same year in which Cyrillus Damian patented the accordion in Vienna; the concertina was much preferred by musicians. An improved patent was registered in 1844.

The experimental basis of such instruments was described by John Tyndall in his book *Sound*, which first appeared in 1867 (I quote the 4th edition of 1908, which has an added account of the microphone, phonograph and telephone), pp. 236ff. Of course, gas was the very popular new lighting fuel: the first gas lamps were installed in London about 1810, but efficient gas lighting was not really available until late in the 1850s.

6 Kastner's father, Emmanuel, had been a composer and a man of letters; Georg Friedrich, who died young (1852–82), is known for a few papers on electricity apart from the pyrophone or *Flammenorgel*, about which he wrote a pamphlet, *Les Flammes chantantes* (Paris, 1873), of which I have not found a copy. The only surviving pyrophone seems to be the one stored in the warehouse of the Science Museum in London, though some of the glass tubes are broken.

7 H[elena] P[etrovna] Blavatsky, *The Secret Doctrine: The Synthesis of Science, Religion and Philosophy* (London, 1888), vol. I, pp. 204f., which claims to be the revelation of a Vedic document that survived only in Chinese and Tibetan translation.

8 Annie Besant and C. W. Leadbeater, *Thought-forms* (London, 1905), see especially pp. 75ff. See also C. W. Leadbeater, *Man, Visible and Invisible* (London, 1902), pp. 70ff.

9 Walter Pater, *The Renaissance* (London, 1924), pp. 135, 140, 144 ('The School of Giorgione'). There are some textual variations between editions and I have taken some liberties with the arrangement of the quotation.

10 Who called his *Orientales*, 'un livre inutile de poésie pure'. The enormously popular *Orientales* went through fourteen 'editions' in January and February 1829; the preface of both the first and the fourteenth edition could be read as manifestos of *l'art pour l'art*. See Victor Hugo, *Les Orientales*, ed. Elisabeth Barineau (Paris, 1952), pp. 5ff., 15ff.

11 'L'Ecole Païenne', an attack on his fellow Parnassians, including his friend Gautier; first printed in *La Semaine Théâtrale* of 1852 and reprinted in *La Revue de poche* in 1866. Baudelaire, *Oeuvres complètes*, ed. Claude Pichois (Paris, 1975), vol. II, pp. 44ff., 1098ff.

12 Théophile Gautier, *Mademoiselle de Maupin* (Paris, 1907), p. 22.

13 The *Idylls* appeared in 1869; the unnamed critic may well have been Swinburne. See Hallam Tennyson, *Alfred Lord Tennyson: A Memoir by his Son* (London, 1897), vol. II, p. 92. And Hallam adds in a footnote: 'He quoted Georges Sand: "L'art pour l'art est un vain mot: l'art pour le vrai, l'art pour le beau et le bon, voilà la religion que je cherche".' On the slogan *l'art pour l'art*, see René Jasinski, *Les Années romantiques de Théophile Gautier* (Paris, 1929), pp. 210ff., and Adolphe Boschot, *Théophile Gautier* (Paris, 1933), pp. 346ff.

14 William Gaunt, *The Aesthetic Adventure* (London, 1945), pp. 53f., 57, where he is said to have been particularly partial to St Alban's, Holborn, by William Butterfield, though there does not seem to have been such a church (St Andrew's, Holborn, is by Christopher Wren). Maybe All Saints', Margaret Street, is intended. It is worth remembering that one of his pupils was Gerard Manley Hopkins, who remained on friendly terms with Pater until his death. His trinity, a malicious contemporary said, were holy light, flowers and incense.

15 Walter Pater, *The Renaissance* (London, 1870; 1924 edn), pp. 249f.: 'Conclusion'. Pater must have been very pleased with that last phrase since he was quoting it from his review of *The Poems of William Morris* in the *Westminster Review*, XXXIV (1868), quoted by Ian Small in *The Aesthetes: A Sourcebook* (London, 1979), p. 20. It is perhaps invidious to ask how a flame might be hard or gemlike, nor is it quite clear where or how the notion of a 'religion of art' was formulated. It was certainly about in the late 1860s and the '70s. See Leon Chai, *Aestheticism: The Religion of Art in Post-Romantic Literature* (New York, 1990).

16 'Sitôt assis, le néophyte entrait en transe, prenait sa tête entre ses mains et ne répondait plus que par monosyllabes exclamatives à ses voisins et copains.' Léon Daudet, *Souvenirs* (Paris, 1920), p. 281. The younger Daudet (son of the more famous Alphonse) was the editor of *L'Action française*.

17 *Les Fleurs du mal*, IV. Charles Baudelaire, *Oeuvres*, ed. Claude Pichois (Paris, 1975), pp. 11, 839ff. He returns to the theme in the last verse of 'Toute entière', XLI, p. 55:

> *O metamorphose mystique*
> *De tous mes sens fondus en un . . .*

18 Philipp Otto Runge, *Hinterlassenen Schriften*, vol. II, pp. 482ff., especially pp. 486f.

19 It is the section on colour. Baudelaire, *Oeuvres* (1976), vol. II, pp. 68ff.

20 E.T.A. Hoffmann, *Werke*, ed. Martin Hürliman (Zürich, 1946), vol. I, p. 406. Since I translate directly from the German, it does not correspond exactly to Baudelaire's beautiful version. The instrument at the end is the *hautbois* in French (as in the sonnet); it is *Bassetthorn* in German – which is in fact the tenor clarinet. Hoffmann became somewhat pedantic about it further on when he spoke of 'wearing a dress which was coloured in C flat so that I had to calm the spectators by wearing a collar of an F major colour'.

There is an extended discussion of this theme in 'Colour Musik' (*sic*) which the Viennese critic-*littérateur*, Hermann Bahr, first published in his *Renaissance* (Berlin, n.d.) and reprinted in the *Hermann-Bahr-Buch* (Berlin, 1913), pp. 129ff. Bahr recalls newspaper reports about Liszt, when conducting, saying to the orchestra: 'This passage, gentlemen should be played more blue, and other the redder.' Bahr maintained that synaesthesia was part of his everyday experience.

Though he was an artist of the Tieck-Wackenroder generation (and a friend of Tieck) Hoffmann made his living as a Prussian civil servant. His music is now largely forgotten but he remains the great fabulist of German Romanticism. In his own time he was read appreciatively in Paris – his collected works were published in French in 1824. Nodier was as much an admirer as Baudelaire. Offenbach made a number of his short stories into the libretto of his last, and one 'serious' opera, *Les Contes de Hoffmann*. It was first performed posthumously in 1881.

While on extended duty in Warsaw, he had founded and directed a music society whose concerts he conducted. He also redecorated the part of the Mniszek palace where it met. For the first opera he composed, Friedrich de la Motte Fouqué himself provided the libretto by dramatizing his own (by-then famous) fairy-tale, *Undine;* it was first performed in 1816; *Undine* was first published in 1811. De la Motte Fouqué was of remote French extraction, but was at the time an officer in the Prussian army.

21 It was written in 1871 and counts as no. XLII of *Poésies; oeuvres complètes* (Paris, 1951), p. 103; comments on pp. 679ff. The variorum texts (Verlaine's and autograph versions in Arthur Rimbaud, *Oeuvres complètes*, vol. I, *Poésies*, ed. Steve Murphy, Paris, 1999), pp. 579ff.

It was not universally welcomed: François Coppé, for instance – a poet whom both Verlaine and Rimbaud knew well – wrote:

> *Rimbaud, fumiste réussi,*
> *Dans un sonnet que je déplore.*
> *Veut que les lettres O, E, I,*
> *Forment le drapeau tricolore*

See *Ballade des Vieux Parnassiens*, quoted by Michel Décaudin in 'Rimbaud et les Symbolistes'; *L'Harne, Cahier Rimbaud* (Paris, 1993), p. 60.

Much ink has been spilt since it was published on the attribution of an allegedly deep knowledge of alchemy and the Kabbalah to an eighteen-year-old Rimbaud – or blaming the analogy on his extreme capriciousness. The most extended commentary is that of (René) Etiemble, *Le mythe de Rimbaud*, vol. II: *Structure du mythe* (Paris, 1952), pp. 81ff. But see a briefer and more sober account in *Rimbaud L'enfant* by C. A. Hackett (Paris, 1948), pp. 116ff. The source of the occult ideas were supposed to have been the writings of 'Eliphas Lévi' (real name, Alphonse Louis Constant), though his most famous work, *Dogme et rituel de la haute magie* (1854–6), does not have such synaesthetic teaching. Rimbaud may have been echoing the teaching methods of his gentle, generous, tubercular musician friend Ernest Cabaner, known in his day as a composer of popular *chansons*, who was developing a complex theory of correspondence between the notes of the scale, numbers and letters – including diph-thongs – so that his sonnet, which he dedicated to Rimbaud, dealt with seven spectrum colours. His curious and cruel relation to Cabaner has been sketched by Jean-Jacques Lefrère and Michael Pakenham, *Cabaner, poète au piano* (Paris, 1994), pp. 48ff. The sonnet, dedicated to 'Rimbald' (a private joke) is reproduced and discussed by Claude Colomer in his *Ernest Cabaner, musicien catalan* (Montpellier, 1993), pp. 114. The sonnet, unknown to Rimbaud's earlier biographers, was part of the papers of Dr Gachet, best-known from a portrait by Van Gogh (now in the Metropolitan Museum, New York) which his son left to the Bibliothèque Nationale.

René Ghil, whose *Traité du verbe* (of 1886) became the most important Symbolist liter-ary theoretical work (it had a preface by Mallarmé, which he also later modified and pub-lished as 'Divigations'), adopted Rimbaud's identification of colour with vowel-sound. Gustav Theodor Fechner's *Vorschule der Aesthetik* (Leipzig, 1876) – of which more later, and which Rimbaud could not have known – has a curious appendix dealing with the colour association of vowels: vol. I, p. 176, vol. II, p. 315; they show no statistical agreement, however, and the letter 'a', which Rimbaud associates with black, seems mostly associated with white and red. Some years later Francis Galton provided an extended account of the association of numbers with geometrical figures as well as with vowels, as I pointed out in note 3.

22 About the turn of the century, and shortly before he fell victim to the General Paralysis of the Insane, Guy de Maupassant, cruising between Cannes and Savona, heard Sunday-night band music from San Remo over the dark and misty sea. He invoked first the Baudelaire and then the Rimbaud sonnets (both of which he transcribed) to acount for the hypersensitivity which he was developing – and it set him off on a meditation about the artist's dependance on sensory data; Guy de Maupassant, *Oeuvres complètes* (Paris, 1909), vol. XXVIII: 'La Vie errante', pp. 18ff. The cruise took place in 1889 and the book first appeared in 1890. He died in 1893.

23 *Orgue-à-bouche*; the French call the mouth-organ *harmonica*. The book was published in 1884.

24 Antoine-Louis Clapisson, a very successful composer of operettas and operas (now largely forgotten), died in 1866.

25 It was named in the 1850s, but clinically described by an American physician, George Miller Beard, in 1886; but see Deborah L. Silverman, *Art-Nouveau in Fin-de-Siècle France* (Berkeley and Los Angeles, 1989), p. 80.

26 J.-K. Huysmans, *A Rebours* [1884] (Paris, 1903), pp. 62ff. 149ff., 166ff. (The country doctor sum-moned by the servants knows nothing of neurasthenia and Huysmans unfortunately does not bother to quote the *quelques termes médicaux* which the confused doctor *bafouille*; and he has the duke reflect [pp. 183f.]: 'A quoi bon bouger, quand on peut voyager si magnifiquement sur une chaise? N'était-il pas à Londres dont les senteurs, dont l'atmosphère, dont les habitants, dont les pâtures, dont les ustensiles l'environnaient?')

27 J.-K. Huysmans quoted by Sven Lövgren, *The Genesis of Modernism* (Bloomington, IN, 1971), pp. 15f.

28 Freud did not get involved in the Parisian art world – though his life-long friendship with the *diseuse* Yvette Guilbert (to whom Madame Charcot introduced him) was touching. She was one of the few people to call him 'Freud' without any suffix. On the friendship, see Ernest Jones, *Sigmund Freud: Life and Work* (London, 1953–7), vol. III, pp. 111, 130, 145f. On the encounter with Nordau (whom Freud found 'vain and stupid'), ibid., vol. I, p. 205. Though her voice has been recorded, Yvette Guilbert was really immortalized in a lithograph by Toulouse-Lautrec.

29 It was dedicated to Cesare Lombroso, the first master of a 'scientific' criminology that was based on classifying the physique of criminal types, and made much of genetic degeneracy.

30 Max Nordau, *Entartung* (Berlin, 1892) trans. as *Degeneration* (London, 1895). As an example of regression, he pedantically instances *pholas dactylus*, a kind of cockle endowed with a very sensitive siphon-duct.

   On Huysmans, ibid., pp. 300ff. On Verlaine's degenerate physiognomy – with reference to Lombroso's criteria, pp. 118ff.; on Rimbaud's *Voyelles* and synaesthesia generally, pp. 139ff.; on Richard Wagner's 'Art-Work of the Future' (an extended attack), pp. 172ff. He also damns Zola, Tolstoy, Ibsen, Rodin and – of course – Nietzsche. Nordau's real name was Simon Maximilian Suedfeld and he had moved to Paris in 1880. He had a second career as a journalist. Soon after 1900 he became very active in the Zionist movement.

31 Charles Darwin, *The Origin of Species* (London, 1876), p. 428; (*The Works of Charles Darwin*, ed. Paul H. Barrett and R. B. Freeman (London, 1988), vol. XVI, p. 446.

32 It was extensively revised in 1887. Haeckel had in fact so named this class of marine creatures with a nuclear body and many fine radiating pseudopods. But more popular books, *Natürliche Schöpfungsgeschichte* (*The Natural History of Creation* – a popular version of his *General Morphology* of 1866) and *Die Welträtsel* (1899, *The Riddle of the Universe*) were also eagerly read by artists.

33 But it continued to inspire artists: the engraver Karl Blossfeldt had begun, in the 1890s, the series of photographs of natural forms, a hundred of which appeared as a book in 1929 as *Urformen der Kunst* with an introduction by Karl Nierendorf. These books went on intriguing artists. You need only look at Amédée Ozenfant's *L'Art* of 1929 or at the photographic decorations which Le Corbusier used in the entry hall of the Pavillon Suisse in Paris of 1931 to see the echoes of that fascination.

34 On the earliest aspiration to a new style, see above, p. 84ff.

35 On their debt to Pugin, see chapter Three.

36 Owen Jones, *The Grammar of Ornament* (London, 1856), p. 154.

37 It was not a new subject. The painter Richard Redgrave had already given a course of lectures on 'artistic botany for ornamentists', though even Dresser's title sounds more scientific than Redgrave's.

38 *The Rudiments of Botany, Structural and Physiological* (London, 1859 and 1860); *Unity in Variety as Deduced from the Vegetable Kingdom* (London, 1859 and 1860); *Popular Manual of Botany* (Edinburgh, 1860); and papers in the *Proceedings* of the Royal Institution and the *Transactions* of the Botanical Society of Edinburgh.

   The term *morphologie* may have been coined by the German biologist K. F. Burdach, but Goethe gave it real coinage in 1817 and became its main proponent.

39 Christopher Dresser, *Principles of Decorative Design* (London, 1873), though it was based on papers published in various periodicals (mostly the *Technical Educator*) from 1870 onwards.

40 John Ruskin, *Seven Lamps of Architecture* (London, 1849).

41 Stated first in his *Psychologie als Wissenschaft*, §30ff. In *Sämtliche Werke* (Hamburg, 1886); Herbart (though a pupil of Fichte) succeeded to Kant's chair at Königsberg in 1809.

42 Gustav Fechner was probably the first to do so systematically. He set out the method in his *Zur Experimentalen Ästhetik* (Leipzig, 1871). On him, see Rudolf Arnheim, 'The Other Gustav

Fechner', in *New Essays on the Psychology of Art* (Berkeley, CA, 1986), pp. 39–49.

43 Born in 1786, he died a centenarian.

44 Eugène Delacroix, considered by many the greatest colourist of his day, had been famously fascinated with the intense yellows achieved by masters like Rubens and Veronese. While painting one of the ceilings in the Luxembourg Palace, he decided to consult those masters in the Louvre. Having summoned a cab, which (like many Parisian ones at the time) was painted canary yellow, he suddenly observed that the shadow it cast was violet. That observation taught him the secret he sought, and the cab was dismissed. The story is told by Charles Blanc, *Grammaire des arts du dessin*, 2nd edn (Paris, 1870), p. 606. In April of the previous year, Goethe is said to have made a similar observation while walking with Eckermann.

His exploration of colour tonalities and contrasts would lead one contemporary critic to maintain that Delacroix 'possessed the mathematical rules of colour'; and Vincent Van Gogh, who loved him, commented that those same ceiling paintings in the Luxembourg 'were a harmony of yellow and violet'; Charles Blanc, quoted by John Gage, *Colour and Culture: Practice and Meaning from Antiquity to Abstraction* (London, 1993), p. 186.

The primary colours – red, yellow, blue – were re-established by the great Edinburgh experimental physicist Sir David Brewster (a somewhat older contemporary of David Hay) early in the nineteenth century, and although their primacy was contested on occasion, that hierarchy soon came to be generally accepted by many painters and colour theorists. Sir David Brewster, who invented many optical devices (including the kaleidoscope) had argued the matter on Newtonian postulates. See his *Treatise on Optics* (a volume of the *Cabinet Cyclopaedia*, 1831; new edition, London, 1838), pp. 72ff. On 'opposite' or 'complementary' colours, pp. 304ff. Another Scots physicist, James Clerk Maxwell, found experimentally that they were red, green and blue. Meanwhile, Thomas Young, an English physician much concerned with the physiology of sight (sometimes called 'the father of physiological optics'), found at the beginning of the nineteenth century that the optical nerves in the retina act as receptors of three other colours: red, green, violet. This was confirmed half a century later by Hermann von Helmholtz.

45 Vitruvius III: 1: iii and Giuseppe Bossi, *Delle opinioni di Leonardo da Vinci* (Milan, 1811).

46 Johann Gottfried Schadow, *Polyklet, oder von Maasen der Menschen nach dem Geschlechte und Alter . . .* (Berlin, 1884). He had already published a comparative anatomy for artists (Berlin, 1830) and would publish a supplement of twenty-nine plates (*National-Physiognomien . . .* (Berlin, 1835)) the following year. He had already published essays on the subject in *Propylaen,* the periodical edited by Goethe and Herder, which were reprinted in 1801. The literature of the whole subject of human proportion is reviewed by Peter Gerlach in *Proportion, Körper, Leben: Quellen, Entwürfe und Kontroversen* (Köln, 1990). The many editions of Schadow's book are listed on p. 214 – including an English reprint of 1947 which is not known to me.

47 He gives a detailed account of that episode in *The Laws of Harmonious Colouring Adapted to Interior Decorations*, 6th edn (Edinburgh and London, 1847), pp. 181ff. On his place in Edinburgh society, see Ian Gow and Timothy Clifford, *The National Gallery of Scotland* (Edinburgh, 1988), pp. 40ff.

48 Mostly remembered for his close association with Constable. See Charles Robert Leslie, *Memoirs of the Life of John Constable* (London, 1951), pp. 269ff. He is quoted in Constable's third lecture at the Royal Institution in 1836, ibid., p. 317: 'whose valuable works on the philosophy of colour are known to most artists, and should be to all' says Leslie.

49 Hussey claimed to have received a key to the cosmological implications of human proportion in a revelation when he was in Rome (a century earlier!). He was very pious and seems to have become a hermit in his old age. His main achievements were a number of highly praised figure-drawings in various private collections. See also Vertue in Horace Walpole, *Anecdotes of Painting in England: With Some Accounts of the Principal Artists; and Incidental Notes on Other Arts*, 5 vols, ed. Rev. James Dallaway (London, 1828), vol. IV, p. 97, note on Vincenzo Damini: 'He returned

to his own country in 1730, in company with Mr Hussey, whose genius for drawing was thought to equal the very great masters'. In fact, Damini seems to have swindled Hussey out of all his possessions once they got to Bologna. Note, ibid. Very interesting notices of Hussey are given by Barry, Fuseli and Edwards. *Chalmers Biog.Dict*.

　　　Hussey's ideas are now known through the work of his biographer, Francis Webb, who translated them into an elaborate chart in which planets, hours, colours and musical tones demonstrate the existence of an all-pervasive universal harmony. On his *Panharmonicon*, see Gage, *Colour and Culture*, p. 235.

50　His father had been brought from Rome by the Adam brothers and worked with them until independently established.

51　It was rather bigger than the one Hittorff had designed for the actress Rachel, see above, chapter Four. Gibson had already coloured other statues. The *Venus* was made for James (?) Preston, and he made replicas for the Marquess of Sligo and a 'Mr Uzielli'. One copy is in the Walker Art Gallery in Liverpool while the original plaster was part of his bequest to the Royal Academy in London. He also did a coloured statue of *Queen Victoria* for the Houses of Parliament which took a long time – 1850–55.

　　　Bonomi was a very successful antiquarian and illustrator. In 1861 he became the second director of the Sir John Soane Museum.

52　Henry James, *William Wetmore Story and his Friends* (London, 1903), vol. II, p. 164.

53　*The Proportions of the Human Figure according to a New Canon, for Practical use; With a Critical Notice of the Canon of Polycletus and of the Principal Ancient and Modern Systems*, by William Wetmore Story (London, 1866). Another American sculptor, Hiram Powers, had already taken an interest in the matter. Story's book is not known to the assiduous Gerlach.

54　Chapter Four, p. 12.

55　Carl Gustav Carus, *Symbolik der Menschlichen Gestalt: Ein Handbuch zur Menschenkenntniss*, 2nd edn (Leipzig, 1858). The first edition appeared in 1853 and was supplemented in 1854 with a folio of ten lithographs. He discusses alternative systems on pp. 48f., 60ff. There was an extended edition in 1925 which was reprinted in 1962. He set himself a problem which, following Goethe, he considers morphological: to find a unit which will work as a module for all human bodies. The head (so prominent in 'classical' systems), as others beginning with Dürer had pointed out, is hardly appropriate, since the human stature develops from four head-heights in the infant to eight head-heights in the adult. His own system is based on a module taken as 1/3 of the spinal column – which is the first element of the embryo to take form – as he argues on pp. 57ff. The first edition of his book had an extended and favourable review in the *Quarterly Review* (CLXXXVIII, September 1856). Carus also published a large folio of anatomical measurements. In that second edition he flatly rejects – on morphological grounds – Zeising's devotion to the Golden Section (pp. 60f.).

56　Euclid II, 11; VI, 13 but especially XIII, 1–6.

57　Brother of the more famous physicist, Georg Simon, after whom the unit of resistance to electric current was named. The label *Der Goldene Schnitt* occurs in his *Reine Elementar-Mathematik* (Berlin, 1834), though he speaks of the label as already customary. See R. Herz-Fischler, *A Mathematical History of Division into Extreme and Mean Ratio* (Waterloo, ON, 1987), pp. 121ff.; see also Richard Padovan, *Proportion: Science, Philosophy, Architecture* (London, 1999), pp. 305ff.

58　Gustav Theodor Fechner (1801–1887), usually described as an 'experimental psychologist', spent his life in Leipzig, first as Professor of Physics. He decided to work on the mind-body relationship on recovering from temporary blindness caused by his colour/vision experiments.

59　Helmholtz devised both the opthalmoscope and the spectroscope, though his work on the perception of tone quality was perhaps the most revolutionary. In spite of the double concern with optics and accoustics, and his involvement in contemporary art, he does not seem to have been interested in synaesthesia.

60 On Fechner's formulation of this law, and his debt to Ernst Heinrich Weber, see Wilhelm Wundt, 'Gustav Theodor Fechner', in *Reden und Aufsätze* (Leipzig, 1913), pp. 298ff. On Fechner and Herbart, pp. 319ff.

61 Robert Vischer, *Über das Optische Formgefühl*, reprinted in *Drei Schriften zum Ästhetischen Formproblem* (Halle/Saale, 1927). See especially pp. 17, 21, where Vischer distinguishes between *Zusammenfühlen*, *Mitfühlen*, *Ausfühlen* and *Einfühlen* and similar transformations of *Empfinden*. He also notes (p. 77) that he had coined the term unaware that Herder had already used it.

62 Ibid., chapter Four.

63 Konrad Fiedler (1841–1895), a collector and patron of the arts; many of his writings appeared posthumously, but his influence worked through Adolf Hildebrand. Art, he believed, offered an autonomous area of experience – which opposed him to the standard neo-Kantian view.

64 He is now chiefly remembered for an essay, 'Das Problem der Form in der Bildenden Kunst', which was first published in 1893 and often reprinted. It made Fiedler's rather complex teaching more accessible and had a much more powerful impact on the history of art than on the work of artists. His father Bruno (no von – Adolf's personal title of 1903 was made hereditary in 1913), a disciple of Herbart's educational ideas, was an important political economist and had been a left-democratic deputy in the 1848 Frankfurt Diet (and later in the 'rump-parliament' in Stuttgart – he was even been spoken of as a possible *Volkskaiser*), as a result of which he was accused of high treason in 1851 and also sought refuge in Zürich. He spent ten years teaching in Switzerland. After 1862 he returned to a chair in Jena.

   By the 1914–18 hiatus, however, his work was considered too bland to be of much interest. though some years later he did become one of Adolf Hitler's favourite artists. Since Adolf's mother, Clementine Guttentag, was Jewish, the Führer's enthusiasm could not have been unalloyed.

65 Its English equivalent, 'empathy', did not appear until after 1910.

66 Theodor Lipps, *Leitfaden der Psychologie*, 3rd edn (Leipzig, 1903), p. 222. Lipps had started his academic career with a critique of Herbart. His doctoral thesis, *Zur Herbartschen Ontologie*, was presented in Bonn in 1874.

67 See Vernon Lee, *The Beautiful* (Cambridge, 1913), pp. 59ff., but especially pp. 66f.

68 See Edgar Wind, *Art and Anarchy* (London, 1963), pp. 49ff. (and notes); Geoffrey Scott, *The Architecture of Humanism*, 2nd edn (London, 1924); his debt to Lipps and Berenson is acknowledged, pp. 212ff. Scott was re-discovered in the 1960s by some apologists of postmodern 'classicism' who seemed quite unaware both of the earlier literature or the criticism of empathy early in the twentieth century.

69 Husserl acknowledges his use of the concept in his *Ideas* (New York, 1962), §79, pp. 204ff., §151, pp. 387, where he relates its intersubjectivity. Yet he was critical of Lipps and conscious of the limitations of the concept. He therefore asked one of his most brilliant pupils, Edith Stein (canonized under her conventual name, St Teresa Benedicta, in 1998), to work on the concept, which became her doctoral thesis in 1916. See Michele Nicoletti, ed., *L'empatia (*translation of *Zum Problem der Einfühlung*) (Milan, 2002), especially pp. 24ff.

70 See above.

71 Friedrich-August Kekulé von Stradonitz (the title was 'retrieved' by his son Stephan, a historian-genealogist and recognized officially) went to London to work as a chemist at St Bartholomew's Hospital. Tetravalent carbon then appeared to him as a series of solids in movement, but when he was called to the chair of chemistry at Ghent university in 1858, he had a vision of a snake biting its tail as it 'whirled mockingly' – which some commentators recognized as *Ouroboros*, the alchemical device figuring Mercury or the *materia prima*. He soon realized that the linkage of atoms in structures could not be represented adequately in a linear way but had to be shown in

a perspective or a three-dimensional model. Since the report of both visions was made late, in 1890 (in the report of a meeting, the Benzol-Fest in honour of Kekulé, his own contribution is prolix and not altogether accurate about dates and places), some doubts have been expressed about whether the account of the dreams has any substance. So John H. Wotiz and Susanna Rudofsky, 'The Unknown Kekulé', in *Essays on the History of Organic Chemistry*, ed. James G. Traynham (Baton Rouge, LA, 1987), pp. 21ff. However, for my purposes the way the dreams were reported seems almost more important than their exact dating.

Kekulé had no real interest in the application of his discoveries. 'As soon as a reaction seemed to offer nothing new theoretically, it had no further attraction for him' reported a collaborator.

Friedrich Bayer established his works in Barmen (now Wuppertal) in 1863, moved to Würzburg in 1880 and then to Leverkusen, since associated with the firm, in 1912; Friedrich Bayer Jr. discovered a process for producing aluminium from bauxite in 1880, while aspirin was synthesized by a chemist working in the firm.

The Badische Anilin und Soda Fabrik was started in Mannheim in 1865 and the Aktien Gesellschaft für Anilinfabrikation in 1867 near Berlin. They were the core of the combine IG Farben which was founded in 1915 and dissolved by the Allied government in 1945.

72 Within a decade (1863–73) a number of chemical enterprises, Bayer, BASF, AGFA, began to apply both the aromatic and colouring derivatives of coal-tar industrially. They were part of that second industrial revolution which made Germany a chemical producer to rival Britain and France. The victory of 1871 and the institution of the Empire propelled them into activity: AGFA into photography and film, Bayer laboratories synthesized Acetylsalicylic acid (and called it aspirin), while Bayer-fils refined aluminium from bauxite in 1889. All this is discussed in much greater detail by Esther Leslie in *Synthetic Worlds* (London, 2005), which did not come to my notice until after this was written.

73 See some rather curious musings on this in Thomas Pynchon's *Gravity's Rainbow* (New York, 2000), pp. 84f., 410ff.

74 Dr Johnson in his *Dictionary* considered the word 'Japan' an adjective for work 'varnished and raised in gold and colours', or anything black and shiny, even shoe-blacking. Any regional reference seemed irrelevant.

75 Siegfried Bing spelt it *Mangua*. I use the Goncourt's transliteration but there were others. A Polish aesthete and collector, Feliks Jasienski, who used the term as his pseudonym (and the title of a *magnum opus* which appeared simultaneously in Paris and Warsaw in 1901) spelt it *Manggha*. His collection of Japanese art, gathered mostly in Paris between 1880 and 1890, is now housed in a special museum in Kraków, designed by Arata Isozaki. See Ewa Miodonska-Brookes and Maria Ciesla-Korytowska, *Feliks Jasienski i Jego Manggha* (Kraków, 1992), pp. 59f. for a biography.

76 Now in the Musée d'Orsay, Paris.

77 The importance of the paper is underlined by its eye-catching appearance in several Impressionist paintings of the time. Cézanne's father, for instance, is shown reading it in a portrait painted in 1866–8.

78 Three enlarged copies after Hiroshige and Kesaï Eisen (one of the Kesaï copies has a combined Hokusai/Utagawa surround) are in the Van Gogh Museum in Amsterdam; but Van Gogh also showed Japanese prints in the background of his late self-portrait with a bandaged ear (Courtauld Institute, London) and several in the background for Père Tanguy (late Niarchos Collection, Athens). See Siegfried Wichmann, *Japonisme* (New York, 1985), pp. 40ff.
    Lautrec, Whistler and other painters also dressed their sitters in kimonos; ibid., pp. 16ff.

79 The Emporium was first called J. and J. Holmes, then Farmer and Rogers; it was at 171–3 Regent Street. The 'Oriental Warehouse' started as a branch of Farmer and Rogers.

80   Alison Adburgham, *Liberty's: A Biography of a Shop* (London, 1975), pp. 12ff.

81   Worried, the Japanese authorities invited some Western 'experts' to advise them about main-taining quality in an industrializing society; Christopher Dresser, who first went in 1876, was 'seconded' by the British Government. Demand continued to grow in spite of any decline.

      The Tokugawa heir, Akitake, visited Paris for the 1867 Exposition and remained to study. His watercolour portrait by the then very fashionable James Tissot (who also gave him drawing lessons) was mounted as a *kakemono* is in the Tokugawa Museum in Mito. Akitake was in Paris in 1877–81.

82   He was encouraged to do so by his brother-in-law, the engraver Seymour Haden.

      Claude Monet was also a rebel student of Gleyre – who looked back not to their master but to Gustave Courbet. Whistler met Courbet and also Manet, and Baudelaire, who praised his first exhibition of etchings.

83   E. R. Pennell and J. Pennell, *The Life of James McNeill Whistler* (London, 1908), vol. I, p. 122. The *Princesse* was a Greek girl, Miss Christine Spartali, later Countess Edmond de Cahen.

84   It had been stripped out of Northumberland House at Charing Cross, which had been demol-ished in 1874 to make way for Northumberland Avenue. Another room from it, also designed by the Adam brothers, is now in the Victoria and Albert Museum in London.

85   From a broadside Whistler had printed for the many visitors to the room while he was work-ing on it; it included grandees, like the Marquess of Westminster and the Prince of Teck, but also the now aged Sir Henry Cole. Quoted by Stanley Weintraub in *Whistler, a Biography* (New York, 1976), p. 176. The fee, agreed verbally, was to be 500 guineas, but Whistler asked for 2,000 and expenses. Leyland – though advised to pay nothing by Rossetti – gave £1,000.

      The room has now been installed in the Freer Gallery in Washington, DC. The episode is described in detail in Pennell and Pennell, *The Life of James McNeill Whistler*, vol. I, pp. 198–202.

86   Whose widow he was to marry in 1888. An excellent (though not altogether successful) 'Gothic' architect, Godwin would branch out to design the most subtle Japanese-style furni-ture of the time. With him Whistler also collaborated on a home for the newly married Oscar and Constance Wilde on the other side of the road.

87   Walter Crane, *Ideals in Art* (London, 1905), pp. 19ff.

      The Aesthetic movement and the Japanese craze associated with it invited mockers: *Punch* started publishing cartoons on the subject in the 1870s, but the most famous and popu-lar was the comic opera *Patience* by W. S. Gilbert and Arthur Sullivan first performed in April 1881, with sets and costumes designed by Gilbert using real Liberty prints, etc., and revised for the gala opening of the Savoy Theatre in the Strand (which became the home of Gilbert and Sullivan operas) in October the same year and opened on the same day in New York. See Elizabeth Aslin, *The Aesthetic Movement* (London, 1969), pp. 112ff. Gilbert and Sullivan produced their Japanese opera, *The Mikado*, with 'authentic' background and costumes – and even gestures – in March 1885.

88   Crane, *Ideals in Art*, p. 272.

89   In the same year, 1886, *La Vogue* first published Rimbaud's *Les Illuminations*.

90   On the importance of this notion, see Jean Starobinski, *Action et réaction* (Paris, 2001), especially pp. 134ff. on reflex action.

91   The *Rapporteur esthétique* was published in 1888, the *Cercle chromatique* in 1889; see Michael F. Zimmermann, *Seurat and the Art Theory of his Time* (Antwerp, 1991), p. 233. In fact, his colour theory depends more on Wilhelm Wundt's experiments and researches, which systematized Goethe's intuitions.

92   In his very laconic letter (28 August 1890) about compositional principles to his friend Maurice Beaubourg, the debt to Superville is obvious. It is discussed in some detail by Zimmermann in his *Seurat and the Art Theory of his Time*, pp. 298ff.

93 When Signac wrote a history of the movement – *D'Eugène Delacroix au Néo-Impressionisme* (Paris, 1899) and new edition 1911 – he also acknowledged having learnt both from Helmholtz and from Humbert de Superville. The text was first published (1898) as a series of articles in *La Revue blanche*.

94 In fact, he warned Van Gogh (who admired Seurat almost as much as he admired Delacroix) against all pretended methods in painting.

95 The quarrel about its origins is described by John Rewald, *Post-Impressionism* (New York, 1956), pp. 191ff.

96 Although this is not the official account, both Gauguin and Cézanne knew it well; Cézanne even remarked angrily once: '[Gauguin] m'a chipé sa petite sensation pour aller la promener sur les paquebots.' Quoted by Charles Chassé, *Le Mouvement symboliste dans l'art du xixme siècle* (Paris, 1947), p. 98.

97 Schuré even claimed to have introduced Lamoureux to the 'true meaning of Wagner's music'. See Alphonse Roux and Robert Veyssié, *Edouard Schuré* (Paris, 1914), pp. 45ff.

98 He was one of the founders of the *Mercure de France*; he died at 27 (in 1892) from typhoid contracted in Marseilles.

99 He may have taken the term from Gauguin, who applied it to his own work as in a letter of 14 August 1888 to Emile Schuffenecker (*Lettres de Gauguin*, ed. Maurice Malingue, Paris, 1946, pp. 134f.). But see Sven Lövgren, *The Genesis of Modernism* (Stockholm, 1956), pp. 102ff., on Aurier and the post-Gauguin artists.

100 Their work turned into a 'school' named after Beuron which was much employed by monastic houses and by publishers of devotional books: it soon degenerated into repetitive kitsch.

101 On the upper Danube; it was a suppressed Augustinian house which the Benedictines were given in 1887.

102 He published his discovery of 'regulating lines' in the chapters on proportion in Josef Durm's *Handbuch der Architektur* (Darmstadt, 1890–1908), vol. IV, p. 1. In the most popular architects' handbook of the inter-war (and even post Second World War years), Ernst Neufert's *Bau-Entwurfslehre*, the Golden Section as applied to the human body is given as an a priori, with reference to Zeising (*sic*): p. 23. Further material on proportion – the 3,4,5 triangle, 1:√2, and Golden Section – are given with reference to Thiersch, Fischer and Moessel. pp. 25f. The young Charles-Edouard Jeanneret, when on his 1910–11 study tour of Germany, was very impressed with Theodor Fischer's buildings and tried to find a job in his office: in spite of a very warm welcome, that proved impossible, and he moved on to Berlin and the larger office of Peter Behrens.

On the encounter with Thiersch and Fischer, see H. Allen Brooks, *Le Corbusier's Formative Years* (Chicago, IL, 1997), pp. 211ff., 417f. Thiersch's teaching, which became familiar to many architects through his *Handbuch der Architektur*, was much admired by Heinrich Wölfflin; see his *Kleine Schriften* (Basel, 1946), pp. 48ff. ('Zur Lehre der Proportion') and his *Renaissance und Barock*, 4th edn (Munich, 1925), pp. 69ff.

103 It was destroyed in 1910.

104 J. K. Huysmans quoted by Silverman, *Art-Nouveau in Fin-de-Siècle France*, p. 288.

105 Oddly enough, fifty years earlier (René Wellek).

106 Gustave Eiffel quoted by Silverman, *Art-Nouveau in Fin-de-Siècle France*, p. 297.

107 François Carco, 'Sur la Tour Eiffel, Deuxième Plateau' in *Chansons Aigres-Douces* (Paris, 1913), p. 69.

108 As, for instance, the Flemings Jan Toorop or Johan Thorn Prikker, whose linear style might seem much more like Horta's ornamental manner: it might almost seem that he cultivated a deliberate discontinuity between 'art' and the 'craft' interior.

109 It was wantonly pulled down by them in 1967.

110 Although she was later known by her married name as Mrs Cochrane, the tea-rooms remained Miss Cranston's.

418

111 The three winning projects for *Das Haus eines Kunstfreundes* (Baillie Scott, Mackintosh and Leopold Bauer, a very successful *Wagnerschüler*) were published as portfolios by the *Zeitschrift für Innendekoration* in 1901. Baillie Scott's *Kunstfreund* was certainly no collector. His house, with widely spread wings on a hexagonal plan, was heavily half-timbered on the interior, with any leftover wall-areas filled with painted and carved decorations. But it was Mackintosh's project which was built in Glasgow in 1890.

112 On the structural use of the catenary curve, see Joseph Rykwert, *The First Moderns* (Cambridge, MA, 1980), pp. 311ff.

113 Many of them were taken by his friend, the caricaturist and painter Ricardo Opisso. He was well known in Barcelona and was even an (unsuccessful) competitor of the young Picasso. Opisso sat as a model for some of the figures, yet Gaudí never asked him for any designs.
　　His faithful disciple-collaborators in this were Catalan mason-sculptors – Llorenç de Matamala (and his son Juan), as well as Emili Fontbona (remembered now chiefly for having taught Picasso clay modelling).

114 On Gaudí and his sculptor/carvers, see R. Descharnes and Clovis Prévost, *Gaudí the Visionary* (New York, 1971), pp. 117ff.

115 Gaudí and a number of the more conservative artists, nationalists though they were, identified that label with *fin-de-siècle* decadence and later with the Modernist heresy which was condemned by Pius X in 1907 – and of which they would certainly have disapproved. They therefore founded a rival pious and 'healthy' – but equally *Catalonista* – Guild of St Luke.

116 An unsatisfactory English version had meanwhile been made by Lord Alfred Douglas which Wilde and Beardsley both 'corrected'. The brilliant youth supplanted Wilde's previously favoured illustrator, Charles Ricketts – whose gentler manner and tonalities were closer to Burne-Jones'.

117 On this episode, see Richard Ellmann, *Oscar Wilde* (New York, 1987), pp. 375ff., 404. Ten years later Richard Strauss turned it into an opera, which was first performed in Dresden in 1905. Wilde had suffered imprisonment in Reading Gaol in 1895.

118 Though there were 'token' paintings in the auditorium building, 'Spring' and 'Autumn' landscapes by the otherwise undistinguished Louis-Albert Fleury; they were installed in the arched blanks on either side of the balcony (where, for the Republican convention of 1888 – held there before the exterior was finished – electrically-framed portraits of Lincoln and Grant looked over the hall). He also provided the decorative contractors of the building, Holloway and Millet, who executed Sullivan's ornament, drawings for paintings in the banqueting hall. The allegorical frieze framing the proscenium arch by the then young Charles Holloway was selected in a competition also run by the contractor.

119 It was opened in 1890 and razed in 1925. Some years later the statue, which had also been used on a building of the *Centennial Exhibition* in Chicago, was moved to the Philadelphia Museum of Art. At the time, it was reputed to be the first sculpture to be lit electrically.

120 Linda Merrill, *The Peacock Room: A Cultural Biography* (Washington, DC and New Haven, CT 1998), p. 316. Pennell and Pennell, *The Life of James McNeill Whistler*, vol. II, p. 132.

121 The surface material, which was also used for the statues, was called 'staff' and was, in effect, a fibrous plaster. One of the statues, Daniel Chester French's *Republic* at 65 feet was the tallest in the United States and was cast in bronze, about a quarter-size, to stand in Jackson Park, Chicago – which was laid out on the exhibition site.

122 Louis Sullivan, *Kindergarten Chats and Other Writings* (New York, 1947), p. 208. Even Gaudí was seduced by the idea and designed a skyscraper as tall as the Eiffel Tower, but shaped by a whole hive of inverted catenary curves, for a hotel promoter in New York.

123 Michael Whiteway, *Christopher Dresser, 1834–1904* (Milan, 2001), p. 26.

124 A *Filmographie* is provided by Giovanni Lista, *Loïe Fuller, danseuse de la Belle Epoque* (Paris, 1994), pp. 638ff.; he considers one of the imitator's films (Annabel Whitford Moore's) made

in 1895 by the Edison company to be the first colour film ever made.

125 'Or cette transition de sonorités aux tissus (y-a-t-il, mieux, à une gaze ressemblant que la musique!) est, uniquement le sortilège qu'opère Loïe Fuller, par instinct, avec éxagérration, les retraits de jupe ou d'aile, insinuant un lieu. . . L'exercise, comme invention, sans l'emploi, comporte une ivresse d'art et, simultanément un accomplissement industriel'; Stephane Mallarmé, 'Autre étude de danse', in *Oeuvres* (Paris, 1945), pp. 308f.

126 They were to get the 1903 Nobel Prize in 1898. On their friendship with Loïe Fuller, and her introducing them to Rodin, see Lista, *Loïe Fuller*, pp. 323ff.

127 Some fifty films and kineographs about her were made in her lifetime, beginning in 1893. The Edison company produced *Annabel's Serpentine Dance* in 1893. Loïe herself was first filmed in 1896 by Georges Mélies. See Lista, *Loïe Fuller*, pp. 30f., 638.

128 Lithography proper was a century old and had attracted many great artists – such as Goya and Delacroix – who liked the fact that the image that appeared in the print was the one they had drawn directly on the stone. Early line and shade lithographs, of which Daumier had been the master, were replaced in the 1880s by images relying on large areas of flat, sometimes transparent and brilliant colour. Other artists were excited by the possibilities and the popular appeal of the street poster: Toulouse-Lautrec was the first master; the young Bonnard and Vuillard both produced them; by the last years of the nineteenth century rollers and photography allowed large areas to be printed.

129 By then the much more stylized tones and gestures of Japanese Nō plays were also known – they were admired by Gordon Craig and Yeats. The first Indian dancers were also appearing in Europe.

130 The Eiffel Tower could not be modified substantially for the occasion, but the Palais des Machines, now entirely run on electricity, was masked by an elaborate oriental-rocaille fountain grotto in ceramic and plaster designed by two well-known Parisian figures, Eugène Hénard (the father of the traffic round-about) and Edmond Paulin, said to be 'inspired by the Louis xv style' – though in fact it was far too clumsy and stiff to deserve the rocaille label. For all that, it was not only lit by rows of light bulbs, but enlivened by an elaborate play of fountains, all of it powered by generators inside the glass building.

131 Though he had another important semi-public commission, the redesign of the Grands Magazins du Printemps in 1910–11 – which unfortunately burnt out in 1921. They were one of the early open, several-storey spaces with elevators connecting the floors.

132 The work of such artists as Josef Fanta and Jan Kotera in Prague, Giuseppe Somarruga in Milan, Bruno Schmitz in the (1910) Monument of the Battle of the Nations in Leipzig (*Völkerschlachtdenkmal* – a Wilhelmine showpiece) show such over-life size figures built into the structure, and are not offered to the viewer as individual works of art, but as a part of the building's vesture. In the monument to the Besenzanica Family in the Monumental Cemetery in Milan (by E. Butti) the figure is the whole tomb.

133 He saw the drawings for the Hôtel Solvay which was still under construction.

134 Humbert de Romans was an early general of the Dominican Order and the hall was financed by an eccentric Dominican friar with monies he had collected from the faithful; it was finished in 1900. When his superiors withdrew their sanction, the building (and the school connected with it) were sold and soon after demolished. It was in the Rue St Didier, not far from Guimard's early school.

135 One of those removed has achieved 'work of art' status and is now in the Museum of Modern Art in New York. But the two small station building pavilions – somewhat smaller but much more florid than the ones Wagner built in Vienna (two at the Etoile and one at the Place de la Bastille) – were demolished after the First World War.

136 Jiři Mucha *et al.*, *Alphonse Mucha* (London, 1971), p. 22 – which, he believes, however, is the proportion of 2 to 3, and which, he seemed to think, corresponded to some fixed perceptual rule.

137 Mucha designed the coat of arms, postage stamps and banknotes of the new republic – all of which he seems to have done without payment. He crossed effortlessly from the role of graphic designer to that of painter and was one of the last to do so: after 1920 the realm of the graphic designer and that of the artist divided sharply.

  Another emigré, the Italian Leonetto Capiello, moved to Paris in 1900 to make his fame at the poster. He went on working there until his death in 1942. Very few important painters made commercial posters after the break of the century: Toulouse-Lautrec, Pierre Bonnard, Raoul Dufy; some poster-artists, however, such as Paul Colin and A. M. Cassandre made their reputation as artists after designing commercial posters which had outstanding formal qualities.

138 Robert Musil, 'Denkmale', in *Gesammelte Werke*, ed. Adolf Frisé (Berlin, 1978), vol. VII, p. 506: 'Es gibt nichts auf der Welt, was nicht so unsichtbar wäre wie Denkmäler.'

139 By the leading New York art critic of the time, Royal Cortissoz, quoted by Burke Wilkinson, *The Life and Works of Augustus Saint Gaudens* (San Diego, CA, 1985), pp. 326f. Antoní Gaudi was one of the very few involved (however marginally) in the design of a public monument – to a Catalanista mayor of Barcelona, Bartomeu Robert, in 1902. See Tokutoshi Torii, *El mundo enigmático de Gaudí* (Madrid, 1983), vol. II, pp. 326f.

140 James was probably echoing Wilde: see Richard Ellmann, *Along the Riverrun* (New York, 1989), p. 145.

141 Of Claude Lorrain for Nancy, for instance, or of Victor Hugo in the gardens of the Palais Royal in Paris (not finished as he wanted) or to President Sarmiento in Buenos Aires.

142 Judith Cladel, *Rodin: sa vie glorieuse et inconnue* (Paris, 1936), pp. 114ff.

143 The Musée des Arts Décoratifs was to be established in the old building of the Cour des Comptes which had been burnt out during the Commune of 1871; it was opened in the Pavillon de Marsan (also damaged in 1871) in 1880.

144 The plaster cast presented at the 1900 Exposition is in the Musée Rodin in Meudon, but stripped of the independent figures. By 1912 he denied any interest in this work. Cladel, *Rodin*, p. 142.

  Two bronze casts ordered by the Philadelphia film mogul, Jules Mastbaum, were made in 1925–8: one for his Rodin Museum in Philadelphia and the second as a gift for the Musée Rodin in Paris – which owned the copyright. Later ones, from the same foundry, are in the National Museum of Western Art in Tokyo. The Zürich Kunsthaus one was bought in 1949 but I do not know the date of the cast. Yet another was cast for the Rodin Exhibition at the National Gallery in Washington, DC in 1978. Since Rodin himself was not interested in the casting process, and neither chisel-finished nor patinated his bronzes, the argument as to which is the authentic work stands. See Rosalind Krauss, *The Originality of the Avant-Garde and Other Modernist Myths* (Cambridge, MA, 1985), pp. 151ff.

145 By Léonce Bénédite (who was to become the first director of the Musée Rodin).

146 Auguste Rodin, *Les Cathédrales de France* (Paris, 1914), pp. 134, 159.

> *Sa douceur (de la moulure) est celle de la nature elle-même; sa vie, la vie de tout l'édifice. Elle contient toute la force de l'architecte, elle exprime toute sa pensée . . . Les moulures sont des symphonie douces. C'est dans mes dernières minutes que je parle . . . je me résigne à la mort de ces édifices, comme à la mienne. . .*

147 His best-known work was the metal-and-glass building for the department store, La Samaritaine, though he also designed the mausoleum of Zola. Jourdain was to speak at Rodin's funeral in 1917 – though as a representative of the Salon d'Automne (of which he was one of the founders) rather than as a personal friend.

  In spite of his passionate involvement with past architecture, Rodin's friends (Jourdain apart) were not architects but patrons, writers, politicians. The bases of his monumental figures he designed himself – he sometimes even modelled them. But *Balzac* was not set up until 1939, on a bare cubic plinth in the central grass verge of the Boulevard Raspail.

148　The plaster model is in the Musée Rodin. *The Benediction* exists in plaster and bronze casts, as well as in a marble version in the Ny Carlsberg Glyptothek, Copenhagen. Rodin's account of his aim exists in manuscript notes now in the Library at Princeton and were published in the Library's *Bulletin* of Autumn 1965 by Howard C. Rice.

　　　　The funding was organized by the American dancer Loïe Fuller, whom I mentioned earlier; she was devoted to Rodin and was involved in the problems of his inheritance.

149　The episode was well known from the *Chronicles* of Jean Froissart. After some early abortive efforts David d'Angers made a project in 1845, just before his death. Jean-Baptiste Auguste Clésinger made another in 1868. There were a number of competitions and fragmentary statues were actually executed.

150　'Je ne voulais aucun piédestal à ces statues. Je souhaitais qu'elles fussent posées, scellées même à les dalles de la place publique . . . et qu'elles eussent à partir de là pour se rendre au camp des ennemis. Elles se seraient ainsi trouvées comme mêlées à l'existence quotidienne de la ville', quoted in Paul Gsell, 'Chez Rodin', *L'Art et les artistes*, XIX/109 (1914), pp. 67f. Rodin also considered an alternative on a very high plinth like the Breton calvaries. The debate round the work is reported in some detail by Cladel, *Rodin*, pp. 152ff.

151　In spite of its size and complexity, the group was cast in bronze several times. One was for a Belgian, another for a Danish collection. The British Government bought a cast in 1911. Rodin helped to site it in the small garden beside the Royal Tower of the Palace of Westminster. Several more casts were made after Rodin's death.

152　Notably by Krauss, *The Originality of the Avant-Garde*, pp. 279f.

153　At the end of the century Rodin overcame his antipathy to Art Nouveau and became involved in a group connected with the Union des Arts Décoratifs; he had always been true to his sense of himself as a craftsman – indeed, he had on occasion described himself as an 'artistic mason'.

154　Klinger (a close friend of Brahms) had specialized in large allegorical canvases (somewhat after Puvis de Chavannes), with elaborate painted, carved and moulded frames – which he renounced for engraving and polychrome sculpture. Ferdinand Avenarius, *Max Klinger als Poet* (Munich, 1921), p. 142f., Willy Pastor, *Max Klinger*, 3rd edn (Berlin, 1922), pp. 142 on the *Brahmsphantasie* engravings.

155　A private letter of Wagner quoted by Carl E. Schorske, *Fin-de-Siècle Vienna* (New York, 1981), p. 84.

156　*Ver Sacrum* with its implication of spring, renewal and separation was appropriate – it could be read almost as a translation of *Secession*.

157　By then Mackintosh was more famous in Germany and Austria than in Britain: his international fame was carried by work he did in Munich and Vienna and his contributions to various exhibitions.

158　Both Adolf Loos and Karl Kraus despised and attacked the Secession generally and Klimt's work particularly as 'decadent'.

159　Klinger's statue is now in the Museum der Bildenden Künste, Leipzig. It was long in the making; the body is of Parian (Inselmarmor) marble, the drape of Tyrolean onyx; Pyranean marble was used for the rock and the eagle; the angle-heads on the throne are of ivory; its background is of true opal – a first version had a simple seat. The elaborate throne in *cire-perdue* bronze was a later addition, and was considered his masterpiece. The monument was compared by contemporaries to Rodin's *Victor Hugo* monument. On all this, see Pastor, *Max Klinger*, pp. 161ff.

　　　　Klimt's frieze is in the Öesterreichische Galerie in Vienna. The term 'visible music' was used by J. O. Lux, the author of the first 'authorized' biography of Otto Wagner, and one of the most authoritative Viennese critics. Quoted by Peter Vergo, *Art in Vienna, 1898–1918*

(London, 1975), p. 69. Vergo's is the most detailed study of that exhibition, pp. 67ff.

160 A brilliant Parisian contribution – and a retrospective of Klimt. After that the society split into two factions and ceased to have its leavening role in Vienna.

161 William Cecil Dampier Dampier-Whetham, *A History of Science and its Relation with Philosophy and Religion* (Cambridge, 1930), p. 382.

162 Which he seems to have read two years earlier; his letter to his friend Emil Freund in 1894 speaks of a remarkable book which would have an 'epoch-making effect' on his life, though he is said to have withdrawn the sub-title *Die Fröliche Wissenschaft* from his third symphony in case it was taken as referring to Nietzsche. See Alma Maria Mahler, ed., *Gustav Mahler: Briefe, 1879–1910* (Berlin and Vienna, 1925), pp. 151ff.

163 Otto Erich Hartleben, *Tagebuch, Fragmente eines Lebens* (Munich, 1906), pp. 117ff. Entry for 22 June 1890; he rightly fears the systematizers who will deny the pleasure in his prose and his wit – so as to iron out his contradictions.

     The first French translations appeared two or three years later and had an almost instant impact. Guy Michaud, *Message poétique du symbolisme* (Paris, 1947), vol. III, p. 518, quoted by Romeo Arbour, *Henri Bergson et les lettres françaises* (Paris, 1955), p. 260. If English and Russian versions were more sluggish, many musicians testified to his overpowering influence. Richard Strauss published his tone-poem, 'Thus Spake Zarathustra' (op. 30) in 1896, and in 1904–5 the British–German composer Frederick Delius used his own anthology of texts from Nietzsche's *Zarathustra* for his *Mass of Life*. It was not performed until 1909 in London. He also used a somewhat man-handled Nietzsche anthology for his Requiem of 1913–16.

164 He makes it clear in the dedication letter of the *Birth of Tragedy*, addressed to Richard Wagner, dated 'end of 1871'. (KSA I, p.23f.). They had met in 1868, when Nietzsche was 24.

165 It first appeared in 1901; a revised and enlarged edition in 1904, and yet another (as part of the collected works) in 1906, and yet another in 1911. The story of the 'editing' has often been told.

     The breach with Wagner was made with the first publication of *Menschliches, Allzumenschliches* in 1878, which contains veiled but critical remarks about Wagner without, however, naming him. Wagner attacked Nietzsche a few months later – though they continued to see each other.

166 *Nietzsche* by the Danish poet and critic Georg Brandes (Copenhagen, 1898).

167 *The Genealogy of Morals*, III §6 (KSA V p. 347); quoting Stendhal (Henri Beyle), *Rome, Naples et Florence*, ed. Henri Martineau (Paris, 1928), vol. I, p. 51: 'La beauté n'est jamais, ça me semble, qu'une *promesse de bonheur*'. He seems to have been well pleased with the phrase which he used again in *de l'Amour* I, 17, n.1: 'La beauté n'est que la *promesse de bonheur*.' (Stendhal's emphasis).

     Nietzsche notes in this context that if aestheticians will continue to maintain 'dass man unter dem Zauber der Schönheit sogar gewandlose weibliche Statuen "ohne Interesse" anschauen könne, so darf man wohl ein wenig auf ihre Unkosten lachen . . . Pygmalion war jedenfalls nicht nothwendig ein "unästhetischer Mensch".' Of course, in both contexts, Stendhal was justifying his aphorism about beauty and about male perception of female beauty.

     Martin Heidegger attempted to reconcile Nietzsche to Kant's ideas of beauty in art by circumventing Schopenhauer's interpretation of Kant – on which, he maintained, Nietzsche based his critique. See his *Nietzsche*, trans. David Farrell Krell (San Francisco, 1991), vol. I, pp. 107ff.

168 *Wille zur Macht*, §822; *The Will to Power* trans. Walter Kauffman and R. J. Hollindale (New York, 1967) p. 435 (slightly modified), where it is dated 1888.

169 *Twilight of the Idols*, §9, ed. G. Colli and M. Montanari (Berlin, 1969). 'Skirmishes of the Untimely Man', p. 11.

Six: The Geometry of Disenchantment

1 The poster was the work of a sculptor, Leonardo Bistolfi; it was also already out of date – Loïe herself was modifying and sobering her dances by then.

2 Vittorio Pica, *L'arte decorativa all'Esposizione di Torino* (Bergamo, 1902–3), English section, pp. 176–209, Scottish section, pp. 211–34; Pica (a leading critic of the time) says that the Scottish rooms are perhaps 'the most outstanding and most surprising for their originality' in the whole exhibition.

3 Raimondo d'Aronco had been a stonemason in Austria before returning to Venice and training as an architect. The Turkish period was his most productive. See Diana Barillari and Ezio Godoli, *Istanbul 1900* (New York, 1996), pp. 52ff. D'Aronco went back to his home city, Udine in the Veneto, when Sultan Abdulhamid II was deposed in 1909, and continued building, but in a stuffy, sober, academic manner.

 The statues were the work of two – now forgotten – sculptors, Edoardo Rubino (b. 1871 – whose best-known work is the figure of *Victory* added after 1918 to the monument of Victor Emmanuel II in Rome) and Augusto Reduzzi. Critics accused D'Aronco of excessive reliance on Viennese models.

 On the importance of the grid as the 'type' of non-narrative, non-sequential structure, see Rosalind E. Krauss, 'Grids', in *The Originality of the Avant-Garde and Other Modernist Myths* (Cambridge, MA, 1985), pp. 8ff.

4 Quoted by Stanford Anderson, *Peter Behrens and a New Architecture for the Twentieth Century* (Cambridge, MA, 2001), p. 33, though his most famous exhibit turned out to be an electric lamp in the shape of a woman whose raised arms support a spread fan of veils which transform into a scalloped dome of Tiffany-like coloured glass. Designed for Ernst-Ludwig of Hesse-Darmstadt, it was still recognizably Art Nouveau, and was reproduced in many manuals about the style. On the place of that design in Behrens' work, see Fritz Hoeber, *Peter Behrens* (Munich, 1913), pp. 20ff. Another famous exhibit was Behrens' own copy of *Also Sprach Zarathustra* in a heavy metal and leather binding, which would also appear in his Darmstadt house, ibid., pp. 83, cat. no. 7. A letter of 6 December 1902, quoted by Jürgen Krause, *'Martyrer' und 'Prophet': Studien zum Nietzsche-Kult in der Bildenden Kunst der Jahrhundertwende* (Berlin, 1984).

5 Behrens and his wife Lili had intended to visit Villa Silberblick in 1898, and had a letter of introduction to Elisabeth Förster-Nietzsche, but had to curtail their journey. Tillmann Buddensieg, *Monographien und Tate zur Nietzsche Forschung* (Nürnberg, 1980), vol. XIV, p. 38.

6 Born in 1872 in Darmstadt, he worked in Stuttgart in 1910–37, when he returned to Darmstadt and carved the sarcophagus of Ernst-Ludwig.

7 *Ein Dokument deutscher Kunst: Die Ausstellung der Künstler Kolonie in Darmstadt* (Munich, 1901). Text signed by Peter Behrens (1901), p. 5: 'Dank gebühret dem, der groszen Willen hat und die Macht, dasz dieser Wille sich in That und schöner Grosze erhebt'; p. 11: 'Wir wollen lächend leben in unserer hellen Zeit, wir haben unsere Träume vergessen, wir sind erweckt, erwacht. – Heil dir Wecker im Sommerglanz.'

 The other, thicker volume, also called *Ein Dokument deutscher Kunst*, edited by Alexander Koch, was published in Darmstadt, also in 1901. An account of the ceremony, the text of *Das Zeichen* (with music), on pp. 56ff.

8 *Das Sinnbild des neuen Lebens*. The distinction between the mechanically working society, based on common interest and convention, *Gesellschaft*, against the organic human grouping, the community, *Gemeinschaft*, is one of the great themes of the time. Ferdinand Tönnies' book *Gemeinschaft und Gesellschaft* was published in 1887 and was much discussed. It is echoed in such books as *The Village Community* by George Laurence Gomme (London, 1890), though he makes no mention of Tönnies. The distinction between contractual and organic association was made by Emile Durkheim in *De la division du travail social* (Paris, 1932) – and

occupies much of the first part of that book, especially pp. 79ff. This distinction is often paralleled by that between mechanical civilization and 'organic' culture – *Kultur* and *Zivilisation*. See Hanno Kersting, *Geschichtsphilosophie und Weltbürgerkrieg* (Heidelberg, 1959), pp. 141ff., 178ff., and Marvin Harris, *The Rise of Anthropological Theory* (New York, 1968), pp. 192ff.

On the role of the crystal, see also Donna Haraway, *Crystals, Fabrics and Fields: Metaphors in Twentieth-Century Developmental Biology* (New Haven, CT, 1976). The transformation of carbon into diamond may also echo Kekulé's alchemical sublimation of coal-tar into aromatic compounds. See above, chapter Five.

9 Anon, ('Ein ehrlicher aber nicht blinder Hesse', i.e. Georg Fuchs), *Was erwarten die Hessen von ihrem Grossherzog Ernst Ludwig?* (Darmstadt, 1873). But the duke was also very influenced by the publisher and patron of the Arts and Crafts movement, Alexander Koch.

Like his friends Dehmel and Fuchs, Behrens gladly accepted the label *Neuromantik* which suggested that (like Goethe and Schiller) they saw the arts as the leaven that would transform society.

10 On the *Mass of Life*, see Julius Bab, *Richard Dehmel: Die Geschichte eines Lebens-Werkes* (Leipzig, 1926), pp. 210ff., 239ff., and Harry Slochower, *Richard Dehmel: Der Mensch und der Denker* (Dresden, 1928), pp. 216ff. Slochower suggests that the oratorio, which was to be like the choralł movement of Beethoven's Ninth Symphony, was the response to the Polish occult-expressionist Stanisław Przybyszewski's *Totenmesse*. Frederick Delius' *Mass of Life* written in 1905 (and mentioned earlier) was anthologized out of *Zarathustra*.

11 Anderson, *Peter Behrens*, pp. 50ff.

12 Reminiscent of the system recommended by William Whetmore Story, on which see above, chapter Five. Hendrik Petrus Berlage, *Grundlagen und Entwicklung der Architektur* (Rotterdam, 1908), pp. 43ff.

13 Adolf Meyer worked with Gropius (and at the Bauhaus) until 1925, when he moved to Frankfurt. He drowned accidentally in 1929.

14 Notably by August Thiersch (whose contribution 'Proportionen in der Architektur', a separate volume of Josef Durm's *Handbuch der Architektur*, was the most widely read manual on the subject) and his pupil Theodor Fischer. The young Charles-Edouard Jeanneret was enchanted by Fischer – his most important Munich mentor in 1910 – who may have introduced him to the mysteries of the Golden Section, though he was already using 'regulating' lines earlier. Another contact with the group was through August Thiersch's son, Paul, who had worked in Behrens' Düsseldorf office from 1906. See H. Allen Brooks, *Le Corbusier's Formative Years* (Chicago, IL, 1997), pp. 212ff., Stanislas von Moos and Arthur Rüegg, *Le Corbusier before Le Corbusier* (New Haven, CT, 2002), pp. 73ff.

The business was given wide currency through Ernst Neufert's *Bau-Entwurfslehre* which was a 'Graphic Standards' equivalent, conveniently in one volume. First published by the German Industrial Standards Authority (Deutscher Normenausschuss) in Berlin in 1936, it has a brief introduction to the German literature on the subject (pp. 29f.) and contrasts the Golden Section – which is in fact the basis of the foolscap/quarto paper sizes – with the $\sqrt{2}$ rectangle adopted by the DIN, which is the basis of 'A' paper sizes.

15 Called after the home of the goddess Freya in the Norse legends: Osthaus was intensely nationalist at this period.

16 Osthaus, who had inherited a vast fortune just out of his teens, commissioned the building proper – for a natural history museum – from a conventional Wilhelmine Berlin architect and only learnt about Van de Velde when the carcass of the building was up. He tells of his change of mind himself in an unrepentantly lyrical monograph: *Van de Velde* (Hagen, 1920), pp. 21ff, though Van de Velde tells the story in greater detail in *Récit de ma vie*, ed. Anne van Loo (Brussels, 1992), vol. I, pp. 389ff. He decided that his museum would house an art collection as well, and bought extremely well from both Parisian and Berlin dealers. Neither Van de Velde nor Osthaus mention Behrens in this context.

17 I have used the notorious term 'Expressionist' as a handy label for 'northern European art *circa* 1910–25'; of course, many of the artists so labelled bridled at it. Ernst Ludwig Kircher found it 'more degrading than ever . . . to be identified with Munch and Expressionism'. That was in 1924. Quoted by John Willett, *Expressionism* (London, 1970), p. 7.

18 On which see Hoeber, *Peter Behrens*, pp. 34ff., and Anderson, *Peter Behrens*, pp. 33ff.

19 The building has not lasted well, moreover – which is why, presumably, the exterior is usually illustrated as a drawn perspective.

20 Emil Robert Weiss considered himself primarily a painter, but his highly successful career as engraver, calligrapher and book-designer overshadowed his painting. See Julius Meier-Graefe, E. R. Weiss in *E. R. Weiss zum fünfzigsten Geburtstage* (Leipzig, 1925), pp. 57ff. The Delsten mosaic had been 'tried out' a year earlier in another Behrens exhibition pavilion in Cologne, where it was set in the apse of a concert hall, over the piano.

21 In a letter to Count Kessler, who collected Maillol, as did Osthaus,

22 The small but very knobbly Russian Orthodox church on the Mathildenhöhe, next to the artists' colony, was also a monument of the occasion – and to an earlier Hesse-Darmstadt tsarina, Maria Alexandrovna, wife of Alexander II.

23 What he meant by that he declared fairly explicitly in the last, the ninth chapter of *Beyond Good and Evil* in *Werke,* ed. Giorgio Colli and Mazzino Montanari (Berlin, 1969) ('*Was ist Vornehm?*, §257ff. KSA, V, pp. 257ff.) and in part I §11 of the *Genealogy of Morals* (KSA, V, pp. 274ff.), the one which describes the 'blond beast' – though it might be worth recalling that he makes it quite clear that between 'us Germans and the ancient Teutons there is no conceptual affinity, never mind any blood relationship' (ibid., p. 276). There is also another aspect to this body and spirit aristocracy in which rank is determined by a capacity to suffer: on which see Wolf Zachriat, 'Nietzsche's Entwurf einer "geistig-leiblichen Aristokratie"' in *Nietzsche-Bibliographie* (Weimar, 2000), p. 182.

 He returns to the matter of nobility in the *Will to Power* (New York, 1967), §935ff. Contemptuous though he is of conventional titles, he does allow a role to birth.

 In fact, the circle of rich, well-born, cultured and influential women in Berlin (Cornelia Richter, Countess Harrach, Princess Radziwill, Princess Bülow – and the Dowager Empress Frederick) welcomed Rathenau and Kessler. See Count Harry Kessler, *Walter Rathenau: His Life and Work* (New York, 1930), pp. 47ff.

24 Nietzsche despised his brother-in-law, Bernhardt Förster, who had gone to Paraguay to found a nationalist German settlement (Neu Germanien). Elisabeth settled in Germany in 1893 (her husband, dogged by failures, committed suicide in 1889). She joined their mother Franziska as guardian of her brother's demented presence – and after Franziska's death – also the shaper of his image.

 In spite of seemingly cordial relations with them, Nietzsche had nothing but rage and contempt for both in his later writings. In *Ecce Homo* in *Werke*, ed. Colli and Montanari (I, 'Why I am so wise', §3), he wrote that 'the thought of being related to such *canaille* would blaspheme against my divine nature', a remark suppressed by Elisabeth when the book was published in 1908 – like many other of his comments which she judged 'untimely'. More coolly, Kessler wrote of Elisabeth many years later that she was the 'Verkörperung gerade dessen, wass ihr Bruder bekämpft hat' (the incarnation of exactly what her brother fought). Harry Graf Kessler, *Tage-Bücher, 1918–37* (Frankfurt, 1961), p. 137.

25 A few months after that other great demented critic of the age, John Ruskin.

 The phrase about 'putrescence' is quoted by Rüdiger Safranski in his *Nietzsche: A Philosophical Biography* (London, 2002), p. 318, though he does not give a source. But see also 'Nietzsche und das Archiv seiner Schwester' in Walter Benjamin, *Gesammelte Schriften* (Frankfurt, 1972), vol. III, p. 323, for the account of the distasteful party she arranged to celebrate Nietzsche's last birthday.

26 Kessler visited the Nietzsche family first in Naumburg in 1895, but saw the demented philosopher a number of times. He introduced his protégé Henry Van de Velde to Elisabeth, and in casting the death-mask, assisted the very young sculptor Curt Stoeving (it is in the Weimar Archiv). Max Klinger based his first bronze heads on a cast of it, and in 1911 the marble Herm was installed in the main room of the Weimar archive. See also Krause, *'Martyrer' und 'Prophet': Studien zum Nietzsche-Kult in der Bildenden Kunst der Jahrhundertwende* (Berlin, 1984), pp. 96ff., pp. 151 f.

Kessler's father, a successful German banker working in Paris, had been ennobled by Wilhelm I; his mother was Irish – though with oriental connections. Having been to an English preparatory school and a German High School and university – to qualify for a diplomatic post – he spent some time in his widowed mother's home in Paris where he became familiar with the art scene; he was already perfectly trilingual. He did not enter the diplomatic service until he took up the post of German Ambassador to Poland in 1918.

27 Van de Velde saw himself as threatened by more powerful rivals, Horta and Seurier-Bovy in Brussels and needed international exposure: *Récit de ma vie*, vol. I, pp. 349ff., vol. II, pp. 19ff.

In fact, the Seurat painting could not be entirely displayed in the apartment, being 2 metres high by 3 metres long, so Van de Velde set it up on two rollers and only one figure was displayed at any one time. It is now at the Barnes Collection near Philadelphia.

28 On the episode, see ibid., vol. II, pp. 153ff. The Klinger bust was paid for by Kessler privately.

The Van de Velde *Zarathustra* was not published until 1908, by Insel-Verlag, and printed on special paper which was water-marked with Van de Velde's 'N', also used throughout the archive interior; Van de Velde had already designed a special typeface for it by 1901. See also Krause, *'Martyrer' und 'Prophet'*, pp.172ff.

29 Her attempt to have her brother buried in the garden (as Wagner had been in Bayreuth) was thwarted by the authorities and his body was taken to the family tomb in Röcken.

The archive was given its present form by Van de Velde in 1902–3 while Mrs Förster-Nietzsche was absent. Krause, *'Martyrer' und 'Prophet'*, p. 176.

30 Goethe's grandson, Walther, who died childless, bequeathed the archive to the Grandduchess Sophie in 1885, and the Schiller archive was incorporated into it, to become the Goethe-Schiller Institute.

31 On being introduced into the 'Nietzsche presence' and for a discreet account of the break, see Rudolf Steiner, *The Story of my Life* (London, 1928), pp. 179ff. His book was *Friedrich Nietzsche: ein Kämpfer gegen seine Welt* (Weimar, 1895).

32 Ten years before his childhood schoolfriend, the critic and historian Roger Fry, managed to arrange one in London.

33 He was present at the meeting of the National Assembly in February 1919 which gave the soubriquet 'Weimar' to the 1919–33 Republic. Weimar remained the centre of many of his activities, and his publishing house took its name, Cranach-Presse, from the street on which he lived until his exile (from all Germany) in 1933. Exile is perhaps too legal a term: at the German Embassy in Paris he was told that were he to return, there was a risk that some hot-headed young men might get out of hand.

34 In 1917 the enemy alien Belgian Van de Velde was forced out. He recommended Walter Gropius as his successor. That is how the Bauhaus began. The buildings were incorporated into the Bauhaus University (founded in 1990).

35 Osthaus, *Van de Velde*, pp. 44f.

36 The placing of the boxes varies in three schemes for Louis Dumont which were shown in London in 1974. So Dennis Sharp, ed., *Henry Van de Velde: Theatres, 1904–1914* (London, 1974). But see Van de Velde, *Récit de ma vie*, pp. 177ff. (especially p. 181 n. 1) on the theatre with a revolving stage built for them in Düsseldorf in 1905.

37 Kessler's private Cranach-Presse published Gerhard Hauptmann's version of *Hamlet* with

woodcuts by Craig in 1928.

38 Kessler did take Maillol back-stage at the Diaghilev Ballet once, and introduced him to Nijinski – but like many of Kessler's patronage proposals, it all came to nothing. Hans Blumenberg, *Höhlenausgänge* (Berlin, 1989), pp. 633ff. (quoting H. F. Peters, *Zarathustra's Sister*, New York, 1977, pp. 269ff.), thinks the 'temple' was to contain an empty tomb or cenotaph. On Van de Velde's project, see Leon Polgaerts in A. Kostka and I. Wohlfarth, eds, *Nietzsche and an Architecture of our Minds* (Los Angeles, CA, 1999), pp. 233ff. On the prehistory of the monument and its relation to the contemporary Bismarck-monument agitation as well as the Leipzig monument to the Battle of the Nations, see Krause, *'Martyrer' und 'Prophet'*, pp. 199ff.

39 Hitler – who visited the archive several times – decided to take the situation in hand. A great deal of money was set aside, partly from his private funds, and a project by Paul Schultze-Naumburg (the father of the *Heimatkunst*, which Nietzsche would of course have despised, though in an earlier life he had been one of the early enthusiasts of an abstract art when writing as art critic in Munich) was approved in 1936. Although the war intervened so that the Memorial Hall was never used as intended, as late as 1943 Mussolini sent a late-antique *Dionysus* statue to be set in its main niche (it is now in the Pergamon Museum in Berlin). See David Marc Hoffmann, *Zur Geschichte des Nietzsche-Archivs* (Berlin, 1991), pp. 111ff. Karl Löwith, *From Hegel to Nietzsche: The Revolution in Nineteenth Century Thought* (New York, 1964), p. 231, wrote of it: 'The Nietzsche Hall of the Third Reich in Nietzsche's Bayreuth, by which Wagner took revenge on Nietzsche'.

40 W. B. Yeats. 'A Prayer for my Daughter' in *Collected Poems* (London, 1933), p. 214. He dated the poem 1919 in fact. The parallel with Nietzsche was pointed out by Alexander Nehamas in *Nietzsche: Life as Literature* (Cambridge, MA, 1985), p. 47.

41 W. B. Yeats, quoted by Christopher Innes, *Edward Gordon Craig* (Cambridge, 1983), p. 119.

42 On Wagner's Bayreuth aims, see Edouard Schuré, *Richard Wagner: son oeuvre et son idée* (Paris, 1920), pp. 291ff., but in fact it was designed by a Berlin architect, Walter Neumann. He was replaced, after delays and disagreements, by Otto Brückwald of Leipzig, who is often credited with the design. Robert Hartford, ed., *Bayreuth in the Early Years* (London, 1980), pp. 25f., 42ff.

43 The last was in fact designed for Georg Fuchs who, disappointed – as was Behrens – with the Darmstadt court, moved back to Munich.

44 Paul Kühn, *Weimar* (Leipzig, 1919), pp. 185ff. Karl Ebert, the first president, was sworn in Weimar on 21 August. Count Kessler reflected: 'The Republic should avoid ceremony. That form of government does not suit it. It's like a nanny dancing a ballet. Nevertheless there was above all something touching about it.'

45 This very condensed warning was not issued until 1918–19, to a student career-gathering in Munich, 'Wissenschaft als Beruf', long after these events, but his earlier work has many such warnings, if less pithily put. In Max Weber, *Gesammelte Aufsätze zur Wissenschaftslehre* (Tübingen, 1922), p. 554. See also Peter Lassman *et al.*, *Max Weber's Science as a Vocation* (London, 1989).

   On the circumstances of that lecture, see Karl Jaspers, *On Max Weber* (London, 1989), pp. 65ff.

46 By the twentieth century Feuerbach and Comte, who did not know each other's ideas, were seen as the two founders of a 'religion of Humanity' (as by T. G. Masaryk, for instance). See S. Rawidowicz, *Ludwig Feuerbachs Philosophie* (Berlin, 1964), pp. 310f. These ideas are still very much alive in the 'Sea of Faith' movement of the Church of England.

47 The sentiment was first attributed to him by the critic Jules Huret in 1891; but he reiterated it in *La Revue blanche* (1 July 1895) and reprinted it as part of '*Etalages*' in *Oeuvres* (Paris, 1945, p. 378): 'Une proposition qui émane de moi tant, diversement, citée à mon éloge ou par blâme – je la revendique . . . ici – veut, sommaire, que tout, au monde, existe pour aboutir à un livre.' Quoted by Bertrand Marchal, *La Religion de Mallarmé* (Paris, 1988), pp. 497, 500.

See Henri Mondor in Jacques Scherer, *Le 'Livre' de Mallarmé* (Paris, 1957), pp. xvf.

As for his Wagnerian enthusiasm, Mallarmé seems never to have actually attended one of the operas. Théophile Gautier, who claimed to have 'discovered' Wagner for the French public, and his followers, even had an influential periodical, the *Revue Wagnérienne*, to which a number of writers I mentioned earlier contributed: Villiers de l'Isle Adam, Barbey d'Aurevilly, J. K. Huysmans, Théophile Gautier's daughter Judith; *Le Wagnérisme* was a pervasive French literary phenomenon: in German there is not even such a word as *Wagnerismus*.

48   '. . . il parlait avec un charme incomparable, voltetant, tel un oiseau rare, à la cime des idées et de formules, faisant du verbe un jeu magnifique'; Léon Daudet, *Souvenirs* (Paris, 1920), p. 145.

49   To Claude Debussy, who told him of the plan to set *L'après midi d'un Faune* to music, he is reported to have said 'but I thought that I had already done that'. The remark may have been apocryphal; having heard the music, Mallarmé was very impressed, or so Debussy reports. Quoted in Stéphane Mallarmé, *Oeuvres* (Paris, 1945), pp. 1464f.: 'cette musique prolonge l'émotion de mon poème et en situe le décor plus passionément que la couleur.' Debussy's music became the famous Nijinski 'neo-classical' ballet for Diaghilev in 1912.

50   Marchal, *La Religion de Mallarmé*, pp. 498f., 520f., 537f. Schérer, *Le 'Livre' de Mallarmé*, pp. The 'celebrant' is called *lecteur/opérateur* (90a), though 106a mentions ballet, songs, *parades*. 111aff. considers permutations of audience and even prices. The *volume* on 119a; the identity of audience numbers and page numbers, 127af.; the ceremony 191aff.:

> *pureté lumière électr –*
> *– le volume, malgré l'im-*
> *pression fixe, devient par ce jeu, mobi-*
> *le – de mort il devient vie*

51   In any case, Mallarmé's distrust of the stage, of the actors and singers interposing between text and auditor, was radical. Fastidiously, he believed that the book rather than an orchestra would challenge the mystery of a reverentially silent audience. Henri Mondor, *Vie de Mallarmé* (Paris, 1943), pp. xixff.

52   *Bogostroitelstvo* was an answer to the instinctive 'God-seeking', *Bogoiskatelstvo*, of Christian thinkers and of the people in general. Anatoly Lunacharsky set these ideas out in his *Socialism and Religion*, 2 vols (New York, 1908–11) when he had a spell out of the Bolsheviks. Gorky gave a much more graphic account of it in a novel, *Ispoved*, 'A Confession', which was published in 1909 (in M. Gorky, *Sobranie Sochinenii*, Moscow, 1961, vol. v, pp. 173ff.) and dedicated to the great Russian base, Feodor Chaliapin. In it Gorky contrasts the disorientated, dirty and often fraudulent *Bogoiskately* (pp. 241ff.) with the much sounder believers in *Bogostroitelstvo* whom the hero finds through a factory, though his account of this curious religiosity includes a miracle 'performed' by an icon of the Virgin (pp. 302f.). But see Leszek Kolakowski, *Main Currents of Marxism* (Oxford, 1978), vol. II, pp. 445ff.; George L. Kline, *Religious and Antireligious Thought in Russia* (Chicago, IL, 1968).

53   Lenin explicitly attacked Lunacharsky's religious ideas in his 'Struggle for a Social Revolution' (German, 1925, p. 282); quoted in Rawidowicz, *Ludwig Feuerbachs Philosophie*, p. 493, n. 3.

54   The internationalist modern Olympic games were first held in Athens in 1892, but various *Turnfeste* were often associated with nationalist movements, notably the Czech Sokol group. By manipulating coloured shields, participants in them were later turned into 'points' in a composition, when, at a signal, the whole display became a slogan or a picture.

55   The Society was founded in 1875 in New York. By the time Mme Blavatsky died – in London – the society had some 100,000 members.

56   Unlike the theosophists, who claimed to receive their revelation from great and veiled masters, Steiner's anthroposophy was the result of personal illumination – helped only by a

429

friendly herb-gatherer. See Steiner, *The Story of my Life*, pp. 39ff. On his visit to the Society's London conference in 1902, when he took over the running of the German section, and his break with them – as a result of the promotion of the young Indian boy Krishnamurti as the world-teacher in 1906, see pp. 295ff.

57 On Ernst Haeckel and his monism, see above, chapter Five. On the place of evolution in Steiner's thinking, see Johannes Hemleben, *Rudolf Steiner und Ernst Haeckel* (Stuttgart, 1965), especially pp. 154ff.

58 On the forms of therapy, see Victor Bott, *Introduction to Anthroposophic Medicine* (London, 2004).

59 J. W. von Goethe, *Gedankausgabe*, ed. Ernst Beutler (Zürich, 1949), vol. I, pp. 516. The Greek word *ev-rhythmia* first appears in Plato's Republic (VII: 522a). It is a familiar and much debated architectural term since its appearance in Vitruvius I:2: iii; as a complement to 'symmetry' – but it is also applied to music and even rhetoric: by Plutarch (*Moralia* 45) and Isocrates (v: 27). According to Diogenes Laertes (*Vit. Phil.* VIII:46), Pythagoras of Rhegium first discovered its laws.

In 1916 Steiner designed the Goetheanum, convinced that no architect could interpret his ideas. It was burnt by persons unknown (right-wing extremists? Catholic zealots?) in 1922 and replaced by a concrete building he also designed, which still stands and which takes up the form of a skull; this, too, is a reference to Goethe, *Die Metamorphose der Tiere* (1949), vol. I, pp. 519. The first building, paid for by free gifts, was made of wood, living stuff, the second, paid for by insurance money, of inert cement, he said. It was completed in 1928, but Steiner died in 1926. See Rudolf Steiner, *The Mission of Spiritual Science and of its Building at Dornach, Switzerland* (London, 1917), pp. 38ff., and his *Ways to a New Style in Architecture* (London, 1927), p. v; also Wolfgang Pehnt, *Rudolf Steiner: Goetheanum Dornach* (Berlin, 1991), and Beat Wyss, *Der Wille zu Kunst* (Köln, 1996), pp. 142ff.

60 'The great wooden houses . . . taught me to move within the picture . . . every object was covered with brightly-coloured, elaborate ornament . . . I felt surrounded on all sides by the paintings which I had thus penetrated'; W. Kandinsky, *Rückblicke*, p. xiv, quoted by Peg Weiss, *Kandinsky in Munich: The Formative Jugendstil Years* (Princeton, NJ, 1979), p. 63. He would later react similarly to Bavarian Rococo churches.

61 Quoted by John Golding, *Paths to the Absolute* (London, 2000), p. 83.

62 It was rescored in 1899 and again in 1917. The larger-scale *Gurrelieder* is the setting of an epic sequence by the Danish Symbolist Jens Peter Jacobsen in 1901. It was ambitiously rescored in 1911 (no opus number).

63 Which appeared in the Schönberg festschrift (Munich, 1912) and is reprinted in *Arnold Schoenberg – Wassily Kandinsky: Letters, Pictures and Documents*, ed. Jelena Hahl-Koch (London, 1984), pp. 125ff.

64 Wilhelm Worringer, *Abstraction and Empathy: A Contribution to the History of Style*, trans. Michael Bullock (London, 1953), pp. 18, 104; original version, *Abstraktion und Einfühlung* (Munich, 1908). He is quoting Arthur Schopenhauer, *Kritik der Kantischen Philosophie* in *Werke* (Grossherzog Wilhelm Ernst Ausgabe) (Leipzig, n.d.), vol. I, p. 546. Worringer was also very influenced by the Viennese art historian Alois Riegl, who had established the historical concept of *Kunstwollen* – the notion that every age has its own complex of formal intentions which constitutes its 'style', so that the style of one epoch cannot be judged by reference to another style, another epoch, to which he added the notion that each region also had its proper formal geography, so that art had a geography, a *Kunstgeographie,* as articulated as its history.

65 He had arrived at this approach gradually and intuitively, though he later formulated a compositional method which became the basis of his very influential 'analytical drawing' class at the Bauhaus.

66　Usually listed as M(ikalojaus) K(onstantino); born in 1880, he studied music in Warsaw and Leipzig, and began painting in 1904, mostly pastels and tempera. Some of the paintings are in cycles (Sonata of the Sun, of Spring, etc.) and are subdivided into 'movements': *allegro, andante, finale*. See Antanas Venclova, *N/Ciurlionis*, 2nd edn (Vilnius, 1964), p. xvi. He died – insane – in 1911.

　　His work was known outside Russia through the advocacy of Boris Anrep, a mosaic artist who settled in London (his pavements in the National Gallery are too little known!) and published an article on him in the Moscow review *Apollon* in 1905 and included his work in the *Second Post-Impressionist Exhibition* in London in 1912.

67　His scenario for the ballet is reprinted in Wassily Kandinsky, *Essays über Kunst und Künstler*, ed. Max Bill (Bern, 1955), pp. 119ff. It was only produced once (and much later), in Dessau, in 1928; such theatrical performances had by then been up-staged by colour film. *Pictures at an Exhibition* is more often heard in orchestral versions, of which the best (or the most performed) is by Maurice Ravel. Victor Gartman or Hartman, an architect, spent the last years of his short life at Abramtsevo, where he had designed workshops and houses. The memorial exhibition of his drawings in the Academy of Arts was organized by Vladimir Stassov, to whom Moussorgsky dedicated the music. Kandinsky's damning of programme music in *On the Spiritual in Art* (Munich, 1911) (which was already translated into English in 1914) is concerned with the imitation of 'natural' noises, not with the finding of musical equivalents for visual phenomena.

　　Inevitably, at the Bauhaus too, Ludwig Hirschfeld-Mack and Kurt Schwerdtfeger experimented with some rather elementary synaesthetic devices – though the idea was so rooted there that it did not need the support of new technology. A student of Kandinsky's, Heinrich Neugeboren, produced a sculpture which showed synaesthesia without either colour or movement – he developed it three-dimensionally from a graphic plotting of some bars in Bach's E-flat minor fugue from the *Well-tempered Klavier*. He proposed that it should be executed on a large scale as a monument to Bach.

68　It was published in Wassily Kandinsky and Franz Marc, *Der Blaue Reiter* (Munich, 1965), pp. 210ff. Kandinsky himself says that the musical part was by Thomas von Hartmann; see Peter Jelavich, *Munich and Theatrical Modernism* (Cambridge, MA, 1985), pp. 217ff.

　　There was in fact only one of these almanacs and the origin of the name is uncertain. Kandinsky maintained that he liked blue riders and Marc liked blue horses; they were inspired by Frau Marc's excellent coffee – and the name seemed obvious. See Kandinsky, *Essays über Kunst und Künstler*, p. 137 n. 1 but also Klaus Lankheit, ed., *Der Blaue Reiter: Hrsg. Von Wassily Kandinsky und Franz Marc* (Munich, 1965), pp. 301, n. 8.

69　Although it was reprinted, the planned second volume never appeared. Lankheit, *Der Blaue Reiter*, pp. 276ff.

70　Sub-titled *Poème du Feu*; it was his opus 60.

71　Of 1900, opus 26. Of 1908, opus 54.

72　Kandinsky and Marc, *Der Blaue Reiter*, pp. 107ff. Scriabin's second symphony, of 1903, was his opus 29 and had no special title.

73　The first 'full' performance (though still not altogether successful) was in New York in 1915, with a keyboard designed by anonymous engineers from the General Electric Company. See Adrian Cornwell-Clyne, *Colour-Music: The Art of Light* (London, 1926), pp. 171ff., The two organs are described on pp. 188ff.

　　Kandinsky, who had commissioned Sabaneyev's article, had long been passionately interested in this idea himself. He attributes his knowledge of it to a Moscow piano-teacher, Mme Sacharin-Unkowsky. She adapted Castel's colour-and-note system to teach her pupils – and her device is still used by various computer programs for piano beginners.

　　Kandinsky implies that this lady suggested the idea to Scriabin, though I think synaesthesia was by then sufficiently familiar and he did not need to derive his ideas from a single source.

74 John Gage, *Colour and Culture: Practice and Meaning from Antiquity to Abstraction* (London, 1962), p. 243.

75 They, and some other less developed experiments are described by Adrian Cornwell-Clyne, *Colour-Music* (London, 1926), pp. 6ff. 183ff. Although he knows Castel's *Claveçin*, he does not seem to have heard of the pyrophone.

76 Claude Bragdon, *The Beautiful Necessity* [1910], 2nd edn (London, n. d.), p. 14.
On 'architecture as frozen music', see above, chapter x, p. x. Bragdon was a follower of the 'reform' theosophist, Vladimir Ouspensky, whose writings on the fourth dimension were to be important later.

77 Adolphe Appia, *Die Musik und die Inscenierung* (Munich, 1899).

78 Fortuny's theatrical ventures began modestly with a production of the Gilbert and Sullivan *Mikado* in his Venetian home in 1899. It led to the invitation to 'design' d'Annunzio's *Francesca da Rimini* which he declined, having realized he was expected to produce it as well, but he then designed the *Tristan* for La Scala. From then on, he worked on his system for using a folding half-dome on which projections 'constituted' the decor, which he patented in 1901. His patent was taken over by AEG. Beleuchtung System Fortuny GMBH. AEG was founded in Berlin in 1906, and the system installed in several German theatres. Anne-Marie Deschodt, *Mariano Fortuny* (Paris, 1979), pp. 209ff. The publicity was designed by Behrens in 1908.
Another project for a 'festival theatre' (with d'Annunzio again, in 1912) using the dome as a velarium for the whole building also failed.

79 Adolphe Appia, *Oeuvres complètes*, ed. Marie L. Bablet-Hahn and Denis Bablet (Basle, 1983–92), vol. II, pp. 276ff., 374ff. ; vol. III, pp. 107ff. And Irwin Spector, *Rhythm and Life: The Work of Emile Jaques-Dalcroze* (Stuyvesant, NY, 1990), pp. 82ff., 152ff.; Mariano Fortuny, *Eclairage scénique* (Paris, 1904); Guillermo de Osma, *Mariano Fortuny: His Life and Work* (New York, 1980), pp. 64ff.

80 Luciano Bottoni, *Storia del teatro italiano, 1900–1945* (Bologna, 1999), pp. 39ff. There was also a project for a theatre on the Gianicolo in Rome.

81 Eadweard Muybridge was the pseudonym of the British photographer Edward James Muggeridge who patented the Zoopraxisope which projected moving pictures of animals. E.-J. Marey's Chronophotograph was perfected about 1890. On these and even earlier mechanisms and Edison's part in the inventions, see Georges Sadoul, *Histoire générale du cinéma* (Paris, 1956), pp. 113ff., which also discusses their failure to achieve an accord with the sound recording phonograph which was being developed at the same time.

82 Eric Rhode, *A History of the Cinema* (Harmondsworth, 1978), pp. 15ff. Siegfried Giedion, *Mechanization Takes Command* (New York, 1955), pp. 17ff.

83 Henri Bergson, *L'Evolution créatrice* (Paris, 1911), p. 331.

> *Au lieu de nous attacher au devenir intérieur des choses, nous nous plaçons en dehors d'elles pour recomposer leur devenir artificiellement. Nous prenons des vues quasi instantanées sur la réalité qui passe, et comme elles sont caractéristiques de cette réalité, il nous suffit de les enfiler le long d'un devenir abstrait, uniforme, invisible, situé au fond de l'appareil de la connaissance pour imiter ce qu'est caractéristique dans ce devenir lui-même. Qu'il s'agisse de penser le devenir ou de l'exprimer, ou même de le percevoir, nous ne faisons guère autre chose qu'actionner une espèce de cinématographie intérieure.*

Many years later, when Bergson attempted a phenomenology of laughter, he suggested that the comic arises analogously in situations when what is general and moral-intellectual is mechanically interrupted by the specific and corporal-mechanical. *Le Rire* (Paris, 1936), pp. 16, 23ff. 152f.

84 The dematerialized voice and its relation to the body fascinated Mallarmé's friend, the novelist Villiers de l'Isle-Adam; in his last novel, *La Nouvelle Eve,* set in Edison's laboratory, he even considers the possibility of an artificial body endowed with a perfect voice which would reflect a perfect intelligence. See Esther Rashkin in *A New History of French Literature,* ed. Denis Hollier (Cambridge, MA, 1989), pp. 803ff.

85 For her first season (1901) she even commissioned a poster from the young Pablo Picasso. The sketch survives, but it was not used. Picasso, anyway, did not care for Japanese art. But the enthusiasm for her was infectious: 'ce fut beau comme Eschyle, simplement', wrote André Gide in *La Vogue.*

     Gordon Craig disapproved of women on the stage – generally (his mother and Eleanora Duse always excepted), nor did he care for what he considered Yakko's excessively westernizing innovations. E. Gordon Craig, *The Theatre Advancing* (London, 1921), pp. 261ff.

86 Though she claimed also to be inspired by two sculptures I mentioned earlier: Rude's *Marseillaise* on the Arc de Triomphe de l'Etoile and Carpeaux's unfortunate *Dance* at the Opéra. She was somewhat disingenuous – there was a great deal of interest in Greek dance during the 1890s in Paris. Maurice Emmanuel's extended and very well illustrated *Essai sur l'orchestique grecque*, subtitled *Etude des mouvements d'après les monuments figurés* (Paris, 1895) was quickly sold out and widely discussed.

87 Though her method – and that of many of her contemporaries and successors – owes a great deal to the first theorist of 'expressive' dance, François Delsarte (1811–1871) who evolved a triple division of the human body; physical (below the belt), emotional (bust and arms), intellectual (neck and head) which corresponded to three movements: opposition, parallelism, succession. On this he based a pantomymic system which he taught to actors: Jenny Lind and Rachel were his most famous pupils.

88 Isadora Duncan, *My Life* (London, 1928), pp. 162f. The mixture of English and German is hers. She gives an account of her first Russian visit in January 1905, and of meeting the funeral procession of the victims of the Revolution on p. 173.

89 Rimsky-Korsakov's *Shéchérezade* was created by Fokine and Bakst, danced by Ida Rubinstein and Nijinski. It was shown in Paris in 1910, two years after Chaliapin's triumph in *Boris Goudunov.* Serge Diaghilev came from Perm in Siberia, and was as conscious of his provincial status as he was determined to make a mark. He described himself lucidly in a letter to his stepmother as: '1. A charlatan, but full of dash; 2. A great charmer; 3. Cheeky; 4. A reasonable man with few scruples; 5. Someone afflicted with a complete absence of talent [who has] found his true vocation, to be a patron of the arts. For that I have everything I need except money – but that will come.' Adapted from Alexander Schouvaloff, *The Art of Ballet-Russes* (New Haven, CT, 1998), p. 42.

90 It was very near the Kremlin and was dynamited and pulled down in 1930–34 to make way for the competed-for but never built Palace of the Soviets, but was in fact replaced by the giant Moskva swimming pool and reconstructed on the site in the years 1995–2001.

91 The Tsarina Alexandra Feodorovna (née Charlotte of Prussia) had preferred Schinkel, who had designed a chapel for her as well as a dream palace in the Crimea. But his Neues Museum was considered 'impractical' by Russian administrators, while Klenze's Munich museums were considered more up-to-date. He was also engaged to complete the interior and build an iconostasis in St Isaac's Cathedral, which the tsar considered both too Byzantine and too Baroque. Klenze's design was rejected in the end. See Adrian von Buttlar, *Leo von Klenze: Leben–Werk–Vision* (Munich, 1999), pp. 39ff.

92 *Peredvizhniki,* though it was not the painters who wandered, but the itinerant exhibitions. The 'realists' left the academy in 1863, but the Stroganov art school in Moscow offered an

alternative training which also taught craft skills.

93 On Overbeck and the Nazarenes, see above. On the meeting with Mamontov, see Eleanora Paston, *Abramtsevo: Iskusstvo I Zizn* (Moscow, 2003), p. 314. Overbeck died, aged 80, in 1869.

94 Abramtsevo had already been a literary resort when it belonged to Gogol's friends, the Slavophile Aksakovs; a part of *Dead Souls* was written there. See Camilla Gray, *The Russian Experiment in Art* (London, 1962), pp. 9ff., 20ff.; Isaiah Berlin, *Russian Thinkers* (London, 1978), pp. 26f., 168.; Paston, *Abramtsevo*, pp. 16ff.

95 On the disputes between Slavophiles and Westernizers, see Berlin, *Russian Thinkers*, pp. 6ff.; and Judith Deutsch Kornblatt and Richard F. Gustafson, eds, *Russian Religious Thought* (Madison, WI, 1996), pp. 7ff. 158f.

96 On the whole episode and the Mamontov circle, see Paston, *Abramtsevo*. On the relation between form-masters and trade-masters at the Bauhaus, see below.

97 His father, Nicolai Benois (he transliterated it from Benua), the son of a French émigré, had won the Russian equivalent of the Rome Prize in 1836, and in the course of his tour had fallen in with the surviving Nazarenes – who fired him with the idea of a possible national revival in Russia. He built in Peterhof and collaborated with K. A. Tron on the Great Palace of the Kremlin in what was considered a 'national' style. Tron (or Thon) produced its major monument, the Cathedral of Christ the Saviour, in 1840–83. Benois was very much in sympathy with the aims of Abramtsevo: he saw the productions there as realizations of the Wagnerian ideal of the *Gesamtkunstwerk*. See Paston, *Abramtsevo*, p. 337.

98 The first Fabergé Easter egg seems to have been made to the order of Alexander III (who had a hand in designing it) in 1885 when the workshop was given the imperial patent. By 1917, when the workers unionized themselves in a council, there were 500 employees between the parent workshop in St Petersburg and those of Moscow, Odessa and London (for more modest products). In 1918 the Fabergé family emigrated. See Kenneth Snowman, *Fabergé: Goldsmith to the Imperial Court of Russia* (London, 1971).

99 Paston, *Abramtsevo*, pp. 278ff., 307ff. The Paris exhibit was Konstantin Korovin and Viktor Vasnetzov, who also designed the Abramtsevo church.

100 Walcot was born (1887) in Odessa to English parents, and studied in Paris as well as St Petersburg. After the Revolution, he lived in Britain (where he died in 1943), and became well known as an atmospheric etcher and a perspective draughtsman for architectural projects and antique restorations which he often exhibited at the Royal Academy. His vivid watercolour style owed something to Vrubel. Paston, *Abramtsevo*, p. 244.

Mamontov had ambitious plans for an arts complex – including two cinemas – which collapsed when he was arrested (for misappropriation of funds); when absolved and released a year later, he had lost most of his financial clout. Even then, he reflected on future developments and was convinced of the demise of the framed easel-picture; he retained Abramtsevo and continued to act as a patron, however. He died in March 1918. Ibid., pp. 359ff.

101 Shukhov had gone to the United States after his Moscow graduation in 1876 to spy out the latest technical achievements. He seems to have been little interested in metal construction, but reported on the Singer sewing machine, the typewriter and the Bell telephone. On his return in 1878, he became involved in a metal construction firm, of which he became the manager when it was nationalized after 1918. A brilliant mathematician, his principal innovations were concerned with lattice design, and he patented several latticed structural devices during the 1890s. The US navy used his observation towers on warships. He became the favoured engineer for many of the structures of that 'Silver Age' (as the pre-1914 flowering was sometimes called) and worked with a concrete specialist, Arthur Loleit. There were no architects working in Russia at the time to equal their brilliance and originality. For a treatment of Shukhov's methods and achievement, see Elizabeth Cooper English, 'Arkhitektura/Mnimosti: The Origins of Soviet Avant-Garde Rationalist Architecture in the Russian Mystical-Philosophical and Mathematical

Intellectual Tradition', PhD thesis (University of Pennsylvania, 2000), pp. 20ff.

102 Nikolai, a scion of this banking family, edited the most luxurious of the art magazines of the time, *Zoloteie Runo* (The Golden Fleece – a successor to the World of Art) at the time the house was built. It included a secluded Old Believer chapel. Art Nouveau had more single-minded epigones – two engineers, R. A. Berzcn and A. K. Montag, who designed the metal-and-stone Petersburg Nimetti theatre in 1901–2 (both seem to have been destroyed) as one of the largest buildings in the style. It was also innovative in that the stage faced two ways – towards a closed auditorium and towards an open-air one – an arrangement taken up by a number of architects after the Revolution. Shekhtel also made a neo-Russian design for the much larger, southward Kazan station in 1911.

103 To music Debussy based on Mallarmé's poem – see earlier this chapter, n. 42.

104 Emile Jaques-Dalcroze was an Austrian musician of French origin, a pupil of the great Austrian composer Anton Bruckner, and of Leo Délibes in Paris. It is not clear whether he or the Steiners first used the word 'eurythmics' for their method, but see note 59.

   In his *Rhythm, Music and Education* (New York, 1921), Duncan is criticized as being dis-continuous, too dependent on the 'poses' found on pottery and sculpture (pp. 242f.), but also praised for the fluidity of her movements (p. 269). But he also found the Nijinski *L'Après Midi* 'distasteful' (his word; pp. 267f.) – also because of the discontinuity.

   Debussy hated the ballet, but precisely 'because it is Dalcrozian, and this to tell you that I consider M. Dalcroze to be one of the worst enemies of music! You can imagine what havoc his method has caused in the soul of this wild young Nijinski!' Letter to Robert Godet quoted by Lynn Garafola, *Diaghilev's Ballets Russes* (New York, 1989), p. 61.

105 It was founded by Wolf Dohrn, whose father Adolf had, for his part, founded the Naples Aquarium where Hans von Marées and Adolf von Hildebrandt had worked thirty years earlier. On Hellerau, see also Peter Guth *et al.*, *Hellerau, Festspielhaus-Ensemble* (Ludwigs-burg, 2002). After 1933 the theatre building was taken over by the ss and after 1945 by the Red Army. It was returned to its original use in 1992.

   The term *eurythmy* was also claimed for the somewhat different methods of Dalcroze and Rudolf Steiner, which last regarded it as the basis of his educational methods – as well as an art, 'a kind of voiceless, visible speech' or 'ensouled gymnastics'. In fact, Marie von Sievers (Mrs Rudolf Steiner) seems to have coined the term in 1912, though her husband had formu-lated the basic ideas about 1908. Rudolf Steiner, *Rhythms of Learning*, ed. Roberto Trostli (Hudson, NY, 1998), p. 299; R. Steiner, *The Renewal of Education*, ed. Eugene Schwartz (Great Barrington, MA, 2001), pp. 103ff.

106 Marco de Michelis, *Heinrich Tessenow, 1876–1950* (Milan, 1991), pp. 13ff., 201ff. C.-E. Jeanneret [Le Corbusier], *Etude sur le mouvement d'Art décoratif en Allemagne* (Chaux-de-Fonds, 1912; reprinted New York, 1968), pp. 49f. Tessenow had by then even patented a system of ventilat-ed hollow walls. In 2002–3 the buildings were restored as a theatre and mediathèque.

107 Diaghilev engaged one of Dalcroze's pupils, Myriam Rambam (also known as Cyvia Ramberg; and Marie Rambert – and Madame Rythmichka by the dancers), and she was in part responsible for Nijinski's choreography of the *Sacre*. She moved to England where she started her own company and dance school that still bears the Rambert name.

   Mary Wingman (originally Wiegmann) and her assistant Hanya Holm (originally Johanna Eckert) introduced his methods in the USA where Holm had a successful career on Broadway and in Hollywood. Her school trained many of the 'modern dance' virtuosos.

108 The Institute was short-lived, closed at (and by) the outbreak of the First World War, by financial problems, and by chauvinism. It was revived by Wolf Dohrn's brother Heinrich after the war, while Jaques-Dalcroze (1865–1950) himself went on to teach both music and his method in Switzerland. He was also a prolific composer: several chamber works, two violin concertos, ballet suites, choral works and several operas are published. And of course there

are a number of writings about his dance-gymnastic method. On Le Corbusier's several visits to Hellerau, his meeting Tessenow and the offer of work on the garden city as well as his support of his brother Albert, see H. Allen Brooks, *Le Corbusier's Formative Years* (Chicago, IL, 1927), pp. 225, 235.

Albert Jeanneret (the brother of Le Corbusier) wrote on the method for *L'Esprit nouveau*, but it was much more popular in the USA. Several books by or on Dalcroze were published there during the 1920s and '30s. But see Irwin Spector, *Rhythm and Life: The Work of Emile Jacques-Dalcroze* (Stuyvesant, MA, 1990).

Tessenow moved to Berlin, where his best-known pupil was Albert Speer. As a life-long socialist, Tessenow disapproved of Speer's colossal projects. Of the Nuremberg stadium he merely said 'You think you have created something? It's just overbearing (es macht Eindruck), that's all'; when shown the Hitler–Speer model for the rebuilding he is said to have remarked 'you are all mad!'. Albert Speer, *Erinnerungen* (Frankfurt, 1969), pp. 40, 159, and Gita Sereny, *Albert Speer: His Battle with Truth* (New York, 1995), p. 147.

Charles-Edouard Jeanneret was a frequent visitor and was as enthusiastic about Hellerau as a properly organized garden city as he was about Tessenow's project. He even considered leaving Behrens' office to work with him on Hellerau. Albert established a eurythmic school soon after 1920 in Paris, in a house designed by his brother, and continued to teach the Dalcroze method.

109 In fact, *Diogen* was a 'free (unrhymed hexameter) version' of a play by Frédéric Pyat published in 1846 and translated into German that same year. Hartleben worked on it spasmodically between 1894 and 1898 and some scenes were published in *Pan* in December 1896; he died before completing it and it was published posthumously (Berlin, 1905).

The performance took place in a garden pavilion, not in the Folkwang hall which Behrens had designed. There was no painted scenery: 'Die Malerei soll eben hier keine Natur darstellen, sondern vielmehr ein schöner . . . Hintergrund sein, vor dem schöne Menschen in prächtigen Gewandungen und mit feinen Bewegungen die Schönste Sprache reden'; Fritz Hoeber, *Peter Behrens* (Munich, 1913), p. 216.

Deirdre Priddin, *The Art of the Dance in French Literature* (London, 1952), quotes in this connection Ortega y Gasset's view that the dancer was to 'dehumanize'; he was to 'vider la danse, autant que se peut, de son humaine matière'.

110 Edward Gordon Craig, *On the Art of the Theatre* (London, 1912), p. 54; this is the chapter called 'The Actor and the *Übermarionette*'. This echo of Nietzsche's *Übermensch* seems to be set by Craig in Heinrich von Kleist's *Marionettentheater*. Heinrich von Kleist, *Sämtliche Werke*, ed. Arnold Zweig (Munich, 1923), vol. IV, pp. 396ff. 'Uber das Marionettentheater'; but see Curt Hohoff, *Heinrich von Kleist* (Hamburg, 1958), pp. 130ff. Ladislao Mittner, *Storia della letteratura tedesca, 1700–1820* (Turin, 1964), pp. 874f. Kleist's ingenious speculation on the puppeteer's jerky movement being related to the puppet's graceful ones as a number is to its logarithm is more subtle than Craig's, but has an analogous motivation, the de-personalizing of the actor. Kleist the playwright and producer had to endure too much 'personality'.

Craig was the son of the great actress Ellen Terry by William Godwin (whom he never met) whom I mentioned in the previous chapter as the favoured architect of the Wilde–Whistler circle, and whose widow Whistler married. But Godwin had also written theatre criticism and having designed some sets, also turned to production: see Innes, *Edward Gordon Craig*, pp. 25ff.

111 Quoted by Frank Kermode in 'Poet and Dancer before Diaghilev', in *Puzzles and Epiphanies* (London, 1963), p. 1. Yeats turned to Japanese Nō drama as a model for his theatre. So Roy Foster, *W. B. Yeats: A Life* (Oxford, 2003), vol. II, pp. 34ff.

112 Although they seem to have corresponded even earlier, in 1899. The older Rathenau, Walter's father Emil, had arranged to manufacture Thomas Alva Edison's incandescent light bulbs

436

after 1881 and soon diversified into other electric equipment.

113   The AEG was 'undoubtedly the largest European combination of industrial units under a centralized control and with a central organization'. So Walter Rathenau in 1907, quoted in Kessler, *Walter Rathenau*, p. 117.

114   Behrens himself suggested that Paul Jordan, one of Emil Rathenau's most trusted associates, should initiate the negotiation, having been impressed with his recent work. The appointment does not seem to have been in Walter's gift. Tilmann Buddensieg *et al.*, *Industriekultur* (Cambridge, 1984), pp. 10ff., 488.

115   Jeanneret, *Etude sur le mouvement d'art décoratif en Allemagne*, p. 44: 'Sa plus récente fabrique, la Turbinen Halle, a même été qualifiée par certains de Kathedrale der Arbeit.' (*sic*).

116   He had, however, inserted a vignette-type relief of a single female figure by Encke into the shorn pediment over the main door of the Mannesmann offices.

117   Jeanneret, *Etude sur le mouvement d'art décoratif en Allemagne*, p. 74.

118   Georg Simmel, *Soziologie*, in *Gesamtausgabe*, ed. Otthein Rammstedt (Frankfurt, 1989), vol. XI, pp. 414ff. Textual variants on pp. 947ff. The text was originally published in 1908 as *Psychologie des Schmuckes*. I have departed at points from the standard translation by Kurt H. Wolff in *The Sociology of Georg Simmel* (New York, 1950), pp. 338ff. But see the grossly unjust dismissal of Simmel by Rathenau in Kessler, *Walter Rathenau*, p. 26.

119   Hermann Muthesius, *Kunstgewerbe und Architektur* (Jena, 1907), pp. 12ff.

120   Burkhardt Rukschcio and Roland Schachel, *Adolf Loos: Leben und Werk* (Vienna, 1989): catalogue no. 4, p. 417; reproduced by Benedetto Gravagnuolo, *Adolf Loos: Theory and Works* (New York, 1982), p. 92. The theatre was to seat 4,000 and Loos returned to it, several times, the last time when he discussed an opera with Schönberg about 1930.

121   'Von einem armen reichen Manne', first published in *Neues Wiener Tageblatt* (26 April 1900); reprinted in *Ins Leere Gesprochen* (Paris, 1921), pp. 159ff. The standard English version mistranslates the title as 'poor little rich man'.

   As late as 1930, Loos on a visit to Darmstadt took his wife to look at the Behrens house: a necktie pattern (*Krawattenmuster*) he calls it, and finds it funny. 'There are others now who laugh at the *Künstlerkolonie* with me'. 'A few years ago', he adds, 'I was the only one' Claire Loos, *Adolf Loos Privat* (Vienna, 1985), p. 104.

122   'Ornament und Verbrechen', in *Franfurter Zeitung*, 1908; reprinted in *Trotzdem* (Innsbruck, 1931), pp. 79ff. It was also published in translation in *L'Esprit nouveau*. The parallel to Simmel's text is evident – though I do not know of any direct contact between them.

123   'The Chippendale chair is so perfect, that it will suit any room that has been created since'; 'Josef Veillich' [1929], in *Trotzdem*, p. 252.

124   Though the direct source for some of the ideas on degeneracy may have been the rather repulsive ideas of Otto Weininger, whose *Geschlecht und Charakter* was published in Vienna in 1903, the year he also, very publicly, committed suicide.

125   In 1922 he designed a department store in Alexandria in Egypt using giant Ionic pilasters, executed by a local architect. Rukschcio and Schachel, *Adolf Loos*, p. 484; a coloured perspective by his pupil Rudolf Wels decorated his office (*Kaminzimmer)* at home, fig. 129. But the Chicago building was more important to him, and he even tried to persuade the Tribune proprietor, on a visit to France, that he had to build it – a beacon of the freedom of the press, the Chicago equivalent of the Statue of Liberty. Ibid., pp. 23ff., 273f. and 562f. Elsie Altmann-Loos, *Mein Leben mit Adolf Loos* (Vienna, 1984), pp. 175ff.

126   'Weiszer Hochpriester der Wahrheit', the opening line of Georg Trakl's poem on Kraus whom he calls *Zörnender Magier*, 'wrathful magician'; in *Dichtungen* (Salzburg and Leipzig, 1938), p. 132.

127   In *Die Fackel*, 389/390, 15, 12 (1913), Walter Benjamin comments on this: 'Loos' primary business was . . . to separate the work of art from the implement; in the same way, Kraus' primary

business is to keep information and the work of art quite separate.' Walter Benjamin, 'Karl Kraus' in *Illuminationen* (Frankfurt, 1969), p. 375.

128 In *Trotzdem*, p. 107. The italics are Loos' own. Loos gave an account of how he weaned the young Kokoschka from his employment at the Wiener Werkstätte, ibid., p. 256. On their complex and emotional relationship, see Rukschcio and Schachel, *Adolf Loos*, pp. 139ff.

129 Though he could be scathing about the label, as in his poem 'Expressionismus', *Worte in Versen* (Munich, 1959), p. 341. In any case, it was not a clear description. In 1912 Roger Fry wanted to call the *Second Post-Impressionist Exhibition* at the Grafton Gallery 'Expressionist' because of the number of Russian works which seemed to him to deserve that label.

130 Rukschcio and Schachel, *Adolf Loos*, pp. 556, no. 145. It was to be a black granite ziggurat with white, raked joints.

131 There was some talk, when Poelzig left the Academy, of offering the position to Gropius. Things fell out otherwise. On the Breslau exhibition buildings, see Jerzy Ilkosz and Beate Szymanski, eds, *Hans Poelzig in Breslau* (Delmenhorst, 2000), pp. 389ff.; on the *Festspiel*, pp. 95ff.

132 Max Berg became a senior building official in Breslau, a post he held until 1925. Poelzig and he would collaborate frequently. There are some rough sketches for the crematorium in Breslau and one large decorative gouache for the decoration. He was very interested in the whole problem of high-rise office buildings in Germany as a means of limiting sprawl. See Véronique Mauron, *Werke der Oskar Kokoschka-Stiftung* (Mainz, 1994), pp. 42ff. Richard Konwiarz, 'Neue Baukunst in Breslau', in *Wasmuths Monatshefte zur Baukunst IX* (Tübingen, 1925), p. 156.

133 Elias Canetti, 'Karl Kraus, Schule des Widerstands' in *Macht und Überleben: Drei Essays* (Berlin, 1972), pp. 33f. In making the extract I have impoverished Canetti's image but also softened his condemnation. An earlier version of this essay was called 'Warum ich nicht schreibe wie Karl Kraus'. On his gradual enchantment by Kraus and his eventual 'liberation', see his *Die Fackel im Ohr* (Munich, 1980), pp. 79, 142, 180ff., and *Das Augenspiel* (Munich, 1985), 124ff., 136ff.

134 Kraus himself was usually respectful about Freud, but reacted violently when his work was 'analysed' in 1910 in a paper to the Vienna Psychoanalytic Circle by a young analyst, Fritz Wittels. Ernest Jones, *The Life and Work of Sigmund Freud* (London, 1955), vol. II, pp. 133f. There were many references in *Die Fackel*, as well as satires, such as 'Die Psychoanalen' (in 1959, pp. 412ff.).

135 The admiration was reciprocal and long-lasting; Loos, never very well off, became one of the financial guarantors of the first performances of *Gurrelieder*. What they did have in common was a conviction about the ethical implication of their activities: in a Loosian note, Schoenberg wrote that he wanted to 'substitute a craftsmanly discipline for the bad aesthetics of musicians'. Preface to the *Harmonielehre* (Vienna, 1911).

136 This, one of the most generally discussed twentieth-century paintings, is now in the Museum of Modern Art, New York. On its genesis, see, with bibliography, John Richardson, *A Life of Picasso* (New York, 1991), p. 55. It is of that picture and its contemporaries that Braque remarked: Picasso was trying to get his viewers to eat pitch and drink petrol.

137 Now in the Museum of Modern Art, New York.

138 Albert Gleizes and Jean Metzinger, *Du 'Cubisme', On 'Cubism', Über den 'Cubismus'*, ed. Fritz Metzinger (Frankfurt, 1993), p. 28: 'Qui comprend Cézanne pressent le Cubisme.'

139 Changes in style and in the modelling of volumes are also said to be due, in Picasso's case, to his encounter with old Iberian sculpture which cultivates distortion and anomaly in contrast to African masks whose stylizing emphasizes symmetry and regularity. Perhaps it is true that the Iberian precedent allowed him the violent distortions which African masks taught him to restrain: they are, one critic maintained, the source of what is calculated (*savant*) in his art. There is therefore a sharp dialectic between the stylizing, geometricizing urge and the coarse,

expressive deformation which marks the *Demoiselles* and much of his proto-Cubist and earliest Cubist work. To Braque, on the other hand, African sculpture acted as a release for his expressive urges, and maybe that was what Picasso meant when he told André Malraux that Braque did not really understand African sculpture 'because he was not superstitious'. Braque's fine collection of African sculpture seems to give the lie to Picasso's jibe.

140 The French term *peintre-décorateur* suggests a whole world of skill which the term house-painter obliterates.

141 Gleizes and Metzinger, *Du 'Cubisme'*, p. 40: 'Un objet n'a pas une forme absolue, il en a plusieurs, il y en a autant qu'il y a de plans dans le domaine de la signification'; p. 32: 'Si l'on désirait rattacher l'espace des peintres à quelque géométrie, il faudrait en référer aux savants non euclidiens, méditer longuement certains théorèmes de Rieman' (*sic*); p. 40: 'La géométrie est une science, la peinture est un art. Le géomètre mesure, le peintre savoure.'

142 *De Caelo* I:4; 271a.

143 However, according to Linda Dalrymple Henderson, on whose book, *The Fourth Dimension and Non-Euclidean Geometry in Modern Art* (Princeton, NJ, 1983), I shall rely for much of what follows, the suggestion that time is a fourth dimension was first made by D'Alembert in his article 'Dimension' in the *Encyclopédie*; her pp. 9f. It does seem as if the term 'fourth dimension' was coined in the circle of the Cambridge philosopher Henry More. On his 'spiritual' use of the term, see C. A. Patrides, *The Cambridge Platonists* (Cambridge, 1970), pp. 31ff.

Descartes had himself suggested the existence of 'superforms', for which he was rebuked by his contemporaries. But some nineteenth-century writers also speculated on it; notably Feodor Dostoyevsky in *The Brothers Karamasov* (written about 1870) has Ivan speculating on other dimensions in the course of his struggle with God.

144 Henri Bergson, *Essai sur les données immédiates de la conscience*, 7th edn (Paris, 1909), pp. 68ff., a passage which also sets out his critique of the Kantian *a priori* space.

145 'On ne rejoindra la durée que par un détour; il faut s'installer en elle d'emblée. C'est que l'Intelligence refuse le plus souvent de faire, habituée qu'elle est à penser le mouvant par l'intermédiaire de l'immobile.' Henri Bergson, *L'Evolution créatrice*, 11th edn (Paris, 1911), p. 323. This is a viewing of the problem against Bergson's general discussion of the subject reading the world from within, by intuition, or from without, by analysis. On the parallel between Bergson and his exact contemporary Edmund Husserl, see Herbert Spiegelberg, *The Essentials of the Phenomenological Method* (The Hague, 1965), pp. 128, 398f. The most recent account of the literature in Leszek Kolakowski, *Bergson* (Oxford, 1985). His view that Bergson's failing is that 'one cannot be Descartes and Schelling simultaneously' seems too radical, however.

146 Christopher Green, *Léger and the Avant-Garde* (New Haven, CT, 1976), p. 27; although Green wrote this about Léger, the same could apply to many artists of the time. John Richardson, *A Life of Picasso* (London, 1991), vol. I, p. 203, notes that Max Jacob, who was a friend and something of a mentor to Picasso from their first meeting in 1901, had read deeply in Bergson as a philosophy student. Bergson criticizes the Kantian space-time discussion at length in *Essai sur les données immédiates de la conscience*, pp. 69ff.

147 On its logical implications, see Léon Brunschvigg, *Les Etapes de la philosophie mathématique* (Paris, 1930), pp. 313ff.

148 'A Square' (i.e. Edwin Abbott Abbott), *Flatland: A Romance of Many Dimensions*, 2nd revd edn (London, 1884), describes a world peopled by two-dimensional shapes, where the mere suggestion of a possible third dimension is considered a crime. It implies that a similar relation exists between inhabitants of the fourth dimension and our space:

Suppose a person of the fourth dimension, condescending to visit you, would say, 'Whenever you open your eyes, you see a plane (which is of two dimensions) and infer a

Solid (which is of three); but in reality you also see (though you do not recognize) a Fourth Dimension, which is not colour nor brightness nor anything of the kind, but a true Dimension, although I cannot point out to you its direction, nor can you possibly measure it . . .

149 Brunschvigg, *Les Etapes de la philosophie mathématique*, pp. 440ff. Bergson called *temps homogène*, time 'spaced' by a pendulum swing, the fourth dimension of space: which allows him to imagine a space without *durée. Essai sur les données immédiates de la conscience*, pp. 83f.

150 The subject was treated much more jokily by Lewis Carroll/Charles Dodgson whose *Alice Through the Looking Glass* suggested the existence of another and quite different world. It was also exploited by occultists: unscrupulous 'mediums' claimed that their visions were figures from other dimensions and this subject entered theosophical speculations. Mme Blavatsky herself may have been sceptical about the matter but 'Bishop' Leadbeater, whom I have quoted on colour-music, connected such visions with an 'Astral plane'.

151 A rather louche personage who seemed to know them all, Maurice Princet, an actuary with some knowledge of mathematics and a chess enthusiast, would certainly have shown Jouffret's book to some painters; if Richardson (*A Life of Picasso*, p. 5) is to be believed, Princet was 'charmless and clever' and lost his wife (with Picasso's connivance) to Derain; but though he eschewed painters after that, he did play chess with Marcel Duchamp. Both Braque and Picasso have denied any contact with him and Daniel-Henri Kahnweiler, in his *Juan Gris: His Life and Work* (London, 1947), p. 71, dismisses him contemptuously. Princet's part in the gener-ation of Cubism (through Max Jacob) may have been exaggerated by their rather unfriendly critic, Louis Vauxcelles; see Dalrymple Henderson, *The Fourth Dimension and Non-Euclidean Geometry in Modern Art*, pp. 71f., 310ff.

152 Most decisively later, by Juan Gris, into 'analytical' (early) and 'synthetic' (late) in the answer to a questionnaire about Cubism reprinted by Kahnweiler, *Juan Gris*, pp. 144f. But Apollinaire himself *Méditations Esthétiques* 1913/50, pp. 83f.) divides the movement into Scientific, Physical, Orphic and Instinctive (in which last he includes Matisse and Marinetti).
     Le Corbusier and Amédée Ozenfant, *La Peinture moderne* (Paris, 1925) set the break at 1912; though they called the earlier period 'hermetic' or 'collectivist'. But see John Golding, *Paths to the Absolute* (London, 2000), pp. 114ff.

153 His real name was Gaston Duchamp, but he assumed the pseudonym Jacques Villon out of admiration for the poet François Villon.

154 On Beuron, and the monks' French disciples, see above, chapter Five.

155 He later devised two chessboards, for one of which he made most of the pieces, while the other was a pocket one; he had an almost obsessive, but also rather aesthetic interest in the beauty of the game which, some critics said, was a handicap. Arturo Schwarz, *The Complete Works of Marcel Duchamp*, 2nd edn (New York, 1970), cat. nos 364, 366, 504, 506.

156 Duchamp himself was quite explicit that he had seen no Futurist works when he started working the 'Nude'. Marcel Duchamp, *Marchand du Sel*, ed. Michel Sanouillet (Paris, 1958), pp. 152ff. The text is taken from a radio interview with James Johnson Sweeny in January 1956.

157 Before leaving for New York, he took a job as a trainee librarian at the Bibliothèque Ste Geneviève.

158 Why *Le Figaro* printed this piece of bombastic prose on its front page is not clear. Was it simply a paid advertisement?

159 F.-T. Marinetti, *Le Futurisme* (Paris, 1911), pp. 83ff.

160 Ibid., p. 8. On the 'Battle of Hernani' and the foundation of the Romantic movement, see above,

161 Described in F. T. Marinetti, *Guerra sola igiene del mondo* (Milan, 1915), pp. 51ff.

162 His celebration of his part in it, the verse-novel *Le Monoplane du pape* (Paris, 1912), must be one of the most distasteful literary productions of the time.

163 Apollinaire had mocked Jourdain (as early as 1907) in a piece of doggerel:

> *Comme architec*
> *On dit 'Quel mec!'*
> *Il a du poil au ventre!*
> *Et on l'assure'*
> *Qu'en fait d'peintur'*
> *C'est un gai dilettante.*

164 On Mare, one of the new profession of *enssemblier*, see Emile Sedeyn, *Le Mobilier* (Paris, 1921), pp. 71, 80 – though it has no word about the Cubist house of 1914; on which see Eve Blau and Nancy Troy, eds, *Architecture and Cubism* (Cambridge, MA, 1997), p. 26ff.

165 'Dès que la sculpture s'éloigne de la nature elle devient de l'architecture . . . L'architecte, l'ingégnieur doivent construire avec des intentions sublimes: élever la plus haute tour, préparer au lierre et au temps une ruine plus belle que les autres . . . Duchamp-Villon a de l'architecture cette conception titanique, il n'y a pour lui que la lumière qui compte . . . la lumière incorruptible.' Guillaume Apollinaire, *Méditations esthétiques: les peintres cubistes* (Geneva, 1950), pp. 79ff. The opening 'salvo' is criticized by Guillaume Janneau in *L'Art cubiste* (Paris, 1929), p. 89, as being too absolute, but by then the work of Jacques Lipschitz and Henri Laurens suggested other approaches to the problem of a Cubist sculpture.

166 Guillaume Apollinaire, 'Antonin Gaudi' of 14 July 1914, in *Chroniques d'Art, 1902–18*, ed. L.-C. Breunig (Paris, 1960), p. 411; Loos, whose exhibition had been announced, appears in the Gaudí text as 'le plus grand architecte Viennois'. A rather unfriendly dismissal of Futurist claims pushed by 'overfilled moneybags' of the movement on p. 262.

167 Raymond Duchamp-Villon was gassed in 1916 and did not recover from its effects, dying in 1918.

168 Muybridge worked mostly in the USA. Both he and Marey published a vast amount of material. But see above, chapter Six, pp. 256ff.

169 Anton Giulio Bragaglia produced his own 'photodynamism' before turning to more conventional set design.

170 They worked under the pseudonyms Arnaldo Ginna and Bruno Corra.

171 Arnaldo and Bruno Corradini signed the Manifesto of Futurist Cinema (with Marinetti, Balla, Settimelli, Chiti) pseudonymously. On their short film, *La vita futurista*, see Pontus Hulten, ed., *Futurism and Futurisms*, exh. cat. Palazzo Grassi, Venice) (London, 1986), pp. 448ff., 455, 485. The links between Futurism, spiritualism and theosophy have been very neglected.

 More adventurous film-makers – Viking Eggeling, Oskar Fischinger, Alexander Laszlo – all tried their hands at semi-abstract colour film during the 1920s and '30s.

172 Boccioni had written a draft architectural manifesto in 1913; but it was not discovered until 1971 when it was published in his collected works, *Gli scritti editi e inediti*, ed. Zeno Birolli, Milan, while Carlo Carrà, having introduced Sant'Elia to the Futurists, showed his first group of drawings in May 1914 when a draft of the Manifesto was published in the catalogue and was revised for the 'definitive' publication two months later. The matter of the authorship is discussed in some detail by Esther da Costa Meyer in *The Work of Sant'Elia* (New Haven, CT, 1995), pp. 156ff. Meanwhile, Prampolini had published his proclamation in the Roman *Piccolo giornale d'Italia* in January.

 Apart from the Manifesto, Sant'Elia's testament are some Olbrichian houses and tombs, as well as 'Romantic' projects done in collaboration. There are some three hundred more or less Futurist drawings, one of which was 'worked up' to make a Sant'Elia monument in his home city, Como in 1930 by Prampolini, whose lack of building skills led to his being replaced by another Comasco, Giuseppe Terragni, the most brilliant member of the anti-Futurist 'Group 7'.

173 Carlo Carrà, *La pittura metafisica*, 2nd edn (Milan, 1945), has an explicit condemnation of pictorial dynamism (pp. 53ff.), but by 1911 Giorgio de Chirico (who first exhibited in the Salon d'Automne in 1912) was writing about 'the call of prehistory': 'In a ruined temple the broken statue of a god speaks a mysterious language . . . It is the cold hour of sunrise in a distant, unknown country'. This text, unknown until it was published by James Thrall Soby in 1916 (the manuscript which belonged to Jean Paulhan), is almost an illustration of De Chirico's paintings of this time.

174 Perret's father had been a Communard refugee there, and they were childhood friends. But see, on this whole episode, Maurice Culot and others, *Les Frères Perret: L'oeuvre complète* (Paris, 2000), pp. 96ff.

175 Institut Français d'Architecture, *Les Frères Perret*, pp. 97ff.

176 Bourdelle may well have modified Perret's treatment as well – so, at any rate, Michel Dufet, 'La Couleur dans la Maison' in *Le Décor d'aujour d'hui* (Paris, 1960), no. 29.

177 As exemplified at the time by the Petit Trianon at Versailles, and Ange-Jacques Gabriel's other work of that date.

178 If not always wholly explicit, Bourdelle was certainly articulate. The texts are quoted by Gaston Varenne, *Bourdelle par lui-même* (Paris, 1937), pp. 166ff.

   The marriage of the panels with the structure was not as perfect as Bourdelle implied, and on the first night some of the reliefs had to be stored and the openings filled with canvas: so Peter Collins, *Concrete* (London, 1959), pp. 185f.

   While Nijinski married, split from Diaghilev and descended into dementia, Isadora Duncan went on dancing and teaching until her own tragic death in 1927. Curiously enough, Adolf Loos and his dancer-wife Elsie Altmann saw her at the Trocadéro in Paris in 1922. An orchestra of 80 musicians (conducted by Reynaldo Hahn) was to play a whole Beethoven symphony, Tchaikovsky, Chopin. Elsie was taken aback:

> I couldn't believe my eyes: a rather fat, elderly lady in a Greek tunic and all too naked, hopped about the stage, tramping when Beethoven growled, skipping when the music got milder. It was an indescribably comical sight.

The public was wildly enthusiastic for all that, and Loos insisted on Elsie applauding the great pioneer of modern dance. They visited the Duncan family dancing school the next day. Altmann-Loos, *Mein Leben mit Adolf Loos*, pp. 154ff.

179 For an outsider's view, see Umberto Boccioni, 'Technical Manifesto of Futurist Sculpture', in P. Hulten, ed., *Futurism and Futurisms* (London, 1987), p. 41.

180 After the First World War, he involved Maurice Denis in a later masterpiece, the church of Nôtre-Dame at Le Raincy, north-east of Paris (of 1922–3) which he conceived like a Gothic building in the sense that thin columns supported a vault – admittedly a very un-Gothic, shallow one – while the walls were, in effect, concrete-fretted stained-glass windows, so that the visual impact of the interior depended entirely on Denis' rather static, but very brightly tinted windows. Bourdelle carved his black basalt bust in 1922.

181 Arnold Haskell, *Diaghileff: His Artistic and Private Life* (London, 1947), pp. 207ff. Alexander Shouvaloff, *The Arts of Ballets Russes* (London, 1997), pp. 74ff., 200ff., 291ff. Moussorgsky's *Khovanshina* was also part of the season. Astruc went bankrupt at the end of the summer, when Thomas Beecham brought the company to London.

   On Bourdelle's contribution, see Emile-Francois Julia, *Antoine Bourdelle: maitre d'oeuvre* (Paris, 1930), pp. 69ff., 131ff. If Julia is to be believed, Bourdelle not only rediscovered the technique of true fresco in these decorations, but virtually designed the building. She quotes

Bourdelle's remark to his students: 'La nouvelle Cathédrale, le nouveau Temple, où ira la foule, ce sera le Théâtre lorsqu'il réunira en lui tout l'Art' (p. 70*).*

Bourdelle was explicit about his role within the building as an organism, about his own archaism (an accusation of which he was proud) and on the models he followed: which were not other sculptures, but living models. The dancer whom he most admired was Isadora Duncan, the avowed enemy of the traditional balletic methods. Haskell, *Diaghileff*, pp. 157ff., 162ff.; Antoine Bourdelle, *Ecrits sur l'art et la vie* (Paris, 1955), pp. 63f., 66ff., 91ff.

Kessler's comment came in a letter to the poet Hugo von Hoffmannsthal, quoted by Laird McLleod Easton, *The Red Count* (Berkeley, CA, 2002), p. 207.

182 Frank Lloyd Wright, *An Autobiography* (New York, 1943), pp. 175ff. It is discussed in all the literature. Neil Levine, *The Architecture of Frank Lloyd Wright* (Princeton, NJ, 1996), pp. 105ff.; William Allin Storer, *The Frank Lloyd Wright Companion* (Chicago, IL, 1993), pp. 181; T. T. Wijdevelde, *The Work of Frank Lloyd Wright*, The Wendingen Edition (New York, 1965), pp. 63ff.; Henry Russell Hitchcock, *In the Nature of Materials: The Building of Frank Lloyd Wright, 1887–1941* (New York, 1942), pp. 62ff.

183 Anthony Alofsin, *Frank Lloyd Wright: The Lost Years* (Chicago, IL, 1993), especially pp. 127ff.

184 Osthaus, *Van de Velde*, pp. 116ff., Van de Velde, *Récit de ma vie*, pp. 354ff.

185 Erich Mendelsohn, *Letters of an Architect*, ed. Oskar Beyer (New York, 1967), p. 33. The letter was written in September 1914, as a reaction to a publication. But his reaction was not unusual. Theodor Heuss, already an influential critic (and later president of the German Republic) wrote: 'Van de Velde fascinates, Behrens disappoints . . .' (in *Maertz*, VIII/27, 1914, p. 207).

186 Paul Scheerbart, *70 Trillionen Weltgrüsse*, ed. Mechtild Rausch (Berlin, 1991), p. 460 for his letters to Taut. One of the typical couplets runs: 'Glück ohne Glas/Wie dumm ist das!'

187 Van de Velde, *Récit de ma vie*. But of course the issue was a burning one and the 1914 annual of the Werkbund carried a paper on Normaliesierung by Wilhelm Ostwald, whose colour system I mentioned earlier, extolling the benefits of standardization (paper sizes, colours) for artists as social operatives; in his memoirs, he gives an account of the preliminary agitation while led to the institution of the Deutsche Industrie Norm in Munich in 1911. *Lebenslinien* (Berlin, 1926), vol. III, pp. 299ff.

188 Giovanni Lista, *La Scène futuriste* (Paris, 1989), pp. 319ff.

189 Garafola, *Diaghilev's Ballets Russes*, pp. 81ff.; Stephen Walsh, *Stravinsky* (New York, 2000), p. 245.

190 Richardson, *A Life of Picasso*, vol. II, pp. 389ff., 419ff. In the article he wrote for the catalogue, Apollinaire used the word 'sur-réaliste' as well as the expression 'un esprit nouveau', which Le Corbusier (then still Charles-Edouard Jeanneret) and Amédé Ozenfant adopted for the title of their review which began publication in 1919. Boris Kochno, *Diaghilev and the Ballets Russes* (London, 1971), p. 101.

191 The intricacies of these conflicts are set out in detail by Richardson, *A Life of Picasso*, vol. II, pp. 419ff. Garafola, *Diaghilev's Ballets Russes*, pp. 81ff. What seemed to infuriate Breton especially were some of the costumes designed by Sonia Delaunay.

192 Mark Polizzotti, *Revolution of the Mind* (New York, 1995), pp. 191f.

193 A. Schwarz (1997), pp. 648ff. 'R. Mutt' is a joke too inane and elaborate even for this footnote. Duchamp writes to his sister Suzanne (11 April 1915) in a tone of hurt innocence: 'une de mes amies [*sic*!] sous un pseudonym masculin, Richard Mutt, avait envoyé une pissotière comme sculpture. Ce n'était pas du tout indécent, aucune raison pour la refuser. Le comité a décidé d'exposer cette chose. J'ai donné ma démission et c'est un potin qui aura sa valeur à New York.' In Francis M. Naumann and Hector Obalk, *Affectionately, Marcel: The Selected Correspondence of Marcel Duchamp*, trans. Jill Taylor (Ghent, 2000), p. 47.

194 Schwarz, no. 306, p. 615.

195 In 2005 another conceptual artist took the joke one further by proposing to line an ironing

board with a reproduction of Duchamp's LHOQ.

196 In 1912, as part of his 'renunciation', he visited Munich, where he seems to have bought a copy of Kandinsky's *On the Spiritual in Art*. The heavily-annotated (perhaps by Raymond) copy survived, together with a sketched translation, in either Marcel's or Jacques Villon's library, and is now in a private collection. The information is conflicting, but see Thierry de Duve, *Nominalisme pictural* (Paris, 1984), pp. 175ff.

He remained on good terms with many painters and in 1943–8 wrote a number of very shrewd appreciations of contemporary artists for the New York collection, *Société Anonyme*, which are reprinted in *Marchand de sel* (Paris, 1958), pp. 116ff.

197 *The Large Glass* is perhaps the most commented work of art ever. But see A. Schwarz, *Complete Works of Marcel Duchamp* (1969), pp. 70.

198 See Thierry de Duve, *Nominalisme pictural* (Paris, 1984), pp. 17ff.

199 Camille Pisarro, who suspected that the painting of the series was Monet's bending to the demands of his dealers, changed his mind radically when he saw fifteen of the 'Haystacks' exhibited in the Durand-Ruel gallery in 1891. See Charles F. Stuckey, *Water-Lilies* (New York, 1993), p. 14; p. 12 on the precedents of the series. On the water-lily series in general, see Marianne Alphant, *Claude Monet: une vie dans le paysage* (Paris, 1993), pp. 649ff. In Daniel Wildenstein's *Claude Monet: biographie et catalogue raisonné* (Lausanne, 1996), vol. IV, nos 1655–1735, 1781–1823, 1846–67, 1883–1903, 1964–83 are practically all *Nymphéas*, including photographs of some of the destroyed pictures taken by Durand-Ruel in Monet's studio. The last group are those which make up the *Grandes Décorations*.

200 '. . . bâti comme une église de hameau': so René Gimpel in his diary in 1918; quoted by Steven Z. Levine, *Monet and his Critics* (New York and London, 1976), p. 365. It was Monet himself who thought it 'an eyesore'; Stuckey, *Water-Lilies*, p. 19.

201 Levine, *Monet and His Critics*, p. 360.

202 The Duc de Trévise, 'Le Pélerinage à Giverny', *La Revue de l'art ancien et moderne*, (February 1927), quoted in Stuckey, *Water-Lilies*, p. 22.

203 Although he is known to have painted some fifty large canvases of water-lilies, only twenty-eight of them survive.

204 So Stuckey, *Water-Lilies*, pp. 22f. André Masson is quoted there on p. 22. Monet preferred the rotunda in the Hôtel Biron which is 18.5 metres in diameter; the ovals at the Jeu de Paume were only 12.5 metres wide, though they were 23 metres long. Lefèvre replaced Bonnier when he was named architect to the Louvre.

Conclusion: After the Wars

1 The term 'cosmic spring' was allegedly coined by Franticek Kupka. John Reed's *Ten Days that Shook the World*, with a foreword by V. I. Lenin (New York, 1919). Reed died in Moscow in 1920. The 1960 edition is quoted here.

2 Vladimir Tatlin, 'The Work Ahead of Us', Report to the VIIIth Congress of the Soviets on 31 December 1920. It is one of the most sober of such statements. Quoted from John E. Bowlt, *Russian Art of the Avant Garde* (Cambridge, MA, 1988), pp. 205ff.

Leon Trotsky, *Literature and Revolution* (Ann Arbor, MI, 1966), p. 110.

3 The visit was certainly proposed but there is some confusion about whether it actually took place. My mother (not an altogether reliable witness on such matters) claimed to have heard a lecture by him in St Petersburg, though when pressed about details said that she did not remember much, since 'she only went for the laugh'.

4 Ivan Aleksandrovich Fomin (1872–1936) also moved from St Petersburg to Moscow after the Revolution and had some reputation as a historian. He had also developed an ambitious

project for the monumental and heavily Italianate rebuilding of the Golodov Island to the north of Petersburg in 1913. Ivan Vladislavovich Zholtovski (1867–1959) was trained in St Petersburg, but spent much of his career in Moscow. He produced a Russian version of Palladio's Treatise in 1938.

5 A study trip in Italy (1923–5) produced another, rather crassly literal counterfeit 'completing' of Palladio's three-bay and three-storey Loggia del Capitanato in Vicenza as a seven-storey and seven-bay apartment building in Mokhovaya Street in Moscow; as late as the 1950s he produced another 'adaptation' of Palladio – the Villa Poiana as a Moscow cinema.

His pupils included Golosov, Umanski, Ladovsky, Melnikov, of course – and even the most adventurous, Leonidov.

6 The best known were Alexander Kuznetsov, Alexei Bubyr, Alexander Nikolsky and N. V. Vassilev. Bubyr died in 1919, Vassilev played no further part after the Revolution. Kuznetsov became a designer of industrial buildings. Only Nikolsky, who had worked with Bubyr, played some part in the development of Soviet architecture. Lidval did few buildings of substance after 1918 but was a teacher in VKHUTEMAS into the 1930s.

7 Tilman Buddensieg, 'Die Kaiserlich Deutsche Botschaft in Petersburg von Peter Behrens', in Martin Warnke, ed., *Politische Architektur in Europa* (Cologne, 1984), pp. 374ff.

8 The most important was called the 'Knave of Spades' (Bubovny Valet). For a while (1910–12) the 'Knave' accommodated various factions of the avant-garde. In 1912 the 'Donkey's Tail' (Osly ogon), broke off as an anti-Paris, anti-Munich, 'nativist' faction in which the Rayonists Goncharova and Larionov joined Tatlin and Malevich. Ossip Brik, an impresario artist, provided the energy. His wife, Lily, was the woman in Vladimir Mayakovsky's life.

9 Peace was made by the wonderful painter-decorator Aleksandra Exter, who was born near Kiev in 1882; she had travelled often to Paris where she befriended Apollinaire and Marinetti as well as Picasso, Braque and Léger. But she had exhibited in most Russian avant-garde shows and returned home in 1914. Exter taught briefly at VKHUTEMAS, collaborated with the Moscow Chamber theatre producer Alexander Tairov, and did sets and costumes for a science-fiction film, *Aelita*. She emigrated to France in 1924 and died at Fontenay-aux-Roses in 1949.

10 Charlotte Doulas in Velemir Khlebnikov, *Collected Works* (Cambridge, MA, 1987), vol. I, p. 178, for an account of *zaum.*

11 It was hung (with his self-portrait) above his death-bed when his body was laid out in his atelier. When he lay in state in the Artists' Union in Leningrad the *Black Square* hung over his body alone. A. Nakov, *Kazimir Malewicz* (Paris, 2002).

12 Known in English as *A Life for the Tsar.*

13 He had been the originator – with Gorky – of *Bogostroitselstvo*, as I mentioned earlier.

14 A. L. Tait, *Lunacharsky: Poet of the Revolution (1875–1907)* (Birmingham, 1984); *Three* – rather symbolist – *Plays* of A. V. Lunacharsky, 'Faust and the City', 'Vasilisa the Wise' and 'The Magi'; were translated by L. A. Magnus and K. Walter (London, 1923). The passage about 'god-building' comes in his history of the October event, *Velikii Perevorot* (St Petersburg, 1919), p. 31, quoted by Tait, *Lunacharsky*, p. 106. And Lunacharsky adds that 'it was the most dazzling and decisive step towards the programme laid down by Nietzsche: "The world is without meaning, but we must give it meaning."'

It is worth remembering, however, that among the things Lenin definitely did not like were 'Bohemianism, religion, Mayakovsky' – or so A. C. MacIntyre, 'The Way Not to Write About Lenin' in *Against the Self-images of the Age* (New York, 1971), p. 44.

15 NARKOMPROS was the *NARodnyi KOMissariat ROSSveshchenya*, National Commissariat of Education, which Lunacharsky headed until 1928. Trotsky, who often worked closely with Lunacharsky, had misgivings about his character: 'imposing in appearance and voice, eloquent in a declamatory way, none too reliable, but often irreplaceable'. He was commenting on Lunacharsky introducing Lenin to the crowd below from the balcony of the Kschesinsska

Villa shortly after his arrival from the Finland Station in April 1917. Mathilde Kschessinska was a *prima ballerina assoluta* of the Imperial company, a dancer whom Nicholas II as heir to the throne much favoured, and who later married Grand-Duke Andrei Vladimirovich. She had her house, near the Peter and Paul Fortress, designed by A. I. von Gogen, and it was one of those Art-Nouveau *palazzine* I mentioned earlier. It was taken over by the Bolsheviks in March 1917. Turned into the Museum of the Revolution, it is now the Museum of Russian Political History. Leon Trotsky, *History of the Russian Revolution* (London, 1967), vol. II, p. 46ff., also vol. III, p. 200. For a somewhat different account of the event, also relying on the memoirs of Nikolai Nikolaievich Sukhanov, a Menshevik – and an attentive although prejudiced (so Trotsky) witness, see Edmund Wilson, *To the Finland Station: A Study in the Writing and Acting of History* (London, 1953), pp. 470ff.

Lunacharsky was never admitted into the inner councils of the Central Committee of the Party, and in fact responsibility for education was taken by Nadezhda Krupskaya, Lenin's wife. He resigned as commissioner in 1929 protesting – by letter – to Stalin at the persecution of the children of those accused in the first 'show trials' and the reduction of technical education. Krupskaya resigned with him, but her resignation was not accepted.

16 *Otdel Izobrazitenykh Iskustv* – literally, Department of Representational Art.

17 The Memorandum (dated 24 July–6 August 1918) set up the project for the sculptures 'with quotations or maxims engraved on the pedestals or surroundings, so that the monuments should appear as street rostra' as a series of competitions to be judged by the general public. About thirty of them were erected – among them to Robespierre, Danton, Garibaldi, Heine, Herzen, Chernyshevsky, Nekrasov, Dostoyevsky, Ogarev and, improbably, the anarchist Bakunin. There was opposition to the project, especially from some architects in the Moscow Soviet, as is clear from a letter Tatlin sent to Lunacharsky later that year. See Larissa Alekzejevna Zhadova, ed., *Tatlin* (London, 1988), pp. 41f., 186ff.

18 Originally founded in May 1919 as SINtineza SKULPTUry i ARCHitektury, its members were Boris Korolyov, Nicolai Ladovski, Konstantin Melnikov, Alexander Rodchenko and Lyubov Popova, but there were a number of sympathizers – Yakov Chernikhov, and the self-proclaimed 'neo-primitivist' Alexander Shevchenko. Since Zholtovski was the director of the architecture section of IZO it was attached to its sculpture section. In December 1919 it became the Kollektiv ZHIvopisno (painterly) – SKULPTurno – ARCHitekturny Syntezy and was joined by Ivan Golosov. It seems to have disbanded after its first exhibition in the summer of 1920. Its members were then incorporated into INKHUK, Moskovski Institut KhUdozennei Kultury, which was founded in 1921 by Kandinsky, and dedicated to the scientific study of the psycho-physiology of aesthetic phenomena. But the emphasis of INKHUK shifted; Kandinsky resigned and left for Germany; and the direction was taken over by Rodchenko.

19 *svobodneie gosudarstvennye khudozhestvennie MASterskie* – Free State Art-workshops. They replaced PEGOSKHUMA (PETrogradskie GOsudarstvennye Svobodno-KHUdozhestviennye uchebnye Masterskie) which were in turn replaced by the old Academy as a title. VKHUTEMAS was the Vyzhshii Gosudarstvennye KHUdezhstvenno-TEChnicheskie MASterskie and Technicheski Institut; VKHUTEIN stood for vyzhii Gosudarstvenny KHUdezhstvenno-TENChnicheski INstitut. In 1930 it reverted to the title of Academy.

Lunacharsky resigned soon after his appointment on hearing that Red Guards had destroyed the Moscow Kremlin monuments, but was persuaded back by Lenin when the rumour turned out to be unfounded.

20 Pseudonym (suggesting a spinning top) of Denis Abramovich Kaufman, born in Białystok in 1896. He studied at the Psychoneurological Institute in St Petersburg in 1916–18, working on sound perception and sound recording, but moved into the Soviet newsreel agency soon after the Revolution. There he developed a theory of the camera as an 'objective' observer, superior

446

to the human eye: it became *kino-oko* (contracted to кinoko), the cinema-eye, where each 'true image', being an element which 'told its own story', had a sense, a *zaum*, beyond anything that could be verbalized or narrated, parallel to the use of the word in formalist and even Futurist poetics. Of course, the stage and theatrical cinema was rejected as bourgeois.

He, his wife and his brother Michael formed a team, and they also worked with the Swedish photographer Eduard Tissé, to become Eisenstein's principal collaborators . They made a number of films based on newsreels, culminating in a thirteen-reel history of the Civil War in 1922. Vertov's knowledge of sound recording came into play when the first Soviet sound films were made, about 1930. Unfortunately, the *Song of Lenin*, made in 1928 before the party *aparat* turned on the cinema avant-garde (Stalin was, unfortunately for them, a cinema-buff), contained footage of Trotsky and after 1930 Vertov was limited to routine newsreel reportage, though he was rediscovered in the 1960s by French movie makers. For this and the following, see Eric Rhode, *A History of the Cinema from its Origins to 1970: Essays in Film Theory*, ed. and trans. Jay Leyda (Harmondsworth, 1979), pp. 86ff; Orlando Figes, *Natasha's Dance* (London, 2002), p. 451. The best collection of Vertov writings remains *Articles, journeaux, projets de Dziga Vertov*, ed. Sylviane Mossé and Andrée Robel (Paris, 1972).

21 Eisenstein, *Film Form*, p. 179. He returns to the matter in much greater detail in (the later, though translated earlier) *Film Sense* (London, 1943), pp. 58ff.; but especially pp. 84ff. He also developed a brilliant theory of montage in *Film Form*, pp. 72ff., and *Film Sense*, pp. 166ff.

The two artists with whom he felt a special affinity were Daumier and Piranesi. He even considered writing a monograph or study of Piranesi.

22 Eisenstein, *Film Form*, pp. 177f.; in 1928 a prophetic statement on sound film by Eisenstein, Pudovkin and Alexandrov appeared in *Zhizn Iskusstva*, but the Soviet film industry took a year or two to adapt to this development; ibid., pp. 257ff.

23 The cinema had energetic government backing, both for internal Agit-prop consumption and for international propaganda. Eisenstein was dispatched on a world fact-finding tour in 1927; it began his (brief) and intermittent international career and gave him some respite from *aparat* pressure – but this belongs to another part of my story. Still, it is true that Soviet – like other film-makers – chafed at the limitation of soundless and colourless film, and made various attempts to produce synthetic sound by 'drawing' music – or sound, at least – on film, as with an inked needle. Sound recording technology had in fact been available since the First World War, but what was lacking was the projection equipment, and that had to wait for the breakthrough which came in 1927–8 in the United States. Soviet colour film had a tragic beginning; the unfinished second part of Eisenstein's *Ivan the Terrible*, made during the Second World War, could not be shown until 1958.

24 Ivan Puni (Jean Pougny) had been advised to become a painter by Ilya Repin, studied in Paris and participated in the various avant-garde shows after his return in 1912. He stayed briefly in Vitebsk and emigrated to Berlin at the end of 1920,via his native Finland. From 1924 until his death in 1956 he lived in Paris.

Lazar Markovich (or Mordechovich) Lissitzky was born near Smolensk, but spent his childhood in Vitebsk. He studied architecture at the Darmstadt Technische Hochschule, which he entered just after Behrens left its direction. On his return he produced a number of Yiddish and Hebrew as well as Russian illustrated books, but his whole outlook changed radically after the meeting with Malevich.

25 Lissitzky's earliest productions, like the two calligraphed versions of the Passover song *chad gadia* (one billy-goat) in Yiddish (MS. 1917) and in Hebrew (Kiev, 1919) were very much in sympathy with Chagall, but the impact of Malevich in 1919–20 seems to have been radical and immediate. He began working with collage and abstraction in late 1919; even though he did one or two more illustrated books (a Yiddish version of Kipling's *Little Elephant* appeared in Berlin in 1922), he aligned himself with Malevich (and later with Tatlin and Rodchenko)

from the break of 1919–20.

26 The dismissal of Chagall was voted in his absence and in spite of student protests, he departed for Moscow. Chagall records his view of the episode in *Ma Vie* (Paris, 1931), pp. 205ff., in
which he speaks of Lunacharsky's kindness, his own mobilizing of the house-painters of
Vitebsk to paint copies of his works, as well as conspiracies against him, including that of an
unnamed 'professor who lived in the academy and surrounded himself with women prey to
"Suprematic" mysticism', as well as his later privations in Moscow and his work at the
Yiddish Theatre.

      Malevich may have been primarily attracted to Vitebsk by the relative plenty of food
and fuel there.

27 Quoted in Mario Perniola, *L'alienazione artistica* (Milan, 1971), p. 252. Wherever he said it,
he was echoing (as he often did) Jean-Jacques Rousseau's advocacy of the popular festival as
a social cement in his *Lettre à M. d'Alembert*; on which see Jean Starobinski, *J.-J. Rousseau: la
transparence et l'obstacle* (Paris, 1971), pp. 116ff. And Timothy Edward O'Connor, *The Politics
of Soviet Culture: Anatolii Lunacharskii* (Ann Arbor, MI, 1983), p. 64.

28 Edward J. Brown, *Mayakovsky: A Poet in the Revolution* (Princeton, NJ, 1973), pp. 198ff.

29 Only an elevational drawing and photographs of the 'city' models have survived. The Khodynka
field had been used as a parade-ground during the Revolution and became the first commercial
airport in the Soviet Union, but in 1913 there had been a plan to build a garden city there.

30 His pseudonym, meant 'God-given' – even if he was no *Bogostroitsel* himself. See John E.
Bowlt, ed., *Russian Art of the Avant-Garde*, pp. 176ff.

31 Biomechanics was a system of movement: on its relation to Constructivism, see the 'actressy'
Juri Elagin, *Vsevolod Meierkhol'd Tsemnyi Genii* (Moscow, 1998), pp. 213ff.

32 Lenin made his personal views public in an article on *Proletkult* which appeared in *Pravda* on
1 December 1920, in which he described avant-garde taste as 'disgusting and degenerate'.
V. I. Lenin, *On Literature and Art* (Moscow, 1967), p. 235. In Hans-Jürgen Drengenberg, *Die
Sowjetishe Politik auf dem Gebiet der Bildenden Kunst von 1917 bis 1934* (Berlin, 1972), pp. 72ff.,
the whole article is reprinted on pp. 331ff. Bogdanov died in 1928, allegedly in an experiment
he was conducting on himself. Lenin regarded Lunacharsky as a slouch in such matters and
wrote indignantly (on 6 May 1921) 'it is nonsense, stupidity, double-dyed stupidity and
affectation . . . as for Lunacharsky, he should be flogged for his Futurism'. The note was not
published until 1957.

      Olga Rozanova, who organized the first workshops, was married to the Futurist poet
Alexei Kruchenykh; she died of diptheria in 1919.

33 Pavlov himself was not a full fledged behaviourist, yet some of his followers (like Western
behaviourists, of whom B. F. Skinner was the most prominent) believed that conditioned
reflexes could be genetically transmitted.

34 See Figes, *Natasha's Dance* (2002), pp. 445ff.; Jean Starobinski, *Action et réaction* (Paris, 2000),
pp. 134ff.; Leszek Kolakowski, *Main Currents of Marxism* (Oxford, 1978), vol. III, pp. 134ff. Also
above, chapter Six, n. 85.

35 Biomechanics owed almost as much to Gordon Craig's belief in the depersonalizing of the
actor as to Dalcroze's eurythmics.

36 Leon Trotsky, *Literature and Revolution* (Ann Arbor, MI, 1966), p. 113.

37 In *Novyi Mir*, no. 9 (1920); quoted by Selim O. Khan-Magomedov, *Pioneers of Soviet Architecture*
(London, 1987), p. 24.

38 Which had been performed in Hellerau in 1913, as I noted in the previous chapter.

39 Claudel's statuesquely pious play was first produced in 1912. Ferdinand Crommelynck was
not much performed outside Russia, while Chesterton's book, first issued in 1908, is a satire
on political conspiracy. These sets, often reproduced, are now better known than the text
which they set. *The World Upside-Down* (*Zemlya Dybom*), also called *The Earth in Turmoil*, is

Sergei Tretyakov's reworking of *La Nuit* by Marcel Martinet.

40 On its astronomic-cosmic implication, see John Milner, *Vladimir Tatlin and the Russian Avant-Garde* (New Haven, CT, 1983), pp. 178ff. On the influence of the rocket-engineer Konstantin Tsiolkovski (whose science-fiction novel, *Beyond the Planet Earth*, was first published in 1920) and his mathematical-philosophical teacher and mentor, Nikolai Fedorov, on Tatlin, see Milner, *Vladimir Tatlin and the Russian Avant-Garde*, pp. 177ff.; Elizabeth English, 'Arkhitektura Mnimosti: The Origins of Soviet Avant-garde Rationalist Architecture in the Russian Mystical-Philosophical and Mathematical Intellectual Tradition', unpublished PHD thesis (Philadelphia, 2000), pp. 30ff., 130ff.

41 An article on Tatlin's recent work in *Zhizn Iskusstva* (19 January 1921), quoted in L. A. Zhadova, ed., *Tatlin* (London, 1984), pp. 342f.

42 On that Moscow showing, Lenin went to see it. According to Tatlin's collaborator, Tevel Markovich Shapiro, 'Vladimir Il'ich asked us two questions: how much it would cost and whether it was technically feasible. Alas, we could not answer his questions.' V. Lovginov, 'Kak poema Metalle', quoted in Zhadova, *Tatlin* (1984), p. 442.

43 It shows Tatlin standing on a stool, holding a wood lathe; by his feet are symbols: a spiral and formulae, as well as calculations – but they are mysterious: $\int \Delta x = \propto$; $+ ? 3?$-0. The portrait was used to illustrate one of Ehrenburg's stories. Milner, *Vladimir Tatlin and the Russian Avant-Garde*, pp. 168ff.

44 See E. H. Carr, *The Bolshevik Revolution* (London, 1966), vol. I, pp. 205, 213ff.; Leon Trotsky, *The History of the Russian Revolution*, trans. Max Eastman (London, 1967), vol. III, pp. 370ff.; and on the renewed interest in NEP during perestroika, Eric Hobsbawm, *The Age of Extremes: The Short Twentieth Century* (London, 1994), pp. 378f.

45 A young architect, Nikolai Kolli (later a collaborator of Le Corbusier), turned the graphic sign into a Moscow monument.

46 S. Frederick Starr, *Melnikov: Solo Architect in a Mass Society* (Princeton, NJ, 1981), pp. 59ff.

47 Melnikov did a number of projects, including a broken-crystal one. The effect he was after, he said, was that of the sleeping princess (Tsarina) waiting for the awakening – a very 'unconstructivist' vision. See ibid., pp. 81ff.

48 V. E. Chazanova, *Sovetskaia Arkhitektura Pervichlet Oktiabria* (Moscow, 1970), pp. 164ff. Selim O. Khan-Magomedov, *Pioneers of Soviet Architecture* (London, 1987), pp. 236f., figs 245, 249, 635ff. The first pyramidal 'thought' was abandoned for a cube; it was not executed, but transformed into a ziggurat between side pavilions topped by a spire; Shchusev's wooden Kourgan replaced it in 1924. Other projects for the monument were produced by Fomin and Lev Rudnev; Joseph Rykwert, *On Adam's House in Paradise* (New York, 1981), pp. 26f. On Shchusev's conviction that the cube, archetypically, represented eternity, and its relation to current Soviet thinking, see Vieri Quilici, *L'architettura del Construttivismo* (Bari, 1969), pp. 278ff. St Petersburg became Leningrad two days after Lenin's death and reverted back to its old name, St Petersburg, on 26 September 2000.

49 See Khan-Magomedov, *Pioneers of Soviet Architecture*, pp. 232ff., Starr, *Melnikov*, pp. 88ff., 192ff. Quilici, *L'architettura del Costruttivismo*, pp. 143ff. El Lissitzky in *Russland* (Vienna, 1930), pp. 13f., hails it as the first 'Western' achievement of Soviet architecture.

50 Selim O. Khan-Magomedov, *Alexander Rodchenko: The Complete Work*, ed. Vieri Quilici (New York, 1986), p. 178.

51 Shchusev's protection probably ensured that Melnikov was left alone in the house he had designed for himself in 1929 until he died in 1957. However, his career declined during the 1930s – he was stripped of professional status and then (1934) dismissed from the architecture institute and barred from participating in competitions. Denounced as an impractical individualist in 1937, he was forbidden to practise or teach.

52 In a big industrial complex like Ivanovo, where much worker housing was built directly after

the Revolution, 'modernity' does not appear among the constructions until after 1926. So Khlebnikov in J.-L. Cohen, M. de Michelis and M. Tafuri, eds, *URSS, 1917–1978: La Ville, l'architecture. les avant-gardes et l'état* (Paris, 1979), pp. 248ff.

53 Ilya Golosov's building won a competition in the same year, 1927, in which Giuseppe Terragni was commissioned to design the formally similar Novocomum apartment block in Como. But while Golosov's block is dynamic in that it encloses a circular staircase, and is interrupted by the orthogonal structure, Terragni's is much more static, the cylinder acting somewhat like the circular corner pavilions in academic plans; moreover, the orthogonal structure caps the cylinder instead of allowing it to break through. The formal device is used for the opposite effect in the building. See Giorgio Ciucci, ed., *Giuseppe Terragni: opera completa* (Milan, 1996), pp. 315ff., and Khan-Magomedov, *Alexander Rodchenko*, pp. 435f.

54 Khlebnikov had imagined that kind of unmanned flight, and Tatlin was very much involved with Khlebnikov's ideas. Following his mentor he gave his invention a title combining his name with the Russian verb *letat*, 'to fly' – 'flying Tatlin', and Khlebnikov composed a poem about it and played variations on the word. See Milner, *Vladimir Tatlin and the Russian Avant-Garde*, pp. 224ff.; Zhadova, *Tatlin*, pp. 147ff., 309f. There are many photographs of Letatlin in art-exhibitions, and even of demonstrations on the ground at air shows, but none that I have seen shows it flying. A semi-technical manual was published by a test pilot, Konstantin Artseulov, for the *State Museum for Applied Arts* in 1932 (translated and quoted by Zhadova in *Tatlin*, pp 408f.) It was Tatlin's last design for a piece of equipment. When he moved from the monastery into a two-room flat in 1937, his friends organized a 'funeral procession' of the remains of the air-bicycle. Milner, *Vladimir Tatlin and the Russian Avant-Garde*, pp. 224ff. and n.

55 Tatlin (who died in 1953) is buried in the Novodevitschy monastery churchyard (as are many distinguished artists and writers: Gogol, Chekhov, Ostrovsky, Scriabin and Prokoviev – as well as politicians: Litvinoff, Khrushchev and Mikoyan).

56 He escaped to the Netherlands on 10 November, but the act of abdication was not signed until 28 November. Having given up the Empire, he tried to hang on to the Kingdom of Prussia, but had to abdicate that as well, and all the German princes abdicated with him.

57 The Sparticists called themselves after Spartacus the gladiator and leader of an extremely successful slave rebellion, which was finally put down by Pompey the Great in 71 BC. Harry Kessler, as I noted earlier, witnessed the Weimar events.

58 In spite of having opposed him on the subject at the Cologne *Werkbund* exhibition in 1914.

59 Alan Windsor, *Peter Behrens: Architect and Designer, 1868–1940* (London, 1981), pp. 156ff.; Stanford Anderson, *Peter Behrens and a New Architecture for the Twentieth Century* (Cambridge, MA, 2001), pp. 222ff.

60 On the separation from Alma Mahler, the Iron Cross and the Weimar negotiations, see Reginald R. Isaacs, *Walter Gropius: Der Mensch und sein Werk* (Berlin, 1983), vol. I, pp. 181ff. Henry Van de Velde's version of the same incidents in his *Récit de ma vie*, ed. Anne van Loo (Paris, 1992), pp. 381ff.

61 Albers (and his wife Anni, who was the originator of the Bauhaus textile 'style') moved to the USA (first to Black Mountain College, later to Yale) and had an immense impact on the development of American art after 1950.

62 The founder of Mazdaznan, O. Z. Hanish, was an American who claimed (as had Mme Blavatsky) to have learned a secret doctrine in the Himalayas: though more improbably, he said that his 'masters' were Zoroastrian. The sect still exists, and even offers on-line ordination to prospective ministers. It involved a diet in which raw garlic was an important component. Itten became a high officer of the German branch of the sect. His account of his beliefs, 'Was ist Mazdaznan', is in Willy Rotzler, ed., *Johannes Itten: Werke und Schriften* (Zürich, 1972), pp. 228f.; he had offered an account of the 'Zoroastrian' and rather yoga-like origin of the founda-

tion course (on which many analogous courses in the world's art schools are based) in his *Mein Vorkurs am Bauhaus* (Ravensburg, 1963), pp. 11f. Mazdaznan itself did not have more than a background influence on its structure, which owed a great deal more to Itten's brilliant and charismatic Stuttgart teacher, Alfred Hölzel (in whose class he first met his later Bauhaus colleague, Oskar Schlemmer), but see Hans Hildebrandt, *Adolf Hoelzel* (Stuttgart, 1953), than to any oriental 'masters'.

63 The episode has often been recounted. The best general introduction may be the collection edited by Hans Richter, *Dada-Kunst und Antikunst* (Cologne, 1964). An excellent but neglected discussion by C. J. Middleton. More recently, Detlef Mertins, 'Architectures of Becoming' in Terence Riley and Barry Bergdoll, eds, *Mies in Berlin* (New York, 2002), p. 111; Huelsenbeck, who went on publishing Dada manifestos after his move to New York, was in fact working as a psychoanalyst.

   What is usually omitted is the dismissive account by Georg Grosz, *An Autobiography* (*Ein kleines Ja und ein groszes Nein)*, trans. Nora Hodges (New York, 1983).

64 A number of his drawings and texts had appeared in no. 2; texts were also circulated and some architects distributed letters on architecture among themselves. They were called, Scheerbartly, *Die Gläserne Kette* – the 'Glass Chain' – and much of the text of *Frühlicht* was drawn from them. It was marked by the posthumous influence of Paul Scheerbart on Bruno Taut.

   The group became the nucleus of a later association, the Ring, which collectively became CIAM in 1928, as I will have occasion to note.

65 The project went through several stages, and the commission came though Einstein's collaborator Erwin Freundlich in July 1918. See Jörg Limberg and Jürgen Staube, *Erich Mendelsohn's Einsteinturm in Potsdam* (Potsdam, 1994), especially pp. 5ff., 51f.

66 On the interaction between these groups, see Regina Stephan, ed., *Erich Mendelsohn: Gebaute Welten* (Stuttgart, 1998), pp. 64ff.; Riley and Bergdoll, *Mies in Berlin*, pp. 110f.

67 See Hermann George Scheffauer, *The New Vision in the German Arts* (New York, 1924), pp. 45ff., on Expressionist cinema; on pp. 142ff he gives an account of a showing of Ruttman's film. For *Berlin, das Bild Einer Stadt*, see Bela Balasz, *Il Film* (Turin, 1957), pp. 151f., 208, and Eric Rhode, *A History of the Cinema* (Harmondsworth, 1977), pp. 179ff. Ruttman was killed working as a photographer on the Eastern front in 1942. Butting had many contacts with the Novembergruppe and collaborated with Hindemith, but as an unyielding left-winger, he had no position and his work was not performed between 1935–45.

68 The Kap-putsch of March 1920 was an unsuccessful right-wing rising in Berlin which spread to some other cities.

69 Mies seems to have been commissioned at the instance of the art historian and collector Eduard Fuchs, then a Communist Party member (on whom see Walter Benjamin, *Angelus Novus: Ausgewählte Schriften*, Frankfurt, 1966, pp. 302ff., who had bought the house which Mies designed for Hugo Perls in 1911 and for which Mies provided an addition).

   The monument was also to carry an inscription, for which there are only sketches. It was damaged in 1933 and completely destroyed in 1935. In 1983 a cube was put on the site, a 'monument for a monument'. There is a vast literature. See most recently, Riley and Bergdoll, *Mies in Berlin*, pp. 162, 218, 228ff. Judith Bartel, Dirk Dorsemagen and Barbara Perlich, 'Das ehemalige Revolutionsdenkmal auf dem Friedhof Friedrichsfelde', in Johannes Cramer and Dorothée Sack, *Mies van der Rohe: Frühe Bauten* (Berlin, 2004), pp. 139ff.

70 R. R. Isaacs, *Walter Gropius: Der Mensch und sein Werk* (Berlin, 1983), vol. I, pp. 264ff.

71 H. P. Berlage, *Amerikaansche Reisherinneringem* (Rotterdam, 1913). The best summary of his principles is *Grundlagen und Entwicklung derArchitektur* [lectures given in Zürich] (Rotterdam, 1908).

   A young Hague architect, Robert van t'Hoff, visited many of Wright's buildings and returned to the Netherlands to design obsessively Wrightian but also obsessively symmetrical villas at Huis ter Hayde in 1916, after which he gave up architecture in favour of occultism, vegetarianism and potato-farming in Norfolk.

72 They also published the review *Wendingen*, best translated as 'New Direction'. On the society and its connection to the masonic lodge Wahana, see Giovanni Fanelli, 'Eenheid in de Vielheid, in *L'architettura completa di Berlage*, ed. Sergio Polano (Milan, 1987), p. 20.

73 He himself cultivated a variety of approaches, as his pseudonyms indicate. As a 'simultaneist' poet, he was Aldo Camini; as a Dadaist I. K. Bonset. Doesburg was, in any case, his stepfather's surname (his 'registry' name was C.E.M. Küpper). On the origin of the names, see Joost Baljeu, *Theo van Doesburg* (New York, 1974), pp. 38f., 46f.

74 The objects included a number of variants on the chair, a sideboard, a child's buggy, a radio, a lamp, etc. On these and his later furniture, see Daniele Baroni, *I mobili di Gerrit Thomas Rietveld* (Milan, 1977). The office was for a medical practice, and the lamp appeared also in Gropius' office at the Weimar Bauhaus in 1921 and reappeared in a number of other interiors of the 1920s.

75 He had meanwhile transformed himself into Mies van der Rohe – it sounded much better than plain Mies – which means 'wretched', 'mean', in German.

76 'G' stands for *Gestaltung* – to signify design as 'form-giving' (but avoiding the classicizing word 'Form'). The word became increasingly important in the language of architecture and the arts at the time.

77 A literature has grown round this incident: see Marcel Franciscono, *Walter Gropius and the Creation of the Bauhaus in Weimar* (Champaign and Urbana, IL, 1971), pp. 38ff., 243ff. Isaacs, *Walter Gropius*, vol. I, pp. 285ff., 486ff. It does not seem to me improbable that Gropius did indeed offer a generic invitation and that Doesburg took him at his rather vague word.

78 The poet-critic Maurice Raynal also officiated. Unlike his more successful (and mercenary) brother Paul (on the two brothers, see Amédée Ozenfant, *Mémoires, 1886–1862*, Paris, 1968, pp. 119ff., 146ff), Léonce Rosenberg was (in spite of his early conflicts with the Cubists), a real enthusiast and had wanted to run a competition between members of the various groups for an art lover's house; only van Doesburg and van Eesteren responded, however. The gallery also showed the colour projects for van Eesteren's failed Rome Prize university hall. Much of the material was also reproduced in the De Stijl special issue of the new periodical, *L'Architecture vivante*.

79 Although he had also fallen out with van Doesburg, J.J.P. Oud went on to build his first full-fledged de Stijl project, the café de Unie in Antwerp, a white facade dominated by a red square with yellow and blue garnishes.

80 A full account of the little building was given by Mildred Friedman, ed., *De Stijl: Visions of Utopia* (Minneapolis and New York, 1982), pp. 136ff.

81 Adolf Meyer, *Ein Versuchshaus des Bauhauses in Weimar* (Munich, 1924). Georg Muche explained why he rather than Gropius designed the house and gives an account of the episode: *Blickpunkt: Sturm, Dada, Bauhaus, Gegenwart* (Munich, 1961), pp. 128ff.; 'weil es ihm nicht gelungen war, mit den nüchternen Plänen und Beispielen . . . die Jugend des Bauhauses zu überzeugen', is the way Muche summed it up much later.

82 Most Bauhaus monographs give little account of the events which underlie the sense of the 'unity of the arts' essential to the ethos of the institution. See, however, Isaacs, *Walter Gropius*, vol. I, pp. 298ff.

83 Heinrich Neugeboren emigrated to Paris after 1930, where he made common cause with Theo van Doesburg, worked mostly as a graphic designer and changed his name to Henri Nouveau. He died there in 1959. The monument was published, with an explanatory text, in the first issue of the periodical *Bauhaus* in 1929. Hans M. Wingler, *The Bauhaus* (Cambridge, MA, 1978), pp. 440f.

84 The best-preserved one is in the Busch-Reisinger Museum, Cambridge, MA. Krisztina Passuth, *Moholy-Nagy* (London, 1985), pp. 53ff., 381. It has been published many times and

shown in many exhibitions.

85 It was produced in 1929 by Erwin Piscator (on whom see below) and conducted by Otto Klemperer.

86 If Johannes Itten is to believed, it was he who induced Gropius to hire Kandinsky and Klee instead of Karl Schmitt Rottluf, Rudolf Belling and 'a completely unknown Russian' in the spring of 1922 – presumably saving the Bauhaus from being overwhelmed by the Expressionists. Letter to Ludwig Grote of 17 March 1950 in Rotzler, *Johannes Itten*, p. 92.

87 At one point there were more Russian-language publishers in Berlin than German ones: Figes, *Natasha's Dance*, p. 528ff; who also points out that the young Nabokov was the goalie of the Berlin Russian football team. Koujevnikov (Kandinsky's cousin and occasional confidant) was to have a revolutionary influence on French thinking during the 1930s and '40s as Kojève. See Dominique Auffret, *Alexandre Kojève* (Paris, 1990), pp. 92ff., on his arrival in Berlin.

88 It was also praised, not altogether accurately (by Ilya – Elias – Ehrenburg) in *Frühlicht* 3 of Spring 1922.

89 Golo Mann, *The History of Germany since 1789* (New York, 1968), pp. 358ff.; A. J. Ryder, *Twentieth-century Germany: From Bismarck to Brandt* (New York, 1973), pp. 220ff. It was the second and more important treaty negotiated in that Riviera resort.

90 A Bauhaus student, Herbert Bayer (who had designed much of the printed material for the 1923 exhibition – which coincided with the beginning of the inflation crash), designed banknotes with denominations of between one and ten million marks for the State Bank of Thuringia.

91 Gustav Hartlaub, preface to *Ausstellung 'Neue Sachlichkeit'*, exh. cat., Städtische Kunsthalle (Mannheim, 1925). In Anton Kaes, Martin Jay and Edward Dimendberg, *The Weimar Republic Sourcebook* (Berkeley and Los Angeles, 1994), pp. 491ff.

92 He had been pulled into the Berlin scene by Walter Gropius, to whom he sent some drawings, and who gave him a special room in the 'Exhibition of Unknown Architects'. He maintained that Hannes Meyer summoned him to the Bauhaus in 1928 to counteract the sterilizing influence of Mies van der Rohe. He died in Stuttgart in 1973.

93 Amédée Ozenfant, *Sur les écoles cubistes et post-cubistes* (Paris, 1926; reprinted Turin, 1975), pp. 121.

94 Harry Graf Kessler, *Tagebücher, 1918–1937* (Frankfurt, 1957), p. 624:

Jamais je n'ai vu cela, C'est la première fois que je vois de l'architecture moderne qui est parfaite. Oui, c'est parfait, il n'y a pas une tache. Si je savais écrire, j'écrirais un article . . . Jusqu'à présent tout ce que j'ai vu d'architecture moderne était froid; mais ceci n'est pas froid, au contraire . . .

95 Ibid., pp. 667f. (28 May 1932).

96 Ibid., p. 712.

97 Mies van der Rohe, ed., *Bau und Wohnung* (Stuttgart, 1927), is the official publication. More recently and critically, see Karin Kirsch, *Die Weissenhofsiedlung* (Stuttgart, 1987). The list of invited architects changed in the preliminaries, when both Mendelsohn and Adolf Loos were dropped. Heinrich Tessenow withdrew – and so on. The details in Riley and Bergdoll, *Mies in Berlin*, pp. 53ff.

98 The parallel development of the two cities was the subject of a large exhibition: *Paris and Berlin, 1900–1933*, Paris, 1978.

99 His term.

100 The Schwobs were of Alsatian-Jewish origin but established at Chaux for some time, where they were among the elite of watchmakers. The villa was not finished when Jeanneret went to Paris and this led to a conflict between owner and architect.

There was some doubt whether a panel was to be left blank or was intended to carry a relief or painting, and this has led to much speculation. One early drawing clearly (if not altogether distinctly) shows the panel filled with a relief, however. Stanislas von Moos and

Arthur Rügg, eds, *Le Corbusier before Le Corbusier*, exh. cat. (New York, 2002), pp. 90ff., 220ff.

101 John Richardson, *A Life of Picasso* (New York, 1996), vol. II, pp. 419ff.

102 I am translating '*gai* Futuristes'.

103 Much came from Pergolesi's comic opera *il Flaminio*.

104 The confiscated (as part of the reparation) collections of the three German collectors of Cubism in France, Daniel-Henri Kahnweiler, Wilhelm von Ude and Goetz, were sold for give-away prices at auction in 1921.

105 Marie-Jeanne Dumont, ed., *Le Corbusier: lettres à Auguste Perret* (Paris, 2002), p. 195.
    Amédée Ozenfant's father, a contractor, had been interested in concrete construction and had been an early supporter of Hennebique as well as of the Perret Brothers.
    The fashion house took the name JOVE and was the scene of several avant-garde presentations. Ozenfant, *Sur les écoles cubistes et post-cubistes*, pp. 93ff.

106 Dermée was the pen-name of Camille Janssen of Bruges, who had moved to Paris in 1910. Tzara established contact with him in 1917 and they issued the short-lived review *z* whose properly Dadaist editorial Dermée signs as a 'Cartesian Dadaist', which seems a bit of a contradiction. He was an editor of *Nord–Sud*, a literary review which also owed its inspiration to Apollinaire. It was edited by another poet, Pierre Reverdy. The title *Nord–Sud* commemorated the Montparnasse–Montmartre link by Métro.

107 Since Mme Jeanneret's maiden name was Perret, it was not a suitable pseudonym for a young architect. Jeanneret thought of the name of his cousins, the extinct Lecorbézier, which Ozenfant claims to have 'corrupted' into Le Corbusier, *Sur les écoles cubistes et post-cubistes*, p. 113.

108 He published the letter he had received from Apollinaire in March 1917 (he claimed that he coined it so as to replace the clumsier 'surnaturalism') in the special Apollinaire number (no. 26) of *L'Esprit nouveau*. Breton, for his part, discusses Surrealism and Super-naturalism in his first manifesto (André Breton, *Les Manifestes du surréalisme*, Paris, 1947, pp. 44ff.) with reference to Gérard de Nerval (dedication of 'Filles de Feu', in *Oeuvres*, ed. Albert Béguin and Jean Richer, Paris 1960–66, vol. I, pp. 158f.) and (improbably) Thomas Carlyle, *Sartor Resartus* (London, 1871), pp. 176ff.

109 Inevitably, the Surrealist relation to the Communist Party was never easy. Maurice Nadeau, *Histoire du surréalisme* (Paris, 1964), pp. 88ff and *passim*, and Gaetan Picon, *Panorama de la nouvelle littérature française*, 2nd edn (Paris, 1960), pp. 42ff.

110 Maurice Culot *et al.*, *Les Frères Perret: l'oeuvre complète* (Paris, 2000), pp. 151ff., 162f. Muter's studio was taken over by Jean Dubuffet in 1944, and he wrote Perret an ecstatic fan-letter about the little building; ibid., pp. 170f.

111 Edmund Wilson, who acted briefly as their press officer during a New York season, records de Maré's sending him to Los Angeles to sound out Charlie Chaplin for a mime part in a ballet which Wilson was to have 'scripted'; it would make Milhaud's and Cocteau's productions 'sound like folk-song recitals', in *The Twenties*, ed. Leon Edel (New York, 1975), pp. 153ff.

112 It had indeed been technically possible even before the war, and various tentative essays to show them had been made in the 1920s, but sound transmission remained prohibitively expensive. The cinema organ, which after 1920 usually incorporated complex coloured lights and could be played like a 'pyrophone', was installed in many of the more opulent cinemas – but was a stop-gap (Rudolph Wurlitzer, who gave his name to this type of organ, bought the patent of a British inventor, Robert Hope-Jones, in 1910). Some 5,000 were produced by his and other companies, most of which had gone out of business by the Second World War. Attempts were also made to produce synthetic sound; in Soviet Russia it was 'drawn' directly on film – with an inked needle. The film industry was thrown into confusion by the instant commercial success of *The Jazz Singer* in 1927, the schmaltzy, but first continuously 'voiced' film. Kevin Brownlow, *The Parade's Gone By* (New York, 1968), pp. 658ff., Eric Rhode, *A History of the Cinema* (Harmondsworth, 1978), pp. 266ff. *The Jazz Singer* marked the victory of the

Vitaphone patent and Warner Brothers over the rest of the film industry.

113 On Léger's involvement with film, see Christopher Green, *Léger and the Avant-garde* (New Haven and London, 1976), pp. 275ff.

114 Pseudonym of the Russian graphic designer Romain de Tritoff, who made most of his money as a designer of film sets. Both he and Lempicka (who added the *particule* 'de' to her name) were enthusiastically revived in the 1980s.

115 Lisa Phillips, ed., *Frederick Kiesler* (New York, 1989), pp. 14, 48ff.

116 The dispute about the priority of the stage project went on for several decades, but see chapter Six.

117 *Oeuvres complètes*, vol. I, pp. 92ff.

118 Green, *Léger and the Avant-garde*, pp 286ff.; William W. Braham, *Modern Color/Modern Architecture* (Aldershot, 2002), pp. 37ff. It was the time of his break with Ozenfant.

119 Gouverekian would design the first formal garden of the time (for the Viscomte de Noailles, one of the – if not the – patron of new art in Paris); it was at Hyères. It incorporated a sculp-ture by Jacques Lipschitz. set on a turntable base. Van Doesburg also designed a room for the Villa (Allan Doig, *Theo van Doesburg: Painting into Architecture*, ed. Jo-Anne Birnie Danzker, Cambridge, 1986, pp. 167f.; *Theo van Doesburg, Maler-Architect* (Munich, 2001, p. 161). On the refusal of the De Stijl participation in the Dutch section, see Doig, *Theo van Doesburg: Painting into Architecture*, pp. 166f.

   Gouverekian, Armenian but with Persian attachments, became the earliest designer of formal gardens for 'advanced' architects. P. Morton Shand, 'An Essay in the Adroit', in *Architectural Review*, LXV (March 1929), pp. 174ff., and Richard Wesley, in *Rassegna* 8 (Milan, 1981), p. 17.

   Both Oud and Wils exhibited in the Dutch pavilion nevertheless.

120 El Lissitzky and Hans Arp, *Die Kunstismen/Les Ismes de l'art/The Isms of Art, 1914–24* (Erlenbach-Zürig, 1925). Lissitzky tried to produce 'the tombstone' of the isms (his term) with Kurt Schwitters, who did not see the point. Margarita Tupitsyn, *El Lissitzky: Beyond the Abstract Cabinet* (New Haven, CT, 1999), pp. 20f.

121 A garrison headquarters building designed in 1764 by Jacques-François Blondel and a protected monument recently restored. Since orders for the garrison were issued at sunrise, *à l'aube*, the building got its name l'Aubette. Blondel had been the teacher of most French architects in the second half of the eighteenth century.

122 Doig, *Theo van Doesburg*, pp. 174ff.

123 On Van Doesburg's break with Mondrian, see Michel Seuphor, *Piet Mondrian* (New York, 1987), pp. 163f.

124 The approach was already suggested in *Die Bühne im Bauhaus* by Oskar Schlemmer, László Moholy-Nagy and Farkas Molnar. The fourth *Bauhausbuch* (Fulda, 1925; reprinted Mainz, 1985) contains a supplement with the *Totaltheater* project. Piscator had his apartment designed and furnished by Gropius and Breuer. The *Totaltheater* was prompted or abetted by a fashionable actress, Tilly Darieux, and her financial backer.

125 When Gropius presented his project, his approach was attacked by the elderly Gordon Craig as well as by Marinetti and the Soviet producer Alexis Tairov (of the Kamerny theatre – the Vesnins' patron) for excessive reliance on 'mechanics': Reale Accademia d'Italia. Walter Gropius, 'Theaterbau' (*Il Teatro Drammatico*), *Estratto degli atti: convegno della Fondazione Alessandro Volta* (Rome, 1935). Perhaps because of his audience, Gropius makes an emotive (and Wagnerian) appeal for a return to the transformative social function of the theatre, the role it had played for the Greeks.

126 Mies' competition scheme for the Deutsche Reichsbank of 1934 is well known; those of Gropius and Hans Poelzig are less familiar; Albert Speer records Hitler's particular detestation of Poelzig.

127 Quilici in *L'architettura del costruttivismo*, pp. 202, 220ff., gives a detailed account of the plans and disputes. See also Khan-Magomedov, *Pioneers of Soviet Architecture*, pp. 335ff.

128 *Assotsyatsya kHudozhnikov Revolutsyi*, the powerful Association of Revolutionary Artists, succeeded some earlier groups in 1928; it had its own periodical, *Iskusstvo v Masy*, but was dissolved in 1932 together with all other 'artistic groups'.

129 Quoted in Quilici, *L'architettura del costruttivismo*, pp. 217, 257.

130 Khan-Magomedov, *Pioneers of Soviet Architecture*, pp. 402ff. But the competition and its after-effects are discussed in every history of twentieth-century architecture.

131 The whole episode is discussed in detail by Jean-Louis Cohen in *Le Corbusier and the Mystique of the USSR* (Princeton, NJ, 1992), pp. 165ff.

132 The catalogue was issued as a book, *The International Style of Architecture*, by Philip Johnson and Henry-Russell Hitchcock (New York, 1932; reprinted with a new preface in 1966).

133 In the form of two articles (December 1926–May 1927) of the periodical *Rassegna italiana*. Their programmatic status was confirmed by their reprinting in the architectural magazine *Quadrante* in March–April 1935. The seven architects were Ubaldo Castagnoli (who soon lapsed), Luigi Figini, Guido Frette, Sebastiano Larco, Adalberto Libera (the only one of the group who worked mostly in Rome), Gino Pollini, Carlo Enrico Rava and Giuseppe Terragni.

134 According to some accounts the first idea of the commission was already documented in 1928 (at any rate, before the Casa del Fascio); with his engineer-brother Attilio, Terragni converted one of Sant'Elia's (who was also a native of Como) electrical transformer drawings into a stone war-monument. I mentioned his first major building, Novocomum, of 1927–9 earlier in connection with Golosov.

135 The Danteum was to be ready for the World Exposition planned for 1942 in Rome, for which a very substantial new suburb E42 was in fact built, and many of the architects I have mentioned participated in the project, notably Adalberto Libera with a large Congress Palace.

Mussolini saw and approved Terragni's plans on 25 October 1938, but a subsequent audience arranged for June 1939 never took place. See Thomas L. Schumacher, *The Danteum* (Princeton, NJ, 1985), *passim*. The documents about the costs and the interviews with Mussolini and his receiving the money for the building are on pp. 155ff.

136 Its programme was written by Paul Valéry, *Oeuvres*, ed. Jean Hytier (Paris, 1957–60), vol. II, pp. 1128ff.

137 The first programme was published by H. T. Wijdeveld, *Eine Arbeitsgemeinschaft* (Santpoort, 1931).

138 Known as the Palais du Trocadéro, after one of Napoleon's Spanish battles which gave its name to the *rond-point* in front of it. Erik Mattie, *World's Fairs* (New York, 1998), pp. 178ff.

139 The original Palais with its cascade had been built for the 1878 Fair by Gabriel, Davioud and Bourdais. It was dismounted only in part; much was left standing and encased in the new structure by Jacques Carlu, Hippolyte Boileau and Léon Azéma. An alternative project by Auguste Perret (who designed the neighbouring Musée des Travaux Publics) was rejected by the authorities. Many sculptors were employed to carve the relief and fountains; most of them are not very memorable.

140 The inscribed walls at Chaillot might be considered the definitive 'publication' of these texts; they also appeared in book form in a limited edition with a lithograph by Aristide Maillol (not Charles Despiau) who did most of the sculptures there. *Quatre Inscriptions* (1938). To introduce them, there is a fifth 'inscription':

> N'entre pas pour trouver ici
> Un abri contre l'eau du ciel:
> La plume est bonne pour celui
> D'esprit stérile et de coeur sec.

456

141 Albert Speer, *Erinnerungen* (Frankfurt, 1969), pp. 94f. He tells of stumbling by accident on the Soviet design which had been kept secret and designing his in direct defiance of it. He points out that the Soviet-Nazi 'classicism' he practised was not totalitarian. London, Paris and Washington were full of such buildings; it was the style of the new epoch.

142 A small bronze copy of the sculpture by Vera Mukhina, 1.6 metres high, is in the State Russian Museum, St Petersburg.

143 The painting was dismounted and is now shown in the Musée d'Art Moderne de la Ville de Paris. The architects, Alfred Aublet, Eric Bagge, Jack Gérodias and René Hartwig, have not been remembered for other work.

144 It was commemorated by a special volume, *Des Canons, des Munitions? Merci! Des Logis . . . s.v.p.* (Paris, 1937). The detailed proposals and projects, their rejection and the negotiations, are told in *Oeuvres complètes, 1934–1938* (Zürich, 1958) pp. 140ff.

145 He had worked for Le Corbusier in 1929–30, when he returned to Barcelona to edit a review; he then emigrated to the United States in 1939 and succeeded Walter Gropius as Dean of the Harvard Design School in 1953.

146 This kind of quasi-organic column was later emulated by Joan Miró. Sanchez-Perez, an auto-didact and friend of Picasso, took refuge in Moscow on the fall of the Republic. He never adapted and died there in 1952.

147 *Guernica* was housed in the Museum of Modern Art in New York, according to Picasso's will, until the fall of Fascism. It was then returned to Spain and is now shown, with models of the building and of the sculptures, in the Reina Sofia museum in Madrid, where it looks – inevitably – de-contextualized.

148 'They were just cheapskates', said Lipschitz. (Personal communication.)

149 It was Diego Rivera who intervened with Cárdenas to welcome Trotsky to Mexico; and (in spite of their political differences) Rivera's summer place in Coyoacán was put at his disposal. After he moved out and after Siqueiros botched a machine-gun attempt, he was in fact murdered in Coyoacán by an OGPU agent in August 1940.

150 Victor Jimenez, *Juan O'Gorman* (Mexico, 2004), pp. 14ff. During the late 1930s it became increasingly common in Latin America for public buildings – theatres, cinemas, official buildings, even churches – to carry paintings and reliefs, remarkable for their size, though not always memorable for their grandeur.

151 It is in the north of Mexico City; now the Diego Rivera Museum, it houses his large Pre-Columbian collection.

152 And the year after, José Clemente Orozco was called by one of the young architects operating in Mexico, Mario Pani, to create a large (six-storey-high) wall painting to cover the cyclorama in the open-air theatre which forms the courtyard of a teachers' college in Mexico City.

153 See Marian Moffett and Lawrence Wodehouse, *Built for the People of the United States: Fifty Years of TVA Architecture* (Knoxville, TN, 1983), *passim*.

154 A recent comprehensive account of this project has not been done. But see Bruce I. Bustard, *A New Deal for the Arts*, exh. cat. (Washington, DC, and Seattle, 1997). It would be a mistake to regard the Project as a charity for the ineffectual. Under its aegis Orson Welles, for instance, staged a very successful run of Marlowe's *Doctor Faustus*, which played for some months in New York; Aaron Copeland gave recitals and so on.

155 On Arshile Gorky's canvases (for Newark Airport, later painted over) for the FAP, see Nouritza Matossian, *Black Angel: A Life of Arshile Gorky* (London, 2001), pp. 260ff.; on his earlier connection with the project, 243ff. In the MOMA 1942 exhibition *Americans 1942: 18 Artists from 9 States*, exh. cat., ed. Dorothy C. Miller (New York, 1942), most of the eighteen had had commissions from the FAP at some point in their careers (pp. 9f.). Guston's later return to figuration does not concern me here.

156 On Stuart Davis' political activities, see Serge Guilbaut, *How New York Stole the Idea of Modern*

Art (Chicago, IL and London, 1983), pp. 20ff.

157 An article by him on Duchamp appeared in *Architectural Record* for May 1937; Francis M. Naumann and Hector Obalk, *Affectionately, Marcel: The Selected Correspondence of Marcel Duchamp*, trans. Jill Taylor (Ghent, 2000), pp. 212f., 233. The Guggenheim gallery is the only building or project mentioned in Duchamp's correspondence.

    Kiesler had written an expository article on the *Large Glass* and had a number of ready-mades in his collection – and even became his landlord for a while during the war.

158 Denis Hollier, *Against Architecture* (Cambridge, MA, 1989), especially pp. xii, 146ff.; to be fair, the French edition (Paris, 1974) was titled *La Prise de la Concorde.* Much of it is an extended commentary on Bataille's essays 'Abattoir', 'Architecture', 'Musée', which appeared in his magazine *Documents*, which was (of course) despised by the Surrealists. However, it is very much the line of argument which Michel Foucault took over first in *Surveiller et punir*, and his paradigmatic building was a prison.

    Of course, Bataille's dual function can be read as a sarcastic echo of Loos' limiting of true architecture to the tomb and the monument.

159 But see Thomas Mical, ed., *Surrealism and Architecture* (London, 2005).

160 It is hard to make any more explicit reference to such matters – Breton's note about 'la très belle et très inutile Porte St Denis' in *Nadja*, 2nd edn (Paris, 1928), p. 38, is about as close as it gets.

161 M. Polizzotti, *Revolution of the Mind: The Life of André Breton* (New York, 1995), pp. 367, 474, 583.

162 Even Salvador Dalí's paranoiac criticism was not applied to buildings until the 1950s, when he fused his ostentatious Catalanism and his passion for virtuosic detail into an enthusiasm for the architecture of Gaudí – by misreading him egregiously. A wholly unsystematic account of Gaudí's relation to the Catalanistas and Dalí's lasting admiration in Roger Descharnes and Clovis Prévost, *La Vision artistique et religieuse de Gaudí* (Lausanne, 1969; English edn New York, 1971). It has a truculent preface by Dalí.

    Karel Teige, the Czech designer-polemicist, found his rigorously anti-lyrical 'functional-ism' challenged when he joined a Surrealist group in 1934 and began to consider the effect of the environment on the unconscious. Rotislav Svácha (1996), pp. 256ff., 330f. Mical, *Surrealism and Architecture*, pp. 24ff.

163 Salvador Dalí records an improbable meeting with Le Corbusier, who (he alleges) asked him what the future of architecture should be like – to which (so he reports), he answered that it should be *molle et poilue* – soft and hairy.

164 A Mexican silver magnate, variously referred to as 'Marquis' and 'Count', he was one of the late investors in the Ballets Russes and the host, in 1951, of a masked ball in the Palazzo Labia in Venice (which he then owned) which is often referred to as the last great ball of the century.

165 Le Corbusier, *Oeuvres complètes*, vol. II, p. 53; Stanislaus von Moos, *Le Corbusier: Elements of a Synthesis* (Cambridge, MA, 1979), pp. 85f., 294, 305ff. Le Corbusier, *The Drawings*, ed. H. Allan Brooks (New York and London, 1982), vol. VIII, pp. 3–147; it is a disproportionate number of drawings for what is, in fact, a one-bedroom apartment. But see, more generally, Daniel Naegele, 'Un corps à habiter: The Image of the Body in the Oeuvre of Le Corbusier', in *Interstices 5* (Auckland, 2000) and his 'Le Corbusier's Seeing Things: Ambiguity and Illusion in the Representation of Modern Architecture', unpublished PhD thesis, University of Pennsylvania (1996).

166 Personal communication.

167 The 'New Bauhaus' was initiated in 1937 but closed in 1938 for lack of financial support; Moholy-Nagy then founded the School of Design in Chicago in 1939, which became the Institute of Design in 1944 and was awarded College Status and incorporated into IIT formally in 1949; Moholy died in 1946.

168 Martin Duberman, *Black Mountain: An Exploration in Community* (London, 1973), pp. 51ff.: describes the origin of the maverick institution which included on its faculty the Albers (fresh

from the Bauhaus), John Cage and Merce Cunningham, Charles Olson and Robert Creeley, Buckminster Fuller, Willem de Kooning, Robert Motherwell and the psychologist-philosopher, Erwin Strauss. Even Walter Gropius visited sometimes. The students included Robert Rauschenberg and Cy Twombly. The insistence on the unity of the arts was not programmatic to the college, but more a by-product of the underlying influence of the 'pragmatic' philosopher of education, John Dewey, as Duberman explains (pp. 32, 40 and on Dewey's visit there, p. 102).

169 J. Rykwert, *The Seduction of Place* (Oxford, 2004), pp. 184ff.

170 The volume which resulted from these deliberations was published by J. Tyrwhitt, J. L. Sert and E. N. Rogers, eds, *The Heart of the City: Towards the Humanisation of Urban Life* (London, 1952), p. 55. A eulogy of the Harkness Center in Sigfried Giedion, *Space, Time and Architecture*, 3rd edn (London, 1954), pp. 502ff.

171 R. I. Isaacs, *Walter Gropius: Der Mensch und sein Werk* (Berlin, 1983), pp. 975f.

172 Gertje R. Utley, *Picasso: The Communist Years* (New Haven, CT, 2000), pp. 147ff.

173 Jacob Baal-Teshuva, *Art Treasures of the United Nations* (New York and London, 1964), pp. 18ff. They were executed from postcard-sized sketches by one of Léger's American pupils, Bruce Gregory.

174 Paulina Villanueva and Macia Pintó, *Carlos Raúl Villanueva* (Seville and Madrid, 2000), pp. 52ff., 76ff.

175 Rose Sélavy (one of his feebler puns – *éros c'est la vie*) was the name of Duchamp's feminine alter ego. The object has now joined the Duchamp-Dreyer collection in the Philadelphia Museum of Fine Arts.

176 Jean-Paul Sartre, 'Qu'est-ce que la littérature', in *Situations*, II (Paris, 1948), p. 216. The essay first appeared in *Temps modernes*. Sartre wrote:

> The primary model of this procedure is offered by the fake sugar-lumps which turn out to have been cut in marble by Duchamp . . . A visitor who handled it was to feel – in a lightning and instant revelation – the auto-destruction of the objective essence of sugar; it was necessary to provide him with this disappointment in all its being, this malaise, this instability conveyed by practical jokes, for instance when the spoon suddenly dissolves in the teacup or the sugar-lumps (by a trick which is the inverse of Duchamp's) swim up to the surface. As a result of this intuition, it is hoped that the whole world will be found to be in fundamental contradiction with itself. Surrealist painting and sculpture have no other end than multiplying such local, imaginary 'strokes' which will act like plugholes through which the whole universe will empty itself. . .

177 The full title of the installation is: *Etant Donnés 1º La chute d'Eau, 2º Le Gaz d'Eclairage*, which might translate: 'Given 1st The Waterfall 2nd Gas for lighting'. See Anne d'Harnoncourt and Walter Hopps, *Etant donnés* (Philadelphia, 1987). The conundrum goes back to a text in the *Green Box*, the notes connected with the *Big Glass*.

178 On a number of occasions I have seen such innocents leave without a second look, assuming the room to be empty.

179 The original, being a series of sheets in ring-binders, may never be published but is part of the Duchamp deposit in the Philadelphia Museum of Fine Art. d'Harnoncourt and Hopps, *Etant données*, pp. 12f. and n. 17.

180 Notably the *Fountain* of 1917: the urinal on its back (proclaimed the most influential work of art of the century by 500 art experts in Britain in 2004) has provoked a number of artists to urinate into it more or less publicly – notably Pierre Pinoncelli in May 1993 on the occasion of an exhibition in Nîmes (for which he was fined 300,000 francs), and Brian Eno and the duo 'performance artists' Youan Cai and Jian Jung Xi in September 2000 at Tate Modern in London). These gestures are symmetrical with the artist's Bernard Bazille's opening of the tin

of Piero Manzoni's excreta in the Galerie Pailhas, Marseilles, in 1989, which allegedly doubled the tin's fiscal value. But see also above, Preface, n. 9.

181 At La Tourette, the composer Iannis Xenakis, still working as a designer-engineer, was responsible for the rhythmic articulation of the façade.

It is said (I report hearsay) that Léger was invited to design the windows for Ronchamp, but asked too high a fee. Since he worked with enthusiasm on other church commissions, he was maybe unwilling to be 'absorbed' into Corbusier's work.

182 It was his only full 'decorative' project in France, though about 1930 he had been commissioned by the collector Barnes to install a sequence of paintings called *The Dance* to decorate his art gallery outside Philadelphia. The buildings had been designed by the French-born and 'academic' architect Paul Philippe Cret, and the exterior was decorated with minuscule neo-Cubist reliefs by Jacques Lipschitz; the experience was not a happy one for Matisse. That collection is to be moved to a new building about 2010 and the fate of the old gallery buildings has not been settled at the time of writing.

It was presumably the vestments which prompted Picasso's bitchy comment about Matisse being a *chapelier modiste*, found among his papers.

183 The Abstract Expressionist ethos seems totally alien to such engagement, yet around 1950 Jackson Pollock worked on black-and-white paintings which he thought of as possible cartoons for stained-glass windows in an unrealized, unrealizable church or chapel designed by his friend and drinking companion, the architect Tony Smith (who had done other settings for his paintings). The project came to nothing nor did Pollock (or any of his contemporaries, for that matter) ever work on another building. Tony Smith abandoned architecture for sculpture in the late 1960s. Stephen Naifeh and Gregory White-Smith, *Jackson Pollock: An American Saga* (New York, 1989), pp. 664ff., 761ff.; Rosalind Krauss, *The Originality of the Avant-garde and Other Modern Myths* (Cambridge, MA, 1985), pp. 232ff.

More recently the painter Enzo Cucchi has chosen to work with the architect Mario Botta on an Alpine chapel overlooking Lago Maggiore in such a way that building and painting are interdependent.

184 See, for instance Marcus Brüderlin, *Archisculpture* (Basle, 2005).

185 Kurt H. Wolff, *The Sociology of Georg Simmel* (New York, 1950), p. 414.

186 By James Wines, *site. Identity in Design* (2005), and popularized by Tom Wolfe.

187 Matthew Arnold, *Literature and Dogma* (London, 1904), p. xix.

188 Le Corbusier, *The Modulor* (London, 1954), p. 72.

189 Donald Sassoon, *The Culture of the Europeans* (London, 2006), especially pp. xxvff.

190 Hal Foster *et al.*, *Art since 1900* (London, 2004), p. 662, fig. 3. The photographer is Andreas Gursky and the architect is Norman Foster.

Bibliography

Abbott Abbott, Edwin, *Flatland: A Romance of Many Dimensions* (London, 1884)

Adam, Robert, *Ruins of the Palace of the Emperor Diocletian at Spalatro in Dalmatia* (Venice, 1764)

—, and James Adam, *The Works in Architecture*, 3 vols (London, 1773–1822; reprinted 1931)

Adburgham, Alison, *Liberty's: A Biography of a Shop* (London, 1975)

Ahern, Geoffrey, *Sun at Midnight* (Wellingborough, 1984)

Alméras, Henri d', and Paul d'Estrée, *Les Théâtres libertins au XVIIIe siècle* (Paris, 1905)

Alofsin, Anthony, *Frank Lloyd Wright: The Lost Years* (Chicago, IL, 1993)

Alpers, Svetlana, and Michael Baxandall, *Tiepolo and the Pictorial Intelligence* (New Haven, CT, and London, 1994)

Alphant, Marianne, *Claude Monet: une vie dans le paysage* (Paris, 1993)

Altmann-Loos, Elsie, *Mein Leben mit Adolf Loos* (Vienna, 1984)

Amaury-Duval, Eugène-Emmanuel, *L'Atelier d'Ingres*, ed. D. Ternois (Paris, 1993)

Anderson, Stanford, *Peter Behrens* (Cambridge, MA, 2001)

Andia, B., de, *et al.*, *Fêtes et révolution* (Paris and Dijon, 1989)

Antal, Frederick, *Florentine Painting and its Social Background* (London, 1947)

Antonowa, Irina, and Jörn Merkert, eds, *Berlin–Moscow* (Munich, 1995)

Apollinaire, Guillaume, *Méditations esthétiques: les peintres cubistes* (Geneva, 1950)

—, *Oeuvres poétiques*, ed. Marcel Adéma and Michel Décaudin (Paris, 1965)

Appia, Adolphe, *Die Musik und die Inscenierung, 1892–97* (Munich, 1899)

—, *Oeuvres complètes*, ed. Denis Bablet and Marie L. Bablet-Hahn, 4 vols (Lausanne, 1983–92)

Arbour, Roméo, *Henri Bergson et les lettres françaises* (Paris, 1955)

Arnason, H. H., *The Sculptures of Houdon* (London, 1975)

Arnheim, Rudolf, *New Essays on the Psychology of Art* (Berkeley, CA, 1986)

Arnold, Matthew, *Literature and Dogma* (London, 1904)

Art and Power: Europe under the Dictators, 1930–45, exh. cat., Council of Europe (London, 1995)

Aslin, Elizabeth, *The Aesthetic Movement* (London, 1969)

Assunto, Rosario, *Stagioni e ragioni nell'estetica del Settecento* (Milan, 1967)

Auerbach, Jeffrey A., *The Great Exhibition of 1851: A Nation on Display* (New Haven, CT, and London, 1999)

Auffret, Dominique, *Alexandre Kojève* (Paris, 1990)

Avant-Garde 1, 1900–1923, exh. cat., Kunsthalle, Tübingen (Stuttgart, 1991)

Avenarius, Ferdinand, *Max Klinger als Poet* (Munich, 1921)

Aymonino, Carlo, *et al.*, *Le città capitali del XIX secolo* (Rome, 1975)

Baal-Teshuva, Jacob, *Art Treasures of the United Nations* (New York and London, 1964)

Bab, Julius, *Richard Dehmel: Die Geschichte eines Lebenswerkes* (Leipzig, 1926)

—,with Harry Slochower, *Richard Dehmel: Der Mensch und der Denker* (Dresden, 1928)

Badt, Kurt, *John Constable's Clouds* (London, 1950)

Bahr, Hermann, *Hermann-Bahr-Buch* (Berlin, 1913)

Balázs, Béla, *Il Film* (Turin 1957)

Baljeu, Joost, *Theo van Doesburg* (New York, 1974)

Baltrusaitis, Jurgis, *La Quête d'Isis* (Paris, 1967)

—, *Aberrations* (Cambridge, MA, 1989)

Balzac, Honoré de, *Un Grand Homme de Province à Paris* (Brussels and Leipzig, 1839)

Bann, Stephen, *Paul Delaroche: History Painted* (London, 1997)

Barillari, Diana, and Ezio Godoli, *Istanbul 1900* (New York, 1996)

Barker, Stephen, *Autoaesthetics: Strategies of the Self after Nietzsche* (Atlantic Highlands, NJ, 1992)

Baron-Cohen, Simon, and John E. Harrison, *Synaesthesia: Classic and Contemporary Readings* (Oxford, 1997)

Baroni, Daniele, *I mobili di Gerrit Thomas Rietveld* (Milan, 1977)

Barringer, Tim, *Men at Work: Art and Labour in Victorian Britain* (New Haven, CT, 2005)

Barry, James, *An Inquiry into the Real and Imaginary Obstructions to the Acquisition of the Arts in England* (London, 1775)

Barthélémy, J.-J. Abbé, *Voyage du jeune anacharsis en Grèce* (Paris, 1789)

Bastide, Jean François de, *La Petite Maison*, trans. and ed. Barbara Briganti (Palermo, 1989)

Baudelaire, Charles, *Oeuvres,* 2 vols, ed. Claude Pichois (Paris, 1976)

Bauer, Hermann, *Rocaille: zur Herkunft und zum Wesen eines Ornament-Motivs* (Berlin, 1962)

Bauquier, Georges, *Fernand Léger: vivre dans le vrai* (Paris, 1986)

Becker, Wolfgang, *Paris und die deutsche Malerei, 1750–1840* (Munich, 1971)

Beckett, R. B., ed., *John Constable's Correspondence*, 6 vols (London, 1962–8)

Behrens, Peter, *Ein Dokument deutscher Kunst* (Munich, 1901)

Bell, Quentin, *The Schools of Design* (London, 1963)

Bellini, Mario, ed., *Album, annuario di progetto e cultura materiale* (Milan, 1981)

Bénédite, Léonce, *Théodore Chassériau: sa vie et son oeuvre* (Paris, 1931)

Benjamin, Walter, *Illuminationen: Ausgewählte Schriften* (Frankfurt am Main, 1955)

—, *Gesammelte Schriften* (Frankfurt am Main, 1972)

—, *Angelus Novus. Ausgewählte Schriften 2* (Frankfurt am Main, 1966)

Bergdoll, Barry, *Léon Vaudoyer: Historicism in the Age of Industry* (Cambridge, MA, 1994)

Bergson, Henri, *Essai sur les données immédiates de la conscience* (Paris, 1888)

—, *L'Evolution créatrice* (Paris, 1911)

—, *Le Rire* (Paris, 1936)

Berlage, Hendrik Petrus, *Grundlagen und Entwicklung der Architektur* (Rotterdam, 1908)

—, *Amerikaansche Reisherrinneringen* (Rotterdam, 1913)

Berlin, Isaiah, *Russian Thinkers* (London, 1978)

Berlyn, Peter, and Charles Fowler, *The Crystal Palace: Its Architectural History and Constructive Marvels* (London, 1851)

Besant, Annie, and C. W. Leadbeater, *Thought-Forms* (London, 1905)

Białostocki, Jan, 'Rafael i Dürer jako Symbole dwóch Artystycznych Ideałów w Dobie Romantyzmu', in *Refleksje i Syntezy ze Świata sztuki, Cykl Drugi* (Warsaw, 1987)

Bidou, Henry, *Paris* (London, 1939)

Bird, Vivian, *Portrait of Birmingham* (London, 1970)

Biver, Marie-Louise, *Pierre Fontaine: premier architecte de l'empereur* (Paris, 1964)

Blake, William, *The Complete Writings of W. B.*, ed. Geoffrey Keynes (London, 1957)

Blanc, Charles, *Ingres: sa vie et ses ouvrages* (Paris, 1870)

—, *Grammaire des arts du dessin: architecture, sculpture, peinture*, 2nd edn, 2 vols (Paris, 1870)

Blau, Eve, and Nancy Troy, eds, *Architecture and Cubism* (Cambridge, MA, 1997)

Blavatsky, H. P., *The Secret Doctrine: The Synthesis of Science, Religion and Philosophy* (London, 1888)

Blossfeldt, Karl, *Urformen der Kunst* (Berlin, 1929)

Blotkamp, Carel, *Mondrian: The Art of Destruction* (London, 1994)

Blühm, Andreas, *et al.*, *The Color of Sculpture, 1840–1910* (Amsterdam and Zwolle, 1996)

Blumenberg, Hans, *Höhlenausgänge* (Berlin, 1989)

Blunt, Wilfrid, *England's Michelangelo: A Biography of George Frederic Watts* (London, 1975)

Boccioni, Umberto, *Gli scritti editi e inediti*, ed. Zeno Birolli (Milan, 1971)

Boehme, Jakob, *Sämtliche Schriften* (Stuttgart, 1730; repr. 1957)

Boetticher, Carl, *Die Tektonik der Hellenen*, 2 vols (Berlin, 1874)

Bolton, Arthur T., ed., *The Portrait of Sir John Soane* (London, 1927)

Bonnet, J. C., ed., *La Carmagnole des Muses* (Paris, 1988)

Bordes, Philippe, *Le Serment du Jeu de Paume de Jacques-Louis David* (Paris, 1983)

—, ed., *Autour de David: dessins neo-classiques du Musée des Beaux-Arts de Lille*, exh. cat. (Paris, 1983)

Boschot, Adolphe, *Théophile Gautier* (Paris, 1933)

Bossi, Giuseppe, *Delle opinioni di Leonardo da Vinci* (Milan, 1811)

Bott, Victor, *Introduction to Anthroposophic Medicine* (London, 2004)

Bottoni, Luciano, *Storia del Teatro Italiano, 1900–1945* (Bologna, 1999)

Boullée, Etienne-Louis, *The Treatise on Architecture*, ed. Helen Rosenau (London, 1953)

—, *L'Architecture: essai sur l'art*, ed. J.-M. Pérouse de Montclos (Paris, 1968)

Bourdelle, Antoine, *Ecrits sur l'Art et sur la vie* (Paris, 1955)

Bourdieu, Pierre, *La Distinction: critique sociale du jugement* (Paris, 1979)

Bowlt, John E., ed., *Russian Art of the Avant-Garde* (New York, 1988)

Bragdon, Claude, *The Beautiful Necessity* (London, 1910)

Braham, William, *Modern Color, Modern Architecture* (Aldershot, 2002)

Breton, André, *Les manifestes du surréalisme* (Paris, 1947)

Brewster, Sir David, *Treatise on Optics* (London, 1838)

Briganti, Giuliano, *I pittori dell'immaginario* (Milan, 1989)

Britton, Karla, *Auguste Perret* (London, 2001)

Brooks, H. Allen, *Le Corbusier's Formative Years* (Chicago, IL, 1997)

Brown, Edward J., *Mayakovsky: A Poet in the Revolution* (Princeton, NJ, 1973)

Brownlow, Kevin, *The Parade's Gone By* (Berkeley, CA, 1968)

Brüderlin, Markus, *Archisculpture* (Basel, 2005)

Brunel, Georges, ed., *Piranèse et les français* (Rome, 1978)

Brunschvigg, Léon, *Les Etapes de la philosophie mathématique* (Paris, 1930)

Büchner, Ludwig, *Kraft und Stoff* (Leipzig, 1876)

Buddensieg, Tilmann, and Henning Rogge, *Geschmackswandel in Deutschland: Historismus, Jugendstil und die Anfänge der Industrieform* (Nürnberg, n. d.)

Buddensieg, Tilmann, and Henning Rogge, *Industriekultur: Peter Behrens and the AEG, 1907–1914*, trans. Iain Boyd-Whyte (Cambridge, MA, 1984)

Burchard, John, and Albert Bush-Brown, *The Architecture of America* (Boston, MA, 1961)

Burke, Edmund, *A Philosophical Enquiry into the Origin of our Ideas of the Sublime and the Beautiful* (London, 1757)

B[urne]-J[ones], G[eorgiana], *Memorials of Edward Burne-Jones*, 2 vols (London and New York, 1904)

Bustard, Bruce I., *A New Deal for the Arts*, exh. cat., National Archives Building, Washington, DC (Washington, DC, and Seattle, WA, 1997)

Buttlar, Adrian von, *Der Englische Landsitz, 1715–1760* (Mittenwald, 1982)

—, *Leo von Klenze: Leben–Werk–Vision* (Munich, 1999)

Cabanne, Pierre and Pierre Restany, *L'Avant-Garde au XXe siècle* (Paris, 1969)

Cameron, Charles, *The Baths of the Romans* (London, 1772)

Canales, Jimena, and Andrew Hersher, 'Criminal Skins: Tattoos and Modern Architecture in the Work of Adolf Loos', in *Architectural History*, 48 (2005)

Canetti, Elias, *Macht und Überleben: Drei Essays* (Berlin, 1972)

—, *Die Fackel im Ohr* (Munich, 1980)

—, *Das Augenspiel* (Munich, 1985)

Carlyle, Thomas, *Sartor Resartus* (London, 1871)

Carr, E. H., *The Bolshevik Revolution* (London, 1966)

Carrà, Carlo, *La Pittura Metafisica* (Milan, 1919)

Carus, C. Gustav, *Neun Briefe über die Landschaftsmalerei Geschrieben in den Jahren 1851–1824 zuvor ein Brief von Goethe als Einleitung* (Dresden, 1831; reprinted 1923)

—, *Symbolik der Menschlichen Gestalt: ein Handbuch zur Menschenkenntniss* (Leipzig, 1858)

Caso, Jacques de, *David d'Angers: Sculptural Communication in the Age of Romanticism* (Princeton, 1992)

Cassirer, Ernst, *The Philosophy of the Enlightenment* (Princeton, NJ, 1951)

Cazes, E., *Le Château de Versailles et ses dépendances* (Versailles, 1910)

Chagall, Marc, *Ma vie* (Paris, 1931)

Chai, Leon, *Aestheticism: The Religion of Art in Post-Romantic Literature* (New York, 1990)

Chassé, Charles, *Le Monument Symboliste dans l'Art du XIXme siècle* (Paris, 1947)

Chatham, Mark A., *The Rhetoric of Purity* (Cambridge, 1991)

Chazanova, V. E., *Sovetskaia Architektura Pervich Let Oktiabria* (Moscow, 1970)

Chénier, André, *Oeuvres*, ed. Gérard Walter (Paris, 1958)

Ciucci, Giorgio, ed., *Giuseppe Terragni. opera completa* (Milan, 1996)

Cladel, Judith, *Rodin: sa vie glorieuse et inconnue* (Paris, 1936)

Clarac, C. de, *Description historique et graphique du Louvre et des Tuileries* (Paris, 1853)

Clark, T. J., *The Image of the People* (London, 1973)

—, *The Absolute Bourgeois* (London, 1982)

—, *Farewell to an Idea* (New Haven, CT, 1999)

Cohen, J. L., *Les Avant-Gardes et l'Etat*, URSS, *1917–1978*, ed. M. de Michelis and M. Tafuri (Paris, 1979)

—, ed., *Le Corbusier and the Mystique of the USSR* (Princeton, NJ, 1992)

Collins, Peter, *Concrete* (London, 1959)

Colomer, Claude, *Ernest Cabaner, 1833–1881: Musicien catalan, grand animateur de la vie parisienne, ami intime de Rimbaud et des Impressionnistes* (Montpellier, 1993)

Colvin, Howard M., ed., *The History of the King's Works*, 6 vols (London, 1963–82)

Cook, Sir Edward T., *The Life of John Ruskin* (London, 1911)

Cornwell-Clyne, Adrian, *Colour-Music: The Art of Light* (London, 1926)

Cousin, Victor, *Du vrai, du beau et du bien* (Paris, 1865)

Cozens, Alexander, *A New Method of Assisting the Invention in Drawing Original Compositions of Landscape* (London, 1786; repr. 1977)

Craig, Edward Gordon, *On the Art of the Theatre* (London, 1912)

—, *The Theatre Advancing* (London, 1921)

—, ed., *The Mask* (New York, 1909–29)

Cramer, Johannes, and Dorothée Sack, *Mies Van der Rohe: Frühe Bauten* (Berlin, 2004)

Crane, Walter, *Ideals in Art* (London, 1905)

Crary, Jonathan, *Techniques of the Observer* (Cambridge, MA, 1990)

Crawford, Alan, *C. R. Ashbee: Architect, Designer and Romantic Socialist* (New Haven, CT, and London, 1985)

Crow, Thomas, *Emulation: Making Artists for Revolutionary France* (New Haven, CT, and London, 1995)

Cruikshank, George, *Phrenological Illustrations; or, An Artist's View of the Craniological System of Doctors Gall and Spurzheim* (London, 1826)

Culot, Maurice, *et al.*, *Les Frères Perret: l'oeuvre complète* (Paris, 2000)

Cuzin, Jean-Pierre, *Jean-Honoré Fragonard, Life and Work* (New York, 1988)

464

Cytowic, Richard E., *The Man who Tasted Shapes: A Bizarre Medical Mystery Offers Revolutionary Insights into Emotion, Reasoning and Consciousness* (New York, 1993)

Daix, Pierre, *Le Cubisme de Picasso* (Neuchâtel, 1979)

Dalcroze, Emile-Jaques, *Rhythm, Music and Education* (New York, 1921)

Dalrymple-Henderson, Linda, *The Fourth Dimension and Non-Euclidean Geometry in Modern Art* (Princeton, NJ, 1983)

Daly, Aedan, *S. Isidoro* (Rome, 1971)

Damaz, Paul, *Art in European Architecture: Synthèse des Arts*, preface by Le Corbusier (New York, 1956)

Dampier-Whetham, William Cecil Dampier, *A History of Science and its Relation with Philosophy and Religion* (Cambridge, 1930)

Danzker, Jo-Anne Birnie, ed., *Theo van Doesburg: Maler-Architect* (Munich, 2001)

Darley, Gillian, *John Soane: An Accidental Romantic* (New Haven, CT, 1999)

Darwin, Charles, *The Origin of Species* (London, 1876)

—, *The Works of Charles Darwin*, ed. Paul H. Barrett and R. B. Freeman (London, 1988)

Darwin, Erasmus, *The Botanic Garden: A Poem in Two Parts* (London, 1789)

Daudet, Léon, *Souvenirs des Milieux Littéraires, Politiques, Artistiques et Médicaux*, 6 vols (Paris, 1920)

David, Louis Jacques, *Le Tableau des Sabines, exposé publiquement au Palais National* (Paris, 1799)

—, *Le Peintre Louis David* (Paris, 1880–82)

Deane, Phyllis, *The First Industrial Revolution* (Cambridge, 1965)

Décaudin, Michel, 'Rimbaud et les symbolistes', in *L'Harne, Cahier Rimbaud* (Paris, 1993)

Décimo, Marc, *Marcel Duchamp mis à nu: A propos du processus créatif* (Dijon, 2004)

Delacroix, Eugène, *Journal, 1822–1863*, ed. H. Damisch (Paris, 1981)

Delafosse, Jean-Charles, *Nouvelle iconologie historique; ou, Attributs Hiérogliphyques qui ont pour objects, les quartre elémens, les quartre Saisons, les quartre parties du monde et les différentes complexions de l'homme* (Paris, 1768)

Delaunay, Robert, *1906–1914, De l'Impressionisme à l'Abstraction: exposition présentée au Centre Georges Pompidou* (Paris, 1999)

Delécluze, E. J., *Louis David: son école et son temps* (Paris, 1855; reprinted 1983)

Denney, Reuel, *The Astonished Muse* (Chicago, IL, 1957)

Descharnes, Robert, and Clovis Prévost, *Gaudí the Visionary* (New York, 1971)

Deschodt, Anne-Marie, *Mariano Fortuny: un magicien de Venise* (Paris, 1979)

Deshairs, Léon, and Jean Laran, *Gustave Moreau* (Paris, 1916)

D'Harnoncourt, Anne, and Walter Hopps, *Etant-donnés* (Philadelphia, PA, 1987)

Diamonstein, Barbaralee, *Collaboration* (New York, 1981)

Diderot, Denis, *Oeuvres complètes*, ed. Roger Lewinter (Paris, 1969–73)

Doig, Allan, *Theo van Doesburg: Painting into Architecture* (Cambridge, 1986)

Doob, Leonard W., *Propaganda: Its Psychology and Technique* (New York, 1943)

Dreijmanis, John, ed., *Karl Jaspers on Max Weber* (London, 1989)

Drengenberg, Hans-Jürgen, *Die Sowjetische Politik auf dem Gebiet der bildenden Kunst von 1917 bis 1934* (Berlin, 1972)

Dresser, Christopher, *Principles of Decorative Design* 2nd edn (London, 1873)

—, *Studies in Design* (London, 1874–6)

—, *General Principles of Art, Decorative and Pictorial; with Hints on Colour, its Harmonies and Contrasts* (London, 1881)

—, *Japan: Its Architecture, Art and Art Manufactures* (London, 1882)

Drexler, Arthur, ed., *The Architecture of the Ecole des Beaux-Arts* (New York, 1977)

Dreyfous, Maurice, *Ce que je tiens à dire: un demi-siècle de choses vues et entendues, 1862–1872* (Paris, 1912)

Duberman, Martin, *Black Mountain: An Exploration in Community* (London, 1973)

Duchamp, Marcel, *Marchand de sel: Ecrits de Marcel Duchamp*, ed. Michel Sanouillet (Paris, 1958)

Dumont, Marie-Jeanne, ed., *Lettres à Auguste Perret* (Paris, 2002)

Duncan, Isadora, *My Life* (London, 1928)

Dunlop, Ian, *Versailles* (London, 1956)

Durand, J.N.L., *Précis des leçons d'architecture* (Paris, 1802–5)

Durkheim, Emile, *De la division du travail social* (Paris, 1932)

Durm, Josef, *Handbuch der Architektur* (Darmstadt, 1890–1908)

Duve, Thierry de, *Nominalisme pictural* (Paris, 1984)

Eastlake, C. L., *A History of the Gothic Revival in England* (London, 1872)

Easton, Laird McLeod, *The Red Count* (Berkeley, CA, 2002)

Easton, Malcolm, *Artists and Writers in Paris* (London, 1964)

Ede, H. S., *Savage Messiah* (London, 1931)

Einem, Herbert von, *Deutsche Malerei des Klassizismus und der Romantik, 1760 bis 1840* (Munich, 1978)

Eisenstein, Sergei, *Film Form*, ed. and trans. Jay Leyda (London, 1949)

—, *Film Sense*, ed. and trans. Jay Leyda (London, 1943)

El arquitecto D. Ventura Rodríguez, exh. cat., Museo Municipal, Madrid (1983)

Elagin, Juri, *Vsevolod Meierkho'd Tsemyi Genii* (Moscow, 1998)

Ellmann, Richard, *Oscar Wilde* (New York, 1987)

—, *Along the Riverrun* (New York, 1989)

Ellul, Jacques, *Propaganda: The Formation of Men's Attitudes* (New York, 1971)

Emmanuel, Maurice, *Essai sur l'Orchestique Grecque* (Paris, 1895)

English, Elizabeth Cooper, 'Arkhitektura Mnimosti: The Origins of Soviet Avant-Garde Rationalist Architecture in the Russian Mystical-Philosophical and Mathematical Intellectual Tradition', unpublished PhD thesis, University of Pennsylvania (Philadelphia, 2000)

Eriksen, Sven, *Early Neo-Classicism in France* (London, 1974)

Escholier, Raymond, *Eugène Delacroix* (Paris, 1926)

Etiemble, [René], *Le Mythe de Rimbaud*, vol. II: *Structure du mythe* (Paris, 1952)

Ettlinger, L. D., *Kandinsky at Rest* (Oxford, 1961)

Evans, Robin, *The Fabrication of Virtue: English Prison Architecture* (Cambridge, 1982)

Faber, Geoffrey, *Oxford Apostles: A Character Study of the Oxford Movement* (London, 1933)

Fechner, Gustav Theodor, *Zur Experimentalen Aesthetik* (Leipzig, 1871)

—, *Vorschule der Aesthetik*, 2 vols (Leipzig, 1876)

Fergusson, James, *The Illustrated Handbook of Architecture* (London, 1859)

—, *History of the Modern Styles of Architecture* (London, 1891)

—, *A History of Architecture in all Countries*, ed. R. Phené Spiers (London, 1893)

Ferrari, Enrique Lafuente, *Goya: The Frescoes in San Antonio de la Florida in Madrid* (Geneva, 1955)

Feuerbach, Henriette, ed., *Ein Vermächtnis* (Berlin, 1911)

Fiedler, Conrad, *Schriften über Kunst*, ed. Hans Marbach (Leipzig, 1896)

—, *Schriften über Kunst*, vol. II, ed. Hermann Konnerth (Munich, 1914)

Figes, Orlando, *Natasha's Dance* (London, 2002)

Finley, Gerald, *Turner and George IV in Edinburgh* (London, 1981)

Flandrin, Louis, *Hippolyte Flandrin: sa vie et son oeuvre* (Paris, 1902)

Fontaine, Pierre-François, *Journal, 1799–1853* (Paris, 1987)

Fortier, Bruno, *Le Métropole Imaginaire: un Atlas de Paris* (Brussels, 1989)

Fortuny, Mariano, *Eclairage scénique: système Fortuny* (Paris, 1904)

Foster, Hal, *et al.*, *Art since 1900* (London, 2004)

Foster, Roy, *W. B. Yeats: A Life* (Oxford, 1997–2003)

Fothergill, Brian, *Sir William Hamilton, Envoy Extraordinary* (London, 1969)

Franciscono, Marcel, *Walter Gropius and the Creation of the Bauhaus* (Champaign and Urbana, IL, 1971)

Franco, Lourdes Cruz González and Zoraida Gutiérrez Ospina, eds, *Guía de murales de la Ciudad Universitaria* (Mexico, 2004)

Freeman, John Grace, *The Maniera of Vasari* (London, 1867)

Friedman, Mildred, ed., *De Stijl: Visions of Utopia* (Minneapolis and New York, 1982)

Fülöp-Miller, René, *Geist und Gesicht des Bolschewismus* (Zurich, 1928)

Gage, John, *Colour and Culture: Practice and Meaning from Antiquity to Abstraction* (London, 1993)

Galbraith, John Kenneth, *The Affluent Society* [1958] (London, 1962)

—, *The New Industrial State* (London, 1967)

Gallet, Michel, 'Jean-Charles Delafosse, Architecte', *Gazette des Beaux-Arts* (March 1963)

Galliot, Marcel, *Essai sur la langue de la réclame contemporaine* (Toulouse, 1955)

Galton, Francis, Sir, *Inquiries into Human Faculty and its Development* (London, 1883)

Gamboni, Dario, *The Destruction of Art: Iconoclasm and Vandalism since the French Revolution* (London, 1997)

Garafola, Lynn, *Diaghilev's Ballets Russes* (New York, 1989)

Gargiani, Roberto, *Auguste Perret* (Milan, 1993)

Garnier, Charles, *Le Nouvel Opéra de Paris* (Paris, 1878)

Gassier, Pierre, and Juliet Wilson, *Goya: His Life and Work* (London, 1971)

Gaunt, William, *The Aesthetic Adventure* (London, 1945)

Gautier, Théophile, *L'Art moderne* (Paris, 1856)

—, *Mademoiselle de Maupin* (Paris, 1907)

Geist, Johann Friedrich, *Arcades: The History of a Building Type* (Cambridge, MA, 1983)

George, Eric, *The Life and Death of Benjamin Robert Haydon* (Oxford, 1948)

Gerlach, Peter, *Proportion-Körper-Leben: Quellen, Entwürfe und Kontroversen* (Cologne, 1990)

Ghil, René, *Traité du verbe* (Paris, 1886)

Giedion, Sigfried, *Space, Time and Architecture* (Cambridge, MA, 1954)

—, *Mechanization Takes Command: A Contribution to Anonymous History* (New York, 1955)

Gilbert, Sir W. S., *The Savoy Operas* (London, 1926)

Gilly, Friedrich, *Essays on Architecture*, ed. Fritz Neumayer, trans. David Britt (Santa Monica, CA, 1994)

Girardin, René Louis, Marquis de, *De la Composition des Paysages; ou. Des moyens d'Embellir la Nature Autour des Habitations, en Joignant l'Agréable à l'Utile* (Geneva and Paris, 1777); as *An Essay on Landscape*, trans. Robert Malthus (New York, 1982)

Girouard, Mark, *Sweetness and Light: The Queen Anne Movement, 1860–1900* (New Haven, CT, and London, 1977)

Gleizes, Albert, and Jean Metzinger, *Du 'Cubisme' / On 'Cubism' / Über den 'Kubismus'*, ed. Fritz Metzinger (Frankfurt, 1993)

Goethe, Johann Wolfgang von, *Werke* (*Gedenkausgabe*), ed. Ernst Beutler, 27 vols (Zurich, 1948–64)

Golding, John, *Paths to the Absolute* (London, 2000)

Gomme, George Laurence, *The Village Community* (London, 1890)

Goncourt, Edmond de, and Jules de Goncourt, *Histoire de Marie Antoinette* (Paris, 1859)

—, *Histoire de la Société Française pendant le Directoire* (Paris, 1880)

Goodison, Nicholas, *Matthew Boulton: Ormolu* (London, 2002)

Gorky, Maxim, *Sobranie Sochinenii* (Moscow, 1961)

Gottfried Semper und die Mitte des 19. Jahrhunderts, Symposium proceedings, ETH, Zurich (Basel, 1976)

Gould, Stephen Jay, *The Mismeasure of Man* (New York, 1981)

Gow, Ian, and Timothy Clifford, *The National Gallery of Scotland* (Edinburgh, 1988)

Graf, Otto Antonia, *Otto Wagner* (Vienna, 1985)

Gravagnuolo, Benedetto, *Adolf Loos: Theory and Works* (New York, 1982)

Gray, Camilla, *The Russian Experiment in Art, 1863–1922* (London, 1962)

Green, Christopher, *Léger and the Avant-Garde* (New Haven, CT, 1976)

Green, Vivien, 'Hiram Powers's "Greek Slave": Emblem of Freedom', *American Art Journal*, XIV (Autumn 1982)

Grimm, Jacob, *Deutsche Mythologie* (Göttingen, 1835)

Grosz, George, *An Autobiography*, trans. Nora Hodges (New York, 1983)

Grunewald, Marie-Antoinette, *Paul Chenavard et la Décoration du Panthéon* (Lyon, 1977)

Gsell, Paul, 'Chez Rodin', *L'Art et les Artistes*, XIX/109 (Paris, 1914)

Guénon, René, *Le Théosophisme* (Paris, 1975)

Guilbaut, Serge, *How New York Stole the Idea of Modern Art* (Chicago and London, 1983)

Gurlitt, Cornelius, *Die Deutsche Kunst seit 1800* (Berlin, 1924)

Guth, Peter, *et al.*, *Hellerau, Festspielhaus-Ensemble* (Ludwigsburg, 2002)

Guyot, M., *Nouvelles Récréations physiques et mathématiques*, 4 vols (Paris, 1772–5)

Gwilt, Joseph, *An Encyclopaedia of Architecture* (London, 1835)

Hackett, C. A., *Rimbaud l'enfant* (Paris, 1948)

Haeckel, Ernst Heinrich Philipp August, *Natürliche Schöpfungsgeschichte, Gemeinverständliche Wissenschaftliche Vorträge über die Entwicklungslehre im Allgemeinen und Diejenige von Darwin, Goethe, und Lamarck im Besonderen* (Berlin, 1866)

—, *Prinzipien der Generelle Morphologie der Organismen, Allgemeine Grundzüge der Organischen Formenwissenschaft, Mechanisch Begründet durch die von Charles Darwin Reformierte Descendenztheorie* (Berlin, 1966)

—, *The Riddle of the Universe at the Close of the Nineteenth Century*, trans. Joseph McCabe (New York, 1900)

—, *Kunstformen der Natur* (Leipzig and Vienna, 1904)

Hahl-Koch, Jelena, *Arnold Schoenberg – Wassily Kandinsky: Letters, Pictures and Documents* (London, 1984)

Hamilton, W. R., *Memorandum on the Subject of the Earl of Elgin's Pursuits in Greece* (Edinburgh, 1810)

Hancarville, Pierre François Hughes, Baron d', *Collection of . . . Antiquities from the Cabinet of the Hon.ble Wm. Hamilton* (Naples, 1766)

—, *Recherches sur l'origine . . . des Arts de la Grèce* (London, 1785)

Haraway, Donna, *Crystals, Fabrics and Fields: Metaphors in Twentieth-Century Biology* (New Haven, CT, 1976)

Harries, Karsten, *The Bavarian Rococo Church* (New Haven, CT, 1983)

Harris, John, *Sir William Chambers, Knight of the Polar Star* (London, 1970)

Harris, Marvin, *The Rise of Anthropological Theory* (New York, 1968)

Harrison, John, *Synaesthesia, the Strangest Thing* (Oxford, 2001)

Harsdoerffer, Georg Philipp, *Deliciae Physicae-Mathematicae*, 3 vols (Frankfurt, 1636–51; reprinted 1991)

—, *Der Geschichtspiegel* (Nuremberg, 1654)

Hartford, Robert, ed., *Bayreuth, The Early Years* (London, 1980)

Hartleben, Otto Erich, *Tagebuch: Fragment eines Lebens* (Munich, 1906)

Haskell, Arnold, *Diaghileff: His Artistic and Private Life* (London, 1947)

Haskell, Francis, *Past and Present in Art and Taste: Selected Essays* (New Haven, CT, and London, 1987)

Hautecoeur, Louis, *Histoire de l'architecture classique en France*, 7 vols (Paris, 1943–57)

Hay, David Ramsay, *The Laws of Harmonious Colouring, Adapted to Interior Decorations with Observations on the Practice of House Painting*, 6th edn (Edinburgh and London, 1847)

—, *The Geometric Beauty of the Human Figure Defined* (London, 1851)

Haydon, Robert, *Lectures on Painting and Design*, 4 vols (London, 1844–6)

—, *The Autobiography and Memoirs of Benjamin Robert Haydon*, ed. Tom Taylor (London, 1926)

Haynes, Deborah J., *Bakhtin and the Visual Arts* (Cambridge, 1995)

Heck, Sandy, 'The Only Possible Word is "Swank"; Restoration and "Reinterpretation" of the Rainbow Room at Rockefeller Center', *Architecture*, LXX/6 (June 1988)

Hector Horeau, 1801–1872, exh. cat., Musée des Arts Décoratifs, (Paris, 1977)

Hegel, G.W.F., *Die Aesthetik*, ed. F. Bassenge after H. G. Hothos (Berlin and Weimar, 1965)

Heidegger, Martin, *Nietzsche*, trans. David Farrell Krell (San Francisco, 1979)

Heinze-Greenberg, Ita, and Regina Stephan, eds, *Erich Mendelsohn: Gedankenwelten* (Stuttgart, 2000)

Helmholtz, Hermann, *Handbuch der Physiologischen Optik* (Leipzig, 1856)

—, *On the Sensations of Tone as a Physiological Basis for the Theory of Music* (London, 1885)

Hemleben, Johannes, *Rudolf Steiner und Ernst Haeckel* (Stuttgart, 1965)

Hensbergen, Gijs van, *Guernica: The Biography of a Twentieth-Century Icon* (London, 2004)

Herbart, Johann Friedrich, *Sämtliche Werke*, ed. Karl Kehrbach and Otto Flügel (Hamburg, 1887)

Herder, Johann Gottfried, *Sämmtliche Werke*, ed. Bernhard Suphan (Berlin, 1877–99)

Herrmann, Wolfgang, ed., *Gottfried Semper: Theoretischer Nachlass an der ETH* (Basel, 1981)

—, *Gottfried Semper: In Search of Architecture* (Cambridge, MA, 1984)

—, ed., *In What Style Should We Build?: The German Debate on Architectural Style* (Santa Monica, CA, 1991)

Herz-Fischler, R., *A Mathematical History of Division in Extreme and Mean Ratio* (Waterloo, Ontario, 1987)

Hildebrand, Adolf von, *Das Problem der Form in der Bildenden Kunst* (Strasbourg, 1893)

Hildebrandt, Hans, *Adolf Hoelzel* (Stuttgart, 1953)

Hitchcock, Henry-Russell, *In the Nature of Materials: The Buildings of Frank Lloyd Wright, 1887–1941* (New York, 1942)

Hittorff: un architecte du XIXème siècle, exh. cat., Musée Carnavalet (Paris, 1986)

Hobhouse, Hermione, *Thomas Cubbitt: Master Builder* (London, 1971)

—, *A History of Regent Street* (London, 1975)

Hobsbawm, Eric, and Terence Ranger, eds, *The Invention of Tradition* (Cambridge, 1983)

—, *The Age of Extremes: The Short Twentieth Century* (London, 1994)

Hoeber, Fritz, *Peter Behrens* (Munich, 1913)

Hoffmann, David Marc, *Zur Geschichte des Nietzsche-Archivs* (Berlin, 1991)

Hoffmann, E.T.A., *Werke*, ed. Martin Hürliman, 4 vols (Zürich, 1946)

Hoffmann, Johann Leonhard, *Versuch einer Geschichte der Malerischen Harmonie ueberhaupt und der Farbenharmonie insbesondere . . .* (Halle, 1786)

Hoggart, Richard, *Speaking to Each Other: Essays* (London, 1970)

Hohoff, Curt, *Heinrich von Kleist* (Hamburg, 1958)

Hollier, Denis, *Against Architecture* (Cambridge, MA, 1989)

—, ed., *A New History of French Literature* (Cambridge, MA, 1989)

Hollinrake, Roger, *Nietzsche, Wagner and the Philosophy of Pessimism* (London, 1982)

Homer, William Innes, *Seurat and the Science of Painting* (New York, 1985)

Honour, Hugh, *Chinoiserie: The Vision of Cathay* (London, 1961)

Hopkins, Eric, *The Rise of the Manufacturing Town: Birmingham and the Industrial Revolution* (Sutton, 1998)

Huebsch, Heinrich, *Über Griechische Architektur* (Heidelberg, 1822)

—, *In welchem Style sollen wir Bauen?* (Karlsruhe, 1828); ed. Wolf Schirmer (Karlsruhe, 1984)

—, *Bau-Werke*, 3 vols (Karlsruhe and Baden, 1838–59)

—, *Die Architektur und ihr Verhältnis zur heutigen Malerei und Skulptur* (Stuttgart and Tübingen, 1847; reprinted Berlin, 1985)

—, *Die Altchristlichen Kirchen nach den Baudenkmalen und älteren Beschreibungen und der Einfluss des Altchristlichen Baustyls auf den Kirchenbau aller Späteren Perioden*, 2 vols (Karlsruhe, 1862–3)

Huebsch, Heinrich, and Franz Heger, *Malerische Ansichten von Athen* (Darmstadt, 1823)

Hueffer, Ford Madox, *Ford Madox Brown* (London, 1896)

Hughes, Peter, *Eighteenth-Century France and the East* (London, 1981)

Hugo, Victor, *Les Orientales*, ed. Elisabeth Barineau (Paris, 1952)

—, *Théâtre*, 4 vols (Paris, 1856)

—, *Les Misérables*, 10 vols (Paris, 1862)

Hulten, Pontus, ed., *Futurism and Futurisms*, exh. cat., Palazzo Grassi, Venice (London, 1986)

Humbert de Superville, D. P. G., *Essai sur les signes inconditionnels dans l'art*, 3 vols (Leiden, 1827)

Husserl, Edmund, *Ideas: General Introduction to Pure Phenomenology* (New York, 1962)

Hussey, Christopher, *The Picturesque: Studies in a Point of View* (London, 1967)

Huysmans, J.-K., *A Rebours* [1884] (Paris, 1903)

Ilkosz, Jerzy, and Beate Szymanski, eds, *Hans Poelzig in Breslau* (Delmenhorst, 2000)

Innes, Christopher, *Edward Gordon Craig* (Cambridge, 1983)

Isaacs, Reginald R., *Walter Gropius: Der Mensch und sein Werk* (Berlin, 1983)

The Italian Metamorphosis, 1943–1968, exh. cat., Solomon Guggenheim Museum, (New York, 1994)

Itten, Johannes, *Gestaltung- und Formenlehre: Mein Vorkurs am Bauhaus* (Ravensburg, 1975)

—, *Werke und Schriften*, ed. Willy Rotzler (Zurich, 1972)

James, Henry, *William Wetmore Story and his Friends: From Letters, Diaries and Recollections* (Edinburgh and London, 1903)

Janneau, Guillaume, *L'Art cubiste* (Paris, 1929)

Jappellli, Paola and Giovanni Menna, *Willem Marinus Dudok* (Naples, 1997)

Jarzombek, Mark, *The Psychologizing of Modernity* (Cambridge, 2000)

Jasinski, René, *Les Années romantiques de Théophile Gautier* (Paris, 1929)

Jaspers, Karl, *On Max Weber* (London, 1989)

Jelavich, Peter, *Munich and Theatrical Modernism* (Cambridge, MA, 1985)

Jimenez, Victor, *Juan O'Gorman* (Mexico, 2004)

Johnson, Dorothy, *Jacques-Louis David: Art in Metamorphosis* (Princeton, NJ, 1994)

Johnson, Philip, and Henry-Russell Hitchcock, *The International Style of Architecture* (New York, 1932; reprinted 1966)

Jones, Ernest, *Sigmund Freud: Life and Work*, 3 vols (London, 1953–7)

Jones, Owen, *The Grammar of Ornament* (London, 1856)

—, *Lectures on Architecture and the Decorative Arts* (London, 1863)

Julia, Emile-François, *Antoine Bourdelle: maitre d'oeuvre* (Paris, 1930)

Julius, Anthony, *Transgressions: The Offences of Art* (Chicago, IL, 2003)

Kadatz, Hans-Joachim, *Peter Behrens: Architekt-Maler-Grafiker und Formgestalter, 1868–1940* (Leipzig, 1977)

Kaes, Anton, Martin Jay and Edward Dimendberg, *The Weimar Republic Sourcebook* (Berkeley and Los Angeles, CA, 1994)

Kahnweiler, Daniel-Henry, *Juan Gris: His Life and Work* (London, 1947)

Kandinsky, Wassily, *Essays über Kunst und Künstler*, ed. Max Bill (Bern, 1955)

—, and Franz Marc, *Der Blaue Reiter* (Munich, 1965)

Kant, Immanuel, *Werke*, ed. E. Cassirer, 12 vols (Berlin, 1922–3)

—, *Critique of the Power of Judgment*, trans. Paul Guyer and Eric Matthews (Cambridge, 2000)

Kaufmann, Emil, *L'Architettura dell'Illuminismo* (Turin, 1966)

Kaufmann, Walter, *Architecture in the Age of Reason* (Cambridge, MA, 1955)

—, *Nietzsche: Philosopher, Psychologist, Antichrist* (Princeton, NJ, 1974)

Kelvin, Norman, ed., *The Collected Letters of William Morris* (Princeton, NJ, 1984)

Kemp, Martin, *The Science of Art: Optical Themes in Western Art from Brunelleschi to Seurat* (New Haven, CT, and London, 1990)

Kermode, Frank, *Puzzles and Epiphanies* (London, 1963)

Kersting, Hanno, *Geschichtsphilosophie und Weltbürgerkrieg* (Heidelberg, 1959)

Kessler, Graf Harry, *Walther Rathenau: His Life and Work* (New York, 1930)

—, *Tage-Bücher, 1918–1937* (Frankfurt, 1961)

Khan-Magomedov, Selim O., *Pioneers of Soviet Architecture* (London, 1987)

—, *Alexander Rodchenko: The Complete Work* (New York, 1986)

Khlebnikov, Velemir, *Collected Works*, trans. Paul Schmidt, ed. Charlotte Douglas (Cambridge, MA, 1987)

Kimball, Fiske, *The Creation of the Rococo* (Philadelphia, 1943; reprinted New York, 1964)

Kirsch, Karin, *Die Weissenhofsiedlung* (Stuttgart, 1987)

Klein, Adrian Bernard, *Colour-Music: The Art of Light* (London, 1926)

Kleist, Heinrich von, *Sämtliche Werke*, ed. Arnold Zweig (Munich, 1923)

Kline, George L., *Religious and Anti-Religious Thought in Russia* (Chicago, IL, 1968)

Koch, Alexander, *Darmstädter Künstlerkolonie* (Darmstadt, 1901, reprinted 1979)

Kochno, Boris, *Diaghilev and the Ballets Russes* (London, 1971)

Koerner, Joseph Leo, *Caspar David Friedrich* (London, 1990)

Kolakowski, Leszek, *Main Currents of Marxism: Its Origins, Growth and Dissolution* (Oxford, 1978)

—, *Bergson* (Oxford, 1985)

Kornblatt, Judith Deutsch, and Richard F. Gustafson, eds, *Russian Religious Thought* (Madison, WI, 1996)

Kostka, Alexander, and Irving Wohlfarth, eds, *Nietzsche and 'An Architecture of our Minds'* (Los Angeles, 1999)

Kraus, Karl, *Worte in Versen* (Munich, 1959)

Krause, Jürgen, *'Martyrer' und 'Prophet': Studien zum Nietzsche-Kult in der Bildenden Kunst der Jahrhundertwende* (Berlin, 1984)

Krauss, Rosalind, *The Originality of the Avant-Garde and Other Modernist Myths* (Cambridge, MA, 1985)

Kris, E., 'Der Stil Rustique: Die Verwendung des Naturabgusses bei Wenzel Jamnitzer und Bernard Palissy', *Jahrbuch der Kunsthistorischen Sammlungen in Wien*, n. s. (Vienna, 1926)

Kristan, Markus, ed., *Adolf Loos: Wohnungen* (Vienna, 2001)

Kühn, Paul, *Weimar* (Leipzig, 1919)

Lancellotti, Arturo, *Storia anedottica della réclame* [1912] (Milan, 1953)

Lanciani, Rodolfo Amedeo, *The Ruins and Excavations of Ancient Rome* (Boston, MA, and New York, 1897)

Lankheit, Klaus, ed., *Der Blaue Reiter*, ed. Wassily Kandinsky and Franz Marc (Munich, 1965)

Lapauze, Henri, *Ingres: sa vie et son oeuvre* (Paris, 1911)

—, *Histoire de l'Académie de France à Rome* (Paris, 1924)

Lassman, Peter, et al., *Max Weber's Science as a Vocation* (London, 1989)

Laumann, E.-M., *L'Epopée Napoléonienne: le retour des cendres* (Paris, 1904)

Lavedan, Pierre, *Histoire d'urbanisme* (Paris, 1959)

Leadbeater, C. W., *Man: Visible and Invisible* (London, 1902)

—, and Annie Besant, *Thought-forms* (London, 1905)

Le Camus de Mézières, *Le Génie de l'Architecture; ou, l'Analogie de cet Art avec nos Sensations* (Paris, 1780)

Le Corbusier [Charles-Edouard Jeanneret], *Etudes sur le mouvement d'art décoratif en Allemagne* (Chaux de Fonds, 1912; New York, 1968)

—, *Architecture d'Epoque Machiniste* (Paris, 1926; reprinted Turin, 1975)

—, *Des canons, des munitions? merci! des logis, SVP* (Paris, 1937)

—, *The Modulor* (London, 1954)

—, *The Drawings* (New York and London, 1982)

Lee, Vernon, *The Beautiful: An Introduction to Psychological Aesthetics* (Cambridge, 1913)

Lefrère, Jean-Jacques, *Cabaner: poète au piano* (Paris, 1994)

Léger, Fernand, *Fonctions de la peinture* (Paris, 1965)

Lenin, V. I., *On Literature and Art* (Moscow, 1967)

Le Roy, J. D., *Les Ruines des plus beaux Monuments de la Grèce* (Paris, 1758)

Leslie, Charles Robert, *Memoirs of the Life of John Constable* (London, 1951)

Leslie, Esther, *Synthetic Worlds* (London, 2005)

Lessing, G. E., *Werke* (Weimar, 1954)

Lethaby, W. R., *Philip Webb and his Work* (Oxford, 1935)

471

Lévi, Eliphas [Alphonse-Louis Constant], *Dogme et rituel de la haute magie,* 2 vols (Paris, 1854–5)

Levine, Neil, *Architectural Reasoning in the Age of Positivism* (Ann Arbor, MI, 1977)

—, *The Architecture of Frank Lloyd Wright* (Princeton, NJ, 1996)

Levine, Steven Z., *Monet and his Critics* (New York, 1976)

Levitine, George, *The Dawn of Bohemianism: The Barbu Rebellion and Primitivism in Neoclassical France* (University Park, PA, 1978)

Limberg, Jörg, *Erich Mendelsohns Einsteinturm in Potsdam* (Potsdam, 1994)

Lindley, John, *The Vegetable Kingdom* (London, 1846)

Lipps, Theodor, *Leitfaden der Psychologie,* 3rd edn (Leipzig, 1903)

Lissitzky, El, *Russland* (Vienna, 1930)

—, and Hans Arp, *Die Kunstismen/Les Ismes de l'Art/The Isms of Art, 1914–24* (Zürich, 1925)

Lista, Giovanni, *Loïe Fuller: danseuse de la Belle Epoque* (Paris, 1994)

—, *La Scène futuriste* (Paris, 1989)

Loos, Adolf, *Ins Leere Gesprochen* (Paris, 1921)

—, *Trotzdem* (Innsbruck, 1931)

Loos, Claire, *Adolf Loos Privat* (Vienna, 1985)

Lövgren, Sven, *The Genesis of Modernism* (Bloomington, IN, 1971)

Löwith, Karl, *From Hegel to Nietzsche: The Revolution in Nineteenth-Century Thought* (New York, 1964)

Lunacharsky, Anatoly Vassilevich, *Three Plays,* trans. L. A. Magnus and K. Walter (London, 1923)

—, *Sobranie Sochinenii; Literaturovedenie, Kritika, Estetika* (Moscow, 1963–7)

—, *Socialism and Religion,* 2 vols (New York, 1996)

McCarthy, Fiona, *William Morris: A Life for our Time* (New York, 1995)

MacIntyre, Alastair, *Against the Self-Images of the Age* (New York, 1971)

Mackail, J. W., *The Life of William Morris* (London, 1901)

Mahler, Alma Maria, ed., *Gustav Mahler: Briefe, 1879–1910* (Berlin, 1925)

Malevich, Suetin, Chashnik, Lissitzky, The Suprematist Straightline, exh. cat. (London, 1977)

Malingue, Maurice, *Lettres de Gauguin* (Paris, 1946)

Mallarmé, Stéphane, *Oeuvres* (Paris, 1945)

Mallgrave, H., *Gottfried Semper, Architect of the Nineteenth Century* (New Haven and London, 1996)

Maltese, Corrado, *Storia dell'arte in Italia, 1785–1943,* (Turin, 1960)

Mann, Golo, *The History of Germany since 1789* (New York, 1968)

Manuel, Frank E., and P. Fritzie, *Utopian Thought in the Western World* (Cambridge, MA, 1979)

Mantoux, Paul, *The Industrial Revolution in the Eighteenth Century* (New York, 1961)

Marache, Maurice, *Le Symbole dans la pensée et l'oeuvre de Goethe* (Paris, 1960)

Marchal, Bertrand, *La Religion de Mallarmé* (Paris, 1988)

Marconi, Paolo, *Giuseppe Valadier* (Rome, 1964)

Marinetti, Filippo Tommaso, *Le Futurisme* (Paris, 1911)

—, *Guerra sola igiene del mondo* (Milan, 1915)

Marx, Karl, and Friedrich Engels, *Selected Works,* 2 vols (Moscow, 1962)

Masson, Frédéric, *Livre du Sacre de l'Empereur Napoléon* (Paris, 1908)

Matisse, Henri, *The Vence Chapel, the Archive of a Creation,* ed. M.-A. Couturier and L. B. Rayssiguier (New York and Milan, 1999)

Matossian, Nouritza, *Black Angel: A Life of Arshile Gorky* (London, 2001)

Mattie, Erik, *World's Fairs* (New York, 1998)

Maupassant, Guy de, *Oeuvres complètes* (Paris, 1903–30)

Maurois, André, *Chateaubriand* (Paris, 1938)

Mauron, Véronique, *Werke der Oskar Kokoschka-Stiftung* (Mainz, 1994)

Mendelsohn, Erich, *Neues Haus* (Berlin, 1932)

—, *Letters of an Architect,* ed. Oskar Beyer (New York, 1967)

Merrill, Linda, *The Peacock Room: A Cultural Biography* (Washington, DC, and New Haven, CT, 1998)

Meyer, Adolf, *Ein Versuchshaus des Bauhauses in Weimar* (Munich, 1924)

Meyer, Esther da Costa, *The Work of Sant'Elia* (New Haven, CT, 1995)

Mical, Thomas, ed., *Surrealism and Architecture* (London, 2005)

Michel, Régis, ed., *David contre David* (Paris, 1993)

Michelis, Marco de, *Heinrich Tessenow* (Milan, 1991)

Mickiewicz, Adam, *Ksiegi narodu polskiego i pielgranymstwa polskiego* (Paris, 1832; Kraków, 1924)

Middleton, Robin, ed., *The Beaux-Arts and Nineteenth-Century French Architecture* (London, 1982)

Millais, John Guille, *The Life and Letters of Sir John Everett Millais* (New York, 1899)

Millet, Jules, *Audition colorée* (Paris, 1892)

Milner, John, *Vladimir Tatlin and the Russian Avant-Garde* (New Haven, CT, 1983)

Miodonska-Brookes, Ewa, *Feliks Jasienski i jego Manggha* (Kraków, 1992)

Mitchell, Timothy Frank, 'Philipp Otto Runge and Caspar David Friedrich', PhD thesis, (Indiana University, IN, 1977)

Mittner, Ladislao, *Storia della letteratura tedesca, 1700–1820* (Turin, 1964)

Mivart, St George Jackson, *The Cat* (London, 1881)

Moffett, Marian, and Lawrence Wodehouse, *Built for the People of the United States: Fifty Years of TVA Architecture* (Knoxville, TN, 1983)

Mondor, Henri, *Vie de Mallarmé* (Paris, 1943)

Mondrian, Piet, *Collected Writings*, ed. and trans. Harry Holtzman and Martin S. James (London, 1987)

Moos, Stanislas von, *Le Corbusier: Elements of a Synthesis* (Cambridge, MA, 1979)

—, and Arthur Rüegg, *Le Corbusier before Le Corbusier* (New Haven, CT, 2002)

Mordaunt-Crook, J., *The Dilemma of Style* (London, 1987)

Morelli, Giovanni, *Italian Painters,* 2 vols (London, 1893; reprinted 1990)

Morris, May, ed., *The Collected Works of William Morris* (New York, 1966)

Moureau, Nathalie, and Dominique Sagot-Duvauroux, *Le Marché de l'art contemporain* (Paris, 2006)

Mucha, Jiři, *et al., Alphonse Mucha* (London, 1971)

Muche, Georg, *Blickpunkt: Sturm, Dada, Bauhaus, Gegenwart* (Munich, 1961)

Müller, Johannes von, *Geschichte der Schweizer Konfederation* (Zurich, 1780)

Muller, Priscilla E., *Goya's 'Black' Paintings: Truth and Reason in Light and Liberty* (New York, 1984)

Münch, Marc-Mathieu, *La 'Symbolique' de Friedrich Creuzer* (Paris, 1976)

Musil, Robert, *Gesammelte Werke,* 9 vols, ed. Adolf Frisé (Reinbek bei Hamburg, 1978)

Muthesius, Hermann, *Kunstgewerbe und Architektur* (Jena, 1907)

Muthesius, Karl, *Goethe und das Handwerk* (Leipzig, 1927)

Myers, F.W.H., *Human Personality and its Survival of Bodily Death* (London, 1903)

Nadeau, Maurice, *Histoire du surréalisme* (Paris, 1964)

Naegele, Daniel, 'Un Corps ? Habiter: The Image of the Body in the Oeuvre of Le Corbusier', *Interstices* 5 (Auckland, NZ, 2000)

Naifeh, Steven, and Gregory White Smith, *Jackson Pollock: An American Saga* (New York, 1989)

Nakov, Andrei, ed., *Malevitch: écrits* (Paris, 1986)

—, *Kazimir Malewicz* (Paris, 2002)

Naumann, Francis M., and Hector Obalk, *Affectionately, Marcel: The Selected Correspondence of Marcel Duchamp,* trans. Jill Taylor (Ghent, 2000)

Nehamas, Alexander, *Nietzsche: Life as Literature* (Cambridge, 1985)

Nerval, Gérard de, *Oeuvres*, ed. Albert Béguin and Jean Richer (Paris, 1960–66)

Neufert, Ernst, *Bau-Entwurfslehre* (Berlin, 1936)

Neufforge, Jean-François de, *Recueil elémentaire de l'architecture* (Paris, 1757–62; Supplement, 1780)

Neumann, Robert Alfred, 'The Evolution of the Concept *Gesamtkunstwerk* in German Romanticism', PhD thesis (University of Michigan, MI, 1951)

Newhouse, Victoria, *Art and the Power of Placement* (New York, 2005)

Newman, Ernest, *The Life of Richard Wagner*, 4 vols (New York, 1933–46)

Nibby, Antonio, *Roma nell'Anno, MDCCCXXXVIII* (Rome, 1838)

Nicoletti, Michele, ed., *L'empatia* [translation of *Zum Problem der Einfühlung* by Edith Stein] (Milan, 2002)

Nicolson, Benedict, *Joseph Wright of Derby* (London and New York, 1969)

Nietzsche, Friedrich, *The Will to Power*, trans. Walter Kaufmann and R. J. Hollingdale, with a commentary by Walter Kaufmann (New York, 1967)

—, *Werke: Kritische Gesamtausgabe*, ed. Giorgio Colli and Mazzino Montanari (Berlin, 1967 onwards)

Nodier, Charles, *Oeuvres* (Brussels, 1832–40)

Nolhac, Pierre de, *Fragonard, 1732–1806* (Paris, 1901)

Nordau, Max, *Entartung* (Berlin, 1895); trans. as *Degeneration* (London, 1892–3)

Novalis [Friedrich von Hardenberg], *Schriften*, ed. J. Minor (Jena, 1907)

O'Brien, David, *After the Revolution: Antoine-Jean Gros, Painting and Propaganda under Napoleon* (College Park, PA, 2006)

O'Connor, Timothy Edward, *The Politics of Soviet Culture* (Ann Arbor, MI, 1983)

Ogden, Charles, I. A. Richards and James Wood, *The Foundations of Aesthetics* (New York, 1925)

Ohmann, Richard, *Selling Culture: Magazines, Markets and Class at the Turn of the Century* (London and New York, 1996)

Osma, Guillermo de, *The Life and Work of Mariano Fortuny* (New York, 1980)

Osthaus, Karl-Ernst, *Van de Velde* (Hagen, 1920)

Ostwald, Wilhelm, *Lebenslinien* (Berlin, 1926–7)

Ozenfant, Amédée, *Sur les écoles cubistes et post-cubistes* (Paris, 1926; reprinted Turin, 1975)

—, *Art*, 2 vols (Paris, 1928)

—, *Journey through Life* (London, 1939)

—, *Mémoires, 1886–1962* (Paris, 1968)

Ozouf, Mona, *Festivals and the French Revolution* (Cambridge, MA, 1988)

Packard, Vance, *The Hidden Persuaders* (New York, 1957)

—, *The Status Seekers* (London, 1959)

Padovan, Richard, *Proportion: Science, Philosophy, Architecture* (London and New York, 1999)

Pascal, Blaise, *Lettres provinciales*, ed. H. F. Stewart (Manchester, 1920)

Passuth, Krisztina, *Moholy-Nagy* (London, 1985)

Paston, E., *Abramtsevo: Iskusstvo i Zhizn* (Moscow, 2003)

Pastor, W., *Max Klinger* (Berlin, 1922)

Pater, Walter, *The Renaissance* (London, 1924)

Patin, Sylvie, *Regards sur Nymphéas de Paul Claudel à André Masson* (Paris, 2006)

Patrides, C. A., *The Cambridge Platonists* (Cambridge, 1970)

Pauli, Gustav, *Die Kunst der Klassizismus und der Romantik* (Berlin, 1925)

Paulson, Ronald, *The Art of Hogarth* (London, 1975)

Pehnt, Wolfgang, *Rudolf Steiners Goetheanum, Dornach* (Berlin, 1991)

Pennell, E. R., and J. Pennell, *The Life of James McNeill Whistler* (London, 1908)

Percier, Charles, and Pierre-François Fontaine, *Recueil de décorations intérieures . . .* (Paris, 1801)

—, *Résidences de Souverains* (Paris, 1833)

Perniola, Mario, *L'alienazione artistica* (Milan, 1971)

Peters, H. F., *Zarathustra's Sister* (New York, 1977)

Petity, Jean-Raymond de, *Manuel des Artistes et des Amateurs ou Dictionnaire Historique et Mythologique . . . Composé en Faveur des Nouvelles Ecoles Gratuites de Dessein* (Paris, 1770)

Phillips, Lisa, ed., *Frederick Kiesler* (New York, 1989)

Phillips, Samuel, *Guide to the Crystal Palace and Park* (London, 1854)

Pica, Vittorio, *L'arte decorativa all'esposizione di Torino 1902* (Bergamo, 1903)

Picon, Gaetan, *Panorama da la nouvelle littérature française*, 2nd edn (Paris, 1960)

Piel, Friedrich, *Die Ornament-Grotteske in der Italienischen Renaissance* (Berlin, 1962)

Piero Manzoni: Paintings, Reliefs and Objects, exh. cat., Tate Gallery (London, 1974)

Piranesi, G. B., *Diverse Maniere d'Adornare i Cammini ed Ogni Altra Parte degli Edifizi Desunte dall'Architettura Egizia, Etrusca e Greca* (Rome, 1769)

Planta, Edward, *A New Picture of Paris* (London, 1818)

Pointon, Marcia, *William Dyce, 1806–1864* (Oxford, 1979)

Poisson, Georges, 'Les Fontaines de Paris sous le Premier Empire', *Urbanisme et architecture* [Festschrift for Pierre Lavedan] (Paris, 1954)

Polak, Ada, *Glass: Its Tradition and its Makers* (New York, 1975)

Polano, Sergio, ed., *L'architettura completa di Berlage* (Milan, 1987)

Polizzotti, M., *Revolution of the Mind: The Life of André Breton* (New York, 1995)

Ponce, [Nicolas], *Description des Bains de Titus; ou, Collection des Peintures trouvées dans les Bains de cet Empereur* (Paris, 1786)

Pospelov, Gleb, *et al.*, *Baranov-Rossiné* (Moscow, 2002)

Pourtalès, Guy de, *Berlioz et l'Europe romantique* (Paris, 1939)

Potts, Alex, *Flesh and the Ideal: Winckelmann and the Origins of Art History* (New Haven, CT, and London, 1994)

Prendergast, Christopher, *Napoleon and History Painting* (Oxford, 1997)

Prettejohn, Elizabeth, *The Art of the Pre-Raphaelites* (London, 2000)

Prévost, Jean, *Eiffel* (Paris, 1929)

Priddin, Deirdre, *The Art of the Dance in French Literature* (London, 1952)

Pugin, A.W.N., *Contrasts* (London, 1836)

—, *The True Principles of Pointed or Christian Architecture* (London, 1853)

Pynchon, Thomas, *Gravity's Rainbow* (New York, 2000)

Quatremère de Quincy, Antoine-Chrysostome, *Dictionnaire historique de l'architecture*, 2 vols (Paris, 1832)

Quilici, Vieri, *L'architettura del Costruttivismo* (Bari, 1969)

Rampley, Matthew, *Nietzsche, Aesthetics and Modernity* (Cambridge, 2000)

Raval, Marcel, *Claude-Nicolas Ledoux, 1736–1806* (Paris, 1946)

Rave, Paul Ortwin, *Genius der Baukunst* (Berlin, 1942)

Ravel, Maurice, *On the Spiritual in Art* (Munich, 1911)

Rawidowicz, S., *Ludwig Feuerbachs Philosophie* (Berlin, 1964)

Redgrave, Samuel, *A Dictionary of Artists of the English School* (London, 1890)

—, and Robert Redgrave, *A Century of Painters of the British School* (London, 1947)

Reed, John, *Ten Days that Shook the World* (New York, 1919)

Reitlinger, Gerald, *The Economics of Taste* (London, 1961)

Rewald, John, *Post-Impressionism* (New York, 1956)

Reynolds, Joshua, Sir, *Discourses on Art*, ed. Robert R. Wark (New Haven, CT, and London, 1975)

Rhode, Eric, *A History of the Cinema* (Harmondsworth, 1978)

Richards, I. A., and James Wood, *The Foundations of Aesthetics* (New York, 1925)

Richardson, John, *A Life of Picasso* (New York, 1991 and 1996)

Richter, Hans, *Dada-Kunst und Antikunst* (Cologne, 1964)

Riesman, David, *The Lonely Crowd* [with Nathan Glazer and Reuel Denney] (New Haven, CT, 1967)

Riley, Terence, and Barry Bergdoll, eds, *Mies in Berlin* (New York, 2002)

Rimbaud, Arthur, *Oeuvres complètes*, ed. Rolland de Reneville and Jules Mouquet (Paris, 1951)

—, *Oeuvres complètes*, ed. Steve Murphy (Paris, 1999)

Ripa, Cesare, *Iconologia*, ed. G. Zaratino-Castelli (Rome, 1604)

Roch, Wolfgang, *Philipp Otto Runges Kunstanschauung (dargestellt nach seinen 'Hinterlassenen Schriften') und ihr Verhältnis zur Frühromantik* (Strasbourg, 1909)

Rodin, Auguste, *Les Cathédrales de France* (Paris, 1914)

Roh, Franz, *Nach-Expressionismus: Magischer Realismus, Probleme der Neuesten Europäischen Malerei* (Leipzig, 1925)

Rohe, Mies van der, ed., *Bau und Wohnung* (Stuttgart, 1927)

Roland Michel, Marianne, ed., *Aspects de Fragonard: peintures-dessins-estampes*, exh. cat., Galerie Cailleux (Paris, 1987)

Rosen, Charles, and Henri Zerner, *Romanticism and Realism: The Mythology of Nineteenth-century Art* (New York, 1984)

Rosenblum, R., 'The International Style of 1800', PhD thesis (New York, 1956)

Rotzler, Willy, ed., *Johannes Itten, Werke und Schriften* (Zürich, 1972)

Roux, Alphonse, and Robert Veyssié, *Edouard Schuré: son oeuvre, sa pensée* (Paris, 1914)

Rukschcio, Burkhardt, and Roland Schachel, *Adolf Loos: Leben und Werk* (Vienna, 1989)

Runge, Philipp Otto, *Farben-Kugel* (Hamburg, 1810, Mittenwald, 1977)

—, *Hinterlassenen Schriften*, 2 vols, ed. Daniel Runge (Hamburg, 1840–41; reprinted Göttingen, 1965)

Ruskin, John, *Seven Lamps of Architecture* (London, 1849)

—, *The Stones of Venice* (London, 1851–6)

—, *Modern Painters*, 5 vols (London, 1860–69)

—, *The Complete Works*, 39 vols, ed. E. T. Cook and A. Wedderburn (London, 1903–12)

The Russian Show, exh. cat., ed. Andrei Nakov (London, 1983)

Ryder, A. J., *Twentieth-Century Germany: from Bismarck to Brandt* (New York, 1973)

Rykwert, Joseph, *The First Moderns* (Cambridge, MA, 1980)

—, *On Adam's House in Paradise* (Cambridge, MA, 1981)

—, *The Dancing Column* (Cambridge, MA, 1996)

—, 'The Constitution of Bohemia', *RES* 31 (Spring 1997)

—, *The Seduction of Place* (Oxford, 2004)

—, and Anne Rykwert, *The Brothers Adam* (London, 1985)

Sadler, Simon, *The Situationist City* (Cambridge, MA, 1999)

Sadoul, Georges, *Histoire générale du cinéma* (Paris, 1956)

Safranski, Rüdiger, *Nietzsche: A Philosophical Biography* (London, 2002)

Sagner-Düchting, Karin, *Monet in Giverny* (Munich, 1994)

Saler, Michael, *The Avant-Garde in Interwar England* (New York, 1999)

Sartre, Jean-Paul, 'Qu'est-ce que la Littérature', *Situations*, II (Paris, 1948)

Sassoon, Donald, *The Culture of the Europeans* (London, 2006)

Saunier, Charles, *Les Conquêtes artistiques de la Révolution et de l'Empire* (Paris, 1902)

Schadow, Johann Gottfried, *Polyclet: oder von den Maassen des Menschen nach dem Geschlechte und Alter, mit Angabe der wirklichen Naturgrösse nach dem Rheinländischen Zollstocke und Metermaase*, 5th edn, 2 vols (Berlin, 1884)

—, *Kunstwerke und Kunstansichten*, ed. Götz Eckhardt (Berlin, 1987)

Scheerbart, Paul, *70 Trillionen Weltgrüsse*, ed. Mechtild Rausch (Berlin, 1991)

Scheffauer, Herman George, *The New Vision in the German Arts* (New York, 1924)

Schelling, Friedrich, Wilhelm Joseph von, *Sämmtliche Werke* (Stuttgart, 1856–61)

Schérer, Jacques, *Le 'Livre' de Mallarmé* (Paris, 1957)

Schirmer, Andreas, and Rüdiger Schmidt, eds, *Entdecken und Verraten: Zu Leben und Werk Friedrich Nietzsches* (Weimar, 1999)

Schirmer, Wulf, ed., *Heinrich Huebsch, 1795–1863: Der Grosse Badische Baumeister der Romantik*, exh. cat. (Karlsruhe, 1983)

Schlemmer, Oskar, Moholy-Nagy, László, and Molnar, Farkas, *Die Bühne im Bauhaus (4th Bauhausbuch)* (Fulda, 1925; reprinted Mainz, 1985)

Schmarsow, August, *Beiträge zur Ästhetik der Bildenden Künste*, 3 vols (Leipzig, 1896–9)

Schmid, Max, *Max Klinger*, ed. Julius Vogel (Bielefeld and Leipzig, 1926)

Schnapper, Antoine, *David: témoin de son temps* (New York, 1980)

476

Schopenhauer, Arthur, *Werke*, Grossherzog Wilhelm Ernst Ausgabe, ed. Moritz Brasch (Leipzig, 1891)

Schorske, Carl E., *Fin-de-Siècle Vienna* (New York, 1981)

Schouvaloff, Alexander, *The Art of Ballets-Russes* (New Haven, CT, 1998)

Schumacher, Thomas L., *The Danteum* (Princeton, NJ, 1985)

Schuré, Edouard, *Le Drame musical: Richard Wagner et son Oeuvre* (Paris, 1894)

—, *Richard Wagner: son oeuvre et son idée* (Paris, 1920)

Schwarz, Arturo, *The Complete Works of Marcel Duchamp*, 2nd edn (New York, 1970)

Scott, Geoffrey, *The Architecture of Humanism: A Study in the History of Taste*, 2nd edn (London, 1924)

Sedeyn, Emile, *Le Mobilier* (Paris, 1921)

Ségalen, Victor, *Les Synesthésies et l'école symboliste* (Paris, 1981)

Seigel, Jerrold, *Bohemian Paris* (New York, 1986)

Semper, Gottfried, *Das Königliche Hoftheater zu Dresden* (Brunswick, 1849)

—, *Der Stil*, 2 vols (Munich, 1878)

Sereny, Gitta, *Albert Speer: His Battle with Truth* (New York, 1995)

Seuphor, Michel, *Piet Mondrian* (New York, 1987)

Shand, P. Morton, 'An Essay in the Adroit', *Architectural Review*, LXV (March 1929)

Sharp, Dennis, ed., *Henry van de Velde: Theatres, 1904–1914* (London, 1974)

Sharp, William, *Dante Gabriel Rossetti: A Record and a Study* (London, 1882)

Signac, Paul, *D'Eugène Delacroix au Néo-Impressionisme* (Paris, 1899)

Silverman, Deborah L., *Art Nouveau in Fin-de Siècle France* (Berkeley and Los Angeles, 1989)

Silvestre, Théophile, *Les Artistes français*, 2 vols (Paris, 1926)

Simmel, Georg, *Gesamtausgabe*, ed. Otthein Rammstedt (Frankfurt, 1989)

Slochower, Harry, *Richard Dehmel: der Mensch und der Denker* (Dresden, 1928)

Small, Ian, *The Aesthetes: A Sourcebook* (London, 1979)

Smiles, Samuel, *Lives of the Engineers* (London, 1874–99; 1905)

Snowman, Kenneth, *Fabergé: Goldsmith to the Imperial Court of Russia* (London, 1971)

Solnit, Rebecca, *River of Shadows: Eadweard Muybridge and the Technological Wild West* (New York, 2003)

Spalding, Frances, *Roger Fry: Art and Life* (London, 1980)

Spector, Irwin, *Rhythm and Life: The Work of Emile Jaques-Dalcroze* (New York, 1990)

Spector, Jack J., *The Murals of Eugène Delacroix at Saint-Sulpice* (New York, 1967)

Speer, Albert, *Erinnerungen* (Frankfurt, 1969)

Spiegelberg, Herbert, *The Essentials of the Phenomenological Method* (The Hague, 1965)

Spurling, Hilary, *The Unknown Matisse* (London, 1998)

—, *Matisse the Master* (London, 2005)

Stafford, Barbara Maria, *Symbol and Myth: Humbert de Superville's Essay on Absolute Signs in Art* (Cranbury, NJ, 1979)

Starkie, Enid, *Petrus Borel: the Lycanthrope* (London, 1954)

Starobinski, Jean, *Jean-Jacques Rousseau: la transparence et l'obstacle* (Paris, 1971)

—, *1789, les emblèmes de la raison* (Paris, 1979)

—, *Action et réaction* (Paris, 2001)

—, *L'Invention de la liberté 1700–1789 suivi de 1789 les emblèmes de la raison* (Paris, 2006)

Starr, S. Frederick, *Melnikov: Solo Architect in a Mass Society* (Princeton, NJ, 1981)

St Clair, William, *Lord Elgin and the Marbles* (London, 1967)

—, *The Mission of Spiritual Science and of its Building at Dornach, Switzerland* (London, 1917)

—, *Ways to a New Style in Architecture* (London, 1927)

—, *The Story of my Life* (London, 1928)

—, *Rhythms of Learning*, ed. Robert Trostli (Hudson, NJ, 1998)

—, *The Renewal of Education*, ed. Eugene Schwarz (Great Barrington, MA, 2001)

Steinhagen, Harald, and Benno von Wiese, *Deutsche Dichter des 17. Jahrhunderts* (Berlin, 1984)

Stendhal [Henri Beyle], *Oeuvres complètes,* ed. Henri Martineau (Paris, 1927–37)

Stephan, Regina, ed., *Erich Mendelsohn: Gebaute Welten* (Stuttgart, 1998)

Storrer, William Allin, *The Frank Lloyd Wright Companion* (Chicago, IL, and London, 1993)

Story, William Wetmore, *The Proportions of the Human Figure, According to a New Canon, for Practical Use; with a Critical Notice of the Canon of Polycletus and of the Principal Ancient and Modern Systems* (London, 1866)

Stuckey, Charles F., *Monet: Waterlilies* (New York, 1993)

Suarez de Mendoza, F., *L'Audition colorée; étude sur les Fausses Sensations Secondaires Physiologiques . . . Objectives des Sons* (Paris, 1892)

Sullivan, Louis, *Kindergarten Chats and Other Writings* (New York, 1947)

Sulzer, Johann Georg, *Allgemeine Theorie der Schönen Künste in Einzeln, nach alphabetischer Ordnung der Kunstwörter auf einander folgenden Artikeln abgehandelt,* 5 vols (Leipzig, 1792–9)

Summers, David, *The Judgement of Sense* (Cambridge, 1987)

Summerson, John, ed., *Concerning Architecture, Essays on Architectural Writers and Writing Presented to Nikolaus Pevsner* (Harmondsworth, 1964)

—, *Georgian London* (London, 1980)

Svácha, Rotislav, *The Architecture of the New Prague, 1895–1945* (Cambridge, MA, 1996)

Szeeman, Harald, ed., *Der Hang zum Gesamtkunstwerk* (Arrau, 1983)

Tait, A. L., *Lunacharsky, Poet of the Revolution (1875–1907)* (Birmingham, 1984)

Taylor, Charles, *Hegel* (Cambridge, 1975)

Tennyson, Hallam, *Alfred Tennyson: A Memoir by his Son,* 2 vols (London, 1897)

Thackeray, W. M., *Roundabout Papers* (London, 1873)

Thévoz, Michel, *Le Théâtre du crime: essai sur la peinture de David* (Paris, 1989)

Thomas, Keith, *Man and the Natural World* (London, 1983)

Thornton, Peter, *Authentic Décor* (London, 1984)

Tieck, Ludwig, *Franz Sternbalds Wanderungen,* 2 vols (Berlin, 1798)

Tild, Jean, *Théophile Gautier et ses amis* (Paris, 1951)

Todorov, Tzvetan, *Mikhaïl Bakhtine: le principe dialogique* (Paris, 1981)

Tomory, Peter, *The Life and Art of Henry Fuseli* (New York, 1972)

Tönnies, Ferdinand, *Gemeinschaft und Gesellschaft* (Leipzig, 1887)

Torii, Tokutoshi, *El mundo enigmatico de Gaudí* (Madrid, 1983)

Trakl, Georg, *Die Dichtungen* (Salzburg, 1938)

Trappes-Lomax, Michael, *Pugin: A Mediaeval Victorian* (London, 1932)

Traynham, James G., *Essays on the History of Organic Chemistry* (Baton Rouge, LA, 1987)

Tripier le Franc, J., *Histoire de la vie et de la mort du Baron Gros* (Paris, 1880)

Trotsky, Leon, *Literature and Revolution* (Ann Arbor, MI, 1966)

—, *The History of the Russian Revolution,* trans. Max Eastman (London, 1967)

Tupitsyn, Margarita, *El Lissitzky* (New Haven, CT, 1999)

Turner, E. S., *The Shocking History of Advertising!* (New York, 1953)

Turquan, Joseph, *The Wife of General Bonaparte* (London, 1912)

Tyndall, John, *Sound: A Course of Eight Lectures Delivered at the Royal Institution of Great Britain* (London, 1908)

Tyrwhitt, J.J.L. Sert and E. N. Rogers, eds, *The Heart of the City: Towards the Humanisation of Urban Life* (London, 1952; reprinted Lichtenstein, 1979)

Uglow, Jenny, *The Lunar Men: Five Friends Whose Curiosity Changed the World* (New York, 2002)

Utley, Gertje R., *Picasso: The Communist Years* (New Haven, CT, 2000)

Valéry, Paul, *Oeuvres,* ed. Jean Hytier (Paris, 1957–60)

Van Zanten, David, *Designing Paris: the Architecture of Duban, Labrouste, Duc and Vaudoyer* (Cambridge, MA, 1987)

Varnedoe, Kirk, *Vienna 1900: Art, Architecture, and Design* (New York, 1986)

—, and Adam Gopnik, eds, *High and Low: Modern Art and Popular Culture* (New York, 1991)

Varenne, Gaston, *Bourdelle par lui-même* (Paris, 1937)

Vasari, Giorgio, *Vite*, ed. G, Milanesi, 9 vols (Florence, 1878–1906)

Velde, Henry van de, *Récit de ma vie*, ed. Anne van Loo (Brussels, 1992)

Venclova, Antanas, *N. čiurlionis* (Vilnius, 1964)

Venturi, Lionello, *Il gusto dei primitivi* (Turin, 1972)

Vergo, Peter, *Art in Vienna, 1898–1918* (London, 1975)

Vidler, Anthony, *Claude-Nicolas Ledoux* (Cambridge, MA, 1990)

Viel de Saint-Maux, C. F., *Lettres sur l'architecture* (Paris, 1787; reprinted Geneva, 1974)

Vietor, Karl, *Geist und Form; Aufsätze zur deutschen Literaturgeschichte* (Bern, 1952)

Vigée-Lebrun, Louise-Elizabeth, *Memoirs of Madame Vigée Lebrun*, trans. Lionel Strachey (New York, 1989)

Villanueva, Paulina, and Marcia Pintó, *Carlos Raúl Villanueva* (Seville and Madrid, 2000)

Viollet-le-Duc, E.-E., *Entretiens sur l'architecture*, 2 vols (Paris, 1863–72)

—, *Dictionnaire raisonné de l'architecture française*, 7 vols (Paris, 1867)

—, *Lectures on Architecture*, 2 vols, trans. B. Bucknall (London, 1877–81)

—, *Les Eglises de Paris* [with E. Quinet, *Le Panthéon*] (Paris, 1883)

—, *Discourses on Architecture*, 2 vols, trans. B. Bucknall (New York 1959)

Vischer, Friedrich Theodor, *Aesthetik: oder Wissenschaft des Schönen*, 6 vols (Hildesheim, 1922–3)

Vischer, Robert, *Drei Schriften zum Ästhetischen Formproblem* (Halle/Saale, 1927)

Vogt, Adolf Max, *Architektur, 1940–1980* (Frankfurt am Main, 1980)

Wackenroder, W. H., and Ludwig Tieck, *Outpourings of an Art-Loving Friar*, trans. Edward Mornin (New York, 1975)

Wagner, Otto, *Modern Architecture*, ed. and trans. H. Mallgrave (Los Angeles, CA, 1988)

Wagner, Richard, *Gesammelte Schriften und Dichtungen* (Leipzig, 1871–83)

—, *Die Hauptschriften*, ed. Ernst Bücken (Stuttgart, 1956)

Wakefield, A. M., ed., *Ruskin on Music* (London, 1894)

Walker, R.J.B., *A Catalogue of Paintings, Drawings, Engravings and Sculpture in the Palace of Westminster* (Croydon, 1988)

Walpole, Horace, ed., with Rev. James Dallaway, *Anecdotes of Painting in England; with Some Accounts of the Principal Artists; and Incidental Notes on Other Arts*, 5 vols (London, 1828)

Walsh, Stephen, *Stravinsky* (New York, 2000)

Ward, Colin, ed., *Vandalism* (London, 1973)

Warnke, Martin ed., *Politische Architektur in Europa* (Cologne, 1984)

Watkin, David, *Sir John Soane: Enlightenment Thought and the Royal Academy Lectures* (Cambridge, 1996)

Watson, F.J.B., *Louis XVI Furniture* (London, 1960)

Weber, Max, *Gesammelte Aufsätze zur Wissenschaftslehre*, ed. Johannes Winckelmann (Tübingen, 1922 and 1988)

Weintraub, Stanley, *Whistler: A Biography* (New York, 1976)

Weiss, E. R., *E.R. Weiss zum Fünfzigsten Geburtstage* (Leipzig, 1925)

Weiss, Peg, *Kandinsky in Munich: The Formative Jugendstil Years* (Princeton, NJ, 1979)

—, *Kandinsky and Old Russia* (New Haven, CT, 1995)

Welch, Evelyn, *Art and Society in Italy, 1350–1500* (Oxford, 1997)

Wellek, René, and Austin Warren, *A Theory of Literature* (London, 1954)

Weston, Nancy, *Daniel Maclise: An Irish Artist in Victorian London* (London, 2001)

Weyegraf-Serra, Clara, and Martha Buskirk, *The Destruction of Tilted Arc: Documents* (Cambridge, MA, 1991)

White, Christopher, *Peter Paul Rubens: Man and Artist* (New Haven, CT, and London, 1987)

Whiteway, Michael, *Christopher Dresser, 1834–1904* (Milan, 2001)

Wichmann, Siegfried, *Japonisme* (New York, 1985)

Wijdeveld, H. T., *Eine Arbeitsgemeinschaft* (Santpoort, 1931)

Wildenstein, Daniel, *Claude Monet: biographie et catalogue raisonné*, 5 vols (Lausanne, 1974–91)

Wilkin, Karen, *Stuart Davis* (New York, 1987)

Wilkinson, Burke, *The Life and Works of Augustus Saint Gaudens* (New York, 1985)

Willet, John, *Expressionism* (London, 1970)

Willis, Carol, *Form Follows Finance* (New York, 1995)

Wilson, Edmund, *To the Finland Station: A Study in the Writing and Acting of History* (New York, 1953)

—, *The Twenties*, ed. Leon Edel (New York, 1975)

Winckelmann, J.-J., *Versuch einer Allegorie, besonders für die Kunst* (Dresden, 1766)

—, *Monumenti Antichi Inediti Spiegati ed Illustrati* (Rome, 1767)

—, *Geschichte der Kunst des Altertums* (Vienna, 1934)

Wind, Edgar, *Art and Anarchy* (London, 1963)

—, *Hume and the Heroic Portrait: Studies in Eighteenth-century Imagery* (Oxford, 1986)

Windsor, Alan, *Peter Behrens: Architect and Designer, 1868–1940* (London, 1981)

Wines, James, *De-Architecture* (New York, 1987)

—, *et al.*, SITE, *Identity in Density* (Mulgrave, Australia, 2005)

Wingler, Hans M., *The Bauhaus* (Cambridge, MA, 1978)

Wolff, Kurt H., *The Sociology of Georg Simmel* (New York, 1950)

Wölfflin, Heinrich, *Renaissance und Barock* (Munich, 1925)

—, *Kleine Schriften* (Basel, 1946)

Woolf, Virginia, *Roger Fry: A Biography* (London, 1940)

Worringer, Wilhelm, *Abstraction and Empathy: A Contribution to the History of Style*, trans. Michael Bullock (London, 1953)

Wright, Frank Lloyd, *An Autobiography* (New York, 1943)

Wundt, Wilhelm Max, *Reden und Aufsätze* (Leipzig, 1913)

Wyss, Beat, *Trauer der Vollendung* (Munich, 1989); trans. as *Hegel's Art History and the Critique of Modernity* (Cambridge, 1999)

—, *Der Wille zu Kunst* (Cologne, 1996)

Yeats, W. B., *Collected Poems* (London, 1933)

Zeitler, Rudolf, *Klassizismus und Utopia: Interpretationen zu Werken von David, Canova, Carstens, Thorvaldsen, Koch* (Stockholm, 1954)

Zhadova, Larissa, ed., *Tatlin* (London, 1988)

Ziller, Hermann, *Schinkel* (Bielefeld and Leipzig, 1897)

Zimmermann, Michael F., *Seurat and the Art Theory of his Time* (Antwerp, 1991)

Acknowledgements

This book has been long in gestation, during which time it has acquired a lot of debts.

The Graham Foundation offered me a generous grant at the beginning of the work. The Centre Canadien d'Architecture allowed me two stints (once as Mellon Fellow) of research, for which I am grateful to the directors, Phyllis Lambert and Mirko Zardini. The library staff really put themselves out for a quirkily demanding customer, as did the staff at the University of Pennsylvania and the London Library.

Much of the material was discussed with doctoral students during seminars at the University of Pennsylvania, and many friends have patiently helped to shape parts of the argument and have read portions of the text and disagreed with – or dealt with my ignorance of – specific points: Valerio Adami, Anthony Alofsin, Stanford Anderson, Bryan Avery, George Baird, the late Giuliano Briganti, Tilmann Buddensieg, Melvyn Charney, David Chipperfield, Jean-Louis Cohen, Michael Craig-Martin, Marina Engel, Elizabeth C. English, Anat Falbel, Maurizio Ferraris, Roy Foster, Celina Fox, Lynn Garafola, Alexander Goehr, Vittorio Gregotti, Niall Hobhouse, Eric Hobsbawm, Jennifer Homans, Barbara Jakobson, Rafael Moneo, Francesco Pellizzi, Deanna Petherbridge, Jean Starobinski, Robert Tavernor, Joe and Joss Tilson, Liliane Weissberg and James Wines.

Richard Sennett's careful examination of the book helped to give it its final shape, while Juan Manuel Heredia was a courteous – though testing – research assistant.

As with all my books, Anne Rykwert has had a share which makes her, in fact, its co-author.

Photographic Acknowledgements

The author and publishers wish to express their thanks to the below sources of illustrative material and/or permission to reproduce it. Locations of artworks or illustration sources not fully credited in the captions are also given below.

Altes Museum, Berlin: pp. 97, 98, 99; Bayerische Staatsgalerie, Munich: p. 85; Peter Behrens, *Ein Dokument Deutscher Kunst* (1901): p. 239; Château de Dampierre (Salon de Minerve), Dampierre-en-Yvelines: p. 121; Jean-Charles Delafosse, *Algemeen Kunstenaars Handboek* (1785): p. 38; Christopher Dresser, *The Art of Decorative Design* (1862): p. 183; Ecole des Beaux-Arts, Paris: p. 102; Emil Engelmann, *Das Nibelungenlied für das Deutsche Haus . . .* (1889): p. 96; James Fergusson, *An Illustrated Handbook of Architecture* (1853): p. 161; Pierre-François-Léonard Fontaine, *Le Palais Royal* (1834): p. 64; Charles Gourlier et al., *Choix d'edifices publics projetés et construits en France depuis le commencement du XIXe siècle . . .* (1825–50): p. 115 (foot); Pierre-François Hughes d'Hancarville, *Collection of Etruscan, Greek and Roman Antiquities from the Cabinet of the Hon.ble Wm. Hamilton . . . ,* vol. II (Naples, 1770): p. 19; David Hay, *The Geometric Beauty of the Human Figure Defined* (1851): p. 187; Jacques-Ignace Hittorf, *Restitution du Temple d'Empédocle à Selinonte, ou l'architecture polychrome chez les Grecs* (1851): pp. 103, 109 (foot); Kunsthalle Hamburg: p. 131; Owen Jones, *The Grammar of Ornament* (1856): pp. 136, 179; Batty Langley, *Gothic Architecture, Improved by Rules and Proportions* (1747): p. 29; Musée des Beaux-Arts, Nantes: p. 6; Musée Carnavalet, Paris: pp. 34, 101; Musée National du Château de Versailles et du Trianon: pp. 47 (Depôt du Cabinet des Desseins du Musée du Louvre, Paris), 48, 57; Museum der bildenden Künste, Leipzig: p. 229; Museum für Kunst und Kulturgeschichte der Hansestadt Lübeck: p. 82; 'Supplement' of 1780 to Jean-François de Neufforge, *Receuil elementaire de l'architecture* (1757-62): p. 38; Charles Percier and Pierre-François-Léonard Fontaine, *Receuil des décorations intérieures . . .* (1801): pp. 61, 63; Giovanni Battista Piranesi, *Diverse maniere d'adornare i cammini* (1769): p. 22; private collections: pp. 202, 355; A.W.N. Pugin, *Contrasts; Or a Parallel between the Noble Edifices of the Fourteenth and Fifteenth Centuries, and Similar Buildings of the Present Day; Shewing the Present Decay of Taste . . .* (1836): p. 90; A.W.N. Pugin, *Floreated Ornament . . .* (1849): p. 180; A.W.N. Pugin, *The True Principles of Pointed or Christian Architecture: Set Forth in Two Lectures . . .* (1853): p. 92; Alfred Rietdorf, *Gilly: Wiedergeburt der Architektur* (1940): p. 78; Royal Society of Arts, London: p. 72; Gottfried Semper, *Das Königliche Hoftheater zu Dresden* (1849): p. 137; Tate, London (photos © Tate, London 2008): pp. 50 (presented by the Earl of Liverpool, 1830), 150 (purchased with assistance from The Art Fund and various subscribers, 1921).

Index

494